Reader's Digest

# Great Adventures That Changed Our World

L'Astrolabe by Ambroise-Louis Garneray
Musée des Arts Africains et Océaniens,
Paris/Photo Edita, Lausanne

*Reader's Digest*

# Great Adventures That Changed Our World

---

## The World's Great Explorers
## Their Triumphs and Tragedies

The Reader's Digest Association, Inc.
Pleasantville, New York • Montreal

Staff for *Great Adventures That Changed Our World*

*Editor:* Peter Lacey
*Art Editor:* Murray Miller
*Associate Editors:* Miriam H. Carroll, Richard Scheffel
*Research Editors:* Rita G. Christopher, Noreen B. Church
*Picture Researchers:* Margaret O. Mathews,
Richard Pasqual, Penelope Ray
*Copy Editor:* Rosemarie Conefrey
*Research Associates:* Pamela Gilbert, Nancy Gilligan
*Assistant Artist:* Craig Carl
*Art Assistant:* Barbara J. Schneit
*Editorial Assistant:* Patricia Selden

---

*Consultant*
J. H. Parry
*Professor of Oceanic History and Affairs, Harvard University*

*Contributing Writers:*
Edmund Morris, Sylvia Morris, Morrow Wilson, Carol Mankin,
Jean Burton Walker, James Cassidy, Edward Sammis

*Contributing Artists:*
George Buctel, Jean Leon Huens, Gloria McKeown,
George Kelvin, Edward Malsberg

The credits and acknowledgments that appear on
pages 382-384 are hereby made a part of this copyright page.

Library of Congress Catalog Card Number 78-52846
ISBN 0-89577-048-2

Printed in the United States of America

# PREFACE

"The people of this island and of all the other islands which I have found and seen, or have not seen, all go naked, men and women, as their mothers bore them. . . . Of anything they have, if you ask them for it, they never say no; rather they invite the person to share it, and show as much love as if they were giving their hearts; and whether the thing be of value or of small price, at once they are content with whatever little thing of whatever kind may be given to them. . . . I gave them a thousand good, pleasing things which I had brought, in order that they might be fond of us, and furthermore might become Christians and be inclined to the love and service of Their Highnesses and of the whole Castilian nation, and try to help us and give us of the things which they have in abundance and which are necessary to us. And they know neither sect nor idolatry, with the exception that all believe that the source of all power and goodness is in the sky, and they believe very firmly that I, with these ships and people, come from the sky, and in this belief they everywhere received me, after they had overcome their fear. And this does not result from their being ignorant (for they are of a very keen intelligence and men who navigate all those seas, so that it is wondrous the good account they give of everything), but because they have never seen people clothed or ships like ours.

"And as soon as I arrived in the Indies, in the first island which I found, I took by force some of them in order that they might learn [Castilian] and give me information of what they had in those parts; it so worked out that they soon understood us, and we them, either by speech or signs, and they have been very serviceable. I still have them with me, and they are still of the opinion that I come from the sky, in spite of all the intercourse which they have had with me, and they were the first to announce this wherever I went, and the others went running from house to house and to the neighboring towns with loud cries of, 'Come! Come! See the people from the sky!'"

From Columbus' Letter to the Sovereigns on His First Voyage,
15 February – 4 March 1493.

*Journals and Other Documents on the Life and Voyages of Christopher Columbus,* published by The Limited Editions Club and The Heritage Club. Copyright © 1963 by Samuel Eliot Morison. Used by arrangement with The Heritage Press, Avon, Conn., and by permission of Admiral Morison as translator and editor.

# CONTENTS

# INTRODUCTION

This book is about the adventure of discovery, about the daring, imaginative, sometimes tragic exploits of the great explorers who unveiled our world. It is a saga that began when the first men cautiously reconnoitered unknown terrain thousands of years ago and that continues today as modern man prepares to launch himself toward the planets of the solar system. Even in the 17th century, when the earth itself was far from fully explored, some men already imagined voyages to the heavens above. In the illustration at left, a fictional explorer of 1687 ascends to the stratosphere in a kind of space capsule; even then men knew that it was technology that would assist them to explore realms beyond the dreams of their ancestors. Within these pages you will see the inventions and developments that allowed the great explorers to map and conquer the earth. There was the astrolabe, an ancient Greek invention that enabled a sailor to find his location by the stars. There was the caravel, that seaworthy but uncomfortable little ship in which Columbus and others began to map a new hemisphere. There was the fearsome arquebus, an early portable firearm that helped such explorers as Champlain to defend themselves against hostile native peoples. There was the chronometer, a marvelous timepiece that aided Captain Cook in his astounding navigation of the Pacific Ocean. There was the steel bathysphere that protected William Beebe in his record-breaking descent into the depths of the Atlantic Ocean. And there was the Apollo 11 lunar module that safely landed two American astronauts on the surface of the moon. It is certain that as man continues to probe his universe, he will create more marvelous machines to assist him in his adventures, for technology is a tool that has shaped our world. As Professor J. H. Parry has written: "A technological attitude to knowledge, an extreme readiness to apply science in immediately practical ways, eventually became one of the principal characteristics which distinguish western civilization, the civilization originally of Europe, from other great civilized societies. The unprecedented power which it produced eventually led Europe from Reconnaissance to worldwide conquest, and so created the world of yesterday, much of which was governed by Europeans, and the world of today, almost all of which has accepted European technology and European techniques of government, even if only to escape from European rule."

But fascinating as the technology of exploration has been, this book is mainly about the adventures of the great explorers and the spirit that drove them to their great achievements. The ancient Greek merchant Pytheas sails his small ship far north beyond the known end of the earth, to "Ultima Thule," because he wants new markets and also because he simply wants to know what the end of the earth looks like. When he returns, few believe his story, but later historians confirm much of what he saw. There is the same skeptical reception for the medieval merchant Marco Polo when he tells of the fabulous Far East, but a later generation of explorers is spurred by his account and finds most of his "wonders" to be true. A fervent desire for fame, fortune, and the spread of the Christian faith animates the explorers of the Renaissance who create the Golden Age of Discovery. Vasco da Gama leads a Portuguese expedition 13,000 miles across unknown seas "in search of Christians and spices." The audacious Spanish soldier Cortés and other conquistadors annihilate the native civilizations of America during their search for gold and glory in the service of their king and church. In the 18th and 19th centuries, desire for empire and adventure motivates such diverse figures as the Frenchman Bougainville, the Scotsman Mackenzie, and the Australian emigrants Burke and Wills. Yet the desire for knowledge itself and for the benefit of mankind has also inspired explorers. These motives are dramatically expressed by the first man on the moon: "That's one small step for a man, one giant leap for mankind" says Neil Armstrong as he puts down the first human footprint on the surface of the moon.

Here then, from ancient mariner to modern astronaut, are the great adventurers who have changed our world.

# Part

# 1

# Exploring From Earliest Times

## Merchants and Marauders

*In the beginning, men had two main motives for discovery: trade and land. The first explorers were engaged in commerce and, sometimes, in conquest.*

Men have been wanderers since time immemorial. They followed the migrations of animals they hunted or fled hostile tribes and encroaching glaciers. By about 10,000 B.C., with the ending of the last ice age, almost every part of the earth except the polar regions had been found and inhabited by our Stone Age ancestors. It remained for the later civilizations of western Europe to rediscover the people and lands of prehistory. This European exploration, aimed at opening up the world and defining its features, began with the countries of the eastern Mediterranean.

In a sense, the emergence of organized trade in the Middle East marked the beginning of "modern" exploration. Expeditions were then sent out to import exotic luxuries or scarce raw materials and to develop foreign markets for local products. In fact, our earliest documentation of a Mediterranean voyage is a notice of 40 shiploads of cedar exported from Lebanon to Egypt about 2600 B.C. History's first recorded voyage into unknown seas was a four-year expedition from Egypt to the mysterious land of Punt in 2500 B.C. to obtain incense, myrrh, gold, ebony, and dwarfs.

The Egyptians never had a great affinity for the sea, and they came to rely on Minoan and Phoenician shipping for their commerce. Settled on the island of Crete, the Minoans were the first naval power in the Western World. They were adventurous, pressing steadily farther westward across the unexplored Mediterranean, apparently using the sun and stars to navigate beyond sight of land. The Minoans were eventually surpassed by the Phoenicians, who ruled the Mediterranean for 1,000 years. So skillful and daring were the Phoenician navigators that they made the first known forays past the Pillars of Hercules (landmasses at the east end of the Strait of Gibraltar) into the forbidding Outer Sea, the Atlantic. One of the great feats in the history of navigation occurred about 600 B.C., when Phoenicians employed by Egypt sailed around Africa from east to west.

### A Millennium of European Discovery

Interested chiefly in commerce, the Phoenicians ringed the Mediterranean with trading settlements and explored and colonized the African coast south of Morocco. The leader of the latter enterprise, probably about 240 B.C., was the Carthaginian admiral Hanno. His city, Carthage, on the coast of present-day Tunis, had been founded in similar fashion four centuries earlier by Phoenicians from Tyre, in Lebanon. Having established their colonies, the secretive Phoenicians circulated stories about boiling seas and other supposed perils of the Atlantic to frighten rival sailors, and they blockaded the Strait of Gibraltar.

The Phoenicians' most formidable rivals—the Greeks—were not put off by tall tales. Beginning in the eighth century B.C., the Greeks became a maritime power, with colonies stretching across the northern Mediterranean and along the Black Sea. In the next few centuries a great number of Greeks accomplished significant feats of exploration. The most famous was Alexander the Great, who led his conquering army through the towering mountains of Afghanistan to the Indus River, the eastern limit of the former Persian Empire, in 310 B.C. He then sent surveyors and scientists to probe the corners of the domain he had seized—from the Caspian Sea to the Arabian Sea, from the Indus River to the Persian Gulf. At the other end of the Greek world, Pytheas of Massalia (Marseille) made a daring journey to the North Atlantic and returned with accounts of his observations.

By the end of the third century B.C., the world known to the West had grown to include southern Asia as far east as India, the Arabian Sea, the northern African coast, the coast of western Europe, and the eastern Atlantic, possibly as far north as Iceland.

The emergence of the Roman Empire (eighth century B.C.–fifth century A.D.) eclipsed both Carthage and Greece and terminated the first great era of exploration. Rome's conquests and its remarkable road-building projects brought northern Europe into focus, and Rome's great wealth created a demand for silks and certain other luxuries obtainable only in India and China. These goods were scandalously expensive as they trickled into Rome via Asian traders, so wealthy Romans began to back Greek and Phoenician shippers to reach India by way of the Red Sea and eliminate the Asian middlemen. Then a Greek navigator learned from an Indian to use the monsoons to cross the Indian Ocean, and by A.D. 40, Roman ships, as well as others, were sailing either from the Persian Gulf or the Red Sea directly across the Indian Ocean. A century later they were calling at the ports of southern China.

Roman authority collapsed in the fifth century when Rome itself was occupied and sacked. The eastern empire, with its capital at Constantinople, survived but was eventually threatened by the growing power of Islam. Its territory shrank effectively to the lands of Greek speech in the Balkans and Asia Minor. Islam itself, originally the faith of primitive desert nomads, was carried by the conquering Arabs east to India, west along the African shore of the Mediterranean, and over into Sicily and Spain. It became not only a world religion but a world civilization that, at least in a cultural sense, united a vast area to the east and south of a shrinking Christendom and cut off western Europe from all contact with central and eastern Asia.

While southern Spain and southern Italy flourished under Moslem rule, the slow recovery of western Europe was threatened by fresh barbarian invasions. In the ninth century the coasts of France and the British Isles were constantly harried by Scandinavian raiders. These marauders called themselves Vikings, or "pirates," but Norsemen could be more than pirates. Increasingly as time went on, they became traders, explorers, and colonizers and conquerors. They settled Iceland and the Faeroes, explored and settled parts of southern Greenland, and found the agreeable country in North America that they called Vinland.

Much more significant for the future were the Norse conquests in Europe itself: Normandy, England, Calabria, and Sicily. Operating from these bases, Christianized, Latinized Norman knights provided vigorous leadership for the first major counterattack of Western Christendom against Islam: the Crusades. From the late 11th century to the late 13th, Western Christians fought a long series of campaigns to control the Holy Places and to maintain Latin principalities in Syria and Palestine. The initial successes of the First Crusade, however, proved hard to maintain, and by the early 13th century the Latin states were reduced to a precarious remnant. They would have gone under much more quickly had not it been for the Mongol invasions.

### Merchants, Mongols, and Marco Polo

The arrival of the Mongols in Asia Minor temporarily diverted the Moslems at the same time as it briefly threatened Europe. Eager to establish peaceful ties with the Mongol overlord, in 1245 Pope Innocent IV sent an emissary, Friar Joannes de Carpini, to the Mongol capital of Karakorum, in Outer Mongolia, northwest of China. A few years later another friar, William of Rubruck, visited Mongolia as representative of the French king. They were the first Europeans to make the overland journey across Asia, and they returned with reports that lured Europeans to the East. Other missions of the sort were made intermittently. They failed in their primary purpose—to convert the Mongols to Christianity—but they helped secure a century of peaceful relations between East and West during which a flourishing caravan route was developed between the West and China, after the Mongols conquered it. The Mongol Empire was the first to encourage direct contact between East and West, and European merchants began to follow the Silk Route to China to purchase directly the luxuries of the Middle Ages. These merchants traveled more extensively in the East than the friars had, often returning to Europe by sea, thus encircling what was then the known world.

Marco Polo, in the late 13th century, was the most famous traveler to make that long and perilous overland journey. His account inspired a fascination with China that endured even after 1340, when the curtain dropped on Asia as the caravan routes across Persia and India were closed off by the Turks. The Mongol Empire collapsed, and the new Ming dynasty in China shut its doors to foreigners.

Changes had occurred in Europe, too. It had been jarred awake by the Crusades, and it had been stirred by the flow of learning from the Arab-Moslem world. As Europe emerged from the Middle Ages charged with new ideas and needs, a sea route to the luxuries of China and the Far East became imperative.

**For the ancient Mediterranean nations,** *the western end of the known world was marked by the Pillars of Hercules at the Strait of Gibraltar, gateway to the Atlantic. Hercules allegedly erected the two "Pillars," Gibraltar (above) and a nearby promontory in Morocco, as* *he sailed out of the Mediterranean into the nether world on a perilous mission (top, opposite page). A hero of classical mythology, Hercules inspired Phoenician and Greek sailors with his bravery and triumphs over evil forces during his voyages, and they hoped for his favor on their own travels. To them, bad luck showed the ill will of the gods. The Roman carving of Jonah and the whale (left) shows Jonah being thrown overboard by superstitious Phoenicians who had blamed him for a violent storm. Yet interest in trade sent many men into the unknown Atlantic, though we know of only two, Hanno and Pytheas. A Greek vase of 500 B.C. (below) shows a trading vessel being overtaken by an oared pirate ship. Such vases were popular Greek trade items, and Pytheas may have carried some.*

*Chapter One. Thousands of years ago only the boldest Mediterranean sailors ventured out into the vast Ocean Sea to the west of Gibraltar. No one knew what dreadful terrors lurked at the edge of the world until two bold men—Hanno, a Phoenician, and Pytheas, a Greek—wrote their amazing accounts of the African coast and fabled northern islands.*

# Beyond the Pillars of Hercules: Hanno and Pytheas

*The accounts of the Phoenician admiral Hanno and the Greek merchant-mariner Pytheas are tantalizingly vague in their origins and contents. Neither of the original documents—Hanno's inscription placed in a temple in Carthage and Pytheas' manuscript—has survived. Both stories have come down to us through the works of ancient and medieval historians, and both have long been doubted by generations of scholars. Yet there is a convincing ring of authenticity about many of their observations that gives credence to the accounts. Though there is no general agreement, Hanno is believed to have sailed as far south on the coast of Africa as Sierra Leone or possibly even down to the Gulf of Guinea. Pytheas' "Ultima Thule" may have been as far north as Iceland. It is possible he may have sighted Norway as well.*

Sometime during the early fifth century B.C., an extraordinary fleet sailed through the Pillars of Hercules, under the command of the Phoenician admiral Hanno. Ship after ship strained against the tidal current that carried chill ocean brine into the balmy Mediterranean waters. The current was like a signal to those aboard: beyond lay the vast uncharted Atlantic. But prospects of new commerical markets provided the venturesome Phoenicians with a motive that overcame their fear.

The fleet had set out from Carthage, the north African coastal city that the Phoenicians had established centuries earlier. That splendid metropolis had so prospered that it now sent forth its own people to establish new colonies for trade.

Ships in that day tended to hug the shores, and Admiral Hanno was undoubtedly experienced in navigating coastal waters. Emerging from the strait, Hanno ordered his expedition around the northwestern tip of Africa and then down the coast of what today is Morocco. Day by day the fleet sailed in and out of favorable harbors. Two days beyond the Pillars, they

founded the first city above the broad valley of the Sebu River, Morocco. Leaving ships and enough supplies to feed the settlers until their first crop ripened, Hanno sailed on. Presently, he reached a headland (most likely Cape Cantin) that seemed so perilous that a temple was duly built and dedicated to the sea god Poseidon. Thirty miles farther on he "came upon a lagoon situated close to the sea and full of tall reedbeds [perhaps the Wadi Tensift]. In those there were elephants feeding and many other sorts of wild animals."

Five more colonies were established along the Moroccan coast. Suddenly, as Hanno continued southward, a shimmer on the horizon foretold the approach to a great desert (the Sahara). Prudently stopping to fill his water barrels in "the Lixos, a large river flowing from [the interior of] Africa" (assumed to be the Wadi Dra), Hanno recorded his expedition's first encounter with other peoples.

"Along it the Lixite nomads [possibly Berbers] were pasturing their herds; and among them we remained for some considerable time, making friends of them.

"From these Lixites we took aboard interpreters and continued our voyage southward past the desert for nine days, whereupon we turned again toward the sunrise for a day's run. And there in the recesses of a gulf we discovered a small island. . . . This we occupied, giving it the name Kerne."

The "gulf" Hanno had chanced upon was most likely the inlet Rio de Oro. At its mouth stands Herne Island, which possibly became the site of another colony.

Hanno's mission was now complete, and he was free to return to Carthage. But he had one or two ships and plenty of supplies left and decided to continue to explore the African coast. Obviously, this was more to his taste than founding cities. Hanno discovered and cruised up the Senegal, which was "great and wide, and swarming with crocodiles and hippopotamuses." In

Map for Pytheas on page 17.

the hilly regions of the interior he found "savages clad in wild beast hides. These drove us off by hurling stones at us and would not let us land."

Sailing back to sea, the admiral proceeded south along an increasingly green and swampy coastline. Incredulous natives gathered on the beaches to watch his ships go by, but whenever the Lixites accompanying Hanno tried to talk to them, they "fled and would not abide us." The fleet rounded Cape Verde, swung slightly southeast with the coast, and, on the 12th day of sailing, moored beneath the cape's great forest-covered hills. Here, at the foot of the hills, Hanno allowed his sea-weary men ashore to stretch their legs and enjoy the fragrant air, for "the wood of their trees was odorous sweet and of great variety."

The final days of the admiral's voyage are best told in his own vivid words. "[After] we journeyed for two days, we found ourselves in an enormous inlet of the sea [the estuary of the Gambia River]. On the landward side was a level plain from which at night we beheld fires leaping up everywhere at varying distances, now greater and now less [grass fires, which may be seen in the dry season].

"We took on water and proceeded thence along the coast for five days until we came to a large gulf that our interpreters said was called Horn of the West [probably the estuary of the Geba River in modern-day Guinea-Bissau.] Therein there was a large island; within the island there was a sealike body of water containing a second island. [These were probably the Bissagos Islands.] Here we landed. And from it by daytime we saw nothing except forest; but at night we beheld many blazing fires and heard the sound of pipes and the rattle of cymbals and drums and an endless shouting. Thereupon fear seized on us, and our soothsayers advised us to quit the island.

"At once putting out to sea, we coasted past a blazing land filled with the odor of aromatic shrubs. And from it, fiery torrents cascaded into the sea. The earth was so hot that we could not see land.

"From there too, fear-stricken, we quickly sailed away, and for four days were carried along, beholding the countryside aflame by night and in the midst thereof a heaven-high fire greater than the rest that seemed to touch the stars. By day this showed as a lofty mountain that was called the Chariot of the Gods [presumed to be Mount Kakulima in the present-day country of Sierra Leone].

"Two days later, having passed these fiery torrents, we reached a bay called Horn of the South [probably Sherbro Sound]. In a corner of this there was an island like the former one, enclosing a body of water in which there was a second island. This was full of savages. Far the most of these were women with hairy bodies, whom our interpreters called gorillas. [Whether they were apes or humans, no one knows.] Although we pursued the men, we were unable to capture these, as all of them eluded us by climbing cliffs and warding us off with rocks; but we caught three of the women, who bit and scratched their captors and would not come along. So we slew and flayed them and brought their skins back to Carthage.

"Provisions failing, we sailed no farther."

With that terse sentence Hanno's document, the *Periplus*, comes to an end, and Admiral Hanno, along with his six African cities, vanish from history. Not for almost 2,000 years were European navigators to venture so far down the west African coast.

For about two centuries after the expedition of Hanno's fleet, Carthage maintained an inflexible blockade of the Pillars of Hercules. No foreign vessels were permitted to sail past them. Determined to protect its thriving colonies on the north shore of Africa and the south shore of Spain, Carthage crammed the thin strip

**"I once went aboard a Phoenician trader,"** *wrote the Greek historian Xenophon about 380 B.C. "What numbers of oars, stretchers, boathooks, marlines, and cleats for bringing the ship in and out of harbor! What numbers of shrouds, cables, hawsers, ropes, and tackle for sailing her! And what a vast quantity of provisions!" All equipment was kept in repair and neatly stowed in strictest order, he noticed, so that everything could be found in an instant. Here a Phoenician ship of the type Hanno probably sailed passes the Pillars of Hercules on her way into the mysterious Atlantic Ocean. Such ships may have reached America.*

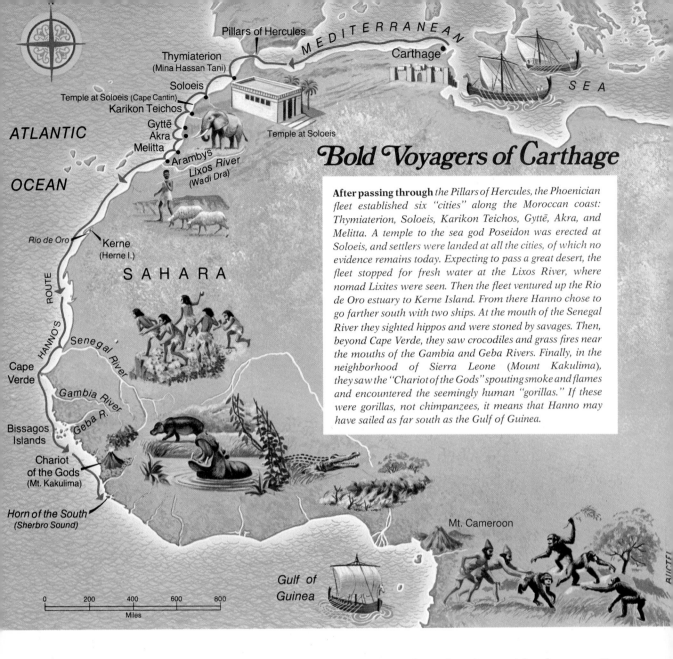

# Bold Voyagers of Carthage

**After passing through** the Pillars of Hercules, the Phoenician fleet established six "cities" along the Moroccan coast: Thymiaterion, Soloeis, Karikon Teichos, Gyttē, Akra, and Melitta. A temple to the sea god Poseidon was erected at Soloeis, and settlers were landed at all the cities, of which no evidence remains today. Expecting to pass a great desert, the fleet stopped for fresh water at the Lixos River, where nomad Lixites were seen. Then the fleet ventured up the Rio de Oro estuary to Kerne Island. From there Hanno chose to go farther south with two ships. At the mouth of the Senegal River they sighted hippos and were stoned by savages. Then, beyond Cape Verde, they saw crocodiles and grass fires near the mouths of the Gambia and Geba Rivers. Finally, in the neighborhood of Sierra Leone (Mount Kakulima), they saw the "Chariot of the Gods" spouting smoke and flames and encountered the seemingly human "gorillas." If these were gorillas, not chimpanzees, it means that Hanno may have sailed as far south as the Gulf of Guinea.

of water between Gibraltar and Algeciras with warships ready to attack on sight.

But at one time during this ancient era a Greek sailor named Pytheas slipped through the Strait of Gibraltar and explored the North Atlantic. There is some controversy as to when he made the voyage. It could have been during the fourth century B.C., when Carthage's attention was diverted by wars in Sicily. But it is more likely that it was during the Punic Wars of the third century B.C., when Rome had weakened Carthage's control of Gibraltar. Pytheas was from the powerful Greek colony of Massalia (modern-day Marseille, France), and Massalia was a loyal ally of Rome.

Because it was strategically situated near the mouth of the Rhone, bustling Massalia was a natural place for trading between the Mediterranean world and that re-

mote source of metal, amber, and furs known as Europe—"land of the setting sun." Copper and silver were available in Spain and Portugal, gold in Ireland, tin in Brittany and Cornwall, amber in Denmark, and the markets of Massalia were filled with these wares, brought in almost daily from the north by Celtic merchants. Where these dark-haired, taciturn people came from was a mystery to the Massalians. They spoke vaguely of an "island" honeycombed with tin and copper and of "beaches" where amber washed up in translucent chunks, so geographers deduced they must live along the northern shores of the Atlantic Ocean.

As Massalia grew and prospered, its demand for Celtic metals began to outstrip supply, and the Massalians started to talk about exploring a sea route to northern Europe, recalling stories of coastal trade as far north as Lisbon before the Carthaginian blockade. Bargeloads brought down the Rhone, they argued, were no substitutes for the huge cargoes that could be brought by ship via the Pillars of Hercules. If only that Phoenician stranglehold could be broken!

Massalia's chance came probably about 240 B.C., when its ally, Rome, had destroyed the naval power of

### Did the Phoenicians Find the New World?

Did Hanno reach North America? The inscribed stone (above), found on Cape Cod near Bourne, Massachusetts, 300 years ago, may prove he did. Dr. Barry Fell, a Harvard zoology professor, believes it is a land claim left by Hanno, written in a language he identifies as Iberian-Punic. The Bourne Stone measures 45 by 5 by 15 inches and is similar to several other stones discovered along the Atlantic coast of North America.

Carthage. Then Pytheas sailed his ship past the Pillars of Hercules without difficulty, explored the North Atlantic, and returned home to write a book about it, entitled simply *The Ocean*. The stories he told, of seas thick as jelly and a land where the sun revolved horizontally, were so fantastic that most men disbelieved them for 2,000 years.

Unfortunately, not a single copy of *The Ocean* survives. Yet, in its time, the book created such a sensation that many ancient writers referred to it and quoted some passages from it. Modern historians have patched together these colorful fragments like a mosaic, filling in the blanks with enlightened guessing; and so, bit by bit, the narrative of Pytheas has been restored. Allowing for some contrary opinions, it goes like this:

Late one spring about the year 240 B.C., Pytheas left Massalia in a 75- to 100-ton trading ship. The citizens of Massalia probably favored this expedition because they were particularly interested in the sources of amber and of tin, so vital for making bronze. They also wanted markets for their own goods. Pytheas himself was more than a practical mariner and commercial entrepreneur. He was also an astronomer and geographer, capable of making careful observations, calculations, and conclusions.

Pytheas' ship was probably a solid, tubby vessel, making up in stability what she lacked in speed. The mariner was in no hurry: Indeed, his whole voyage seems to have been so leisurely one can only assume he

was enjoying his opportunity to explore. He was accompanied by about 25 sailors and—possibly—a Carthaginian pilot lured aboard with bribes.

For a while he cruised west and then south past the familiar flatness of Gaul, until the Pyrenees rose jaggedly to starboard. After a brief visit to the Greek colony of Emporion (now Ampurias, Spain), Pytheas sailed on, hugging the rocky shoreline and keeping a watch for Carthaginian warships. Abruptly, his course veered to the west. The snowy summits of the Sierra Nevada appeared, and soon a mass of limestone began to rise out of the sea. It continued to rise until it seemed to wall off half the sky. Pytheas had reached the European Pillar of Hercules (Gibraltar Rock).

Anchoring in its shadow until night fell, he handed over command to his pilot, and the slow, silent journey through the strait began. The Greek crew tensely watched the square sail of the ship strain against the easterly wind that filled it. Swiftly, the craft glided over the darkly foaming water that rushed beneath the painted eyes of her prow. Dawn found Pytheas' ship far out to sea, rocking on the cold swell of the Atlantic.

Having passed through the Pillars, Pytheas began sailing to the northwest and soon reached Gades (Cádiz). Five days later, he rounded the headland at Cape St. Vincent, Portugal, and began his journey due north, generally staying within sight of land. For navigation, he had only the stars to guide him, but his knowledge of astronomy proved useful. Once he had rounded the northwestern tip of the Iberian Peninsula, he got his bearings by measuring the latitude with an astrolabe. When he realized that he was consistently at the same latitude as Massalia (roughly 43° N), he knew that he was sailing due east! Only when he was less than 400 miles from Massalia did the coastline turn north again. Thus did Pytheas discover that Iberia is a peninsula, attached to Europe only by the few-hundred-mile strip of the Pyrenees.

Making perhaps 50 miles a day (a slow speed even in

**Increased trade** *in the Mediterranean world led to the development of coinage in the seventh century B.C. Each city issued coins with its own symbol. The one here, minted about 500 B.C. in Zancle, a Greek colony in Sicily, shows a dolphin in the city's harbor. The dotted line indicates a breakwater.*

those times), the Greek explorer cruised peacefully along the Atlantic littoral of Gaul (France), by now lush with summer. At Corbilo (St. Nazaire), a Celtic port at the mouth of the Loire River, he was able to replenish his stocks of food and water. He would have had no difficulty with communication here, since the Celtic speech had been heard in Massalian markets for centuries and Pytheas probably spoke it.

The bulge of Brittany led him west again, until he

**This island** (*St. Michael's Mount*) *off the Cornish coast of England was an international center for the tin trade long before Pytheas' visit. Foreign merchants preferred to trade on islands off the wooded coast, fearing the wild British mainland tribes.*

rounded a spectacular promontory that he named Cape Kabaion (Pointe du Raz). Beyond it lay the forlorn, foam-fringed island of Uxisame (Ile d'Ouessant), off the westernmost point of France.

Pytheas now decided to quit the comforting shores of the continent and sail out to sea. Possibly, he had learned from the sailors of Corbilo of the ocean trade routes to Cornwall's tin mines. As the continent of Europe disappeared from view behind him, Pytheas was intrigued to note that summer daylight in these northern latitudes lasted a full 16 hours.

A few days after leaving Brittany, the Massalians saw a dark green line staining the horizon ahead of them. They had discovered the island of Britain. Drawing nearer, Pytheas found it to be a wild place of forests and swamps. The air was loud with an indescribable medley of bird song. For a while, he could see no signs of human life. Then, on the summits of grassy hills that rose here and there above the vegetation, he made out a few villages surrounded by circular walls. Dark-haired, long-headed men and women were already emerging and making their way down to the seashore.

When they hailed him, Pytheas was delighted to hear the familiar sounds of Celtic. They told him that their part of the island was called Kantion (Kent). Asked about neighboring regions, they said that hills rich with tin lay to the southwest. Pytheas sailed on to investigate and came upon the rocky headland of Bolerium (Land's End, Cornwall). Its inland slopes were scarred with hundreds of mines, which were a novelty to Pytheas. Fascinated, the Greek mariner went ashore and was welcomed by the Cornish miners. His description of that British industry has come down to us through the Greek historian Diodorus:

"They [the natives of Britain] have a clever process for extracting tin from its bed, which is of rock with earthy veins. Along these veins they dig galleries. . . . After they have smelted and refined the tin, they hammer it into the shape of knucklebones and transport it

to an adjoining island named Iktis [St. Michael's Mount in Penzance Bay]. Having waited until the ebb-tide lays bare the intervening channel, they bring entire loads of tin across on wagons."

As he stood watching the ingots being piled ready for pickup by Celtic ships from Gaul, Pytheas realized that this was the source of the tin that had been finding its way to Massalia for centuries.

The Britons proved to be friendly and "very mannerly." Pytheas seems to have accepted some hospitality, because he wrote approving descriptions of their fermented barley liquor (beer) and honey wine (mead). He also remarked, as generations of subsequent visitors have done, that Britain was densely inhabited and that its weather was terrible.

How much of Britain Pytheas visited is not known—one ancient writer says he explored all of it on foot—but we next hear of him sailing north through the Irish Sea. Curiously enough, Pytheas does not seem to have visited Ireland, although he must have seen its emerald hills on his port bow. Maybe he had heard Celtic ru-

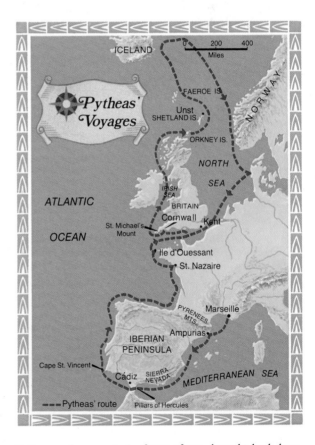

**Pytheas, whose route is shown above,** *brought back long-sought information about the "Tin Islands" (England) and the northern sea. In the fifth century B.C., the Greek historian Herodotus had lamented that he could get no firsthand account of these places, for "it cannot be disputed that tin and amber do come to us from what one might call the ends of the earth."*

## A Curtain of Fixed Stars and Moving Planets: How the Ancients Measured Their Universe

Thousands of years ago the earth was thought to be a flat disk encircled by the ocean and domed by the sky. Generations of early observers, particularly Egyptians and Babylonians, watched the moving curtain of stars for omens. While their study of the heavenly bodies was remarkably accurate (especially since they had no telescopes), they did not question the idea of a flat earth and arched sky. Then, in the sixth century B.C., the Greek philosopher Pythagoras asserted that the earth was a sphere, though he believed it to be the center of the universe around which the heavenly bodies traveled. At first ridiculed, his idea later won the support of the respected thinker Aristotle. It seemed to explain the roundness of the earth's shadow on the moon during a lunar eclipse and the changing pattern of stars in the sky when going north or south.

Men still believed the earth formed the center of the universe, when in 280 B.C. Aristarchus of Samos put forth a disturbing theory that was forgotten for more than a 1,000 years. He said that it was in fact the sun around which the earth and all other planets moved.

In the second century B.C., the Greek scientist Eratosthenes estimated the earth's circumference, using a gnomon, a device much like a simple sundial. Eratosthenes observed that when the summer sun was directly over Aswan,

Egypt, the pin of the gnomon cast no shadow, while in Alexandria, about 500 miles north, the shadow fell at an angle of one-fiftieth of the gnomon's circle. He concluded that the earth's circumference was 50 times the distance between the cities—25,000 miles—the most accurate measurement until modern times. He also made an important mistake: Knowing that there were tides on the shores of both Europe and Asia, he assumed that only one sea lay between.

It was Ptolemy of Alexandria, in the second century A.D., who compiled data and developed geographical concepts (though many were misconceptions) that became articles of faith for the next 1,400 years. One important error he passed on was to assume the earth was smaller than it is and its land surface vaster. This view underestimated the width of the ocean, which he, like Era-

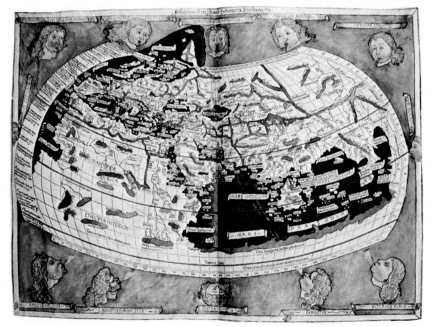

mors, popular at the time, that Irish aboriginals were "wild" and ate human flesh. Sailing ever northward, he watched the trees of Scotland yielding to heather, heather to grass, grass to bare rock. Finally, Britain, as Europe had done before it, disappeared from sight.

Courageously, Pytheas pushed north through increasingly gray and chilly seas. At times his sluggish Greek boat was pounded by 60-foot waves; still he would not stop. The Orkney Islands loomed up to starboard, then, after a long interval, the Shetlands. Putting in at Unst Island, the northernmost of the Shetlands, Pytheas now measured daylight at 19 hours. He had passed the then unbelievable latitude of 60° N.

The shepherds of Unst, who welcomed their spray-soaked visitors with hot food and no doubt sold them sheepskin jackets, told Pytheas that yet another island—a large one—lay to the north six days away, on the very edges of the Frozen Sea that marked the end of the world. Its name, they said, was Thule, and they "pointed to the sleeping place of the sun."

Pytheas of Massalia then went on to make his greatest—and most mysterious—discovery. To this day scholars argue over whether Thule was Iceland, one of the Faeroes, or even part of Norway. All that is certain is that the Greek explorer reached it, after sailing northward for six days, and that he stayed there a considerable time. While exploring this place, the "ultimate" as he called it, the man of the Mediterranean observed a phenomenon that must have filled him with awe, the midnight sun.

References by others to this "ever-shining fire" and the island's "immense summit" seem to indicate that Thule was indeed the volcanic outcrop of Iceland.

Before turning south and sailing for home, the insatiable explorer ventured another 100 miles north, across the Arctic Circle and into "regions in which there was neither land properly so-called nor sea nor sky, but a sort of mixture of all three, like a jellyfish, in which earth and sea and everything are held suspended in a sort of compound of all the elements, upon

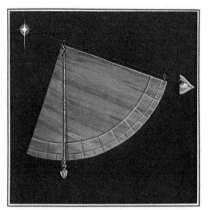

tosthenes, believed reached around the rest of the globe. This notion was ultimately the basis of Columbus' optimistic belief that only one 2,500-mile ocean lay between eastern Asia and Europe.

Ptolemy did contribute much to geographical method by placing many cities of the Mediterranean area in relation to arbitrary, but usable, lines of latitude and longitude into which he divided the world. As late as the 1500's maps based on his specifications were still being published. The copy at left is from a German book of the fifteenth century.

The instruments available to ancient scientists were usually simple. Nevertheless, they helped establish our knowledge of the universe. The most important known ones were the astrolabe, the armillary sphere, and the quadrant.

The earliest astrolabe is thought to have originated with the Babylonians in the fifth or fourth century B.C. It consisted of a ring with its edge marked off in degrees and a pointer fixed to its center. By sighting along the pointer, the altitude of the sun or stars could be read in degrees above the horizon, giving a basis for reckoning latitude. Astrolabes remained in use until after A.D. 1600. The one shown at left is the oldest astrolabe found to date, believed to be of Greek make from about A.D. 250.

As early as 300 B.C., astronomers began adding refinements to the astrolabe, such as a cross-ring representing the Equator and other movable rings, which allowed them to map the stars, predict eclipses, and correct the crude calendars of the day. The elaborate instruments that resulted are called armillary spheres. A picture of one is shown in the 17th-century illustration below.

Before 200 B.C., the mariner's astrolabe began to be supplemented by the

quadrant (above)—actually a quarter of a circular astrolabe—which was fitted with a plumbbob and two pinhole sights along the side that had to be alined between the eye and the star. The star's altitude could be read where the plumbline cut the scale on the curved side. More accurate than a simple astrolabe of the same size, it was used and unchanged until 1595, after which a series of modifications transformed it into the modern navigator's sextant.

Despite the relative lack of practical navigational instruments and charts, mariners were finding their way by the sun, stars, winds, and currents. By Ptolemy's time they were sailing from Africa to Asia. Methods of calculating latitude were developed by then, but the mystery of longitude did not fully clear up until the 18th century, following the invention of the telescope and the chronometer.

---

which one can neither walk nor sail."

This surrealistic description, which for centuries gave Pytheas the reputation of an imaginative liar, has been convincingly explained by the modern Arctic explorer Fridtjof Nansen. What Pytheas encountered, he says, was a combination of "ice sludge," formed by grinding floes, and the characteristic fog such sludge produces. It is a measure of Pytheas' supreme courage that he continued exploring until he could "neither walk nor sail."

On his way home Pytheas crossed over into the North Sea and discovered another source of European merchandise, the "Amber Isle" of Sanland, off the coast of Denmark. By now it was probably early autumn, but Pytheas returned to Britain (it seems) to complete its exploration. No more is known about his great voyage, but he must have reached home safely and once again dropped anchor in the harbor of Massalia.

Did the Massalians believe Pytheas when he announced he had voyaged more than 7,000 miles or when he described a land where the sun shone at midnight, in a region Greeks "knew" was dark and uninhabitable? In any case, no other Mediterranean explorers or merchants seem to have followed in his wake for several hundred years, whether because the Carthaginians reimposed their blockade or because no one else felt the journeys were worth the risks. Within a few generations, Pytheas' account was being discounted as a sailor's yarn.

Yet not by all. During this era the Greeks were establishing geography as a science, and two of the most learned Greek scientists, Eratosthenes and Hipparchus, credited Pytheas for his information. Later generations granted him priority in such matters as his observation of the pole stars or the relationship between the moon and the tides. Only recently has Pytheas of Massalia been accorded his rightful place among great explorers. With neither maps nor compass to guide him, he singlehandedly pushed the boundaries of knowledge to the Arctic Circle!

*Hanno and Pytheas*

**As early as the first century A.D.,** *the Roman historian Tacitus described the ancestors of the Vikings as well armed and skilled at sailing ships "with a prow at each end." Seven centuries later the Norse warriors slashed through the seas in their longships to pillage the British Isles and continental Europe. Eager for farmland as well as plunder, they were especially drawn by the green fields of Ireland. They ravaged the country, but they also founded towns, including Dublin. In the following years Vikings reached Baghdad and Istanbul, where they traded furs, amber, and blond slaves for oriental silks and Arab silver. Many settled down in Asia and Europe, but others turned westward into the Atlantic, discovering and colonizing Iceland and Greenland. Eventually, almost 500 years before Columbus, a group led by Leif Ericsson reached North America and allegedly established a colony in Newfoundland. A manuscript illumination by English monks of the 12th century (far left) shows typical Viking raiders. Monasteries such as Lindisfarne (below), on England's coast, were especially vulnerable to these marauders. The beautiful ship (near left), found in Oseberg, Norway, in 1904, was built for some ceremonial occasion, perhaps a Viking chief's burial, and probably never sailed on the high seas.*

*Chapter Two. In the Middle Ages the Vikings spring from their Scandinavian homeland in search of land and booty, striking a hammerblow at Europe and Asia from the north. In the course of their widespread conquests, they discover and abandon the forested border of the New World. But the memory of their adventures remains in their folk sagas.*

# Islands in the West:
# The Vikings Seek New Lands

*After years of controversy, it is now generally accepted that the Vikings did indeed reach the coast of North America sometime around the year A.D. 1000. Though the Greenland Vikings under Leif Ericsson deserted their New World settlement after only a decade or so, the history of their great discovery was preserved in the old verses of* The Greenlanders' Saga. *In the past century the saga has come to be seen as evidence of an exploration that was unknown to the great navigators of Columbus' time. Though they set foot on the edge of North America and probably built a settlement, the Vikings, like many early explorers, assumed that they had encountered another island, like Greenland or Iceland. Neither they nor any of the earliest explorers of the New World could imagine what they had discovered.*

A June morning, A.D. 793, English sunshine bathes Lindisfarne Holy Island, just off the wild shores of Northumbria. Black-robed monks potter quietly about their hilltop monastery, sluicing out the kitchen, polishing the sacramental silverware, tossing bales of hay down to their cattle. Chores over, they retire to their cells to read, write, and meditate. The cold blue expanse of the North Sea surrounds the island, but the busy monks do not glance at it. They do not see the bright, square sails rise over the horizon as the dragonships glide toward shore. The serpentine prows are pointing directly at Lindisfarne, and they are moving fast across the sparkling sea.

Inside the monastery there is no sound except the click of rosary beads, the soft scratching of quills on parchment. Then, from the beach below, comes the hiss of a falling sword, followed by the agonized bellow of a dying cow. A harsh voice shouts orders in a foreign language. The monks rush out and gaze upon a sight that freezes their blood. The high-prowed longships are drawn up on the sand, and a hundred or more bearded men are leaping from them. Dressed in leather breeches and mail armor tunics, they brandish iron swords and axes. With military precision they encircle the monastery and begin to scramble rapidly up the slopes toward it.

By early afternoon the wealthiest monastery of Britain has been stripped of its treasures, and pools of blood coagulate on the bare floor of the sanctuary. Every barrel of Lindisfarne's famous mead has been rolled out of the brewhouse. Every cow has been speared, hacked into portable chunks, and stowed aboard the long, black ships. Without a backward glance, the marauders shove off into the surf and sail for the horizon. There will be feasting and drinking on the North Sea tonight.

The news of the rape of Lindisfarne sent waves of shock throughout the Christian world. "Never before in Britain," wrote the ecclesiastical scholar Alcuin, "has such a terror appeared as this we have now suffered at the hands of the heathen. Nor was it thought possible that such an inroad from the sea could be made." It was some time before the identity of the heathen was discovered. They were, to use their own word, *vikingr—*"pirates and traders." Worshipers of the warlike god Odin, they came from Scandinavia, a vast, cold region somewhere north of Europe, somewhere east of Britain—a region that, despite its size, had run out of tillable land by the middle of the eighth century. So the frustrated farmers and trappers turned pirate and began to explore the North Sea.

A year after their attack on Lindisfarne, the Norsemen struck again, at the nearby monastery of Jarrow, and followed up with profitable raids on the coasts of Scotland, Wales, and Ireland. By the early ninth century the North Sea and English Channel were swarming with Viking ships. "These pagans come like stinging hornets," wrote one chronicler, "and spread on all sides

It was along such deep, *narrow fiords as this one (Geiranger) in Norway that the Vikings originally lived. In time, increased population and limited arable land forced many to migrate far beyond Scandinavia. Pillage and conquest gained them a fearsome reputation. Indeed, the name* Viking *is Norse for "pirate."*

In the year 930, *Icelandic Vikings held the first session of their althing, or "parliament," now the oldest democratic body in the world. Outdoors on the grassy plain edging the lake in the background above, disputes were settled and laws were voted on by all landowners long before a proper meetinghouse was built.*

like fearful wolves." Fleets of 40 or 60 vessels, and occasionally many more, ravaged the shores of Europe. Some enterprising pirates passed through the Pillars of Hercules into the Mediterranean Sea. Others penetrated as far as Paris by sailing their shallow-drafted ships up the Seine. The defenseless Parisians watched helplessly as the blond visitors camped on midstream islands and feasted on stolen cattle. Occasionally, the Vikings would impale a live hostage on a spit and roast him along with their beef: They were not cannibals, but they knew the power of terror.

Scandinavia prospered with the rich hauls of gold, silver, clothes, and livestock brought back after raids, and a romance began to attach itself to the seagoing life. To "go Viking" promised a young man adventure, wealth, and fame. Successful pirates were dubbed with heroic nicknames, such as Sword-Leif, Eric Bloodax, and Thorfinm Skull-splitter. Tales of their exploits were relayed in the form of "sagas"—memorized stories told through the centuries until scribes transformed them into written history.

But even as they plundered and raped, the pirates began to long for the things they could not carry away: the apple orchards of France, the wheatfields of England, the rich pastures of Ireland. Land hunger gave rise to another breed of emigrant Vikings, Norsemen who wanted not to steal but to settle. They established themselves by force in areas from which they could not

easily be dislodged and proved to be surprisingly peaceable when left alone. Gradually, they blended into the neighboring populations and put their bloody history behind them.

The larger of these Norse communities were in the upper Seine Valley (Normandy) and along the eastern coast of England, while smaller settlements were established in Ireland, the Orkneys, the Shetlands, and the Faeroes. Swedish Vikings known as Rus sailed down the Volga and settled in a vast country to which they gave their name: Russia. By the mid-ninth century all the available lands of northern Europe had been settled. And still there were Vikings with land hunger.

About 860 some storm-blown sailors reported that a large, mountainous, and apparently uninhabited island lay seven days west of Norway. Although its heights were snowy, they praised the land enthusiastically and said that fertile plains, birchwoods, and fields of blueberries lay along its southern shore.

A major reconnaissance expedition with three ships was soon dispatched from Norway. Its commander was a Viking named Floki Vilgerdarson. On board ship with Floki were two freemen, Thorolf and Herjolf, and Faxi, a Hebridean. "Floki had taken three ravens to sea with him. When he loosed the first, it flew aft astern; the second flew high into the air, then back to the ship; the third flew straight ahead in the direction in which they found land. . . . 'This must be a big country we have found,' said Faxi. 'There are big rivers here.' "

The explorers cruised west along a summer-green coast shining with fiords. Inland, white mountains thrust upward like a solid wall. Raven-Floki rounded a volcanic promontory and anchored in a fiord "full of fish and seals." Here he established his base camp, but "because of the fishing they overlooked the need to make hay, and all their livestock perished during the winter. The spring was very cold. Floki walked up onto a high mountain, and north beyond the mountain could see a fiord full of drift ice, so they called the country Island, 'Iceland,' the name by which it has been known ever since. . . . When men inquired about the country, Raven-Floki gave it a bad name, Herjolf had both good and bad to say of it, while Thorolf swore that butter dripped from every blade of grass."

Thorolf's report was enough for the cramped peasants of Norway, who began to arrive en masse in the 870's, bringing their belongings and noisy cargoes of pigs, sheep, and cattle with them. They settled along the southeastern fiords and spread across the lush grassland around Reykjavik, "Smoky Bay." Prospectors were startled to find the nearby hills inhabited by Christian hermits. "But later they went away," says *The Book of the Icelanders*, "because they were not prepared to live here in company with heathen men. They left behind Irish books, bells, and croziers, from which it can be seen that they were Irishmen."

At first, Iceland's virgin spaces intoxicated the new arrivals, and it became necessary to limit their claims. It was arranged "that no one should settle land more widely than he and his crew could carry fire round in one day." And a woman could claim only as much land as "a two-year-old heifer . . . might be led around on a spring day between the rising and the setting of the sun." But by 930 there were close to 20,000 settlers, and all the arable land on the island was occupied.

Among the latecomers were a peppery Norwegian called Thorvald and his teenage son, Eric. They came reluctantly, exiled from Norway "because of some killings." Eric was nicknamed the Red because of his flaming russet hair and beard.

The pair settled on the bare northwestern peninsula of Hornstrandir and hacked out a miserable living fishing and hunting for seals. Here they heard from

**A grim king** *and an alarmed queen are pieces from a 12th-century walrus-ivory chess set found on the Isle of Lewis, off Scotland's northwest coast. The game, which probably originated in India, was a favorite pastime of the warlike Norsemen, and many chessmen have been found on Viking sites.*

neighbors of the remarkable discovery made some years before by an Icelander, Gunnbjorn Ulf-Krakason:

Sometime between 900 and 930 Gunnbjorn had apparently been returning home from a trip to Norway when a terrific storm blew him past Iceland and out into the western sea. Before fighting his way back, he came upon a group of "skerries" (rocky islets) and saw through curtains of sea spray a white blur that might have been a new land.

Young Eric never forgot this story. He married and settled on better land among his wife's kin in Haukadal. There he became involved in a blood feud and again committed murder. The Vikings, though brutal in conquest, condemned killings in their settlements, and Eric was summarily expelled from Haukadal. He eventually moved to Breidafjord, where he killed two of his neighbor's sons in a quarrel. As a result, he was exiled from Iceland for three years.

Not daring to return to Norway, the enterprising redhead made good use of the time. He decided to seek out Gunnbjorn's white land and see whether it could be colonized. In the early summer of 982, he headed his *knarr* ("ship") west into the uncharted ocean. With the exuberant self-confidence of a born explorer, he took with him about 30 would-be settlers, including his own family and neighbors as well as a menagerie of farm animals. Clearly, he did not doubt that he would find land and that it would be habitable.

For about four days Eric sailed due west, crossing 450 miles of cold water before sighting the coast of the world's largest island. But alas, it was as white and sterile as Gunnbjorn had reported: a dazzling mass of glaciers, stony mountains, and snow, good only for walruses. Disappointed, Eric followed the coastline south "to discover whether the land was habitable in that direction."

The whiteness came to an end as Eric rounded a

### The Mysterious Viking Monuments of Gotland Island

The carved Viking stone at left, dating from the eighth century, is one of several found on Gotland, an island near Sweden. The scenes, including battles, unidentified rituals, and a longship carrying Viking warriors, are from Norse mythology, but their meaning has not yet been determined. The lapidary work shows the influence of contemporary Christian art in Europe. Cut in bas-relief as well as carved, the limestone was probably brightly painted. The stone shown here stands 11 feet high.

**The Viking "knarr"** (above) was the stocky working cousin of the long and elegant striped-sailed dragonship (right background) used for war. It was probably with such boats that the Norsemen made their voyages of discovery and kept frequent contact between Scandinavia, Iceland, and Greenland. Mention of them in the sagas had enabled scholars to guess about their design, but it was not until 1962 that archeologists found, patiently salvaged, and reconstructed the crushed remains of a knarr found in the Roskilde Fjord, northwest of Copenhagen, Denmark.

The sturdy cargo vessel, which now rests in the Roskilde museum, has been carbon-dated at about A.D. 1000. It is 54 feet long and nearly 15 feet in the beam—much shorter and a little narrower than the warships. The Roskilde knarr has neatly beveled and overlapping planks of pine and a keel and ribs of oak caulked with animal hair soaked in tar. Both stem and stern curve gently, and there is no terrifying figurehead because

it was designed for commerce, not war. Unlike the longships, it was dependent almost entirely upon its sail (a large, woolen square) and had a fixed mast. The rigging was of plaited walrus hide. The crew, stationed upon the decks fore and aft, could sit and row if necessary. The steerboard, or rudder, was on the right side. The vessels that carried settlers to Iceland and Greenland, and then to North America, may have been larger than the Roskilde ship and may have been capable of carrying horses and other livestock in the hold. They probably had a halfdeck for protection from rain like the ship in this illustration, and buckets were on hand for bailing out water. On those long, dreary voyages the Vikings lacked the comfort of a fire—they had only cold food and drink and snuggled into their sleeping bags to keep warm and dry. Offsetting the discomforts, perhaps, was the remarkable seaworthiness of the knarr. Such sturdy ships were capable of sailing from Iceland to Newfoundland in extremely heavy seas for weeks at a time.

crenellated cape (Cape Farewell) at the southern tip of the great island and suddenly saw patches of green. He landed and formed a temporary base camp at Eriksey, near the entrance to Eriksfjord, and spent the next three years hunting, fishing, and birding. Summers he went exploring, finding peaceful fiord after peaceful fiord, each one surrounded by green pastureland thick with flowers. Birds sang and fish flashed by in water warmed by the northern currents of the Gulf Stream, although more whiteness loomed in the interior.

At the end of this three-year exile Eric returned home to Iceland, but he promptly got into trouble again. He needed elbowroom, and his new land could provide it for him. Deciding to promote a colony there, Eric "called the country he had discovered Greenland, for he argued that men would be drawn to go there if the land had an attractive name."

It was a shrewd inspiration. Eric had no difficulty recruiting settlers, for times were bad in Iceland: There was not enough land to go around, and there had been a cruel famine. In 986, 25 ships set out, but only 14, with about 450 people, arrived in Greenland. The others did not complete the difficult crossing; they "were forced back and some perished."

The red-bearded discoverer established himself at Brattahlid, near the head of the lovely inlet known to this day as Eriksfjord. Here he raised three sons and a daughter, ate and drank hugely, and presided over the affairs of the colonists whose farms lined the fiords along 120 miles of coast. A few years later a new settlement was begun farther north, and eventually the Greenland colony numbered some 3,000 souls.

His settlers, however, found life harder than they expected. Winters were cold in a country where trees grew a stunted 10 feet high, if they grew at all. The sheltered fiords, for all their beauty, provided only the thinnest strips of grasslands.

Once again the Vikings began to search for more land. Men sailed the western coast and climbed the snowy heights of Greenland, but all they found was ice.

In 986 a Norwegian trader named Bjarni Herjolfsson, sailing from Iceland to Greenland to join his father for the winter, was swept off course. Drifting southwest, he discovered a "flat country . . . covered with woods." Realizing this was not Greenland, he turned to the northeast and sailed back, passing more land before reaching his destination. But when he reached Greenland, the news of his adventure invited someone hungry for wealth, fame, and land to follow his course. In 1001 Eric the Red's son and heir, Leif, announced that he planned to set out on a most ambitious voyage of exploration. His objective was the flat, wooded land that Bjarni had glimpsed 15 years earlier.

A rugged young man in his twenties, Leif Ericsson was already a formidable sailor and a natural leader. *The Greenlanders' Saga* describes him as "big and strong, of striking appearance, shrewd, and in every

respect a temperate, fair-dealing man." Thirty-five men agreed to sail with him in the seasoned *knarr* he had purchased from Bjarni Herjolfsson. As a gesture of respect before leaving Greenland, Leif invited his father to take command of the expedition. The old man agreed, but on the way down to the ship he fell off his horse and was badly hurt. "It is not in my destiny," said Eric the Red, "to discover more lands than this. . . " So he watched his son put out to sea and vanish into the midsummer haze.

*The Greenlanders' Saga* tells nothing of the long, dull days Leif and his crew spent as their ship plowed westward through the green sea. Only a few of the crew had been on Bjarni's earlier voyage and had some knowledge of their destination. Leif visited Baffin Island en route, but he "could see no grass there" and called it Helluland, "Flatstone Land," before sailing on.

A few more days at sea, sipping beer or mead and eating cold provisions; a few more nights tossing under the halfdeck in leather sleeping bags; then, silently and slowly, the mainland of the North American continent slid into view. The indescribable immensity of its size, wealth, and promise remained hidden beyond the forested shore. The saga of Leif Ericsson routinely records that first landing of Europeans on the American continent: ". . . They sailed to land, cast anchor, then put off a boat and went ashore. The country was flat and covered with forest, with extensive white sands wherever they went, and shelving gently to the sea. 'This land,'

---

### Effective Instruments for Viking Navigation

Norsemen could navigate by the stars at night, but during the day they may have relied on the *sol-skuggafjol* or "sun shadow-board" (below), a miniature gnomon or pin fixed upright in the center of a wooden disk scored with concentric circles. The disk floated in a tub of water to keep level. As the Vikings sailed north or south, the pin's shadow at noon lengthened or shortened accordingly. On reaching a particular place, they noted the circle that the tip of the shadow reached on the scored disk. When returning there, they sailed north or south until the pin's shadow reached that same circle again and then sailed east or west along the latitude until they reached the desired port. In a heavy fog the Vikings would be lost and would have to wait for the sun to reappear to get their direction.

At a later period they may also have used a bearing dial. The one above is based upon part of a dial found in Greenland, constructed about 1200. From the shadow of the pin, a navigator could find due north at midday and check his course against the compass marks on the dial.

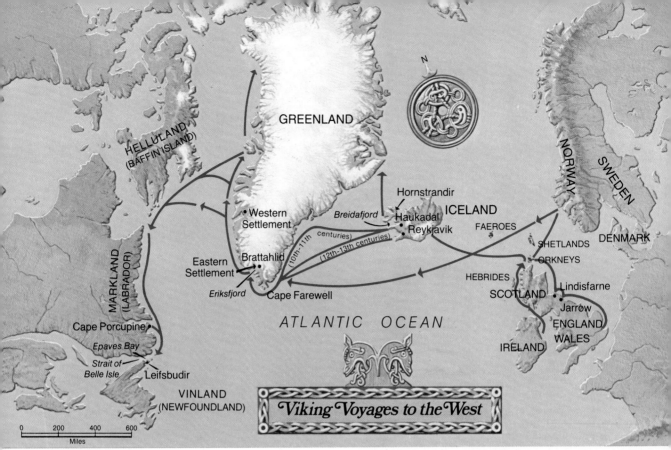

Viking Voyages to the West

**Sailing from their homeland** *about A.D. 800, the Vikings ransacked the British Isles and swept into continental Europe. Later boldly turning west, they reached the Faeroes and, by 870, Iceland, which the Norsemen settled. In 986 Eric the Red took colonizers from Iceland to Greenland. Others quickly followed, many sailing directly there from Norway, clustering along the great island's southwestern coast. Then, in 1001, Leif Ericsson, hearing talk of new land to the west, sailed to Baffin Island and down Labrador's coast to Newfoundland, the "Vinland" of the sagas. In 1965 a storm of controversy arose over the publication of the "Vinland Map" (right) as the earliest map to show part of the New World. Supposedly based on Viking cartography, it includes Vinland. The map has since been proved a forgery by analysis of its paper and ink. Yet few scholars dispute that the Vikings did reach the New World.*

said Leif, 'shall be given a name in accordance with its nature, and be called Markland, "Wood Land."'"

Something about the vastness of this evergreen wilderness (the coast of Labrador flanking Cape Porcupine at 54° N) seems to have frightened the Vikings, because "they got back down to the ship as fast as they could." Sailing out to sea again, Leif Ericsson set a course south and two days later visited an island (Belle Isle) covered with dewy grass. According to *The Greenlanders' Saga,* "They set their hands to the dew, then carried it to their mouths, and thought they had never known anything so sweet as that was." According to some scholars, what these men wanted was pastureland for their cattle, and now they had found some of a

quality beyond their experience. South of the island, across a strait of sparkling water (Strait of Belle Isle), lay the landmass of Newfoundland. Its low green hills were so seductive to the sea-weary explorers that Leif ran his ship aground on some shoals in Epaves Bay in his hurry to get there. Undeterred, he rowed to shore in one of the ship's small boats and found a perfect camping site: a crescent beach, a broad grassy meadow, and a lake-fed stream full of salmon "bigger than they had ever seen before." Leif liked the site so well he decided to spend the winter there and ordered the construction of a great house, or hall, to be built of turf, timber, and sod, like the Viking houses in Greenland. The settlement was called Leifsbudir.

Once the hall was finished, the Vikings began to reconnoiter the countryside. According to *The Greenlanders' Saga*, Tyrkir the German discovered wild grapes growing at some distance from the camp. Leif delightedly ordered his crew to bring in a harvest of the fruit. The Vikings were encamped several degrees north of North America's grape belt, but perhaps in that warmer century vines were able to thrive there. Or, more likely, the "grapes" were wild berries. The Vikings spent the mild winter fishing and logging, and "in the spring they made ready and sailed away." Behind them foamed a towboat full of "grapes." As Newfoundland disappeared from sight, "Leif gave the land a name in accordance with the good things they found in it, calling it Vinland, 'Wineland'; after which they sailed out to sea and had a good wind until they sighted Greenland and the mountains under the glaciers."

The next year Leif's brother Thorvald sailed back to Vinland and wintered at Leifsbudir. When summer arrived, he and his companions explored the Labrador coast, and they came upon a headland so lovely that Thorvald wanted to make his home there. But on the shore the Norsemen encountered native Americans for the first time: Napping under their canoes were nine Indians. The Vikings quickly killed all but one. He escaped, and soon great numbers of Indians paddled into the inlet and attacked in retaliation. Thorvald was the only casualty—he died from arrow wounds. The following spring his friends returned to Greenland.

Nevertheless, in 1009 a serious attempt to colonize Vinland was made by Thorfinn Karlsefni with 250 men and women from Greenland, including Karlsefni's bride, Gudrid, and Eric the Red's formidable daughter, Freydis. Soon fights broke out with the Skraelings, as the Greenlanders called the American natives, who were probably Beokuk Indians. In a pitched battle the fierce and courageous Freydis grabbed a sword and "pulled out her breasts from under her shift and slapped the sword on them, at which the Skraelings took fright, and ran off to their boats. . ." As time went by and the Indians continued their harassment, it became apparent that Karlsefni's colony was doomed in a land where grain sowed itself, fruit grew wild, and trenches dug at high tide quickly filled with fish. In the summer of 1013, Karlsefni and the other colonists abandoned the colony and sailed for home, taking with them Gudrid's son, Snorri, the first white child to be born in America.

Freydis inspired and directed the last attempt at settlement in Vinland. But once there, she channeled her energies into treachery against her partners, two brothers of Icelandic descent. Her schemes culminated in her goading her pliant husband into murdering them, while Freydis herself singlehandedly massacred the five women in their party. This gruesome episode brought the settlement at Leifsbudir to an end. We hear no more of Vinland in the Viking sagas after that.

Greenland, too, proved to be a doomed colony. After 1200 the North Atlantic weather grew steadily colder, and frozen seas began to isolate that great island. Abandoned by Europe and succumbing to malnutrition, epidemics, Eskimo invasions, and the effects of intermarriage, the descendants of Eric the Red dwindled in number. Finally, toward the end of the 15th century, the last member of the colony faced his lonely death. By then the Age of the Vikings was long since over, and other explorers were sailing the northern seas. John Davis, sailing past the tip of Greenland in 1586, saw no traces of white men, "nor saw anything, save only gripes [vultures], ravens, and small birds, such as larks and linnets."

**On this invitingly green** *point of land* (*above*), *near the Newfoundland hamlet of L'Anse aux Meadows, Leif Ericsson and his companions are believed to have built their Vinland settlement, Leifsbudir. Large wooden sheds now shelter the sites of their houses to protect the excavation. The largest building (50 by 75 feet) was probably a Viking longhouse and was flanked by several others, some 30 feet long. (The lower walls of many were fashioned from turf, and wood was used for the upper walls and roof.) The wooden longhouse (top) boasted a great hall with a central hearth as its focal point, around which the settlers probably gathered for work, meals, and social events, such as singing and exchanging tales. To keep the hearth continually warm, some dwellings had small, slate-lined ember pits in their earthen floors. Here, coals could burn all night to light the fire the next day. Burned and fire-cracked stones may be evidence of a steam bath in one of the dwelling sites. A few rusty nails led archeologists to believe the Vikings even smelted iron for their needs; searching for a smithy, they finally excavated a broken anvil.*

**Marco Polo's Venice** (*left*) *was built on a lacework of canals that mirrored palaces and the elegant residences of international merchants like the Polos. Many ships came to its great harbor with goods from the Orient. To get to the source of these goods, the Polos traveled to China, crossing the 1,500-mile-long Great Wall above) erected 15 centuries earlier in a futile effort to keep out the neighboring Mongol tribes.*

**The Mongol emperor** *of China, Kublai Khan (left), was a gracious host to his European visitors. Impressed by Marco's intelligence and linguistic ability, the khan employed him as an emissary and, for a time, as his special agent in the large, important city of Kinsai (above). Like Venice, it was a city of canals, but to Marco, Kinsai (modern-day Hangchow) was unmatched "in point of grandeur and beauty, as well as from abundant delights, which might lead an inhabitant to imagine himself in paradise."*

*Chapter Three. A young merchant of Venice travels through Asia to Kublai Khan's China and brings back an account that inspires and amazes medieval Europe. For centuries the "Travels" of Marco Polo are thought to be fabulous; yet others come to realize that the incredible riches of the Orient can be reached—if not by land, then by sea.*

# The Splendor of the East: Marco Polo's Journeys

*Some 700 years ago, the 17-year-old Marco Polo embarked from Venice for Cathay, then ruled by the Mongol Yuan dynasty, whose symbol is shown above. He would spend the next 24 years exploring a world as remote and mysterious to Europeans of his day as the planets are to us. The tales of what he saw there, later put into book form, still makes one of the most engrossing travel narratives of all time. Born in the year 1254, while his father and uncle were on their first trip to China, Marco was an adolescent when he set out on his great journey. A natural observer, he kept a diary of his experiences during his remarkable odyssey. By his death in 1324, his story had passed into European legend, and much of it was thought to be myth. Yet for more than 200 years, his book was the main source of information about the fabulous Orient.*

In the autumn of 1298 a middle-aged Venetian war prisoner named Marco Polo found himself in a Genoese jail. There he passed the time by telling of an extraordinary journey he had once made. News of his past spread through Genoa, and people began coming to the prison to hear him speak of the legendary lands of the Great Khan Kublai, emperor of the Mongols. He told of golden temples and ruby mines and other wonders he had seen on his travels in the East and of the sumptuous palaces and the dazzling court life of the Great Khan that surpassed anything known in medieval Europe in sophistication and elegance.

Among Marco's fellow inmates was a man named Rustichello, a professional romance writer from Pisa. As enthralled as the others by the adventures, he persuaded Marco to send to Venice for the notebooks that he had kept for Kublai. Using these stories and notes, and adding various literary embellishments of his own, Rustichello completed a manuscript on the travels just before Polo's release from prison in 1299.

Soon afterward, several translations of it were made and circulated in Europe. At first the book was simply called *A Description of the World*, for it was just that, covering more lands than any other book of its time. But it soon became known as *The Book of Milione About the Wonders of the World*, in mocking reference to the great numbers Polo gave when mentioning the khan's revenues and wealth. Even though many readers were incredulous, Polo's narrative generated a centuries-long European fascination with the riches and marvels of the fabulous Far East.

In the 13th century, as it began to emerge from the isolation of the Dark Ages, Europe was busily engaged in a growing commerce as well as with war in the Near East. Its rapidly growing population and urban development had increased the demand for goods, and since feudal lords disdained trade, a new middle class of merchants had arisen in the towns and cities. No city was better suited for commercial enterprise than Venice, ideally situated on the Adriatic, facing the East. It was in this prosperous, sophisticated city that Marco Polo was born in 1254.

A few months before Marco's birth, his father, Nicolo, and uncle, Maffeo, who were jewel merchants, set out on a business trip to Constantinople. As the years passed, the Polos' trading ventures took them eastward until finally they reached Bukhara, deep into the lands ruled by the Mongols, or Tartars as Europeans commonly called them. The Polos spent three years there, afraid to move because the region was infested by war parties and bandits. Finally, the envoy of a local lord invited Nicolo and Maffeo to accompany him to Kublai Khan's court in China. Quick to see the unique opportunity to open direct trade with the Far East (bypassing the Arab and Persian middlemen) and happy to leave Bukhara in safety, the Polos accepted the lord's offer.

In 1265, after a year's arduous journey, Nicolo and Maffeo Polo were received by Kublai, grandson of the great empire builder Genghis and the most powerful emperor the world had ever known. Other Europeans—merchants and friars—had preceded them into Mongol territory during the previous 20 years, but Nicolo and Maffeo Polo were the first to visit China and be presented at the imperial court.

Inquisitive about the world at large, Kublai showed an interest in Christianity, perhaps for political reasons. When the Polos were ready to leave, he asked them to take a letter to the pope requesting that he send 100 learned priests to the Mongol court. He cordially invited the brothers to return to China with these men and gave them an inscribed gold tablet to guarantee their safe passage home.

In 1269 the Polo brothers arrived back in Venice. Only then did Nicolo learn that his wife had died after giving birth to a son, Marco, leaving the infant to the care of relatives. Now 15, Marco proved to be a fine, alert lad, and Nicolo decided to take him along on his return to Kublai's court.

Two years later Marco sailed from Venice with his father and uncle, headed for Cathay, or China, a third of the way around the world. At Ayas, a port in southeastern Turkey, the Polos organized a small caravan with camels, horses, and attendants. Finally, their preparations made, they started their journey. It would be a test of their courage and physical endurance: Before them stretched all of Asia.

The pope's efforts to meet Kublai's request for a hundred priests had failed: Only two friars had volunteered to join the Polos. But now that they were on their way, the friars were overtaken by panic and feared for their safety. Feigning illness, they turned back, and the Venetians continued on alone.

Marco, a serious youth with a love for nature, began keeping a journal of the expedition. Since he had an eye for practicalities and business as well as an impressionable, lively, inquiring mind, he did not dwell on the personal discomforts of the long trek. Instead, he noticed everything that seemed strange and marvelous: oil "fountains," exotic game birds, salt sands, ferocious porcupines, and ruby mines, among others.

Hoping to avoid the areas where the Crusaders and Moslems were fighting, the small caravan struck out northward. On drawing near the Black Sea, they veered eastward, passing close to Mount Ararat, where it was believed Noah's Ark had come to rest, and on through the hills of Russian Georgia. All of this territory was familiar to European merchants, but not to Marco, and he was struck by the sight of a fountain that discharged great quantities of oil. This oil was not used for food, he added, but as an unguent for treating mange in men and camels and for burning in lamps. The Mesopotamians and Persians had long used fossil oil (petroleum) for lighting and heating in their civilizations, but to a medieval European this was something new: They and the Romans and Egyptians before them had used the less effective olive oil.

Moving into Iran, the Polos stopped at Saba, from whence the Three Magi had followed a star to Bethlehem. Hearing that their bodies were perfectly preserved in a tomb there, Marco tried in vain to find them.

The Polos were now in a remote, forbidding region, and the discomforts and dangers of travel were great. The caravan covered only 10 to 20 miles a day, crossing cold mountain passes, rocky deserts, and burning hot saltpans where the only drinking water was a bilious green. On reaching Kerman, the Polos thought to continue by sea to China, and so they turned south to Hormuz, a port on the Persian Gulf. Along the way they passed villages hidden behind high mud walls—protection against the Karaunas, notorious marauders. Suddenly, the Karaunas swooped upon the caravan in the middle of a blinding duststorm. These robbers, Marco related, had "acquired the knowledge of magical and diabolical arts, by means of which they are enabled to produce darkness. . . [so] that persons are invisible to each other, unless within a very small distance." He

### Dancing Mongol Shamans Dealt With Spirits

The Mongol nomads had a simple folk religion, believing that the spirits of both good and bad ancestors lived in stones, trees, and other things about them. These spirits were thought to be responsible for death and other unfortunate events; so the Mongols would call upon their shamans, or priests, to mediate with the spirits to ward off misfortune. To do this the shamans went into a trance induced by drum or fiddle music and frenetic dancing, as shown in the 14th-century Mongol painting above. While in the trance, the shaman would communicate with the spirits through the medium of the special animal that represented his power. Thus a shaman whose alter ego was the fox would "communicate" through that animal to the spirits. Following Genghis Khan's death, many Mongols believed his guardian spirit resided in his black banner. His grandson Kublai, who had a more sophisticated outlook, was influenced by Chinese civilization and fostered the spread of Buddhism.

**Commissioned to make a world atlas** *for Charles V of France in 1374, a Jewish cartographer worked a scene from the "Travels" of Marco Polo into his map of Asia. Here the Polos travel with a caravan for security against the hazards of crossing Asia's great wastelands. A passport from the khan insured their protection against ruthless bandits and scheming tribal rulers along the way: These marauders feared the Mongol ruler and the vast army of mounted warriors that rigorously maintained his law.*

and his uncle and father had the good fortune to escape, fleeing to a village, but many of their companions were "taken and sold, and others, were put to death." Marco, with characteristic understatement, concludes, "Now let us turn to other matters."

Finally, the Polos arrived in sultry Hormuz, but a glance at the flimsy vessels, their planks "sewed together" with a yarn made from coconut fibers, was enough to change their minds about sailing, and they turned back to Kerman. There they picked up the Silk Route, which eventually brought them to Balkh in northern Afghanistan.

Once Balkh had been a city of marble palaces, the capital of ancient Bactria, and it was there that Alexander the Great had married the daughter of the Persian king Darius. But the Venetians found it in charred ruins, leveled by Genghis Khan 50 years earlier.

Leaving Balkh, the Polos traveled on to Badakhshan, a mountainous province north of the Hindu Kush that boasted women who padded their hips to make themselves attractive, magnificent ruby mines, and the finest lapis lazuli in the world. Marco wrote: "It is in this province that those fine and valuable gems the Balas Rubies are found . . . in certain rocks among the mountains. . . . The stones are dug in the king's account, and no one else dares dig in that mountain on pain of forfeiture of life as well as goods; nor may anyone carry the stones out of the kingdom . . . for if the king were to allow everybody to dig, they would extract so many that the world would be glutted with them, and they would cease to bear any value."

The region was also famous for its healthy climate. "On the summits of the mountains, the air [was] so pure and so salubrious that it was known to restore health." Marco attested to this out of his own experience, "for having been confined by sickness, in this country, for nearly a year, he was advised to [ascend] the hills: when he presently got well."

Moving on from Badakhshan, the Polos crossed over Kashmir through the Pamir highlands. Marco commented on the "wild sheep of great size, whose horns are a good six palms in length. From these horns the shepherds make great bowls to eat from, and they use the horns also to enclose folds for their cattle at night." These remarkable animals, called Marco Polo sheep, are still prized by big game hunters today.

The Polos continued along the 12,000-foot-high plateau that is called the Roof of the World. It is nestled among ranges so lofty "that no birds are to be seen near their summits" and fires "do not give the same heat as in lower situations, nor produce the same effect in cooking food."

Leaving the mountains, they descended into Sinkiang, a mild region with verdant oases and riverbeds of chalcedony and jasper. Coming to Lop, they prepared to cross the southern edge of the Takla Makan Desert. According to Marco: "Such persons who propose to cross the desert take a week's rest in this town to refresh themselves and their cattle; and then they make ready for their journey, taking with them a month's supply for man and beast. On quitting this city, they enter the desert.

"The length of the desert is so great that 'tis said it would take a year or more to ride from one end of it to the other! And here where its breadth is least, it takes a month to cross it." The Takla Makan Desert was believed to be the abode of evil spirits that lured travelers to their destruction, calling to them by name and assuming the appearance of their companions. Taking precautions, the Polos successfully made their way across a wasteland infamous for its singing sands and mirage-producing heat waves.

For several weeks they skirted the southern edge of the Gobi Desert. After reaching Kumul, they entered Mongolia, at the eastern end of Asia. They were now traveling through regions inhabited by the Tartars. Marco recorded everything he saw or heard of, from the true source of asbestos (which medieval Europeans had thought was the wool of salamanders) to a giant statue of a reclining Buddha. He also made one of the first accurate observations of the Mongols:

"The wealthy Tartars dress in cloth of gold and silks, with skins of the sable, the ermine, and other animals, all in the richest fashion.

"[The Tartars] are brave in battle, almost to desperation. . . . They are capable of supporting every kind of privation, and [when necessary] can live for a month on the milk of their mares, and upon such wild animals as they may chance to catch. . . . The men are trained to remain on horseback during two days and two nights, without dismounting; sleeping in that situation whilst their horses graze. No people upon earth can surpass them in fortitude under difficulties, nor show greater patience under wants of every kind. . . .

"Should circumstances render it necessary . . . they can march for 10 days without lighting a fire or taking a meal. During this time they subsist upon the blood drawn from their horses, each man opening a vein, and drinking from his own [steed]."

The Polos were nearing their destination. They had traveled some 8,000 miles over difficult terrain during the three and a half years since leaving Venice. Having notice of their approach and realizing how weary they must be, the Great Khan "sent forward to meet them at the distance of 40 days' journey, and gave orders to prepare in every place through which they were to

## The Magnificent Nomadic Horsemen of the Steppes of Asia

"The Tartars never remain fixed," wrote Marco Polo, "but as the winter approaches remove to the plains of a warmer region, in order to find sufficient pasture for their cattle; and in the summer they frequent cold situations in the mountains, where there is water and vegetation. . . ." This was the timeless way of life of the people of the Mongolian steppe to the north of China.

Everything they had was designed for mobility. Their yurt, or tent, still made today, was cleverly designed with a latticed framework (right) "exactly round," Polo explained, so that it could be collapsed and gathered into a single bundle to be carried on camelback. The covering, heavy felt waterproofed with tallow, was easily folded. Ox-drawn carts with great platforms conveyed the largest yurts intact (some were 30 feet in diameter), while felt-covered wicker chests bound onto carts carried cooking pots, bedding, and other belongings.

The idyllic scene at far right of an *orda*, a yurt encampment, is from a 14th-century scroll showing a Chinese lady captured by a nomad. Here the nomads rest beneath a canopy in front of a yurt enclosed by felt screens. A smaller yurt can be seen in the foreground and chest carts in the rear. The Mongol word for an encampment is the origin of the English word "horde," first applied to the Mongol armies. The *orda* of a wealthy nomad

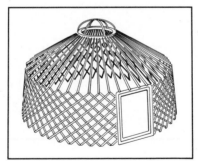

resembled a town, since each of his wives had her own yurt. The wives took great interest in beautifying their homes, decorating the tops and hanging colorfully appliqued felt rugs over the doorways.

While the women ran the camp and performed their chores, the men went on hunting or military expeditions. On long outings they subsisted mainly on dried milk, an innovation that intrigued Polo. Every morning each man put half a pound of the dehydrated milk "into a leathern bottle, with as much water as is thought necessary. By their motion in riding the contents are violently shaken, and a thin porridge is produced, upon which they make their dinner." They were superb horsemen, and their horses were so well trained that they wheeled instantly in any direction upon a given signal; such rapid maneuvering gained them many victories. A fine mount was greatly prized, as suggested by the 14th-century painting of a Mongol and his horse below.

For centuries the Tatars and the Mongols, tribal groups whose names are often used interchangeably, feuded for control of Mongolia's grasslands. About 1200 a powerful Mongol leader emerged, and after defeating the Tatars, he became ruler with the title Genghis Khan. Uniting the nomads, Genghis began a series of conquests. Waves of Mongol warriors, seemingly attached to their small horses, pounded across Asia, razing cities and slaughtering whole populations. To those in their path they seemed to ride "straight out of hell," *ex tartaro*, and so "Tatar" became "Tartar." At his death in 1227, Genghis' empire, which extended from Peking to Russia, was divided among his successors. They continued westward until they reached the Danube River. When Arghyn, the Mon-

pass, whatever might be requisite to their comfort."

Finally, in the summer of 1275, they entered the Mongol city of Shangtu. The khan's magnificent stone and marble summer palace there was situated in 16 square miles of parkland that was watered with many rivulets and roamed by deer and other game animals, which the khan hunted with cheetahs and falcons. Awaiting them in a great gilded hall sat one of the most remarkable rulers in history. His empire, the largest the world has ever seen, stretched from Hungary to the seacoast of China. Kublai Khan, then about 60, was a well-built man of average height with rosy cheeks and "black and handsome" eyes. Dressed in a silk robe stiff with gold embroidery, he was an imposing figure. When Nicolo introduced young Marco as "your servant, and my son," the khan replied, "He is welcome, and it pleases me much," whereupon he ordered a great feast and celebration.

Shangtu was the khan's summer residence. The main capital of Kublai's realm was about 200 miles to the

south at Cambaluc (present-day Peking). It was a more splendid a city than Shangtu, with still more magnificent palaces. At the end of August, Kublai and his court moved back to Cambaluc, as they did each year, and the Polos moved there, too.

Now a member of Kublai's retinue, Marco had an intimate view of the imperial household. Kublai lived graciously. He had adopted many Chinese ways, and he entertained in the grandest Chinese style. At banquets, the often thousands of guests would be served at least 40 dishes of meat and fish, 20 varieties of vegetables, 40 kinds of fruits and sweetmeats, and huge quantities of milk and rice wine.

Kublai had four legitimate wives, each with 10,000 people in her own court. Each of these wives bore the title of empress, and at state affairs one of them sat in honor at the khan's side on a throne of equal height. In addition, Kublai had hundreds of concubines, and every two years or so he acquired 30 or 40 more. They were carefully screened for beauty, Marco learned, and

gol khan of Persia, offered Jerusalem to France in return for its assistance against Egypt, European rulers were jolted into quick recognition of this new world power that had so suddenly emerged from the remote East.

Kublai, who became Great Khan in 1260, was chiefly interested in southeast

Asia. He moved his capital to Cambaluc, conquered the rest of China, and proclaimed the Mongol dynasty, giving it the Chinese name Yuan. Kublai's empire was the largest the world has ever known, but the Mongols had no administrative experience, and it soon began to crumble. One of Kublai's Chinese advisers sar-

donically commented: "I have heard that one can conquer the empire on horseback, but one cannot govern it on horseback." Following Kublai's death in 1294, the Chinese began to reclaim their country. Finally, in 1368 the Mongols were expelled from the Chinese paradise of Marco Polo and Kublai Khan.

attentively observed at night "to ascertain . . . that they sleep tranquilly, do not snore, have sweet breath, and are free from unpleasant scent in any part of their body." Parents regarded it as an honor for their daughters to be chosen, for the khan often gave his concubines in marriage to nobles in his court.

Also serving the khan was a corps of diabolical astrologers. Marco Polo expressed strong disapproval of them: "They exhibit themselves in a filthy and indecent state. . . . They are addicted, moreover, to this beastly and horrible practice, that when any culprit is condemned to death, they carry off the body, dress it on the fire, and devour it. . . . So expert are they in their infernal art, they may be said to perform whatever they will and one instance shall be given, although it may be thought to exceed the bounds of credibility. When the Great Khan sits at meals, in his hall of state . . . the table which is placed in the center is elevated to the height of eight cubits, and at a distance from it stands a large buffet, where all the drinking vessels are ar-

## The Meeting With Kublai Khan at Shangtu

Marco Polo's historic meeting with the Mongol emperor Kublai Khan took place in the year 1275 at the khan's summer palace in Shangtu, a short distance north of the Great Wall. When the Polos approached the khan, they prostrated themselves on the floor to pay respect. Then, commanded to rise, they gave him the letters and presents sent by Pope Gregory X, including a vessel of sacred oil from the lamp above the Holy Sepulcher in Jerusalem. The scene, as imagined by a medieval European, is shown below in an illumination for a French manuscript of about 1400. In contrast is a modern painting of the same meeting at left, based on historical research. It shows Marco's father presenting his son to Kublai. The khan instantly took a liking to the intelligent young man of 21, matured and seasoned by three and a half years of travel across a third of the earth. Standing behind Marco is his uncle, holding one of the pope's gifts, a crystal vase embellished with gold and jewels.

Kublai, who gradually abandoned Mongol ways, is wearing the robe of a Chinese emperor embroidered with the five-clawed imperial dragon. He is surrounded by his most important officials, including Mongol military leaders and Persian administrative assistants; Kublai employed many foreigners to help oversee his empire. On the step below Kublai stands one of his generals. Also present are a few Chinese scholars; such men were encouraged to slump and look venerable rather than maintain an erect military posture. At the far right, one of the khan's four empresses stands with three of her handmaidens. Servants hold large ornamental fans to stir the warm summer air.

Beyond the gallery the royal park can be seen; it abounded with cranes, herons, deer, and other wildlife, which the khan occasionally hunted with cheetahs and falcons. In the center of the park Kublai built a great pavilion, which Marco called the Cane Palace: a colonnade of gilt pillars supporting a roof of bamboo cane that was tied down with more than 200 silken tent ropes, a nostalgic reminder of a yurt. In the park the khan also kept the thousands of snow-white horses sent to him each year on New Year's Day, a holiday celebrated in Mongolian style with the giving of white presents.

Shangtu was the first Mongol capital in China, though Kublai later decided to move his court to Cambaluc. But because of its pleasant summer weather, he built this summer residence amid miles of walled parkland at Shangtu, close to his native Mongolia.

ranged. Now, by means of their supernatural art, they cause the flagons of wine, milk, or any other beverage to fill the cups spontaneously, without being touched by the attendants, and the cups to move through the air the distance of 10 paces until they reach the hand of the Great Khan. As he empties them, they return to the place from whence they came."

The khan was so impressed by these sorcerers, who were said to control the weather, that he told the Polos Christianity would not interest him unless it produced similar miracle men for his enjoyment.

Equally magical to Western eyes was the administration of the khan's vast empire. Its 34 provinces were governed by 12 barons responsible only to the khan. An elaborate system of comfortable posthouses spaced at intervals of 25 or so miles, fast horses, and speedy couriers connected the provinces to the capital and ensured that the khan's orders were promptly executed. This communications network was so efficient that a single courier could travel 250 miles a day, and "in the

## Silk, Paper, and Porcelain: The Wonders of China That Marco Polo Saw and Europe Sought

From all parts of the khan's empire, "everything that is most rare and valuable" found its way to Peking to supply the thousands of functionaries obliged to live there, wrote Marco Polo. He was overwhelmed by what he saw: jade and other gemstones, gold, silver, and clay all worked into exquisite objects by artisans whose techniques and craftsmanship were unknown or unequaled in Europe. Also, there were glorious silks weighted with threads of gold and sometimes "garnished

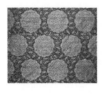

with gems and pearls." The weavers of Venice, just learning the silk industry, were unable to match the opulent gold brocade at left, made in China about 1300. The blue-glazed vase above, believed to have been brought back to Venice by Marco Polo, is a fine sample of Chinese craftsmanship. Groping for a word to describe the hard, resonant pottery, Polo used an Italian word for a kind of shell, *porcellana*, hence our term "porcelain." Porcelains and silks were often fancifully patterned with figures of birds and beasts and floral designs. The Venetian merchant was amazed that even the most valuable goods could be paid for with paper money (below), a Chinese innovation that the khan had adopted. The blackish paper was made from the bark of mulberry trees and then cut into pieces of various sizes and stamped in vermilion with the royal seal. (Paper itself was a Chinese invention. The secret took 1,000 years to reach Europe, where it was first produced in Spain about A.D. 1150.) Polo undoubtedly brought a lot of merchandise back to Venice. Sixteen years afterward he still had some to sell, including Tibetan musk, the costly base of fine perfumes. It was such treasures that later European explorers sought in travels to the East.

fruit season, what is gathered in the morning at Cambaluc is conveyed to the Grand Khan, at [Shangtu], by the evening of the following day; although the distance is generally considered as 10 days' journey."

Travelers had no difficulty with currency in most of the empire. Paper money printed in the khan's mint at Cambaluc was accepted everywhere except in the far south and far west. Marco Polo described how the notes were made from mulberry trees by craftsmen:

"He [takes] that thin inner rind which lies between the coarser bark and the wood of the tree. This being steeped, and afterward pounded in a mortar, until reduced to a pulp, is made into paper, resembling . . . that which is manufactured from cotton, but quite black. . . . He has it cut into pieces of money of different sizes, nearly square. . . . The principal officer . . . having dipped into vermilion the royal seal committed to his custody, stamps with it the piece of paper. . . . And the act of counterfeiting it is punished as a capital offence." It would be 600 years before paper money became common in Europe.

Despite some harshness, the khan was in many respects a most benevolent despot. If famine or pestilence afflicted any part of the empire, he supplied grain and cattle from his own stocks to the victims. If lightning struck a merchant ship, the khan waived his right to collect cargo duty. If he admired the social and economic structure of any of his conquered territories (as in the case of China), he left it intact.

Marco Polo did not learn all this at the outset but in the course of many years. (Nicolo and Maffeo settled down to commercial affairs in Cambaluc and rarely appear in Marco's account of the years they all lived in China, although they must have traveled extensively.)

The receptive young Polo had quickly adopted Tartar manners and customs and learned to read and converse in at least four languages of the Mongol Empire. The khan was so impressed by his intelligence and accomplishments that he decided to test Marco's business talents and sent him on a mission into southwestern China, Burma, and Bengal. "Perceiving that the Great Khan took a pleasure in hearing accounts of whatever was new to him . . . [Marco] endeavored, wherever he went, to obtain correct information and made notes of all he saw and heard."

**On his journeys** *for the khan, Marco Polo often used riverboats like the one in this contemporary Chinese woodcut. Cities edging a river or lake were required to keep three or four boats and crew in constant readiness for the needs of travelers.*

In short, during the 17 years that Marco continued in the khan's service, he rendered himself so useful that he was employed on confidential missions to every part of the empire and its dependencies; and sometimes he also traveled on his own private account, but always with the consent of the Great Khan.

These missions for the khan took Marco Polo north to Mongolia, south to Burma and Bengal, west to Tibet, and east to China's great coastal towns. For three years he was the khan's agent in the beautiful city of Kinsai (Hangchow), just south of the Yangtze River.

Kinsai, like Venice, was built on canals, but its size and magnificence made Venice seem provincial. Kinsai, Marco reported, was 100 miles in circumference. No fewer than 12,000 bridges spanned its waterways, and the main street, which ran from one end of the city to the other, was 40 paces broad. This street was interrupted by 10 enormous squares surrounded by tall houses and shops selling wines, spices, jewels, and pearls. Some 50,000 merchants and customers converged on each square two or three times a week. Marco wrote:

"There is an abundant quantity of game of all kinds, such as roebucks, stags, fallow deer, hares, and rabbits, together with partridges, pheasants, quails, common fowls, capons, and such numbers of ducks and geese as can scarcely be expressed. . . .

"At all seasons there is in the markets a great variety of herbs and fruits, and especially pears . . . weighing 10 pounds each, that are white in the inside, like paste, and have a very fragrant smell. There are peaches also . . . both of the yellow and white kind. . . . There is daily a vast quantity of fish [from the sea]; and in the lake also there is abundance. . . . The sorts are various according to the season of the year."

Marco Polo was fascinated by Kinsai's unheated public baths, in which the Chinese bathed daily. Apparently, they considered bathing in cold water "highly conducive to health." Baths with hot water were, however, available "for strangers, who cannot bear the shock of the cold."

He also described Kinsai's craft guilds and reported that Kublai Khan did not enforce the ancient Chinese law that each man must continue practicing the craft of his father. Rather, "they were allowed, when they acquired wealth, to avoid manual labor, provided they kept up the establishment and employed persons to work at their paternal trades."

Marco by no means confined his journeys to the comfort and safety of the great cities. He traveled all over China and probably got to know it better than most Chinese or their Mongol overlords. His most ambitious trip was to the southwestern provinces of Szechwan and Yunnan and a region he called Tibet. Traveling through these parts, he missed the comfortable Chinese inns and noted the paucity of food and the pervading scent of musk. He was fascinated by the salt

**Each year Kublai Khan** *spent the spring hunting. Attended by "full 10,000 falconers," he pursued small game in the countryside. The scene at top, painted in his time, shows Kublai, robed in ermine, with a female hunting companion and several attendants. The oriental sport of falconry to attack fowl or game had been popular in Europe for centuries. But—as the smaller painting shows—Europeans had only slight knowledge of oriental life. The scene is based on a Kublai Khan falcon hunt described in Polo's book.*

currency in circulation in Tibet. "In this country there are salt springs, from which they manufacture salt by boiling it in small pans. When the water has boiled for an hour, it becomes a kind of paste, which is formed into cakes of the value of twopence each. These, which are flat on the lower, and convex on the upper side, are placed upon hot tiles, near a fire, in order to dry and harden. On this latter species of money the stamp of the Great Khan is impressed, and it cannot be prepared by any other than his own officers."

Considerable risk attended these missions, not only from brigands but also from wild beasts. Travelers, forced to camp in the open at night, protected themselves by making fires with branches of green bamboo that grew along the rivers. Warped in the fire, the bamboo often "burst with loud explosions" that could be heard two miles away and frightened off animals.

Marco continued into Burma, an area unknown to Europeans and unexplored until six centuries later. In this remote region Marco encountered the most exotic

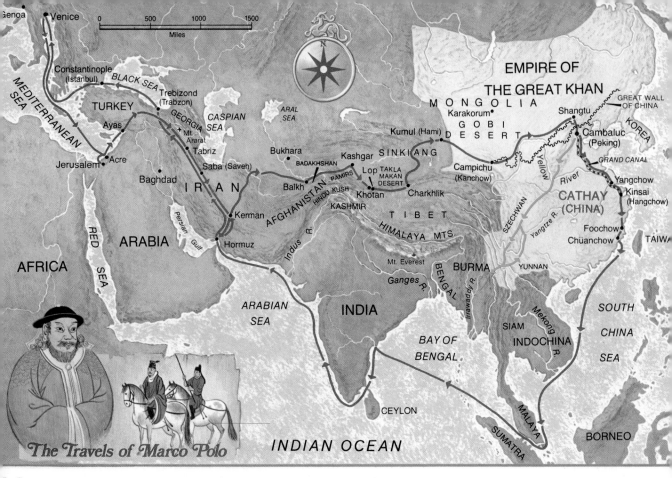

The Travels of Marco Polo

In 1271 the Polos sailed *from Venice on an epic journey to the court of Kublai Khan in Cathay. From Ayas, they plunged into Asia, crossing Armenia, Persia, northern Afghanistan, and Sinkiang, passing through regions only partially charted even today. In 1275 they reached Shangtu, north of Chi-* na's Great Wall. For the next 17 years Marco Polo traveled extensively throughout China, Tibet, and Indochina on missions for the khan. Then the Polos sailed for home. Reaching Hormuz on the Persian Gulf, they crossed overland to the Black Sea, where they boarded ship again and arrived back in Venice in 1295.

sights of all: people who covered their teeth with gold; men who tattooed themselves all over. He learned of a singular custom in one area: "As soon as a woman has been delivered of a child, and . . . has washed and swathed the infant, her husband immediately takes the place she has left, has the child laid beside him, and nurses [tends] it for 40 days. . . . The woman . . . suckles the infant at his side."

For 10 more years Marco Polo traveled on the khan's business while his father and uncle enriched themselves buying and selling jewels. But they were longing to see Venice again. And, Marco explained:

"It became the more decidedly their object, when they reflected on the very advanced age of the Great Khan, whose death, if it should happen previously to their departure, might deprive them of that public assistance by which alone they could expect to surmount the difficulties of so long a journey. . . .

"Nicolo Polo accordingly took an opportunity one day, when he observed him [the khan] to be more than usually cheerful, of throwing himself at his feet, and soliciting on behalf of himself and his family . . . his

majesty's gracious permission for their departure."

The khan appeared hurt. They could have anything they wanted, he said, but, "from the regard he bore to them, he must positively refuse their petition." The Polos were, in effect, prisoners and had it not been for a subsequent stroke of luck, history might never have heard of Marco Polo.

About 1286 one of Kublai's relatives, Arghyn Khan, ruler of Persia, sent envoys to the Great Khan requesting a new wife. A "handsome and accomplished" 17-year-old girl was selected, and the envoys set off overland with her. About a year later the caravan reappeared in Cambaluc, forced back by warring tribes in central Asia. As it happened, Marco had just recently returned from a voyage to the East Indies, and the envoys now asked the Polos to guide their party by sea. When this plan was presented to the Great Khan, he reluctantly consented to let the Polos leave, giving them letters to be delivered to the kings of Europe.

In 1292 a fleet of 14 ships set sail from China with hundreds of men and women, including the three Polos, the envoys of Arghyn Khan, and the young bride-to-be. They sailed down the coast of China, around Vietnam down to Sumatra, over to Ceylon and India, and then north to Hormuz. As usual, Marco's all-embracing curiosity inspired accounts of lands, peoples, and other matters that Europeans up to that time simply did not know about—from a description of rhinoceroses (which he called unicorns) to a sympathetic life of Buddha.

Eventually, the fleet arrived at Hormuz on the Persian Gulf, the very port the Polos had decided not to sail from 20 years earlier. The voyage had taken some two years and was not without its discomforts and perils, whether from the elements or from the ever-present threat of pirates: Marco described one lot of corsairs that forced captured merchants to drink a purgative so that they would regurgitate jewels they had swallowed to hide. Many of the party died en route, but the Polos' indomitable will, strength, and luck held up. The young bride was safely delivered, but Arghyn had died and so she was married to his son. The Polos, still far from home, made their way overland and by sea to Constantinople. They must have been relieved to be heading west when they heard of the khan's death in 1294.

Finally, in 1295 Marco, Nicolo, and Maffeo Polo sailed into the harbor of Venice after a 24-year absence. If no one recognized them at first, it was understandable, for, as it was later explained, they had assumed "a certain indescribable smack of the Tartar both in air and accent." Neighbors related that to prove their tales of the great wealth they had seen and acquired, the Polos gave a banquet for their kinsmen. After the feast the travelers ripped open the seams of the coarse garments they had worn home from Asia and spilled quantities of diamonds, pearls, rubies, em-

**Mongol guards** *escort a princess in this painting from the time of Genghis Khan. The Polos accompanied such a princess to the khan of Persia on their way back to Venice. Their hazardous journey there, mostly by sea, took two years and cost 600 lives.*

eralds, and other precious stones on the table.

Marco Polo was still only in his early forties, but his later years are scantily documented. Evidently, he never traveled far from Italy again. Three years after his return, he was captured by the Genoese. Following his release from prison, Marco married and had three daughters. He must have enjoyed the celebrity that resulted from the circulation of his book, although many readers accused him of telling "tall tales."

Strangely, when Marco Polo died in 1324, he was no millionaire, although he left a modest estate to his heirs. His last testament freed the Tartar servant he brought back with him. Inevitably, many more legends grew up around the Venetian and his travels. According to friends, as Marco lay dying someone asked if he would now like to remove from his tale "everything that went beyond the facts." He replied, "I have not told half of what I saw."

But Marco Polo was not responsible for the many additions that others must have made to the accounts in his book. Over the years he was criticized for many errors, omissions, and wild claims, but his were nothing compared with those in other books of the time. Whatever their limitations, his observations were undeniably real, and they had considerable impact on subsequent generations of mapmakers, geographers, travelers, and scholars of all kinds. Even his erroneous placement of Japan between China and Europe became significant: Some 200 years later, one of Marco Polo's readers set sail to search for a western route to the Orient, carrying his carefully notated copy of the "Travels." Christopher Columbus did not find Japan or China, but Marco Polo's inspiration led him to another new world.

**Marco Polo**—*with a medieval interest in the grotesque—wrote of natives near Sumatra who supposedly had doglike tails. An early illustrator of the "Travels" added his own imaginative creations. Polo's credibilty was not enhanced by these unlikely fantasies.*

# Part

2

## Discovering New Worlds

## Navigators in Unknown Seas

*In the space
of only half a century,
bold European captains find
a sea route to India,
discover America, and
circle the earth.*

By the dawn of the 15th century Europe was embarking on its most dramatic era of change since the fall of the Roman Empire. New ideas of all kinds—political, religious, economic, and social—were challenging the provincialism of medieval life. A growth in population had caused new lands to be cultivated, new towns to be established, and had created a need for more food and goods. A new middle class of merchants had arisen that prospered from the thriving commerce of the towns.

Europe now needed precious metals to mint coins for this increased commerce. Inevitably, it looked to the East for gold and for other riches that the Crusaders had seen Arab merchants selling in Middle Eastern markets: silks from China and Persia; emeralds, rubies, and sapphires from India, Burma, and Ceylon. But what Europe wanted most of all was spices, the condiments used for preserving and seasoning meat. The plant *Piper nigrum*, the source of black and white pepper, grew only in India and Sumatra, and other spices—cinnamon, nutmeg, and the much-prized clove—were indigenous to the East as well. And they were outrageously expensive.

Although these spices were readily available in the markets of western India, by the end of the 14th century Arab traders controlled both the land and sea routes from there to the Mediterranean. They brought their precious cargoes to Alexandria and other Levantine ports, where they sold them to Venetian and Genoese merchants with whom they had exclusive trade agreements. By the time these commodities reached Europe, they commanded prices so high that the profits of one Arab shipload of spices, so it was said, handsomely paid the expenses of five other spice ships, if they were lost at sea. The potential profits from Far Eastern trade had become especially attractive to the rulers of the young kingdoms of Iberia—Aragon, Castile, and Portugal—where the costs of fighting the Moors and administrating newly conquered territory required a steady flow of money.

If these compelling economic factors were not sufficient, religion provided an additional incentive. Although by 1400 most of Europe had lost its crusading zeal, the spirit was still flourishing on the Iberian Peninsula, where centuries of struggle against the Moors had left an abiding animosity toward the Moslem faith.

The Renaissance thirst for personal fame, glory, and recognition of individual achievements also contributed to the burst of exploration in the 15th century. For example, Christopher Columbus demanded a variety of lofty titles in return for his services to the Spanish crown, while other ambitious captains and skilled crewmen could be hired by any country if the rewards were sufficient.

Beyond all of these incentives, the explorations of the 15th century would never have been possible without the revival of Greek scientific learning, the construction of seaworthy ships, and the development of a technology to navigate at great distances from shore.

To begin with, Moslem universities on the Iberian Peninsula, in Constantinople, and elsewhere had preserved and studied works of ancient Greek scholarship that had been lost or forgotten in Europe. Along with this theoretical knowledge, navigators acquired new instruments. The magnetic compass had been familiar for 200 years or more. In the course of the 15th century, two additional basic instruments became available: the quadrant and a smaller astrolabe. None of these devices was entirely reliable over long passages in open water. The north point of the compass differed from geographical, or "true," north by an unknown inconstant angle: the variation. The quadrant and the astrolabe—used for measuring the height of the polestar or the sun in order to ascertain latitude—were unavoidably less accurate on a rolling ship than they were on firm ground. Nevertheless, these new devices enabled European sailors to navigate with enough accuracy and confidence to begin their historic conquest of the Ocean Sea. Explorers were also assisted by some improvements in chartmaking. Although cartography had not advanced as much as sailing and shipbuilding, Mediterranean sailors had gained some experience in plotting a course on a chart.

Another technological advance was the development of more effective and reliable types of firearms. The availability of cannon and arquebuses allowed the Europeans to explore and settle by force. They could now successfully defend themselves against enemies—whether hostile natives or Arab shippers—that might otherwise have discouraged their explorations and establishment of trading posts.

### A New Portuguese Ship for Discovery

In the early 15th century, on the eve of their voyages of exploration, the Portuguese developed a new kind of ship, the caravel. In the beginning it was a small craft, combining Arab lateen (pointed) sails for speed and maneuverability with the broader, deeper hull of the northern European traders, which had more cargo space and were sturdy enough to weather the open Atlantic. As the century progressed, caravels became steadily larger and more elaborate, with full decks, a moderate-sized poop to provide for cabin and steerage, and sufficient room below to carry provisions for a long voyage. New types of rigging were also devised, and taller masts and various combinations of lateen and square sails were used for greater sailing efficiency.

These, in essence, were the historical developments that converged in the early 1400's to bring about Europe's Great Age of Exploration. Now governments rather than individual adventurers were ready to pursue exploration in a systematic way, using the new technology of the age to help them. Of all the countries in Europe, Portugal was in the best position to launch this Great Age of Exploration. Traditionally, it had always been a gateway to Africa, the first destination of these new ventures. Lisbon and Oporto, both excellent natural harbors, were thriving centers of commerce. Politically, Portugal was reasonably stable: It was not engaged in the Hundred Years' War that wracked France and England; it did not have rivalries between city-states as did Italy; and it was no longer fighting the Moors as were the Spanish in Granada.

### Cargoes of Slaves, Gold, and Spices

Eventually, it was through the vision of a single man—Prince Henry of Portugal—that the awesome task was actually begun. He sent forth mariners to explore and trade along the west African coast and to search for a river passage to Prester John's alleged Christian kingdom in east Africa. Inevitably, his work was carried on by others interested in the gold and slave trade of west Africa. Once that trade had been firmly established, Portugal sent Cão and Dias farther south on voyages of discovery until, finally, Dias reached the southernmost tip of Africa. In 1497 Vasco da Gama sailed with specific instructions to reach India and negotiate with Christians there for a share in the spice trade. With that great voyage, the Portuguese at last broke the Arab monopoly in the Orient, greatly increasing their own power and wealth and helping to revitalize the economic life of Europe as a whole.

The example of Prince Henry and his successors was not lost on the other nations of Europe. By the latter part of the 15th century, the newly united kingdom of Spain had caught the same spirit of adventure and, desiring a share in the Far Eastern trade, sent Columbus to find a westward route to the Indies.

The result was the most famous and important voyage in the history of exploration. But this voyage also precipitated a dispute between Spain and Portugal about their right to new lands. The pope, at the request of the Spanish government, issued a bull in 1493 supporting a Spanish monopoly of exploration in the Atlantic, west of an arbitrarily fixed line. The Portuguese government objected, and as a result of negotiation, the two governments agreed in the Treaty of Tordesillas in 1494 to move the line farther west.

The discovery and subsequent colonization of the New World transformed Spain into the most wealthy and powerful nation in Europe, with political consequences that were felt for centuries. It also provided geographers and navigators with their first hint of the earth's true size, which had been vastly underestimated by Columbus and his contemporaries. It was fully revealed in Magellan's excruciating journey of 1519–21, and it had a dramatic effect on the European imagination, creating a growing fascination with new lands. For Europe, it was as if a curtain had just been lifted, revealing endless vistas and opportunities. The earth was suddenly far larger than had been known, but it was also far less mysterious.

**Portugal's determination** *to sail south to unknown seas originated in the time of these leaders, painted by the 15th-century
artist Nuno Goncalves. At right, wearing a black hat, stands
Prince Henry the Navigator with hands folded. The child next
to him is the future King John II, at whose urging Bartolomeu
Dias and Vasco da Gama would press past the southern tip of
Africa. Knowledge of the world beyond the Mediterranean Sea
was still fragmentary at the beginning of the 15th century, but
the desire to learn more was rapidly growing. The map, at top
left, drawn as a tribute to Henry's accomplishments by Fra
Mauro, an Italian monk, shows the discoveries along the west
coast of Africa made during the prince's lifetime. But ambition
to know more of the world had to combat the terror of sailing
into uncharted waters. Terrible monsters, like the one shown
in the woodcut above right, were believed to dwell in the
depths of the ocean. The intrepid Portuguese, nonetheless, continued to adventure beyond the limits of the known world. An
ivory carving of a Portuguese seaman in the crow's nest of a
ship (top right) stands as a symbol of the venturesome spirit of
the early age of exploration. Carved by a craftsman of Benin,
Nigeria, in the 17th century, the statue is evidence of the lasting
impact of the Portuguese explorers on Africa.*

# *Portugal Opens the Age of Discovery: Henry the Navigator*

*Called the Navigator because he actively fostered the great Portuguese discoveries of the 15th century, Prince Henry never led an exploration. He preferred to remain at his headquarters at Sagres on the southwestern tip of Portugal, and from there he directed his captains and crews in their gradual reconnaissance of the west African coast over a period of almost 40 years. Born in Oporto in 1394, Henry was the third son of King John I and his English queen, Philippa. A deeply religious leader, Henry saw Portugal's explorations as a means to the conversion of heathens as well as to the development of economic and political power. Henry died at the age of 66 in 1460 in his palace on the rock of Sagres. He had seen his captains round the great bulge of western Africa and begin to head south toward the continent's tip.*

Before the Age of Discovery the world of Europe, the civilization of the Middle Ages, ended at Cape St. Vincent, a promontory that juts from the southwestern corner of Portugal. There bushes give way to coarse grass, and grass to scrub. Finally, only cliffs remain—sheer, honey-colored limestone heights that reverberate with the thud of Atlantic breakers below. Suddenly, dizzyingly, Europe drops off into the sea.

For centuries men had stood on Cape St. Vincent and gazed at the horizon. To most, that meetingplace of sea and sky had seemed to mark the outer limit of life. But in 1419 a contemplative young Portuguese prince stood on Cape St. Vincent and saw the horizon differently. It filled him with fascination, not fear, and an urge to know what lay beyond.

According to Prince Henry's contemporary biographer, Gomes Eanes de Zurara, the prince's horoscope destined him to "toil at high and mighty conquests, especially in seeking out things that were hidden from other men, . . ." and Zurara attributed Henry's interest in scientific navigation and exploration to this "incli-nation of the heavenly wheels."

Little is known of Henry's youth except for his early interest in Africa and his determination—shared by his two older brothers—to be knighted in battle. This was realized when the three princes finally persuaded their father to plan a crusade for them to carry out against the Moroccan port of Ceuta. At daybreak on August 15, 1415, they attacked the city, and Henry soon took the lead. Fighting like a man possessed, he broke through the city gates and, largely due to his prowess, the banner of St. Vincent, the flag of Lisbon, flew above the captured Moslem port that night. A few days later, Henry and his brothers were knighted.

When the Moors tried to retake Ceuta in 1418, Henry rushed back to its defense. His father, perhaps wary of Henry's zealousness and ambition, ordered him home after three months, but not before the prince had heard the reports of Arab merchants and prisoners: They spoke of Negro kingdoms south of the great desert; of cities that were centers of trade and learning; of a "Western Nile" that flowed to the Atlantic, with an estuary marked by two tall palm trees; of gold-laden caravans that crossed the Sahara to Ceuta. Henry already knew of the trans-Sahara gold trade, for the little gold that the Portuguese had came from Morocco. He had also heard since childhood of the priest-king Prester John, whose Christian empire supposedly existed somewhere in Africa. Now Portugal needed allies, both for commerce and crusades against Islam.

When he returned to Portugal, Prince Henry's mind was filled with questions. How far south did Moslem control extend? Just where did they get their gold? Could trade be established with regions to the south? What lay beyond Africa's Cape Bojador and the Canaries? Was there a sea route to India as Herodotus and the best cartographers of his own time suggested? Realizing that neither merchants nor mariners would

*Map for Henry the Navigator on page 50.*

**Medieval mariners faced frequent peril** *as their ships challenged wind and water. In this early-15th-century painting, a group of terrified sailors pray to St. Nicholas to save them from a stormy sea in which their ship's mast has been broken. Although St. Nicholas is best known today as the jolly Santa Claus, sailors in the Middle Ages regarded him as their patron saint.*

"sail to a place where there is not a sure and certain hope of profit," Henry decided to find the answers.

In 1419 his father made him governor of the Algarve and Administrator of the Order of Christ. The first honor enabled him to live in Portugal's most southerly seaward-facing region. The second obliged him, in his 26th year, to adopt a life of celibacy—but it also gave him revenues to finance exploratory expeditions. The prince settled down at Lagos, a few miles from Cape St. Vincent, and planned his life's work.

These events marked the dawn of the Great Age of Discovery. For the rest of his life, whenever affairs of state permitted, Prince Henry devoted his energies to organizing expeditions to probe southward along the mysterious coast of Africa.

Henry lost no time getting started. During the 1420's he dispatched two unsuccessful colonizing expeditions to Grand Canary Island and urged exploratory expeditions to round Cape Bojador on the northwestern coast of Africa. (Possibly, this cape was the one known today as Cape Juby, about 140 miles north of modern-day Cape Bojador.) But for 12 years his reluctant sailors would only go as far as the Canaries and then return, driven back by the fear that prevailing winds and a strong current might prevent their return to Portugal. They also hesitated to venture into the unknown when they thought they could more profitably trade and plunder in familiar waters. Henry's chronicler, Zurara, phrased their fears: "How are we, men said, to pass the bounds that our fathers set up, or what profit can result to the Infant [Prince Henry] from the perdition of our souls as well as of our bodies—for of a truth by daring any further we shall become willful murderers of ourselves? . . . For, said the mariners, this much is clear, that beyond this cape there is no race of men nor place of inhabitants: nor is the land less sandy than the deserts of Libya, where there is no water, no tree, no green herb—and the sea so shallow that a whole league from land it is only a fathom deep, while the currents are so terrible that no ship having once passed the cape will ever be able to return."

The cape referred to was a low sandspit protruding from the edge of the Sahara into the ocean. Although in itself it was not a fearsome sight, it lay on the fringe of the so-called Burning Zone: It was said the bay beyond was a cauldron of death, where the sea boiled over razor-sharp reefs and maneating monsters lay in wait on the steaming rocks.

The mariners' fears were not entirely fanciful, however—a reef at the foot of old Cape Bojador churns the water and throws up clouds of spray, while heat haze mingled with windblown desert sand darkens the sky and obliterates the sun, creating a "Sea of Darkness."

The years passed as captain after captain returned with tales of unseen horrors. Henry listened with polite disbelief, rewarded them from his rapidly dwindling revenues, and implacably sent them back. Clearly, he hoped that familiarity and entreaty would conquer superstition in the end. But when one of his most esteemed men, Gil Eannes, returned in 1433 with the usual excuses, Henry became impatient. The following year Henry had Eannes' *barcha* (a small craft, not fully decked, with oars and sails) readied and, summoning him, "charged him earnestly to strain every nerve to pass that cape." Zurara recaptured the prince's words:

---

### King Prester John: A Possible Ally in Africa

The legend of Prester John grew in fame from the 12th century. Marco Polo claimed he had traveled through the lands of the fabled Christian king. So real was the blind faith in Prester John's kingdom, at first thought to be in Asia and later in Africa, that cartographers often drew it on their maps. The picture at right, for example, comes from the Catalan Atlas of 1375. Prince Henry believed the mythical king was emperor of Ethiopia, a kingdom that had been Christian since the fourth century, and he hoped to find him to enlist his aid in fighting the Moslems. The Portuguese finally reached Ethiopia in 1520.

**Henry the Navigator** *won the first and most famous of the north African clashes between Christian and Moslem, the Siege of Ceuta in 1415. Fired by Moorish tales of African exploration and profit, Henry returned to Portugal determined to put his nation in the forefront of trade and discovery. A devout Christian, he re-* *solved to combine this expansion with a crusade to convert the infidel. This 16th-century picture shows Spanish forces taking a Moslem stronghold in Palma de Mallorca, off the coast of Spain. This battle is similar to those Henry fought. Firearms did not exist then, though primitive cannon were occasionally used.*

"You cannot find a peril so great . . . that the hope of reward will not be greater, and in truth I wonder much at the notion you have all taken on so uncertain a matter—for even if these things that are reported had any authority, however small, I would not blame you, but you tell me only the opinions of four mariners, who come but from the Flanders trade . . . and know nothing of the needle [compass] or sailing chart. Go forth, then . . . with the grace of God you cannot but gain from this journey honor and profit."

Even Henry's lightest remonstrance carried weight, and Eannes, shamed by his failure, vowed not to return to his prince until he could bring tidings of success: "And as he purposed, so he performed—for in that voyage he doubled the cape, despising all danger, and found the lands beyond quite contrary to what he, like others, had expected." Instead of boiling waves and monsters, Eannes found only a gentle bay full of fish. When he lowered a small boat and approached the desolate shore, he found no signs of human life, but on stepping ashore he found, to his delight, a few familiar plants growing in the desert sand bordering the sea.

A few weeks later he proudly presented them to his prince: "Since, my lord, I thought that I ought to bring some token of the land since I was on it, I gathered these herbs, which we in this country call Roses of St. Mary."

Prince Henry was jubilant. He knighted and rewarded Eannes and immediately sent him and another captain, Goncalves Baldaya, on a second mission to the cape. This time they sailed 191 miles beyond Cape Bojador and, when they landed, found the footprints of men and camels in the sand.

Thus, with the discovery of some rosemary and a few footprints, a great wall of superstition came crumbling down. A turning point in the history of exploration had been reached, and the whole curve of the world now lay open to Portugal and its brave navigators.

About 1436 Prince Henry sent Baldaya south once again, hoping to capture some of the men who had left footprints in the sand in order to learn about their land. This time his sailors did see natives but were nearly

killed when they tried to capture them. They were more successful in killing seals, however, and took home a valuable load of skins—the first commercial cargo any of Henry's pilots brought back from Africa. Baldaya also discovered a crack in the Sahara coastline, an inlet that he supposed was a river. There the Portuguese were able to obtain a small amount of gold dust, and so they named the inlet Rio de Oro, "River of Gold."

More pressing matters—an unsuccessful attempt to capture Tangier in 1437 and near civil war over his brother Pedro's regency—diverted Henry's attention from exploration for the next five years. Finally, in 1441 he was able to return to his work at Cape St. Vincent. A steady stream of visitors poured into his residence, and Henry's court became a clearinghouse for geographical information. Merchants conferred with English and Italian seamen; Jewish and Arab cartographers pored over maps. Presiding over all this excited give-and-take was the prince, who seemed, according to Zurara, never to sleep.

That year Henry dispatched two expeditions from Lisbon: One ship, under the command of Antão Goncalves, was to return to Rio de Oro for seals; the other, under Nuno Tristão, was to explore farther south and try once again to capture some natives. Tristão was given a caravel, a newly developed type of craft that hopefully would be more suitable for long voyages than the little *barchas* and barinels Henry's mariners had used on earlier expeditions.

Meeting near Rio de Oro, the captains joined forces and took a dozen captives. Then Goncalves returned home with sealskins and half of the captives, leaving Tristão to continue south. Tristão was now well over 1,000 miles from home. Seeing that his "caravel needed repair," he calmly proceeded to have it careened "and mended her as far as was needful . . . as if he had been in front of Lisbon harbor, at which boldness of his there was much marvel." The feat was to prove to Prince Henry that in its caravels Portugal now had ships capable of sailing any distance. Tristão proceeded southward and reached Cape Blanc, a gleaming white headland. Unable to capture any more men, he sailed back home to Portugal.

Although Henry thought of captives as sources of information and—ever a crusader—as lost souls to be saved, other men quickly realized they were a source of wealth. Before long, navigators licensed by Henry were

## Moslem Learning Aided European Discovery

Moslem and Christian were not always antagonists in the medieval world. Europeans in the Age of Discovery gained much of their knowledge of geography from the work of Moslem scholars. Islamic influence in Europe was at its strongest in Spain and Portugal, since large areas of both countries had been conquered by Moors from north Africa in the eighth century. By the 12th century the Spanish and Portuguese had learned from the Arabs of the works of Ptolemy, the greatest of the ancient geographers, whose notions of the size and shape of the world dominated scientific thinking for more than 1,000 years. (Ptolemy's *Astronomy*, in fact, is still referred to by its Arabic name, *Almagest*, meaning "the greatest.") The Moslems, however, did more than simply transmit the works of classical scholars. They also had their own historian-travelers in the 14th century: Ibn Khaldun recorded journeys into areas unfamiliar to Europeans; and Ibn Batuta, the most famous of medieval Moslem travelers, made a 26-year journey that took him through Africa, Asia, and parts of China. The Jew Abraham Cresques, who drew the Catalan Atlas, one of the most famous of medieval guides, got much of his information on Africa from Ibn Batuta. The Islamic world, in addition, produced brilliant astronomers and mathematicians, such as al-Battani, whose work influenced Columbus. Ironically, the Moslems were driven from Granada, their last stronghold in Spain, in 1492, the year Columbus set sail on his first historic voyage.

regularly raiding the coast for natives to be sold in Portugal as slaves. Thus, one grim side effect of Henry's explorations was European participation in the west African slave trade, a cruel commerce that would truly flourish for Europe once Columbus discovered the West Indies and labor was needed there. When Tristão returned to Cape Blanc and rounded it in 1443, he found a sheltered bay with several islands. Landing on one of them, Arguin Island, he easily enslaved a number of natives. Henry soon had his first small overseas fort and trading post built on Arguin, and while a modest trade in gold dust and ivory soon developed, the major trade eventually was in slaves, or black gold as they were called in Lisbon.

In 1444 the valiant Tristão set out again and coasted past Cape Blanc. At last, the arid Saharan coastline began to give way to green countryside with many palms and people on the shore. But bad weather prevented a landing, and so he returned to Portugal with the news that he had found the "Land of the Negroes."

Upon Tristão's return to Portugal, Dinis Dias determined to explore farther. Sailing 300 miles beyond Cape Blanc before ever lowering his sails, Dias continued on until, near the Senegal River, he captured some men in canoes. Eager to discover as much as possible, he then pushed on another hundred miles and discovered Cape Verde, a cape so lushly vegetated that it cast green reflections on the water. Rounding the cape, he landed on Gorée Island before returning.

Back in Portugal, Dias described to Henry various landmarks along the coast, including two tall palm trees. The prince was greatly excited—these were the palms the prisoners at Ceuta had said stood near the mouth of the "Western Nile." Now he was able to give his men explicit directions: Eight miles beyond those trees they should look for the great river.

In 1445 a large squadron of caravels under the command of Lançarote Pessanha (simply known as Lançarote) left Lagos to avenge the killing of two captains who had been slaving on Tidra Island near Rio de Oro. Afterward, Lançarote, Gil Eannes, and four other captains continued on, heading for the Guinea coast. Presently, they spotted the two palms and sniffed the heady perfume of fruit trees so fragrant that "it seemed to them that they stood in some gracious fruit gar-

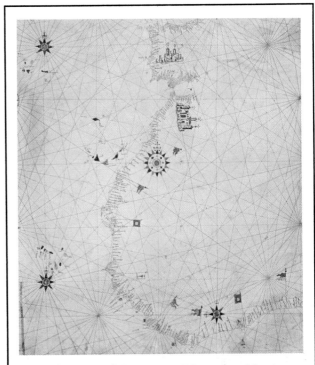

### Coastlines and Compass Lines for Mariners

Steering a course in the open sea was a perilous task for early mariners, but by the 13th century, navigators had "portolani" charts to guide them. Coastlines were indicated on these charts in black, while red flags marked important harbors. Intersecting compass lines helped mariners chart a course. The portolan chart above, dated 1470, depicts the coast of Iberia and includes Africa as far south as the Gulf of Guinea. Maps with latitudes and longitudes appeared much later.

den. . . ." Coasting on as the prince had directed, they soon spied a current of clay-colored water and on tasting it found it sweet. In a short time they landed at an estuary of the Senegal River, thought to be a branch of the Nile. After kidnaping two small children there, they sailed on a bit and then returned home.

One of the captains on Lançarote's expedition was the young and daring Alvaro Fernandes. His uncle, who had outfitted him, had instructed him not to join in the slave hunts but to go to Guinea and bring back something new to please the prince. And so he took from the Senegal two drums of water before passing on. South of Cape Verde he discovered another cape, which he called the Cape of Masts because of its stand of bare palms. Having sailed farther south than any other explorer, Fernandes turned back and proudly gave the prince one of the drums of water. And as Zurara noted, "Perhaps not even Alexander drank of water that had been brought from so far."

Determined to be among those who had passed "the Nile," Tristão set out again in 1446 and sailed on to the Gambia River. There he lowered a couple of rowboats, and he and 21 of his crew made their way upstream.

**Cabin boys** *in the Age of Discovery had the very important job of turning the ship's glass every half hour, as soon as the last grain of sand had run out, singing aloud the number of the glass as they did so. This was the only way to determine the changes of watch. It is unlikely that full hourglasses were carried on ships because they were too heavy to be practical. Ship's glasses were used until a reliable marine clock, the chronometer, was developed in the 18th century by the Englishman John Harrison.*

## Slave Trade Was a By-product of Exploration

Prince Henry observed with great interest the profit Arab merchants made from their monopoly of the slave trade along the west coast of Africa. When he returned to Portugal after the conquest of Ceuta, he encouraged his captains to seize part of this lucrative trade. Accordingly,
in 1441 Antão Goncalves brought the first African slaves back to Lisbon. Soon, slaving caravans led by Arab traders raided the interior of west Africa to supply Portuguese demand. The traders brought their captives to the coast, where they were confined to stockades while awaiting the arrival of Portuguese caravels. The colorful flamingos flying over the coastline of present-day Mauritania (above right) give no clue that near this tranquil area the Portuguese established the first of their forts where African captives were imprisoned. Slaving soon became one of the most profitable activities of the Portuguese adventurers. Between 1441 and 1500, 50,000 slaves were brought back to Portugal. With the colonization of the Americas in the 16th century, the demand grew, and the number of Africans sold into slavery increased dramatically in decades.

Although some of the captured Africans came from such sophisticated cultures as the Benin of Nigeria, Europeans viewed them as primitive children of nature, as the early-16th-century woodcut at left shows. The man wields fish spears.

They were met by a great number of Guineans in boats and were showered with poisoned arrows. Tristão and 19 others died of the lethal poison. Of the entire crew only nine survived, and four of them had been disabled. They were mostly boys who knew little about the art of navigation. Weeping from fear and sorrow, they turned their ship toward Portugal. For 60 days they sailed out of sight of land, not knowing where they were. Finally, they were sighted by a pirate who told them, to their great joy, that they were just north of Cape St. Vincent.

Henry was deeply upset by the deaths of Tristão and so many others whom he had brought up, and he saw that their families were cared for. Realizing then that slave-snatching had made enemies all along the African coast, Henry advocated that his men trade rather than raid for slaves in the future.

Undaunted by Tristão's disaster and bent on going even farther, young Alvaro Fernandes sailed again that same year and went more than 400 miles beyond Cape Verde, passing Sierra Leone. Only a troublesome wound in his leg from a poisoned arrow caused him to turn back. The prince, ecstatic over this great advance, handsomely rewarded Fernandes and his crew.

Further disruptions in the royal family of Portugal, a complicated dispute with Castile over ownership of the Canary Islands, and above all, lack of money prevented Henry from sending out any expeditions for several years. In 1455 and again in 1456, however, a skilled Venetian seaman, Alvise da Cadamosto, sailed for Henry, going twice beyond Cape Verde. Primarily interested in trade to bring Henry some revenues, he attempted little exploration. However, he did discover the Cape Verde Islands, and he managed to sail a short distance up the Gambia River—the first time Portuguese ships penetrated the interior of Africa.

Cadamosto's accounts are valuable because of their fine descriptions not only of landscapes and wildlife but of the customs, life, and governments of the tribes he became acquainted with. (He was especially impressed by hippos and elephants; he even brought Henry a piece of salted elephant meat.) Above all—and in contrast to most of the Portuguese explorers—he was genuinely interested in Africans as people and spent four weeks as the guest of King Budomel, at a place about 50 miles below the mouth of the Senegal River and 25 miles inland.

"These Negroes, men and women, crowded to see me as though I were a marvel," he reported. His European clothing and his white skin seemed equally unbelievable. The bewildered Africans "rubbed me with their spittle to discover whether my whiteness was dye or flesh," he commented, and added, "Finding that it was flesh, they were astounded."

Equally astonishing to the Africans were the bagpipes that one of Cadamosto's sailors played to a delighted audience of natives. Thinking at first "that it was a living animal that sang thus," they finally concluded "that it was a divine instrument, made by God with his own hands, for it sounded so sweetly with so many different voices."

Touched by their reaction to the bagpipes and also to a burning candle that struck them as "beautiful and miraculous," Cadamosto showed them how to make candles from beeswax. "On seeing this," he related, "they showed much wonderment, exclaiming that we Christians had knowledge of everything."

By this time Henry's fame had become so great that men from far and wide begged to sail for him. Wherever Henry's explorers landed, they proudly carved his initials on trees and rocks. Year after year, trading vessels sailed confidently down the African coastline past the now familiar series of landmarks: Cape Bojador, Cape Blanc, the Senegal River, Cape Verde, and beyond. And in Lisbon and Lagos, where Henry lived most of the time, the markets began to fill up with exotic imports: gold dust, ivory, sugarcane (Henry had started sugar plantations in Madeira), pepper, ostrich eggs, brilliantly plumed parrots, and other birds.

But then, with the support of his nephew King Alfonso V, the aging prince decided to lead yet another Moroccan crusade. His attack on Alcácer Ceguer in 1458 was a brilliant personal triumph, but it diverted his attention once again from exploration. It probably was also too great a strain on the 64-year-old prince. On November 13, 1460, Henry the Navigator died at Sagres. With him as he died was one of his navigators, Diogo Gomes, who had just returned from an expedition to the Gambia River area.

During the last months before his death, Henry apparently had made plans for a voyage to be captained by Pedro da Sintra, which his nephew, King Alfonso, soon carried out, sending Da Sintra on his way. Passing Mount Auriol, Da Sintra named it Sierra Leone ("Lion Mountain") because of thunder growling like a lion around its summit. Next he discovered a promontory higher than any he had ever seen, and he named it Cape Sagres. Reaching a latitude of 6° N, he saw a "great green forest," and beyond that a river overhung by great clouds of smoke, the Rio dos Fumos, which Hanno may have had described.

After Henry's death, however, it seemed for a time as if the great age of Portuguese exploration would also die. King Alfonso V was far more interested in sponsoring crusades to Morocco than in spending money on expeditions. Yet he seems to have shared at least a hint of Henry's passion "to know what lands were beyond."

## "The Best Sailers That Ever Traveled Upon the Open Sea"

Without the caravel, the Portuguese exploration of the African coast might not have taken place. It gave seamen a new speed and maneuverability that was not possible in earlier ships. Reflecting the confidence that the caravel's improved design gave to mariners, 15th-century Venetian navigator Alvise da Cadamosto wrote: "I see no reason why these ships should not go anywhere in the world. For I believe that they are the best sailers that ever traveled upon the open sea."

Unlike the large, round-bottomed carracks that were used in Mediterranean trade, the caravel had a slimmer hull, which made for greater speed as it cut through the waves. More important, the caravel had a very shallow keel, which permitted navigators to sail into small harbors and narrow inlets as they voyaged down the coast of Africa. Not only was this a more effective way to learn about uncharted waters, but it also allowed the mariners to sail within sight of land, which allayed their fears of the sea.

The speed and maneuverability of the caravel resulted from both its hull construction and the design of the sails. Older craft had been square-rigged, with their rectangular sails set at right angles to the mast. The caravel, however, adopted the lateen rig of the Arab boats that plied the Mediterranean and the Indian Ocean. The triangular lateen sail could be set on either side of the mast to take advantage of the direction of the wind. The ability to change the position of the sails enabled the caravel to make much better time in opposing winds than the square-rigged ships. This was an immeasurable advantage when the ship faced into the prevailing winds on much of their return trip from Africa to Portugal. Most early caravels had two masts, each with its own lateen sail. Later, caravels often had a third mast, which carried a square-rigged sail to give a wider area of canvas to take advantage of stiff ocean breezes.

The ships rarely exceeded 50- or 60-ton capacity and about 70 feet in length. Living conditions on board were extremely cramped, especially since the handling of the sails required a larger crew than earlier ships had used.

lier ships had used.

Seamen were not only experienced navigators but also experts in the repair and upkeep of their ships. Often, on long voyages, the ships would be brought into shallow water so the bottoms could be scraped and recaulked. This operation (left) was known as careening.

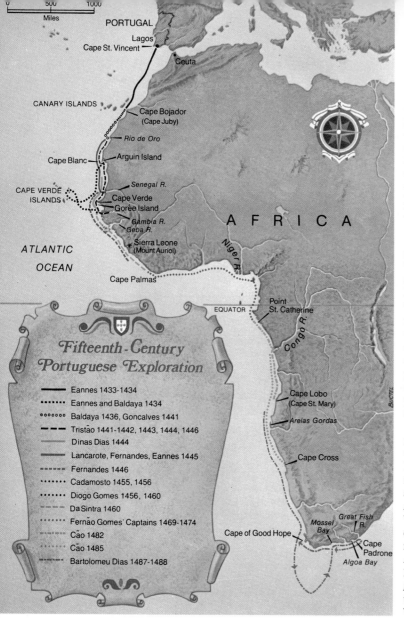

PORTUGAL
Lagos
Cape St. Vincent
Ceuta

CANARY ISLANDS

Cape Bojador
(Cape Juby)
*Rio de Oro*
Cape Blanc
Arguin Island

*Senegal R.*
CAPE VERDE
ISLANDS
Cape Verde
Gorée Island
*Gambia R.*
*Geba R.*
Sierra Leone
(Mount Auriol)

ATLANTIC
OCEAN

A F R I C A

*Niger R.*

Cape Palmas

EQUATOR
Point
St. Catherine

*Congo R.*

Cape Lobo
(Cape St. Mary)
*Areias Gordas*

Cape Cross

Great Fish
R.
Mossel
Bay
Cape of Good Hope
Cape
Padrone
*Algoa Bay*

### Fifteenth-Century Portuguese Exploration

—— Eannes 1433-1434
••••••• Eannes and Baldaya 1434
ooooooo Baldaya 1436, Goncalves 1441
– – – Tristão 1441-1442, 1443, 1444, 1446
——— Dinas Dias 1444
——— Lancarote, Fernandes, Eannes 1445
••••••• Fernandes 1446
••••••• Cadamosto 1455, 1456
••••••• Diogo Gomes 1456, 1460
——— Da Sintra 1460
••••••• Fernão Gomes' Captains 1469-1474
••••••• Cão 1482
——— Cão 1485
——— Bartolomeu Dias 1487-1488

## Tracking the Long African Coast

For more than 50 years a series of Portuguese expeditions made their way cautiously down the west coast of Africa from Cape Bojador in 1434 to the rounding of the Cape of Good Hope in 1488. Keeping their shallow-hulled vessels close to shore, Portuguese captains established trading posts and forts at intervals along the way. The most coveted trade was in slaves, gold, ivory, sugarcane, and pepper. Though a passage to India was undoubtedly a long-range purpose of these voyages, it was Africa itself that was of principal interest to the Portuguese through most of the 15th century. After Gil Eannes had finally dispelled the terror of the "Sea of Darkness" that supposedly lay beyond Cape Bojador, further expeditions inched down the arid coast past new capes and rivers. Then, in 1444, Nuno Tristão passed the end of the desert and reached lush Cape Verde at the west tip of Africa's great bulge.

At the time of Henry's death in 1460, the prince's navigators had pushed as far south as the Gambia River. In 1469 King Alfonso V of Portugal signed a five-year contract with the merchant Fernão Gomes. Gomes was granted almost exclusive right to the by-then lucrative African trade in return for exploring southward. When his contract expired in 1474, Gomes and his captains had reached Point St. Catherine, adding nearly 2,000 miles of coastline to the map of Africa. Yet it was not until 1488 that Bartolomeu Dias succeeded in placing a stone pillar, or *padrão* (top right), on the African shore beyond the Cape of Good Hope. A decade after that, Vasco da Gama finally reached India.

---

In 1469 he signed a five-year contract with a wealthy merchant, Fernão Gomes, granting Gomes exclusive rights to most of the African trade in return for an annual rent and a promise to continue exploration beyond Sierra Leone.

Gomes fulfilled his pledge. Year after year he sent his pilots farther and farther into the unknown. Sailing southeast from Cape Verde and on past Sierra Leone, his ships soon reached Cape Palmas in modern-day Liberia. And there, no doubt to their great surprise, his captains discovered that the coast trended almost due east. They had rounded the bulge of Africa.

Continuing their voyages, a year or two later Gomes' explorers reached the great delta of the Niger River, and a little beyond it found the coastline to turn again, this time abruptly south. By the time Gomes' contract expired in 1474, one of his navigators had pressed on to Point St. Catherine, two degrees south of the Equator. In five years Gomes' explorers had added nearly 2,000 miles of coastline to the map of Africa.

Although the African trade continued to flourish— more and more gold was flowing into the royal treasury—the outbreak of a bitter war with Spain in 1475 brought exploration to a temporary halt. It was revived in earnest when Henry's ambitious great-nephew, John II, acceded to the throne in 1481, for John cherished a scheme far grander than any of Prince Henry's.

Many geographers had by then rejected Ptolemy's notion that Africa and Asia were connected somewhere to the south, completely enclosing the Indian Ocean. They believed instead that Africa was surrounded by ocean, making it circumnavigable. And so Africa appeared, on a map by Fra Mauro, commissioned by the Portuguese throne in 1459 (see page 42).

The current geographical thinking and the successful exploration of Africa's west coast led King John to pin his hopes on reaching the kingdom of Prester John in east Africa and enlisting his aid against the Moslems. Then Portuguese ships would sail right on to India itself for a share in the lucrative spice trade.

John II sent Capt. Diogo Cão south to test this optimistic theory in 1482. On board his caravel Cão carried a number of *padrãos*, carved stone pillars bearing the date and the coat of arms of Portugal. Cão's orders were to erect these monuments on prominent points in any lands he discovered to establish possession. By the time he returned to Lisbon in 1484, the shore of the Congo River was graced with a stately column, and another stood on Cape Lobo (Cape St. Mary today), well down the coast of present-day Angola.

For some reason, Cão seems to have concluded that he had all but reached the tip of Africa. The king, delighted, showered rewards and a title on his navigator and sent him back in 1485 to make the final leap into the Indian Ocean. This time Cão went a short way up the Congo River, but when he continued down the coast past Cape Lobo, he discovered to his dismay that the coast ran south, ever south, with no end in sight. His last *padrão* was erected on the arid shore of Cape Cross in modern-day South-West Africa, almost 1,000 miles north of the continent's southern tip.

Though Cão must have been profoundly discouraged, King John was not. Two years later he sent yet another navigator, Bartolomeu Dias, to seek the route around Africa to the Indian Ocean. Little is known about this momentous voyage and still less about the discoverer; yet the plain facts are filled with drama.

Dias left Lisbon in August 1487 with two caravels and a stubby storeship. (Cão had found provisions were hard to come by along the arid coast of southwest Africa.) Early in December he moored the storeship in a sheltered bay in southern Angola and proceeded south at a leisurely pace. Appalled by the blasts of heat and the desolate sandhills that formed the coastline, he named the area Areias Gordas, "Broad Sands."

Then, according to legend, in mid-January 1488 the caravels were hit by a tempest lasting 13 days, driving them far to the south. But northerly winds of such duration are rare there, and it seems likely that, skilled seaman that he was, Dias deliberately set out to sea to avoid contrary winds and currents close to shore. As soon as he found a favorable wind—perhaps about 40° S—he ran to the east to regain the coast. But, to his bewilderment, he found nothing but open water. Gradually, he realized that he had sailed beyond the elusive tip of Africa. Changing course, he sailed northward until finally "lofty mountains" appeared on the horizon. Anchoring in what is now known as Mossel Bay, about midway along the blunt southern end of the

**Discovering the southernmost tip** *of Africa, near the rockbound Cape of Good Hope, fulfilled a goal of Prince Henry and the early Portuguese seamen. Once around the cape, the adventurers could make for India and the lands of gold and spices that they hoped to find. Bartolomeu Dias first rounded the cape in 1488, but his cautious crew, frightened by the enormity of the Indian Ocean, forced their captain to return to Portugal.*

continent, he stepped ashore on February 3, 1488.

Hottentot cowherds, frightened by the appearance of the ships, pelted the Portuguese with stones. The Portuguese in turn killed one of their number, and the natives quickly retreated with their cattle before Dias could learn anything about them.

Continuing eastward, Dias reached Algoa Bay, and there his men began to protest—the coastline went on and on, India was still far away, their provisions were low, and their storeship was weeks behind them. Dias bowed to the decision of his crew to turn back but requested that they "let him sail for a few more days along this new shore." Granted two or three days, Dias reached a latitude of 33°30' S, probably at Great Fish River. Seeing the coast trending in a northeasterly direction, Dias had no doubt that he was now in the Indian Ocean, but he was obliged to heed the wishes of his crew. They turned about, and as their ship passed the *padrão* they had erected on Cape Padrone, one of the men noticed Dias' face—it was contorted by bitter disappointment: He saw "the land of India, but, like Moses and the promised land, he did not enter it."

On his way home Dias saw for the first time the most majestic of all capes and there erected another *padrão*. Tradition holds that Dias called it Cabo Tormentoso, "Cape of Storms," and that it was later renamed by the king. But a witness stated the facts quite differently: "Note, that in December of this year, 1488, there landed at Lisbon Bartolomeu Didacus [Dias], the commander of three caravels . . . who reported that he had sailed . . . as far as a cape named by him the Cape of Good Hope. . . . This voyage he had depicted and described from league to league upon a chart, so that he might show it to the king; at all of which I was present."

The witness was Christopher Columbus.

**Genoa was the birthplace** of the discoverer of the New World. Shown above in a late-16th-century painting, the city had been a major port and center of maritime commerce since the 10th century. It was also notable for its mapmakers, merchants, and navy, as well as its towering lighthouse known as the Lanterna (at far left). Two hundred years before Columbus' voyage, the Venetian Marco Polo had been held in a Genoese jail as a prisoner of war. During his imprisonment, the memoirs of his extraordinary adventures in the East were written. Columbus (left), avid in his research of the known geography of the world, made a close study of Polo's text. It was Polo's Cipangu, or Japan, that he expected to encounter at the other side of the Ocean Sea. Columbus' own annotated copy of Marco Polo's famous book is shown below.

*Chapter Five. A visionary Italian navigator sails west from Spain into the unknown Atlantic in search of the fabulous East. Instead of the Orient, he finds a hemisphere unknown to Europe and changes the course of history; yet to his death, the great captain believes he has discovered a new route to the East Indies rather than a new world.*

# The Enterprise of the Indies: Columbus Discovers America

*Even Columbus' failures and his mistaken belief that he had reached "the Indies" cannot detract from his immense skill and achievements. Born in Genoa, Italy, in 1451, young Christopher probably had little formal education. Though he was the son of a master weaver, he was inexorably drawn to the sea and the swift Genoese ships that plied the city's trade across the Mediterranean. Later, in Lisbon, he joined his brother Bartholomew as a chartmaker, while continuing his career as a master mariner. In that period Columbus sailed in Portuguese ships as far north as Iceland and as far south as west Africa. From 1483 on, he devoted himself to his "Enterprise of the Indies," finally achieving success in Spain. Then came the four great voyages, triumph, disappointment, and finally, death on May 20, 1506.*

In 1476 a tall, redheaded, 25-year-old Genoese seaman swam to safety from a shipwreck and landed on the shores of Portugal. There he remained, and over the next few years he prospered moderately, married well, and became a father. When his young wife died, he could have continued, secure and successful, in his career as a merchant-mariner, mainly in the ocean waters off Portugal. But there was always that horizon out there to the west, mysterious, tantalizing Christopher Columbus with dreams of wealth and glory.

Columbus was dead certain that somewhere over that western horizon—2,500 miles away, to be exact—lay Marco Polo's wondrous, golden land of Cipangu (Japan) and the fabulous, spice-rich "Indies" (in Columbus' day, a vague, catchall term for all eastern Asia). For years the Portuguese had been searching for an eastward route to all those riches; Columbus was certain that the shortest route was to the west.

As we now know, there were a few flaws in his cal-culations. Like most educated people of his time, Columbus believed the world was round. But no one understood exactly how big it was. By combing the writings of learned cosmographers for facts and figures that supported his theories, Columbus convinced himself that the globe was much smaller than it really is. And, by fitting together various bits of information and misinformation, he had come to the conclusion that Asia extended much farther east than it actually does. It was by wrapping his oversized Asia around his undersized globe that he came up with the—to him—very logical estimate of a 2,500-mile-wide Ocean Sea—an easy sail for any first-rate navigator.

In fact, the distance from Portugal to Japan is some 10,600 miles, and the North American continent blocks the way. But, Columbus' guess at the width of the Atlantic Ocean was reasonably accurate, and to the end of his life he remained convinced that the lands he found were parts of Asia.

For years Columbus mulled over his theories, discussing his western shortcut to the Indies with anyone who cared to listen. Finally, in 1484 the brash, blue-eyed immigrant managed to present Portugal's King John II with a proposal to test his route. The king's advisers answered with an emphatic "No," claiming—correctly—that Columbus had vastly underestimated the distances involved.

Frustrated but still haunted by his dream, Columbus soon quit Portugal to seek the patronage of Ferdinand and Isabella of Spain. He was presented at their court in May 1486, and from the start the queen supported him. The story that she pawned her jewels to finance his exploration is a myth, but as one contemporary observed, "In truth, she more than the king ever favored and defended him."

The editors gratefully acknowledge that this account is based on the following works of Samuel Eliot Morison: *Admiral of the Ocean Sea* (Little, Brown and Co.); *Christopher Columbus, Mariner* (Little, Brown and Co.); *Journals and Other Documents on the Life and Voyages of Christopher Columbus* (The Heritage Press); *The Caribbean As Columbus Saw It*, with Mauricio Obrejon (Little, Brown and Co.).

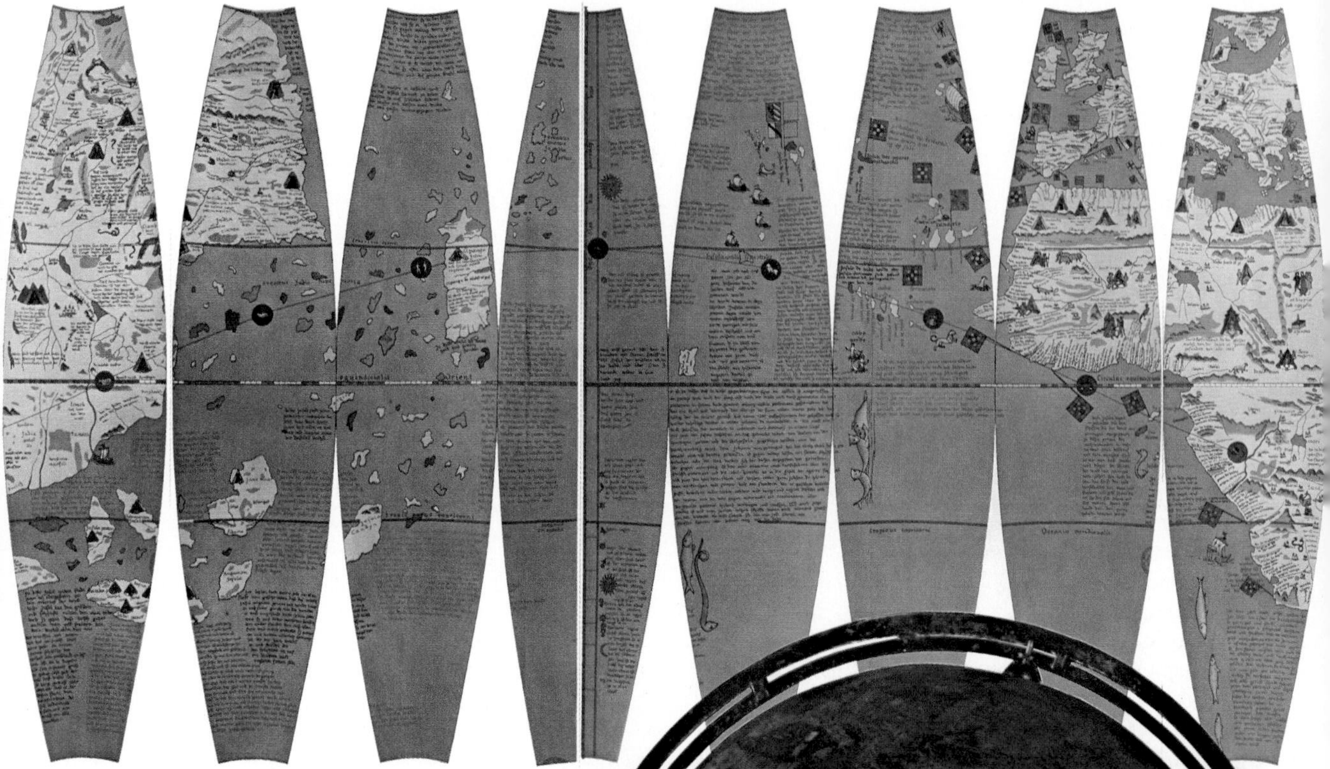

This earliest known terrestrial globe, made in Nuremberg in 1492, the very year of Columbus' voyage, does not show the Western Hemisphere, since no one knew it existed. It was the work of Martin Behaim, a German who was official map-maker to the Portuguese court. In its assembled form at right, the lands known about in Columbus' time—Africa, Europe, and the Near East—are in view. A modern copy of the flattened sections is shown above: Europe, Africa, and the Atlantic are at the right; Asia is at the left; and the island of Japan (Cipangu) stands between (third panel from left). Behaim's theories of the size of the earth and the proximity of Asia and Europe were based on the miscalculations of the ancients. Furthermore, considering the knowledge of the west coast of Africa brought back by the Portuguese explorers, even his portrayal of that continent was outdated. Columbus reckoned the Ocean Sea even narrower than indicated on this map, thus enforcing his belief in the feasibility of a westward route to the East.

The monarchs listened gravely as Columbus explained his project, citing all the ancient authorities who seemed to support his ideas. (Had not the Romans, for instance, written that it was possible to sail west from Spain to India in just a few days?) The king and queen were impressed by their petitioner's honesty and self-confidence as well as his vast geographical learning. They were also titillated by the prospect of beating Portugal in the race for a sea route to the wealth of the East Indies.

Before long, they appointed a board of "learned men and mariners" to study Columbus' proposal and awarded him a small annuity. But the commission took its time. When by 1488 it still had not reached a decision, Columbus impatiently went back to Lisbon to try again for King John's support. He arrived just in time to witness the return of the Portuguese navigator Bartolomeu Dias with the news that he had rounded the southern tip of Africa. With a way around Africa now open, Portuguese discovery of an eastern route to Asia was all but assured. King John immediately lost all interest in Columbus.

Since overtures to the kings of England and France had also been unsuccessful, Columbus had no choice but to wait for the report of Isabella's commission. It finally came in 1490: The royal advisers pronounced his scheme totally impracticable.

Although the monarchs refused to finance Columbus' project, Isabella still had faith in the persistent Genoese and hinted that it might be worth trying again in a few months. By late 1491 Columbus was back at court, reciting all his arguments once more. A new commission was appointed and this time reported promptly and favorably on the Enterprise of the Indies, as Columbus called his scheme.

But the long years of waiting in limbo, far from humbling Columbus, had made him bolder than ever. Self-confident to the point of arrogance, he now stated his demands for compensation, insisting that, if successful, he be made Admiral of the Ocean Sea, Viceroy and Governor of all lands he discovered, and recipient of 10 percent of all future colonial revenues. The monarchs replied with a firm "No."

Fortunately for Columbus, Luís de Santángel, a trusted courtier and keeper of Isabella's privy purse, now intervened and persuaded the queen that the cost of the expedition would be small compared to the potential profits. On April 17, 1492, the royal couple ended Columbus' eight years of frustration by signing a document agreeing to all his demands.

By early August the Enterprise of the Indies was ready to begin. Moored on the Río Tinto in the little port of Palos in southwestern Spain was the most famous fleet ever to sail the Ocean Sea: Columbus' flagship, the *Santa María*, and two trim caravels, the *Pinta*, under command of Martín Alonso Pinzón, and the *Niña*, captained by his brother, Vicente Yáñez Pinzón. The crew, about 90 able seamen, mostly from Andalusia, included an Arabic-speaking linguist who, Columbus hoped, would act as interpreter when he met the Great Khan of China. (Arabic was thought to be the mother of all languages.) Below decks lay a year's supply of food and great stores of glass beads, hawkbells, and other trinkets to barter for gold in Cipangu.

On August 3, 1492, long before dawn, Columbus boarded the *Santa María* and gave the order to weigh anchor. With hardly a breath of wind stirring, all sails hung limp as the three ships glided slowly down the Río Tinto on the silent ebb of the tide. By the time they reached the open sea, the sun was high enough to warm the groups of sailors that clustered on the decks to

**The union of Ferdinand II** *of Aragon and Isabella of Castile bound factions of the 15th-century Spanish nobility under a "Catholic Sovereignty," which secured Spain as a power.*

catch a parting glimpse of Spain.

Nine days later the fleet put in at the Canary Islands, off the coast of Africa, to make a few repairs and take on extra supplies and firewood. The sailors enjoyed their shore leave in the time-honored fashion; even Columbus is said to have indulged in a stately flirtation with Doña Beatriz de Peraza y Bobadilla, the beautiful young widow who ruled Gomera Island. Morale was high. Although desertions at the first port of call were common in the 15th century, all crewmen reported for duty when the time came for Columbus to set sail.

The fleet left the Canaries on September 6, and three days later the last of the islands' volcanic peaks faded from view. The course Columbus set was west, directly west. Years before, on trading missions to Africa, he had noticed that winds off the Canaries blew from the northeast—ideal for carrying his fleet across the open sea to Cipangu.

Day and night, the winds blew the fleet steadily to the west, sometimes 150 miles or more in 24 hours. Day and night, the empty horizon unrolled, revealing only more emptiness beyond. Before long the crew settled down to the monotonous routine of life at sea. From the saying of prayers at daybreak to the singing of "Salve Regina" at sunset, the passage of time was punctuated every 30 minutes by a ship's boy, who chanted a pious refrain as he turned the half-hour glass and the sand grains renewed their endless trickle through the instrument's narrow waist. Every four hours the watch changed, and sailors not on duty lolled on deck and chatted or curled up in some shady corner to sleep as best they could. (On the tiny ships of the late 15th century, only the captain and one or two top officers enjoyed the luxury of a cabin and bunk.)

For Columbus, the early days of the voyage were sheer delight. He reveled in the freshness of the mornings, the balmy afternoons "like April in Andalusia," and the calm, friendly seas. Yet he sympathized with the anxieties of his superstitious sailors, who had no real idea what lay ahead. From the start he kept two logbooks: a secret one recording his estimates of the actual distance covered each day, and a public one recording much slower progress "so that the crews should not lose heart or be alarmed if the voyage grew long." (Ironically, he so consistently overestimated his speed that the falsified log was more accurate than his private reckoning.) And when, two weeks out, the wind temporarily shifted and the fleet had to battle a brisk headwind, he found cause for comfort. "This headwind was very necessary to me," he confided to his journal, "since my people were very much excited, because they thought that in these seas no winds ever blew to carry them back to Spain."

The crew was less easily consoled when "they began to see many tufts of very green seaweed. This was the Sargasso Sea, a vast expanse of the mid-Atlantic covered by floating masses of sargassum weed.

Afraid that the ships might run aground on hidden shoals or become entangled in the all-embracing growth, the men began to fear for their lives. But the weeds, stretching as far as the eye could see, parted easily before the ships' prows, and from then on Columbus' log simply noted, "saw plenty weed," without further comment.

Fortunately, there were promising signs as well, or so everyone thought. When a sailor caught a crab clinging to a bit of seaweed, Columbus kept it, confidently announcing that "these were certain signs of land, because they are not found [more than] 80 leagues from land." In fact, it was undoubtedly a little gulfweed crab, which flourishes throughout the Sargasso Sea.

On September 25 it seemed as if the moment of discovery had arrived. At sunset, Martín Alonso Pinzón on the *Pinta* cried out that he saw land ahead. Seamen on the other ships immediately scrambled up the rigging

**Columbus declared** *his flagship* Santa María *a poor ship for reconnaissance. Broad, heavy, and slow, the little merchantman probably carried 3,500 square feet of sail and a square rig that was ideal for running before the mid-Atlantic trade winds. This reconstruction shows she had little room for a 40-man crew and provisions for a long journey. The cross section looks aft from the mainmast; from top to bottom there is the poop deck (1), quarterdeck with captain's apartment (2), main deck (3), and storage deck above the stone ballast in the hold (4). Guns, carried for defense, were included on board. Light swivel guns (5) and heavier lombards (6) were among the ship's weapons.*

**After 33 days** *of uncharted ocean, the sight of the Bahama Islands brought tears to the eyes of the sea-weary voyagers. First seen were the white sands and coral beaches of the island shown here. "To the first island I discovered I gave the name San Salvador . . . everything is so green that it is a pleasure to gaze upon it," wrote Columbus. The land lay just where he had predicted it would but wasn't the wealthy country of Cipangu he sought. In fact, the island is quite small (it is 13 miles long, 5 wide) and was inhabited only by primitive Arawak Indians. The British renamed the island Watling. A century ago Columbus' original name for it was restored by the British.*

and shouted that they too could make out an island—or something—on the horizon. Columbus, overjoyed, "fell on his knees to give thanks to our Lord" and ordered the men to sing "Gloria in Excelsis Deo."

But when he tried to find the "island" the next day, it had disappeared. Martín Alonso Pinzón was not the first seaman to mistake a low-lying storm cloud for a landfall, nor would he be the last.

As September gave way to October—by then the fleet had been sailing for three weeks without sight of land—the strains of isolation began to show. The sailors, their faces now covered with unruly beards, their woolen clothing caked with sweat and salt spray, began to mutter openly about the folly of this so-called Enterprise of the Indies. A few were so terrified that they even whispered plots to throw the captain-general overboard and head for home.

Columbus ignored their grumbling and sailed resolutely on to the west. He did not waver in his course until October 7, when another supposed island proved to be nonexistent. That day a great flock of small birds flew overhead toward the southwest—and they were definitely land birds. With that, Columbus decided to let the birds be his beacons and gave the order: Head west by southwest. Follow the birds.

He correctly guessed that the birds were "flying from the winter which was about to come to the lands whence they came." The annual autumn migration of warblers, tanagers, orioles, and countless other birds from North America to the islands of the Caribbean and to South America was then at its peak. The next day, he noted with satisfaction, the crew sighted "many land birds," and on October 9, "All night they heard birds passing."

But on October 10 he was faced with open rebellion. Sailing before a brisk wind, the fleet covered the miles so rapidly that "the men could now bear no more." They were certain they were being swept to their doom. Somehow, Columbus managed to placate them with

reassuring words and promises of oriental gold. Then, in a speech undoubtedly laced with a good many "By San Fernandos!" (according to his son, the strongest oath he ever uttered), "he added that it was vain for them to complain, since he was going to the Indies and must pursue his course until, with the help of our Lord, he found them."

The next day all the grumbling faded away. Floating on the waves were so many signs of land—a leafy twig, a branch covered with flowers, a piece of wood that seemed to have been carved by human hands—that "all breathed again and rejoiced."

At sunset Columbus led his sailors in the ancient Benedictine chant "Salve Regina" and reminded them that the crown had promised an annuity of 10,000 maravedis to the first man to sight land. He himself added the pledge of a silk doublet. The galley fires were put out, lanterns were hung astern to keep the ships from losing track of each other, and at 7 o'clock the first night watch began.

The sea was rough that night, and the fleet bobbed dizzily across waves whose crests glistened in the moonlight. The captains on all three ships paced the decks nervously, straining their eyes to scan the western horizon. At about 10 o'clock Columbus saw a faint light, far in the distance, "like a small wax candle which was raised and lowered." The glow rose and fell for a time and then disappeared and was seen no more.*

The flurry of excitement over the captain-general's false alarm soon died down, and the ships sailed on into the silent, starry night. Then, at 2 o'clock on the morning of October 12, Rodrigo de Triana, a sailor on the *Pinta*, cried out, *"Tierra! Tierra!"* And land it was, white sandy cliffs glowing pale in the moonlight.

So began the greatest day in Christopher Columbus' life. He was no longer a mere explorer. He was a discoverer. He had found his western shortcut to the East Indies. His theories now were proven fact. He had earned the right to the titles he had demanded, Admiral

---

*\* Mrs. Rose Malvin, an American resident of San Salvador, is the first
to explain what Columbus saw: It was Indians lighting brush fires on the eastern coast of the island to keep sand flies out of their huts.*

of the Ocean Sea, Viceroy and Governor of the Indies.

(The island shimmering with ghostly pallor on the horizon, of course, was not part of the Indies, but one of the Bahama Islands, whose low, sandy profiles dot the sea in a broad arc off the southern tip of Florida.)

The sun rose that day on the virginal beauty of the New World. Six miles ahead, a necklace of coral reefs and sparkling beaches encircled a gently rolling island covered with such a lush growth of tropical hardwood that Columbus pronounced it "so green that it is a pleasure to gaze upon" and named his find San Salvador—"Holy Savior."

Quickly and almost quietly, one of the great events in the history of exploration took place. From his ship Columbus saw naked humans emerging from the green trees along the shore. Excitedly, he called his captains, Martín and Vicente Pinzón, gathered up the royal standards of Spain, and set out for land in an armed boat. Then, leaping ashore, he and his companions planted the fluttering banners in the sand, and as the natives watched their strangely jubilant visitors from a distance, he formally took possession of the island.

Almost immediately, Columbus was surrounded by dozens of the curious inhabitants, "naked as their mothers bore them." (Thinking he was in the Indies, Columbus called them Indians, and all indigenous Americans have been so known ever since. These and all the Indians he encountered on his first voyage were Arawaks, belonging to a group of peoples then widespread in the islands and along the north coast of South America.) Columbus was highly impressed by their trim physiques ("they have no bellies but very good figures"), by their hospitality (they "became so entirely our friends that it was a wonder to see"), and by their quick wits ("they very soon say all that is said to them"). Ever an evangelizer, he also noted their apparent lack of religion ("I believe that they could easily be made Christians"). And observing their docility, he commented—prophetically—that "with 50 men they could be kept in subjugation and forced to do whatever may be wished."

But most of all, he was impressed by the little glittering pendants of pure gold that dangled from their noses. In the two days the Spaniards remained on San Salvador, a brisk trade developed in red woolen caps, glass beads, and other trinkets bartered for food, fresh water, parrots, balls of cotton thread—and those little gold pendants.

Columbus' Arabic interpreter, naturally, proved quite useless in the Bahamas. Even so, by means of sign language, the Spaniards managed to extract a good deal of information from the gentle Arawaks. For one thing, they gathered that to the south and west the sea was strewn with countless islands. Better still was the news that in the south "there was a king who had . . . much gold."

This was thrilling news. According to some of the highly imaginative maps of the time, the sea to the east of Asia *was* dotted with islands, including that big one, Cipangu, where, according to Marco Polo, gold was so plentiful that palaces were roofed and floored with the precious metal. "So," Columbus declared, "I resolved to go to the southwest, to seek the gold and precious stones . . . and see if I can make the island of Cipangu."

With six captive Arawaks as interpreters and guides, the little fleet cruised to the southwest for nearly two weeks, discovering new islands along the way. Wherever the fleet stopped, bewildered natives, once they overcame their fear of the explorers, made it clear that they believed the Spaniards had come from heaven. The Spanish, in turn, were the first Europeans to taste sweet potatoes, maize, and cassavas, and the first to admire the Indians' strange beds, "like nets of cotton." These queer contraptions—hammocks—were soon to be enthusiastically adopted by European sailors.

But the only gold to be found in the Bahamas was those little nose ornaments. The only encouraging signs were garbled hints of a much bigger island to the south,

## Hammocks, Pineapples, and Other Novelties

If Columbus was disappointed that he had not found great quantities of gold and silver, his journals give no evidence of it. Instead, he rejoiced over the discovery of plants and animals previously unknown to Europeans. Columbus lamented his inability to identify "many trees which are worth a lot for medicine and spicery, but I don't recognize them, which gives me great grief." Among the plants new to Columbus were the sweet potato, the tobacco plant, and the pineapple, described by one of his men as "a fruit the shape of a pine cone but twice as big." Columbus also noted the customs and unusual inventions of the Caribbean Indians, including the hammocks in which they slept. These hammocks were soon adopted by European seamen, who had previously slept on the hard planks of ships' decks. The 16th-century woodcut at left is the first European illustration of an Indian hammock. It appeared in 1535.

called Coiba or Cuba, where, the Indians seemed to be saying, there were many large ships. This, Columbus optimistically concluded, had to be "the island of Cipangu, of which marvelous things are recounted."

The mariners caught their first glimpse of Cuba as the sun set on October 27. It certainly looked different from the little, low-lying Bahamas. Covered with lofty blue mountains, it seemed to stretch endlessly to the east and west. When the fleet anchored along the north coast the next day, Columbus was immediately struck by the island's beauty. (Unlike most of the early explorers, he had an eye for landscapes.) Calling Cuba the most beautiful island he had ever seen, he had nothing but praise for its excellent harbors and inviting streams, its lush green trees quite unlike anything that grew in Spain, its flocks of colorful birds singing sweetly on every side.

But instead of merchant ships and gold-roofed palaces, all he found on shore were dugout canoes and a village of small, round huts. And their conical roofs were thatched not with gold but with palm leaves.

This scene was very confusing. Had Marco Polo exaggerated the riches of Cipangu? However, within a few days the perplexed Columbus solved the riddle. Whenever he showed any native Cubans a bit of gold, they pointed inland, where there may have been a little of the metal, and pronounced their word for the center of the island, "Cubanacan."

Cubanacan? -can? -khan? That was it! They could mean nothing but "the Great Khan." Columbus was not in Cipangu at all. He had stumbled on some impoverished corner of Asia. He was in China!

The admiral immediately dispatched a diplomatic party, complete with an official letter from Ferdinand and Isabella, on a mission to meet with the Great Khan. But they found no gold-domed city—just a village of about 50 native huts. Although the local cacique, or chief, politely entertained his guests from heaven, he could not understand a single word spoken by the Arabic interpreter. Even the names of the famous Chinese cities of Kinsai and Zayton failed to ring a bell. When Columbus' disgruntled ambassadors returned to the coast, about the only interesting thing they could report on was the natives' strange habit of inhaling smoke from rolled *tobacos,* which they stuck in their nostrils. Little did the Spaniards suspect that this weed one day would prove as valuable as gold.

Columbus cruised along the north coast of Cuba for five weeks and in that time found not a scrap of gold. Somewhere along the line his Arawak guides changed their tune and began insisting that they got the metal from yet another island to the east. Its name was Babeque and its beaches, they seemed to be saying, were studded with pure gold nuggets. This tale proved too tempting for Martín Alonso Pinzón. One night the *Pinta*'s sails disappeared over the horizon as her captain set off to do some exploring on his own. He would not be seen again by Columbus for more than six weeks.

By December 5 the *Niña* and the *Santa María* reached the easternmost tip of Cuba and continued east across the open sea. The next day the explorers made the most important discovery of their voyage: a vast, heavily populated island of breathtaking beauty. With characteristic enthusiasm, Columbus wrote eloquently of its "beautiful, fertile plain" and its "very lofty mountains which seemed to touch the sky, and which were very beautiful, full of green trees." A practical mariner, he also took note of its many harbors, which he declared to be the finest he had ever seen. All hands, in short, agreed that the island was every bit as beautiful as Spain—perhaps even more so—and Columbus accordingly named it La Isla Española, "The Spanish Isle." (Later renamed Hispaniola, it is now shared by Haiti and the Dominican Republic.)

In the next two weeks the Spaniards explored about a third of Hispaniola's northern coast, which Columbus mapped with fair accuracy. Here and there they paused to visit large settlements of corn- and cassava-growing Arawaks and to look for signs of gold. As they headed east, it seemed to become more plentiful.

On December 20 the ships dropped anchor in Acul Bay, a mountain-fringed harbor so magnificent that Columbus confessed himself completely at a loss for words to describe it. Better still, the local natives proved to be extraordinarily friendly. They passed out gold trinkets with such a free hand that Columbus piously commented, "It is easy to know when something is given with a great readiness to give." One chief, Guacanagari, sent a particularly handsome gift of finely embroidered cotton cloth decorated with hammered gold. Dazzled by such generosity, Columbus promptly set sail to visit the chief, whose village was a few miles to the east—closer, perhaps, to Cipangu.

The result was an accident that led to the establishment of the first Spanish settlement in the New World. Toward midnight on Christmas Eve, as the two ships sailed into the bay off Guacanagari's village, the sleepy helmsman on the *Santa María* took a nap, leaving the tiller in the hands of an inexperienced boy. In no time at all, there was a sickening crunch as the ship ran aground on a coral reef.

The first Europeans ever to spend Christmas in the New World had little time for celebration. They worked the whole day desperately trying to save the ship. But the hull was so full of holes that water gushed in faster than the men could pump it out. Columbus finally had to admit defeat and salvage what he could of the supplies before transferring his flag to the *Niña.*

He was soon consoled by the discovery that Guacanagari's subjects had plenty of gold ornaments and were willing to part with them for practically nothing. The chief, moreover, assured Columbus that there was lots more gold where that came from, in an interior region called Cibao. Columbus, in another lin-

guistic lapse, jumped to the conclusion that the Indian was mispronouncing Cipangu. The Spanish Isle could be none other than Japan, here in the sea to the east of China, just where the maps said it should be.

The admiral decided then and there that the shipwreck had been a blessing in disguise. In this island paradise he had discovered a boundless source of wealth for his monarchs. With the broken timbers of the *Santa María*, he built a fort on shore and named it Navidad to honor Christmas. Then, in the first attempt at colonizing the New World, he left about 40 men behind to work Hispaniola's gold mines and, on January 4, 1493, set sail for Spain. With him, he took his haul of gold trinkets, all sorts of island souvenirs, and six Indians as proof of his discoveries.

Two days later he sighted the *Pinta* cruising west along the coast. The reunion with Martín Pinzón must have been a bit tense. Columbus was distinctly annoyed with the insubordination of one who "had parted from him against his will." Pinzón, he now

### Fierce Caribs Battle Determined Spaniards

Tranquil and luxuriant that day, the Salt River Bay on the coast of St. Croix (now one of the American Virgin Islands) provided the setting for one of the first armed clashes between Europeans and Indians in the New World. The battle took place on November 14, 1493, during Columbus' second voyage to America. A party of sailors returning to the Spanish fleet from shore reconnaissance sighted and pursued a canoe of belligerent Carib Indians with Arawak captives. The seamen, a rough lot, wore no armor in the steamy tropical heat. None of them carried guns, a luxury only wealthy gentlemen could afford, but several men were armed with pikes and swords. The seamen's round shields, made of heavy leather, did not offer great protection from arrows shot at such close range. The shield of the sailor in the stern, in fact, had been pierced by a Carib arrow as the seaman was leaning forward to fire his heavy crossbow. The warlike Caribs, who originated in South America, had only recently immigrated to the Lesser Antilles, where they had conquered the peaceful Arawaks who inhabited the islands. The English word cannibal actually comes from the Arawaks' term to describe the Carib practice of eating their captives. The captive Arawaks who paddled this Indian canoe, however, had been enslaved rather than killed. Carib women often held positions of power in tribal society, and two fought alongside the warriors in this canoe. One of Columbus' lieutenants, Michele da Cuneo, described the battle, the first of many such encounters between European and Indian: "The Caribs began shooting at us with their bows in such a manner that, had it not been for the shields, half of us would have been wounded. But I must tell you that to one of the seamen, who had a shield in his hand, came an arrow which went through the shield and penetrated his chest three inches so that he died in a few days. We captured the canoe and all the men, and one Carib was wounded by a spear in such a way that we thought he was dead and cast him into the sea, but instantly saw him swim. In so doing we caught him and with the grapple hauled him over the bulwarks of the ship where we cut his head with an ax." One of the women was captured and given to Cuneo, who—after thrashing her—made her his mistress. Cuneo's eyewitness description contrasts with the peaceful rendition of Columbus' landing in the New World in the late-15th-century picture at right. Here docile Indians line the shore as the Europeans disembark.

learned, had sailed on to Babeque (Great Inagua in the southern Bahamas), where he had found no gold, then proceeded to Hispaniola, where (so he said) he had found a source of it. This good news presumably did much to quell Columbus' anger. About a week later the two ships let the mountains of Hispaniola drop below the horizon and headed out into the Atlantic.

The homeward voyage was plagued by violent storms and raging seas, which caused the ships to become separated off the Azores. Even so, by March 4

Columbus found his way into the harbor of Lisbon, where he paused for repairs and paraded his gold and the captive Arawaks before a not very enthusiastic King John. At last, on March 15, 1493, the *Niña* came to anchor in the Río Tinto, and the admiral strode ashore at Palos. A few hours later Martín Pinzón followed him into port with the *Pinta*. The weary discoverers had been away for 7 months and 12 days.

The next few months were among the happiest in Columbus' life. Summoning him to court at Barcelona in mid-April, Ferdinand and Isabella honored the admiral with a reception that surpassed his wildest dreams. "The king received him with much honor and favor," reported Columbus' son, "and bade him be seated and not doff his cap." (To be allowed to sit in the royal presence was an honor indeed.) The monarchs listened with rapt attention to Columbus' tales of his adventures and his glowing descriptions of the New World. They gasped in awe at the captive Arawaks, the squawking parrots, the odds and ends of gold. Overnight, Columbus became a national hero.

Anxious to secure their claim on his discoveries, the king and queen ordered Columbus to return to Hispaniola as soon as possible. Within five months a fleet of 17 ships carrying more than 1,200 men—the largest colonizing expedition to that time ever sent out by a European nation—was equipped and ready to set sail. Columbus' instructions were to convert the natives, establish a permanent trading colony, and find out whether Cuba was really part of Asia. To assist him in these tasks, the admiral took along his younger brother, Diego.

Columbus' first departure had been from an unimportant little river town. This time trumpets blared and cannon boomed across the water as his armada moved majestically out to sea from the splendid port of Cádiz. The date was September 25, 1493.

From the Canaries, Columbus set his course farther south than he had on his first voyage. His aim was to find some of the large islands his Indian interpreters claimed lay to the southeast of Hispaniola. (One especially quick-witted Arawak, who had been baptized Diego Colón, had picked up a good deal of Spanish during his visit in Castile. He was to prove infinitely more useful than the Arabic interpreter had been.)

The easy Atlantic crossing ended when a lookout sighted an extremely lovely island on November 3. Since the day was Sunday, *dies Domini*, Columbus named his new discovery Dominica. The island, located about halfway down the Lesser Antilles, which form a chain south from the Virgin Islands nearly to South America, marked the beginning of the world's first-known Caribbean cruise.

Pausing briefly at Marie-Galante, named after Columbus' flagship, the fleet sailed north and landed next at the lush volcanic island of Guadeloupe. There a shore party was aghast to discover that Arawak tales of their dreaded enemies, the Caribs, were true. Hanging in hastily abandoned huts were joints of human flesh. The Caribs were cannibals, fierce warriors who raided nearby islands to satisfy their sinister appetites. The explorers also came across captive women, whom the cannibals kept to provide them with their favorite morsels—plump, succulent babies. The Spaniards, for their part, preferred pineapples, which they tasted here for the first time.

Continuing north, the armada sailed past an exquis-ite group of islands—Montserrat, Antigua, Redonda, Nevis, St. Kitts—many of them still bearing names based on those that Columbus gave them. On November 13 the fleet put in at St. Croix. The next day the explorers had their first serious fight with Caribs. On past the seemingly countless Virgin Islands they sailed, along the mountainous southern coast of Puerto Rico, and then across the Mona Passage on November 22 to their first landfall on Hispaniola.

There the idyllic island-hopping cruise abruptly ended. While coasting west toward Navidad, a shore party found four corpses, all so badly decayed that it was impossible to tell if they were whites or Indians. But one had traces of a beard—and the Arawaks, like most Indians, were beardless.

When the armada reached Navidad on November 28, the explorers made an even more alarming discovery: The fort had been burned to the ground, and not a Spaniard was to be seen anywhere. Columbus soon learned that instead of mining for gold his settlers had spent their time rampaging over the island, stealing from the natives, and appropriating their women. Before long, they had run afoul of a fierce inland chief, whose subjects ran down the greedy colonists and murdered every last one of them. So much for the myth of the timid Arawak.

Appalled by this outcome, the Spaniards gave up the plan of settling Navidad and founded a new colony at Isabela, about 100 miles to the east. Over the next few months Columbus explored enough of the island's interior to realize it was not Japan. But he did manage to collect a fair haul of "that thrice-blessed gold" to send to Spain with a fleet going back for supplies.

Late in April the admiral set out for Cuba "to explore the mainland of the Indies." Leaving the garrison at Isabela under command of his brother Diego, he sailed with a fleet of three small caravels, headed by the trusty little *Niña*. This time he planned to probe Cuba's southern shores, since, according to notions of the day, things of value were more likely to be found in the south than in the north.

The Indians he encountered in Cuba proved hospitable enough, but they had no gold. That, they explained, came from a large island to the south called Jameque. Jameque? Could they mean Babeque, the island with the gold-paved beaches?

Speeding south to find out, on May 5 the explorers sighted a lush tropical island—Jamaica—and another gap on the map of the Caribbean was filled in. But the Indians were unfriendly and had no gold. After cruising west along Jamaica's coast for about a week, the disappointed Spaniards returned to Cuba.

The next month provided a real test of the admiral's skill as a navigator. Hugging the coast lest he miss any signs of oriental splendor, he guided his fleet slowly and painfully through narrow, twisting channels between the treacherous shoals and islets that dot Cuba's

**There are no portraits** *of Columbus painted during his lifetime. However, the "Virgin of the Navigators" (above) was done not long after his death by Alejo Fernández, a Spanish artist who knew the admiral. The man in the rich robes with a sharp aquiline nose, at lower left, has often been identified as Columbus.*

At that point his little fleet was perhaps 50 miles short of the western tip of Cuba. But how was Christopher Columbus to know that? For the rest of his life he remained firmly convinced that Cuba was a peninsula of Asia, the goal he had sought by sailing west.

The homeward journey, beating against constant headwinds, was painfully slow. Even so, instead of returning directly to Isabela, Columbus took the time to veer south and explore and map the southern coasts of both Jamaica and Hispaniola. He did not reach Isabela until September 29.

When he got there, he found that in the five months he had been away the fledgling colony had fallen into utter chaos. Bands of Spaniards were roaming all over the island, terrorizing the natives, stealing their gold, and enslaving captives. Soon open warfare broke out, with Columbus himself leading his troops in battle. This was in sorry contrast to his monarchs' orders to be kind to the Indians. The cruelty of the Spaniards was so great, in fact, that Hispaniola's Arawaks, who numbered in the hundreds of thousands in 1492, were virtually exterminated within 50 years.

Eventually, complaints about Columbus' inept and arbitrary administration reached the crown. In October 1495 a Spanish inspector visited the colony and took a report back to the sovereigns. Columbus, correctly assuming that its contents were unflattering, realized he had better return to Spain to defend himself. Leaving the colony in charge of his brother Bartholomew, who had joined him there, Columbus set sail in March 1496, along with 30 Indians and 225 disillusioned colonists. Impossibly crowded into two small ships and badly underfed en route, the group reached Cádiz on June 11. According to one observer, mere skeletons with "faces the color of lemon or saffron" struggled down the gangplanks.

Two years passed before Columbus was able to drum up support for another venture to the New World. Though cooperative, Ferdinand and Isabella were not quite as enthusiastic as before, and their attention was diverted by other interests. The expedition, as finally approved, consisted of six ships and a motley crowd of colonists, including many criminals who were promised pardons in return for working in Hispaniola. For the first time, a number of women also were included. One purpose of the voyage was to deliver men and supplies to Hispaniola, but Columbus also planned to search for more new lands, particularly to the south of the islands he had already discovered.

Invoking the blessings of the Holy Trinity, he left Spain on May 30, 1498. From the Canary Islands three of the ships sailed directly for Hispaniola, while the rest continued south to the Cape Verde Islands. There Columbus headed southwest on the most southerly of all his voyages across the ocean.

No land was seen until July 31, when the crew sighted a cluster of peaks that, as if by miracle, "had

southern coast. Yet the agonies of the voyage seemed worthwhile. According to the maps he had seen, the sea off southern China was peppered with islands. And, though he found no great cities, Indians told him that the territory to the west was called Magón, which sounded encouragingly similar to Marco Polo's Chinese province of Mangi. For good measure, the Indians added that their own land was so big that it would take years to reach its end. When a shore party saw a couple of fair-skinned natives dressed in flowing white robes, Columbus jumped to the conclusion that he had stumbled on the kingdom of Prester John, a Christian prince who supposedly lived somewhere in Africa or the Far East. There might be no gold, no spices, no splendid cities; yet all the signs seemed to indicate that Cuba was indeed the Asian mainland.

But Columbus was too weary to prove it. By June 12 he calculated—incorrectly—that he had sailed about 650 miles along the coast of Cuba. And no one, the crew agreed, had ever heard of an island *that* long. So Columbus had all his men sign depositions swearing that Cuba was part of Asia and then turned back.

*Map for Columbus on page 66.*

the appearance of three mountains joined at the base." Giving thanks to the Holy Trinity, Columbus named the island Trinidad. The next day he made out the long low profile of what seemed to be another island on the misty horizon to the south. Columbus named it Isla Sancta. Although he did not know it, he had just discovered South America.

Sailing into the Gulf of Paria between Trinidad and the mainland, Columbus spent two weeks exploring the lush green coast of present-day Venezuela. He was much impressed by the sophistication of the Venezuelan Indians, expert cotton weavers who wore huge ornaments of gold-and-copper alloy as well as strings of magnificent pearls. (Within a year the Spanish would begin to exploit the region's lucrative pearl fishery.)

But by August 15, afraid that his cargo of food and wine was spoiling in the tropical heat, he decided to leave his new discoveries behind and sail north to Hispaniola.

By then Columbus realized that his "Isla Sancta" was much bigger than an island. The seawater in the Gulf of Paria was so fresh (it is diluted by the outflow of the great Orinoco River) that he concluded that it had to receive the drainage of a really immense landmass. In his journal Columbus declared, "I believe that this is a very great continent, which until today has been unknown."

But even a continent was not a big enough find for the Admiral of the Ocean Sea. A shore party had discovered four large rivers flowing into the gulf (actually four of the many mouths of the Orinoco); Columbus in

---

## Dead Reckoning a Course Across the Ocean: How Columbus Navigated His Way to America

The discovery of America is only part of Christopher Columbus' achievement. It is equally remarkable that he found his way back across the Atlantic to bring the news of his discovery to Spain. Even more noteworthy, on his subsequent voyages Columbus was able to relocate previously discovered islands, although they were scattered across a wide area of the virtually unknown Caribbean.

Columbus' ability to find the correct landfall was not a matter of luck. He was an excellent navigator who employed only the most basic of marine instruments: a compass (an enclosed circular card—marked with the points of direction—mounted on a pin, with a lodestone beneath the North point), assorted navigational charts, a pair of dividers, a straightedge, and a sandglass to reckon time. Although Columbus had an astrolabe and a quadrant, both of which help determine latitude, he was unable to take correct readings with either. The movement of the ship made accurate sightings impossible. Like most experienced mariners of his day, Columbus relied on dead reckoning, navigating a ship by periodic estimates of speed and direction. In dead reckoning, a navigator multiplies the estimated speed of his ship by the length of time it has been sailing in a particular direction. He then places one point of his dividers on the starting location of the vessel, and measuring along the correct course with a straightedge, he pricks a hole with the other point at the approximate place his calculations indicate the ship has reached.

Navigators still use dead reckoning to determine the position of their ships, but today, sophisticated instruments can check their calculations. Dead reckoning in the 15th century, however, involved much guesswork. There were no accurate methods to gauge time, speed, or distance. Mariners in the 16th century began to employ a line with knots tied at regular intervals to determine a ship's speed. By counting the number of knots played out in a half hour, approximate speed could be calculated. Today, we still

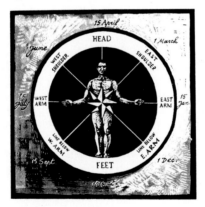

use the term knots to denote speed at sea. Columbus, however, had no such device to help him. As a result, he overestimated his speed, which threw off his calculations of distance.

On his first voyage Columbus recorded the distance his ships traveled every day in his personal logbook. In a logbook kept for the crew, he reduced the distances, so the men would not know how far they had sailed from land. Ironically, the crew's logbook was a more accurate record of the distances Columbus covered than his own personal calculations, in which he consistently overestimated the distances by about 9 percent.

Reckoning time at sea also presented problems. The ship's sand clock had to be adjusted periodically as the vessel traveled through the changing time zones of the Atlantic: The clock could be checked against the elevation of the sun at local noon. At night sailors could tell time by the stars. One method well known to 15th-century mariners was to determine the position of Kochab, the brightest star in the Little Dipper, in relation to the North Star. The Little Dipper rotates around the North Star every 24 hours like the hands of a clock. A diagram of a man, similar to the one at left, with the North Star at the center of his body, could therefore be used as a kind of heavenly timepiece. Lines radiated from the center of the diagram to the edges of a circle where dates were indicated. On April 15, for example, midnight could be determined by noting when Kochab appeared above the head of the man. In his journal Columbus noted that he told time in this manner.

But dead reckoning depended on more than just estimating time and distance. It also depended on the innate skill of the navigator, his own individual sense of the sea. And no mariner of the age surpassed Columbus in his ability to "read" the wind, sky, and waves. Michele da Cuneo, who sailed with the second voyage, paid tribute to Columbus' genius: "In my humble opinion, since Genoa was Genoa, no other man has been born so magnanimous and so keen in practical navigation as the above mentioned Lord Admiral; for when navigating by only looking at a cloud or by night at a star, he knew what was going to happen and whether there would be foul weather."

a breathtaking leap of the imagination decided that they were none other than the four rivers of Paradise. South America was the Garden of Eden!

(The idea, in fact, did not seem as farfetched in the 15th century as it does today. In Columbus' time, most scholars agreed that the Earthly Paradise lay somewhere off the southeastern corner of Asia—and that is exactly where Columbus thought he was.)

On August 31, 1498, the fleet arrived at Santo Domingo, the new capital of Hispaniola, which Columbus' brother Bartholomew had founded during his absence. He soon discovered that Bartholomew was no better than Diego at governing the fractious colonists and spent the next two years trying to establish order in the chaotic colony. The Spanish sovereigns, however, eventually concluded that Columbus was a good admiral but a poor governor. When he returned from an inland tour in August 1500, he found himself replaced by a royal commissioner, Francisco de Bobadilla.

Bobadilla immediately seized Columbus' house, his gold, and his papers. And, as if that were not brutal enough, he had Columbus and his brothers clapped into chains for alleged crimes and improprieties and summarily shipped them back to Spain. During the voyage the ship's captain offered to take off the bonds, but Columbus refused. He was determined to wear them until Ferdinand and Isabella personally ordered them removed. According to his son Ferdinand, "he was resolved to keep those chains as a memorial of how well he had been rewarded for his services. . . . And this he did, for I always saw them in his bedroom, and he wanted them buried with his bones." The chains were still in place when the Admiral of the Ocean Sea arrived in Cádiz at the end of October 1500.

His condition caused an instant sensation. The monarchs soon had him freed and invited him to court. When he was ushered into the royal presence, Columbus fell on his knees and wept. Deeply touched by his humiliation, Ferdinand and Isabella "received him with friendly and affectionate greetings, assuring him that his imprisonment had not been by their wishes or command." Although they made no mention of sending Columbus back to administer Hispaniola, they did send another royal commissioner, Nicolás de Ovando, to replace Bobadilla. Eventually, the admiral's confiscated property was restored as well.

Months passed, and Columbus gradually recovered his dignity. Though he was 50—an old man by 16th-century standards—and suffering from arthritis and poor eyesight, he was still eager to explore. Early in 1502 he asked his monarchs' permission to set out on yet another voyage of discovery. They promptly agreed, and on May 11 he embarked from Cádiz with a fleet of four caravels. Accompanying him this time were his brother Bartholomew and his 13-year-old son Ferdinand, who later chronicled the voyage.

Columbus' plan was characteristically grandiose: to

### "Nobody Objected"

Returning from his first voyage, Columbus wrote immediately to the Spanish rulers via his benefactor and friend Luís de Santángel, keeper of the privy purse for the queen: "Forasmuch as I know that you will take pleasure in the great triumph with which Our Lord has crowned my voyage, I write this to you from which you will learn how . . . I reached the Indies. . . . And there I found very many islands filled with people without number, and of them all have I taken possession for their highnesses . . . and nobody objected." He related the richness and beauty of the islands, the gentleness of the people he called Indians, the outpost he built at Navidad, and his wish to return and reap the wealth for their majesties. Printed in Barcelona, the letter created such a stir that six editions soon followed, and an illustrated translation appeared in Basel that year. The admiral's ship in one version (above) copied a 1486 woodcut. Columbus' logbooks have been lost, but this map of the north coast of Haiti, which he called La Isla Española, is his. Columbus made the drawing during his second voyage to America.

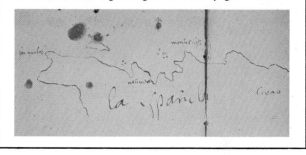

sail west between the south coast of China (Cuba) and his recently discovered Earthly Paradise (South America) until he reached India, and then continue on back to Spain via the other side of the world. Always thinking of a new crusade, he intended to use the profits of the voyage to liberate Jerusalem from the Turks.

On June 15 Columbus discovered Martinique, the next island south of his 1493 landfall at Dominica. Two weeks later the fleet made an unscheduled stop at Santo Domingo and then, continuing across the Caribbean, found its way blocked by Central America.

Assuming this obstacle to be Indochina, known to jut south from eastern Asia, Columbus spent the next several months trying to find a way around it or through it. From his landfall in present-day Honduras, he sailed laboriously south past Nicaragua and Costa Rica as far as modern-day Panama, battling headwinds, contrary currents, and storms every inch of the way.

Sailing conditions were among the vilest Columbus had ever endured. One storm that blew up on December 6 and lasted for a month he declared to be the worst he had ever experienced: "The wind not only prevented

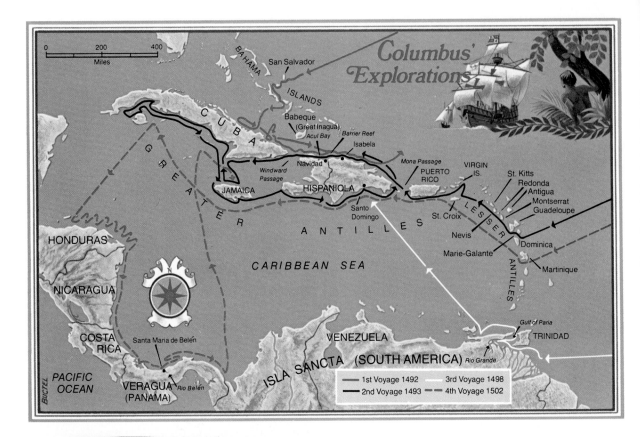

Columbus' Explorations

1st Voyage 1492
2nd Voyage 1493
3rd Voyage 1498
4th Voyage 1502

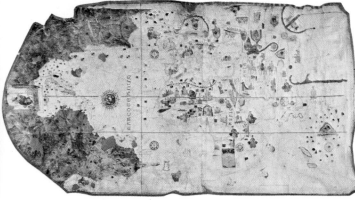

**Columbus' four encounters** *with the New World took place in the Caribbean. The very first landfall (San Salvador in the Bahamas) was the happiest, for to Columbus it was indisputable proof of his belief that the Indies lay across the Ocean Sea. Then followed the meandering and increasingly frustrating course along the coasts of Cuba and Hispaniola. When he returned to Spain in 1493, Columbus and his sponsors were sure he had fulfilled his mission. The succeeding three voyages, in 1493, 1498, and 1502, uncovered many new islands and what appeared to be extensive mainland, but no sign of Japan or China. Left, the first-known map to show the New World (islands at far left) in relation to the Old World was drawn by Columbus' shipmate Juan de la Cosa in 1500.*

our progress, but offered no opportunity to run behind any headland for shelter; hence we were forced to keep out in this bloody ocean, seething like a pot on a hot fire. Never did the sky look more terrible; for one whole day and night it blazed like a furnace, and lightning broke forth with such violence that each time I wondered if it had carried off my spars and sails; the flashes came with such fury and frightfulness that we all thought the ships would be blasted. All this time the water never ceased to fall from the sky; I don't say it rained, because it was like another Deluge. The people were so worn out that they longed for death to end their dreadful sufferings."

As for food, Ferdinand vividly described the situa-

tion. "What with the heat and dampness," he recalled, "our ship biscuit had become so wormy that, God help me, I saw many who waited for darkness to eat the porridge made of it, that they might not see the maggots; and others were so used to eating them that they didn't even trouble to pick them out, because they might lose their supper, had they been so nice."

Through it all, Columbus kept optimistically probing rivers and bays, hoping each one would turn out to be the strait he was looking for. All were dead ends. By the time he reached the vicinity of modern-day Panama, he learned, through an Indian interpreter who developed a remarkably quick command of Castilian, that he was standing on an isthmus between two oceans. Possibly,

**An embittered** *Columbus appears in this portrait painted some years after his death. Feeling that fate had dealt harshly with him, Columbus wrote, late in his life: "I have lost my youth and the part which belongs to me of these discoveries and the glory of it. . . . I was despoiled of my honor and estate without cause. . . . Weep for me whoever has charity, truth, and justice!"*

he was also told that no waterway connected the two seas, for he here gave up his search for a strait and resumed his favorite occupation: looking for gold.

Indians all along the coast had plenty of gold ornaments. When Columbus learned that most of the ore from which the ornaments were fashioned came from a rugged stretch of the isthmus that he named Veragua, he hurried there to establish a settlement. In the hopes of finally having made a truly profitable discovery, in January 1503 he anchored his fleet in the Río Belén, planning to leave one ship and her crew behind to mine a load of the precious metal. But the local Guaymi Indians had other ideas, and after a few fierce battles Columbus wisely decided to give up the project. In mid-April he quit both the would-be settlement and a caravel that had become stranded behind a sandbar.

Before long, a less violent but equally dangerous enemy—shipworms—destroyed another of the caravels, riddling her planks with borings. Multiplying rapidly in the tropical heat, these silent destroyers soon attacked the other two caravels as well. By the time the ships reached Jamaica late in June, six pumps were working night and day to keep the rotting hulks afloat.

Realizing that the ships would never make it to Hispaniola, Columbus beached them in a sheltered bay. And there the explorers remained for a year, surviving as best they could on shipboard.

The admiral soon sent two volunteers, Diego Mendez and Bartolomeo Fieschi, across the open sea by canoe to seek help at Santo Domingo. As months dragged by, no sails appeared on the horizon, and the marooned men waited helplessly in their stricken vessels. Columbus took to his bed with arthritis, forbidding his men to go ashore lest they terrorize the Jamaican Indians who were supplying them with food.

By early January the shipboard atmosphere, always claustrophobic, grew explosive. Mutiny erupted, and about half the men abandoned ship to set out for Hispaniola by canoe. Rough seas soon brought them shamefacedly back to Jamaica, where they set up camp in the wilderness.

The relief ship did not appear until June 29, 1504. Columbus by then had made peace with the mutineers, and with immense relief, they all set out for Hispaniola. The ordeal of Columbus' fourth voyage was over.

From there Columbus, his son Ferdinand, his brother Bartholomew, and 22 members of the expedition chartered a vessel to Spain. By the time Columbus arrived in November 1504, he was a mortally tired man. When his revered Queen Isabella died three weeks later, the loss must have seemed to the aging explorer like an omen of his own death. In the last year of his life he suffered increasingly from arthritis and public indifference to his great achievements. On May 20, 1506, he died in the presence of his brother Diego, his two sons, and a few faithful friends, including the valiant canoeists, Mendez and Fieschi, who had delivered him from the indignity of an unmarked grave.

He died convinced that he had accomplished exactly what he had set out to do 14 years before. Certain that he had succeeded in sailing west to Asia, he never once suspected that he had in fact made the greatest geographical discovery of all time. Instead of the Indies, he had opened up the way to a whole new world.

## Why It's "America"

Not only was Columbus frustrated in his desire to reach the Indies, but the great discovery he did make was to be named after another explorer: Amerigo Vespucci (left), an Italian who sailed for Spain and Portugal to coastal South America in 1499, 1501, and 1503 and claimed the great landmass to be a continent. It was first shown in a map of 1507 with an introduction stating: "This fourth part of the world, in as much as Americus discovered it, be called Amerigo, or . . . land of Americu, that is AMERICA." Gradually, the name became accepted. In an allegorical engraving (below), Vespucci meets a lady called America.

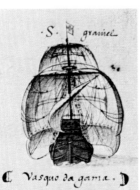

**News swept across Europe** *that Da Gama's voyage had linked the sumptuous markets of India to a western world eager for trade. European art and writing on the discovery relied mainly on the embellished tales of seafarers, with some whimsical results. In the Flemish tapestry above, woven about 1525, Indians in western garb celebrate Da Gama's arrival on the Malabar Coast in 1498. The oriental buildings of tropical Calicut are here transformed into towers and turrets of a European city, while children ride a horselike elephant and giraffes, the latter native to Africa rather than India. Calicut is not Calcutta but the Malabar city of Kozhikode, situated near the southern tip of the peninsula. Returning to India twice, Da Gama died there in 1524, only four months after arriving as viceroy (far left) at the trading post at Cochin. The flagship* São Gabriel *of his landmark voyage was probably a square-rigged nao (left), less than 100 feet long. She probably made a maximum of eight miles an hour on the 13,000-mile outbound journey.*

*Chapter Six. After a half century of African reconnaissance, the Portuguese finally reach the Orient in a momentous 13,000-mile voyage from Lisbon to the Malabar Coast. The success of the bold two-year mission breaks the Arab monopoly of the lucrative spice trade and establishes European power in the Far East for the next four centuries.*

# *A Sea Route to India: Vasco da Gama Sails to Calicut*

*Little is known of Vasco da Gama's early years after his birth in Sines, southern Portugal, in 1460. King John II of Portugal originally chose his father to command an expedition to sail around the Cape of Good Hope to India, but both the king and Da Gama's father died before their plans could be completed. The new king, Manuel I, gave a similar command to Vasco, whose four-ship expedition left Portugal on July 8, 1497. On May 20, 1498, he reached Calicut (now Kozhikode) on the Malabar Coast of India. There Da Gama made contact with the local zamorin, or king, purchased a moderate quantity of spices, and returned to Lisbon a hero. Da Gama went back to India twice, the last time in 1524 as viceroy. That same year he died in the city of Cochin. To this day, he is a national hero of Portugal.*

The letter King Manuel I of Portugal received in July 1499 went right to the point: "Vasco da Gama, a gentleman of your household, came to my country, whereat I was pleased. My country is rich in cinnamon, cloves, ginger, pepper, and precious stones. That which I ask of you in exchange is gold, silver, corals, and scarlet cloth."

That brief message, written on a palm leaf, had been dictated by the ruler of Calicut, a city on the west coast of India, more than 13,000 miles from Lisbon by sea. It offered the first opportunity in 150 years to open direct trade between East and West.

The news excited King Manuel. Spain had been boastfully quoting letters of Christopher Columbus since 1493. But Columbus, after three voyages to his so-called Indies, had found no spices and only scraps of gold. Now Portuguese ships had discovered a direct sea route to India itself—and had returned with samples of all sorts of spices and jewels to prove it.

Manuel lost no time in gleefully communicating his good news to Ferdinand and Isabella of Spain: "Most

high and excellent Prince and Princess, most potent Lord and Lady!

". . . Your Highnesses already know that we had ordered Vasco da Gama, a nobleman of our household, and his brother Paulo da Gama, with four vessels to make discoveries by sea, and that two years have now elapsed since their departure. . . . From a message which has now been brought to this city by one of their captains, we learn that they did reach and discover India, and other kingdoms . . . among whom is carried on all the trade in spices and precious stones. . . ."

After dwelling on the riches to which Portugal now held the key, Manuel could not resist adding, ". . . we are aware that your Highnesses will hear of these things with much pleasure and satisfaction."

The news, as Manuel expected, spread like wildfire through Europe. As one Florentine merchant living in Lisbon wrote to a friend in Italy, ". . . all the wealth of the world seems now to have been discovered." And Portugal had direct access to all the wealth.

For the previous century and a half, all eastern goods destined for sale in Europe had been carried across the Arabian Sea by Indians, Arabs, or Persians. Sailing from India to the Persian Gulf and Red Sea, they then transported precious goods by caravan to Alexandria and other ports on the eastern Mediterranean. There Venetian and Genoese merchants bought them for sale throughout the rest of Europe. Now Portugal had found a route enabling it to eliminate all the middlemen and buy the precious jewels and spices directly at their source.

Portugal had not achieved this coup with one bold voyage. For more than a century its ships had been probing farther and farther south along the unknown west coast of Africa, seeking the continent's southern tip. One of its mariners, Bartolomeu Dias, finally found the tip of Africa in 1488. But after rounding the Cape of

**Already a busy port,** *Lisbon was galvanized by the results of Da Gama's successful voyage to India. Its warehouses were soon filled with eastern wares, for Portugal dominated the Indian Ocean route to the East for the next hundred years. Its merchantmen sailed under the guard of warships like these great carracks, shown here in a 1564 engraving of the busy harbor. Unwieldy seagoing fortresses, they were heavily armed and manned and were almost invulnerable to boarding attacks.*

Good Hope, he had given in to the demands of his frightened crew and turned back.

This sign of weakness may have caused the king to pass over the experienced Dias and select Vasco da Gama to lead the new expedition that was to round Africa, sail up its east coast, and then challenge the unknown Indian Ocean as he headed for the bustling ports of the Orient. Though little is known of Da Gama's early career, he was obviously a decisive leader and skilled navigator. By all contemporary accounts, he was also harsh, masterful, and "fearfully violent in anger." He was, the king no doubt realized, the kind of man who would get to India.

The fleet that Da Gama commanded was the biggest, best organized commitment to overseas exploration that Portugal had ever made. Two of the four ships had been built specifically for the expedition under the skillful supervision of Bartolomeu Dias. They were equipped with cannon and supplied with the most up-to-date charts and navigational instruments available. The *São Gabriel,* commanded by Gonçalo Alvares, was Vasco da Gama's flagship. Da Gama's brother Paulo went as captain of the *São Raphael,* Nicolau Coelho of the *Berrio.* The fourth vessel, a storeship to carry extra provisions, was under the command of Gonçalo Nunes, who would have the melancholy duty of scuttling her when the holds were empty.

No one watching the storeship being loaded could believe that scuttling would ever come. Up the gangplank went cask after cask of wine and water; ton after ton of such staples as ship biscuits, dried cod, and

salted pork and beef; and even a few niceties, such as honey, sugar, garlic, plums, and almonds. In all, there were said to be supplies enough to last three years.

While the storeship was being loaded, Da Gama was busy recruiting sailors. Estimates of the size of the crew vary from 118 to 170 men, including a number of veterans of Dias' voyage. Besides the usual sailors, soldiers, carpenters, and ropemakers, he took along priests, interpreters, and even trumpeters. There were also the *degradados,* convicts condemned to death, who would be assigned to particularly hazardous missions on shore. If successful, they would be granted pardons on their return to Portugal.

The embarkation of Da Gama's fleet on Saturday, July 8, 1497, was an impressive affair. Luís de Camoens, the great Portuguese poet who chronicled the voyage, expressed the pride of the crowd of well-wishers who gathered that morning on the white beach of Restelo, four miles downriver from Lisbon:

"We are Portuguese who from the Sunset hail
And to find out the Sunrise lands we sail."

The fleet finally got under way when a fresh breeze sprang up late in the afternoon. A traditional "Make Sail" trumpet fanfare sounded across the water; white sails emblazoned with red crosses of the Order of Christ bellied out from all the masts; and the ships glided slowly downriver toward the open Atlantic. And then, in the words of Camoens:

"Little by little was exiled our sight
From hills of our own land that lay behind. . . .
Until at length all vanished utterly,
And we saw nothing but sky and sea."

The first part of Da Gama's voyage followed the usual route of Portuguese trading ships to Africa: south along the Moroccan coast; past the Canaries to the Cape Verde Islands, where they stopped for repairs, provisions, and drinking water; and then southeast around the great bulge of Africa. But somewhere in the vicinity of Sierra Leone, a little north of the Equator, Da Gama headed away from the familiar coast. He was well aware of the contrary winds and currents that slow the passage of any ship trying to hug the coastline from that point south to the Cape of Good Hope, so he boldly swung *southwest* and headed out into the empty blueness of the Atlantic.

As it happened, his decision was a wise one. The winds and currents of the South Atlantic are such that the best sailing route to south Africa is via a gigantic arc away from the coast. Sailing southwest, Da Gama and his fleet crossed the Equator at about 19° W and probably came within 600 miles of the as yet undiscovered coast of Brazil in South America before sweeping back toward the southeast. His route, in fact, is more or less the one followed to this day by ships sailing from Europe to the tip of Africa.

Da Gama's astonishing maneuver no doubt was also disquieting to his men. From the time they left the Cape

Verde Islands on August 3, three months passed before they again sighted land, a record for the time. On October 22, however, Da Gama's weary sailors were encouraged by the sight of birds flying vigorously to the southeast "as if making for the land." Seals and whales were sighted on October 27; gulfweed, "which grows along the coast," on November 1; and finally on November 4, the west coast of Africa. Everybody was so relieved that the sailors put on their best clothes, decked the ships with flags, and shot off cannon to celebrate sighting a landfall and to salute Da Gama's skill and daring in bringing them to safety.

Four days later the fleet anchored in the sheltered waters of St. Helena Bay, about 125 miles north of the Cape of Good Hope. There the men had their first contact with south African natives. According to the only firsthand account of the voyage in existence (a diary kept probably by Alvaro Velho, a man-at-arms), a party went ashore, captured a native, and brought him aboard Da Gama's ship, where "being placed at table he ate of all we ate."

"On the following day," the diarist added, "the captain-major had him well dressed and sent ashore." History does not record the reaction of the Hottentot's naked colleagues when he reappeared in their midst wearing a Portuguese doublet and hose. The gift of clothing seems to have overcome any shyness, and soon parties of Hottentots were venturing down to shore for three successive days to trade with the sailors. But then, when a sailor somehow offended some Africans who had invited him to dine, a quarrel broke out, and several Portuguese, including Da Gama himself, were wounded by lances hurled by angry natives.

It was a prophetic incident. This pattern of initial welcome, followed by resentment, was to mark nearly every stage of Da Gama's voyage to India.

After eight days of "cleaning the ships, mending the sails, and taking in wood," the fleet left St. Helena Bay

for the Cape of Good Hope. They sighted Table Mountain and the Cape Peninsula on November 18. But the monstrous promontory was in one of its stormy moods: Rounding the cape took four days of fighting gales and heavy seas.

On November 25 Da Gama anchored in Mossel Bay, some 300 miles east of the cape, to replenish his water supply and erect his first *padrão* (stone column surmounted by a cross). He also emptied the storeship of her remaining provisions and destroyed the creaky craft. They remained in the bay until December 8, helping themselves to water at their leisure. Just before setting sail, however, they saw a group of angry natives demolish the *padrão* Da Gama had erected on shore.

Continuing east along the blunt foot of Africa, on December 16 the expedition sailed past the last *padrão* Bartolomeu Dias had set up in 1488, appearing golden-gray and tall on the sandy cliff of Cape Padrone. Later that day they passed the mouth of the Great Fish River, the farthest point Dias had reached before turning back to Portugal. From that point on, the "charming and well wooded" coastline curved invitingly northeastward. Da Gama's tiny fleet was now venturing into waters where no European ship, so far as it is known, had ever sailed before.

By Christmas Day, Da Gama's diarist noted with satisfaction, "we had discovered 70 leagues [about 250 miles] of coast," which Da Gama named Natal in honor of the birth of Christ. Soon, however, the water supply was running so low that food had to be cooked in salt water, and each man's daily ration of drinking water was reduced to less than a pint. Seeking a port for fresh water and repairs, the fleet anchored off Delagoa Bay, at the southern end of modern-day Mozambique, in early January and remained there for five days. For once, Da Gama's relations with the natives remained cordial throughout the visit. He was so impressed by the courtesy of his tall black hosts that he named

---

## Steering Toward Discovery: Rudders, Tillers, and Helmsmen

When the stern rudder and high fore and aft towers became part of ship design in the mid-14th century, helmsmen moved below deck to work the tiller and stayed there for almost the next 400 years. On the *São Gabriel*, the tiller ran from the rudderhead through the open tiller-port to a compartment below the aft castle, just below the quarters of Captain-Major da Gama. Aided only by a lighted compass and commands shouted from the open quarterdeck above him, the helmsman steered a blind and hazardous course, drenched by a following sea whenever the ship moved in the direction of the tide. It took great strength to hold the tiller in a storm, and a dozen strong

men might handle the helm together on larger ships. The Portuguese poet Camoens, whose *Lusiad* celebrates Da Gama's voyage, wrote of the difficulty even strong men had steering in rough weather. Not even "the robustest arms" or the "firmest knees," he said, "can guide the starting rudder." When another lever called a whip-staff was added to the tiller, the helmsman's lot improved. He moved up one deck and forward of the mizzenmast, where he could see the set of the sails. Later in the 16th century, blocks and tackles running from the tiller to a winch eased the tremendous pull. But the ship's wheel didn't come into use until the 18th century.

the region the Land of Good People.

His next landfall, on January 25, was at the broad harbor near modern-day Quelimane, well up the coast of Mozambique. He spent a full month there, taking on water, cleaning the hulls of his ships, and repairing a cracked mast. Although the banks of the river were thick with "tall trees yielding an abundance of various fruits," it seems that the Portuguese did not take advantage of this natural supply of vitamin C: Soon many of the men were suffering from scurvy. Camoens vividly described the horrifying effects of the disease:

"The gums within the mouth swelled horribly
And all the flesh about it tumid grew,
And as it swelled apace, it rotted too."

Scurvy would be the bane of long-distance mariners for at least the next two centuries.

During his stay at Quelimane, Da Gama was encouraged by signs that he had reached the fringes of the Arab trade domain. Instead of wearing skins or going naked, some of the natives here wore pieces of cotton cloth. In fact, he was approached by two blacks offering to barter some material. One wore a cap "with a fringe embroidered in silk, and the other a cap of green satin"—both obviously of Moslem origin. Most interesting of all was the boast of a boy with them who "had come from a distant country, and had already seen big ships like ours." Da Gama realized the boy could only be referring to Arab trading vessels. Encouraged by these signs that he was approaching his destination, Da Gama named the river that empties

A west African *Benin bronze of a Portuguese soldier shows how native artisans respected European weaponry: The armor and arquebus are finely detailed, while the face is merely a mask. The Edo people of Benin held a powerful kingdom at the Niger Delta when slavers discovered it. The Portuguese traded with them for pepper, slaves, and native crafts. Benin's advanced culture died out by the 17th century, and its fine bronzes are now valuable works of art.*

into Quelimane harbor the River of Good Omens.

On February 24 the fleet proceeded up the increasingly tropical coastline. Six days later, when they were nearly halfway up the east coast of Africa, the Portuguese sighted a bay dominated by the island of Mozambique. Now they realized they were definitely trespassing in Arab trading waters. On the island, instead of a village of cowherds and farmers, they found a busy town full of prosperous, Arabic-speaking black merchants wearing gold-embroidered silk caps and gowns of fine, colorfully striped linen and cotton. In the harbor were several large Arab dhows with rakish bows, sewn planking, and lateen sails. Da Gama's diarist was impressed by their mariners' use of compasses, quadrants, and navigational charts.

The ships, the Portuguese soon discovered, were laden with rich cargoes of "gold, silver, cloves, pepper, ginger, and silver rings, as also with quantities of pearls, jewels, and rubies." Much to the delight of the credulous Europeans, the Africans readily volunteered that in India all these goods "were so plentiful that there was no need to purchase them as they could be collected in baskets."

The sultan of Mozambique soon made his appearance on the *São Gabriel*, where Da Gama regaled him with a lavish dinner and presented him with hats, gowns, coral, and other gifts; but, Da Gama's chronicler noted, the wealthy sultan was "so proud that he treated all we gave him with contempt." When the sultan later discovered that his visitors were not some exotic sect of Moslems, but Christians, his initially cool reception turned definitely frigid. Nonetheless, the meeting was not a complete failure. Prior to leaving Mozambique, Da Gama maneuvered the sultan into lending him two Arab pilots for the remainder of the voyage.

So on March 11 Da Gama set sail to the north. But powerful currents soon dragged his ships back, and the

## Portuguese Guns Against Arab Monopoly

The Portuguese naval achievement of a cape route to India did not ensure their control of the spice trade: Rival Arab trading ships had to be stopped by force. In 1502 Da Gama won the first naval battle in the struggle for control in the East, using guns like the one below. Breech-loaded, they were made of welded iron staves, bound with hoops of iron, and lashed to the bulwarks on wooden frames. This haphazard construction gave limited range and striking power, and gunners were in danger of the cannon exploding when overcharged. Despite this, they usually overwhelmed the lighter and less heavily armed Arab ships.

*Navigators in Unknown Seas*

fleet was forced to lie at anchor off Mozambique for two weeks waiting for favorable winds. During this time open hostility broke out—once again over drinking water for the ships—and the Portuguese bombarded the town with cannon before setting sail on March 29.

Sailing now with the assistance of the Arab pilots, on April 7 the fleet reached Mombasa, on the coast of Kenya, and anchored just outside the fine harbor because Da Gama, suspecting treachery, was reluctant to take his fleet into the harbor itself. His fears were well founded: That night a party of 100 armed men tried to board his ships to see whether they could easily be captured. Torturing a couple of captives "by dropping boiling oil upon their skin," Da Gama discovered that the king had heard about the bombardment of Mozambique and was anxious to tempt the Portuguese into the harbor and capture them in revenge for the attack on his ally.

Although the next day the local king sent out gifts (including large quantities of oranges, which quickly cured the scurvy victims in the crew), and Da Gama in turn sent the king a string of coral beads, the Portuguese still refused to enter the harbor. Despite a second attempt by the Moslems to damage his ships on the night of April 10, Da Gama defiantly remained at anchor outside the harbor for two more days before setting sail again on April 13.

The following evening the fleet reached Malindi, its last port of call on the African coast. By now the expedition had reached a point about 3° S. The town, with its stately whitewashed houses surrounded by palm groves and grainfields, reminded Da Gama's chronicler of a village near Lisbon. The fleet's nine-day visit there proved a pleasant interlude.

The sultan, as it happened, was a bitter enemy of the sultan of Mombasa and, following an exchange of gifts, promised to supply Da Gama with an additional pilot and anything else he needed. Then followed an interview on the open water of the harbor, the king in a dhow, Da Gama in a ship's boat specially decorated for the meeting. The sultan cut quite an impressive figure. Seated on a cushioned chair of bronze beneath a crimson parasol, he wore "a robe of damask trimmed with green satin" and a richly embroidered cap. Accompanying him were a page and musicians who played small trumpets and two huge, elaborately carved ivory instruments "of the size of a man, which were blown from a hole in the side, and made sweet harmony." The meeting lasted for three hours, but despite the king's obvious goodwill, the suspicious captain-major refused to step ashore. Nevertheless, the king amused the crew with an exhibition of horsemanship on the beach.

The Portuguese were more interested in other foreign visitors they met in the harbor: four ships manned by Hindu merchants from India. All along the coast they had been titillated by tales of Christian settlements in the interior of Africa and for a time had even hoped to find the kingdom of Prester John, a legendary Christian potentate rumored to live somewhere in east Africa. (In fact, there was a Christian kingdom in Ethiopia.) So when the Indians mistakenly bowed and prayed before a Christian altarpiece on one of the Por-

**The palm-fringed coast** *of Malabar, situated along a 450-mile stretch of southwestern India, screens fields of pepper and cardamon and inland forests of ebony, teak, and sandalwood, which have attracted traders for a thousand years. The inhabitants have kept their distinctive culture in spite of successive domination by the Arabs, Portuguese, Dutch, and British. The harbor at Cochin, which Da Gama established as a Portuguese outpost during his second voyage, still handles Indian trade today.*

**Triangular and baggy, lateen sails** *have ridden the seasonal winds of the Indian Ocean since ancient times. Arab merchants sailed on the northeast monsoon in winter, carrying cotton and beads to Africa; when the wind reversed in summer, they returned to India with ivory and slaves. By the 15th century Europeans had combined the lateen with square sails on ships, improving their efficiency in sailing to windward. In Da Gama's time, dhows did not have jibs, as shown in the picture above.*

tuguese ships and greeted Da Gama with cries of *"Krishna"*—which does sound something like the Portuguese word for Christ—the Portuguese optimistically assumed their visitors were indeed fellow Christians. The Indians, in turn, apparently assumed the Portuguese were Hindus. With the sultan's permission, they entertained the fleet one evening with cannon salutes and a display of fireworks.

The steady succession of "fetes, sham fights, and musical performances" on shore pleased the crew, but Da Gama was becoming impatient. The sultan seemed to be taking his time in providing the pilot he had promised. With characteristic abruptness, Da Gama took drastic action. On April 22 he seized a servant of the royal court and held him hostage. The king hurriedly responded by sending out an experienced pilot whose presence on board the *São Gabriel* virtually assured the successful completion of Vasco da Gama's mission. At last, after almost 10 months at sea, the Portuguese could relax in his experienced hands.

Leaving Malindi on April 24, the fleet was caught up by the southwest monsoon, which blows steadily across the Indian Ocean from Africa to India during the spring and summer months. (These winds very conveniently reverse direction in winter and so were perfect for shuttling Arab trading vessels back and forth across the Indian Ocean.) Pushed on by the gentle rush of air, the ships completed the last leg of their voyage—a distance of almost 2,500 miles—in less than a month. Finally, on May 18, 1498, sailors stationed high on the masts spied land rising ahead, and in the words of the poet Camoens:

> "Cheerily the Malindian pilot spake,
> 'That land is Calicut, or I mistake.'"

Calicut, now called Kozhikode, was then the richest and most powerful of the string of ports along the lush Malabar Coast near the southern tip of India. It was a trading center where goods imported from lands farther to the east were resold to Moslem traders for the European and African markets. Its large warehouses and many shops were fairly bursting with all the exotic merchandise the Portuguese longed for: fine silks and porcelains; pearls, sapphires, and rubies; gold and silver; and tall sacks filled with cloves, nutmeg, cinnamon, pepper, ginger, and other fragrant spices.

Into this centuries-old marketplace of Asia stepped Vasco da Gama's first envoy, one of the convicts who had been brought along for dangerous assignments. Met by two Moslem traders from Tunis who spoke Spanish, he was astonished to be greeted with the

---

## Silver for Pepper and Gold for Nutmeg: Europe's Expensive Appetite for Oriental Spices

The West's almost insatiable need for exotic spices probably began with the jaded tastebuds of wealthy Romans in the first century A.D. and increased in the Middle Ages when Crusaders brought home aromatic plants of the East. Medieval herbals proclaimed the oriental plants' medicinal as well as culinary value. Because spices were scandalously expensive, their presence at an elegant table was as much a symbol of status as courtly manners and elaborate menus. In addition, the need to season and preserve meat made spices desirable in an age before refrigeration. Livestock was slaughtered in autumn, then salted and dried with pepper and cloves.

Although exact amounts of spices were seldom specified in medieval and Renaissance recipes, it may not be true that sauces of nutmeg, cinnamon, ginger, and mace were spicy and hot to hide the rancid taste and smell of bad meat. Sauces were possibly mild and enhanced the flavor of well-smoked and dried food. Spices were also brewed for drinks and medicines. In perfumes and pomanders they appealed

to a populace unaccustomed to baths.

Because of the great demand and small supply, pepper was as valuable as silver, and nutmeg was measured in gold. Prices could rise 500 percent because of middlemen along the overland-sea route and still yield merchants a profit in the West. The Portuguese, despising dependence on Arab traders, determined to find the all-sea path to India's marts. But Da Gama's discovery hardly eased the exorbitant prices in Europe. Some buyers still preferred wares arriving at Venice and Aleppo, fearing spoilage in goods carried for months in the leaky holds of ships.

The Dutch and English made importing more economical, but by the 17th and 18th centuries agricultural reforms were lowering demands for spices. Crop rotation had increased the fodder supply, allowing livestock to survive the winter.

This tapestry in Lisbon's Marine Museum shows Portuguese commerce in the 16th century. Bales of Indian spices are delivered from shore by longboat and hauled aboard ship for the long ocean voyage to Europe.

**India was a land** *of splendid courts and grandiose architecture when the Portuguese arrived. Its culture was 3,000 years old and richly infused by the Hindus, Buddhists, Moslems, Christians, and Jews who mingled in every city. Early 16th-century Moslem emperor Baber in this miniature is surrounded by the various kinds of exotic luxuries that Europe sought in the East.*

words, "May the Devil take you! What brought you here?" "We have come," the convict explained, "in search of Christians and spices." Then, after a brief tour, the Moslems took him to their home and fed him with great hospitality before returning him to the ship. There one of them exclaimed: "A lucky venture, a lucky venture! Plenty of rubies, plenty of emeralds! You owe great thanks to God, for having brought you to a country holding such riches!"

Surprised and delighted, Da Gama sent a message to the zamorin, or king, of Calicut, announcing that he was the ambassador of the king of Portugal and had letters to present. Within a few days he received word that the zamorin would see him. Surrounded by 13 bodyguards dressed in their best and carrying trumpets and flags, the captain-major stepped grandly into a covered litter that had been provided for him.

Proceeding along the road to Calicut, the Portuguese caused quite a sensation. "The road was crowded with a countless multitude anxious to see us," reported Da Gama's diarist. Before progressing to the zamorin's palace, the Portuguese were taken to a Hindu temple "as large as a monastery," where once again there was confusion over religions. (Da Gama returned to Portugal firmly convinced he had visited a Christian land.) The "church" was decorated with pictures of what the explorers took to be saints, despite the fact that "they were painted variously, with teeth protruding an inch from the mouth and four or five arms." In the center of the temple was a sanctuary containing an image of a maternal Hindu figure. Assuming it represented the Virgin Mary, Da Gama led his men in prayer before it, much to the pleasure of the attendant Hindu priests.

Climbing back into his covered litter, Ambassador da Gama rode on to the beating of drums, the wail of Hindu pipes, and the firing of guns by 2,000 armed men who lined the processional route. "They showed us much respect," noted the diarist, "more than is shown in Spain to a king." By now the crowds were so dense that spectators even climbed to the rooftops to catch a glimpse of the strangers. Finally, they came to the palace itself. Passing through the gate, they crossed a vast courtyard and went through room after room until at last they reached a small interior court. There they beheld the zamorin, holding a large golden cup as he lounged among thick cushions on a green velvet couch beneath a gilt canopy.

Da Gama greeted the king politely, and the king in turn offered his guests a selection of exotic fruits, including one that "resembled a fig, and tasted very nice." (It was a banana.) After this exchange of courtesies, Vasco da Gama made a highly imaginative speech. He said that he represented a king whose wealth exceeded anything in that part of the world; that for 60 years Portugal had been searching for a sea route to India; that he had been ordered to discover Calicut "on pain of having his head cut off"; and that King Manuel wished to be the friend and brother of the zamorin. In reply, the zamorin welcomed Da Gama and assured him that he would send ambassadors to Portugal. The conversation lasted four hours into the night and concluded on a note of mutual friendliness.

After such a promising beginning, however, relations between East and West quickly deteriorated. King Manuel had not provided Da Gama with gifts befitting the zamorin. His offerings—12 pieces of striped cotton cloth, 4 scarlet hoods, 6 hats, 4 strings of coral, 6 washbasins, a case of sugar, 2 casks of oil, and 2 casks of honey—were received by the king's agents with in-

credulous laughter. On his next audience, Da Gama was kept waiting for hours outside the palace door. When he was finally admitted, the zamorin remarked sarcastically "that he had told him that he came from a very rich kingdom, and yet had brought him nothing." Da Gama protested that he was an ambassador, not a merchant, and that plenty of rich gifts would come on future Portuguese missions.

When the Moslem traders of Calicut heard of this, they launched a desperate campaign against their new Christian competitors. "These Portuguese are thieves," they warned the king and threatened never to return to Calicut if he opened trade with them. They added that Portugal had nothing worth trading, "but would rather take away, and that thus his country would be ruined." Negotiations continued throughout the summer, while the Moslems became so hostile that they spat at the feet of any Portuguese who stepped ashore.

But the zamorin undoubtedly realized that he had the upper hand. If the Portuguese competed with the Moslems for the merchandise of his kingdom, his trade revenues would become greater than ever. Eventually, he relented. He promised to erect a Portuguese pillar in Calicut to commemorate the historic visit and then dictated his letter to King Manuel, offering to open direct trade with Portugal.

Moreover, the zamorin permitted Da Gama to purchase a small quantity of cinnamon and pepper. Although the amount was unimpressive, the price of pepper had become so inflated in Europe that it could be sold there for 27 times its cost in India.

And so, on August 29, according to Da Gama's diarist, the captains concluded that "inasmuch that we had discovered the country we had come in search of . . . it would be as well to take our departure. . . . We therefore set sail and left for Portugal, greatly rejoicing at our good fortune in having made so great a discovery."

The journey back across the Indian Ocean was nearly disastrous. The ships were poorly provisioned. They had no native pilots to guide them. And they were sailing at the wrong time of year: Instead of steady winds carrying them straight to Africa, foul storms alternated with long enervating calms. The men did not sight the coast of Africa until January 2, 1499. By then scurvy had taken a dreadful toll of the company. Thirty sailors died during the long crossing of the Arabian Sea, and the rest were so weak they could barely sail. "I assure you," asserted the diarist, "that if this state of affairs had continued for another fortnight, there would have been no men at all to navigate the ships."

Five days later the little fleet was welcomed back at Malindi, where the king lavished gifts of oranges and fresh meat on the scurvy victims. But in many cases the cure came too late, and even more men succumbed to the disease. (Nearly half of the original crew was dead by the time the voyage ended.) A few days later Da Gama sadly set fire to his brother Paulo's ship, the *São Raphael*, "as it was impossible for us to navigate three vessels with the few hands that remained to us."

Continuing down the coast of Africa, the two surviving ships stopped here and there for fresh provisions, and gradually most of the crew recovered. When they reached the Cape of Good Hope on March 20, in fact, "those who had come so far were in good health and quite robust, although at times nearly dead from the cold winds which we experienced."

Paulo da Gama did not fare as well. By the time the ships reached the Cape Verde Islands, he was gravely ill. Vasco, a devoted brother, hired a caravel to take Paulo and himself to Lisbon because it would be faster than sailing aboard the *São Gabriel*. While under way, it became clear that Paulo was too ill to travel at all; so

Vasco ordered the caravel to land at the Azores, where Paulo died the following day.

On July 10, 1499, exactly two years and two days after the start of the expedition, the *Berrio* dropped anchor in Lisbon harbor, and Captain Coelho triumphantly announced his safe return to the king. The *São Gabriel* followed in mid-August, and a few weeks later Vasco da Gama himself arrived in Portugal.

Immediately hailed as a national hero, he was greeted with a tumultuous welcome. With consummate skill and fierce determination, he had proved once and for all that there was a navigable sea route to India—and that Portugal had ships and men equal to the hazards of the voyage. With a commercial and administrative capital at Goa in India, Portugal's eastern empire soon became a source of national pride, while its official policy of secrecy on trade and navigation kept vital records, charts, and sailing instructions to India out of the hands of its European rivals who might attempt to follow Vasco da Gama's lead.

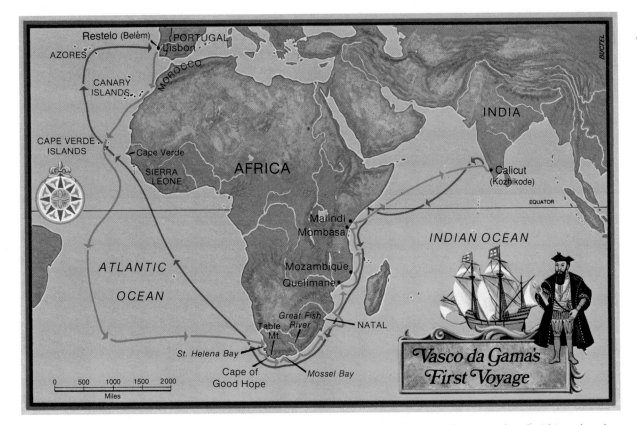

**In the half century preceding** *Vasco da Gama's great voyage, Portuguese sea captains, initially under the direction of Prince Henry the Navigator, cautiously mapped the entire west African coast from Morocco to the Cape of Good Hope. Those expeditions had slowly beaten their way southward against prevailing winds and currents. By the time Da Gama set sail for India in 1497, the New World had been discovered, and it was known that the winds and currents of the South Atlantic favored a southerly*

*passage. Thus Da Gama chose not to hug the African shore but to sail south from the coast of Sierra Leone until he reached the latitude of St. Helena Bay. Then he would turn east to the tip of Africa and sail before the prevailing winds. Da Gama's skill brought his fleet safely to the bay after three months out of sight of land—an amazing feat. Beyond there, despite storms and battles, the voyage—an incredible 13,000 miles—was completed with relative ease, due to the seasonal Indian Ocean monsoon winds.*

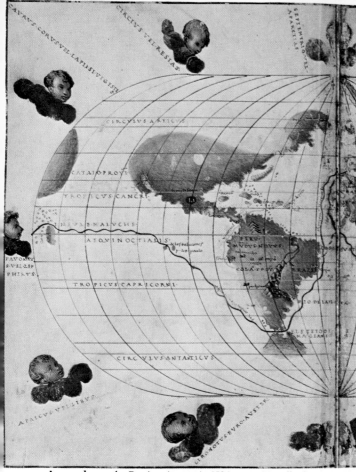

A map drawn *by Battista Agnese in 1536 traces Magellan's route. The boundaries of North and South America are not clearly defined, and the continent of Australia, not to be discovered for another 200 years, is absent from the map. Nonetheless, when compared to the charts used during Henry the Navigator's era, the map shows the astonishing increase in man's knowledge of world geography.*

FERDINAN:MAGAGLIANES

Ferdinand Magellan *(above), rejected by the ruler of his native Portugal, presented Spain with his plan to reach Asia by sailing west. The Spanish were eager to find their own route to the East Indies to compete with Portugal for the enormously profitable spice trade. Magellan's voyage was chronicled in the journal of Antonio Pigafetta (left), a gentleman from Vicenzia, Italy. The illustration shows an outrigger boat of the Mariana Islands in the Pacific. The adventurous Pigafetta was one of only 18 men of the original 250 who survived the journey around the world.*

*Chapter Seven. A Portugese soldier-navigator, spurned by his own king, leads five ships on an expedition west for Spain. He is the first European captain to find a way past the New World, through the strait that bears his name, and across the vast Pacific. After his death, a few survivors in one ship complete the first circumnavigation of the earth.*

# Beyond the New World: Magellan's Great Venture

*A brilliant navigator and a taciturn but determined leader, Ferdinand Magellan was born of a noble family in northern Portugal about the year 1480. Having served as a page in the royal court of King John II, he joined one of the annual Portuguese fleets to India. After eight years of soldiering in the Indies and Africa, he returned to Portugal, lamed by a wound received fighting the Moors in Morocco. Refused by King Manuel I, Magellan turned to Spain and its young ruler Charles I, later emperor of the Holy Roman Empire. Charles entrusted Magellan with a fleet of five ships to seek a westward passage to the Indies—the Portuguese dominated the eastern passage. Magellan had completed the most difficult part of his voyage when he was killed in a campaign against a native king at Mactan Island in the Philippines in 1521.*

One autumn day in 1516, a crippled soldier knelt awkwardly before his king, Manuel I of Portugal. The sovereign gazed with some distaste at the man, one Ferdinand Magellan. In recent years superior officers with whom Magellan had dared to disagree had been circulating malicious reports about his conduct. Yet there was no denying his noble birth, his brilliant military exploits, and his unswerving loyalty to the crown. Reluctantly, King Manuel nodded for him to speak.

Magellan announced that, at the age of 36, he was impoverished by eight years of navigating, exploring, and fighting battles for the crown in Africa and the Portuguese Indies. What was more, he had suffered three serious wounds in his majesty's service, including a lance wound in the knee that had left him permanently lame. He humbly begged an increase in his pension. Manuel, who was not by nature a rewarder, denied the request.

Surprised and hurt, Magellan remained on his knees. Then might he be granted command of a caravel to the Indies and perhaps restore his fortunes? No, said his

majesty, there was no place at all for him in Portuguese service. The humiliated soldier could make only one final request: to be allowed to serve some other king. Manuel waved him away and snorted that he did not care in the least where Magellan went or what he did.

Bitterly humiliated, Magellan brooded over these harsh words for months. Gradually, he began to form a plan. For years his friend Francisco Serrano, who had settled in the Moluccas, had been urging Magellan to join him. These islands, lying just to the west of New Guinea, were also known as the Spice Islands, for they were the primary source of most of the spices that Europeans desperately coveted. And, Serrano added, the profits to be made in the spice trade were fabulous.

Eventually, Magellan wrote to his friend: "I will come to you soon, if not by way of Portugal, then by way of Spain." At the back of his mind as he penned those momentous words were recollections of maps and globes he had seen in the royal chartroom at Lisbon, as well as the widespread rumors that suggested the existence of an unexplored strait through the South American continent into Balboa's recently discovered "South Sea" (the Pacific). If he could discover the strait, he might open a western alternative to Portugal's lengthy—and fiercely defended—route around Africa and across the Indian Ocean to the Indies.

Fortunately for Magellan, several influential men in Spain were considering the same possibility. And Ferdinand Magellan, with his wealth of experience in the Indies, they all agreed, was just the man to carry out their plan. When they summoned him to Spain, Magellan left his native Portugal immediately.

In due course Magellan's backers arranged an audience with Spain's 17-year-old King Charles I, who would have to approve the expedition. From the start everything went well. The youthful king was impressed by the limping veteran's passionate ambition, his geographical logic, and his personal knowledge of the Indies. Most likely, Magellan's past exploits and the drama of the proposed voyage itself also appealed to the young king's sense of adventure. In any case, he was well aware of the profits Spain could expect to reap if it broke the Portuguese monopoly of the spice trade by opening a new westward route to the Indies. On March 22, 1518, King Charles approved the financing of "a voyage to discover unknown lands" by way of the unexplored strait and appointed Magellan captain-general of the expedition.

At Seville, preparations for the voyage took a full 18 months to complete. The long delay was partly the result of the machinations of King Manuel's consul at Seville. Although the expedition's destination was an official secret, Manuel's spies had found out the truth, and the king was determined to undermine this Spanish attempt to poach on the wealth of what he considered his personal realm in the Indies. Even more sinister were the plots of Don Juan de Fonseca, bishop of Burgos and counselor to the Spanish king, and German bankers who were financing the expedition. Appalled by the generous rewards King Charles had promised Magellan and fearing that the expedition was becoming too "Portuguese," they planned to limit Magellan's authority. In the course of several months of intrigue, Bishop Fonseca succeeded in having his illegitimate son, Juan de Cartagena, appointed captain of one of the ships (the others were commanded by Portuguese officers) and sympathetic Spaniards placed in a number of other key positions.

Through it all, Magellan worked methodically at the task of equipping his fleet for exploration. Five ships were purchased: the *Trinidad* (Magellan's flagship), the *San Antonio*, the *Concepción*, the *Victoria*, and the *Santiago*. "They are very old and patched," the Portuguese consul wrote contemptuously to King Manuel, "and I would be sorry to sail even for the Canaries in them, for their ribs are as soft as butter." He did not realize that Magellan, who was as much a sailor as a soldier, was having the ships expertly reconstructed to withstand the hazards of the coming voyage.

One of the greatest problems was recruiting enough sailors to man the fleet. Haughty Castilian seamen were reluctant to serve under a foreign-born commander. More important, the taciturn Magellan refused to say exactly where he was going, and professional mariners balked at signing up for a voyage of at least two years "to an unknown world." The only really willing recruit, in fact, seems to have been Antonio Pigafetta, a young Italian nobleman who wanted to see "the very great and awful things of the ocean." Secretly, he may also have been a spy for Venetian merchants interested in the spice trade. Whatever the case, history is in Pigafetta's debt. His lively, detailed diary is a first-hand account of Magellan's momentous voyage.

Despite the difficulties, the captain-general even-

**A 16th-century** *Spanish artist captured the activity of the port of Seville as it looked when Magellan embarked on his historic voyage. Ship bottoms are being careened at lower left, while on the far right, heavy, square-rigged carracks, like those Magellan sailed, ride at anchor. In the center of the harbor, lateen-rigged*

tually managed to sign up a full complement of about 250 men, including Italians, Frenchmen, Germans, Flemings, Moors, and blacks, as well as Spaniards and Portuguese. He seemed confident that his iron personality would weld this motley assembly into a disciplined corps of explorers.

On September 20, 1519, everything was finally ready. Cannon thundered and banners waved as the five ships glided out into the Atlantic from the port of San Lúcar de Barrameda at the mouth of the Guadalquivir River. On September 26 they put in at the Canary Islands for last-minute supplies and fresh water. Within hours a packet followed them into port with an urgent letter for Magellan from friends in Spain. The message was ominous: It warned him of the plot of Cartagena and his henchmen to mutiny and murder their leader. Magellan coolly decided for the moment to do nothing more than watch Cartagena closely. He was confident that, when the time came, his military training would be more than a match for any insubordination.

*galleys of the sort that plied the Mediterranean, their sails furled, glide along propelled by oarsmen. At a dockyard (upper right), timbers are piled high awaiting the construction of new ships. Carts carry provisions to vessels about to sail. Along the waterfront, crowds promenade, admiring the rows of ships and pick-*

*ing up the latest maritime news. Men wishing to sign on as sailors seek information about proposed sailings from ships' captains. In just this way Magellan recruited part of his crew. The powerful shipowners of Seville were eager to get a share of the lucrative spice trade and financed voyages of exploration themselves.*

A few days later the little armada headed south along the coast of Africa. Magellan's sailing orders were characteristically terse: "Follow my flag by day and my lantern by night." Silently limping to and fro on the quarterdeck of the *Trinidad*, he divided his attention between the empty ocean up ahead and the four ships foaming along behind him. Every evening at sunset he had his captains draw near the flagship and shout the traditional greeting: "God save you, Sir Captain-General and Master and good ship's company." By this simple procedure Magellan regularly reminded every man in the expedition of his absolute authority.

Chafing with resentment, Cartagena waited for a chance to challenge the captain-general. It came when Magellan, true to his Portuguese training, followed Da Gama's course and hugged the bulge of Africa for a while before heading west across the Atlantic. Cartagena asked sharply why the expedition was not following a diagonal "Spanish course" to the southwest. He was stunned by the response. Magellan simply warned

him to mind his own business and follow orders.

After enduring violent storms off the coast of Sierra Leone, the fleet finally altered course and headed southwest, but was soon becalmed in the equatorial doldrums. For three weeks the ships lolled idly on the glassy sea. Tar melted, timbers split in the baking heat, and the men began to grumble about the futility of the voyage. But the little captain-general remained wrapped in a private cocoon of silence.

Some time after the wind returned and the ships resumed their journey (reports on the incident are vague and contradictory), Cartagena again challenged Magellan's authority. One evening, instead of personally calling out the customary salute, he turned the duty over to his boatswain, who rudely addressed the captain-general simply as "captain." Magellan sharply upbraided the sailor but took no immediate action against Cartagena. Three days later, however, in a face-to-face confrontation, Cartagena abruptly announced that he would no longer obey Magellan's orders. This was an act of open mutiny—exactly what Magellan had been waiting for. Grabbing Cartagena by the shirtfront, he icily declared that the Spaniard was his prisoner. The rebel was placed in custody of another officer, and that evening a new captain shouted obeisance in his stead.

Favorable winds now blew the ships steadily across the Atlantic, and before long the shores of Brazil were sighted. Sailing south past jungle-clad coasts, the fleet finally dropped anchor in mid-December in the spectacular bay that would in time become the site of Rio de Janeiro. There Magellan allowed his weary sailors two idyllic weeks ashore.

The local Indians, Pigafetta noted, were cannibals. Fortunately for the Europeans, they were greeted as gods and regaled with banquets of suckling pig and fresh pineapples—certainly a welcome change from pickled pork and ship biscuit. There was also much delighted chasing of Indian girls who wore no clothes and whose parents were more than willing to give them up as slaves in exchange for a knife or an ax.

Magellan, who had recently married a Spanish woman, remained aloof from the revels until the time came to drag his reluctant men back to their duties.

---

## Mysterious Big-Footed Giants of Patagonia

Wintering in Port St. Julian on the bleak southern coast of Argentina, Magellan's ships were approached by men that Antonio Pigafetta described as "large as giants." They were so tall, according to Pigafetta, that the Europeans did not even come up to their waists. Because of the fact that they wrapped their already sizeable feet in thick bundles of animal skins stuffed with grass, the giants were called Patagonians, from the colloquial Spanish word for "big feet." Pigafetta recorded words in their languages, as well as their medical practices. For an upset stomach, the Patagonians swallowed thistles, which caused them to vomit. "When their head aches," Pigafetta reported, "they give themselves a slash in the forehead and also on the arms and legs." A half century after Magellan's voyage, Sir Francis Drake put in at Port St. Julian. A narrative of his voyage disputes the highly exaggerated claims of the Patagonians' size: "They generally differ from the common sort of men, both in stature, bigness and strength of body, as also in the hideousness of their voices. But yet they are nothing so monstrous or giantlike as they were reported." In 1767 a British magazine published the picture at right of a European with two Patagonians. It was based on accounts of British Adm. John Byron's experiences in Argentina. Since then, however, the Patagonians, whose origins are shrouded in mystery, have disappeared.

There were fouled water casks to scour and refill, worn timbers to repair, torn sails to stitch. On December 27, to the tearful farewells of native girls, the captain-general ordered his men to weigh anchor and continue south in search of the strait.

New Year's Day 1520 passed almost unnoticed as the explorers scanned Brazil's impenetrable coast for any sign of the strait. Hopes soared when, after two weeks and more than 1,200 miles of sailing, they discovered a broad westward channel at just about the latitude where all the charts indicated the strait would be. But the channel rapidly narrowed to nothing more than a river, the modern-day Río de la Plata.

Bitterly disappointed, Magellan concluded that the charts were wrong. The strait had to be farther south in the frozen regions of Terra Australis, the legendary landmass presumed to exist at the bottom of the globe. Many sailors were so discouraged they wanted to turn back, but Magellan's iron will and contempt for cowardice drove them on. Sailing headlong into the approaching autumn and winter of the Southern Hemisphere, the five ships were beaten by brutal seas, violent winds, and persistent hailstorms. Ice began to clog the rigging faster than the sailors could hack it away. The captain-general himself slept no more than a couple of hours at a time and, like the rest of the crew, ate not even one hot meal for weeks on end. "The fool is leading us to destruction," Cartagena is said to have muttered. "He is obsessed with his search for the strait. On the flame of his ambition he will crucify us all."

At the end of March, Magellan took pity on his frozen crew and decided to winter ashore. The fleet anchored in a forbidding but sheltered bay he named Port St. Julian, near the southern tip of Argentina. There were no friendly welcoming natives: only gray cliffs and desolate beaches. A mood of general depression settled down like a fog. After six months at sea the explorers had reached nowhere, found nothing. Of what use was this sterile coast to Spain? they asked. Where was this imaginary strait to the Spice Islands?

The captains pleaded with Magellan to return home or at least go back to the milder latitudes of Río de la Plata for the winter, but Magellan stubbornly "refused even to discuss the matter." In no time at all the mutiny he had so long expected broke out. According to Pigafetta, the ringleader in the plot was Juan de Cartagena. Gaining control of three ships, he apparently planned to make a dash for the harbor entrance and head for Spain, but he proved no match for Magellan. Slipping some of his own men aboard one of the mutineers' ships, Magellan quickly took possession of her and with three ships formed a blockade across the harbor's mouth and regained control of all five of his ships.

Magellan immediately court-martialed the leaders of the plot, and they were found guilty of mutiny. Then, displaying a grim sense of drama, he staged a ritual execution against a background of jagged rocks in the

**Magellan found** *what had eluded Columbus: a way to reach the Orient from the west. The Strait of Magellan (above) is a torturous, cold, often stormy passage between the southern tip of the South American continent and the Tierra del Fuego Archipelago. The 16th-century map at left shows two ships about to enter the strait. Though the dangerous waterway was long unused as a regular trade route, it was the gateway to the Pacific for both Magellan and Sir Francis Drake.*

presence of officers and men. One of the mutinous captains was led to the block, where his own servant cut off his head. His body and that of another captain who had been killed in the fighting were drawn and quartered, and the pieces hung from four gibbets erected on the shores of the bay. Magellan's authority was reestablished beyond question. As for Cartagena, he and a mutinous priest would be marooned when the fleet eventually left the desolate bay.

The fleet was at Port St. Julian for two months before the Europeans saw any natives. Then, "One day, suddenly we saw a naked man of giant stature on the shore of the harbor, dancing, singing, and throwing dust on his head. . . ." This strange creature, with hair painted white and face daubed with red and yellow, Pigafetta added, "was so tall that we reached only to his waist."

The first giant soon was followed by others, who became friendly with the explorers and went so far as to dance with them, leaving footprints four inches deep in the sand. The skins they wrapped around their feet were apparently packed with dry grass for added warmth. Consequently, Magellan called the giants *Patagones* (Spanish and Portuguese for "big feet"), and the

name of their country soon became Patagonia.

Anxious to continue his exploration, Magellan now sent the *Santiago* south to reconnoiter the coast. The ship was wrecked in a storm—fortunately with only one life lost—but the survivors reported the discovery of a much more favorable harbor. So, after five months in their grim anchorage at Port St. Julian, the four remaining ships set sail late in August for their new port, where they remained until October 18.

By then, spring in the Southern Hemisphere was fast approaching, and Magellan was eager to resume his search for the elusive strait. Three days later and about 100 miles farther south, the fleet rounded a sandy headland and found yet another vast bay. The captains protested that it was useless to waste time exploring there: There could be no strait through the bay's western end. But the captain-general would not pass by any possibility. He ordered the captains of the *Concepción* and *San Antonio* to seek a western outlet in the bay.

A sudden storm swept the two ships out of sight behind a rocky promontory jutting into the bay, and for two days rough weather prevented Magellan from following. When he finally was able to round the headland himself, the two lost ships soon reappeared, with flags waving and cannon booming. Clearly, they had good news to report, but with his usual self-control, the captain-general neither laughed nor shouted. He simply bowed his head and crossed himself. Soon the *San Antonio* drew near enough for her captain to announce joyfully that the ships had sailed more than 100 miles into a deep narrow channel with strong tides and no sign of fresh water. This was no mere river mouth—it had to be the strait to the great South Sea.

The fleet then sailed majestically west into an awesome passage between towering mountains. "And they thought that there was no better nor more beautiful strait in the world than this one," Pigafetta declared enthusiastically. The Strait of All Saints, as the captain-general called it—it now rightfully bears his own name—proved to be no ordinary channel. Varying from 2 to 20 miles in width, it is a watery labyrinth that veers and twists and fans out into countless false bays and narrows. Except for a group of huts filled with mummified corpses and a brief visit by a boatload of natives that disappeared mysteriously in the night, the explorers saw few signs of human life. Yet later in the passage they saw many lights of campfires twinkling and glowing to the south. Magellan accordingly named the place Tierra del Fuego, "Land of Fire," and so the vast island south of the strait is called to this day.

Coming upon a large island in the channel, Magellan ordered the captain of his biggest ship, the *San Antonio*, to explore its southern side while the rest of the fleet continued along the north shore. Soon they found a good anchorage at the mouth of a river teeming with sardines. Magellan set his crew to work salting down a supply of the fish. Then, instead of risking a ship in the unexplored waters ahead, he sent some sailors in a longboat to search for an outlet to the sea. A few days later the boat returned, with its crew screaming, "We found it! We found it!" The news about the outlet so overwhelmed Magellan that, according to Pigafetta, the iron man actually cried.

But the *San Antonio* did not return. Fearing that she had been wrecked, Magellan wasted almost three weeks vainly searching for her, until the bitter truth dawned that the crew had deserted and returned to Spain—along with a great share of the fleet's scant provisions. Although this catastrophe left Magellan dangerously low on supplies, he resolved to sail on west through the mists, turns, and seething waters of the strait. Finally, on November 28, the three ships sailed out of the 310-mile-long channel and into a wide and peaceful ocean. After an appropriate ceremony of thanksgiving, Magellan announced to his officers: "Gentlemen, we now are steering into waters where no ship has sailed before. May we always find them as peaceful as they are this morning. In this hope I shall name this sea the Mar Pacífico."

Instead of sailing boldly northwest into the great blank of the Pacific Ocean, Magellan began to sail north for a while, parallel to the coast of present-day Chile. Although this course was only postponing the agony of finally entering the void, it did bring one welcome bonus: warmth. Magellan's weary sailors, who had been shivering ever since their arrival at Port St. Julian over eight months before, rejoiced as sun and milder air began to caress their skins.

The ships foamed steadily north for almost three weeks before Magellan, worried about his dwindling supplies, issued the momentous order: "Northwest!" The signal passed from ship to ship; three tillers swung to starboard; and the fleet moved out into the open Pacific. Magellan had no way of knowing that his course would bypass most of the islands that dot the mid-Pacific or that an ocean covering one-third of the earth's surface still separated him from the Moluccas.

As 1520 passed unobtrusively into 1521, day after day, week after week, lookouts hopefully scanned the horizon. But the expected islands did not appear. All sense of progress was lost; the three ships seemed to be wallowing in a vast unchanging disk of blue water with no end in sight.

The threat of starvation soon became horrifying reality. Pigafetta vividly recalled: "They ate biscuit, and when there was no more of that they ate the crumbs, which were full of maggots and smelled strongly of mouse urine. They drank yellow water, already several days putrid. And they ate some of the hides that were on the largest shroud to keep it from breaking. . . . They softened them in the sea for four or five days, and then they put them in a pot over the fire and ate them and also much sawdust." In time the starving, scurvy-wracked sailors were reduced to vying with each other for rats caught in the hold.

The suffering of his men opened an unsuspected reservoir of compassion in Magellan. Every morning he would limp from victim to victim, nursing those who had escaped death in the night. Pigafetta noted with admiration that the captain-general "never complained, never sank into despair."

Mercifully, on January 24, after nearly two months of sailing without sight of land, a tiny uninhabited atoll appeared on the horizon. There the famished sailors gorged on sea birds and turtle eggs and replenished their supply of drinking water. A couple of weeks later another small island was sighted, but the wind swept the fleet helplessly past it.

The weeks continued to drag by. On March 4—the 97th day of the voyage across the Pacific—the men on the *Trinidad* ate their last scrap of food. Two days later one of the few men still strong enough to climb the rigging screamed hoarsely from the crow's nest: "Praise God! Land! Land! Land!"

The little fleet had hardly dropped anchors off the island now called Guam when Magellan was greeted by a flotilla of outrigger canoes full of excited, light-

## Sailor Life Aboard Early Ships of Discovery

On an extended voyage like Magellan's, shipboard life, uncomfortable at best, could become a nightmare. Boredom destroyed men's spirits. Foul water and rotting food sapped their strength. Cramped quarters made tempers flare. To fight the tedium, Magellan included among his supplies "5 drums and 20 tambourines for the diversion of the crew of the fleet." For the most part, however, off-duty hours were whiled away in the time-honored practice of swapping sea tales. Captains often tried to limit the number of veteran sailors, preferring to take new men who would not retell the same familiar stories to distraction. But a number of old salts were needed, literally to teach the new men the ropes.

Experienced seamen, with a penchant for second-guessing the captain's orders, also increased the possibility of mutiny. The terrors of sailing unknown seas, combined with the discomforts of life aboard ship, made discipline hard to maintain. Obedience to orders was not automatic, and a captain had to work hard to enforce his control over an unruly crew. As a result, drastic punishment was sometimes needed. In the picture above right, one sailor is being repeatedly dunked from a platform at the stern, a second is being keel-hauled (dragged on ropes beneath the ship's hull), and a third sailor's hand is pinned to the mast with a knife.

The crew was a rough-and-ready lot, drawn from the lowest ranks of society. (They could also be of diverse nationalities. On Magellan's ships there were Italians, Frenchmen, Germans, blacks, and one Englishman, in addition to the Spanish and Portuguese.) They were divided into rotating watches of four hours each. (The completion of eight half-hour sand clocks marked a full watch. The ship's bell or the cabin boy's calls marked the turning of the glass. The ship's bells of modern times originated in this custom.) Their tasks while on watch included setting sails, swabbing decks, and handling rigging, as the picture below shows. At the end of their watch, the men bedded down on the hard planks of the deck, with neither mattresses nor hammocks to sleep on. Only officers had cabins with bunks. Wooden cages suspended over the rails, known as jardines or gardens, a reminder of the usual 16th-century location of the privy, served as latrines. In rough seas, however, the men used the bilges at the bottom of the ship. As a result, the ship constantly reeked of noxious odors even though the bilge

was cleaned and scrubbed several times during a voyage.

The crew ate only one hot meal a day, usually around noon. Because there were as yet no galleys aboard ships, meals were cooked over a fire kindled in a box of sand on the open deck. When it rained, food was eaten cold, but hot or cold, a sailor's diet was monotonous. It consisted of salted pork, a bit of cheese, some beans, onions, and the staple of all nautical diets, ship biscuit. Supplies, stored in leaky barrels, soon went bad. The meat putrified and weevils attacked the biscuit. Antonio Pigafetta described the food Magellan's crew subsisted on: "They ate biscuit and when there was no more of that they ate the crumbs, which were full of maggots and smelled strongly of mouse urine." When even the crumbs gave out, men captured the ship's vermin and auctioned them off as food. Pigafetta reported that "a mouse would bring half a ducat or a ducat."

To wash down their unappetizing meals, the crew had water and wine, both of which quickly spoiled in their wooden casks. The wine turned to rancid vinegar. The water became so foul and smelly that sailors held their noses while drinking it.

The lack of fruit and vegetables led to violent outbreaks of scurvy, caused by the absence of vitamin C in the sailors' diet. Scurvy, in fact, killed more seamen than all other maritime disasters combined. The disease caused gums to blacken and swell, teeth to fall out, and joints to become so weak that it was impossible to stand. A 16th-century sufferer described the ravages of the disease: "Many of our people died of it every day, and we saw bodies thrown into the sea constantly, three or four at a time. For the most part they died with no aid given them, expiring behind some case or chest, their eyes, and the soles of their feet gnawed away by rats."

Officers, whose personal supplies often included some dried fruit, suffered less often from scurvy than the men. Captains knew that fruit and vegetables maintained the crew's health, but in the 16th century there was no way to keep fresh foods from spoiling aboard ship. The appalling suffering scurvy created was not relieved until 1795 when British seamen were ordered to drink a daily ration of lime juice. The juice not only remedied the vitamin C deficiency but also gave British sailors the nickname Limeys, by which they are still known today.

But on Magellan's voyage there were no cures for scurvy. Pigafetta reported that 19 men died of it on the Pacific crossing alone. Yet enlisting for a long voyage in the face of the hazards of shipboard life was not as foolish as it might seem. The ordinary poor, unskilled 16th-century seaman would not have had measurably better living conditions on shore. And on every voyage there was the possibility not only of adventure but of shared booty, if a sailor could survive long enough to collect it.

fingered natives who rushed on board and carried off everything they could lay their hands on. The pilferage continued until some maddened sailors fired their crossbows. Magellan contemptuously named his discovery the Isle of Thieves.

Keeping the islanders at bay by the simple technique of setting their huts on fire, the captain-general managed to send a land party ashore to do some looting of its own. The Europeans helped themselves to the natives' water and the fresh food that the scurvy victims craved, then enjoyed an orgy of feasting on roast pork, chicken, rice, yams, bananas, and coconuts. A few days later they paused at another island for more provisions—this time obtained by barter—and before long the ravaged sailors' health began to return. Ulcers healed; loose teeth became firm; swollen gums slowly began to recede.

With bodies strengthened and morale restored, the explorers sailed on to the west. On March 16 yet another large island came into view, and in the days that followed more and more islands appeared on the horizon. Magellan gradually realized he had stumbled upon a huge unknown archipelago. It was the Philippine Islands. Although no spices grew there, the islanders had plenty of gold and pearls. In time, a valuable transpacific trade would develop between the islands and Spanish ports on the western coasts of Central and South America.

While anchored off one of the islands, Magellan received dramatic proof that he had practically circumnavigated the globe. When a canoe full of islanders put out from shore, Black Enrique, the captain-general's slave since his youthful days in the Far East, hailed the natives in Malay, the language used throughout the

Indies. The islanders understood and responded in Malay. Magellan had left the East Indies eight years before, in 1513. Now, after continuously moving away from them, he was again drawing near.

This supreme moment in the captain-general's life seems to have had an extraordinary effect on him. Always deeply religious, he became obsessed with missionary zeal. Postponing the final stage of his voyage to the Moluccas, he put in at the large island of Cebu, improvised an altar on shore, and began to preach to crowds of fascinated natives. "The Captain told them they should not become Christians out of fear," reported Pigafetta, "nor to please them, but voluntarily." His sermons, interpreted by Black Enrique, must have been extremely effective. On a single Sunday, April 14, Magellan baptized dozens of local chieftains, including the rajah of Cebu himself, as well as hundreds of ordinary citizens. A "holy alliance" was then negotiated with the rajah, effectively establishing the authority of Spain over the Philippines.

Only one chief, a ruler on the tiny island of Mactan, balked against Magellan's peaceful conquest. Intoxicated by his evangelistic and political success, the captain-general threw aside his customary caution. Hastily crowding 50 or so volunteers into three small boats, he set off on a foolhardy attempt to force compliance upon the island.

On April 27, 1521, the little Christian army waded ashore on Mactan Island. Hundreds of warriors awaited them, massed behind a series of deep, defensive trenches. Even with their arquebuses, crossbows, and steel armor, the Europeans were no match for the horde of shrieking Filipinos that let loose volleys of "arrows, javelins, lances with points hardened in the fire, stones, and even filth, so that we were scarcely able to defend ourselves." Before long the Christians were fleeing headlong for their boats. Bringing up the rear were the limping captain-general, by now wounded by an arrow in his leg, and a handful of soldiers. For an hour the little band fought desperately at the water's edge, reported Pigafetta, "until at length an islander succeeded in wounding the Captain in the face with a bamboo spear. He, being desperate, plunged his lance into the Indian's breast, leaving it there. But, wishing to use his sword, he could draw it only halfway from the sheath, on account of a spear wound he had received in the right arm. . . . Then the Indians threw themselves upon him, with spears and scimitars and every weapon they had, and ran him through—our mirror, our light our comforter, our true guide—until they killed him."

After the death of Magellan, relations between the explorers and their hosts on Cebu deteriorated rapidly. Suddenly, men with white skins seemed less godlike, more vulnerable. The rajah, goaded by a disgruntled member of the expedition, suspected the Spanish expedition of treachery. On May 1 he invited 27 officers of the fleet to a banquet, encouraged them to eat their fill,

**As Magellan's small fleet** *approached the Philippine Islands, his ships were met by natives paddling canoes like the ones above. On one occasion, a local ruler had his carved wooden throne placed in a canoe to enable him to greet his visitors with dignity. Here natives bring fresh food for Magellan's crew.*

*Navigators in Unknown Seas*

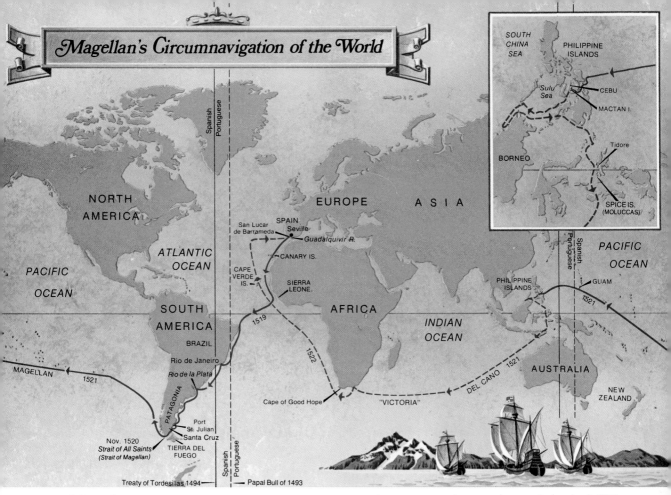

**Magellan left Seville's ocean outlet,** *San Lúcar de Barrameda,* *on September 20, 1519, in search of the New World strait that* *would lead west to the Indies. The expedition consisted of five* *ships and some 250 men. Three years later, on September 8, 1522,* *one ship with 18 men—the sole survivors—limped into San Lúcar.* *Magellan himself had been killed at Mactan Island.*

and then had most of them slaughtered.

This catastrophe reduced to 114 the manpower of an expedition that, at the outset, had numbered some 250 men. There were now too few sailors to man three ships; so hastily stripping and burning the *Concepción,* the survivors consolidated themselves in the *Trinidad* and *Victoria* and fled from Cebu.

Bereft of Magellan's leadership, the two ships wandered aimlessly about the South China and Sulu Seas for six months, committing random piracies on local traders, before happening on the island of Tidore in the Moluccas. There they loaded up with such a heavy cargo of spices, especially cloves, that the *Trinidad* began to split along the seams. Leaving her behind for repairs (she was later captured by the Portuguese and only a handful of her crew ever returned to Spain), the *Victoria,* under the command of Juan Sebastian del Cano, sailed southwestward into the Indian Ocean in December 1521.

The long voyage home was not a happy one. Del Cano, who had been involved in the mutiny at Port St. Julian, proved to be an unpopular captain. There were petty mutinies and desertions en route. Storms im-

peded progress around the Cape of Good Hope. While sailing up the west coast of Africa, sailors continued to die of scurvy and starvation. It was not until September 8, 1522, almost exactly three years since her departure from Spain, that the *Victoria* creaked wearily into Seville's harbor. A silent crowd watched in amazement as only 18 survivors staggered ashore. Gaunt and barefooted, the next day they carried lighted candles to give thanks at Magellan's favorite shrine in the church of Santa Maria de la Victoria.

Having thus honored his dead leader, Del Cano accepted from King Charles the ultimate reward of the expedition: a coat of arms depicting the globe and bearing the motto *Primus circumdedisti me,* "You first circumnavigated me." Yet historians have never been able to decide which man rightfully deserves that honor. Was it Magellan who, some say, had already visited the East Indies as a youth? Was it his humble slave Black Enrique? Or was it Del Cano? But the loyal Antonio Pigafetta, who survived to write the story of the voyage, had no doubts. Of Magellan he stated flatly: "The best proof of his genius is that he circumnavigated the world, none having preceded him."

# Part

3

## Seeking Gold in the Americas

## The Conquistadors

*In their relentless search for treasure, Spanish soldiers conquer Indian empires and explore New World lands.*

What kind of men could endure the hardships of the earliest exploration and conquest in the Americas? They had to spend years—not months—in tropical conditions of the worst sort. Almost constant rain; hordes of insects, snakes, and vermin; hostile natives; often inadequate food; the jealousy of fellow explorers; and isolation from Europe were their lot. Life was short in the New World; men could usually expect to live no more than a few years there, at best, before they died from disease, overexposure, malnutrition, or Indian attacks. Yet in their ruthless zeal for "gold, glory, and the Gospel" (as one historian has put it), these bold men subdued half a hemisphere and changed the course of human history in a short 50 years. They were indeed conquerors, or "conquistadors."

Most of the conquistadors were Spanish, and many had fought in the wars of Europe, north Africa, and Asia. Most were landless in an age when the possession of land was the basic requirement for rank and fortune. The New World was full of "empty" land and Indians to work it. Moreover, it was believed to have gold and silver in great but elusive quantities. A discoverer or conqueror could gain glory and wealth. It was for these reasons that Hernando Cortés, according to his secretary, Gómara, chose to seek his fortune in the Indies rather than in Naples, "because it struck him as the more promising on account of the quantity of gold that was being brought from there." Others felt the same. They could also convert souls to Christianity; the Church was with the conquistadors from the beginning, sharing in the hardships and profits of the New World as it was explored and settled.

Columbus could be called the first conquistador. He had returned from his initial trip with scraps of gold jewelry gathered from the natives of Hispaniola, and this small amount inspired a feverish search for more. Within two decades nearly all the major islands of the Caribbean had been explored and several settlements established, the largest ones on Hispaniola and Cuba. From these outposts the conquistadors made their first forays onto the American mainland, beginning some of the most stunning military exploits in history.

### Civilizations and Savages

In the lands awaiting them the Spanish found an unusual mixture of Stone Age technology, high cultural development, and primitive religious practices. The Indians had tools of stone, for instance, and they had never learned to use wheels for transportation—but they had developed quite sophisticated architecture, farming techniques, and communication systems and had produced intricate crafts and works of art frequently rendered in gold. The Spaniards, however, were appalled to find that certain Indian tribes practiced cannibalism, while others sacrificed human beings in ritual religious ceremonies.

Most of the American Indian societies were loosely

organized, but the Aztecs of Mexico and the Incas of Peru were powerful and prosperous tribes that had extended their authority over large areas and developed elaborate political structures comparable to the empires of the Old World. They boasted cosmopolitan capitals as well, with the Aztec center at Tenochtitlán rivaling Seville, Spain's largest city, in population.

The Aztecs and Incas also posed the greatest challenge to the Spaniards, and their conquest offered the greatest rewards. During the first half of the 16th century, the conquistadors toppled these two great civilizations against terrific resistance and enormous odds. Meanwhile, they had discovered enough gold and silver to make Spain the richest nation on earth and carved out an empire that endured 300 years.

### Indian Life Under the Spanish

The Spaniards who first made passage to the New World, viewing themselves as conquerors and rulers, considered common labor beneath their dignity. So they turned to the natives, whom they subjected to the most brutal sort of slavery. (The men were forced to work in the fields and mines; the women were taken as mistresses or sold as servants.) For the wretched Indians, who were no more used to backbreaking toil than their captors, life under Spanish occupation became a nightmare, and their numbers were soon decimated in their revolts against slavery and by mining accidents, suicide, and the white man's diseases to which they had never before been exposed.

This widespread and almost casual abuse grew out of the Spaniards' belief that the Indians were an inferior, barbaric race, a belief that was little altered even when the Spaniards saw the remarkable accomplishments of the Aztec and Inca civilizations. For years, in fact, it was heatedly debated whether the Indians were human at all and therefore worthy of conversion to Christianity. This was a crucial matter to the Europeans, whose zeal to spread the Gospel was nearly as important a motive for conquest as their appetite for gold. It was finally decided that the Indians did indeed have souls, and as a result of the insistent pleas of Bartolomé de las Casas and other missionaries, the Spanish court eventually issued a series of decrees protecting them against excessive brutality. Even so, the majority of Indians that survived the early Spanish occupation had little to look forward to but chronic poverty and hardship.

The Spaniards divided the conquered population into *encomiendas*, administrative units comprising one or more Indian towns. Some of these were reserved for the crown, the rest granted to the higher ranking officers, who exercised virtually absolute local authority and demanded tribute from the natives, often in the form of forced labor. (As for the common foot soldier who failed to attach himself to the personal retinue of an *encomendaro*, he could only hope to win enough distinction in the next campaign to secure an *encomienda* of his own.)

For all their faults the conquistadors were not merely ruthless butchers or petty tyrants. They were also men of exceptional courage and endurance. The best of them displayed the qualities of truly great commanders. Vasco Núñez de Balboa, one of the first Spaniards to explore the American mainland, won control of the Panamanian isthmus as much by diplomacy as by force. Similarly, Cortés' campaign against the Aztec empire—whose forces outnumbered his own by some 200 to 1—was a model of tactical and psychological genius. Less than 10 years later Francisco Pizarro began his conquest of Peru with an "army" of 180 soldiers and all but guaranteed his victory during a single day when he captured the Inca ruler Atahualpa. To be sure, the conquistadors had advantages beyond their own daring and resourcefulness. The Spanish conquest of the Americas marked a confrontation between two different cultures, one equipped with more advanced weapons and technology.

### Twilight of the Conquistadors

In the end the era of the conquistadors proved as brief as it was tumultuous. By the late 1530's Mexico and Central America were being administered as the viceroyalty of New Spain; De Soto, Coronado, and others had begun exploration of what is now the southern United States; Pizarro had conquered the Incas, leaving other Spaniards to create the only turbulence in Peru. About the same time, the discovery of rich silver mines in Mexico and Peru brought about a steady increase in transatlantic shipping and immigration of Spaniards to the New World.

With such enormous wealth waiting to be taken out of the ground, the Spanish crown—which was entitled to a "royal fifth" of all revenues—was naturally anxious to establish firm control over its new territories. For this reason governmental authority was entrusted not to those who had done the actual fighting but to royally appointed officials—whether soldiers, ecclesiastics, or lawyers—who could be relied upon to do as they were told. Ironically, the very qualities that brought the conquistadors such dramatic success made them singularly unfit to serve as peacetime administrators. Though they differed widely in background and character—from the relatively cultured Cortés to the illiterate cutthroat Pizarro—they were without exception strong-willed, impulsive, fiercely independent men. In short, they were warriors, not bureaucrats, and by the 1540's the Spanish court simply had no further use for them. So the conquistadors fell into eclipse as suddenly as they had emerged. Many, in fact, died at the hands of other Spaniards, and those who survived found themselves stripped of any real authority and were left, like Cortés, to end their days in idleness and bitter frustration.

**Equipped with steel helmets** *and ornate swords (left), like soldiers who were off to fight the infidel, Balboa and his men instead fought a fatiguing battle against the thick Panamanian jungle. Hacking their way through the dense undergrowth, they emerged on the western side of the Isthmus of Panama and became the first Europeans to see the Pacific Ocean (top), which Balboa called the South Sea. Throughout their journey across the isthmus, the Spaniards were accompanied by their faithful but fierce war dogs. The dogs exhibited their ferocity when Balboa discovered a chief with a harem of young men dressed in female clothing. This so enraged the Spaniards that they set the dogs upon the Indians, and the hounds killed the entire group. The engraving above depicts this grisly scene, with Balboa at center. Some Spanish war dogs, like Balboa's bloodhound, Leoncico, were even given a share of the booty captured from the Indians. Usually, though, Balboa's relations with the Indians were much more diplomatic than those of the other conquistadors.*

## Chapter Eight

A bold, red-haired Spanish soldier of fortune pioneers in the first European settlement on the American mainland. From there he leads an expedition through dangerous Panamanian jungles and swamps to the shore of the Pacific Ocean, becoming the first explorer to see the great "southern sea" that lies between America and the Orient.

# *Across the Isthmus: Balboa Discovers the Pacific*

*In 1501 Vasco Núñez de Balboa stowed away in a vessel bound for the New World. He claimed that he was born in 1475 to an illustrious family of Jerez de los Caballeros, in the region of Estremadura, Spain. The young man, who was fleeing his creditors, settled on the island of Hispaniola and tried to make a living raising hogs, but sank more deeply into debt. Again he stowed away, this time on an expedition to establish settlements on the Caribbean coast of the Isthmus of Panama. Arriving there in 1510, Balboa spent the next eight years exploring the isthmus, establishing towns, quarreling with rivals, and looking for gold and pearls. In 1513 he and his expedition discovered the Pacific. In 1519, shortly after a voyage to the Pearl Islands, he met his fate at the hands of a rival who had replaced him as governor of Darién.*

Vasco Núñez de Balboa was not much of a farmer. As a young man in the early 1500's, he struggled hard to make a living raising hogs on the Caribbean island of Hispaniola, but he succeeded only in slipping deeper and deeper into debt. No doubt convinced he was cut out for something nobler than pig farming, he decided that his best course would be to escape his creditors and make a new start somewhere else.

Balboa thought he found a solution in the fall of 1510. Martín Fernández de Enciso was organizing an expedition to take new settlers and supplies to the recently founded Spanish settlement of San Sebastián on the Gulf of Urabá, just east of the present-day Panama-Colombia border. But because of his financial problems Balboa was refused permission to join the fleet.

Bold and aggressive, the 34-year-old redhead was not a man to take no for an answer. When some provisions for the fleet were requisitioned from his farm, he loaded a large barrel not with flour but with himself and his big tawny bloodhound, Leoncico. The barrel was duly loaded on the flagship, the fleet put out to sea,

and Balboa said farewell to Hispaniola—and his cursed creditors—forever.

The stowaways did not crawl out of their cramped container until the ships were well out at sea. When Balboa appeared on deck, Enciso, enraged by his audacity, threatened to maroon him on a deserted island. Balboa, however, described as a "clean-limbed and strong" man "of gallant mien and . . . handsome," had friends on board. Some of the settlers vouched for him as an "outstanding swordsman." Such a fighter and such a war dog, they argued, could be very helpful in battles against hostile Indians. Besides, as a youth in search of adventure, Balboa had visited the coast near San Sebastián on a Spanish expedition in 1500. His knowledge of the area could prove very helpful.

Almost immediately, it did. Entering the Gulf of Urabá, the flagship was wrecked on treacherous inshore shoals. Although most of the colonists were able to struggle ashore, the bulk of their supplies was lost. Worse still, they found that Indians armed with poisoned arrows had wiped out most of the Spaniards at San Sebastián and burned the little settlement to the ground. (Among the few survivors was Francisco Pizarro, the future conqueror of Peru, who was also destined to play a role in Balboa's fate.)

Bewildered, Enciso had little choice but to defer to the experience of his stowaway. Balboa recalled that on visiting the area in 1500 he had seen an Indian village surrounded by cultivated fields on the opposite side of the gulf. This village, which adjoined a large river, sounded inviting indeed, but, more pertinent, Balboa added that its inhabitants did not use poisoned arrows. That news was enough for most of the settlers, who immediately abandoned San Sebastián and followed Balboa in small boats across the gulf.

The village was still there on the Río Tanela, and the settlers found, to their relief, that Balboa was right

## Smoking Tobacco Leaves Was an Indian Pleasure That Soon Became a European Obsession

The conquistadors hoped that the discovery of large amounts of gold would justify the cost of their expeditions. Ironically, it was not gold but a common plant native to the Americas that would become a greater source of wealth in the New World. It was, of course, the tobacco plant. Columbus gave the first account of Indians smoking. He described "women and men with firebrand in the hand, and herbs to drink the smoke thereof, as they are accustomed."

Tobacco cultivation was soon exported to Europe, where the "fad" of smoking quickly caught on, though some vociferously opposed it. France began to grow tobacco in 1556, Portugal in 1558, Spain in 1559, and England in 1565. In fact, the genus of the tobacco plant, *nicotiana*, was named for Jean Nicot, a

16th-century French ambassador to Portugal. It was in the New World, however, that tobacco cultivation formed the basis of much of the economy; in some places tobacco was used as money. The first American tobacco plantation was started at Jamestown, Virginia, in 1612.

A 17th-century English traveler noted

how tobacco was smoked by the Indians of Panama, who first rolled the leaves into a kind of cigar: "A boy lights one end of a roll and burns it to a coal, wetting the part next to it to keep it from wasting too fast. The end so lighted he puts into his mouth and blows the smoke through the whole length of the roll into the face of everyone of the company or council. Then sitting in their usual posture upon forms, they make with their hands held hollow together a kind of funnel round their mouths and noses. Into this they receive the smoke as it is blown upon them, snuffing it up greedily and strongly as long as ever they are able to hold their breath. . . ." The engraving here, dating from 1699, shows Panamanian Indians smoking their cigars in a large hut constructed especially for the purpose.

about the local arrows. With the help of their guns and bloodhounds, the Spaniards easily routed the Darién chief and his warriors and promptly took over the settlement. It was a pleasant spot. The clearings where the Indians had grown corn, cassavas, pineapples, and potatoes formed a comforting buffer zone between the riverside town and the jungle beyond, where howler monkeys, tree frogs, and mysterious tropical birds filled the air with strange sounds. As the months passed, the Spaniards decided that they could not do much better than this readymade village for a "capital," so they christened it Santa María la Antigua del Darién. It was to be, in fact, the first colonial capital on the mainland of the Americas.

Before long, friction arose in the new colony. Enciso, a lawyer by profession, was more at home in the study than as a leader of men, and his arbitrary administration soon provoked active opposition. Excluding Enciso from the voting, the settlers elected his nemesis, Balboa, and another man as coadministrators of the settlement. With this, Enciso made such a pest of himself that, much to Balboa's satisfaction, the colonists banished him and shipped him off to Spain. (In a later report to King Ferdinand, Balboa advised his monarch "that no doctor of laws or anything except medicine should come to these parts . . . because no [lawyer] comes here who is not a devil.") In April 1511 Balboa's coadministrator also left for Spain to defend the two against Enciso's slanders, and Balboa found himself the effective leader of the colony.

After months of building, trading, and administrative work, Balboa, who "could not be still even while his bread was baking," was eager to set about the true business of a conquistador—to explore and exploit the lush surrounding countryside. Early in May 1511 he

went off with a party of 100 men on an expedition to Careta, an Indian province about 80 miles north of Santa María on the Caribbean shore of the isthmus.

Although Balboa first established his authority over the Careta Indians by force, he soon won their friendship by skillful diplomacy. (This pattern—unusual among the conquistadors—was typical of many of Balboa's dealings with Indians.) In the case of the Caretans, his success was especially impressive. Their chief, Chima, converted to Christianity and even presented to Balboa his beautiful young daughter as a mistress. He also agreed to supply the Spaniards with food, gold, and farm laborers if they would subdue his enemies, the neighboring Ponca tribe.

When Balboa led his force on the Ponca stronghold, the Indians wisely fled and let the Spaniards burn their village and take any gold they had left behind. Though the victory was undramatic, Chima was so delighted that he agreed to send an envoy to introduce Balboa to Comogre, chief of Comogra, another large and fertile province to the north.

In the Comogran village Balboa and his men first glimpsed the New World as Europeans had fantasized it: a land of ceremony, of the exotic, of gold. They were graciously received by the chief, who wore a crown of gold. Surrounded by his seven sons, he escorted the Spaniards to a large and splendidly decorated timbered "palace" and regaled them with a feast of smoked venison and roast peccary meat, with wine and maize beer served in handsome, gold-trimmed cups fashioned from gourds or woven with fiber.

The Spaniards also were delighted with the small slender Comogran girls, who bathed five times a day and rubbed their naked bodies with perfumed ointments. (To the chagrin of local youths, the girls soon showed a distinct preference for Spanish lovers.) Relations between the Spaniards and the Comograns became so cordial, in fact, that the visitors were honored with the rare privilege of being shown the sacred Hall of Ancestors.

There, suspended from the roof, dangled the fire-dried bodies of dead chiefs attired in gold masks and sumptuous pearl-trimmed garments. The Spaniards were appalled by the grisly spectacle but were also obviously tempted to plunder the riches. The chief's eldest son, sensing the Spaniards' thoughts, advised his father to appease the conquistadors. Comogre quickly arranged to present his guests with 70 laborers and a selection of the gold ornaments they had seen.

With undiplomatic greed, the Spaniards could not resist weighing their loot then and there, to the contempt of Comogre's son Ponquiaco. Sweeping the scales aside, he exclaimed: "What then is this, Christians? Is it possible that you set so high a value on so little gold? . . . If your thirst for gold is such that to

**Though the Isthmus of Panama** *is extremely narrow, its eastern side is covered with dense, tropical rain forest. It was this tangled natural barrier that caused Balboa's expedition such trouble in its journey to the Pacific. At times it was easier to wade down rivers than to hack through the impenetrable jungle.*

satisfy it you molest peaceable people and bring misfortune and calamity among them, if you exile yourselves from your own country to search for it, I will show you a land where it abounds, and where you can satisfy your thirst." Probably with the idea of getting rid of the Spaniards, he went on to tell Balboa of a great ocean beyond the hills to the south, a sea bordered by rivers running with gold and shores studded with pearls. This had to be that legendary Other Sea, the South Sea. Although Balboa first perceived it as his chance to gain glory and wealth, it eventually provided him with a greater destiny.

Balboa itched with ambition to find that fabulous ocean and gain new territories and wealth for Spain, but he could not begin his search at that time. Ponquiaco had said that the way was barred by treacherous mountains and hostile cannibal tribes. Balboa needed to carefully organize such an expedition, for he was an explorer, not a rash adventurer. Eventually, two years passed before he could make the attempt.

Returning to Santa María in November 1511, he soon was preoccupied with the problems of the growing settlement—crop failures, fractious settlers, and an Indian conspiracy against him. When floods completely wiped out the crops later that month, Balboa sent an assistant, Juan de Valdivia, to Hispaniola for fresh provisions. Among his cargo was the royal fifth of treasure to be sent to King Ferdinand in Spain. However, the ship was wrecked, and the authorities received no news from Balboa; had Ferdinand received that gold, he might have been more influenced in Balboa's favor.

Despite these setbacks, Balboa did find time to explore. In March 1512 he led an expedition south of the Gulf of Urabá, where he discovered the Río Atrato and explored the surrounding country. The trip lasted seven brutal months in intense heat and humidity and cost the lives of 30 men. Besides extending knowledge of the Spanish Main, it provided Balboa with invaluable experience as an explorer.

Unlike many colonial administrators who described the Americas as a virtual paradise in order to coax more funds from the crown, Balboa provided vivid and accurate descriptions of the new land. In a long letter-report to King Ferdinand in January 1513, he commented: ". . . the land is very difficult to travel over on account of the many rivers and extensive marshes and mountains where many men die from the great toil suffered." Describing the realities as one who knew them firsthand, he added: "Your Royal Highness should not believe that the swamps of this land are such light affairs that we move along through them joyfully, for many times it happens to us to go naked through swamps and water for one, two, and three leagues with the clothing collected and placed on the shield on top of the head." He even admitted that he had not been able to travel everywhere "for man arrives as far as he can, and not as far as he wishes."

That June, Balboa received a letter from King Ferdinand announcing his appointment as governor and captain of the colony of Darién, which extended along the eastern coast of modern Panama from Río Tanela to the end of the Gulf of Urabá. However, there was an ominous qualifier to the appointment: It was only temporary. The king would eventually appoint a permanent governor. Balboa was well aware of the constant power plays and subtle manipulations that took place in the royal court to gain potentially lucrative appointments. He knew that unless he did something spectacular to impress the king, someone else eventually would be sent from Spain to replace him and take away the glory—and the gold—he felt he deserved. Now, he realized, was the time to find that great ocean no European had ever seen.

Balboa chose Careta, the home of his old friend Chief Chima, as the jumping-off point of his quest for the unknown sea. The force that set out from Careta on September 6, 1513, included 92 colonist-soldiers (among them, Francisco Pizarro), 2 priests, Indian guides, and hundreds of Indian porters who carried the expedition's armaments, food, and other supplies. There was also a pack of bloodhounds, including the battle-scarred Leoncico, who now wore a gold collar and drew a soldier's pay. Balboa's main purpose was discovery, but he was prepared to fight if he had to.

The explorers rested at the nearby Indian town of Ponca for 12 days, then plunged into the interior. This was the start of the hardest stage of the journey. Although the Isthmus of Panama is only 45 miles wide where Balboa's men crossed it, much of it is covered by mountains shrouded with tropical rain forest so dense it hides the sky. At times the exhausted men found it easier to swim down rivers and wade through shallows than hack a path through impenetrable jungle. After five days of toil the weary explorers at last emerged in a region of hills less thickly overgrown with vegetation.

There the explorers were confronted by 600 Quarecan warriors. As usual, the Indians' gold breastplates, fur-covered shields, and bows and arrows proved scant protection against the determined Spaniards with their guns, swords, and attacking dogs. The Indians were quickly routed, and the explorers took over their main village. (There the Spaniards were astonished to find that the chief kept a harem of young men dressed as women. Horrified by this evidence of mortal sin, the Catholic conquistadors let loose their ferocious war

---

## Panamanian Indians Wrought Gold in the Forms of the Animals and Insects of Their Forests

the precious metal. Sixteenth-century chronicler Gonzalo Fernández de Oviedo noted the Indian attitude toward gold: "They make it into jewels and ornaments with which men and women adorn their bodies. In fact, it is the thing which they esteem and prize above all others."

Some Indians wisely realized that if

The Spaniards were unimpressed by the beauty of the Indian gold objects that they so greedily amassed. In their eagerness to weigh and measure their treasure, they completely ignored the delicate workmanship of the finely wrought pieces that they quickly melted down into solid gold ingots. Smelting tools were often carried on expeditions so the beautifully crafted articles could be reduced to solid gold bricks on the spot. The Indians, unlike the conquistadors, did not consider gold primarily as a form of currency. Instead, they valued the graceful objects that were created from

the Europeans' lust for gold could be satisfied, their people would suffer far less from the fearful weapons the invaders carried. The son of a powerful chief whom Balboa met exploring the isthmus played upon the Spaniards' fascination for gold to lure the expedition away from his tribe's territory. After presenting many gold objects to Balboa, the Indian told him of a land far to the south called Biru, where far greater quantities of gold could be obtained. Biru, which was Peru, was later conquered by one of the men who served with Balboa, Francisco Pizarro.

dogs, who tore the young men to pieces.)

Leaving part of his force in Quareca, Balboa pressed on with 66 men and the Indian guides and porters. At about 10 o'clock on the morning of September 25, 1513, they approached "a bare high hill." From its summit, the Indians said, the great ocean was visible. As the expedition neared the peak, Balboa called a halt and, taking only Leoncico with him, moved out ahead of his men and climbed the slope. At the top the land fell away before him, and in the distance, across thousands of treetops, he saw a long shining strip of blue water shimmering on the horizon.

In the words of the chronicler Oviedo: "Immediately he turned toward the troops, very happy, lifting eyes and hands to heaven . . . and then he knelt down on both knees and gave much thanks to God for . . . allowing him to discover that sea. . . ." After planting a great cross on the top of the hill, Balboa "commanded that the names of all the men who were there with him should be written down so that the memory should remain of him and of them, because they were the first Christians who saw that sea." The little ceremony ended with all hands joining in a "Te Deum," a pious hymn of praise.

Two days later Balboa and 26 selected companions arrived at a great inlet, which he named the Gulf of San Miguel, to take possession of the ocean he called Mar del Sur, the "South Sea." The tide was out, however; only a seemingly endless stretch of sand confronted him. There was nothing to do but sit in the shade and wait for the ocean to come to him. Suddenly, "the water rose exceedingly in the sight of all with great impetus" as the tide came rushing in. Balboa, in a full suit of armor, plunged into the waves brandishing his sword and the banner of Castile and, as the water foamed around his knees, proclaimed: "I take and assume royal possession . . . of these [southern] seas and lands and coasts and islands. . . ." Swearing to defend this huge western extension of Spain's domain, he and his men then cut crosses on many trees in honor of the Holy Trinity.

Even discovery of the Pacific Ocean was not accomplishment enough for Balboa, however. The Indians had told him of the enticingly named Pearl Islands offshore. He was determined to investigate them, but bad weather thwarted all his attempts to reach them. Vowing to return one day, Balboa contented himself with exploring the hinterlands to the north for gold and other valuables. Along the way he also managed to

---

The goldwork of the Panamanian Indians has not received the attention given to Peruvian artifacts, but the craftsmen of the isthmus achieved great skill in the fabrication of fine ornaments. Most of these small gold objects were pendants or nose ornaments. They were cast in molds, sometimes with gold-copper alloys, usually in the forms of small figures of the birds and animals that inhabited the jungles of Central America. The stylized eagle (column one) was among the most common objects made by Indian goldsmiths. Columbus, who discovered the Isthmus of Panama in 1502, noted the abundance of golden

eagle ornaments. The hummingbird (column two) was also a favorite subject for Indian smiths. The intricate golden monkey (column three) is surrounded by a delicate circlet of gold.

Even the most humble creatures were transformed into objects of great beauty by skilled Indian artisans. A lowly spider laying eggs (column four), a frog (column five), and a beetle (column six) were all rendered imaginatively in gold. Often the figures were designed to be worn as amulets. Sometimes the object was hollow with a small clapper inside, making the figure a delicate golden bell.

Oviedo described how the Indians mined gold. American Forty-niners used a similar process more than 300 years later when they panned gold from the streams of California during the famed

gold rush. "If a lode or vein is located on a savanna or clear place, the Indians clean away everything on the surface of the ground over a square of eight or ten feet; then they dig down a distance of one or two spans. Then without digging deeper they wash all the loose dirt of that area. If they find the gold within that area they follow the vein, if not they dig down the same distance and wash the gold as before. This they continue until gradually, washing all the dirt, they strike solid rock. If they have not discovered gold before reaching the rock, they discontinue mining that area."

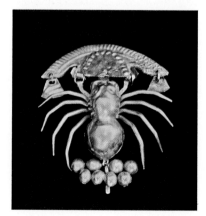

persuade a number of tribes to acknowledge the sovereignty of Spain.

By this time Balboa and his men were exhausted and feverish; he himself had to be carried for a time in a hammock. It was not until January 19, 1514, that the explorers returned in much deserved triumph to Santa María la Antigua. Men had traveled longer and farther and had endured greater hardships. But as a planned, political expedition, this was exploration at its finest.

Balboa immediately wrote to the king, announcing his discovery and asking to be made permanent governor of Darién. Accompanying his letter was another royal fifth, 200 beautiful pearls, and a petition from the colonists requesting Balboa's promotion. But by the time these letters reached Spain, King Ferdinand had already effected a major reorganization of the isthmus. Because Balboa's principal defenders were in Darién, he had not been able to protect himself against plots at court, nor was he able to stake his claim there along with others vying for power and riches. The result couldn't have been more offensive to Balboa if Enciso had masterminded it himself: An armada was already on its way to the colony, bringing some 3,000 new settlers. (Among them were De Soto, Coronado, and a number of others who later made history themselves.) There was also a new administrative staff headed by a 70-year-old courtier, Pedrarias Dávila, whom Ferdinand had appointed permanent governor of Darién.

Pedrarias arrived at Santa María on a steamy tropical day late in June 1514. As if to intimidate the man he was replacing, he entered the sweltering town at the head of a procession of 2,000 soldiers in dazzling armor, horses in brilliant trappings, chanting friars, and Moorish slaves. Despite the heat and humidity, the governor and his wife were bedecked in rich, heavy silk clothing. Awaiting him were 500 settlers in simple cotton clothes and hemp sandals. Quelling any resentment he may have felt, Balboa strode forward and bowed to his pale, sick-looking successor.

The following day Balboa fulfilled the new governor's request for a detailed written report on the land and people of Darién. Pedrarias repaid him by appropriating his house and ordering an investigation of his administration. Although a routine examination was normal for all departing Spanish colonial governors, Pedrarias and a few disaffected settlers prolonged the inquiry by dragging in every possible accusation against Balboa. It was not until December 1514 that Balboa was officially acquitted of any criminal misconduct. Even then Pedrarias would not allow other minor charges to be dropped. Balboa must have read with wry amusement a letter he received about that time from King Ferdinand assuring him that the monarch was instructing Pedrarias "to look to your affairs with care and to favor you as a person whom I greatly desire to gratify."

But Pedrarias was a tyrannical old man, interested only in gratifying and enriching himself. He allowed his troops to rampage for gold and to torture and enslave the Indians whose friendship Balboa had so carefully cultivated. Most rankling of all, he prevented Balboa from doing any more exploring.

Suddenly, events turned in Balboa's favor. In March 1515 King Ferdinand appointed him *adelantado* of the Pacific coast and governor of Panama and Coiba. The first title authorized him to administer his Pacific discoveries; the second permitted him to govern and explore the uncharted territory to the north of Darién. Although these honors surpassed Balboa's wildest expectations, his authority was nullified by Pedrarias' greater power. The old man not only denied him the men and supplies he needed to carry out his new responsibilities but even sent his own lieutenants to explore some of Balboa's new domain.

In desperation, Balboa appealed directly to the king: "[Pedrarius] is very old to serve in these parts, and he suffers greatly from a serious illness so that he has never been well for a single day since he came here. . . . He is a man who does not much care even if half the troops are lost on the expeditions. . . . The governor is a person who is delighted to see discord between people, and if there is none he creates it. . . . He is a man who, absorbed in his profit-getting and greed, does not remember that he is governor. . . . He is a man ruled by

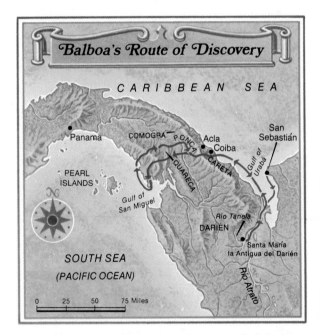

**Balboa set out from the province** *of Careta to find the Great Ocean on September 6, 1513, after traveling there from the "capital" of Darién. Stopping briefly to vanquish Quarecan warriors whom they met along the harrowing trail, the explorers pressed on. Though the Isthmus of Panama is only 45 miles wide where Balboa crossed it, it was not until September 25 that he sighted the Pacific from a hill near the Gulf of San Miguel.*

*The Conquistadors*

## Balboa Found a Wealth of Pacific Pearls for Europe's Women

On the Pacific coast of the Isthmus of Panama, Balboa discovered oysterbeds that produced huge pearls. This news created as much sensation in Spain as did the discovery of the Pacific itself. High-born Spanish ladies, such as the sister of conquistador Hernando Cortés pictured at right, prized the pearls not only for earrings and necklaces but also as decoration for their dresses and headpieces. A 16th-century commentator rejoiced: "Spain may henceforth satisfy the desire of Cleopatra for pearls."

The Spaniards learned of the great oysterbeds by chance. At the village of an Indian chief called Comogre, Balboa and his men were stunned to find the mummified bodies of former chiefs decorated with gold masks and garments trimmed with pearls. By following the instructions from Comogre's son, Balboa located the tribes that gathered the pearls. The chief of one of the tribes presented Balboa with a basket of 240 pearls whose luster, unfortunately, was dimmed since the chief had steamed the oysters before removing the pearls. The historian Gonzalo Fernández de Oviedo described how the Indians fished for pearls: "The Indians use two large stones tied together with a cord, which they place over their shoulders, one on each side, and enter the water. . . . Since the stones are heavy, an Indian can remain on the bottom. When he wants to rise to the surface, he merely drops the stones."

all envy and covetousness in the world."

Pedrarias, in fact, was planning to establish settlements in Balboa's territory. Indignant, Balboa tried to recruit an expedition of his own. The wily old Pedrarias countered by accusing him of conspiracy and rebellion and had Balboa locked in a cage outside his house. There the explorer remained for two months until the protests of his friends brought about his release.

This was followed by an extraordinary turn of events: Pedrarias announced that Balboa had been married by proxy to his daughter in Spain! Apparently the governor, who had just learned of King Ferdinand's death, was uncertain whom a new regime might favor. Taking no chances, he decided to ingratiate himself with his former prisoner.

Although Balboa now was theoretically free to return to the South Sea, Pedrarias ordered him first to build a fort at Acla, up the coast, to protect the mountain passes to the Pacific. Though short on manpower, Balboa completed not just the fort but a supporting settlement as well in just six months. It proved to be so well organized that one delighted visitor reported, "One eats there as well as in Seville."

In August 1517 Balboa set off once more for the South Sea, accompanied by 235 Spaniards. (Leoncico, however, was missing—he had been poisoned by one of Balboa's enemies.) This time the Spaniards carried their own supplies, including local lumber with which to build ships to sail to the elusive Pearl Islands. They took the wood in the mistaken belief that it was impervious to the depredations of shipworms. Balboa himself reportedly carried a plank weighing almost 100 pounds. When the expedition finally reached a river leading to the South Sea, a sudden flood swept the lumber away, and the Spaniards escaped death only by climbing nearby trees.

In spite of this heartbreaking setback, not one man voted to give up. Reasoning that inferior wood was better than none at all, they began to hew new planks on the spot. By May 1518 two small ships had been built and were on their way down the river and out to sea. After a long, difficult voyage they reached the Pearl Islands just in the nick of time. The ships, badly built and honeycombed with worm borings, sank soon after their arrival, leaving the Spaniards stranded.

The explorers quickly learned that the islands had few inhabitants and fewer treasures. Disappointed but undeterred, they built new ships, left the islands in late September, and spent the next several weeks exploring the Pacific coast of the isthmus. Balboa's dreams of easy riches may have faded, but he was still the master of an uncharted realm.

In November, Balboa received some surprising news: Pedrarias was about to be replaced as governor of Darién. Having decided to establish a settlement in his own domain, Balboa invited his soon-to-be-deposed father-in-law to join him in the venture. When he received word in December that Pedrarias wished to discuss matters of mutual interest, he assumed the old man was interested in his offer. Balboa hurried back to Acla—and was greeted by an arresting party that included Francisco Pizarro. He was informed that his proposed settlement was a sign of disloyalty.

Before his departure, Pedrarias in a final act of treachery accused Balboa of a variety of fictitious crimes, ranging from cruelty to the Indians to plots against the crown. Balboa was summarily tried, found guilty, and condemned to death. (According to some accounts, Pizarro presided over the execution.) On January 15, 1519, Vasco Núñez de Balboa, discoverer of the Pacific, walked "valorous and serene" into the public square at Acla and was beheaded.

**In their quest for gold and glory,** *Hernando Cortés and his men confronted a complex Indian civilization of large cities, well-built roads, and disciplined warriors as the mural (above) by Mexican artist Juan O'Gorman shows. It portrays the conquest of Michoacán by Nuño de Guzmán and his men. Above the conquistadors are scenes of Aztec life. The stone and steel contrast between the Indian and Spanish civilizations is dramatically shown by the human skull inlaid with lignite, seashell, and turquoise (bottom right) and the Spanish military helmet (bottom left). Montezuma, ruler of the Aztecs, is believed to have presented the bejeweled skull to Cortés. The helmet is one worn by Emperor Charles V of Spain, in whose name Cortés' conquest of Mexico was made.*

*Chapter Nine. European explorers finally find what they have been looking for: a golden kingdom in the New World. With great bravery and ruthless determination, a Spanish captain leads his men and Indian allies against the powerful Aztecs. With his victory, an Indian civilization is destroyed, and a land is colonized for centuries to come.*

# The Wrath of Quetzalcoatl: Cortés Conquers Mexico

*Hernando Cortés was born of noble parents in 1485 in the town of Medellín, Spain. At 14, he was sent to the University of Salamanca but returned home without a degree. After a year or two of wandering, he decided to seek his fortune in the West Indies, arriving in Hispaniola in 1504 and eventually settling in Cuba. There he held a succession of official posts and gathered a sizable estate, but not the vast wealth he craved. In 1518, in the wake of two unsuccessful expeditions to Mexico by other leaders, Cortés bought the captaincy of a third. Following his conquest of the Aztecs, he founded the colony of Mexico, establishing towns and fostering agriculture. His palace still stands in the town of Cuernavaca. After falling into disfavor with the Spanish court, Cortés eventually returned to Spain, where he died in 1547.*

On a November day in 1518 Hernando Cortés strode into a slaughterhouse in Santiago, Cuba, and bought up its entire stock of meat. In payment, he hung a heavy gold chain around a startled butcher's neck. Cortés needed the meat to supply a trading expedition that he was leading to Mexico's recently discovered Yucatan Peninsula, and he had already used up all his other resources. Now, in shedding the last of his personal valuables, he committed himself to the life of adventure he had long craved.

Cortés, who was 33 years old, had been in the New World for 14 years. Working as a farmer and minor government official, he had so far failed to find the fame and fortune that had tempted him to leave Spain. When Diego Velázquez, the governor of Cuba, offered him a chance to command a trading expedition, he had accepted immediately. Secretly wishing to conquer and settle, Cortés was, in fact, so impatient to be away—and so fearful the governor might change his mind—that he ordered the captains of his six ships to weigh anchor at midnight on November 18, 1518, without lingering for the governor's farewell blessing.

Cortés was described by Bernal Díaz, chronicler of the expedition, as a man "of good height and strongly made, with a somewhat pale complexion and serious expression." Although he lacked experience as either a sailor or a soldier, he had a knack for manipulating people, and command came naturally to him. Sailing for the next three months along Cuba's southern coast, he succeeded in recruiting many other settlers to join him and seek their fortunes. By the time the fleet headed across the Yucatan Channel at the western tip of Cuba in mid-February 1519, the expedition's force had swollen to 100 sailors, 508 soldiers, 200 porters, a few Indian women, 16 horses, and 11 ships.

The fleet's first landfall was the little island of Cozumel, just off the Yucatan mainland. Friendly Mayan Indians welcomed them and brought them two Spaniards who had been shipwrecked on the island eight years earlier. One of them, Jerónimo de Aguilar, eagerly joined the expedition as an interpreter.

Continuing west around the Yucatan Peninsula, the fleet reached the Tabasco region on the Gulf of Campeche toward the end of March. There the Indians were not so friendly. The Spaniards had to fight for possession of the town and soon learned that the Indians were prepared for a full-scale battle.

The thousands of warriors who ranged across a nearby plain fought valiantly with their primitive weapons against Spanish swords and cannon. However, when Cortés' cavalry appeared, some of the Indians, who had never seen a horse before, fled in terror, thinking that horse and armored rider were a single beast. Powerless against such monsters, the Indians soon called a truce. That night the Spaniards, who were short of oil and salt for cauterizing their wounds, made do with fat rendered from some of the hundreds of Indian corpses strewn across the plain.

The next day the conquered Tabascans respectfully presented Cortés with gifts of gold and 20 female slaves. Asked where the gold came from, they pointed westward to the purple mountains of the interior and said: "Mexico." One of the prettiest of the slave girls also came from the interior, and her knowledge of languages was soon to prove invaluable to Cortés. Kind and intelligent, she quickly charmed the Spaniards, who named her Doña Marina.

Cortés was interested in the gold, but he decided to sail farther up the coast before attempting any exploration of the interior. On April 20, 1519, he anchored near the site of the present-day city of Veracruz and received a deputation of Indians from shore. They seemed friendly but spoke a dialect Aguilar could not comprehend. Then someone remembered Doña Marina, who understood their language perfectly.

As she translated into Mayan and Aguilar translated into Spanish, Cortés listened with growing excitement to the Indians' description of an island-city in a great lake less than 200 miles inland. Called Tenochtitlán, it was the capital of the fearsome Aztecs, to whom all neighboring tribes had to pay tribute. The ruler of the Aztec empire and of all Mexico, the Indians said, was the god-king, Montezuma.

Realizing that he had stumbled upon a civilization far richer and more advanced than any yet discovered in the New World, Cortés decided to go no farther. He set up camp on shore and exchanged gifts with his visitors. The very next day more gifts arrived, this time from the chief of the province. Obviously pleased and hoping for more, Cortés sent the envoys away with these words: "I and my companions suffer from a dis-ease of the heart, which can be cured only with gold." The Indians took the message to Montezuma, along with paintings they had made of the Spaniards and their ships, horses, and weapons.

Within a week envoys from the emperor himself arrived, and this time the gifts were magnificent. They included two carved gold and silver disks as big as carriage wheels, exquisite pearl and turquoise ornaments, jeweled robes, and intricate fans and crests of elaborate featherwork. The envoys declared that Cortés was welcome to any treasures he desired, but Montezuma would not meet him. The emperor was sick, they said, and could not travel. The journey to his capital, they added, was across mountains and sterile deserts—much too hazardous for strangers to attempt. Cortés replied that these obstacles only increased his desire to meet the great Montezuma and with that message sent the envoys on their way.

Some historians believe that Montezuma was thoroughly puzzled by the Spaniards who had so suddenly appeared in his realm. According to Aztec myth, one of their gods, Quetzalcoatl, the feathered serpent, had long ago been driven from the shores of Mexico by a rival, but he had promised to return out of the eastern sea in the guise of a bearded, fair-skinned stranger. The year of his return was to be 1519.

Was Cortés Quetzalcoatl or some invading plunderer from an unknown land? Should he be worshiped or wiped out? Montezuma simply could not decide.

Before long Cortés met Indians of the Totonac tribe and discovered that they and many other tribes resented Aztec domination and demands for tribute. The Mexican empire, it seemed, was by no means united.

**Hernando Cortés** (far left, in a painting done after his death) was only 33 when he and his daring soldiers landed in Mexico. Contemporary Spanish chronicler Diego Durán recorded the event in his history of the conquest, illustrated with his own simple drawings (above). The Indian perched in the treetop is a spy, who sent word of the Spanish landing to Montezuma. Cortés' banner with a picture of the Virgin (left) is preserved today in Mexico's National Museum of Anthropology.

Cortés soon realized that, with the help of Indian allies, it might be possible to conquer all of Montezuma's realm. No longer interested in a mere trading expedition, he immediately abandoned his marshy encampment and established a permanent settlement a little farther up the coast. Named Villa Rica de Vera Cruz ("Rich City of the True Cross"), it was to be the beachhead for the Spanish conquest of Mexico. A municipal council and attorney were appointed, and Cortés was elected captain-general and chief justice.

On July 26, 1519, Cortés dispatched his largest ship to Spain with many of Montezuma's gifts and a request that Charles V make him governor of the new colony. He soon discovered, however, that a few of his men, convinced that he was usurping the titles and privileges of Governor Velázquez, were plotting to take one of the ships back to Cuba with their complaints. The captain-general's reaction was swift. Two of the ringleaders were promptly hanged, and the rest were whipped.

Cortés then took an even more drastic action. He declared 9 of his 10 remaining ships unseaworthy, beached 5 of them, and sank the other 4 after salvaging their iron, nails, cord, and equipment. Then, according to his secretary, in order to find out which of the men were disloyal, he invited "those who were unwilling to wage war in that rich country, and who did not like his company" to return to Cuba in the remaining ship. As it turned out, half the malcontents were simply "sailors who preferred sailing to fighting." Nonetheless, "Cortés ordered the ship scuttled, thus removing all means of escape." After this daring move, Cortés was more feared and respected than ever. When he announced his intention to march to the Aztec capital, there were no more voices of dissent.

On August 16, 1519, Cortés left a garrison of 150 Spaniards at Vera Cruz and set out for Tenochtitlán. His army included 15 horsemen, 400 foot soldiers, 300 Indian volunteers, and 200 porters. Passing quickly through lush, mosquito-infested coastal forests, they soon encountered rising land that sloped upward toward the high interior. Gradually, the vegetation thinned and the air grew cooler. At 7,000 feet the little army reached a plateau ribboned with meticulously cultivated fields of cactuses and aloes.

Here Cortés rested for a few days at the imposing town of Zocotlán and learned more of the Aztec capital "where the houses are built over water, and where the only means of passing from one to the other is by bridges or in canoes." The island-city, he also learned, was connected to shore by three causeways, each equipped with drawbridges "so that when one is raised it is impossible to enter the city." Clearly, this fortress-city could be a major military obstacle or a trap should Montezuma prove hostile.

To reach Tenochtitlán, Cortés had to cross the territory of Tlaxcala, the only part of Mexico that was completely independent of the Aztecs. Anticipating a

**Aztec warriors made an impressive sight** *but proved no match for Cortés' men. The Indians fought valiantly, but their spears and swords, set with razor-sharp edges of obsidian, were ineffective against the Spaniards' guns, steel armor, and cavalry.*

friendly reception, he was surprised when the Tlascalans greeted him with a shower of arrows instead. After a day of skirmishing, the warriors withdrew, and the Spaniards set up camp outside their capital. A strict disciplinarian, Cortés that night ordered his men to sleep with their boots and armor on and their horses saddled and ready for any suprise attack.

Increasingly fierce battles in the days that followed convinced Cortés that a major confrontation was imminent. On September 5, tens of thousands of warriors massed across a vast plain. Bristling with feathered headdresses and armed with spears and jewel-encrusted shields, they filled the air with what one Spaniard called "the most frightful whoopings and whistlings in the world." The size and bravery of the Tlascalan army was such that even the "thunder and lightning" of Spanish guns failed to deter them. "In war they are the most cruel people possible," the soldier concluded, "because they give quarter to no one . . . nor do they allow any prisoners to live, except young and pretty women, killing and eating all others." Only a dispute among the chiefs eventually caused the determined Tlascalans to retreat.

They attacked again the following night, surprising

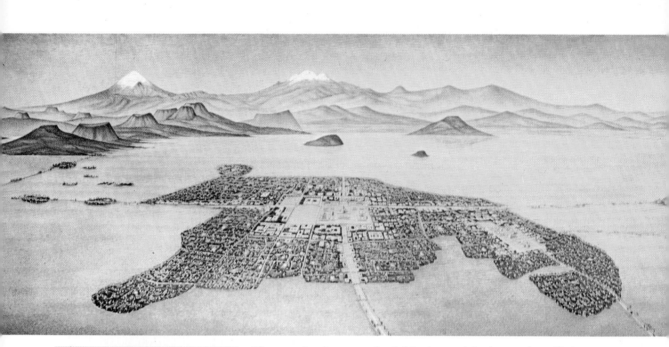

**The conquistadors** *were dazzled by the beauty of the Aztec capital (above), known to the Indians as Tenochtitlán, "Place of the Prickly Pear Cactus." The city (now Mexico City), surrounded by a lake that was later filled in, had a larger population than any city in Spain then. In its center stood the temple of the god of war (below), where the Aztecs sacrificed thousands of captives.*

**Montezuma,** *in this Aztec portrait, wears a feathered headdress and circlets of gold and silver on his arms and legs. He bears ceremonial weapons with barbed tips.*

the Spaniards in their camp. Weary horsemen managed to drive the Indians off, but some of the soldiers began to doubt that they could ever win the war. One of them later recalled: "When we awoke and looked at ourselves, all wounded, many of us two or three times, tired out, in pain, and clothed in rags, with 45 dead in battle or from sickness, Cortés . . . sick with fever, we began to wonder what would be the outcome of all this fighting. We said to each other that if we could be brought to this point by the Tlascalans, who our friends of Cempoala told us were peaceful, what would happen when we met the great forces of Montezuma?"

Sick or not, Cortés fought on, slowly eroding the enemy's strength. After three weeks of fighting, the Tlascalan chiefs gave in and agreed to make peace. On September 23 Cortés entered their capital and concluded a treaty making the Tlascalans his allies in the conquest of Mexico.

Meanwhile, Montezuma, who had heard of Cortés' victory against such overwhelming odds, was beginning to think him superhuman. He sent more lavish gifts, along with a message: The emperor wished to be Cortés' friend and would pay him a yearly tribute of gold, precious stones, and slaves. However, there was one condition: The Spaniards must stay out of Mexico. Once again the message fell on deaf ears.

The vanquished Tlascalans now welcomed the Spaniards with gifts of chickens, tortillas, and prickly pears, and even gave their daughters to Spanish captains. They also nicknamed Cortés Malinche, Captain of Marina, because the pretty Doña Marina, now his mistress, was always at his side. Cortés, for his part, urged the Indians to renounce their idols in favor of Christianity. When they declined, he prudently decided not to press the issue, for he needed their friendship.

In mid-October the Spaniards resumed their journey, accompanied now by several thousand Tlascalan warriors. Soon they reached the ancient and holy Aztec city of Cholula. A major religious center, its broad streets were lined with many temples, including a shrine to Quetzalcoatl that attracted pilgrims from all over the Aztec empire.

At first the Cholulans housed and fed their visitors, but after three days they cut off the food supply and informed Cortés that Montezuma forbade him to proceed any farther. Cortés defiantly ordered his troops to prepare to march the next day to Tenochtitlán, by then less than 50 miles away.

That night an old chief's wife who had taken a liking to Doña Marina revealed that Cholulan warriors planned to ambush the Spaniards as they left the city. At dawn Cortés astounded the Cholulan chiefs by announcing that he knew all about their conspiracy, confronting them with his knowledge of boiling pots "already prepared with salt, pepper, and tomatoes" in anticipation of the Spaniards to be added. He gave a signal, and Spanish artillery fire rang out over the quiet city. A furious battle began. Cannonballs crashed, buildings were plundered and burned, and at the end of the long hot day thousands of Indian corpses littered the streets of Cholula. Triumphant, the Spaniards and their Tlascalan allies set off for Tenochtitlán.

News of Cortés' ruthless progress through Mexico led to a flurry of prayers and sacrificial offerings in the imperial city. Montezuma himself, as both spiritual and political leader of the Aztecs, was plunged into an agony of indecision over the true identity of his visitor. He could receive the Spaniard—and risk losing his empire. Or he could repulse him—and risk the wrath of Quetzalcoatl. Montezuma agonized until November 8, 1519, when he no longer had any choice. The invincible Cortés was already at his gates.

Cortés halted his army halfway out on one of the causeways radiating from the hub of Tenochtitlán, and there awaited Montezuma. Thousands of curious Aztecs thronged the roadway and came out on the lake in canoes to glimpse the strange invaders. Soon a great procession of Aztec lords approached, all adorned with brilliant feathered cloaks, golden nose rings, and turquoise collars and bracelets. When they reached the Spaniards, they set down a sumptuous, silver-fringed palanquin and spread embroidered tapestries on the ground to receive Montezuma.

Cortés at last stood face to face with the emperor, whom Bernal Díaz depicted in his chronicle of the conquest: "The Great Montezuma was about 40 years old, of good height and well proportioned, slender and spare of flesh, not very swarthy, but of the natural color and shade of an Indian. He did not wear his hair long but so as to cover his ears; his scanty black beard was well shaped and thin. His face was somewhat long, but cheerful, and showed in his appearance and manner both tenderness and, when necessary, gravity. He was very neat and clean."

The long awaited encounter went smoothly. Cortés, in the Spanish custom, stepped forward to embrace

### Aztec Sacrificial Rites

When the sun, to which the Aztecs offered human sacrifice, was high in the sky, the victim climbed the 114 steps of the great temple. At the top, waiting priests held his body while one of them plunged a sharp stone knife through the victim's ribs and tore out the still-beating heart. Then, in a grisly ceremony, the priests ritually ate pieces of the victim's flesh.

Montezuma, but two courtiers stopped him—the great god-king was too sacred to be touched. Then Montezuma spoke, solemnly welcoming Cortés in a speech translated by Doña Marina. Cortés, in turn, presented the emperor with a necklace of pearls and cut glass. Ceremoniously approaching the city itself, Montezuma responded with a gift of two snail-shell necklaces, each decorated with eight golden shrimps. The golden shrimps were sacred symbols of the god Quetzalcoatl.

Continuing through the city, the Spaniards were led to the palace of Montezuma's dead father, which had been freshly festooned with green branches and bright flowers. Cortés was amazed at the luxury of its vast halls. The floors were paved with polished stone, the walls were hung with elaborate featherwork, and the scented cedar ceilings were intricately carved with figures from Aztec mythology. "A very sumptuous native meal was already prepared," Díaz noted gratefully, "and we ate at once." Montezuma, meanwhile, returned to his own marble and alabaster palace and dined, as he always did, alone.

## Mexican Indian Sculpture Reveals a Vanished Way of Life

Aztec civilization was at its zenith when Cortés conquered Mexico, yet 200 years earlier the Aztecs had been a migrant tribe, coming from the north of Mexico in search of better farmland. Unable to gain a foothold on the shores of the fertile lake region in central Mexico, they retreated to an island where they founded the city of Tenochtitlán. There the Aztecs prospered and eventually conquered the tribes on the shores of the lake. As their conquests expanded, the tribe came to rule a vast area of central Mexico extending from the Atlantic to the Pacific coasts. (The Aztecs could not match their military prowess with equal administrative ability, however; the subject kingdoms were often in revolt, and some aided Cortés in his conquest.)

The Aztecs did not impose their own civilization on the foes that they had conquered. Rather, their culture borrowed heavily both from the tribes they vanquished and from the Olmec and Toltec civilizations, which had ruled Mexico in the centuries before Aztec domination. While the Aztecs always established an altar to their own supreme god, Huitzilopochtli, in the cities they conquered, they also adopted from the surrounding tribes such deities as Xipe-Totec (below), the god of spring and fertility. Every spring victims were flayed alive as a sacrifice to Xipe-Totec, and priests donned the bloody human skins and paraded through the streets. This statue of Xipe-Totec shows the god clutching the severed head of a victim.

The Aztec social structure resembled a tightly organized pyramid with the ruler

at the top. Each individual below the king knew his place and his function in society. The entire nation was divided into large clans called calpulli, many of which had 20,000 members. The calpulli apportioned farmland, and every man

---

Within a few days the Spaniards were given a tour of Tenochtitlán. With a population estimated at more than 60,000, it was a vast and shimmering metropolis, surrounded by water and crisscrossed with a maze of canals. The fascinated Europeans were led past white-washed houses and terraced gardens, great temples and monumental public buildings, huge market squares teeming with people and overflowing with a wide selection of goods. Finally, they were taken to the great teocalli, or temple, a five-story pyramidal structure that dominated the center of the city. Climbing the steep stairs of the temple, Cortés was ceremoniously greeted at the top by Montezuma, who "took him by the hand and bade him look at his great city and at all the other cities rising from the water, and the many towns around the lake."

Cortés may have enjoyed the view, but he was not at all impressed by the "cursed idols" and the ceremonies that took place atop the teocalli. The Aztec religion included frequent human sacrifices in which the hearts were torn from living victims to appease the gods. Montezuma led his guests into a room at the top of the temple where they found two altars topped by grotesque, jewel-encrusted figures of gods. There were also, Díaz noted with disgust, "braziers with copal in-

cense, and they were burning in them the hearts of three Indians they had sacrificed that day. All the walls and floors were black with crusted blood, and the whole place stank."

As Díaz recounted: "Our captain said to Montezuma, half laughing, 'Lord Montezuma, I do not understand how such a great prince and wise man as yourself can have failed to come to the conclusion that these idols of yours are not gods but evil things. . . . Let us put a cross on top of this tower and . . . set up an image of Our Lady; and you will see how afraid of it these idols who have deceived you are.'

"The two priests with Montezuma looked hostile, and Montezuma replied with annoyance, 'Señor Malinche, if I had thought that you would so insult my gods, I would not have shown them to you.' Cortés said, 'If it is really like that, forgive me, sir.' Then he went down the steps."

Although the Spaniards were denied their own chapel in the temple, they were allowed to set up an altar in their own quarters. While searching for a suitable spot, they noticed a patch of fresh plaster shaped like a doorway. Curious, they drilled a hole in the wall and saw a chamber full of "so many jewels, bars and plates of gold, and other riches that they were so ex-

had his own plot to work, though he was also expected to work a certain number of days a year on the state land. The ordinary Aztec farmer wore only a loincloth and went barefoot (left).

Women did not help in the fields. Their chief occupation was weaving on small looms, one end of which was tied around their waists (below). This type of loom had been used in Mexico for centuries and was common in South America.

In time of war every Aztec man was required to serve in the army, which was highly organized and at full strength

numbered in the hundreds of thousands. All young men attended special schools called *telpochalli* to learn the art of warfare. Soldiers wore armor made of quilted cotton stiffened by dipping in brine. Shields and helmets decorated with brightly colored feathers indicated commanders (above).

Outstanding warriors were often given increased civic duties; however, hereditary nobles filled the higher state offices. Nobles were easily distinguished by their

elaborate dress and haughty bearing. Special schools trained their children for governmental functions, which included making long orations on state occasions. Orators assumed a rigid stance (below) and used highly ornate language. Bernal Díaz noted the elaborate Aztec courtesy that Montezuma displayed toward the conquistadors: "We spoke of the good manners and the breeding which he showed in everything."

cited they did not know what to say." Cortés, suspecting that this was the treasure of Montezuma's father, decided to say nothing about the discovery and ordered the wall sealed for the time being.

Meanwhile, the emperor continued to be hospitable. He showed the Spaniards his splendid rooftop gardens, his aviary of exotic birds, and his menagerie of Mexican animals, but Cortés began to feel uneasy. Tenochtitlán was a natural prison. If Montezuma chose, he could raise the bridges, cut the causeways, and starve the Spaniards into submission.

Then news arrived that one of Montezuma's chiefs had attacked the garrison at Vera Cruz, killing seven Spanish soldiers. It was time to act, and as usual, Cortés acted audaciously. With five captains and a number of soldiers he went to Montezuma's palace, brazenly shouldered past the imperial guard, and accused the emperor of ordering the attack on Vera Cruz.

Until the attackers were punished, said Cortés, Montezuma was under arrest. Frightened by the threats of the burly Spanish captain—who was obviously no god after all—and his ruthless compatriots, Montezuma eventually agreed to spend "a few days" with Cortés in his quarters on the pretext that it "would be good for his health." Then, wearing no shackles, the emperor of

the Aztecs was carried on a litter into captivity.

Montezuma agreed to let Cortés execute the chiefs who had attacked Vera Cruz. (They were burned at the stake.) If he hoped this would win his freedom, he had

**The earliest European pictures** *of Aztecs were drawn in 1529 by the Austrian artist Christoph Weiditz. The nimble juggler at left is lying on his back and tossing a log with his feet. Cortés brought this Indian with him to Spain in 1528, where he performed for Charles V. The Aztec woman at right wears a feathered cloak that is tied at the shoulder, as the Aztecs possessed neither pins nor buttons. The colorful birds of Mexico provided the plumage.*

misjudged his captor: Cortés was not about to release such a priceless hostage. Instead, he forced Montezuma to acknowledge the king of Spain as lord of Mexico, hand over his father's walled-up treasure as tribute, and demand further tribute from all the cities of the Aztec empire. The booty was so immense it took three days to sort it out. The Spaniards melted the gold and silver down into bars and divided it on the spot.

Montezuma was allowed to live much as he had in his own palace, with two wives and a retinue of servants. He even went hunting with Cortés on his private game preserve across the lake. Wherever he went, though, he was accompanied by a few Spanish guards. Cortés eventually offered him his freedom, but the emperor replied sadly that he had lost the respect of his nobles and feared the wrath of his people.

The bloodless conquest of Tenochtitlán now seemed complete, except for one thing: The Aztecs still worshiped their "damnable idols." Cortés again demanded permission to install a Christian altar in the great teocalli, and this time Montezuma reluctantly agreed. One of the sanctuaries of the temple was scraped clean of blood, perfumed with incense, and consecrated by chanting Spaniards.

The Aztecs simmered with resentment at this violation of their most sacred place. Doña Marina began to hear talk of uprisings in the streets, and even Montezuma warned Cortés to get out of Mexico while he could. But the captain-general, who had now been in Tenochtitlań for six months, had previously scuttled all his ships at Vera Cruz.

Just as he sent a work party to the coast to build new ships, he learned that a rival, Pánfilo de Narváez, had landed near Vera Cruz. The treasure ship Cortés had sent to Spain had stopped at Cuba en route. Alarmed by reports of Cortés' activities, Governor Velázquez apparently feared that the young conquistador was accumulating too much power and had sent Narváez with 19 ships and more than 900 men to discipline him.

Cortés, for his part, set out immediately for Vera Cruz with 100 soldiers, leaving 200 men under the command of Pedro de Alvarado to guard Tenochtitlán. When he came upon Narváez' army at Cempoala, Cortés outwitted his foe by attacking at night in a torrential downpour. Narváez, who lost an eye in the battle, was promptly seized and clapped into prison. Placated with liberal promises of gold, most of his troops happily switched their allegiance to Cortés.

As Cortés prepared to return to Tenochtitlán, a courier arrived with devastating news: The Aztecs were besieging Alvarado's garrison. Hastening back with his much enlarged army, Cortés entered Tenochtitlán on June 24, 1520, and found the great city ominously quiet. He reached his quarters unmolested and learned that Alvarado's troops had massacred more than 600 unarmed Indians during a ceremonial dance. Nervous and impetuous, Alvarado had feared the Indians were preparing for an attack.

In retaliation, the Aztecs had cut off the Spaniards' food supply, and the mood in the capital was ugly. The commander, with more than 1,200 troops and several thousand Tlascalans to feed, was speechless with rage. To make matters worse, the Indians now destroyed the drawbridges on one of the causeways, and distant war cries indicated that they were massing for battle.

Cortés, who had originally occupied Tenochtitlán with such contemptuous ease, now found himself in danger of being trapped there. However, his defenses

---

## Aztec Artists Chronicled the Progress of the Invaders' March From the Sea to the Capital

Above, Montezuma meets Cortés. Behind Cortés is his interpreter, Doña Marina. In the foreground are gifts from the seated Montezuma.

Below, the Spaniards are besieged in the palace of Axayacatl in the Aztec capital after Alvarado massacred 600 unarmed Indians at a harvest festival during Cortés' absence.

Above, Cortés and his men fight their way out of the palace of Axayacatl and capture the temple of Huitzilopochtli in the center of the city. Spanish cavalry and weapons were a crucial advantage.

were strong. The Spanish quarters were surrounded by a stone wall, buttressed at intervals by towers, and cannon and arquebuses covered all approaches.

Early the next morning lookouts reported that a warlike mob was moving in. The Tlascalans, who were bivouacked in the courtyard, took up their spears and prepared to meet their ancient enemies once again. As soon as the Aztecs came within gunshot range, Cortés ordered the artillery to fire. The first column of Mexicans fell into disarray, but others pressed on over the dead and wounded, shrieking and firing burning arrows, and women and children on nearby rooftops hurled showers of stones down on the Spaniards. The battle raged all day, but the wall proved impregnable.

The next day, under cover of a storm of artillery fire, Cortés led his cavalry and several thousand Tlascalans out into the city. Their charge met with such crippling opposition that they succeeded only in setting fire to a few buildings before returning to their fortress.

This fiasco convinced Cortés that attempting to leave the city would be suicidal. Frightened for perhaps the first time in his life, he sought Montezuma's help. "I do not believe that I can do anything to end this war," replied the emperor. "[They] have decided not to let you out alive."

Even so, he wearily agreed to beg his people to allow the Spaniards to leave peacefully. Donning his imperial robe, he climbed the steps to the roof of the palace and walked out along the battlements. At the sight of their leader, still majestic in his humiliation, the roaring crowd below fell silent.

Then, according to Díaz, "Montezuma began to speak to the Mexicans in very affectionate terms, asking them to stop the war, and telling them we would

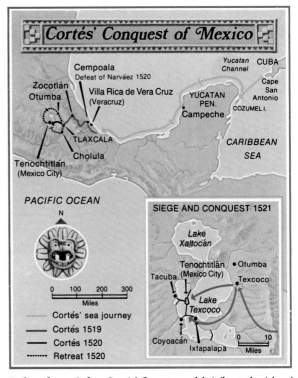

**Sailing from Cuba,** *Cortés' fleet stopped briefly at the isle of Cozumel and on the coast of the Gulf of Campeche. Then it sailed along the coast, landing the expedition near modern Veracruz.*

leave Mexico." A few of his subjects, crying, approached and wailed, "Oh lord, our great lord, how greatly we are afflicted by your misfortune!" They added, however, that they had promised the gods to go

## of the Empire. Spanish Cavalry and Cannon Were Pitted Against Aztec Clubs and Spears

Below, the Spaniards withdraw from the city, suffering heavy losses as they fight down the causeways. Here a Spaniard attempts to rescue his horse on that *noche triste,* "night of sorrow."

Weary after their battles on *noche triste,* the Spaniards sleep on the march (above left). After the Aztecs drove them from Tenochtitlán, Cortés and his men retreated to the territory of the friendly Tlascalan Indians. Above right, the conquistadors gather fresh provisions to march again on Mexico City. The Spaniards' Indian allies carry supplies from their villages to Vera Cruz, the settlement of the True Cross, which Cortés had founded when he landed on the shores of Mexico. Cortés also instructed the Indians to make boats with which he planned to besiege the island capital of Mexico in a third attempt to vanquish the Aztecs.

This 17th-century Spanish painting *shows Cortés, his men, and their Indian allies recapturing Tenochtitlán. The final assault was long and bloody. Bernal Díaz relates that "during 90 and 3 days that we besieged this strong and great city we had war and combats every day and every night." The Aztecs tore up sections of the causeways that led to the island and dug deep holes in the canals that ran through the city to trap unwary Spaniards who attempted to wade across. Cortés himself was nearly killed when he was ambushed at one of these underwater trenches. In addition, the Aztecs drove stakes beneath the water so that the 13 small ships Cortés had made would not be able to provide close support for his troops. An Aztec drawing of the Spanish victory (right) shows the fighting alongside the canals. In the water float the severed heads of warriors.*

on fighting until every one of the Spaniards was dead. "They had hardly finished this speech," added Díaz, "when there was such a shower of stones and javelins that Montezuma was hit by three stones, one on the head, another on the arm, and a third on the leg." His body battered and his will to live broken, the rejected emperor was carried back to his apartments. Within three days the great Montezuma was dead.

Díaz, in moving words, described the reactions of the Spaniards, who had grown fond of their captive during the months he had lived with them: "Cortés wept for him, and all of our captains and soldiers. There were men among us who cried as though he had been our father, and it is not surprising, considering how good he was. It was said he had ruled for 17 years, and that he was the best king Mexico ever had."

If the Spaniards' situation had been critical before, it now seemed hopeless. "Powder was giving out and so was food and water," said Díaz. "In short, we could see death in our eyes." After a few more days of desperate fighting, Cortés decided that his only hope was to sneak away at night. Hurriedly building a portable bridge to cross the sabotaged causeway, the Spaniards stole out of their fortress toward midnight on July 1, 1520.

They did not get far before the Aztecs sounded the alarm. Canoes swarmed across the lake, and Indians thronged out on the causeway. "We saw so many squadrons of warriors bearing down on us and the lake so filled with canoes that we could not defend ourselves," reported Díaz, adding morosely, "One calamity followed another." Horses slipped and fell into the lake, taking their armored riders with them. Wounded

Spaniards drowned beneath the weight of immense loads of gold they greedily clung to. Arrows and lances flew. Swords slashed blindly into human flesh. Shrieks and gunfire filled the air. "The passage and the open water," said Díaz, "were quickly filled with dead horses, Indians, baggage, and leather trunks."

Cortés eventually escaped from his prison, but at the cost of the lives of 450 Spaniards, 4,000 Tlascalans, and uncounted Aztecs. He also lost most of his treasure, supplies, artillery, and ammunition, half his horses, and all of his personal papers on the night called by the Spaniards *noche triste*, "night of sorrow."

On the desperate retreat to Tlaxcala, vengeful bands of Aztecs steadily eroded the Spaniards' numbers. By the time the army reached Otumba, 10 miles east of the lake, on July 7, its strength was one-fifth of what it had been at the height of the conquest, and not so much as one musket remained of its original firepower. Here the combat-weary Spaniards and Tlascalans were challenged in pitched battle by a horde of Aztecs. Fierce fighting raged all day, but in the end Spanish cavalry prevailed. With only swords for protection, Spanish horsemen plunged into the thick of the fray, picking off the Aztec chieftains, who were easily distinguished by their feathered headdresses. Leaderless, the Indian army fell into disarray and finally fled. Bleeding and exhausted, the little Spanish army staggered on to safety in Tlascalan territory.

Few of the Spaniards, as they recuperated in the hospitable atmosphere of Tlaxcala, doubted that their expedition was at an end, but they underestimated their leader, whom Díaz described as "headstrong in all that had to do with war, listening to no one because of danger when there was no rational hope of success." Neither his military losses nor the severe head wounds he had suffered during the retreat could dim the sweet memories of the wealth and power he had known so briefly at Tenochtitlán. Cortés was already planning the reconquest of Mexico.

In the months that followed, Cortés enlisted new troops and horses from ships arriving at Vera Cruz. (Some had been sent to help Narváez; others were manned by soldiers of fortune who had heard fabulous tales of Mexican gold.) On December 28, 1520, Cortés gave the order to march on Tenochtitlán. His army included 600 Spaniards, 40 horses, and 10,000 Tlascalan warriors anxious to crush their age-old enemies once and for all.

Among the supplies were the parts for 13 armed launches, carried by relays of sweating porters. Cortés intended to put them together at Tenochtitlán and launch them on the lake as a defense against marauding canoes. Once he had control of both the lake and the causeways, he planned to besiege the capital.

On December 30 the fabulous city once again came into view. Cortés spent the early months of the new year reconnoitering the surrounding valley, subduing towns around the lake, and cutting off supplies to the capital. After a series of skirmishes, the brigantines were launched, three separate forces sealed off the entrances to the causeways, and on May 26, 1521, the siege began in earnest.

Almost daily, bands of Aztecs forayed out along the causeways, harassing the camps at the entrances and whittling away at the Spanish forces. By late July, Cortés concluded that the only way to take Tenochtitlán was to break right through into the main square, securing the approaches behind him, and then to fight for the city street by street.

On the very first attempt Cortés slipped at a gap in one of the causeways and, as he struggled in the water, was attacked by a swarm of Indian canoes. Hundreds of Tlascalans and 25 Spaniards were killed, and 66 others were captured as the captain-general was dragged to relative safety.

That night a mournful chorus of drums, conch shells, and horns drifted across the lake to Cortés' camp. Díaz vividly described the grisly ceremony that followed: "All of them together made a terrifying sound, and as we looked up at the high temple from which it came, we could see our companions who had been captured in the defense of Cortés being forced up the steps to be sacrificed. When they had them up on the open space before their cursed idols, we saw them put plumes on the heads of many of the prisoners, and with some things like pitchforks they made them dance before Vichilobos [a god of war]. After the prisoners had danced, the Mexicans bent them backward over some narrow stones that they used for sacrificing, and with stone knives they sawed through their chests, took out their beating hearts, and offered them to their idols. Then they kicked the bodies down the steps." There butchers dismembered the bodies. Some of the victims' heads were preserved for fiestas, while others were thrown back into the Spanish ranks.

Though this display of vengeance may have temporarily boosted Aztec morale, the siege was taking its toll. An epidemic of smallpox introduced by Cortés' army was causing enormous mortality. Furthermore, starving Indians, later described by Díaz as "so thin, yellow, and dirty that it was pitiful to see them," were reduced to groveling for roots and stripping the bark from trees for food. By early August their resistance had so weakened that Cortés' army was able to break through into the center of the city. From then on, Aztec surrender was only a matter of time. On August 13 Montezuma's successor, Guatemotzin, was captured and presented to Cortés.

"I have assuredly done my duty in defense of my city and my vassals," sobbed Guatemotzin, "and I can do no more. . . . Take the dagger that you have in your belt, and strike me dead immediately." Cortés did not strike this final blow. He did not need to. The Aztec empire was at an end, and Mexico was his.

**Francisco Pizarro** (*far left*) *was lured down the west coast of South America by tales of an Indian kingdom even wealthier than the Aztec empire. The conquistadors did not realize, however, that they would have to struggle across the snow-capped peaks of the Andes (*above*) to reach the fabled kingdom of the Incas. The Incas, who ruled an area from modern Chile to Ecuador, adopted many of their arts and customs from tribes they had conquered. The water jug at left, shaped like the head of a warrior, is an example of pottery of the Mohicas, a nation included in the vast Inca Empire.*

# A World of Four Corners:
# Pizarro Destroys the Incas

*Francisco Pizarro was more than 50 years old when he finally embarked on his conquest of Peru in January 1531. Born about the year 1475 in Trujillo, Spain, the illegitimate son of a poor Spanish soldier, Pizarro seems to have spent much of his youth as a swineherd. He had no known education and never learned how to read or write, but he did have physical stamina, courage, cunning, and the ability to lead men. Arriving in the New World in 1502, he later joined an expedition to Colombia and then to Panama. He was with Balboa on his epic march to the Pacific in 1513 and witnessed Balboa's execution less than six years later. Not content with farming in Panama, Pizarro, in collaboration with two other Spaniards, explored for gold along the coast of South America, eventually discovering Peru in 1527.*

The Pacific coast of Colombia is a place for plants, not people. With an annual rainfall in some locations of up to 415 inches (nearly 35 feet), it is one of the wettest regions in the world. Almost daily, warm rains pelt down on the sweltering mangrove swamps and dense lowland jungles that flourish in the unending equatorial heat and constantly high humidity.

The rain has been falling like this for centuries, and it was falling in 1527 on a group of Spanish adventurers marooned on the little inshore island of Gallo. Weary, hungry, and ill, their sodden clothes were in tatters, their mildewed boots half rotted. More than a year earlier they had set out from Panama to explore the forbidding, mosquito-infested coast in search of a rumored golden civilization said to exist somewhere to the south in a land called Peru. They had found a fair amount of gold, as well as Indians who told fascinating tales of cities where palace walls were covered with solid sheets of the precious metal.

The co-commanders of the expedition had decided that they needed more men and supplies to explore the coast properly. One of them, Diego de Almagro, had returned months before to Panama for reinforcements. The other, Francisco Pizarro, remained on Gallo with the rest of the expedition to await his partner's return. When two ships finally arrived, however, they came not with reinforcements but with stern orders from the governor to return to Panama at once. (Some of the men had smuggled out a letter with Almagro's ship, complaining of the hardships they had endured and hinting that they were being held against their will.)

Now most of the men welcomed the chance to escape their island ordeal. Gold or no gold, they wanted to go home and take up quiet, safe, peaceful lives as farmers. But not Francisco Pizarro. He had had enough of the quiet life. Poor, illegitimate, and illiterate, he had spent most of his youth in Spain in smalltown obscurity. In the 25 years he had been in the New World, he had so far failed to earn either gold or glory.

He refused to give up now. He was already 50 years old and probably feared his time was running out. Reinforcements would come, he insisted. Almagro and their partner in this venture, Father Hernando de Luque, would raise more money for supplies, he claimed, but the men were unconvinced.

In desperation, Pizarro challenged them to remain. With a bold sense of drama he strode out on the beach, drew his sword, and slashed a furrow in the sand. Glaring at his men, he made a speech that has been preserved by his secretary, Francisco Xeres, who chronicled Pizarro's career. "Friends and comrades!" he said, "on that side are toil, hunger, nakedness, the drenching storms, desertion, and death; on this side, ease and pleasure. There lies Peru with its riches; here Panama and its poverty. Choose, each man, what best becomes a brave Castilian. For my part, I go to the south."

Thirteen men stepped across the line. The rest—more than 100—remained where they were. Pizarro con-

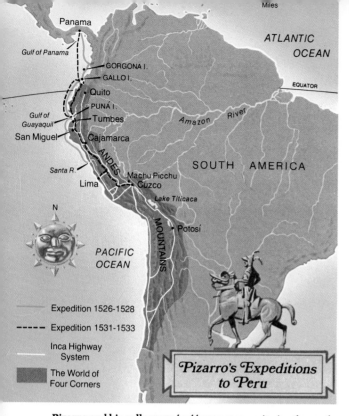

**Pizarro's Expeditions to Peru**

Expedition 1526-1528
Expedition 1531-1533
Inca Highway System
The World of Four Corners

**Pizarro and his colleagues** *had begun reconnoitering the north-west coast of South America as early as 1524 but did not discover Peru until 1527. The Inca Empire that they encountered was then three centuries old. Enveloping many other (and somewhat older) Indian cultures, it extended more than 2,000 miles along the coast of the continent. Its capital at Cuzco was linked to the rest of the empire by an amazing system of stone-paved highways that encompassed most of the World of Four Corners.*

temptuously bade them farewell as they sailed off in the rescue ships. Then, with his little band of volunteers, he settled down for another long, hot, wet wait.

He did not remain on Gallo for long. Probably on the advice of two Indians who had joined the expedition, the men soon set out on a balsa raft for Gorgona, a somewhat less forbidding island about 75 miles to the north. There, weeks dragged into months as the castaways desperately searched the northern horizon for signs of the relief ship's sails.

Only Pizarro gazed obstinately to the south, where the long jagged profile of the Andes Mountains faded into the equatorial haze. Years before, he had accompanied the great Balboa when he discovered the Pacific Ocean and listened to Indian tales of the "land of gold" somewhere in that south. Now he sat in rotting clothes, patiently waiting for the means to get there.

Seven months passed before his faithful pilot, Bartolomé Ruiz, came to his rescue. One of the 13 volunteers, Ruiz had returned to Panama with the defectors for aid. He rejoined his comrades in a small ship with a crew of sailors and fresh supplies. He also carried a message from the governor ordering Pizarro to return

to Panama within six months—a message that Pizarro was ultimately to ignore.

Almost immediately, the little band of explorers set sail for the south. Hugging the coast with its dramatic backdrop of mountain ramparts, their ship passed the shores of modern-day Ecuador, crossed the Equator itself, sailed across the great Gulf of Guayaquil, and within a few weeks came to anchor off the Inca city of Tumbes, near the present-day Ecuador-Peru boundary.

There they discovered that the tales of a golden empire were true. Welcomed by friendly Indians who served them food on gold and silver dishes, they were dazzled by the sight of a temple that one man described as "blazing with gold and silver" and by ornamental gardens "planted" with lifelike gold and silver models of fruits and vegetables.

But Pizarro realized that his party was too small to risk making off with any treasure. Not yet a conquistador, he decided for the moment simply to reconnoiter the fringes of this empire that the Indians explained was ruled by a god-king—the Inca—who lived in a fabulous city high in the mountains. Continuing south along the arid coast of Peru, the explorers eventually reached the mouth of the Santa River, about 500 miles south of Tumbes, before turning back. It was 1528, some 18 months after his escape from Gorgona, when Pizarro arrived back in Panama with news that the mythical golden kingdom of Peru really did exist.

The return of the adventurers, who had been given up for dead, created a flurry of excitement in Panama. Their samples of gold and silver, several Peruvians, and (according to one chronicle) a few live llamas were convincing proof of their discovery. When Pizarro, Almagro, and Luque proposed mounting an army to conquer the Indian empire, however, the governor balked. Such an expensive, dangerous expedition, he felt, was the business of the crown, not the responsibility of a mere colonial administrator.

Pizarro was chosen for the task of pleading the case in court. Charles V, who had not forgotten how much gold flowed into Spain after Cortés had conquered Mexico, was impressed by Pizarro's reports of an even richer Indian civilization. But affairs of state take time. It was not until late July 1529 that the queen mother, Joanna the Mad, authorized the expedition, making Pizarro, among other things, governor and captain-general of the new colony, which was to be named New Castile. To Almagro was promised the minor office of governor of Tumbes, and Luque was to be bishop of that city. (Almagro, who felt he deserved rewards equal to those granted Pizarro, was not at all pleased by this arrangement. His resentment smoldered for years and, in time, contributed to Pizarro's death.)

With royal endorsement, Pizarro eventually raised enough money and recruits to finance and man the expedition. In command of an "army" of just 180 men and 27 horses, he set sail from Panama with a fleet of three ships in January 1531. With him were his brothers Juan and Gonzalo, his half-brother Hernando Pizarro, and his teenage cousin Pedro Pizarro, who later wrote an account of the conquest of Peru. Almagro, who remained in Panama, was to follow as soon as he could enlist reinforcements.

Within two weeks foul weather forced Pizarro to abandon his original plan of sailing directly to Tumbes, still some 350 miles to the south. Instead, he rashly decided to march overland, while the ships paralleled his course near the coast. Raiding an Indian village, he soon came off with a good haul of gold ornaments, which he sent back to Panama with the ships to convince reluctant reinforcements to join him.

The gold was won at dreadful cost. Dressed in armor and heavy quilted doublets, the troops endured unending agonies from heat, rain, insect bites, and festering, ulcerative sores as they hacked their way through mile after mile of swamp and lowland jungle. Instead of weeks, it took months to reach the island of Puná in the Gulf of Guayaquil, where Pizarro's weary army settled down to recuperate and await new recruits. (One group of volunteers that joined him there was led by Hernando de Soto, a popular young cavalry officer who later won fame for his exploration in North America.)

When Pizarro finally mounted his attack on Tumbes in January 1532, he met with bitter disappointment. The splendid city was in ruins. Most of its inhabitants—and all its gold and silver—were gone.

Pizarro soon learned what had happened. Two years before, the god-king of the golden empire, Huayna Capac, had died, and for the first time in Peruvian history the kingdom had been shaken by a struggle for the throne. Tumbes was a casualty of the bloody civil war that followed between partisans of the rival half-brothers, Atahualpa and Huáscar. The victor was Atahualpa, not the oldest of Huayna's sons, but by far the most formidable fighter. At the end of the war Atahualpa had been crowned the 13th Inca, and the vanquished Huáscar had been thrown in prison.

The civilization Pizarro was about to conquer was far grander than anything even he imagined. In all his years of exploring South America, he had never ventured far beyond the coast. The heartland of the Inca Empire was high in the Andes, whose ranges run in double, sometimes triple rows down virtually the entire Pacific coast of South America. Slung between the mountains, like hammocks fringed by undulating crests of stone, are a series of fertile plateaus. Tapestries of meadows, plains, and reedy lakes, they are among the world's most beautiful landscapes.

It was here, according to one Peruvian legend, that the first Lord Inca was born about A.D. 1200, when the sun kissed the waters of Lake Titicaca. For 13 generations these semidivine emperors ruled over Peru, gradually extending Inca power south to the snows of Chile, north to the volcanoes of Ecuador, west to the waters of the Pacific, and east to the jungles of Brazil. It seemed impossible to go beyond such natural limits, so they named their self-contained empire Tavantinsuyu, "World of Four Corners."

At its zenith, just before the arrival of Pizarro, the Inca Empire covered 380,000 square miles and included some 16 million people, a figure recorded by the

## Master Inca Engineers Created Enduring Buildings and Roads With Massive Fitted Stones

inserted between the stones (left). One conquistador wrote: "In all of Spain I have seen nothing that can compare with these walls." Solid Inca structures have survived earthquakes that have felled more modern ones.

Thousands of miles of highway (right) connected all parts of the Inca kingdom with the capital at Cuzco. These roads, which spanned swift-running rivers with

The Incas were master engineers. Without mortar, they built walls so perfectly fitted together that a knife could not be

footbridges like the one at left, were so solidly built that many are still in use. Ironically, this magnificent highway system made it easy to move troops and thus aided Pizarro and his men in their rapid subjugation of the Inca Empire.

### Atahualpa, Inca of Peru

In this 16-century watercolor, Atahualpa rides on a litter carried by men of noble birth. It was painted by a Spanish priest, Fray Martín de Murúa, who wrote an account of the conquest sympathetic to the Incas. Often a curtain was hung around the litter to shield the Lord Inca, who was believed to be a living god, from the gaze of his curious subjects. It was in such a litter that the monarch was carried to his capture in Cajamarca. On his forehead Atahualpa wears the borla, the red fringe symbolic of royal authority. In one of his ears he wears a large gold earplug similar to the ones below, the sign of an Inca noble. The Spaniards referred to the noble Incas as *orejones,* "big-eared ones."

One of Atahualpa's earlobes had been torn in battle sometime before he became Lord Inca. As a result, he could wear only one earplug. So great was the emperor's shame that he hid his damaged ear under a cloak on formal occasions.

Incas' sophisticated annual census system. Each of the Four Corners, or provinces, had a distinctive way of life and style of dress. Even Cuzco, the central capital, was divided into four quarters, one for each segment of the population. A single language, Quechua, linked all Peruvians together, as did their common worship of the sun, father of the Incas.

Symbolic of this worship was Cuzco's great stone Temple of the Sun, the most magnificent structure in the entire Inca Empire. Huge and austere without, the temple was all radiance within. Its walls, cornices, and ceilings were encrusted with gold and silver, and one eastward-facing wall was a solid mass of gold and emeralds worked into a gigantic effigy of the sun. Thus, when the real sun rose each morning, the effigy burst into reflected flame, filling the temple with light. In the evening, when the tired god sank into the sea, aromatic lamps were lit in a silver side temple of the moon, wife of the sun. There the lamps flickered mournfully through the night until the sun rose again the next day.

The Inca, as son of the sun, was worshiped with complete adoration by all Peruvians. Common people were forbidden to look upon his face, lest his glory blind them. Even members of his court had to take off their sandals and carry burdens symbolizing their subservience when they approached him. Because his power was absolute, all of his commands were expected to be obeyed without question.

Although the Inca could propagate his line only by marrying his sister, he traditionally had thousands of concubines who entertained him on his travels through the empire. One night with the Inca was enough to fill a peasant girl with divinity, and for the rest of her life she and her child (if she had one) were maintained by the state as members of the royal family. Over the centuries this family had proliferated into tens of thousands, forming an aristocratic class of administrators and officials that could be distinguished from the millions of ordinary peasants by their great golden earplugs and lustrous robes of vicuña wool.

The peasants tilled their land and paid their taxes in the form of useful labor, such as building roads or carrying baskets of nitrogen-rich sea-bird droppings up from the coast for use as fertilizer. Every man was given, as his birthright, an equal unit of land; as his family increased or diminished, so did his share of units. The tablelands themselves were terraced cornucopias brimming with at least 40 different crops, including white and sweet potatoes, corn, tomatoes, peppers, squash, cotton, and tobacco. A network of canals irrigated every square mile of tillable land, while aqueducts, some of them 500 miles long, carried excess water to the arid flats along the coast.

Peruvian public architecture was uniformly massive. Fortresses and temples were built of granite blocks, some so enormous they had to be dragged by teams of 20,000 men. The blue-gray fortress of Sacsahuama at Cuzco dwarfed even the pyramids of the Aztecs. Some of its stones were 38 feet wide, yet their edges were ground to fit with such geometric precision that, as an astonished Pedro Pizarro observed, "the point of a pin could not be inserted in one of the joints." Cities were spacious, with straight paved streets, brightly painted houses, and—always—an empty mansion for the sun, should he weary of his travels overhead.

Perhaps the most brilliant achievement of the Inca civilization was the imperial road system, which excelled anything in contemporary Europe. This network of paved highways swept across plateaus, around mountains, and down to the sea. No physical barrier could defeat the Peruvian engineers: Swamps were crossed by elevated causeways, gullies filled in with masonry. Even the deep chasms that split the Andean landscape were spanned by sturdy ropework bridges, as they are to this day.

The main artery—up to 24 feet wide and 3,250 miles long—ran the entire length of the empire, from Quito in Ecuador south to central Chile. Paved with smooth stones, it could have been designed for carriages, yet everyone in this horseless, wheelless society went on foot. Connecting roads at frequent intervals allowed the speedy delivery of fresh fish to the uplands, vegetables to the coast, and gold, silver, and emeralds from the mines to the cities.

Every five miles or so along the roads there was a royal posthouse. Here liveried runners transmitted messages coded on knotted string devices called quipus, which they carried in relays at the rate of 150 miles a day. This great highway was the spinal cord of Peruvian communication, and its nervelike network of secondary roads linked even the remotest extremities of the World of Four Corners.

As a result, the Inca was able to sense the slightest tremor of the unusual at any point on his borders. Thus it was that in 1527 the aging Huayna Capac had heard of the approach of the Spaniards when Pizarro had first reconnoitered the coast, and thus it was that in 1532 Atahualpa was aware of Pizarro's return to Tumbes.

Once he had occupied Tumbes, Pizarro spent the next few months exploring the irrigated valleys that sliced across the coastal desert south of the city. In May he founded San Miguel, Peru's first Spanish settlement.

With this nucleus for colonial government established, he was at last ready for the business of conquest. According to local Indians, Atahualpa was settled at the moment in the mountain city of Cajamarca, some 350 miles to the southeast. The time for action had come. On September 24, 1532, Pizarro marshaled his forces—a mere 177 men—and set off for the interior.

Before long, however, Pizarro sensed an undercurrent of fear among his men. Calling a halt, he announced that all who wanted to return to the coast

could do so immediately. "He would proceed with his conquest," he continued, "with those that were left, whether they were few or many." Nine embarrassed soldiers detached themselves, and the little army marched on, its numbers now reduced to 106 infantry and 62 cavalry, but with its morale strengthened.

Several days later Pizarro received an envoy from the Inca himself. His message was surprisingly friendly: Atahualpa welcomed his visitors and looked forward to entertaining them at his lodgings in the mountains. As a gift he sent two ceramic vessels exquisitely cast in the shape of fortresses, some vicuna fabric embroidered with gold and silver thread, and a sample of a prized Inca perfume made from dried and powdered gooseflesh.

By early November the Spaniards had scaled the high wall of the Andes and entered a series of passes leading to Cajamarca, 9,000 feet high on the plateau. Unaccustomed to the low oxygen content in the rarified mountain air, the soldiers bowed under the weight of their armor. And it was cold. "Trees are few and stunted," complained Francisco Xeres, "and water is so cold it cannot be drunk without being first warmed."

Finally, on November 15, 1532, Pizarro's exhausted

## With Gold for the Sun and Silver for the Moon, Inca Artists Crafted Their Many Treasures

The Incas seldom offered human victims to the sun, which they worshiped. Still, on occasion, a particularly attractive child would be sacrificed. Unlike the Aztecs, however, the Inca ritual did not require the bloody removal of the victim's heart. The eight- or nine-year-old boy below was found with gold objects on El Polma peak in Chile in 1954. He had been left to die of exposure as an offering to the sun more than 500 years ago. A feathered pouch hanging from his waist contained coca leaves, which the boy could chew to make him drowsy and ease his suffering. More often, however, a llama would be sacrificed to insure a fertile harvest. A golden knife (column two, top) was used to cut the animal's throat.

Inca temples contained expressive statues like the small silver and turquoise man playing a pipe that resembles a harmonica (column two, bottom) and the graceful silver figure of an Inca maiden (column three). The silver statue at right shows a boy astride a llama. Unfortunately, the animals were not strong enough to carry grown riders, though they could bear light bundles. They are still used today as beasts of burden.

Much of the Inca treasure was collected to fill the rooms of precious metals demanded for Atahualpa's ransom. The conquistadors then destroyed priceless works of art by melting all the objects into gold and silver bars. Nevertheless, some objects, such as these, have survived.

army emerged from a pass and gazed down on the plain of Cajamarca, an immense oval bowl checkered with plots of green and golden vegetation. At their feet lay the city itself, its buildings sharply etched in the crisp, clear mountain air. There was no movement within: Atahualpa had evacuated the town and bivouacked around a misty patch of hot springs some three miles to the south, where thousands of tents dotted the plain. For the first time the Spaniards realized how hopelessly outnumbered they were. "The specta-

cle caused something like confusion and even fear, . . ." one soldier later wrote. "But it was too late to turn back. . . . So, with as bold a countenance as we could, after coolly surveying the ground, we prepared for our entrance into Cajamarca."

Late that afternoon Pizarro's troops clattered into the empty streets of Cajamarca and found shelter in some buildings around the main square. Pizarro then sent De Soto with a detachment of 20 horsemen to convey his compliments to the Inca.

*The Conquistadors*

### An Abandoned City Awaits Its Conquerors

On a cool November day in 1532, Pizarro's conquistadors finally sighted their goal: the Inca city of Cajamarca. After struggling through winding mountain passes, the Spaniards had emerged in a luxuriant valley, green with fields of potatoes, corn, and tobacco. At the center of the fertile farmland stood Cajamarca, a city of impressive plazas and well-planned streets lined with straw-thatched adobe cottages. Two fortresses of pale gray limestone guarded the city, one in the central square, the other, with a spiraling tower, on the edge of the city. The fortresses, to the Spaniards' relief, were empty. The whole town, in fact, was deserted as the fading light of the autumn afternoon filtered through the silent streets. All the inhabitants had fled to Atahualpa's camp. The Lord Inca had come to Cajamarca to bathe in its mineral springs on a hillside three miles beyond the city. In this reconstruction, Pizarro and his men view the scene as a messenger from Atahualpa points to the distant white tents of the Inca encampment, where Atahualpa and a force of 30,000 warriors waited uneasily for their first glimpse of the bearded strangers.

Pizarro sent a mounted detachment to the Inca's camp, but Atahualpa refused to enter Cajamarca immediately. He sent word that the Spaniards were to camp in three long buildings lining the central square. Atahualpa's army did not begin to move until noon the next day. Then, late in the afternoon, the Incas stopped just before entering Cajamarca. Pizarro, fearing a night attack, again sent emissaries to urge the Lord Inca to enter the town. Planning an ambush, Pizarro hid his men in the barracks Atahualpa had assigned them. As the Lord Inca stepped into the central square of Cajamarca, he did not know that in little more than half an hour his army would be decimated and he himself would be a prisoner. When Pizarro gave the signal his men attacked, and the once-silent streets of Cajamarca echoed with the noise of battle. Less than 24 hours after they entered Cajamarca, Pizarro and his forces had crippled the most splendid Indian civilization that had ever flourished in South America. Back in Europe the engraver Theodor de Bry later published a lively but inaccurate engraving of Pizarro's victory at Cajamarca (right). At center, Pizarro pulls Atahualpa from his litter. The only Inca structure left in Cajamarca is the room that held Atahualpa's enormous ransom.

De Soto and his men galloped off across the plain. As they approached the outskirts of the Indian camp, they gathered speed, ignoring the stares of amazed warriors who had never seen a horse before. When they reached a stream, De Soto, who delighted in flamboyant horsemanship, plunged through in a shower of spray and reined up at the entrance to the emperor's quarters.

"The tyrant was at the door of his lodging, sitting on a low stool," reported Xeres, "with many Indians before him, and women at his feet, who almost surrounded him." He was, according to one observer, "a man of 30 years of age, good-looking, somewhat stout, with a fine face, handsome and fierce, the eyes bloodshot." When De Soto, through an interpreter, invited him to visit Pizarro, the inscrutable Inca "gave no answer, nor did he even raise his eyes to look at the captain."

According to one account, the exasperated De Soto then spurred his horse forward until its breath fanned the crimson fringe of Atahualpa's ceremonial headdress. Atahualpa did not move. (He did, however, later

**Without an alphabet** *the Incas relied on the quipu (left), a series of cords knotted at regular intervals, both to count and keep records. Quipu mayocs ("clerks") chronicled harvests, tributes and Inca history on the multicolored strands. Completed quipus were kept in "libraries" in Cuzco. A simplified quipu is still used in Peru today (right), but the meanings of the Inca ones remain a mystery.*

---

behead several bodyguards who shrank back in terror at the monster in their midst.)

The impasse was broken by the arrival of a more experienced diplomat, Hernando Pizarro. Introducing himself as the governor's brother, Hernando respectfully repeated the invitation. At last Atahualpa looked up, and the Spaniards saw, with surprise, that he was smiling. "Tell your captain," he replied, "that I am keeping a fast, which will end tomorrow morning. I will then visit him with my chieftains. In the meantime, let him occupy the public buildings on the square, and no other, until I come, when I will order what shall be done." After exchanging toasts of a native corn liquor served in huge golden goblets, the Spaniards left.

A deep melancholy settled over Pizarro's men that night. Exhausted by their seven-week march, intimidated by the size of Atahualpa's army, whose many campfires sparkled in the darkness, the men slept fit-

fully in the silence of the empty city.

In the morning Pizarro shocked them by announcing a plan so audacious it seemed suicidal. The drama was to begin on an empty stage. When the Inca arrived at the head of his army, only Pizarro; a priest, Father Vicente Valverde; and a few others would be in the plaza. The rest of the army and all the horses were to remain hidden in the surrounding buildings until they heard the signal: *"Santiago!"* At the sound of the old battle cry, every gun was to fire, every sword swing into action, until the Inca himself had been captured.

As the hours dragged by on the morning of November 16, there was no sign of Atahualpa's approach. What the soldiers, anxious in their hiding places, did not know was that Atahualpa probably had fears of his own. Before his death, his father had predicted that the Spaniards, who had been sighted on their first probes of the coast, would one day conquer Peru. And, like the Aztecs of Mexico, the Incas had a white god, Viracocha, who had disappeared into the sea. Could these strange invaders be Viracocha's envoys returning to Peru? On a more practical level, the Inca's closest military advisers—and much of his army—were off in Cuzco where they could not help him. So Atahualpa hesitated as he pondered the novel situation.

Time played on the Spaniards' nerves. When a seemingly endless procession finally began to issue from Atahualpa's camp at noon, the number of warriors amassing on the plain seemed, to one horrified observer, to be at least 50,000. Just outside the city, Atahualpa paused again, deliberating whether or not to enter. After a fresh invitation from Pizarro, Atahualpa's vanguard of 6,000 troops entered the city.

By the time the Inca arrived it was almost sunset,

---

## The Vicuna, Rare Relative of the Llama, Provided Inca Royalty With Superbly Light Wool

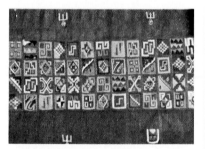

On simple handlooms (left), Peruvian women wove fabrics of complex design and great beauty. Cloth made from the luxurious wool of the vicuna was the most prized of all. Related to the llama, the vicuna (below) grazed wild in the Andean highlands. A decree of the Lord Inca forbade anyone killing them under penalty of death. Each year, in a large roundup, the vicunas were driven into corrals, where they were shorn and then released. Vicuna cloth (above)—extremely light, yet very warm and soft—was so treasured among the Incas that only nobility wore it. Pizarro sent some of the cloth to Spain, where it was believed to be a new kind of silk.

**After the killing of Atahualpa,** *all that remained to complete Spanish control of the Inca Empire was the capture of its capital at Cuzco. Here the Spaniards had to overcome determined Inca military resistance for the first time. It was led by Quisquis, who had been one of Atahualpa's most experienced commanders. Theodor de Bry's engraving (right) is of Pizarro and Almagro's victory at Cuzco. Although De Bry shows the Incas fighting with bows and arrows, the Indians actually preferred to use deadly slingshots and maces similiar to the one pictured above.*

with rich, late-afternoon light flooding down on the plaza. "First came a squadron of Indians dressed in a livery of different colors, like a chessboard," wrote Pizarro's secretary, Xeres. "They advanced, removing the straws from the ground and sweeping the road. Next came three squadrons in different dresses, dancing and singing. Then came a number of men with armor, large metal plates, and crowns of gold and silver. Among them was Atahualpa in a litter lined with plumes of macaws' feathers of many colors and adorned with plates of gold and silver. Many Indians carried it on their shoulders on high."

When the Incas were assembled in the plaza, Pizarro sent Father Valverde forward to offer a welcoming sermon. Speaking through an interpreter, the Dominican friar immediately launched into an impassioned speech, lecturing Atahualpa on the error of his religion and demanding his allegiance to the Christian faith and the Spanish crown. His discourse was somewhat hampered by the interpreter, who translated a long passage on the Trinity as "The Christians believed in three Gods and one God, and that made four." Atahualpa apparently understood the gist of the sermon.

Listening with growing irritation, the emperor finally roared, "For my faith, I will not change it!" Then, pointing at the setting sun, he added, "Your own God, as you say, was put to death by the very men he created. But mine, my God, still lives in the heavens and looks down on his children."

Undaunted, Father Valverde handed Atahualpa a Bible, explaining that it contained the authority for his sermon. At first curious, the Inca, who had never seen a

book before, leafed clumsily through it. Then he lost interest and tossed it to the ground.

Using this unwitting sacrilege as the pretext for ambush, Pizarro strode up to Atahualpa, grabbed him by the arm, and gave the signal: "*Santiago!*" Trumpets blared, and with a burst of gunfire the cavalry and infantry charged out of their hiding places into the plaza. Many of the Indians were so terrified by the stampeding horses that they fled in panic, breaking right through one of the walls around the square. "The infantry made so good an assault upon those that remained," wrote Xeres, "that in a short time most of them were put to the sword."

In barely half an hour the battle was over. Atahualpa was seized, stripped of his rich robes and emerald necklace, and dragged off to captivity. At sundown Atahualpa's god sank behind the mountain peaks, and darkness fell upon the 2,000 Indian corpses that littered the now silent square.

As soon as he recovered from the shock of his capture, Atahualpa began to bargain for his release. From the first he had noticed that gold, which the Indians prized simply for its beauty, had some greater significance for the Europeans. In exchange for his freedom, he offered to fill a room 22 feet long and 17 feet wide to a depth of 7 feet with gold. Pizarro, wanting a ransom that could never be met, demanded that another room be filled twice over with silver.

Atahualpa and Pizarro agreed to the bargain, and within days Indians throughout the empire were frantically stripping gold and silver from their buildings and giving up their jewelry. Some 700 sheets of gold

EL TER3ERO MES MAR3O
PACHIADVM

**Machu Picchu, lost city of the Incas,** *had been abandoned a long time before the arrival of the Spanish. The latter never found it, because the city, high in the Andes, is hidden from view by overhanging ledges. It was discovered in 1911 by Hiram Bingham, an American archeologist. Describing the awe that filled him as he gazed at the ruins of a great temple, Bingham wrote: "I could scarcely believe my senses as I examined the large blocks in the lower course and estimated that they must weigh between 10 to 15 tons each. Would anybody believe what I had found?" An Inca altar at Machu Picchu (far left) is similar to one in a 16th-century Peruvian drawing (left) of a worshiper kneeling at a shrine.*

were torn from the reflecting walls of the Temple of the Sun at Cuzco; ornamental gardens of gold and silver plants were uprooted; whole flocks of miniature silver llamas were rounded up. As the weeks passed, a steady stream of porters began to flow into Cajamarca with baskets full of treasures. They deposited their bright burdens in the appointed rooms, then hurried back along the highways for more. One Spanish patrol, puzzled by the sight of "a golden line shining in the sun" on a mountainside, soon discovered that it was a file of Indians carrying gold sacrificial jars.

Betraying the conquistadors' usual propensity for valuing art by weight alone, Xeres noted: "Thus, some days 20,000, on others 30,000, on others 50,000 or 60,000 pesos of gold arrived." A magnificent golden bench on

which the sun god was meant to sit was inventoried at 25,000 pesos, and the entire contribution of Cuzco, including golden fountains decorated with movable gold birds and "straws made of solid gold, with their spikes, just as they would grow in the fields," was listed under the blanket description, "178 loads."

At last, the gigantic ransom was paid. Although Pizarro had promised to treat the roomfuls of ornaments as art, not bullion, he now decided to liquefy his assets. Nine forges were put into operation in May 1533, and soon gold and silver treasures were being melted down into bars and ingots at the rate of 60,000 pesos a day. When the smelting was finished, the ransom weighed in at 13,265 pounds in gold and 26,000 pounds in silver. After the crown's royal fifth had been set aside, every

Spaniard who had participated in the conquest was paid according to his rank, with Pizarro taking the lion's share of about one-seventh of the total.

Having paid for his freedom with the bulk of the Inca cultural heritage, Atahualpa now awaited his release. But it never came. Pizarro realized that, if freed, the Inca could call up an overwhelming army to crush the invaders. With cold, grim logic, he decided that the Inca must die. On August 29, 1533, the ruler was sentenced to a heretic's death—burning at the stake.

To save himself from this humiliating—and agonizing—fate, the resigned Atahualpa agreed at the last moment to be baptized as a Christian. Pizarro, in turn, "ordered that he should not be burnt, but that he should be fastened to a pole in the open space and strangled." Xeres reported: "He died with great fortitude, and without any feeling, saying that he entrusted his children to the governor."

With Atahualpa out of the way, Pizarro was free to continue the conquest of Peru. Some four months earlier his partner Almagro had joined him in Cajamarca with fresh reinforcements. With a combined force of 600 Spaniards, the two leaders set out in September 1533 to occupy the former Inca capital at Cuzco. They entered the city in triumph on November 15, 1533—a year to the day after Pizarro's arrival at Cajamarca—and soon appropriated most of what remained of the city's wealth.

There Pizarro also crowned his own Inca, Manco, a half-brother of Atahualpa, realizing that he needed a puppet ruler if he was to govern his reluctant subjects. (Another Inca he had appointed some time before had died mysteriously, possibly murdered by one of Atahualpa's generals.) At first Manco proved tractable and endorsed Pizarro's efforts to establish Spanish law and order over Peru, but eventually the Spaniards' greed and cruelty sickened him. Escaping Cuzco, he led a widespread Indian revolt and in 1536 successfully besieged the Spanish forces in Cuzco for several months. Food shortages finally forced him to give up the siege, but until his death in 1545, he continued to lead guerilla attacks on the conquistadors.

Long before that, Pizarro had been moving on many fronts to establish his authority. In 1535 he founded Lima and played an active role in making it the proper capital of a Spanish colony. He sent out many expeditions to explore his new domain. Pizarro also switched much of the Indian labor force from the fields into the mines, producing regular shipments of gold and silver for the Spanish crown and the Church.

The grateful Spanish monarch made Pizarro a marquis and greatly extended his realm, while naming Almagro governor of the southern province of Chile. (The luckless Father Luque, third partner in the original venture, had died before even learning of the success of the conquest.) Almagro soon discovered that Chile had few riches to offer. Feeling shortchanged by the crown

once again, he claimed that Cuzco was part of his domain—as did Pizarro. Eventually, in 1538 he led his army in a fierce battle against Hernando Pizarro for possession of the city. The incident ended with Almagro's capture and execution on charges of treason.

Almagro's supporters paid dearly for their rebellion. Although streams of adventurers were arriving from Spain to share in the wealth of New Castile, Pizarro left the Almagrists penniless, landless, and unemployed. Their resentment festered into open hatred. A few decided to take the ultimate risk on June 26, 1541. Storming into the governor's palace in Lima where Pizarro was dining with a few friends, they burst into his chamber with swords drawn. In the furious battle that followed, Pizarro, though more than 65 years old, defended himself like a tiger until he was cut down.

According to one account, as he lay dying he traced a cross on the blood-smeared floor. If so, it was a fitting end for a conquistador, a mixture of piety and violence. Thus Francisco Pizarro had lived, and thus he died. The colony then fell into the hands of his brother Gonzalo. Resisting orders from the Spanish crown, Gonzalo was defeated and killed by royal forces in 1547.

**An Indian noble of 1599,** *caught between two worlds, wears Spanish dress but sports traditional Inca gold ornaments in his nose and ears. The original Inca noble families gradually disappeared during the ensuing centuries of Spanish rule.*

**The wealth of the Aztec capital,** *Tenochtitlán, made the conquistadors dream of capturing other cities similarly laden with treasure. A 16th-century map of America (left) is dotted with drawings of imposing castles, each one of which was supposed to mark the location of a rich city. The actual cities that Coronado discovered, however, did not conform to the images on the map. Acoma pueblo (above), which remains today the oldest continually inhabited dwelling place in North America, was at least 300 years old when Coronado visited it in 1540. To the conquistador's disappointment, the Indians of Acoma presented him with turkeys, tanned deerskins, pine nuts, bread, and corn, but no gold. Unwilling to abandon the dream of discovering the Seven Cities of Gold, Coronado and his men pushed forward, only to be disappointed again and again. Not even the discovery of the Grand Canyon of the Colorado River (left) could convince Coronado and his men that their expedition had been a success, for they had not found the treasure they had sought. Nevertheless, the Spanish colonized the American Southwest for more than 200 years.*

*Chapter Eleven.* *Lured by tales of Indian cities brimming with gold and turquoise, a large Spanish expedition heads north from Mexico into the unknown American Southwest. Their fruitless quest for treasure drives the explorers far into the heart of the continent, revealing natural wonders that amaze them in the course of their arduous journey.*

# The Seven Cities of Cíbola: Coronado's Trek to Kansas

*A seer once told Francisco Vásquez de Coronado that one day he would visit faraway lands, gain power and high position—and be permanently injured in a fall. The young Spaniard, who was born in Salamanca about 1510, must have found the first part of the prophecy encouraging; his position as second son of a minor nobleman meant he would have to make his own way. So, like many another well-born young Spaniard, he went to the colonies to seek his fortune. In Mexico he prospered as an officer of the viceroy and married the daughter of the former royal treasurer. His appointment to head an expedition into the northern desert was an attempt by the viceroy to forestall Cortés, who was still in Mexico. Having failed to find any cities of gold, Coronado returned to Mexico, where he lived until his death in 1554.*

"He is lacking in many of his former fine qualities, and is not the man he was," said a Mexican judge, assessing the governmental service of Francisco Vásquez de Coronado in 1545. "They say this change was caused by the fall from a horse."

Francisco Vásquez de Coronado had been an outstanding captain in the regime of Mexico's viceroy, Don Antonio de Mendoza. Just 25 years old when he arrived in the colony in 1535, in the ensuing five years he quelled a slave revolt, put down an Indian uprising, was appointed to the council of Mexico City, and served honestly and efficiently for two years as governor of New Galicia, Mexico's northwesternmost province. He was, in short, exactly the sort of man Mendoza needed to investigate reports of fabulously wealthy Indians far to the north, the inhabitants of the legendary Seven Cities of Cíbola.

For several years rumors of this mysterious realm had been flying throughout Mexico, and Mendoza had already sent a missionary monk, Fray Marcos, on a preliminary reconnaissance to check them out. True,

Fray Marcos had not actually seen the cities themselves, but he had come close enough to learn the most extraordinary things about them. The cities, he reported, consisted of "very large houses, as high as 11 stories," and that was taller than most buildings in Spain. The entrances and, sometimes, entire facades of the main buildings were said to be studded with gleaming turquoises, and gold was so plentiful that the Indians even made it into "little blades with which they wipe away their sweat."

Intoxicated by visions of discovering another Peru, Viceroy Mendoza personally provided more than half the money needed to finance an expedition to conquer this new land. Coronado's wife, Doña Beatriz—the wealthiest heiress in all of Mexico—provided the rest.

With money in hand, the expedition was speedily and lavishly equipped. Recruitment was an easy matter. According to one chronicler, Coronado could "take advantage of many noble people who were in Mexico, and who, like a cork floating on water, went about with nothing to do." By February 22, 1540, the streets of Compostela, capital of New Galicia, were overflowing with Coronado's army of 336 soldiers, 1,300 Indian volunteers, about 5 priests, and 559 horses. (Coronado, who loved riding, personally provided "23 or 24 horses.") According to Pedro de Castaneda, a soldier who later wrote an account of the expedition, "It was the most brilliant company ever assembled in the Indies in search of new lands." Prominent among the "brilliant company" were Capts. López de Cárdenas and Hernando de Alvarado, the scout Melchior Díaz, and Fray Marcos, the expedition's official guide. Five other missionaries joined the force to add moral tone, including the quick-tempered Juan de Padilla, who was determined to stamp out swearing and womanizing; a lay brother, Luis de Ubeda, whose only possessions were an adze and chisel for erecting crosses; and big,

*Map for Coronado on page 128.*

barefoot Fray Daniel, who would teach the Indians embroidery. At the head of the expedition was Coronado himself, resplendent in gilded armor and a plumed helmet.

The expedition was well organized. Viceroy Mendoza, who had ordered that the Indian volunteers be treated "as if they were Spaniards" and not forced to carry baggage, had provided more than 600 packhorses and mules to carry supplies and equipment. Herds of sheep and cattle were included as a sort of walking commissary. In addition, two ships carrying extra supplies were to sail up the Gulf of California under the command of Hernando de Alarcón. If the unexplored river at its head (the Colorado) curved northeast—as everybody hoped it would—then Alarcón's supply ships would be able to rendezvous with Coronado's party somewhere in the interior.

On February 23, 1540, with Fray Marcos as official

### Fray Marcos Led a Quest for Gold and Souls

Telling tall tales is part of the heritage of the West—and no wonder, for some of the most whopping stories of all were told by Fray Marcos, the first European priest to travel across the American Southwest. Accompanied by Estebanico, a Moorish slave, Fray Marcos reconnoitered in advance of Coronado's party. Estebanico went ahead of the priest, but the two had agreed if Estebanico found cities rich with gold he would send a messenger back to Fray Marcos with a cross. The size of the cross would indicate the amount of the treasure. It is easy to imagine Fray Marcos' excitement when Estebanico sent back a cross as tall as a man, but unfortunately, the slave was killed by Zuñi Indians before Fray Marcos could join him. Fearing for his life, the priest fled to Mexico City with highly exaggerated tales of the Seven Cities of Cíbola. Despite Fray Marcos' misadventures, however, Spanish priests were instrumental in the early settlement of the Southwest. Above, one baptizes an Indian convert. They also founded missions and schools throughout the area. One of the oldest missions, established at Taos, New Mexico (right), still stands.

guide, the expedition set out from Compostela and headed north along the west coast of Mexico. Slowed by the pack animals and herds of livestock, the caravan did not reach Culiacán, about 300 miles to the north, until March 30. At this northernmmost Spanish settlement Coronado received disturbing news: A scout reported that Indians along the way had told him that Cíbola, though it indeed had plenty of turquoises, contained absolutely no gold. Yet Coronado was not discouraged: The friar cheerfully continued to assure everybody that he would "place them in a country where their hands would be filled."

Impatient to find out the truth, the captain-general soon quit Culiacán with an advance party of 100 of his best men, some Indians, and the zealous friars, leaving the rest of his army to march at a more leisurely pace. His route for the next month was over rough, rocky terrain, interrupted here and there by thickly wooded valleys and alligator-infested rivers.

The hooves of the plodding sheep and cattle accompanying the advance party soon became so badly injured that many of the precious animals had to be left behind. Even so, Coronado was determined not to abuse the hospitality of friendly Indians along the way. At night he insisted on camping outside their villages and refused to commandeer their food supplies. After a spartan supper and a game of cards, his troops would settle down to fitful sleep, with the passing hours punctuated by the distant howling of coyotes.

It was an uncomfortable policy, but the men respected it. One veteran soldier later recalled that he had never known a commander who treated Indians better than Coronado.

After about a month the group emerged into the broad and lushly fertile Sonora Valley in northern Mexico. Following Fray Marcos up the gorge of the Sonora River, the explorers soon reached the border of modern Arizona and headed north along the San Pedro River, then east along the Gila.

The baking deserts of Arizona were nothing like the fertile plains Fray Marcos had described, and the first Indian "city" they encountered—a red earth pueblo whose praises the priest had sung—turned out to be a roofless ruin. The men were even more alarmed to learn that the Gulf of California, which Fray Marcos had assured Coronado could be viewed from the pueblo, was in fact a 15-day march away, separated by the highest mountains in North America. "The curses that some hurled at Fray Marcos were such that God forbid they may befall him," commented one of the soldiers. Their only consolation was the fray's assurance that this was not one of the Seven Cities. Cíbola, the priest explained, lay still farther north.

Finally, on July 8, 1540, after 135 days and some 1,500 miles of traveling, the weary, half-starved army reached Háwikuh, capital of the Seven Cities, in what is now the Zuñi Indian Reservation in New Mexico, about

**As hope of finding the legendary cities** *of gold diminished, Coronado's imagination was captured by tales of Quivira, an Indian kingdom in what is present-day Kansas. An Indian guide, nicknamed the Turk by the Spaniards, promised that Quivira was rich in gold and silver. The Turk, in fact, was lying, but Coronado did not discover that until his troops had marched across miles of flat and monotonous prairie. The party grew restive as the Great Plains seemed to stretch endlessly into the horizon. Pedro de Castaneda, chronicler of the expedition, de-scribed the scene. "In traversing 250 leagues, the other mountain range was not seen, nor a hill, nor a hillock which was three times as high as a man. The country is like a bowl, so that when a man sits down, the horizon surrounds him all around at the distance of a musket shot." This illustration by Frederic Reming-ton shows Coronado's men crossing the Great Plains. In the lead are an Indian guide and two conquistadors carrying arquebuses and the forked rests that supported these early firearms. At the right, his cassock pulled up to his knees, is a priest.*

half the way up the present Arizona-New Mexico border. Anyone still expecting to find another Cuzco was sadly disillusioned. Rising from the treeless plain, like a low pyramid, was a bleak adobe structure three or four stories high, with portable ladders connecting the various levels. And that was all. Far from the jewel-studded buildings of Fray Marcos' tales, there was nothing more than "a little cramped village looking as if it had been all crumpled up together."

Nor were the inhabitants the least bit friendly. Outside the town they had sprinkled a sacred line of cornmeal on the ground, warning the Spaniards not to come any closer. The army, however, was desperate for food. Approaching on foot and on horseback, the troops were greeted by showers of arrows and stones hurled down from the rooftops. Coronado, in his glittering armor, was the principal target. By the time the pueblo was taken, he was unconscious and had to be dragged to safety by two of his men. "His helmet was dented," wrote Capt. López de Cárdenas, Coronado's chief aide, "and had it not been of such excellent quality, I doubt that he would have escaped alive. . . . He received many stone blows on his head, shoulders, and legs, two slight wounds on his face, and an arrow shot in his right foot."

Inside the pueblo, Cárdenas reported, the famished soldiers "found something we prized more than silver or gold, namely, much maize, beans, and chickens" (which were probably turkeys).

In the days that followed, having made peace with the Indians, the Spaniards soon discovered that the fabled Seven Cities of Cíbola were nothing more than a series of dusty pueblos stretching across the Zuñi River Valley. All were equally poor, and Fray Marcos came in for much abuse. Coronado eventually concluded that it was unsafe for the unfortunate friar to remain in Cíbola, since "the kingdoms he had told about had not been found, nor the populous cities, nor the wealth of gold, nor the precious stones." In August he sent the hapless priest back to Mexico, along with a letter complaining to Mendoza that "he has not told the truth in a single thing that he said."

Cíbola had some compensations. The climate was dry and sunny. Nearby pasturage was good, and the Indians, Coronado observed happily, "make the best tortillas that I have ever seen anywhere."

Tales of daring exploits *in the New World were a source of inspiration for writers and artists in Europe. Often, however, the accounts that reached Europe were sketchy and much of the detail had to be created by the artist. For example, in 16th-century Dutch artist Jan Mostaert's rendition of Coronado's attack on the pueblo of Háwikuh (above), the painter has shown the Indians with beards, as though they were Europeans. Mostaert's landscape also shows the influence of firsthand descriptions of Caribbean foliage, and in addition, he has placed some cows, grazing placidly as they did on Dutch farms, in the foreground. A more realistic version of an attack on an Indian pueblo in the Southwest is shown at left. There were usually only one or two entrances into a pueblo, and by concentrating their forces at the entryways, Indians could mount stiff opposition to attack.*

Tortillas, however, would not be enough to support the Spaniards when the main body of the army arrived. What Coronado needed were the supplies on Alarcón's ships. A group of men, under the scout Melchior Díaz, had been sent west in search of the Colorado River. In October they found it—"a mighty stream, . . . half a league wide"—about 90 miles inland from its mouth, but there was no sign of the supply ships. Trekking downstream for three days, Díaz finally spotted a message blazed on a tree trunk: "Alarcón reached this place. There are letters at the foot of this tree." Alarcón, Díaz discovered, had sailed as far as he could up the turbulent river and waited as long as he dared before sailing back to Mexico.

Díaz does not seem to have been in a hurry to return with the bad news. Instead, he spent the fall and early winter exploring the country across the great tawny river as far as the plains of Lower California. Then, suddenly, at the end of December tragedy struck.

"One day a greyhound belonging to a soldier took a notion to chase some sheep, which they had brought along for food, and as Melchior Díaz saw it, he started in pursuit throwing his lance at the dog on the run. The lance stuck in the ground, and not being able to stop his horse, the rider ran upon it in such a way that the lance pierced his groin, tearing his bladder." The scout was in terrible pain but insisted on treating himself. "If I only had a silver tube, I could get along," he said wistfully. His men ferried him gently back across the river, but on January 18, 1541, Melchior Díaz died. His men buried him somewhere in the desert between the Colorado and Sonora Valleys.

Meanwhile, back in Háwikuh, Coronado was digesting the report of another of his captains. On August 25 he had sent out a party under López de Cárdenas to investigate Indian stories of "a great river" about 200 miles northwest of Cíbola. If the men thought that this "great river" was the upper reaches of the Colorado, they were to follow it and try to rendezvous with Alarcón's supply ships.

Riding across a high plateau "covered with low and twisted pine trees," Cárdenas and his 25 horsemen found their way blocked one crisp fall day by the world's most spectacular canyon. From the brink, they reported with awe, "it looked as if the opposite side must have been three or four leagues away by air." It was unbelievable. The little stream of water glittering at the bottom looked no more than a few feet across, yet "according to information supplied by the Indians, it must have been half a league wide."

Short on water (and no doubt curious as well), "the men spent three days looking for a way down to the river." Finally, "at a place which seemed less difficult, Captain Melgosa, a certain Juan Galeras, and another companion, being the most agile, began to go down." By late afternoon they were back—waterless—with reports that the river was every bit as wide as the Indians claimed, but "because of the many obstacles they met," they were unable to reach the bottom. These "most agile" men were the first Europeans ever to attempt a descent into the Grand Canyon of the Colorado River.

While Cárdenas was away in the west, Coronado sent yet another expedition, under Hernando de Alvarado, to the east to look for a rumored "country of cows." Visiting Indians from Cicúye had given him the hides of cowlike animals with woolly hair and had even drawn sketches of the strange creatures, which, of course, were bison. Coronado realized that these "cows" might solve his food problem.

Alvarado left Háwikuh on August 29 with about 20 men. They paused briefly at the ancient, fortresslike pueblo of Acoma, perched atop an enormous mesa, where Indians gave them gifts of turkeys and turquoises. Continuing east, the group entered the broad fertile valley of the Rio Grande and followed it north. Just above modern Albuquerque, they came to Tigeux, a group of 12 pueblos surrounded by lush fields of corn, beans, and melons.

The air cooled noticeably as the Spaniards marched north toward the jagged peaks of the Sangre de Cristo Mountains. All along the way, Fray Padilla erected crosses and taught the Indians to worship them. "They did it with such eagerness," wrote Alvarado, "that some climbed on the backs of others in order to reach the arms of the crosses to put plumes and roses on them."

Reaching Taos, the most northerly of the Rio Grande pueblos, Alvarado sent a messenger to Coronado, urging him to winter the army at Tigeux, with its plentiful food supplies. Then he swung southeast to Cicúye. The largest pueblo in 16th-century New Mexico, it was a major trading center for Indians of the pueblos and those of the southern Great Plains. There he met two Indians who agreed to guide him out into the "country of cows" to the east. Sopete, the younger, said that he came from a distant land called Quivira (in Kansas). The other, whom the Spaniards nicknamed El Turco, the Turk, "because he looked like one," was from an

even more remote region, Harahey (in Nebraska).

In early October the Spaniards and their newly recruited guides left Cicúye. Once in the rippling grasslands of eastern New Mexico, they caught their first glimpse of the mysterious cows. "There are such quantities of them," wrote one astonished soldier, "that I do not know what to compare them with unless it be the fish of the sea." Observing that "the best weapon for killing them was a spear for hurling at them, and the arquebus when they are standing still," he also noted with satisfaction that "their meat is as

## Wonders of the New World

The first pictures Europeans saw of America's flora and fauna were woodcut illustrations in books. The ear of corn appeared in the 16th-century volume *Navigations and Voyages* by the Italian publisher of travel narratives Gianbattista Ramusio. Samples of the plant had been brought back to Europe by Columbus in the 1490's. Corn was the staple food of the pueblo-dwelling Indians, but the Plains Indians relied for their sustenance on the buffalo. In addition, they built their shelters and made their clothes from buffalo skins, using the animals' sinews as thread. (The ramlike specimen above is from a 17th-century book.) Coronado and his men were amazed by the huge numbers of the animals—then in the millions—that roamed the Plains. Castaneda recorded a practice of the buffalo-hunting Querochos: "When the Indians kill a cow, they clean a large intestine and fill it with blood and put it around their necks to drink when they are thirsty." Coronado's party adopted the Indian practice of using buffalo dung for fuel.

good as the cattle of Castile, and some said that it was even better."

The explorers did not linger for much hunting. Alvarado had promised to return to Coronado within 80 days, and his time was running out. Besides, the Turk had confided that there was gold—lots of it—in Quivira, and Alvarado was anxious to deliver the good news.

Back in Tigeux, Alvarado found that Coronado was already settled in one of the pueblos. By the time the main body of the Spanish army finally caught up with them, it was December and the Sangre de Cristo peaks were covered with snow. Any expedition to Quivira obviously would have to wait until spring.

The winter was a difficult one. The army made huge inroads into the Indians' food and other supplies, and relations soon became tense. A Spanish soldier brought matters to a head when he attempted to violate an Indian woman during a visit to a neighboring pueblo.

Within a few days the Indians of the pueblo revolted. They stampeded the Spaniards' horses and mules, killed several, and then chopped off their tails to wave defiantly at Coronado's men. Cárdenas and 60 horsemen had to fight for several hours to quell the uprising. Finally, after smoking the Indians out of the pueblo, he had them tied to stakes and burned alive. When a rebellion broke out at another pueblo, the Spaniards had to besiege it for 50 days, until its well ran dry and the Indians were forced to surrender.

Coronado's only comfort in the long cold winter was the Turk's enticing tales of the riches of Quivira. The king, he claimed, not only ate from golden tableware but also napped each day under a tree that tinkled with the sound of golden bells hanging from its limbs. Enraptured by the prospect of such luxury, the whole restless army was relieved when on April 23, 1541, the captain-general at last gave the order to march.

With the Turk and Sopete as guides, the long column of soldiers, horses, and pack mules trailed north along the Rio Grande and then, skirting the still-frozen moun-

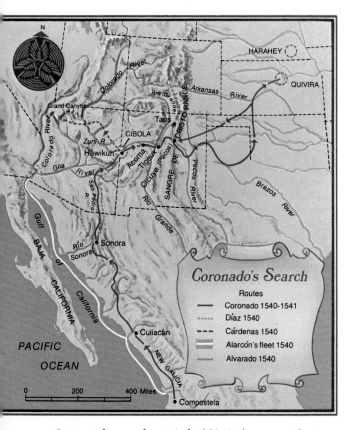

**Compostela was the capital** *of Mexico's most northwestern province when Coronado set out to search for Cíbola. Though no gold was found, the Spanish expedition discovered the Colorado River and the Grand Canyon on its rambling trek to Kansas.*

tains, headed east into the sunny warmth of the Pecos River Valley. Continuing east, in early May near the Texas-New Mexico border, the Spaniards had their first encounter with a tribe of nomadic Plains Indians, possibly Apaches. "They are far more numerous than those of the pueblos," Castaneda declared, "better proportioned, greater warriors, and more feared." Completely dependent on bison for food, clothing, and shelter, they lived in tepees made of bison skins and followed the great herds on their wanderings across the plains. Lacking horses, the Indians used "packs of dogs harnessed with little pads, packsaddles, and girths to transport their belongings on their travels. When the dogs' loads slip to the side," Castaneda added, "they howl for someone to come and straighten them." The Spaniards were also impressed by the Indians' use of the sign language that was the lingua franca of the Great Plains. "These people were so skillful in the use of signs," wrote one surprised soldier, "that it seemed as if they spoke. They made everything so clear that an interpreter was not necessary."

Wandering on across the empty vastness of the Texas plains, the Spaniards now and then encountered more tepee villages of nomadic Indians. And bison—everywhere there were bison. "There was not a single day . . . that I lost sight of them," Coronado later reported. Aside from witnessing a bison stampede and enduring a storm when "hailstones as big as bowls, or bigger, fell as thick as raindrops," they found little to relieve the endless monotony of trudging across the dusty flatlands. With no trees, no hills, no mountains, or other conspicuous landmarks, stragglers were constantly getting lost, and as Castaneda noted, "It was impossible to find tracks in this country, because the grass straightened up again as soon as it was trodden down."

As every mile of march revealed only another mile of emptiness ahead, skeptics began to wonder if the Turk really knew where Quivira was. Their doubts grew even stronger when the expedition came upon a settlement of Tejas Indians. Quivira, the Tejas insisted, contained no gold, no silver, no great buildings—just poor villages of little houses made of straw and hide. They doubted that the Spaniards would even find enough food and water for their army. Sopete, the junior guide, who had been calling the Turk a liar all along, now accused him of leading the army in the wrong direction.

Shocked and outraged, Coronado immediately clapped El Turco in chains, but he was not yet ready to give up the dream. Sending most of his army back to Tigeux, on May 29, 1541, he set off with 30 men to find out for himself exactly what Quivira had to offer.

Swinging northeast under the guidance of Sopete and a few Tejas Indians (with the hapless Turk bringing up the rear), the explorers marched across the sweltering plains of Texas and Oklahoma for 31 days. "We went without water for many days," Coronado later wrote, "and had to cook our food on cow dung." On

## How Spanish Horses Changed the Lives of the Plains Indians

Indians had inhabited the Great Plains for centuries before the arrival of the Spanish. Nothing, however, so changed their life on the Plains as the coming of the Spanish with their horses. How the Indians acquired the Spanish horses is not clear. Some animals that were lame or injured may have been turned loose, and others were probably stolen. Coronado's expedition records having lost three horses in 1541, presumably taken by the Indians. In later years Indian raiders often stampeded Spanish horses to capture them. These horses flourished and multiplied on the Great Plains. Two hundred years after Coronado's expedi-

tion to Kansas, virtually all the Plains Indians were skilled horsemen. An Indian petroglyph at Newspaper Rock in Utah (above) is one of the earliest pictures of an Indian on horseback.

Once horses became available to the Indians, they no longer had to trek across the flat prairie on foot searching for food and water. Riding on swift ponies, they could hunt buffalo much more effectively. Special horses, in fact, were trained to be ridden on buffalo hunts. Other horses were trained for battle, and new mounts were always sought. In the Alfred Miller painting at left, mounted braves pursue a herd of wild horses with lassos. Astride their war ponies, the Plains Indians became the most formidable opponents of white settlers.

June 29 the Spaniards reached the Arkansas River in southwestern Kansas and crossed over at last into the great territory of Quivira.

For the next 25 days the little band of explorers roamed through central Kansas, possibly getting as far north as the Nebraska border. Juan Jaramillo, a well-traveled soldier in the group, liked what he saw. "This country has a fine appearance. . ." he observed. "It is not a hilly country but one with mesas, plains, and charming rivers." Then, prophetically, he added, "I am of the belief that it will be very productive for all sorts of commodities." Castaneda, too, saw the region's potential for settlement.

Coronado, however, cast a jaundiced eye on Quivira's round, thatched houses and tall, tattooed Wichita Indians, whom he pronounced "barbarous." He was looking for gold, not farmland, and in all of Quivira he found not a trace of treasure—just "plains so vast that in my travels I did not reach their end."

On those "plains so vast" El Turco finally paid for his lies. Caught in a plot to persuade some Wichitas to murder the Spaniards, he made a last desperate attempt to save his life by finally admitting the truth. There was no gold in Quivira. The chiefs at Cicúye, he confessed, had asked him to lead the Spaniards astray on the plains, hoping they would die or return from the ordeal so weakened that they could easily be slaugh-

tered in revenge for wrongs they had done to the Indians. The enraged captain-general had the Turk strangled on the spot.

Coronado and his men arrived back in Tigeux halfway through September, in time to begin another miserable winter on a meager diet of maize and buffalo jerky meat. The captain-general tried to boost morale by promising to return to Quivira in the spring and spoke optimistcally of founding a settlement there. But this was not to be. According to Castaneda: "It happened that on a holiday [December 27, 1541] the general rode out on horseback as he often did, to find recreation. Riding a spirited horse, he raced by the side of Capt. Don Rodrigo Maldonado. His servants had used a new girth, which, because of being kept so long, must have been rotten. It burst during the race, and the general fell on the side where Don Rodrigo rode, and on passing over him the horse struck him on the head with a hoof. As a result, Francisco Vásquez was on the point of death, and his recovery was long and uncertain."

The captain-general was never the same again. He became melancholic, listless, and as spring approached, increasingly homesick. In early April, Coronado gave the order for the long march back to Mexico to report their sad news to a very disgusted Viceroy Mendoza. The vast prairies and herds of buffalo were left—for a while—to the Indians.

# Part 4

# Searching for a Northern Passage

## Captains and Colonists

*England, Holland, and France seek an alternate route to the Orient. They fail, but their explorers discover the waters, forests, and Indians of North America.*

With Portugal dominating the sea route around Africa, and Spain controlling the South Pacific, the countries of northern Europe viewed the New World as an obstacle in their path to India and China. Determined to reach the Orient, they inspired and directed attempts to cross to Asia by a northeast passage (above Russia) or a northwest passage (above the Americas).

English efforts to find a passage had started in 1495 when a certain John Cabot (Giovanni Caboto in his native Genoa) had appeared at the English court of Henry VII with a plan for discovering a route to Asia by sailing northwest. Henry was mildly interested and gave Cabot permission to explore, "subdue, occupy, and possess . . . regions or provinces of the heathen and infidels . . . unknown to all Christians."

Cabot rediscovered North America in 1497 (Leif Ericsson had seen it in the 11th century) but believed it to be China. Returning there in 1498, he probably died in a shipwreck on the North Atlantic. Although England sent other expeditions to the North Atlantic in the following decades, no silks or spices filled the holds of the returning vessels. Explorers had found only fish off the northern shores of America, and royal interest in the exploration of that coast soon faded.

By the 1540's English merchants were hungering more than ever for a portion of the oriental spice trade, and English intellectuals were yearning to learn more about the great world that improved navigation techniques had made more accessible. Exploration enthusiasts abounded; adventurers and sea captains published lively narratives of exploration for an avid readership. In 1533 the Muscovy Company had been founded to finance voyages that not only would open up new routes to the Orient via a northeast passage but would also reap immediate profits by selling English woolens in the cold countries along the way.

In 1553 a three-ship expedition headed by Sir Hugh Willoughby sailed for the Muscovy Company into the North Sea and reached the northern coast of Russia. Willoughby died, but Richard Chancellor, commander of the third ship, anchored off Archangel and from there traveled overland to Moscow, where he was received at the court of Czar Ivan IV and given permission to trade. His efforts resulted in a brisk, lucrative commerce between the two nations.

Although several attempts were made to open a northeast passage, the route was found extremely hazardous. "The piercing cold of the gross thick air so near the Pole . . . the air . . . so darkened with continual mists and fogs. . ." made navigation almost impossible, wrote Sir Humphrey Gilbert, arguing for a renewed effort to find a northwest passage instead. Voyages were made, first by Martin Frobisher, who in 1576 discovered Frobisher Bay in Canada; by John Davis, a remarkable Tudor mariner who sailed up the western coast of Greenland in 1587; and later by Henry Hudson, whose exploration of Hudson Bay in 1610 led to the formation of the Northwest Company and more futile efforts to find a passage to China through Canada.

While English explorers were struggling through the ice and mists of the North, English sailors were daring the southern seas at last, for in the Elizabethan Age "freeborn Englishmen," Catholics no longer, were disinclined to honor the Spanish-Portuguese division of the world established in 1494. In addition, England had expanded its navy and built faster, more seaworthy, and better-armed ships. Now a major seapower, it could begin to break the old rules. In 1562 John Hawkins of Plymouth entered the slave trade, selling African natives to Spanish planters in the Caribbean for gold, silver, and a delightful new plant, tobacco. Queen Elizabeth was greatly pleased.

### Singeing the King of Spain's Beard

On a voyage to the New World in 1568, Hawkins, accompanied by his kinsman Francis Drake, was treacherously attacked by Spaniards in the Mexican seaport of San Juan de Ulúa. Although relations between Spain and England had been friendly, this incident precipitated England's desire to "singe the king of Spain's beard" and unleashed the Elizabethan lust for adventure. Francis Drake and other English seadogs plundered the Spanish Main, seizing Spanish treasure ships. In 1577 Drake began the voyage in the *Golden Hind* that was to end, three years later, with his circumnavigation of the globe—an affirmation of England's newly won mastery of the seas. Settlement in North America soon followed when the first English colony was attempted by Sir Walter Raleigh at Roanoke Island, North Carolina, in 1585.

Although the 16th-century Dutch were preoccupied with winning their independence from Spain, they too sought a northern passage to China. As early as 1565 the Hollander Oliver Brunel had established a Dutch trading settlement on the White Sea, north of Russia. The three Arctic voyages of the mariner Willem Barents (1594–97) were a continuation of Brunel's earlier efforts. Barents succeeded no more than the English in finding a way through the polar pack ice and died off the Russian coast. Hudson's probe for the Dutch in 1609 also failed to find a northeast passage, ending the quest for more than two centuries.

An enterprising, seafaring people, the Dutch were the chief shippers of Eastern goods from Portugal to Europe. In 1580, however, the Spanish king Philip II seized the Portuguese throne and denied the Dutch their old trading privileges. Determined to capture for themselves the Far East lands that had enriched Portugal, the Dutch in 1595 boldly sent an armed fleet around the Cape of Good Hope and were not stopped. This first expedition proved so profitable that by 1602 the Dutch East India Company had been formed, sending ships east to create a maritime empire that would make the tiny provinces of the Netherlands the most prosperous country in 17th-century Europe.

Despite the Dutch successes in using the Portuguese route to Asia, the dream of northern passages persisted for them, too. In 1609 the East India Company employed Henry Hudson to seek the elusive passage in America. Hudson discovered the river that bears his name on that voyage, giving the Dutch their claim to their short-lived empire in North America.

### Searching for China in Canada

France, involved in a series of European wars, was slow to seek a new route to the Orient, but by 1523 King Francis I had dispatched the Florentine mariner Giovanni da Verrazano to look for one. Verrazano sailed along the American coast from Georgia to Maine, searching for a passage to China through this "barrier of new land." He never found it.

A decade after Verrazano's voyage, Jacques Cartier discovered the Gulf of St. Lawrence and, on a second voyage, the St. Lawrence River. Believing that the river was the sought-for route to China, he penetrated 1,000 miles into the continent, reaching the site of present-day Montreal. Here Cartier saw his passage vanish, as the river narrowed into a series of rapids. This was as close as Cartier came to the Orient, and official French interest in exploration lapsed for a generation. But Basque fishermen had discovered the Grand Banks, the richest fishing grounds in the world; and while curing their catches on Newfoundland's shores, they bartered with the Indians for furs, merchandise that was to prove nearly as valuable as Spanish gold. The fur trade and religious motives finally brought the French back to North America in the 17th century, led by the visionary explorer Samuel de Champlain, who had visited the Spanish Caribbean empire and dreamed of as great an empire for France in the New World.

Champlain made 12 voyages to Canada; founded the first permanent French settlement, Quebec, in 1608; and organized a thriving fur industry. Other explorers followed and, still seeking the China passage, charted the geography of inland America: Jean Nicolet sailed to Lake Michigan in 1638, Jacques Marquette canoed the Mississippi south to Arkansas in 1673, and fur traders penetrated the wilderness to the western shores of Lake Superior. Robert Cavelier, sieur de La Salle, completed mapping the new French empire by sailing down the Mississippi to the Gulf of Mexico, claiming "Louisiana" for King Louis XIV in 1682.

The dream of the northern passages, which had sent England, France, and the Netherlands on futile voyages for a century and won them overseas empires instead, persisted into our century. The Northeast Passage was finally navigated in 1878, when Nils Nordenskjold sailed the tortuous route across the top of Asia. Then, from 1903 to 1906 Roald Amundsen, sailing from Baffin Bay west to Nome, Alaska, finally traced the Northwest Passage.

**Sir Francis Drake** (*top*), *privateer turned English national hero, circled the globe and plundered a fortune from the Spanish in his 100-ton ship, the* Golden Hind. *A modern replica is shown above. Drake's drum, emblazoned with his coat of arms (opposite page), is the focus of a popular legend—if the drum is beaten when England is in great danger, Drake himself will return.*

*Captains and Colonists*

*Chapter Twelve. A marauding English captain in the service of Queen Elizabeth I is the first great navigator to complete a westward voyage around the world. On the way, his expedition braves the Strait of Magellan, ravages the treasure ships and ports of New Spain, unsuccessfully seeks the Northwest Passage, and sails through the Spice Islands.*

# The Devil at Sea:
# Drake Circles the Globe

*A legend in his own time, Francis Drake was born about 1540 in Devon, England. He earned his sea legs on a coastal trading vessel and became commander of his own ship on a slave-trading mission to South America in 1567–68. For the next few years he was a privateer, plundering Spanish ships and ports in the West Indies and South America. From 1577 to 1580 he led an expedition that sailed around the world, for which he was knighted by Queen Elizabeth I in 1581. In 1585–86 he again plundered the Spanish Main, and in 1587 he led an attack on Spain itself. He was vice admiral of the fleet that destroyed the Spanish Armada sent to crush England in 1588, and in 1589 he led an attack on Lisbon. Drake died at sea in 1596 on a final mission for plunder in the West Indies. He is honored as one of England's great heroes.*

On a February day in 1573 a stocky young sea captain stood on a hilltop in Panama, where he had been boldly looting treasure from Spanish warehouses. Encouraged by some Cimarron natives, the man climbed a tree and saw the vastness of the blue Pacific shining on the horizon. Thus Francis Drake became the first Englishman to see the world's greatest ocean.

It must have been an emotional experience. There and then, according to a sailor who was with him, "he besought Almighty God . . . to give him life and leave to sail once in an English ship in that sea."

Since the time of Ferdinand Magellan, the Pacific had been regarded as the exclusive territory of Spain. Trading galleons shuttled between the Philippines and Spanish America, depositing Asian silks and spices in warehouses already crammed with Peruvian gold and silver. As Drake sat in the tree and gazed at that distant sea, he burned with the desire to plunder it and so revenge himself for an act of Spanish treachery that had rankled him for a long time.

Five years earlier, in 1568, Drake had been sailing in the Caribbean, ostensibly on a slave-trading mission commanded by his cousin John Hawkins. Hurricanes damaged the English fleet, and Hawkins requested permission to repair his five ships in the Mexican port of San Juan de Ulúa, near modern-day Veracruz. Local authorities agreed only reluctantly, since their Catholic king, Philip II, violently disapproved of any contact with heretics. While the English ships lay at anchor, a much larger fleet arrived from Spain bringing the new viceroy of Mexico. At first the viceroy promised to tolerate the presence of Englishmen in his harbor, but a few days later he suddenly ordered an attack on Hawkins' crippled fleet. Three ships were captured, and every Englishman found on shore was put to death. Drake and Hawkins themselves escaped with the survivors and fled, beaten and disgraced, out to sea.

It was this incident, with its combination of cowardliness and deceit, that fueled Drake's ambition to sail in King Philip's private ocean, the Pacific, and "annoy him in his Indies." Queen Elizabeth, unwilling to provoke a war, allowed Drake to work off some of his hatred on short marauding raids on Spanish Atlantic shipping, which he did with such bravado and daring that Spaniards became terrified of him.

Finally, in 1577, the queen felt confident enough to sanction a full-scale expedition into the Pacific by way of the Strait of Magellan at the southern tip of South America. Drake's instructions were to reconnoiter the Pacific coast of South America. Apparently, he also intended to look for the mysterious continent of Terra Australis, believed to lie at the bottom of the globe; to establish trade with friendly natives; to annex any lands not already held by Spain or Portugal; and to sail "by the same way homeward as he went out." There was no mention of circling the globe. As for piracy en route, Drake's backers (who included the queen herself) refused to accept any responsibility. On the other hand, their sizable investments assured him they would cheerfully accept "any profits thereof."

By November 1577 a splendidly equipped fleet was ready to sail from Plymouth harbor. Drake's flagship was the *Pelican*, a 100-ton man-of-war armed with 18 guns. The other four ships were the *Elizabeth*, the *Swan*, the *Marigold*, and the *Christopher*.

Drake, who was of modest origins, surrounded himself with luxuries for his Pacific expedition. Up the gangplank of the *Pelican* went "expert musicians, rich furniture (all the vessels for his table, yea, many belonging even to the cook-room, being of pure silver) and divers shows of all sort of curious workmanship."

The voyage did not start auspiciously. Setting sail from Plymouth on November 15, 1577, Drake had to seek shelter from a storm in nearby Falmouth, where two of the ships were damaged. Forced to return to Plymouth for repairs, the fleet finally got under way on December 13. Favorable winds soon brought the ships to the coast of Morocco, where Drake announced to his astonished sailors (who, for security reasons, had been told they were on a trip to the Mediterranean) that their

real destination was the remote, mysterious Pacific.

Farther down the coast of Africa, off the Cape Verde Islands, Drake captured a Portuguese ship and relieved her of her cargo of wines, fine linens, and woolen cloth. For good measure, he added the ship herself to his fleet, although some months later he was to destroy the leaky hulk. But his most valuable prize was the ship's pilot, Nuno da Silva. A first-rate navigator who knew the South Atlantic well, this old man's valuable charts and nautical know-how were to serve his captor well all the way to the Strait of Magellan.

On April 5, 1578, after a tedious 63-day crossing of the Atlantic, a long, low line of land slid into view over the horizon. As the ships drew nearer, the men saw Indian fires burning and knew they were off the wild coast of Brazil. Foul weather and a lack of suitable harbors prevented Drake from landing until April 14, when he put into the estuary of the Río de la Plata, between present-day Uruguay and Argentina. There the crew killed seals on a rocky island in the bay to replenish the fleet's dwindling food supply.

On May 18 Drake reached the Gulf of St. George, about two-thirds of the way down the Argentine coast, where he destroyed the storm-damaged *Swan*. Going ashore to search for Magellan's reported Patagonian giants, he only found Indians who ran away when he approached. But curiosity soon got the better of them. Before long, the "exceedingly delighted" Indians were dancing to the tune of English trumpets and viols. One of them, carried away by the festivities, even snatched Drake's bright gold and scarlet cap from his head.

Somebody then offered one of the Indians a glass of strong Canary wine. "Taking the glass into his hand," wrote Francis Fletcher, the *Pelican*'s captain, "it came not to his lips when it took him by the nose and so suddenly entered into his head . . . that he fell flat upon his buttocks." The Indian then drank the wine, "from which time he took such a liking to wine that having learned the word every morning he would come down the mountains with a mighty cry, wine, wine, wine, till he came to our tent and would in that time have devoured more wine than 20 men could have done."

Relations with the Patagonians did not remain friendly very long. On June 20 the fleet anchored at Port St. Julian, just a little north of the dreaded Strait of Magellan. Anxious to replenish his water supply, Drake went ashore with six men, including Robert Winterhey, a gentleman-volunteer who carried a bow and arrow, and master-gunner Oliver, who brought along a fowling piece. When two young Patagonians approached, Winterhey set up some targets and organized an archery contest. The youths seemed pleased, until three older Indians appeared and suddenly made angry gestures. Just at that moment, Winterhey's bow string broke, and one of the Indians, "supposing there were no other engine of war in the world but bow and arrows . . . took present advantage, and charging his bow clapt

**Sir John Hawkins** (*above*), *a relative of Drake's, was a famous admiral in his own right. Drake served with Hawkins on the disastrous voyage of 1568, when English ships laden with African slaves were treacherously surprised and defeated by the Spanish off San Juan de Ulúa near Veracruz on the coast of Mexico.*

*Captains and Colonists*

## Masterpieces for Mariners: As Navigation Science Advanced, So Did the Quality of Its Tools

henaer appeared in English. The book combined a nautical manual with marine charts, and it soon became an indispensable part of a navigator's equipment. The seamen on the title page hold plumblines; above them hang astrolabes and quadrants. Marine instruments were also becoming both more elaborate and more accurate. Below is a 16th-century Spanish box containing a sundial and a compass of a type Drake might have captured from a treasure-laden galleon. At right is an intricate and finely deco-

One of Drake's first moves upon taking an enemy ship was to appropriate her marine charts and often to take her pilot aboard the *Golden Hind*. There were, however, less aggressive methods of obtaining marine information in the 16th century. In 1588 *The Mariner's Mirror* (above) by Dutch seaman Lucas Wag-

rated instrument called an astronomical compendium. The compendium contains five different faces, with tables showing tides, phases of the moon, and latitudes, as well as a calendar, a nocturnal for telling time by the Great Bear constellation at night, and a compass. A 19th-century English tradition claimed the instrument belonged to Drake, but this claim is difficult to prove. The compendium was made by Humphrey Cole, a leading British instrumentmaker, in 1569, so it is possible that Drake used it on his historic circumnavigation.

---

an arrow in the body of him and through his lungs." The horrified Oliver aimed his gun, "but the torch being dankish would not fire." He, too, received an arrow "in the breast and through the heart and out of the back of a rib a quarter of a yard at least."

Drake immediately took charge, ordering the rest of his companions to "shift from place to place" and shield themselves as best they could until the Indians ran out of arrows. He then seized Oliver's gun and "made a shot at him that began the quarrel, and striking him in the paunch with a hale shot, sent his guts abroad; it seemed by his cry, which was so hideous and horrible a roar, as if 10 bulls had joined in roaring, wherewith the courage of his partners was so abated they were glad by flying away to save themselves."

Another tragedy followed 10 days later. On June 30, 1578, Drake summoned all the ships' companies, lined up all the men, and announced his decision to bring one of them to trial. The man's name was Thomas Doughty. The charge: incitement to mutiny.

Ever since the fleet left England, this brilliant courtier had been a thorn in Drake's side. Some historians speculate that the queen's chief minister, Lord Burghley, worried that the expedition might provoke Spain, had sent Doughty along to undermine Drake's authority and thwart his attacks on Spanish ports and ship-

ping. Others feel that their differences were more a function of class conflict—Doughty was a gentleman, Drake was not. Whatever the truth may have been, witnesses attested that Doughty had tried to corrupt them, and a jury pronounced him guilty.

Drake seems to have offered Doughty three choices: He could be set ashore on the mainland; he could be sent back to England to face the wrath of the Privy Council; or he could be tried by the entire crew and possibly suffer execution on the spot. Doughty chose to be tried there and was sentenced to death. And so on July 2, after taking Communion and dining "at the same table together," the two men toasted each other "as if some journey only had been at hand." Then, "without any dallying or delaying the time," Thomas Doughty was beheaded. "This," roared Drake as the bloody head was held aloft, "is the end of traitors!"

Ironically, this same Port St. Julian had been the scene of the execution of Magellan's mutineers 58 years earlier. Drake's men actually found a gibbet, "fallen down, made of a spruce mast, with men's bones underneath." With Doughty's death, the English sailors named the place of execution the Isle of Blood.

Determined to restore unity in his ranks, Drake assembled all his men on shore a few days later and ad-

*Text continued on page 138.*

# The Golden Hind: A "Perfect Sailer" of 100 Tons

*Above, a likeness of Drake seated at the carved oak table in the Great Cabin. Here he held councils with his officers and took meals "served on silver dishes with gold borders and gilded garlands."*

Francis Drake's skill as a mariner was matched by the seaworthiness of his ship, the *Golden Hind*. Called a "perfect sailer" by a captured Spaniard, the ship was 90 feet long, 19 feet wide, weighed 100 tons, and carried a crew of approximately 80. In the cutaway painting below, two standing officers, dressed in the garb of 16th-century gentlemen, confer over a map in Drake's cabin. To the right of them, the helmsman, his head peeping out of a small hatch on the quarterdeck, works the tiller. In front of him, a sailor, cross-staff in hand, reads a small compass mounted on the rail and calls out the ship's bearings to the helmsman. Below, crewmen strain to turn the capstan, which raised the *Golden Hind*'s heavy anchor. Another seaman climbs the rigging as his shipmates swab the deck. Below decks, the ship's holds are crammed with supplies and captured Spanish gold and silver. Above the ballast, a cook labors over the open hearth of the cookroom. The photographs that accompany the picture of the *Golden Hind* were taken aboard a 20th-century reconstruction of Francis Drake's famous ship.

*Above, a golden hind, or female red deer, decorated the ship's stern and, below the painting, a bright, gaily decorated gallery gave officers a place to take a private stroll.*

*Drake's private cabin (top) contained his sea chest, with his armor resting on top of it, and a table with a half-hour glass and compass. A sea chart hung on the wall. Hand-carved knights heads (above) were used to fasten the rigging of the* Golden Hind's *mainmast.*

*The* Golden Hind's *cabins (top) were only for officers. Seamen bedded down on the decks, since hammocks were not yet in general use. When fully armed, the ship carried 18 guns (above), 7 mounted on each side and 4 in the bow.*

*From the crow's nest (top), sailors could spy treasure-laden Spanish ships and fire muskets and crossbows at the fleeing galleons. The head of a golden hind (above), the emblem of Sir Christopher Hatton, one of Drake's financial backers, adorned the ship's bow.*

137

**Naval warfare underwent great change** *during Drake's lifetime. The Spaniards still favored medieval-style battles in which boarding parties from rival ships engaged in hand-to-hand combat. The English, however, had begun to equip their ships with heavier guns, which were mounted below deck with portholes cut for the barrels, as shown in the battle scene here. In addition, English ships were lighter and therefore more maneuverable.*

*Discussing the defeat of the Spanish Armada, a contemporary chronicler named William Camden wrote: "For the English ships being far lesser than theirs, charged the enemy with agility and nimbleness and having given their broadsides, presently stood off at a distance from them and leveled their shot without missing at those great ships of the Spaniards which were heavy and altogether unwieldy." Drake, himself, helped defeat the Armada.*

dressed them in a ringing Devon burr. "We must have these mutinies and discords that are grown amongst us redressed," he declared, "for by the life of God it doth even take my wits from me to think of it; here is such controversy between the sailors and the gentlemen, and such stomaching between the gentlemen and sailors, that it doth even make me mad to hear it. But, my masters, I must have it left; for I must have the gentlemen to hale and draw with the mariner, and the mariner with the gentlemen."

Then, after offering the *Marigold* to any men who wanted to return home, he added in a menacing tone, "but let them take heed that they go homeward; for if I find them in my way I will surely sink them."

His words had their intended effect: Not a single man was for turning back. With a pledge to reward them well, Drake ordered the anchors raised and

headed for the Strait of Magellan. By now he had destroyed the *Christopher;* she was constantly becoming separated from the rest of the ships and getting lost for days or weeks at a time. Of his original fleet of five, only the *Pelican,* the *Marigold,* and the *Elizabeth* remained.

Sobered yet somehow united by their grim experience on the Isle of Blood, Drake and his men sailed into the cold, rainy maze of channels and islands at the tip of South America. Their old Portuguese pilot was of no use now: The strait had not been navigated for more than half a century. On August 20, 1578, they entered the strait, passing "high and steep gray cliffs . . . against which the seas beating." There Drake ordered his captains to strike topsails "in homage to our sovereign lady the Queen's Majesty" and ceremoniously renamed his flagship *Golden Hind* in honor of his friend and backer, Sir Christopher Hatton, whose coat of arms included the figure of a golden deer, or hind.

At first, the little fleet made slow headway, but Drake pushed steadily southwest, painstakingly maneuvering his ships between the mountains of Patagonia and the ominous landmass of Tierra del Fuego.

After four days the fleet put in at a group of islands. A landing party found plenty of plump birds charmingly described by one seaman as "fowl whose flesh is not unlike a fat goose in England." Noting that "they have no wings," he also observed that "They walk so upright, that afar off a man would take them to be little children." In a daylong orgy of killing, the landing party cudgeled some 3,000 of these penguins.

Drake continued along the strait through "turnings, and as it were shuttings up, as if there were no passage at all," until he found channels lined with banks of lichen-covered trees. Finally, early in September, he reached the strait's southernmost point. (Freezing in their woolen clothing, the sailors noticed with astonishment naked Indians "of mean stature" slipping through the forests.) Then the strait turned northwest, and a helping wind blew Drake's ships quickly toward its outlet, where the crews gazed in awe one night at the spectral appearance of a volcano.

The following day, September 6, 1578, the *Golden Hind* sailed into the limitless blue of the Pacific Ocean. But rain, snow, hail, and fog almost immediately obliterated it from view as "an intolerable tempest" unleashed itself on the English fleet. The stormy weather continued for an incredible 52 days.

Drake at first attempted to lead his ships up the coast of Chile, but contrary winds slammed into them with such force that they were swept helplessly southward toward the pole. On the night of September 30, shrieks of drowning men were heard on the wind. The next morning there was no sign of the *Marigold:* The Pacific had swallowed up its first English victims. On October 7 the *Elizabeth* managed to anchor in the strait, and the *Golden Hind* passed out of sight. John Winter, captain of the *Elizabeth*, awaited Drake's return for the rest of the month, but in vain. Concluding that his commander was dead, Winter then abandoned the expedition and returned home.

Although Drake continued to hope that the *Elizabeth* would rejoin him at a rendezvous along the coast of Chile, from that point on the *Golden Hind* sailed alone. As one sailor ruefully observed, if the ship had still been named the *Pelican*, "she might have been now indeed said to be as a pelican alone in the wilderness."

Once Drake lost sight of the *Elizabeth*, he was swept southward with such speed it seemed as if the fates were conspiring to make him discover Terra Australis whether he wanted to or not. "We were rather to look for present death than hope for any delivery," wrote one terrified observer as the ship heaved and men were tossed about "like a ball in a racquet."

Then, suddenly, on October 28, "God did wonder-

## A Mountain of Silver Was Mined for Spain

Much of the silver Drake captured came from the mines of Potosí, the richest in South America. According to legend, the mines (located in what is today Bolivia) were unknown to the Incas. They were discovered in 1545 by an Indian who uprooted a small tree and noticed silver ore clinging to the roots. Spurred on by his find, the Spaniards sunk mines in the area, which were soon producing great quantities of high-grade ore. The mountain of Potosí is shown in the top picture below, looming over the small Spanish colonial town in the foreground. Augustín de Zárate, who wrote a history of Peru in 1555, claimed the Indians who worked the mines grew rich on their wages. Other visitors to Potosí maintained the miners were little better than slaves. They worked underground in oppressive darkness relieved only by the flickering light of candles. Great gusts of wind swept the dark interior of the mines, and noxious vapors rising from the mine shafts added to the discomfort. One visitor to Potosí wrote of the miners: "There is no week that passes but some of them die, either by divers accidents that occur as the tumbling down of great quantities of earth and the falling of stones, or by such other casualties." The 16th-century picture at bottom, by Theodor de Bry, shows Indians laboring in the interior of the mines at Potosí. Drake's plunder included more than 26 tons of refined silver.

fully free us." The gale blew itself out, and the *Golden Hind* came to anchor off a group of southern islands. As one account of the voyage put it: "The uttermost cape or headland of all these islands [probably Cape Horn] stands near in 56°, without which there is no main nor island to be seen to the southward, but that the Atlantic Ocean and the South Sea [Pacific] meet in a most large and free scope." Thus, almost casually, Drake's chronicler announced the most momentous discovery of the voyage: that South America tapers off into nothingness. Terra Australis, if it existed at all, was far beyond the cold horizon to the south.

Drake was obviously moved by the sight of the intercontinental channel that now bears his name. Going ashore on the southernmost of the islands, he threw himself on the grass and embraced it, then returned to the ship and boasted to his crew "that he had been upon the southernmost known land in the world, and more further to the southward upon it than . . . any man as yet known."

After two days of rejoicing in the stability of dry land and marveling at the 22-hour subantarctic day (it was then late spring), the explorers set sail again and glided north along the mountainous coast of Chile in King Philip's "private sea."

On November 25, nearly a year after the voyage began, Drake approached an island "named of the Spaniards Mucho, by reason of the greatness and large circuit thereof." Going ashore for provisions, he re-

ceived a none-too-subtle reminder that other Europeans had been there before him. The Indians of Mucho, who had been driven from the mainland by Spanish cruelty, were friendly enough to Drake's party at first, presenting them with "fruits and other victuals as they had and two very fat sheep"—until one man, asking for water, let drop the Spanish word *agua*. With that, the Indians concluded that their visitors were Spaniards, and their hospitality instantly turned to rage. Hundreds of warriors brandishing bows and arrows fell upon the bewildered sailors, killing two and wounding nine. Drake himself received a shaft "under his right eye, and close by his nose, the arrow piercing a marvelous way in under *basis cerebri* [the seat of the brain], with no small danger to his life." Miraculously, neither his sight nor his sanity was affected, and his party managed to escape and sail on.

The throb of Drake's wound seems to have reawakened all his old hatred of Spain. Coasting north, he brazenly sailed into the port of Valparaíso on December 5 and looted a trading vessel anchored in the harbor. To the Spaniards on shore, this appearance of an English ship in "their" ocean was so astounding that they fled in terror. Drake remained in port until December 8 and calmly helped himself to a "great store of wine," provisions, and gold and silver from the church, including "a great cross of gold beset with emeralds."

Continuing north, the triumphant Drake saw New Year's Day in Salada Bay, well up the coast of Chile. There the *Golden Hind* was tipped, scraped, greased, and freshly rigged. The expedition sailed on at a leisurely pace, pausing to loot a silver caravan here, a trading bark there. On February 13, 1579, in Callao, the large port of Peru's capital city of Lima, Drake caused havoc by the simple technique of cutting anchored ships adrift. He stacked another 1,500 bars of silver in his rapidly filling hold but did not yet consider the score of San Juan de Ulúa settled. What Drake wanted was a major prize, a trophy that would both humiliate Spain and enrich him for the rest of his life.

He had to cross the Equator to find it. On March 1 the treasure ship *Cacafuego* appeared on the horizon. Crammed with gold and silver, she was sailing ponderously north to Panama. With catlike stealth, Drake held off until dusk—and then he pounced.

The *Cacafuego*'s captain, San Juan de Anton, was taken completely by surprise as the *Golden Hind* glided swiftly across his course and drew up alongside. When the English ordered the Spaniards to strike sail and De Anton refused, a whistle sounded on the *Golden Hind*, trumpets blared, and "a volley of what seemed to be about 60 arquebuses was shot, followed by many arrows . . . and chainballs shot from a heavy piece of ordnance." In no time at all, English archers were swarming all over the *Cacafuego*. They quickly seized San Juan de Anton and presented him to Drake, who, according to the official Spanish account, embraced his

**While the "Golden Hind" was being careened** *and repaired near San Francisco Bay on the California coast, Drake struck up friendly relations with the neighboring Miwik Indians. He even visited an Indian village "to see the manner of their dwelling and to be better acquainted with the nature and commodities of the country." This De Bry engraving, showing Drake and his men at an Indian village, is one of the first European views of a tepee.*

*Captains and Colonists*

## The Controversial Brass Plate Found Near Drake's San Francisco Area Landfall

Where did Sir Francis Drake land in California? The mystery has never been solved. Although several areas have claimed the distinction, the two principal contenders are San Francisco Bay and Drake's Bay (right), several miles farther up the coast. Some recent discoveries have only compounded the questions that already existed. In 1936 a man named Beryle Shinn discovered an eight- by five-inch brass plate inscribed with Drake's name (below) near Point St. Quentin in the San Francisco Bay area. The inscription states that Drake and his men had put into shore to repair the *Golden Hind* and

left the plate to lay claim to the surrounding territory. Subsequently, a chauffeur named William Caldeira claimed he had found the same brass plate in 1933 near Drake's Bay but discarded it where Shinn had picked it up. In addition to the dispute over its place of discovery, some scholars believe the plate is a clever forgery. They maintain that the brass is less than 400 years old and that the phrasing is not Elizabethan in style. Other finds have deepened the mystery. In 1974 an anthropologist reported discovering a small silver coin dated 1577 bearing a likeness of Queen Elizabeth I (upper left) in the excavation of a Miwik Indian village 30 miles north of San Francisco. The coin may offer evidence of Drake's visit, but it leaves scholars none the wiser about the location of Francis Drake's New Albion, his only encampment in North America.

captive "saying: 'Have patience, for such is the usage of war,' and immediately ordered him to be locked up in the cabin in the poop, with 12 men to guard him."

It took several days to transfer the *Cacafuego*'s treasure to the *Golden Hind*. In addition to "a certain quantity of Jewels and Precious Stones," the booty included 80 pounds of gold, 13 chests of silver coins, and 26 tons of uncoined silver, "value about 360,000 pesos."

Drake and his men, saying they had done Captain de Anton "a kindness, in freeing him of the care of those things with which his ship was laden," set their captives free and continued north. They passed the shores of Costa Rica just in time to witness one of that country's notorious earthquakes, "the force whereof was such that our ship and pinnace . . . were shaken and did quiver as if it had been laid on dry land."

On April 4 yet another treasure ship, the *Espírito Santo*, hove into view. Once again Drake struck by moonlight, and once again he was rewarded with a great load of loot. The *Espírito Santo*'s captain's embarrassed report of the piracy included a fascinating description of Drake the man, seen through Spanish eyes. "He is called Francisco Drake," wrote the captain, "and is a man of about 35 years of age, low of stature, with a fair beard, and is one of the greatest mariners that sails the seas, both as a navigator and commander." Observing that the *Golden Hind* "is a perfect sailer," he added that each crewman "takes particular

pains to keep his arquebus clean. He treats them with affection, and they treat him with respect." Clearly impressed by Drake's sumptuous lifestyle, he also reported that "He is served on silver dishes with gold borders and gilded garlands, in which are his arms. He carries all possible dainties and perfumed waters. . . . He dines and sups to the music of viols."

Reasoning, perhaps, that Drake could not steal any more gold without sinking, the Spanish authorities now began to debate which way El Draco would return home. Drake himself appeared to be undecided. He had no desire to tempt fate and go "by the same way homeward as he went out." He could head west across the Pacific like Magellan, but the distance deterred him. "He has an intense desire to return to his own country," wrote the captain of the *Espírito Santo*, and correctly predicted that Drake would seek the quickest way home—the unexplored Northwest Passage presumed to exist somewhere to the north. Drake's men also realized that if they discovered the passage and proved it navigable, "we should not only do our country a good and notable service, but we also ourselves should have a nearer cut and passage home."

On April 16 Drake sailed away from Spanish America and veered northwest. Within three weeks he was as far north as present-day Oregon, but "extreme and nipping cold" and "most vile, thick, and stinking fogs" forced him to abandon his search for a passage across

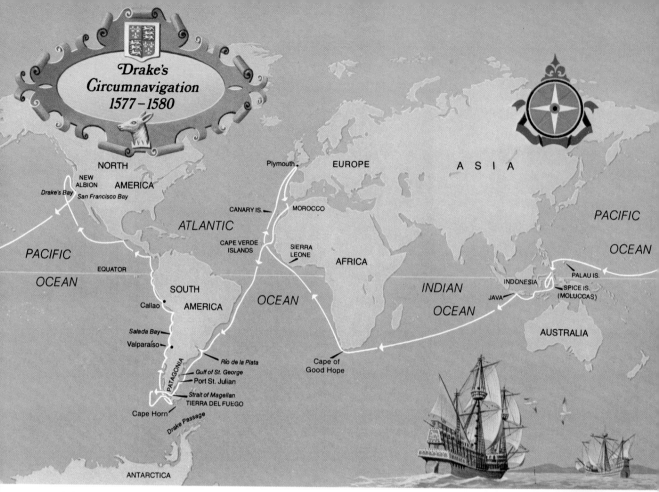

**Drake's Circumnavigation 1577–1580**

NORTH AMERICA
NEW ALBION
Drake's Bay
San Francisco Bay
Plymouth
EUROPE
ASIA
PACIFIC OCEAN
ATLANTIC
CANARY IS.
MOROCCO
CAPE VERDE ISLANDS
SIERRA LEONE
AFRICA
PACIFIC OCEAN
EQUATOR
SOUTH AMERICA
OCEAN
INDIAN OCEAN
INDONESIA
PALAU IS.
SPICE IS. (MOLUCCAS)
JAVA
Callao
Salada Bay
Valparaíso
Río de la Plata
Gulf of St. George
Port St. Julian
PATAGONIA
Strait of Magellan
TIERRA DEL FUEGO
Cape Horn
Drake Passage
Cape of Good Hope
AUSTRALIA
ANTARCTICA

**Drake's great voyage** *was as much a business venture as it was an exploration. A group of highly placed English investors, as well as Queen Elizabeth I and Drake himself, financed the expedition. Though he did a certain amount of legitimate trading, such as the purchase of tons of cloves in the Moluccas,*

*Drake's primary source of revenue came from the plunder of Spanish treasure ships, especially from the silver (right) they carried. His single ship (of the five that set out) returned with a profit of more than £500,000.*

the top of North America. The coast, his chronicler noted, ran "continually northwest, as if it went directly to meet Asia" and sadly concluded "that either there is no passage at all through these northern coasts (which is most likely), or if there be, that yet it is unnavigable."

Disappointed, Drake gave the order to turn about and returned south to warmer latitudes. Thus it was that Francis Drake, after some 18 months at sea, "sailed into a convenient and fit harbor, and on June 17, 1579, came to anchor therein."

Whether or not this "convenient and fit harbor" was San Francisco Bay or the nearby inlet now named Drake's Bay has never been decided by historians. What is certain is that Drake's sailors were the first Englishmen to land in California and that Drake named his "discovery" New Albion. Not realizing that a few Spanish explorers had been this way before him, he "caused to be set up a monument of our being there, as also of Her Majesty's and successors' right and title to that Kingdom; namely, a plate of brass, fast nailed to a great and firm post; whereon is engraven Her Grace's

name, and the day and year of our arrival."

Dazzled by Drake's fair complexion and rich clothes, the local Miwik Indians greeted him with a joy that soon turned into religious hysteria. Apparently under the impression they were being visited by a god, they "used unnatural violence against themselves, crying and shrieking piteously, tearing their flesh with their nails from their cheeks."

Frightened by this spectacle, Drake ordered his men to sing Christian psalms. Once again he proved that music does indeed have charms. The Indians lapsed into reverent silence and requested repeat performances throughout Drake's five-week stay.

Giving up all hope of discovering the elusive Northwest Passage, Drake now concluded that circumnavigation of the globe was the only way home. On July 23, 1579, the *Golden Hind* sailed out into the open ocean and for 68 days foamed steadily southwest across the Pacific. The first landfall was an island of the Palau archipelago, a little east of the Philippines. Unfortunately, the islanders proved inhospitable and "thought whatever they could finger to be their own." Disgusted, Drake christened the place Island of Thieves and sailed on to the Moluccas, the fabled Spice Islands, off the west end of New Guinea.

Although he was now trespassing in Portuguese territory, native spice traders welcomed him with open arms. The sultan of one island, claiming the Portuguese were his enemies, went so far as to sail out to greet the *Golden Hind* in person. Touched, Drake honored him with a cannon salute, "among which sounding out trumpets and other instruments of music." This so delighted the sultan that, in order to hear the music better, he had his boat tied to the *Golden Hind* "and was towed at least a whole hour together."

The Englishmen stayed in the Spice Islands for a week, loading up with cloves. On November 9, however, Drake, conscious that Queen Elizabeth must be wondering about her long-gone expedition—and unrealized investment—set off again.

As 1579 turned to 1580, the ship struggled through the tricky channels of Indonesia. Then, suddenly, on the night of January 9, the *Golden Hind*, wallowing under her load of treasure and spice, crunched into a coral reef. "She herself lying there," wrote one of the crew, "upon the hard and pinching rocks, did tell us plain, that she continually did expect her speedy dispatch." However, inspection proved that her magnificent timbers had sprung no leak. Drake lightened the load by tipping off eight guns and making the sea fragrant with jettisoned spice, and with the next tide the *Golden Hind* rolled off into deep water.

For another month the ship continued to flounder through bad weather among dangerous reefs and shoals. When conditions finally improved, Drake visited several islands to trade for fresh provisions. At Java his musical seamen exchanged serenades with local gamelan bands, and then on March 26 the *Golden Hind* put out to sea on a west by southwest course.

From that point on the voyage home was relatively untroubled. Off South Africa on June 15, the crew beheld the Cape of Good Hope, "a most stately thing and the fairest cape we saw on the whole circumference of the earth." In Sierra Leone on July 22, 1580, they observed such wonders as "great store of elephants, and oysters upon trees." The Cape Verde and Canary Islands were sighted and then the cliffs of Cornwall. And so, concluded Drake's chronicler, "on the 26th of September . . . we safely with joyful minds and thankful hearts to God, arrived in Plymouth, the place of our first setting forth, after we had spent 2 years, 10 months, and some few odd days beside, in seeing the wonders of the Lord in the deep, in discovering so many admirable things, in going through with so many strange adventures, in escaping out of so many dangers and overcoming so many difficulties in this our encompassing of this nether globe."

## A Fortune and Honors Came to Drake After His Voyage, but He Was a Captain to the End

When Francis Drake returned from his circumnavigation of the globe, he became a hero and a wealthy man. Drake was knighted by Queen Elizabeth I (right), who honored him by dining aboard the *Golden Hind*. The socially ambitious captain bought a country estate, Buckland Abbey (far right), in his native Devon. (Now a museum, the house was owned by Drake's family for more than 300 years.) Drake, however, was not to spend too much time in his new home. In 1585 he was once again back in the Caribbean, sacking the Spanish cities of Cartagena and Santo Domingo. Drake's raids aggravated the growing hostility between England and Spain. That hostility came to a climax when he led a daring attack against the Spanish fleet as it lay at anchor in Cádiz harbor. Outraged, King Philip II of Spain quickened his preparations to outfit a great armada to sail against England. In 1588, with much fanfare, the Spanish Armada put to sea. Spanish hopes for an easy victory, however, were dashed when the Armada was defeated in the

English Channel. The Spanish ships were badly outmaneuvered and outgunned in a battle that has become one of the most famous in naval history. Drake, whose actions had done so much to provoke the Spanish, was vice admiral of the vic-

torious English fleet at the time.

After the great triumph over the Armada, Drake's luck deserted him. Following an unsuccessful attempt to capture the Portuguese capital of Lisbon, he again set sail for the Caribbean. This time, however, his attempts to raid Spanish shipping ended in failure. Drake himself contracted a fever and died on the 28th of January 1596 off the coast of Panama. Appropriately enough, the great captain was buried in the blue waters of the Caribbean, where his desire to circle the globe had first occurred.

**Explorers of the far north** *had to dodge the ice floes that clogged the freezing waters (above). Hudson's path was often blocked by floating ice as he pushed his way into Hudson Bay on his final trip to the New World. His third voyage, up the Hudson River, had no such obstacles. Instead, he and his crew were the first Europeans to see the magnificent scenery along the Hudson Highlands (right).*

**Adam Willaerts, a 17th-century** *Dutch artist noted for his marine paintings, depicted the colorful life of an English port at the time Hudson set out on his quest for a northwest passage. Like many mariners of his day, Hudson sailed for those who* *would back his voyages, whether or not they were his own countrymen. Although English, he made his third trip to explore for the Netherlands. A picture from his journal of that voyage, published in Amsterdam in 1663, is shown opposite.*

*Captains and Colonists*

## Chapter Thirteen

*An English sea captain, voyaging for the Netherlands, discovers a great river in North America as he seeks the fabled Northwest Passage to the Orient. Later, sailing on a similar mission for England across the top of the New World, he encounters mutiny and abandonment on the desolate waters of a huge bay in Canada.*

# Daring Northern Waters: Hudson's Voyages

*A man of mystery, Henry Hudson first appeared on the stage of history in 1607 and disappeared just four years later. Nothing is known of his early career, but in the last years of his life this persistent English navigator made four attempts to find a northern shortcut to the Orient. In 1607, working for the English Muscovy Company, he sailed north between Greenland and Spitsbergen in an attempt to find a northeast passage across the North Pole. He came within 10 degrees of the pole when impenetrable pack ice forced him back. In 1608 he tried again, unsuccessfully seeking a route to the Orient along the northern coast of Asia. It is on his two last voyages— to North America in 1609 for the Dutch East India Company and in 1610–11 for some English merchants—that Henry Hudson's fame rests.*

The wily merchants of the Dutch East India Company liked the things they heard about Henry Hudson. In just two years that English sea captain had sprung from obscurity to international repute for his exploits in Arctic seas. Though his two attempts to forge a northern route to the spice-rich islands of the Orient had both ended in failure, he had sailed within 10 degrees of the pole, farther north than anyone had reached before. In addition, his skill and daring in battling icebound northern seas had earned him quite a reputation as a navigator of difficult passages.

When the Dutch summoned Hudson to Amsterdam to discuss the possibility of sailing for them, he went immediately. By then he was obsessed by a dream of discovering the elusive northern passage to the Far East. Since his English backers were unwilling to finance any further exploration, he was ready to sail for the Dutch or the king of France or anyone else who would foot the bills.

On January 8, 1609, Hudson signed a contract with the Dutch East India Company agreeing "to search for

a passage by the North, around by the north side of Novaya Zemlya" to the Orient. Novaya Zemlya, an island barrier jutting from the northern coast of Russia into the Arctic Ocean, had blocked Hudson's passage to the East in 1608, but, undiscouraged, he was eager to try again to find a way around it or through it.

About April 6, 1609, Henry Hudson set sail from Amsterdam in a little yachtlike vessel named the *Half Moon*. Included in his 16-man crew of Dutch and English sailors was an aging mariner from London, one Robert Juet. He had been mate on Hudson's 1608 voyage and would in time play a sinister role in Hudson's fate. Fortunately, he kept a journal—Hudson's own log has disappeared—and Juet's terse commentary is the only firsthand account we have of Hudson's venture for the Dutch East India Company.

Sailing up the west coast of Norway, the crew sighted its North Cape on May 5, and the *Half Moon* veered east into the hazardous waters of the Barents Sea. There the temperature plummeted below freezing. Violent gales alternated with thick, all-enveloping fogs, and great chunks of ice heaved on the swells around the ship. Before long the decks were slick with ice, and even the sails and rigging were frozen stiff.

Sailing through "close stormy weather, with much wind and snow" was thoroughly familiar to Hudson and his English seamen, but it came as a shock to the Dutchmen in the crew, who were accustomed to cruising through balmy tropical seas en route to the Indies. As the temperature dropped, so did their spirits. Soon they were grumbling about the folly of risking their lives on such a voyage. By the middle of May they rebelled openly, resolutely refusing to sail any farther north. Henry Hudson was faced with mutiny.

It was not the first time Hudson had had trouble with a crew. The year before, sailing in these same waters, his men had forced him to return home and compelled him to cover their insubordination by signing a certificate testifying to his "free and willing return, without persuasion or force."

A vacillating, ineffective leader of men—a fatal flaw in any explorer—Hudson once again gave into his crew's demands. Disregarding the terms of his contract, he abandoned the search for a northeast passage before he had even sighted Novaya Zemlya and turned the *Half Moon* back toward Norway.

The decision may not have been a difficult one. Apparently, Hudson had doubts about the feasibility of a northeast passage. Before leaving Amsterdam, he had met with learned geographers and eagerly discussed the possibility of a northwest passage through America. He had also received letters and maps from his friend Capt. John Smith at the infant settlement at Jamestown, Virginia. Smith had fired his imagination with suggestions that there might be a strait to the Pacific somewhere to the north of the Virginia colony. Showing the crew Smith's letters and charts, Hudson persuaded them to probe the North American coast for a passage to the Indies.

Heading southwest, the *Half Moon* made a stormy

### Compasses Behaved Strangely in the Arctic

Nothing so thoroughly changed the art of navigation as the discovery that lodestone, a magnetic iron ore, or a piece of iron touched by lodestone would unerringly point toward magnetic north. From this discovery came the compass, the most valuable of all marine instruments. Western Europeans were using the compass as early as the 12th century, and the Arabs employed it a century later. The earliest compasses were simple affairs in which a piece of magnetized iron attached to a wood splinter was floated in a bowl of water. By the 16th century compasses were far more elaborate, such as the one pictured below. A magnetized iron needle was suspended on a pin above a marked card, which sailors called a wind rose. The card itself was enclosed in a bowl that was held in place by gimbals, hinges that held the compass level so accurate readings could be taken despite the pitching and tossing of the ship. Still, the compass was not unfailingly correct. There is a variation between magnetic north and true north that transoceanic explorers starting with Columbus noticed. The problem was most acute for those like Hudson who explored the Arctic, since the

compass variation increases as one goes farther north. William Baffin, another Englishman who searched for a northwest passage, complained in 1616 about his compass "whose wonderful operation is . . . increasing and decreasing so suddenly and swift, a thing almost incredible and matchless in all the world." It was the powerful fluctuation of the magnetic pole.

crossing of the North Atlantic and reached the coast of Maine in mid-July. The ship then coasted south past Cape Cod, across the dangerous Nantucket Shoals, and by mid-August was off the mouth of Chesapeake Bay, the "entrance into the King's River in Virginia, where our Englishmen are."

Perhaps because he was sailing under the Dutch flag, Hudson made no effort to contact Smith at Jamestown. Instead, he turned about and sailed north to examine the coast more closely for the rumored strait to the Pacific. He paused briefly to probe the mouth of Delaware Bay, but it was so full of treacherous shoals and sandbars that he concluded it could not be the passage he was looking for. Continuing up the New Jersey coast, he rounded the glistening sandbars of Sandy Hook and on September 2, 1609, found himself at the mouth of a vast open bay—the lower bay of New York harbor. (Many years before, in 1524, Giovanni da Verrazano, an Italian sailing for the king of France, had discovered this same bay and spent a few hours exploring it. But no one had followed up on his voyage, and his discovery was soon forgotten.)

Hudson's spirits must have soared at the sight of the forest-fringed harbor. Judging from the strength of the current flowing out of the bay, he realized that it had to be the mouth of some great river or strait. Perhaps this was the road to the riches of the Orient so many explorers before him had sought and had failed to find.

"This is a very good land to fall with," Juet exclaimed with delight, "and a pleasant land to see." Indeed it was. For several days the crew puttered around the lower bay, fishing, taking soundings, going ashore here and there. The bay, they quickly decided, "was a very good harbor," teeming with "salmons, and mullets, and rays, very great." (One day they "caught 10 great mullets, of a foot and a half long apiece, and a ray as great as four men could hale into the ship.") Venturing ashore, they "saw great store of very goodly oaks" and admired areas "as pleasant with grass and flowers and goodly trees as ever they had seen."

Here, too, they encountered Indians of the many tribes that lived around the bay. Obviously impressed by the strange white men and their gigantic canoe, the Indians came aboard dressed in their finest: "some in mantles of feathers, and some in skins of diverse sorts of good furs." Juet also noted covetously that "they had red copper tobacco pipes, and other things of copper they did wear about their necks." Although the Indians seemed "very glad of our coming . . . and are very civil," Juet guardedly added, "we durst not trust them."

The next day his suspicions were justified when five men set out in the ship's boat to take soundings in the bay. As they returned in the evening, they were attacked for no apparent reason by two canoes filled with Indians. Two sailors were injured in the fray and a third, John Coleman—the only casualty of the voyage—was killed when an arrow pierced his throat. Un-

## It Was a Golden Age for Holland's Mariners and Mapmakers

Incredible energy flowed out of Holland in the 17th century, making that small nation both the cultural and financial center of the European continent. In 1609 a truce was concluded with Spain that temporarily gave the Netherlands its long-sought independence. With their country no longer preoccupied by war, the Dutch focused national attention on the expansion of their mercantile empire. Maritime trade became the lifeblood of Holland, whose borders are washed by the sea. In 1602 several small companies were consolidated to form the Dutch East India Company, which grew to dominate the spice trade with the Far

mariners were taught the use of the cross-staff, astrolabe, and compass, as well as the latest geographic intelligence from globes and charts (below). In addition, the Dutch were the most important mapmakers of the 17th century, replacing the Italians and the Portuguese who had earlier dominated the field. Mapmaking acquired prominence in the Low Countries with the publication of the famous world map by Flemish cartographer Gerardus Mercator in 1569. The Dutch East India Company also maintained its own mapmaking division, which helped to insure Dutch superiority in the field of cartography. Finely printed

came one of the most respected in Europe. The Dutch rationalist Benedict Spinoza was among the best known philosophers of the age. A Dutch shopkeeper with no formal scientific training, Antonie van Leeuwenhoek was the first man to observe bacteria under a microscope and became one of the pioneers of modern biology. Holland's lively intellectual life, combined with its commercial dominance, gave a new adventurousness to Dutch society. As a result, the Netherlands successfully competed with much larger powers in exploration for new territories and expanded overseas trade.

East during the 17th century. The company not only promoted trade but also actively encouraged the acquisition of new territory. Henry Hudson, in fact, was sailing in the employ of the Dutch East India Company on his third voyage when he discovered the great river that today bears his name.

Amsterdam, the headquarters of the Dutch East India Company, became the most important maritime center of 17th-century Europe. All arts related to navigation flourished in that busy city. There were schools where ambitious

Dutch atlases and maps (such as the one below right of the New England area) were the best made. Jan Vermeer, one of the most famous Dutch artists of the century, painted a geographer poised thoughtfully over a map (above right).

In 17th-century Holland, commerce and art blended with remarkable harmony. Noted artists, such as Rembrandt and Frans Hals, often painted portraits of the solid merchants who dominated Dutch society. Intellectual life also thrived amid the hurly-burly of the marketplace. The university at Leiden be-

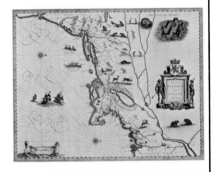

able to find the *Half Moon* in the dark, the terrified survivors spent the night paddling randomly about the bay waiting for dawn.

Sobered by this experience, the next day the crew built up the sides of the little boat with boards "for defense of our men." They became so wary they were scarcely willing to let Indians on board the *Half Moon*. Even so, they continued to trade for tobacco, beans, corn, and "great store of very good oysters . . . which we bought for trifles."

Passing through the Narrows, the *Half Moon* entered the sheltered upper bay of New York's wasp-waisted harbor. There she anchored overnight off the shore of a gently rolling, densely forested island "on that side of

the river that is called Manna-hata." Some have suggested that her anchorage was near the west end of modern Manhattan's 42nd Street.

Then began the journey up the Hudson River itself, a vast estuary where, even 150 miles inland, the water level rises and falls over four feet with the ebb and flow of the tide. The trip, in "fair sunshining weather," must have been a pleasant one, though Juet's comments are sparse. Beyond Manhattan Island, the men undoubtedly admired the spectacular cliffs of the Palisades, the broad expanse of the Tappan Zee, and the abrupt narrowing of the channel where the river is hemmed in by the ancient, deeply eroded peaks of the Hudson Highlands. Past the site of present-day West

## Ice, Fool's Gold, and Eskimos: First Attempts to Find a Northern Passage

Never were there more resolute adventurers than the explorers who sailed small wooden ships across Arctic seas in an attempt to find a northern passage to the Orient. Such a passage was particularly important to England and Holland, both of which wanted a share of the Far East trade controlled by Spain and Portugal. The latter monopolized the southern routes to India and China.

A Dutchman, Willem Barents, led three of the best known expeditions to find a northeast passage, a waterway above Scandinavia and Russia leading to the Far East. Although Barents' voyages aroused initial hope of success, all ended in failure. On his last trip, in 1596, Barents and his men were trapped by polar ice and forced to spend the winter on Novaya Zemlya, a group of frozen islands off northern Siberia. As winter closed in, the crew built a small shelter on land, a sketch of which was made by a member of the crew (below left). When spring came, only 15 men had managed to survive the unbelievable rigors of the Arctic winter. Yet amazingly, in 1871, more than 250 years after Barents' party had left the inhospitable northern wasteland, a Norwegian fisherman found the ruins of their rude shelter, complete with a device to tell time, a gun barrel, and a flute. Even the sailors' clogs were well preserved (top left).

Barents' failure to find a northeast passage refocused attention on a northwest passage, a possible strait cutting through the top of America to China. Martin Frobisher (right), an Englishman,

Point they sailed, through the fertile valley beyond, and north past the undulating mass of the Catskill Mountains. "There," Juet noted, "we found very loving people, and very old men: where we were well used."

Three days later Hudson himself went ashore with an old chief "who carried him to his house and made him good cheer." One of the few surviving fragments of Hudson's own commentary on the voyage may refer to this landing. "The land is the finest for cultivation that I ever in my life set foot upon," he declared and noted that it was "very abundant in all kinds of timber suitable for shipbuilding and for making large casks or vats." He observed that his hosts were drying corn and beans "enough to load three ships, besides what was growing in the fields" and wrote, "On coming nearer the house, two mats were spread out to sit upon, and immediately some food was served in well-made red wooden bowls; two men were also dispatched at once with bows and arrows in quest of game, who soon after brought in a pair of pigeons which they had just shot." He was regaled by his Indian hosts with a feast of freshly killed game and "a fat dog" skinned "in great haste, with shells which they had got out of the water."

Unlike his suspicious crew, Hudson was sympathetic and amicable in his dealings with Indians. "The natives are a very good people," he concluded, "for when they saw that I would not remain, they supposed that I was afraid of their bows, and taking the arrows, they broke them in pieces and threw them into the fire."

On September 19 Hudson anchored the *Half Moon* near the site of present-day Albany, New York, about 150 miles north of New York harbor. By this time he must have begun to doubt that the Hudson River was the Northwest Passage leading to the Pacific Ocean. The next day he sent a boat upstream to take soundings and learned that the river grew narrower and more shallow. He planned to test the channel even farther upstream the following day but was prevented when "much people resorted aboard."

Determined to find out "whether they had any treachery in them," the Europeans plied the Indians with "so much wine and aqua vitae [whisky] that they were all merry." One chief, in fact, became so drunk that he slept quietly all night on board the *Half Moon*.

confidently proclaimed "Frobisher's streytes, like as Magellanus at the South-west end of the world." The Englishman's "straits," however, proved to be only a bay. Since winter was approaching, Frobisher returned to England without exploring the entire bay, vowing to return the next year. He brought back a sample of Arctic rock that the backers of his expedition had tested for gold. Although an assayer declared the rock contained the precious metal, in reality it contained only iron pyrites, or "fool's gold." On his two subsequent voyages, however, Frobisher mined this worthless Arctic rock and filled the holds of his ship with it. While the rock proved valueless, his second voyage provided valuable anthropological information.

Frobisher's crew may have included John White, the first European artist to draw pictures of Eskimos, the inhabitants of the far north. His drawing of an Eskimo man is shown at right. One of Frobisher's sailors described the Eskimos as "Men of large corporature, and good proportion; their colour is not much unlike the Sunne burnt countrie man." Frobisher's relations with the Eskimos were not always cordial. White painted a scene (opposite right) of Eskimos who "fiercely assaulted our men with their bowes and arrows." Although Frobisher discovered Greenland and explored southern Labrador, he and a host of later explorers searched in vain for a northwest passage to the Orient. One was not discovered until the 20th century, when Norwegian explorer Roald Amundsen found a way through the ice-strewn polar sea on his 1903–06 expedition to the far north. The Northeast Passage had been negotiated in 1878–79 by Nils Nordenskjold, a Swede.

had led the earliest serious attempts to find this fabled passage. Frobisher's first expedition left England in 1576, and on July 21 of that year, he sailed into a large body of water off Baffin Island that he

Though mystified by the powers of the white men's potent drink, the Indians proved friendly. The next afternoon they returned and brought Hudson gifts, including a great platter full of venison that they ate with the explorers in a display of friendship.

This pleasant interlude ended very abruptly that evening with the return of the ship's boat, which Hudson had sent up the river again "to try what depth and breadth it did bear." The news was disheartening. Hudson's men reported that just a few miles upstream the river became so shallow that they "found it to be an end for shipping to go in."

Clearly, the Hudson River was no northwest passage, yet the trip was not a total failure. Thanks to Hudson's voyage, the Dutch soon established a claim to the entire Hudson Valley. Within a few years they had settled New Amsterdam on Manhattan Island, set up a trading post near Albany, and were reaping the profits of a brisk fur trade. Even today, the region's Dutch heritage is evident in such place names as Staatsburg and Staten Island (originally Staaten Eylandt), Spuyten Duyvil Creek, Kinderhook, and Rensselaer.

But thoughts of settlement were no consolation to Hudson. On September 23 he weighed anchor and began a leisurely return down the great river. Here and there he stopped to trade with Indians, to gather chestnuts, to stroll on shore. Viewing the countryside around the present-day city of Newburgh, Juet noted, "This is a very pleasant place to build a town on." He scanned the mountains too, commenting that they looked "as if some metal or mineral were in them." The only excitement came from a couple of skirmishes with unfriendly Indians. By October 4 the *Half Moon* emerged from the great river and steered off into the sea.

Hudson arrived in England early in November and immediately sent his Dutch employers a report on the voyage and a proposal to lead another expedition. But the English government, realizing what a prize it had lost by letting Hudson sail for the Dutch, forbade him to leave the country.

Instead, a group of wealthy English merchants formed a private syndicate to finance Hudson's next voyage. He had tried—and failed—to find a route to the Far East along the north coast of Asia and through the

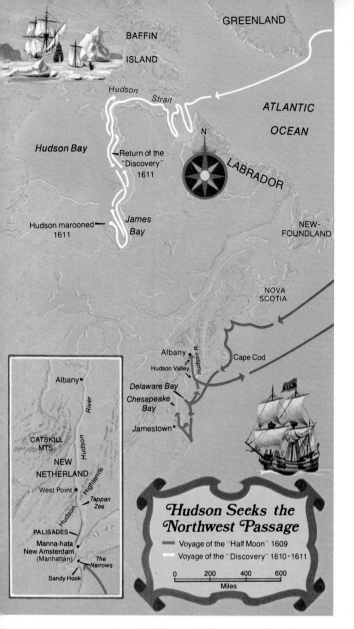

GREENLAND

BAFFIN
ISLAND

Hudson Strait

ATLANTIC
OCEAN

N

Hudson Bay

Return of the
"Discovery"
1611

LABRADOR

Hudson marooned
1611

James
Bay

NEW-
FOUNDLAND

NOVA
SCOTIA

Albany
Hudson Valley

Hudson R.

Cape Cod

Delaware Bay
Chesapeake
Bay

Jamestown

**Hudson Seeks the
Northwest Passage**

— Voyage of the "Half Moon" 1609
— Voyage of the "Discovery" 1610-1611

0    200    400    600
Miles

Albany

Hudson River

CATSKILL
MTS.

NEW
NETHERLAND

West Point

Hudson Highlands

Tappan
Zee

PALISADES

Manna-hata
New Amsterdam
(Manhattan)

The
Narrows

Sandy Hook

**Though Hudson did not achieve his goal** *of finding a northern passage to the Orient, his third voyage ultimately led to the founding of New Netherland, Holland's first colony in the New World. The* Half Moon's *route up the Hudson River more or less traced the area of the eventual Dutch settlement that began in 1621, 12 years after Hudson's voyage. The fate of the explorer in Hudson Bay on his fourth voyage—this time for the English in the* Discovery—*did not encourage further ventures into the north.*

North American continent. This time his orders were to probe dimly known straits and inlets in the Canadian Arctic to see if "any passage might be found to the other ocean called the South Sea."

On April 17, 1610, the indefatigable navigator set sail for the fourth time in as many years to seek the elusive shortcut to the Orient. Young John Hudson accompanied his father, and the enigmatic Juet once again was mate. Also on board was Abacuk Prickett, whose

sprightly account of the voyage provides most of the known details of the strange events that took place on Hudson's new ship, the *Discovery*.

There seems to have been friction among the crew from the very outset, which slowed the Atlantic crossing. Within a few days Hudson dismissed one crewman and sent him back to London. Pausing at Gravesend, he took aboard a final crewmember, Henry Greene, a young ne'er-do-well. Despite Greene's "lewd life and conversation," Hudson for some reason took the young wastrel under his wing.

By mid-May the *Discovery* reached Iceland, where contrary winds forced a two-week delay. There Greene picked a fight with the ship's surgeon, "which set all the company in a rage." Hudson condoned the incident, however, blaming it on the surgeon's caustic tongue.

Juet was incensed, darkly warning that the expedition would end with "manslaughter, and prove bloody to some." When at last they got under way again, Hudson learned that Juet had also been spreading a tale that Greene had been put aboard to spy on the rest of the crew. Hudson was tempted to set Juet ashore at Iceland to find his way to England as best he could but, unfortunately, was persuaded not to do so.

Rounding the southern tip of Greenland, the *Discovery* threaded westward through ice-clogged seas. Late in June she was at the mouth of Hudson Strait, a 450-mile-long channel between the Canadian mainland and the southern end of Baffin Island. Despite dense fog and heaving ice floes drifting south toward the open sea, Hudson resolutely headed his ship into the strait. Nosing between huge masses of ice "as between two lands," the ship tacked north and south wherever Hudson could find an opening in the ice. Gradually working his way northwest, he christened new islands and headlands with such optimistic names as Desire Provoketh and Hold With Hope.

But the crew was less optimistic, and soon another rebellion was brewing. Hudson quelled the discontents by letting the men vote "whether they would proceed any further; yea, or nay." After much argument the yeas carried the day, and the ship continued on her way. A tiny, lonely, and fragile vessel, the *Discovery* poked her way between rock-cliff shores that loomed and disappeared like phantoms in the fog. In contrast to the lush beauty of the Hudson Valley, the desolate shores of Hudson Strait were lined with rock and ice and snow. An oppressive silence was interrupted only by the screams of sea birds nesting in the cliffs, their calls reverberating in the fog.

Yet Hudson's indomitable faith in his goal of finding a passage seemed justified when, early in August, he sailed between two towering headlands into a vast open sea that looked as if it might stretch all the way to Asia. Repressing the jubilation he must have felt, on August 3 he wrote the last entry in the fragmentary remains of his journal: "Then I observed and found the ship at noon in 61°20′ and a sea to the westward."

That "sea to the westward," of course, was Hudson Bay, and it leads not to Asia but deep into the Canadian wilderness. To Hudson, however, it had the look of a dream come true. Confident that success was at hand, he sailed swiftly south along the eastern shore of the great body of water.

Instead of sailing into the Pacific, early in September he sailed into the pocketlike recess of James Bay, the southernmost extremity of Hudson Bay. It must have been a bitter blow, and Hudson reacted bitterly when Juet now openly criticized his actions. Placing him on public trial before the rest of the crew, Hudson proved Juet guilty of "many and great abuses, and mutinous matters against the master." Juet, in disgrace, was replaced as mate by Robert Bylot.

Like an angry lion pacing in its cage, Hudson spent the next several weeks tacking back and forth, north and south, east and west "in a labyrinth without end." By now it was clear to the weary, frightened crew that Hudson intended to winter on the bay. "And it was time," Prickett noted sourly, "for the nights were long and cold, and the earth covered with snow." On November 1 the ship was hauled into shallow water at the southern end of James Bay, and by the 10th she was frozen in until spring.

The prospect of wintering in this desolate wilderness with insufficient supplies was frightening, and everyone's temper was on edge. When the ship's carpenter refused to build a house on land for the crew to winter in, Hudson had a falling out with him, "calling him by many foul names, and threatening to hang him." Then he quarreled with his onetime favorite, Henry Greene, railing at him "with so many words of disgrace" and declaring "that all his friends would not trust him with 20 shillings." He soon made peace with the carpenter, but Greene nursed his grudge and "did the master what mischief he could in seeking to discredit him."

Tension mounted steadily as the long, bitterly cold winter wore on. With food supplies low and constant exposure to the dampness and cold, the crew was wracked with illness. Though the men managed to shoot more than 1,000 willow ptarmigan, provisions were so short that Hudson had to ration them. By spring, despite the return of migrating ducks and geese, the crew was close to starvation. "Then we went into the woods, hills, and valleys," Prickett dolefully reported, to search for "all things that had any show of substance in them, how vile soever." In desperation the men ate frogs—"as loathsome as a toad" in Prickett's estimate—and even moss, which Prickett pronounced as appetizing as sawdust.

Early in June the ice on the bay broke up, and the *Discovery* set sail. Hudson by then had appointed his third first mate of the voyage. He had replaced Bylot with John King, an illiterate sailor. His purpose, some muttered darkly, was to be able to sail the ship wher-

**A 19th-century painting shows** *Hudson and his son in the small boat in which they and seven sailors were abandoned by the mutinous crew of the* Discovery. *They faced a certain death from starvation and exposure on the bleak, icy waters of Hudson Bay.*

ever he chose and without interference—perhaps even to resume his futile search for a northwest passage.

With just two weeks' rations left, the only passage that mattered to the crew was the one that led home. Finally, the tension on the ship broke. Never wholly committed to Hudson, some of the men were now convinced he was playing favorites and distributing their meager rations unequally. Hudson, in turn, suspected that some of the sailors were hoarding food and ordered a search of their lockers.

On June 22, 1611, all the fears, suspicions, and hatreds of the crew erupted into open mutiny. Led by the wily Juet and Henry Greene, who declared "he would rather be hanged at home than starved abroad," the crew seized Hudson as he emerged from his cabin. One by one, Hudson, his son, John King, and six sailors were lowered into the tiny, open ship's boat being towed astern. With that, the rope was cut, and the little boat was set adrift on the icy water of the bay.

And with that fatal act, the career of a great explorer came to an end. His memorials are the river, the strait, and the great bay that bear his name. The *Discovery* and her traitorous crew returned to England, where the story was revealed and the ringleaders punished.

**Samuel de Champlain,** *the father of New France, was not only a successful colonizer but also one of the most accomplished navigators of his day. He drew the map above, considered the most accurate rendition of Canada for many years after it was published in 1632. Champlain's map includes the New England coast, an area he had once reconnoitered for a site to found a French colony.*

**Champlain wrote** *many books on New France, hoping to gain more settlers for his colony. At left is the title page of one of his works. French settlers in Canada, often surrounded by Indians, relied on firearms to defend themselves and protect their fledgling colony. At far left is an early 17th-century French soldier, musket in hand.*

## Chapter Fourteen

*An extraordinary* capitaine ordinaire *establishes a French settlement in North America and maps the land's forests, lakes, and rivers. He also befriends many Canadian Indian tribes and aids them in their wars with the dreaded Iroquois. That alliance will influence the eventual fate of the colony he has so carefully founded.*

# Father of New France: Champlain in Canada

*"Would God that all the French who were first come into these regions had been like him," wrote a 17th-century chronicler paying tribute to Champlain's relations with the Indians of Canada. Born at Brouage, France, about 1570, Samuel de Champlain made his first visit to Canada in 1603, after several voyages to the West Indies. He sailed up the St. Lawrence River as far as present-day Montreal and later (1604–07) joined a group of colonists trying to set up fur-trading posts on the shores of the Bay of Fundy. He also explored and accurately mapped the New England coast from Nova Scotia to Cape Cod. Following the founding of Quebec in 1608, he continued to explore the vast Canadian interior. He died in Quebec on Christmas Day in the year 1635, leaving three adopted Indian daughters: Faith, Hope, and Charity.*

With white sails billowing before the wind, a tiny ship foamed steadily up the St. Lawrence River in the summer of 1608. It was not the first ship to pass this way. Some 73 years earlier, Jacques Cartier had discovered the "Great River of Canada" and claimed it for France. Even before that, European fishermen harvesting cod off the coasts of Newfoundland had been anchoring along its banks each summer, but none remained for long. After drying their fish and trading with local Indians for beaver, marten, and other precious furs, they rigged their sails and headed for home.

This ship was different. Her 38-year-old commander, Samuel de Champlain, not only intended to pass the winter in the Canadian wilderness but also planned to establish a permanent French settlement there.

Champlain had already spent three winters in the New World, attempting to set up trading posts on the shores of Nova Scotia's Bay of Fundy. Those attempts had ended in failure. Now, with the backing of a wealthy merchant, he was about to try again, this time on the forested banks of the St. Lawrence, where his trading post would be closer to the source of the furs—the unmapped, unknown interior of North America.

And who could tell? Perhaps the St. Lawrence was the gateway to the Northwest Passage, that rumored water route across North America to the Orient. If so, Champlain's settlement would control a route to the most lucrative trade ever discovered.

Champlain had no intention of setting up his post near the river's mouth. Up to 70 miles wide, the channel there is too broad to defend against intruders. As the river curves around the Gaspé Peninsula, however, it tapers like a funnel until, about 350 miles inland, it is nearly blocked by the Island of Orleans. Southwest of the island, the St. Lawrence abruptly narrows to less than a mile across. "Here," Champlain noted, "begins the fine, good country of the great river."

This spot the Indians called Kebec, their word for "the narrowing of the waters." Champlain later commented: "I looked for a place suitable for our settlement, but I could not find any more suitable or better situated than the point of Quebec," as he translated the Indian term.

So, on July 3, 1608, he had his crew anchor and ordered the men ashore on a point of land jutting into the river beneath tall rocky cliffs. On that day began the founding of the city of Quebec and of a great nation that ultimately spanned the continent.

Throughout the summer Champlain's men toiled to clear an area of trees and sawed the logs into stout planks. The fortress they built was no mean, temporary affair. Around a central courtyard were a storehouse "with a fine cellar six feet high" and three two-story dwellings. A towering dovecote rose between the buildings, and on one of the roofs was a sundial and a mast to hold the fluttering banner of France. Surrounding all the buildings at second-story level, and pierced with loopholes for guns, was a gallery that Champlain called

*Map for Champlain on page 160.*

"a very convenient thing." For added protection a moat, complete with drawbridge at the entrance, ran around the entire settlement, and outside the moat was a wooden palisade with platforms for cannon. Champlain was ready to face any intruders.

Despite all his preparations, winter took a gruesome toll of the settlers. Huddled in their drafty lodgings and living mainly on vegetables and salted meat, the men were inevitably afflicted with scurvy. Champlain's own mournful words tell the dreadful tale of the ordeal . By June he reported: "Of our company now only 8 of the 28 remain, and half of these were ailing."

Champlain survived the winter in good health and now left the settlement. On an exploratory trip up the St. Lawrence, he encountered a party of Indians and plied them with questions about the lands upstream. If he was to explore Canada's interior, he knew he would need their assistance.

Before visiting the French fort in Quebec (the Indians had insisted on seeing the "wondrous" stockade for themselves), they agreed to guide Champlain into new territories, but on one condition—that the French help them fight their wars. The Montagnais and their upriver allies, the Hurons and Algonquins, were perpetually at war with the fierce Five Nations of the Iroquois.

The party sped swiftly south along the Richelieu until it reached a stretch of foaming rapids, where Champlain and two French volunteers transferred from their clumsy shallop to Indian canoes. A few days later the group reached the river's source, a lake stretching before them that extended directly south. The silent shores showed no signs of the Iroquois.

Champlain was elated by the scenery around the lake, which now forms part of the boundary between Vermont and New York. "In it are many beautiful low islands covered with very fine woods and meadows with much wild fowl and animals to hunt," he reported. The shores were lined with lush forests festooned with grapevines, and the lake teemed with fish. Completing the scene of pristine grandeur were the mountains rising abruptly beyond the lowlands along either shore— to the east, the Green Mountains of Vermont, to the west, the Adirondacks of New York.

With pardonable pride, the normally modest Champlain named his discovery after himself. Though he later placed the lake a bit too far to the east on his maps of America, he called the glistening expanse of water Lac Champlain, "Lake Champlain."

As the war party of some 60 Indians and three Frenchmen paddled down the lake, the Indians dem-

## Champlain's Astrolabe Was Lost—and Found 250 Years Later

In 1867, more than 250 years after Champlain had explored the area, a Canadian farm boy happened upon a buried cache consisting of copper kettles, silver cups, and a bronze astrolabe dated 1603. The astrolabe, five inches in diameter, is almost surely one that belonged to Champlain. He probably dropped it and the other articles on a difficult portage between Green and Muskrat Lakes during a 1613 canoe trip up the Ottawa River. The astrolabe itself was used to measure the vertical angle between the sun and the horizon at noon. When the observer had lined up the two sights of the astrolabe with the sun, he could read his latitude from tables inscribed on the outer ring of the instrument. Champlain, describing the demanding requirements of a master mariner, noted: "He should be a good celestial navigator, skilled in taking altitude with the cross-staff or astrolabe."

From their strongholds in present-day New York State, the Iroquois traveled north to make yearly raids in the St. Lawrence Valley. If Champlain, armed with his miraculous guns, would accompany the northern Indians into the Iroquois' domain, they were sure they could crush their foes.

Champlain had readily agreed to the plan, since ships had arrived from France with fresh supplies and new recruits to man the settlement. He set out to war with the Indians. Traveling up the St. Lawrence— Champlain and his men in a shallop, or ship's boat, the Indians in birchbark canoes—they soon reached a tributary flowing in from the south. This, the modern-day Richelieu River, the Indians explained, was "the river of the Iroquois," for it led directly into the country of those formidable tribesmen.

onstrated their detailed knowledge of the country to the south. At the end of the lake, they explained, they would portage to another lake, and at its southern end they would portage again to "a river which descends to the coast." The second lake was Lake George, and the river was the mighty Hudson. In fact, at that very moment Henry Hudson was cruising along the Atlantic coast in his *Half Moon*. On September 3 he would enter New York harbor, and by the end of the month he would reach the site of present-day Albany on the shores of the river that bears his name—less than 100 miles from the southern tip of Lake Champlain.

The two explorers never met. On the evening of July 29, near what would become the site of Fort Ticonderoga, the Indians spotted the dim forms of birchbark canoes moving up the lake toward them. It was a war

**A 1546 map of New France** (*which, like many maps of the period, has north at the bottom and south at the top) shows Jacques Cartier leading the first French colonists into Canada's forests in 1535. Cartier was chiefly an explorer and gold seeker, and not* *until his third voyage, in 1541, was there an attempt at settlement—led by Sieur de Roberval. After one harsh winter the colonists returned to France. Cartier himself was drawn to the New World in hopes of finding the Northwest Passage to the Orient.*

party of approximately 200 bellicose Iroquois braves.

The meeting that followed was brief and decisive. Champlain's Indians sent two canoes over "to learn from their enemies whether they wished to fight." The Iroquois replied that they did, but added—very sensibly—"that for the moment nothing could be seen and that it was necessary to wait for daylight in order to distinguish one another."

Both sides spent the night singing, dancing, and hurling insults back and forth across the water, Champlain and his allies from their canoes, the Iroquois from a barricade they had built on shore. At dawn Champlain's Indians landed and advanced on their foes. Keeping Champlain hidden, they pointed out three Iroquois chiefs and begged him to kill them. As they neared the enemy, the Indians finally parted ranks and revealed the dazzling figure of Champlain.

The Iroquois must have been astonished by the apparition that boldly marched within 30 yards of them: Champlain was clad in steel armor that glistened in the morning sun, and his bearded, fair-skinned face was framed by a steel helmet topped by a jaunty plume. It was a spectacle such as the Iroquois had never seen before.

When Champlain lifted a harmless-looking metal rod to his cheek and took a bead on one of the three closely grouped chiefs, the Iroquois were in for another surprise. Champlain had loaded his small matchlock musket with four bullets. With a flash of light and a deafening explosion, they felled all three chiefs, killing two and mortally wounding the other.

Champlain's jubilant Indians "began to shout so loudly that one could not have heard it thunder." With a few more shots and a flurry of arrows from both sides, the battle was over. Frightened nearly out of their wits by this strange weapon that could pierce their shields, the Iroquois fled in terror. After a brief celebration, the triumphant Canadian warriors pointed their canoes north and headed for home.

Soon after his return to Quebec, Champlain set out for France on one of the long series of trips he made between the mother country and his beloved colony. (In all, he shuttled back and forth between France and New France a total of 23 times.) In France he did his best to drum up support for a colony at a court whose interest in the venture was halfhearted at best. When in New France he continued to negotiate with the Indians and labored to bring order to the fur trade.

Returning to Quebec for the summer of 1610, he helped the Indians in another successful skirmish with the Iroquois. In 1611 he was back again, this time laying the foundations for a trading post farther inland at a site that eventually became the city of Montreal.

Champlain was unable to visit Canada the next year but did manage to write an impressive book about his adventures. (He was an inveterate publicist for the colony.) Meanwhile, he had plenty of time to mull over stories the Indians had told him of "a place where there is such a large sea, that they have not seen the end of it." The sea presumably was Hudson Bay, the vast saltwater gulf that pierces the heart of northern Canada. But for all Champlain knew, it might be some eastern

*Champlain in Canada*

155

branch of the Pacific Ocean. Could this be the long-sought way to the Northwest Passage?

Champlain's excitement was increased when in 1612 a young Frenchman, Nicolas de Vignau, returned to Paris from New France. Vignau, who had been exploring Canada's interior and had wintered with some Indians, reported that he had actually seen the northern sea. He claimed it was possible to travel from Montreal to the sea and back in just 17 days. And, he added, "he had seen pieces of the wreck of an English ship which had been lost on that coast."

This bit of information jibed neatly with reports filtering through Europe of the 1610–11 voyage of Henry Hudson, who had indeed discovered Hudson Bay and had then been marooned there by a mutinous crew. So, on March 6, 1613, Champlain set sail once again to "search for the northern sea."

Finding the colony at Quebec prospering nicely, he rushed upriver to Montreal. Then on May 27, amid "a farewell salute being given me with a few rounds from small pieces," he set out with Vignau, four other Frenchmen, and an Indian guide. Their immediate

## "Shouts of Astonishment" at Fort Quebec

Silhouetted by the setting sun, the rocky cliffs of Cape Diamond loomed dramatically over the small French fortress in the Canadian wilderness at Quebec. A party of Huron, Algonquin, and Montagnais Indians were performing a war dance around the leaping flames of a fire just outside the walls, while a flag emblazoned with the fleur-de-lis of France waved bravely above the stockade. Settlers lined the fort's palisades and a small balcony to watch the fearsome war dance of the savages who were armed with spears and clubs. A prudent Frenchman near the fire held his musket close to him as he watched the violent ceremony. His comrades no doubt felt reassured by the cannon mounted at a corner of the fort, even though the dancing Indians had just concluded an alliance with Champlain. The French leader had not sought such a treaty, but in late spring of 1609, while reconnoitering the St. Lawrence, he had met some 300 Indian braves. The Indians had demanded to see the Frenchmen's settlement at Quebec before launching an attack on their traditional enemies, the Iroquois. Vastly outnumbered, Champlain and his men had no choice but to bring the large band of warlike Indians to the small French outpost. Once at the settlement, several Frenchmen fired their muskets into the air, making a show of strength to impress their guests. The gesture was necessary, since there were very few of the original settlers in the fort at the time. When they heard the volley, the Indians, according to Champlain, "uttered loud shouts of astonishment." The guns, in fact, so impressed the Indians that they asked Champlain to be their ally against the Iroquois. Champlain, realizing it would be dangerous for the French settlement to antagonize the neighboring Indian tribes, agreed to the request. It was a fateful decision for the future of New France. Champlain's alliance did provide a buffer of friendly Indian tribes behind which his small settlement could grow and prosper. But, by allying themselves with the Huron confederation, the French also permanently alienated the Iroquois, who were both more numerous and more powerful than the Hurons. The Iroquois later allied themselves with the British, and their aid was a factor in the defeat of France by England in the French and Indian War more than a century later.

At right is Champlain's drawing of the fort at Quebec, which had been built on the Cape Diamond promontory to effectively command the St. Lawrence River from its banks. The stockade included a storehouse, workmen's lodgings, an apartment for Champlain, and the "Sieur de Champlain's garden."

destination was the Ottawa River, which branches off to the west of the St. Lawrence several miles beyond the Lachine Rapids at Montreal. Portaging the rapids, Champlain grumbled, was "no small labor for those who are not used to it." Yet this first dose of white water gave only a hint of the hardships to come. Entering the Ottawa River on May 30, they soon encountered rapid after rapid, like a series of steps, where the river foams dizzily downward toward the St. Lawrence and the sea. "Great dexterity is needed to pass these rapids," Champlain observed, then added respectfully, "This the Indians do with the very greatest skill, seeking byways and safe places which they recognize at a glance." He was not so fortunate. On June 1 the party came upon a rapid strewn with rocks and islets where "so great is the swiftness of the current that it makes a dreadful noise and . . . produces everywhere such a white foam that no water at all is seen." Paddling against such a current was useless, and the surrounding woods were too dense for portaging. So the men jumped overboard, tied ropes to the canoes, and began to haul them upstream against the roaring current.

**Wearing body armor and a plumed helmet,** *Champlain fires his musket into a mob of hostile Iroquois. This picture, drawn by the explorer himself, is his only contemporary portrait. It shows him at the head of the band of Canadian Indians he accompanied in an attack on Iroquois tribesmen near what would become the site of Fort Ticonderoga on Lake Champlain. The guns of*

*Champlain and other Frenchmen (top center) were decisive in defeating the Iroquois and also incurred their lasting enmity. The Iroquois were fearsome warriors who usually preferred surprise attacks to staged battles: A French observer wrote that "they approach like foxes, fight like lions, and disappear like birds." One purpose of their warfare was to obtain prisoners to torture.*

"And in pulling mine I nearly lost my life," Champlain recalled. Whisked sideways by a whirlpool, the canoe lurched downstream, knocking him down between two boulders. The towrope, still twisted around his hand, "hurt . . . very much," and he added, "nearly cut it off." Fortunately, the canoe soon drifted into a gentle eddy, and he was able to get free.

Despite this mishap, his enthusiasm for the river's beauty was undiminished. Passing the site of the present-day city of Ottawa, he marveled at "the wonderful waterfall" at the mouth of the Rideau River. "It falls with such impetuosity that it forms an archway nearly 400 yards in width," he commented, and noted that "The Indians, for the fun of it, pass underneath this without getting wet, except for the spray made by the falling water."

So they continued upstream, and by June 6 the explorers reached the rapids at the head of a widening of the river called Lac des Chats. Here the Indian guide advised Champlain to leave the river and portage to a chain of lakes to avoid dangerous rapids up ahead. When Vignau disagreed, insisting "there was no danger by the rapids," the Indian replied scornfully, "You are tired of living," and cautioned Champlain not to believe his protege. Trusting in the Indian's greater experience, Champlain took the portage and thought no more of the incident—for the moment.

The portage, as Champlain put it, caused "much trouble." The men were plagued by hordes of mosquitoes, whose "pertinacity is so great that it is impossible to give any description of it." The going proved no easier as they continued by land through difficult country, but their ordeal was soon over. When they reached an Indian encampment on a pond called Muskrat Lake, they received a hearty welcome. The chief, said Champlain, "was astonished that we had been able to pass the rapids and bad trails on the way to their country" and told his people that "we must have fallen from the clouds; for he did not know how we had been able to get through." Though tired and hungry, the Frenchmen must have been proud of their endurance and their accomplishments.

The following day the explorers skimmed down Muskrat Lake, portaged overland several miles at its head, and emerged once more on the Ottawa River. There, on Allumette Island, they entered the village of the Algonquin chief Tessoüat, with whom Vignau had spent a winter.

Again the weary explorers were greeted warmly. Gathering in the chief's bark-covered lodge, they were honored with a great feast, followed by the solemn smoking of a peace pipe. Then Champlain explained the reasons for his visit: "to assure them of my affection, and of my desire to aid them in their wars," to visit

*Captains and Colonists*

the Nipissing Indians farther upstream, and to see the lakes and sea beyond.

The chief listened gravely but was reluctant to escort the explorers any farther. The river was too dangerous, he claimed, and the Nipissing were vile sorcerers. Why not wait a year, he counseled. Then he would be happy to show Champlain the way.

Disappointed, Champlain pointed to Vignau "who had been in that country and had not noticed all the difficulties they represented, nor found those tribes as bad as they were saying." The chief eyed Vignau and asked, "Nicolas, is it true that you have been in the Nipissing country?"

Vignau hesitated a moment, then replied, "Yes, I have been there."

With that, the Indians suddenly flew into a rage and rushed at Vignau "as if they would have eaten him or torn him asunder."

Glaring at Vignau, Tessoüat declared scornfully: "You are a brazen liar; you know well that every night you slept alongside of me and my children, and rose every morning at that place. If you visited those tribes, it was in your sleep."

Thoroughly confused, and perhaps recalling the incident at des Chats Rapids, Champlain drew Vignau aside and began to question him. Vignau finally admitted that he had never gone any farther than Tessoüat's village. He had made up the story simply to get Champlain to bring him back to Canada. He had hoped Champlain would not make the trip to find the great northern sea or, if he did, that he would find the journey too difficult and soon turn back.

"In a transport of rage at this I had him removed," confessed the normally placid Champlain, "being no longer able to endure his presence." Though eventually he forgave Vignau, he publicly branded the hapless imposter "the most impudent liar that has been seen for a long time." (Some historians now suspect that Vignau may in fact have seen Hudson Bay, or at least heard of it from Indians who had been there. They guess that he may have changed his story because he was intimidated by the wrath of the Indians, who did not want the French to know all about their domain.)

His summer wasted "and without any hope of seeing the sea in those parts," the disgruntled Champlain left Tessoüat's village on June 10. On June 17, just three weeks after his departure from Montreal, he arrived there again, and by August 26 he was back in France. Though he had not discovered the Northwest Passage, however, time would prove that he had forged the first link in an important new trade route.

Late in the spring of 1615 Champlain returned to Quebec, this time accompanied by four Recollet friars, who came to establish Christianity in Canada and convert the Indians. Champlain thus completed the pattern that would dominate France's Indian policy for decades to come. As historian Francis Parkman has

summed it up: "With French soldiers to fight their battles, French priests to baptize them, and French traders to supply their increasing wants, their [the Indians'] dependence would be complete."

One of the priests, Father Joseph Le Caron, was so zealous to convert the Indians that he headed into the wilderness to live among the Hurons. Champlain was soon to follow. When he arrived at Montreal, the Indians, gathered there for the annual fur-trading rendezvous, as usual begged him to help them fight the Iroquois. And Champlain as usual agreed, "both to engage them the more to love us and also to provide the means of furthering my . . . explorations."

In mid-July, Champlain set out to meet the Indians near a great freshwater sea they had long been telling him about. With 10 Indians and 2 young Frenchmen, he quickly retraced his route up the Ottawa River to Tessoüat's village. Then, paddling, portaging, and hauling their two canoes past rapids, the men continued upstream through an area Champlain dismissed as "an ill-favored region . . . very rocky, and in many places rather hilly." About 75 miles beyond Tessoüat's village, the party headed west on the Mattawa River and soon arrived at Lake Nipissing.

The lake delighted Champlain, who wrote glowingly of its many "pretty islands" and the "very fine woods"

### An Iroquois Village Attacked by Champlain

Gunfire and European siege tactics did not terrify the Iroquois when Champlain and a large party of Huron Indians attacked one of their villages in 1615. Near Lake Oneida, in present-day central New York, the town was strongly fortified, the bark-covered houses surrounded by a high wooden wall. Champlain's siege tower can be seen at right. When allies failed to join him, the wounded Champlain gave up the attack and returned to Canada. Indian villages were often large and strongly defended, like this one. One early visitor wrote: ". . . the greatest towns of Muscovy are of no greater magnificence."

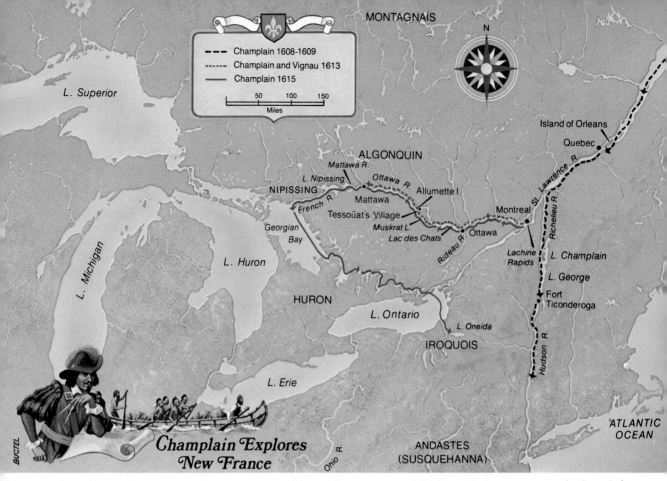

BUCTEL

## Champlain Explores New France

**Champlain could not have made** *his explorations of the North American wilderness without the aid of the Indians he had befriended. He attempted to understand their ways and accompanied them on long canoe trips, living on "salmagundi," a stew the Indians made from whatever animals or fish were available. He* *was one of the first explorers to venture to the Great Lakes region, where he noted the lush meadows and farmlands of the Huron and Algonquin tribal areas. In spite of this, it was the lucrative fur trade, not farming, that drew later explorers and then settlers into New France around the Great Lakes.*

and "fair meadows" on its shores. And contrary to Tessoüat's ominous reports, the local Indians proved friendly. As Champlain reported, they "feasted us on several occasions, according to their custom, and took the trouble to go fishing and hunting in order to entertain us as daintily as they could."

He had good reason to be grateful for their hospitality. Two days later, as he left Lake Nipissing and headed down its outlet, the French River, he found himself running seriously low on supplies, even though he limited his men to one meal a day. Fortunately, the countryside abounded in blueberries and raspberries "in such plenty that it is marvelous." Noting that the local Indians "dry these fruits for their winter supply, just as we do plums in France for Lent," he added gratefully that without the wild fruits "we should have been in danger of starvation."

Before long the two canoes emerged from the French River into a huge bay studded with rocky islands and stretching as far as the eye could see—the Indians' great freshwater sea.

Champlain was on Georgian Bay, a vast expanse of

water along the northeast side of Lake Huron. He had discovered the most direct route between Montreal and the western Great Lakes—up the Ottawa River and then down again via the French River. It was no northwest passage, but it was the route that generations of fur traders would follow to penetrate the lake country and the vast plains spreading beyond.

Champlain did not go any farther west; his destination was the Huron territory to the southeast between Lakes Huron and Ontario. Feasting on huge sturgeon, which he pronounced "marvelously good," he headed the canoes toward the eastern end of the bay, about 100 miles away. On August 1 he landed and began traveling on foot through Huron country.

Throughout the area, thousands of Indians lived in palisaded villages and raised corn, squash, and other crops. As he passed from settlement to settlement to summon his allies to war, Champlain was delighted by the rolling landscape dotted with cultivated clearings. "This country is so very fine and fertile," he enthused, "that it is a pleasure to travel about in it."

He also visited the village where Father Joseph had

settled down. With a few soldiers who had accompanied Father Joseph, Champlain proceeded to another village, where the war party was to rendezvous. By early September several hundred warriors were threading their way by canoe down rivers and ponds toward Lake Ontario. They also dispatched an advance party to inform the Andastes (Susquehanna) Indians of their departure. The Andastes, who lived near the present New York-Pennsylvania border, were also at war with the Iroquois and had promised 500 warriors to assist in the attack.

By October 5 the entire party had crossed the eastern end of Lake Ontario and beached the canoes on the southern shore. Hiding the crafts in the forest, they set out on foot into the Iroquois' domain. Four days later they captured a small fishing party of Iroquois and the next afternoon arrived at a large Iroquois village near Lake Oneida in central New York.

Champlain planned to remain hidden and launch a full-scale attack the following day, but the Hurons and Algonquins, impatient for battle, immediately began to skirmish with their enemies. Champlain quickly put an end to that and, after reprimanding the Indians for their disorganized tactics, proceeded to instruct them in European techniques of warfare. The Iroquois village was surrounded by a wooden palisade 30 feet high with a gallery at the top where warriors shot arrows and heaved stones at attackers. To surmount this barrier, Champlain proposed to build a movable tower with a walled platform at the top where soldiers could shoot down into the village. He also ordered the Indians to build a portable wooden shelter in which they could safely approach the barricade and set it on fire. "This they thought a good idea and very much to the purpose," he reported, and within four hours the next morning, the rickety contraptions were built.

On October 11 the battle began in earnest. Although the 500 Andastes reinforcements had not arrived, Champlain was confident that his men "were numerous enough to take the fort without other help." The tower was hauled up to the walls of the fortress, and the Frenchmen opened fire. With that, the Indians immediately forgot their lessons in European siege techniques. Whooping and shrieking "to such a degree that one could not make himself heard," they began shooting arrows at random, which, Champlain noted sourly, "in my opinion did no great harm to the enemy." The Indians then abandoned the other shelter and set fire to the downwind side of the village, where the Iroquois quickly extinguished the flames with the ample supplies of water they had gathered within the stockade for just such purposes. After three hours of frantic—and fruitless—confusion, Champlain's forces reluctantly withdrew.

Safely beyond range of Iroquois arrows, they counted the wounded: 2 chiefs, 15 warriors, and Champlain himself with two arrow wounds in his leg. Deciding not to make a second assault until the reinforcements arrived, the Indians settled down at the edge of the forest to wait. Now and then they skirmished with small bands of Iroquois, who taunted the French for interfering in Indian battles. But five days passed and still the Andastes did not arrive. (They turned up two days after Champlain's departure.)

Weary and disheartened, Champlain and the Indians gave up the battle on October 16 and headed for home. Champlain, unable to walk, had to be carried on the back of an Indian, trussed up in a crude basketlike contraption—a punishment he found even more painful than the wounds in his leg.

He had been deeply humiliated by the defeat. The Indians had seen for themselves that their fair-skinned friend, despite his guns and armor, was not invincible. Even so, they did not lose faith in the value of his friendship, and Champlain continued to strengthen their dependence on the French. He wintered with the Hurons, traveling from village to village, mediating disputes between the tribes and urging them to come to Montreal in the spring to trade their furs for French goods. Champlain returned to Montreal late in June 1616 and was back in Quebec on July 11.

With that trip, the aging warrior's exploring days were over. He never found his northwest passage to the Orient, but in the long run he accomplished something far more valuable. He spent the rest of his life building up the settlement at Quebec, and by the time he died in 1635 he had, almost singlehandedly, firmly established France's claim to its New World colony.

**A hundred years after Champlain** *had founded Quebec, his small settlement had grown to include a walled citadel, a cathedral, a seminary, and a hospital. In 1629 the English captured Quebec and occupied it until 1632, when it was returned by treaty to France. The French then held Quebec until 1759, when a British force commanded by Gen. James Wolfe defeated the French garrison under Gen. Louis-Joseph de Montcalm on the Plains of Abraham. New France then became a British colony.*

**"The waters foam and boil** in a frightful manner," wrote Father Louis Hennepin, a missionary attached to La Salle's 1678 expedition, "making a continual thundering which can be heard when the south wind is blowing, at a distance of more than 15 leagues." This is certainly a reference to Niagara Falls. Hennepin is the first European confirmed to have seen the mighty cataract, although colonists had heard tales of the great falls since Champlain's time. Hennepin, however, greatly exaggerated the size of the cataract, claiming it was more than 500 feet high (it is actually only 176 feet). Such busy beavers as these building a dam near the falls in an 18th-century engraving provided the wealth of New France. Their luxurious pelts were in great demand in Europe for men's hats. Hopes of growing rich in the fur trade lured young French adventurers like La Salle to the new colony. The imposing geometry of the dam and the beavers' lionlike appearance indicate that the European artist who created the illustration was working from secondhand reports. Just above the dam, at right center, is a domed beaver den, as geometrically unrealistic as the dam. Such pictures answered an insatiable European curiosity about the New World.

**Louis XIV** (*left*), *known as the Sun King, was the ruler of France for whom the territory of Louisiana was named. His astute finance minister, Jean Baptiste Colbert, regulated New France's fur trade and encouraged colonization. One colonizer who dreamed of a vast French empire in North America was La Salle. Though his attempt to establish a colony near the Mississippi River failed, France did take possession of a huge area of the continent, based largely on his explorations along the great river south to the Gulf of Mexico. Above, La Salle claims land at the mouth of the Mississippi after descending the river by canoe in 1682.*

# Visionary in the Wilderness: La Salle Claims Louisiana

*Little of La Salle's life in France prior to his arrival in Canada seems to have prepared him for a career in the wilderness. Born of an upper class family in Rouen in 1643, the young gentleman entered a school for the training of priests when he was 15. For seven years he studied with the Society of Jesus. During that time he made several requests to be sent abroad as a missionary, but his superiors refused. He was too young, they said. Time enough for missionary work when he took his final vows at 25. But La Salle, at 22, could not wait. Restless for new horizons, he resigned his novitiate and sailed for Canada. Once in North America, La Salle quickly proved his extraordinary ability to survive, even thrive, in the forbidding forests. Moreover, few explorers had such steady rapport with the Indian tribes of the wilderness.*

The King's Girls, as they were known in Montreal, received no proposals from Robert Cavelier, sieur de La Salle, when he arrived in Canada in the spring of 1666. The idea of a free wife, offered to all new settlers by Louis XIV as an inducement to emigrate to New France, did not appeal to the ascetic young man who had just quit a Jesuit seminary. Nor was he interested in the rest of the king's offer: one cow, two pigs, two chickens, two barrels of salted meat, and "11 crowns in money." La Salle's ambitions went beyond Montreal's single dirt street and few ramshackle buildings. Something about that primeval forest, stretching away green and silent on all sides, stirred his soul.

Unlike most immigrants, he did not arrive penniless and friendless. His wealthy family provided him with a small annuity, and his brother Jean was already in Montreal, serving as a Sulpician monk. Through Jean's influence, La Salle was able to buy a large tract of land from the order for almost nothing. It lay nine miles southwest of town on the St. Lawrence River.

Within three years the dark, broad-shouldered young immigrant cleared the trees, built fortifications and storehouses, and brought in settlers to farm, trap, and trade. Before long, he had transformed his small holding into a successful fur-trading post. Yet he soon grew bored with his static existence.

A few probes in the area of Lake Ontario convinced him that his future lay to the southwest. Then, too, there were tantalizing Indian rumors of a River Ohio, "Beautiful Water," somewhere beyond the lake. It also flowed more or less southwest and was said to empty into a warm sea. If, as La Salle hoped, this meant the river extended all the way to the Pacific, he could perhaps even open up a trade route to the fabulous cities of China. This dream of a northwest passage through the heartland of America rapidly consumed all of his thoughts. Though taciturn by nature, he talked about China so much that his settlement came to be called La Chine, "China."

In 1669, determined to find the mysterious river, La Salle sold his land and committed himself to the life of an explorer. On July 6 he set off up the St. Lawrence with a motley assembly of tough young woodsmen, Iroquois guides, and several Sulpician missionaries who were hoping to find Indian tribes as yet unconverted by their rivals, the Jesuits. The missionaries assumed that La Salle, like them, was heading directly west: Their secretive leader made no mention of his plan to veer south in search of the Ohio.

Skimming swiftly up the St. Lawrence in nine birchbark canoes, the expedition reached Lake Ontario on August 2. Seneca Indians on the lake's south shore greeted the explorers with a none-too-friendly welcome: They skinned, roasted, and ate a Shawnee prisoner in what could only be interpreted as a threatening manner. Unable to find guides there, the Frenchmen moved on to the western end of the lake a month later.

There came the expedition's parting of ways. The

missionaries insisted on going northwest in search of converts, but La Salle, affecting cowardice, said he wanted to return to civilization. No sooner had the Sulpicians paddled out of sight, however, than La Salle told his men that, far from returning to Montreal, they were heading south.

No one knows exactly what happened next: The records are sparse and contradictory. La Salle may or may not have discovered the Ohio River, but he and his handful of French companions certainly spent the next few months roaming through the unknown, uncharted territory south of Lake Erie.

According to one account, an Indian guide led the group to the Ohio River, and they actually canoed down the broad, glassy-smooth ribbon of water until progress was suddenly—and frustratingly—halted by the foaming rapids at present-day Louisville, Kentucky. If so, La Salle and his companions were the first white men to navigate the Beautiful Water. And if so, he must have been elated to discover that it flowed in ex-

actly the direction he had hoped—southwest. He must also have been encouraged if Indians told him, as they probably would have, that farther downstream the Ohio merged with an even greater river, the Mississippi, "Father of Waters."

Wherever La Salle was, he seems to have had a difficult time when winter arrived. Apparently, his men lost heart and deserted, taking the expedition's supplies. But La Salle, living on his wits, managed to survive. Eating game and herbs, befriending Indians, blazing trails, exploring streams and lakes, he began to understand just how immense—and potentially profitable—the North American wilderness really was.

By the time La Salle returned to Montreal late in 1670, he was laden with furs and filled with dreams of further exploration. But eight years were to pass before he could do anything about them.

In the meantime, others, too, were titillated by Indian tales of the Mississippi. If, as everyone hoped, it emptied into the Pacific, it might indeed be the long-sought, never-found Northwest Passage. In the summer of 1673, Louis Jolliet, a fur trader, and Father Jacques Marquette, a Jesuit priest, set out to discover the truth. By the time they reached the mouth of the Arkansas River, however, they realized the Mississippi flows not into the Pacific but into the Gulf of Mexico.

The news must have come as a bitter disappointment to La Salle. Yet even as he mulled over the significance of the new discovery, he began to form a grand scheme to exploit it. Here, he realized, was the place to found a vast French-American empire, and in his mind he began to map out its future shape and extent. It would stretch from the Great Lakes in the north to the Gulf of Mexico in the south, from the Appalachians in the east to the great river's farthest sources in the west. The central lifeline of the empire would be the Mississippi River itself, in whose fertile valley La Salle correctly envisioned riches far greater than anything English, Dutch, or Spanish colonists had yet dreamed of.

Winning the powerful support of Count Frontenac, New France's ambitious "governor general," La Salle was appointed governor of Fort Frontenac, a trading post at the junction of the St. Lawrence and Lake Ontario. This step westward developed immensely profitable new fur trade for both La Salle and Frontenac, and in 1677 the explorer was sent to France to present the concept of a western empire to King Louis.

Lusty, leathery-skinned, and eloquent, La Salle made a great impression on the French court as he enthusiastically described the beauty and fertility of the new country, "so free of forests . . . so abounding in fish, game, and venison . . . [and] all that is needful for the support of flourishing colonies." The crown gave him some of the concessions he wanted. On May 12, 1678, he was granted a five-year patent to build more forts and trading posts in the west, as well as a monopoly to explore and trade in the Mississippi Valley.

## Chevaliers and Chieftains Dined Together

La Salle made friends with great ease among the Indians. When he sighted an Indian village, he would approach bearing a calumet, or peace pipe (above). After both sides had smoked the pipe, a meal would often be served, as shown in the 17th-century French drawing below. An Indian meal tested not only the explorers' friendship but also their digestion. A contemporary chronicler noted: "Sometimes the meat is only half-cooked. Sometimes it is very tough." The Illinois, as a mark of respect, placed food in La Salle's mouth with their own hands.

*Captains and Colonists*

## Martyrs to Their Faith: The Incredible Courage and Tenacity of the Explorer-Missionaries

No story of the exploration of New France would be complete without the exploits of Jesuit missionaries, who first arrived in Canada in 1611. In their zeal to win converts, they learned Indian languages and compiled the first dictionaries of native dialects. The priests often accompanied explorers on their treks into the wilderness. Some, such as Father Marquette, became noted explorers in their own right. Every year the Jesuits in North America compiled a record of their activities that was sent to their superiors in France. The accounts, published annually as the *Jesuit Relations*, give the most accurate contemporary picture of the Indians of New France and the changes that Europeans brought to their traditional way of life. Inevitably, the Jesuits' efforts to christianize the Indians were responsible for many of these changes. And they also cost the lives of many Jesuit missionaries. This painting, done in 1665, shows the torture of Jesuits during the Iroquois uprisings in the 1640's. At center are Fathers Gabriel Lalemant and Jean de Brébeuf, who

were burned at the stake in March 1649. Father Brébeuf wears a necklace of red-hot tomahawk heads as one Indian pours boiling water over him and another cuts

a piece of flesh from his arm. In the background, a mission church is burned. The missionaries endured these terrible tortures as martyrs to their faith.

The king, however, declined to finance the venture, and La Salle's wealthy relatives once again had to come to his aid. Before leaving for Canada, La Salle recruited 30 artisans to build a pair of trading vessels in America, one to ply the Great Lakes, the other to venture down the Mississippi in an attempt to reach the Gulf of Mexico. He also appointed an Italian, Henri de Tonty, as his second in command. Handsome and dandified, Tonty concealed inside his right glove an artificial hand that earned him the nickname Iron Hand.

Bad luck began to haunt La Salle almost from the moment he arrived in Canada late in 1678. A boat carrying precious shipbuilding supplies capsized in the Niagara River, and only a few parts were saved. Instead of two grand trading vessels, La Salle had to settle for a single 45-ton bark. Throughout the winter his carpenters worked on the boat on the frozen riverbank within two miles of Niagara Falls.

By summer the ship was ready for launching. Tonty named her the *Griffon* in honor of Governor Frontenac, whose coat of arms included two of those mythical beasts. In August 1679, with 30 men aboard, the *Griffon* became the first sailing ship to cross Lake Erie. At the west end of the lake, she entered the Detroit River, passed into Lake Huron, and continued northwest to the trading center of Michilimackinac at the junction of Lakes Huron and Michigan.

It was in this shantytown of lopsided cabins, smelly warehouses, and wigwams that La Salle received his

first intimations of trouble brewing. Apparently, Jesuit missionaries, jealous of his royal patent, were trying to stir up tribal warfare in the Illinois Valley, which he hoped to follow to the Mississippi. La Salle pondered this ominous news; then, leaving Tonty behind to round up some men who had deserted, he sailed on to Green Bay on the western shores of Lake Michigan.

By then the *Griffon* was heavy with a rich cargo of furs and pelts, so in mid-September La Salle sent her back to Niagara for badly needed supplies. With his remaining men, he continued south by canoe to the southern end of Lake Michigan, where he hoped to rendezvous with Tonty, who was marching overland from Michilimackinac. The two men planned to join forces and build a base from which the expedition could push on south to the Mississippi in the spring.

As weeks passed with no sign of either Tonty or the *Griffon*, the men occupied themselves building Fort Miami on the St. Joseph River in present-day southern Michigan. Tonty finally arrived on November 20, but there was still no sign of the *Griffon*. Impatient to get on with the expedition and hoping the ship would soon arrive with supplies, La Salle left Fort Miami on December 3 and headed toward the Illinois River.

Canoeing and portaging through a desolate winter landscape, the explorers reached the Illinois Valley in mid-December. On January 5, 1680, the Frenchmen reached an Indian village in the area of present-day Peoria. Welcomed by friendly tribesmen who feasted them and rubbed their feet with bear grease, the exhausted explorers stayed on for several days until a shrewd blow, aimed hundreds of miles away by La Salle's rivals, struck without warning. The chieftain of a group of Miami Indians, evidently sent south by the Jesuits, arrived to warn his Illinois cousins that the explorer was an agent of their enemy, the Iroquois.

However, the Jesuits had underestimated La Salle's uncanny way with Indians. He calmed the frightened Illinois, assuring them he was their ally and friend, and begged permission to stay for the winter. His hosts reluctantly agreed but their mood remained suspicious, and six Frenchmen, afraid of being massacred, deserted. In order to stave off further desertions, La Salle decided to build his own winter camp a short way downstream. Bitterly, he named it Fort Crèvecoeur, "Fort Heartbreak," after his disappointment.

By March 2 La Salle was desperate for supplies, worried about the fragility of his chain of stockades reaching back to Fort Frontenac, and increasingly anxious about the *Griffon*, which he believed had been lost. Leaving Tonty in charge of the fort, he and four companions headed back toward Montreal. On March 24 they reached Fort Miami and then proceeded east in brutal weather across the wilds of southern Michigan. La Salle later wrote a graphic account of this journey, in which he told of pushing for two and a half days through thickets of thorns and brambles so dense that at the end "our faces were so covered with blood that we hardly knew each other."

Continuing on in incessant snow and hail, the men came to Lake Erie about a week later. By then La Salle's companions were feverish, but they managed to build a canoe and paddle eastward across the heaving gray lake. On Easter Monday they reached Niagara and heard the news La Salle expected—the *Griffon* had never returned. Presumably, the vessel, with her enormous cargo of furs, had sunk somewhere en route from Michilimackinac to Niagara.

Finally, on May 6, in driving rain, La Salle reached Fort Frontenac, exhausted and sick, after traveling more than 1,000 miles in 65 days—a notable achievement even in good weather. It was, in the opinion of historian Francis Parkman, "the hardest journey ever made by Frenchmen in America."

Amazingly, La Salle recovered from his ordeal so quickly that by summer he had collected the needed supplies, staved off his disgruntled creditors with more borrowed money, and was on his way back into the wilderness. Hurrying to rejoin Tonty, he was met en route by two trappers who brought sickening news. Most of the men at Fort Crèvecoeur had mutinied, and 12 of them were on their way to Fort Frontenac to kill him. Their motive, apparently, was to escape punishment for destroying and sacking two of La Salle's forts. Because mutiny was mutiny, La Salle ambushed them on Lake Ontario, killing two and imprisoning the oth-

ers. Then, anxious for Tonty's safety, he hurried back to join him. As he neared the fort, he soon realized that the dreaded Iroquois had at last struck against the peaceful Illinois. One of La Salle's chroniclers described the scene:

"On the 1st of December he reached the village, where he found nothing but signs of fire and of the rage of the Iroquois. There remained standing only some charred stakes, showing what had been the extent of the village. Upon most of these stakes the heads of the dead had been fixed to be devoured by the crows. There were more skulls at the gate . . . with a mass of burnt stones and some remains of utensils and clothing. . . . The horror of the scene was increased by the howls and screams of the wolves and the crows. . . . One after another he inspected all the heads of the dead, which he recognized by the hair to be the heads of women or of savages, whose coarse hair is worn close-cropped. It was not pleasant business, but he was bound to do it in order to learn the fate of M. de Tonty and his men. . . . All through the following night he pushed on, and the next day about noon, when nearing the mouth of the river, saw in a prairie on the north side the remains of lodges and figures like men and children, but motionless. . . . What had been observed from a distance proved to be heads and entire bodies of women and children, empaled and roasted, and then set up in the field." There was no sign of survivors.

Continuing his agonizing search nearly to the mouth of the Illinois River, La Salle still found no sign of Tonty. Before turning back, he nailed a letter to a tree telling his missing lieutenant where to find hidden supplies should he still, miraculously, be alive and pass that way. Then, in black despair, the thwarted explorer went back up the Illinois to winter at Fort Miami.

To his profound relief and delight, La Salle found Tonty alive and still loyal at Fort Michilimackinac in June 1681, and heard of his capture and lucky escape from the Iroquois. Together, they returned to Fort Frontenac during the summer to seek the funds for a final great expedition down the Mississippi, offering to claim the whole tremendous river basin for Louis the Magnificent. Governor Frontenac gave his approval, and by February 1682 the two explorers were standing at the confluence of the Illinois and Mississippi, ready to begin their descent. With them were 23 Frenchmen, 18 Indian braves, 10 squaws, and 3 children.

For a week the expedition was unable to embark on the Father of Waters, since dangerous chunks of ice were still drifting down from the north. La Salle chafed impatiently, aware that only 15 months remained of his royal patent. Eventually, the great river cleared and a flotilla of canoes pushed out onto the murky flood.

Almost immediately, they passed the broad mouth of the muddy Missouri, and a few days later they were swept beyond the flood of water streaming out of the Ohio. At first reedy swamps clogged with foam made

**La Salle canoed down—and up—***the mighty Mississippi River. Not the first European to have seen it (De Soto discovered it in 1541), La Salle recognized the river's potential use as a highway of trade and settlement. In 1682 he explored the Mississippi from its con-* *fluence with the Illinois. Sailing south, he sent Father Hennepin and a group of men to explore the river to the north. Hennepin's party was captured by the Sioux in Minnesota (above in a painting by 19th-century artist George Catlin) but was later rescued.*

shore landings difficult, but within a few days the explorers began to see many inviting nooks on the wooded banks. La Salle, however, preferred to camp on islands. He knew that his flotilla was being watched by unseen eyes and that word of his progress was probably traveling ahead of him. Although still confident of his matchless ability to befriend Indians, he had no desire to court danger by recklessly camping in strange territory where he was unknown.

Pausing only to establish a small stockade he named Fort Prudhomme, La Salle rapidly descended to the mouth of the Arkansas River, the farthest point Marquette and Jolliet had reached in 1673. There, on March 13, thick fog halted the flotilla, and as the explorers groped for a campsite on shore, they heard ominous sounds of Indian war cries coming from somewhere in the distance. They spent an anxious night in a hastily improvised stockade and, when the fog lifted next morning, saw Quapaw Indians paddling across the river toward them. Fearing that they might be hostile, La Salle cautiously held up a calumet. Its effect was immediate. The Indians delightedly accepted gifts of tobacco and invited him to visit their village.

Once there, La Salle formally took possession of Quapaw territory by planting a cross emblazoned with the arms of France. The Frenchmen shouted *"Vive le*

*Roi!"* while the Indians sang and danced excitedly, ignorant of the significance of the ceremony.

Continuing downstream, the expedition glided into the balmy warmth of the southern spring. As they passed luxuriant swamps and groves of towering cypresses, the explorers gazed in wonder at the magnificence of the landscape. Brilliant with blossoms, loud with cries of colorful birds, sweet-smelling and fertile, it seemed a paradise indeed to eyes accustomed to the austere scenery of Canada.

La Salle paused regularly to go ashore and appropriate Indian villages for the greater glory of France. He never had any trouble winning the confidence of tribal councils, which were dazzled by his gifts and shrewdly phrased speeches.

Delighted by the speed with which his inland empire was being assembled, La Salle arrived on April 6, 1682, at the goal he had dreamed of for nearly a decade: the shining blue emptiness of the Gulf of Mexico. Collecting his party at a site just above the mouth of the Mississippi, La Salle erected a cross, a "leaden plate," and a column carved with the words: "Here Reigns Louis the Great, King of France and Navarre; the Ninth of April 1682." Then, in a ceremonial speech, he named the whole vast territory he had opened up after his king. "I now do take, in the name of His Majesty . . . possession

*La Salle Claims Louisiana*

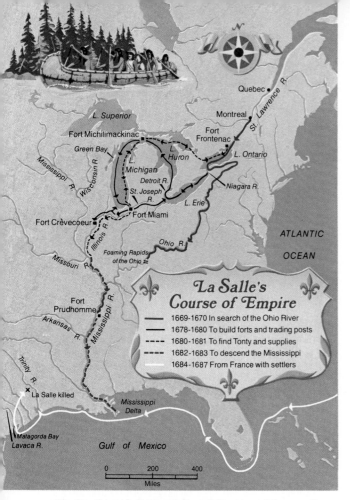

**Moving through dense, uncharted forests** *and down swift, un-known rivers, La Salle and his companions explored thousands of miles of territory in the present-day United States. They traveled mainly on the rivers and lakes that were later to bear many thousands of settlers. La Salle's successful expeditions were made in Indian birchbark canoes or on foot. His two attempts to explore by ship were disastrous: The* Griffon, *which he built for the Great Lakes, was lost with all hands; and of the four ships that left France in 1684, one was pirated in Hispaniola (not shown), one returned, and two were wrecked off the Texas coast.*

ship to France, knowing that the only hope for carrying out his great scheme lay in the royal court itself.

Once again La Salle's oratorical gifts won him a sympathetic hearing. The king's ministers, seeing the strategic value of a colony at the mouth of the Mississippi, authorized him to return and found the colony with full official support. La Salle was delighted, for he could now be free of his irritating enemies in Canada—and on August 1, 1684, he left France for the last time. Under his command were four ships: the *Joly*, the *Aimable*, the *Belle*, and the *St. Francis*.

On board were La Salle's brother Jean Cavelier; his nephew Moranget; a friend from Rouen, Henri Joutel; and 280 would-be settlers.

According to one witness, the founding fathers of Louisiana were not an impressive group. La Salle's soldiers were "mere wretched beggars soliciting alms, many too deformed and unable to fire a musket." As for the carpenters, engineers, and laborers who were presumably to build the new colony from scratch, "the selection was so bad that when they came to their destination and they were set to work, it was seen that they knew nothing at all."

Disaster struck La Salle's expedition even before it reached America. At the lusty port of Santo Domingo on Hispaniola, where the fleet stopped for supplies, pirates made off with the *St. Francis*. La Salle fell sick with fever, men deserted, and, according to one friar, "most of the crew, having plunged into every kind of debauchery and intemperance . . . were so ruined and contracted with dangerous disorders that some died in the island, and others never recovered."

On January 1, 1685, the fleet sailed into the Gulf of Mexico, but in those strange waters, nobody spotted the Mississippi Delta. By early February 1685, La Salle was forced to conclude that he had overshot the river's mouth. Ordering the fleet to turn around, he resumed the search for his elusive prize. Meanwhile, the weather was worsening, and La Salle's frustrated colonists were clamoring to quit their claustrophobic, heaving quarters. Losing patience, the commander finally agreed to put ashore with an advance party of 150 settlers at Matagorda Bay on the barren coast of modern-day Texas, about 400 miles west of the Mississippi.

The rest of the expedition rapidly disintegrated. The *Aimable* was wrecked on offshore shoals. The *Joly* returned to France with many disillusioned settlers. Only the *Belle* managed to anchor safely nearby. The weary La Salle attempted to build a fort on the banks of the Lavaca River. When his artisans proved incompetent, he himself "marked out the lengths, the tenons and the mortises, and made good the defects of the workmen."

At first, life at the river site seemed likely to be pleasant enough. There was an abundance of turkeys, geese, and partridges; plenty of oysters, eels, and tortoise eggs; as well as tart, fleshy grapes. Yet despite all this native prodigality, imported French seeds failed in the

of this country of Louisiana," he declared. Thus, in one stroke, La Salle claimed for France a colony many times larger than France itself.

Despite the ease with which Louisiana had been opened up, however, La Salle realized he could not colonize it with only 23 white men and a handful of Indians. He must return to Canada and then sail to France to solicit investors, recruit settlers, and report his good news to the king.

The voyage up the Mississippi was far more difficult than the easy glide down, and it was November 1683 by the time La Salle reached Quebec. There he discovered that his merchant rivals had been more than successful in prejudicing La Barre, the new governor of Canada, against him. (Frontenac had been recalled.) The official climate was so hostile that he took the first available

merciless sun, and drought killed off the livestock. As the months wore on, men who had contracted syphilis in Hispaniola wasted slowly away, while others died of snakebites and poisonous herbs. By August 1686 only about 44 of La Salle's original 150 settlers remained alive. The bitterest blow of all was the loss of the *Belle*, which ran aground while exploring the Texas coast. With the ship and her crew went most of La Salle's papers, his remaining stores, and his last means of contact with the outside world.

Meanwhile, all efforts to find the Mississippi had failed, and La Salle's despondency spread inevitably to the other men. "We regarded this agreeable country," wrote Jean Cavelier, "only as a tedious resting place and a perpetual prison."

On January 6, 1687, La Salle made a last desperate effort to save the colony. Taking his 20 ablest men, he set off to find the lost river, determined to ascend it all the way to Canada for help. Week after week the party trekked northeastward across vast plains, great tracts of forest, and, worst of all, seemingly endless swamps. "The water was sometimes up to our knees and sometimes higher," complained Joutel, "a thing no way agreeable to our shoes, which were no other than a piece of bullock's hide or goat's skin, quite green. . . . When those wretched boots were dried by the heat upon our feet they hurt us very much, and we were obliged to set our feet in the water to soften them."

In March they reached "a pleasanter country" near the Trinity River in eastern Texas. By then the strains of the journey were beginning to tell. La Salle's customary reserve, often taken for haughtiness, began to irritate some of his companions. Three of them, Duhaut, Liotot, and L'Archevêque, were particularly resentful. To relieve tension, La Salle sent them with a small hunting party to look for food. Two bison were shot, and La Salle sent his hot-tempered nephew Moranget to help drag back the carcasses. But when Moranget arrived at the hunters' camp, he found that the bison were already being smoked and that Duhaut and Liotot had set aside the choicest parts for themselves, "to which, by woodland custom, they had a perfect right." Nonetheless, Moranget flew into a rage, accusing them of greed. That night Liotot took an ax and split Moranget's head as he slept.

Next day, March 18, 1687, the worried La Salle went to look for his nephew. The sight of vultures disturbed him as he drew near the scene of the kill, and he fired a shot to announce his arrival. "This," wrote Joutel, "was the signal of his death." The conspirators, who were hiding in some high reeds, allowed him to walk into pointblank range where he had no chance to defend himself. Then "the traitor Duhaut fired his piece and shot M. de La Salle through the head, so that he dropped dead on the spot, without speaking one word." The murderers stripped their leader's body and left it for the vultures. "Such was the end," lamented his old colleague Tonty, "of one of the greatest men of his age."

## Father Louis Hennepin: A Wily Explorer Who Saw Much and Claimed to Have Seen More

Of all the tales of adventure written by the intrepid explorers of New France, none proved more popular or more entertaining than the works of the Franciscan friar Father Louis Hennepin (above), who had been with La Salle on the Great Lakes. Hennepin never suffered from modesty in describing his own achievements. "I was led to the discovery of a vast and large country," he bragged, "where no European ever was before myself." After La Salle's death, Hennepin claimed that he, not La Salle, had first traveled to the mouth of the Mississippi. He explained that he had not publicized the trip during La Salle's lifetime "because I was as good as sure the M. La Salle would slander me." However, Hennepin's own account would have given him little more than a month to travel to the mouth of the river and return, a feat no 17th-century voyager in a canoe could have performed.

Above are two illustrations from an 18th-century edition of Hennepin's book. One engraving shows the construction of the *Griffon*, the vessel La Salle's men built on the shores of Lake Erie in 1679. The second shows La Salle being ambushed near the Trinity River.

# Part

# 5

## Charting the Pacific

## Sailors and Scientists

*The last great
unexplored ocean is revealed
by teams of seamen and scholars
who resolutely
brave dangerous waters
and hostile islands.*

The Pacific Ocean is the greatest body of water on the globe. Its more than 64 million square miles of deep sea are sprinkled with groups of tiny islands that are lost in its vastness like grains of salt in a large bowl of soup. Although it covers a third of the surface of the world, the Pacific was, before Columbus, not only unknown but undreamed of by Western geographers. The immense extent of the ocean was a mystery until well after the discovery of the New World.

For centuries it had been believed that there must exist, in southern waters, a landmass—Terra Australis Incognita (the "Unknown Southern Land")—that, by providing a necessary balance to the northern continents, prevented the earth from tipping over into the void. The Pacific, it seemed, must bound that evasive Southern Land. Certain passages about a land rich in gold and spices in Marco Polo's "Travels" encouraged the dream; some 16th-century geographers even sketched the outlines of Terra Australis on their maps.

### Searching for a Southern Continent

But the search for the Southern Continent—and for the wealth and rich trading opportunities it might offer—was hampered by extraordinary difficulties. Ships entering the Pacific from the east encountered the prevailing southeast trade winds and were pushed steadily northward toward the Equator. Thus the Spanish, who were the first to search systematically for the Southern Continent from their bases in South America, were in a sense banished from the South Pacific area and consistently made their landfalls far north of Australia. But the Dutch—who from 1595 were determinedly engaged in taking over the bulk of the East Indies spice trade from the Portuguese—came around the Cape of Good Hope to meet the western winds of the Indian Ocean. Their customary course brought them into the latitudes of Australia, and they were the first to explore its waters and to discover the only true Southern Continent.

There was no way of determining longitude with any accuracy. A Pacific island, once discovered, might disappear again for decades, since its location could not be charted with precision: The art of navigation remained relatively primitive until the 18th century. When important discoveries were made, the news was sometimes suppressed, particularly by Spain and Portugal, neither of which desired to share with the rest of Europe knowledge of faster or safer passages to their Asian and South American holdings.

Yet the siren vision of the Southern Continent lured two centuries of adventurers into the Pacific. Each new discovery, hailed at first as the true Australis and then found to be yet another group of islands, pushed the illusory coasts of the ghost continent farther into the ocean's southern reaches. About 1567 the Spaniard Álvaro de Mendaña de Neyra sailed from Peru in search of the Southern Continent, covering 120 degrees of longitude—and one-third the circumference of the earth—before reaching a landfall in a group of large islands. Assuming them to be "children" of Terra Australis where, he believed, King Solomon had his legendary mines, he named them the Solomon Islands. Mendaña, on a second voyage, could not refind them, and although they were later rediscovered and renamed several times, they were not recognized as Mendaña's Solomons for some 200 years.

The visionary search continued. A lieutenant of Mendaña's, Pedro de Quirós, persuaded Spain's King Philip III to mount another continent-seeking expedition "among these hidden provinces and severed regions . . . destined to win souls to heaven and kingdoms to the crown of Spain." In 1605 Quirós discovered the New Hebrides, a group of islands he mistook for the outlying reaches of the Southern Continent. His second in command, Luis Vaez de Torres, determined to find the continent himself, discovered a passage between New Guinea and Australia and established that New Guinea is an island. Torres Strait provided a quicker and safer way for ships coming from the east toward the Philippines. (Northeast winds had formerly pinned vessels against New Guinea's northern coast.) But his discovery, suppressed by Spain, did not find its way onto nautical charts for more than 150 years.

By the early 1600's the Dutch were firmly established in the Malaysian archipelago and increasingly curious about what lay to the south. In 1605 Willem Janszoon sailed into Australia's Gulf of Carpentaria, becoming the first European to sight Australia, which he called New Holland. A generation of Dutch captains followed, charting the western and parts of the northern and southern Australian coasts. This forbidding and barren land, utterly void of the riches hinted at by Marco Polo, was thought to be simply another island; Terra Australis must lie still farther south. In 1616 Willem Schouten and Jakob Le Maire, attempting to find a more southerly route that would take them closer to the elusive continent, made the first voyage around Cape Horn at the tip of South America. Abel Tasman in 1642 voyaged far south of Australia to discover Tasmania and New Zealand.

## A Great Century of Exploration

In the frigid reaches of the northern Pacific, exploration of another kind took place in the early 1700's. Peter the Great of Russia, ambitious to extend the limits of his empire, engaged the Dane Vitus Bering to explore the eastern edges of Siberia and the waters around it and to discover what, if anything, lay between Asia and America. Between 1725 and 1741 Bering explored and mapped Siberia and its coastal waters. His discovery of a strait between Asia and America (Bering Strait) and his scientific exploration of Siberia, Alaska, and the Aleutians established Russian influence as far east as North America.

The first half of the 18th century saw a series of wars between England, France, and Spain over colonial possessions, trade, and seapower. The thirst for empire grew and, with it, the need to reach out and claim new lands. In addition, by the mid-1700's a growing technology had provided navigators with the chronometer, which, unlike any previous ship's clock, kept accurate time on the ocean and could thus help determine longitude; and the sextant, which could accurately determine latitude by measuring the altitude of the sun or a star. Essential navigation aids, such as the English *Nautical Almanac* (first published in 1767), which gave positions of the sun, moon, and planets for all latitudes and longitudes, also helped the sailor chart his course.

In 1764 England's King George III, encouraged by the Royal Society, dispatched the first seaborne scientific expedition to the South Pacific; when it returned without having made any significant discoveries, a second was sent. Its captains, Philip Carteret and Samuel Wallis, found Pitcairn Island and Tahiti in 1767—the latter at first mistaken for Terra Australis. Just one year later the French chevalier Louis de Bougainville, accompanied by an astronomer and a botanist, set out in search of the Southern Continent, refound Tahiti for the French, coasted by the Great Barrier Reef, and rediscovered Samoa.

But the enigma of the Southern Continent remained. Despite almost two centuries of exploration, discovery, and disappointment, belief in the necessary existence of Terra Australis remained as strong as ever. Only its probable location had changed to somewhere south of latitude 50°— dangerously close to the Antarctic Circle. It was left for the greatest explorer of his era, and the first of the new age of scientific voyagers, to end the dream forever. Capt. James Cook—supreme craftsman of the arts of navigation, exploration, and command, whose Pacific revelations left little for those who followed him to discover—sought but did not find Terra Australis. And only then could Europe accept the fact that it did not exist.

The death of the Terra Australis legend marked the beginnings of modern Western domination in the Pacific. The last half of the 18th century saw the first permanent European settlement and colonization of Australia, New Zealand, and the major Pacific islands. In the 1780's the United States, too, began to sail the 10,000-mile-long sealanes between its coast and China, later establishing the clipper ship routes that returned silk, spices, and fortunes to the young republic. Yankee whalers ploughed through all the regions of the Pacific until, by the 1860's and the advent of the first steamships, almost no area of that vast ocean—except the polar seas—remained unknown.

*During the 17th century, Archangel* (above) *was Russia's only ocean port. Situated on the White Sea leading to the Arctic Ocean, its harbor is frozen over half of the year. When Peter the Great ascended the throne, one of his major objectives was to establish a Russian outlet on the more southern Baltic Sea, and to that end he had St. Petersburg built in 1703. As the nation's boundaries moved east with the conquest of Siberia, Pacific coast ports became desirable as well. One of the first was Petropavlovsk, founded by Bering in 1740.*

*Vitus Bering was a tall, stout Dane with dark, quiet eyes and an air of competence. The overwhelming responsibilities and hardships of his explorations destroyed his health.*

*Bering had the duty of supplying the admiralty with information about Siberia. The map detail above, prepared by Bering's cartographers, shows a variety of Siberian natives in traditional costume. One man is astride a dogsled, while two others ride reindeer.*

*Chapter Sixteen. In one of the first explorations in history to include scientists, Russia seeks to define its northern Pacific coastline. Led by a Danish mariner, the ambitious expedition crosses Siberia, finds the strait separating the Old World from the New, and reaches Alaska before disaster strikes at a barren island on the return journey.*

# The Isle of the Foxes: Bering Sails the North Pacific

*Vitus Bering was born of a poor but respectable family in Horsens, Denmark, in 1681. Joining the navy at an early age, he made his mark as a navigator after several long expeditions. Returning from the East Indies in 1703, he went to Amsterdam where he was befriended by Adm. Cornelius Cruys. A Norwegian by birth, Cruys had been hired by Peter the Great to help him establish the Russian Navy. Bering accepted the admiral's offer of a sub-lieutenancy in the czar's new fleet. After a distinguished career, Bering resigned from the Russian Navy in 1724, but because of his ability and daring, Czar Peter urged him to lead Russia's first great expedition to its Pacific coast. During that expedition (1725–30) and a more ambitious second one (1733–41), Bering succeeded in mapping much of Siberia as well as the northern Pacific.*

On August 16, 1728, a Danish sea captain in the service of the czar of Russia found the answer to an old question. Guiding his ship, the *St. Gabriel*, northward through rain, wind, and fog, he had reached a position opposite East Cape, the northeasternmost promontory of Siberia. Vitus Bering, looking ahead and to the east, could see only open water. Bering was now satisfied that he had fulfilled his commitment to the czar. What he saw convinced him that North America was indeed separated from Russia by water. Now he had to choose. Either he could sail on and explore the Asian Arctic northwest of East Cape, or he could turn back at once before the Arctic winter closed in.

It was already mid-August, and seasonal headwinds, due any day now, could seriously hamper the voyage home. Provisions were running low. The men were ill prepared for the possibility of passing the winter on a harsh and unknown shore among the vicious Chukchi, the northeast Siberian natives. Bering's concern for the safety of his ship and crew was stronger than his desire to challenge the unknown; so he ordered the *St. Gabriel*

to continue north a few more days and then reverse her course once she had reached a latitude of 67°18' N.

On the return voyage Bering sailed once more by East Cape, discovering Big Diomede Island. But the fog was so thick that he never saw America beyond, although at this point (eventually to be called Bering Strait) the continents are only 53 miles apart and visible in clear weather.

Less than two weeks after passing St. Lawrence Island at the south entrance to the strait, the ship encountered a storm so violent that Bering's forebodings were justified. Yet he managed to bring the ship safely back to the Kamchatka Peninsula in Siberia on September 2. He spent the following summer exploring by ship off the eastern coast of Kamchatka, as the czar had ordered. Then he returned to St. Petersburg in 1730 to report to the Russians.

St. Petersburg at that time was the capital and cultural center of the "new" Russia that Czar Peter the Great had created out of the vast medieval realm he had inherited. By the end of the 17th century the decline of the Mongols and the rise of Russian power had extended Russia's rule to the shores of the Pacific, several thousand miles from its old eastern borders. Yet the immense land between—Siberia—was virtually unknown. Its seemingly endless stretches of forest, tundra, and mountains were generally cold, forbidding, and desolate. Small, often hostile bands of nomads were the only inhabitants.

Beginning in the 16th century, Cossacks had explored and claimed Siberia for Moscow's czars, but the territory was still unmanned and undeveloped. Czar Peter the Great had been anxious to know the farthest extent of his new lands, and it was for this purpose that he had hired Vitus Bering. But Peter the Great and his successor Catherine I had died before Bering returned from his reconnaissance of the North Pacific. The Dane

## A Dynamic Czar Shaved Old Russia's Beard

The early years of Czar Peter the Great (born in Moscow, 1672) were marked by his absorption with war games and ships, interests that shaped his future and Russia's. Defeat in his first real-life campaign, against Turkey in 1695, impelled him to build a navy. He went to Holland and lived briefly in disguise (left) in Saardam, apprenticing as a ship's carpenter before traveling to Amsterdam and England to study naval shipbuilding.

Peter returned home brimming with ideas for a new Russia and collided instantly with the long-bearded conservatives of his court. The young czar's anger with these "beavers," as he called them, erupted at a reception when, grabbing scissors, he snipped off their beards. The contemporary cartoon (right) illustrates his campaign for beardlessness. In 1703 Peter founded St. Petersburg (now Leningrad) on the Baltic coast, and it replaced Moscow as Russia's capital. Peter's reign launched Russia as a power, while his interest in expansion resulted in Bering's first voyage. He died in 1725 and was succeeded by his widow, Empress Catherine I.

now found the government under Czar Peter II unappreciative of his achievement.

In the Russian capital he was kept waiting a while before being summoned to appear before the admiralty. Their questions shocked him: How, they wanted to know, could he be certain that the continents were separated by water? Why hadn't he sailed on northwest beyond the East Cape and explored for the possible land bridge more thoroughly?

There was worse to come. Certain recognized but highly imaginative cartographers in the Academy of Science—a body created by Czar Peter the Great to attract scholars from western Europe—believed that off Kamchatka lay a large landmass that they called Gamaland. Why hadn't Bering found it? Since Bering had not confirmed Gamaland's existence, they sought to discredit him. Their accusations, far from crushing the Dane's spirit, strengthened his determination to vindicate himself. He prepared and submitted a proposal that he command a second and more far-reaching northern expedition to be launched forthwith.

The timing of his request favored him. The national mood of Russia was one of ebullience and expansion. The Empress Anna, ascending the throne after the death of Peter II in 1730, had resumed the innovative programs of Peter the Great, and influential members of her court saw economic advantages in the expedition. The empress herself envisioned it as a means of enlisting the foremost scientific talents of the Western World to reflect glory on Russia and her reign.

Bering's plan was ambitious enough: He proposed a triple expedition to explore the North American coast and, if possible, establish trade relations there; to open a sea route to Japan for trade; and to travel to the north of Russia by way of the Lena and Ob Rivers and map the Arctic coast of Siberia.

As the proposals passed through bureaucratic corridors of the admiralty, the Academy of Science, and the royal court, they were expanded until they had reached unrecognizable proportions. The Great Northern Expedition, as it came to be called, was to be the most all-embracing scientific exploration ever undertaken anywhere. Scientists were to investigate and report fully on every facet of Siberian life: the geography and climate of the rivers, streams, forests, mountains, and coasts, as well as the origins, customs, and languages of the nomad Siberian tribes.

Bering, reading his revised orders, which were published on December 28, 1732, found that in addition to systematically exploring all of Siberia and the Kamchatka Peninsula, he was expected to develop the Siberian hinterland as well. En route across the Siberian river system to his port of embarkation, he was to establish iron foundries and shipyards, found nautical schools, introduce cattle raising, and inaugurate a postal system between Kamchatka and St. Petersburg. In addition to these responsibilities, he had to arrange to house and feed a small army of people in Siberia.

Assigned as Bering's assistants were two veteran aides of the first expedition—Martin Spanberg and Alexei Chirikov. Chirikov and Bering were to captain two ships to America; Spanberg with three other ships was to explore the Pacific toward Japan and farther south. Bering's authority, perhaps because of his foreign origin, was stringently limited. Not only did he have to submit all critical decisions to a vote, but Chirikov's approval was required for all important moves. Over the scientists Bering had no jurisdiction whatsoever; he was only expected to coordinate their efforts and provide for their needs.

Most of the scientists regarded Bering with condescension or outright antagonism. The presence of one of them—a young, German naturalist, botanist, mineralogist, and physician named Georg Steller—however, was to prove a boon both to the expedition and to Bering himself.

The enormous expedition set out from St. Petersburg in detachments early in 1733. On March 18 Bering himself departed on the journey toward the rivers and marshy tundra of Siberia with an entourage that had grown to nearly 600: his wife and daughter; shipwrights and carpenters; blacksmiths and ironmongers; sailors, soldiers, and priests; cartographers and agriculturalists. Spanberg had preceded him in order to build ships at Okhotsk for his probe to Japan. Chirikov, the rest of the supplies, and the main body of the scientists from the academy would come later.

Traveling slowly on the flat-bottomed riverboats that were the principal vehicles of transportation across Siberia, Bering and his retinue stopped at Tobolsk, the westernmost Siberian provincial capital, to wait for their supplies to catch up with them. During the year Bering spent there, he had a large two-masted schooner built and on May 14, 1734, sent forth a group charged with exploring the Ob River to the Arctic coast.

Five days later Bering was ready to set out for Yakutsk, a provincial Siberian capital on the Lena River. Two-thirds of the way to Kamchatka, it had been selected as the construction headquarters for the remainder of the expedition. On the journey there, swarms of biting black flies made every hour a torment, and when portages were necessary, treacherous bogs in the tundra threatened to swallow up both men and horses.

Yakutsk, when they finally reached it that October, was no more than a dreary little subarctic village, the coldest town in Siberia. Although advance preparations were supposed to have been made for the expedition's arrival, Bering found that nothing had been done. Furthermore, the local officials were totally unprepared to handle such a sudden avalanche of personnel and unfamiliar affairs. Throwing himself into his work, Bering directed the erection of barracks, warehouses, an iron foundry, and a shipyard in which were constructed four barges for the eastward journey and two riverboats. The latter he dispatched down the Lena for additional exploration of the Arctic coast. By the end of the first winter, he had miraculously transformed Yakutsk into a humming hive of activity.

In the spring of 1735 Chirikov arrived with his tons of supplies, all to be checked, inventoried, stored, or shipped ahead. By October the main body of the scientists descended on Yakutsk, swelling the population of the expedition to 2,000. The amount of their equipment was equally awesome: They had brought 9 cartloads of instruments, including telescopes 15 feet long, 27 bulky barometers, drafting tables, and libraries. With the scientists came their retinues of assistants, secretaries, draftsmen, and bodyguards. Expecting to maintain their accustomed lifestyle in the Arctic wastes, they brought delicacies, including whole wine "cellars" to assure them the proper drink for each meal course. They considered Bering responsible for seeing that their demands were met and that they were comfortable. It was almost too much for one man. Peter Lauridsen, a Bering biographer, wrote of him:

"More just than arbitrary, more considerate than hasty, more humane than his position called for, he nevertheless had one important quality, an honest, genuine, and tenacious spirit of perseverance, and this saved the expedition from dissolution."

Four years went by, and Bering was still in Yakutsk, exerting superhuman effort to cope with the many responsibilities that had been thrust upon him. Meanwhile, his enemies—dissident naval officers, disgruntled local officials, and opinionated scientists—were using the postal system he had founded to send back accusations against him.

In St. Petersburg, when the expense of the expedition was scrutinized in 1738, it was found that it had skyrocketed to more than 300,000 rubles. The imperial cabinet demanded that the ruinous drain on the treasury be terminated. The explorer's future hung in the balance, but too much had been spent with nothing to show for it for the government to pull back. The admiralty, in a gesture of futile exasperation, put Bering on half pay but allowed him to proceed with his work.

Meanwhile, Bering had already moved his headquarters to Okhotsk on the Siberian coast, ostensibly to build his two ships and to see how Spanberg was getting along with his but possibly also to escape the unrelenting pressure of Yakutsk. He found that Spanberg had completed his ships, and during the summer of 1738 Bering dispatched him to explore the route to Japan. Beginning work on his own ships, he finished them two years later. In June 1740—more than seven years after Bering had left St. Petersburg—two 80-foot wooden sailing craft, the *St. Peter* and *St. Paul*, slid down the ways into the Sea of Okhotsk.

Bering's plan, previously approved by the admiralty, called for him to be at sea for two years, wintering in North America. During the winter at Okhotsk, he made meticulous preparations, which included seeing that

**Clouds obscured** *the horizon on the morning of July 16, 1741, but at midday they suddenly parted, revealing Alaska's snow-covered mountains dominated by Mount St. Elias (above). The men on the* St. Peter *wept and shouted with joy. Bering limped from his cabin, gazed at America's sparkling coast, and shrugged.*

enough ship's biscuits were baked to last the entire voyage. Finally, everything was ready and only needed to be transported from Okhotsk to Avacha Bay on the Pacific coast of the Kamchatka Peninsula—Bering's final headquarters and point of embarkation. Then a supply ship ran aground on a sandbar, and the store of biscuits was soaked and ruined.

The loss of the ship's biscuits—along with serious delays in receiving other vital supplies that were being transported overland across the Kamchatka Peninsula—forced Bering to alter his plans. He would have to confine his voyage to America—out and back—to the span of the following summer. Also, at the insistence of the academicians in St. Petersburg, Bering was to try once more to find Gamaland.

According to plan, the expedition spent a comfortable winter at Petropavlovsk, the village on Avacha Bay erected for their arrival. The ice in the bay didn't break until late spring, and it was June 4, 1741, before the two ships could embark. Captain-Commander Bering was aboard the St. Peter, his flagship, with Sven Waxell, a Swede, as his second officer, and a crew of 77. Captain Chirikov was in charge of the St. Paul with a crew of 76. The ships were to sail together, keeping in touch by coded flags and cannon shots or, when close, by shouting through a speaking trumpet.

For eight days the two ships sailed in fine weather on a course southeast-by-east in search of Gamaland. When they reached the 46th parallel without discerning any landmass, the officers of both vessels conferred by speaking trumpet. They had arrived at the southernmost latitude specified in the orders and decided to change course east-northeast to North America. In an all too short summer, they had already lost eight days in their attempt to find the nonexistent land of the academy's imagination.

On June 20 the fair weather ceased abruptly. Fog closed in, and the ships lost sight of each other. Bering spent valuable days combing the seas for the St. Paul with no luck. Only later was it learned that Chirikov went on to Alaska's coast but encountered a series of disasters, losing a number of men and his longboats. The St. Paul finally did get back to Avacha Bay safely, but Bering would never know that.

Meanwhile, alone, the St. Peter sailed on to the east-northeast, groping her way through the mist and fog. The water supply was already getting low, and Bering's chief concern now was to find land so that the casks could be refilled. At noon on July 16, the clouds lifted and the men on deck cheered, for they could see Alaska's distant Mount St. Elias, 18,000 feet high, its snow-covered expanse dazzling in the sunlight. Officers went below to rouse Bering, who, since leaving Avacha, had spent most of his time in his bunk, worn out by years of toil and responsibility. Suffering from the beginnings of scurvy, he was more seriously ill than anyone was aware. The crew watched as Bering tottered painfully up from his cabin to view the sight of the mountain.

The men looked at their wary captain for some expression of exultation or at least satisfaction. Instead, as Steller noted in his journal, Bering "received it very indifferently and without particular pleasure, but in the presence of all he even shrugged his shoulders while looking at the land."

Upon finding a suitable place for landing, the St. Peter dropped anchor off a stretch of beach (on what is today known as Kayak Island), and a longboat was ordered to explore for a better anchorage in the strait between Kayak Island and the mainland or farther north. Steller stood watching, aquiver with excitement. His own great moment was at hand. Almost within reach lay a new world ready to disgorge its natural treasures: strange plants, animals, sea creatures, and, perhaps, human beings. He would be the first to find them, to write reports, and to bring back specimens. His discoveries would make him famous.

With these thoughts, Steller asked Bering's permission to join the exploring party. To Steller's shock, Bering refused, informing him that he could not allow him to risk his life on an unknown shore. All of Steller's frustrations boiled up in a violent rage. In an extraordinary act of insubordination, he castigated his captain in front of the crew and threatened to report him for violation of his orders. Bering listened in silence, his face expressionless. Then, with an indulgent smile, he gave Steller permission to join the watering party that he was sending to the island in a small boat.

While the watering boat was preparing to leave, Bering summoned the ship's trumpeters. As Steller's boat pulled away, he ordered them to play the kind of fanfare usually reserved for high naval dignitaries.

Steller put every minute of his few hours ashore to the greatest use, gathering specimens of plant, bird, and animal life. Then, seeing in the distance a column of smoke that could signal the presence of natives, he dispatched an urgent message to Bering. He asked not only that he be allowed more time ashore but that another boat be sent to bring back his specimens. Bering's indulgence had reached its limit. He gave Steller his ultimatum: "Come aboard or remain behind." A deeply frustrated Steller returned, and the St. Peter weighed anchor. As they left, Bering reminded his officers that no more than three weeks remained for them to explore and chart the American coast.

Then, in early August, 26 of the crew reported sick and 5 were unfit for duty. The assistant ship's surgeon diagnosed the outbreak as scurvy, the perennial scourge of seamen. Bering himself, having shown symptoms since July, fell a victim, leaving Sven Waxell, his second in command, increasingly more in charge. When a council of officers was called, the consensus was to waste no more time probing the fogbound coast but to head for home. But before going on, they would have to put in somewhere for more water.

## *Steller's Jay Heralded Arrival at the American Shore*

identification of a blue-plumaged bird his assistant handed him. Steller excitedly recalled a colored print of the bluejay of eastern America (top left) that he had seen years before. He realized the bird he held was a relation ("Steller's Jay," beneath), proving that the expedition really had reached the shores of America.

The signs of habitation Steller found, including a hollowed-out log used to cook meat on hot stones, indicated a mode of life exactly like that on Kamchatka (bottom). The natives of Kayak Island (right), he deduced, were of Asiatic origin. They were of "medium stature, strong and stocky," with flat, brownish faces and eyes "black as coals."

During his months on Bering Island, Steller spent much of his time studying the marine life. For days he knelt behind a blind and took meticulous notes in Latin on the habits of the sea otter, whale, and "Steller's Sea Cow" (below), a northern

The outstanding member of Bering's second expedition was the brilliant German naturalist and physician Georg Steller. While employed as personal physician to Archbishop Novgoroff in St. Petersburg in 1734, the 25-year-old Steller learned of Russia's planned expedition to the far northeast. Eager to be the first

manatee averaging 28 to 35 feet in length and resembling, Steller wrote, an animal above the navel and a fish below it. His description of an 8,000-pounder is the only record of that extinct animal.

Steller never returned home. Fearing the new antiforeign sentiment in St. Petersburg (he had sharply criticized Russia's treatment of Siberian natives), he exiled himself at Kamchatka. Time passed with no acknowledgment of the valuable manuscripts he had sent to the Russian capital, and he became bitter at the lack of recognition. In 1746 he was charged with having aided some rebellious Siberians. Steller started for St. Petersburg to vindicate himself but died from pneumonia along the way.

scientist to report the natural life of that remote area, he applied to be sent to Kamchatka as a botanist. Seven years later, the temperamental and outspoken scientist stared at the American mainland from ship deck, enraged because Bering, afraid for Steller's life on an uncharted shore, wouldn't let him land.

Steller eventually got a few hours on Kayak Island, two miles offshore. He hurriedly collected plants and searched for natives while his Cossack assistant hunted for strange birds. In the late afternoon he spread his specimens around him and, while waiting for the ship's longboat, completed the first treatise ever written on Alaska's flora and fauna. The most impressive demonstration of his remarkable memory that day was his

Off bleak, unforested Nagai Island, due south of the Alaska Peninsula, the *St. Peter* finally found a safe anchorage. A longboat with Steller, Waxell, and other crewmembers was sent ashore, but in their haste, Waxell and the sailors—against Steller's stern warnings—filled the casks from a brackish tidewater pool. It was an act that was to be regretted later, for the salty water dehydrated the scurvy victims, making them even weaker. On Nagai the first of the sick, a sailor named Shumagin, died while being taken ashore for some fresh air. His shipmates buried him there and named the island in his memory.

Nevertheless, the five days spent anchored off the island awaiting the return of a side expedition afforded a welcome rest for the explorers. Steller busied himself collecting antiscorbutic herbs for the scurvy victims, but most of the seamen, fed up with his angry outbursts, scorned his cure. Unable to get the sailors' cooperation, Steller collected the herbs for Bering, himself, his servant, and his artist, checking the course of the disease at least temporarily. Under Steller's ministrations, the depressed, bedridden captain was able to walk a few steps.

Steller himself was in his element, studying and recording the rich variety of sea life. His excitement reached a new pitch one day when he saw some natives—they turned out to be Aleuts—approaching the *St. Peter* in their kayaks. Neither the men on the *St. Peter* nor the Aleuts knew what to make of each other. After giving the natives some trinkets, the crew offered them brandy and tobacco. The Aleuts rejected both with scorn but beckoned the men ashore for food and water. During a 15-minute landing, Steller furiously took the first anthropological notes to be made on these people.

Toward the end of September, a wild and vengeful kind of storm struck with full force; the 80-foot vessel was tossed about the sea like a chip, while water poured over the decks, soaking the men with freezing brine. The storm struck again and again, sometimes with St. Elmo's fire (electricity) flickering about the masts, adding to the crew's terror.

Drenched, ill, half-frozen, and half-starved, with only a few soggy, half-burned biscuits to eat, the crew clung to life more by instinct than by will. Every day more died, and their corpses were unceremoniously tossed overboard. Scarcely enough able hands could be mustered to man the ship. One of the strongest, the second mate, Yushin, wrote in his log: "I have such pains in my feet and hands owing to the scurvy that I can with difficulty stand my watch."

Throughout October they sailed as the wind willed, now south, now west. It was impossible to keep a course. The ship was lost, and more men were dying every day. On November 5 the explorers saw a range of hills, which persuaded them they had reached the vicinity of Avacha Bay. But when the sun came out and they took a reckoning, their jubilation turned to despair: They were two degrees north of their destination.

The next day Waxell and the junior officers realized that the rigging on the ship would have to be repaired before continuing farther and that no men were strong enough to do the work. They dropped anchor off a sandy beach in what appeared to be a safe harbor to decide what to do next. But their "harbor" was only a space between two of the Commander Islands, and with the turning of the tide, a violent sea began to run. The *St. Peter*, torn from her moorings, was heading straight for an ugly reef when a huge breaker lifted her over it and put her down in still water. Later storms soon drove the ship ashore, and it became evident that the *St. Peter* would go to sea no more.

The crew found itself in a chillingly desolate place. Aside from a few half-frozen sticks of driftwood, there was no timber with which they could build a shelter. On a hillside they found some crevices in the frozen sand, and by stretching sailcloth over them, they could create at least some protection from the elements. But there was fresh water from nearby streams, and the ptarmigans and sea otters were so tame they could be killed with a stick, assuring the castaways fresh meat.

Bering, too weak to stand, was carried ashore on an improvised stretcher. Sven Waxell recalled: "Men were continually dying. Our plight was so wretched that the dead had to lie for a considerable time among the living, for there was none able to drag the corpses away, nor were those who still lived capable of moving away from the dead. They had to remain lying all mixed up together in a ring with a little fire in the center."

**Worn down by the burdens** of the expedition, wracked with pain, and longing for his home 6,000 miles away, Bering died of scurvy on the desolate island named for him off the Kamchatka Peninsula. "His corpse was tied fast to a plank and thrust down into the ground," wrote the lieutenant who assumed command.

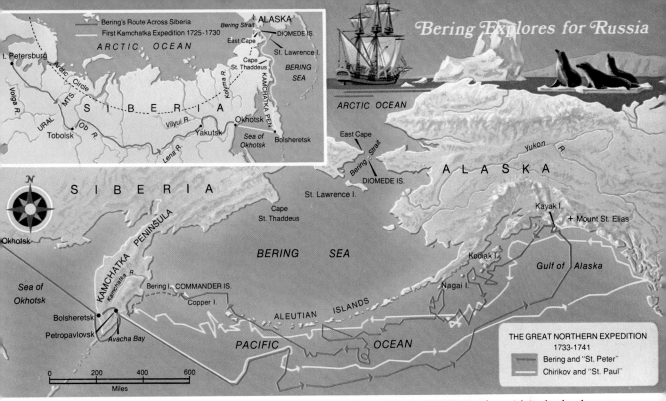

*Bering led two expeditions* (1725–30 and 1733–41) across the plains of Siberia to Okhotsk, using the routes of the Cossacks, and from there by sea to Kamchatka. In 1728 Bering, sailing north from Kamchatka to learn whether Asia and North America joined, passed through Bering Strait in inclement weather.

*Reaching a latitude of 67° 18′ N without sighting land to the east, he decided that the two continents did not join and turned back. Bering sailed eastward in 1741 and sighted the Alaskan coast. Homeward bound, he was shipwrecked on Bering Island and died. The survivors finally reached Kamchatka the next year.*

With the chief officers incapacitated, the chain of command dissolved. The able ones, led by Steller, his artist, and his Cossack servant, organized a kind of cooperative community that nursed Waxell and the other sick back to health and distributed responsibilities among the stronger men. Besides burying the dead and caring for the sick, most of their energy was consumed in beating off the persistent foxes. Snarling and yapping, these animals were always among them, making off with everything movable, even nibbling the toes and fingers of the dead.

Meanwhile, the wind sifted the sand into the crevice where Bering lay, covering him up to the waist. As his shipmates dug it away, Bering stopped them, protesting that only where he was covered was he warm. He knew now that he was dying and, what he dreaded more, that he would be buried on an alien shore far from his native Denmark. Having made up his mind to the inevitable, he showed a composure that impressed Steller, who wrote of him: "That intrepidity and seriousness with which he prepared to meet his death was most worthy of admiration." Vitus Bering died in the early morning of December 8, 1741, and was buried on the isle of the foxes, now named after him.

With the coming of spring, the 46 survivors, whose health, hope, and vigor had in some measure been restored, built from the timbers of the *St. Peter* a new

vessel about half her size. In the new *St. Peter* they finally reached Avacha Bay, sighting the beautiful harbor on August 27, 1742.

By that time the Russian Senate had lost interest in the North Pacific, and politics forced the survivors to wait six years for their recall to St. Petersburg. Waxell was the only commanding officer to live to be honored for his troubles. (Steller died en route to St. Petersburg, leaving other scientists to make use of his reports, which he had sent ahead.)

Although the expedition's Arctic probes had been stopped by scurvy and ice and Chirikov's mission had failed, Bering's overall achievements were significant: The interior of Siberia had been scientifically examined; part of Russia's Pacific coast had been charted; a route had been opened to a newly discovered segment of the Western World. In addition, Spanberg had made two successful voyages to Japan.

For decades, however, Bering's reports lay neglected in the Russian Admiralty's files. Only years later, as curious scientists of western Europe dug them out and brought them to light, did Bering begin to receive his due. His achievement was not fully appreciated, however, until Captain Cook, having sailed the same seas, verified the accuracy of Bering's maps and paid tribute to them. But for Bering, long since dead on a lonely island in the North Pacific, it was too late.

*"Seeing that the North* was closed to us, I thought of means to give my country in the Southern Hemisphere what she no longer possesses in the northern one." So wrote the chevalier de Bougainville (left) after he had witnessed France's loss of Canada to England in the Seven Years' War (1756–63). When he embarked on his expedition in 1766, the Pacific was a vast unknown, and Bougainville did not have accurate charts to guide him. The French encountered both the friendly natives of Tahiti (right) and the unfriendly ones of Melanesia (below in a painting made during Captain Cook's later expedition). The first part of the long Pacific crossing was fairly smooth, but the final leg was marked by hunger, disease, and violence.

*Chapter Seventeen. Seeking to enhance his nation's overseas empire, a French army officer takes command of a ship and boldly sails around the world in search of new lands to claim for France. Voyaging through the South Pacific, he encounters noble savages, cannibals, adventure, and starvation in his quest for unknown isles and continents.*

# From Paradise to Purgatory: Bougainville in the South Pacific

*Aristocrat, diplomat, mathematician, soldier, sailor, and amateur philosopher, Comte Louis Antoine de Bougainville was very much a man of his time, the period of French Enlightenment. Born in Paris in 1729, he gained great fame with his circumnavigation of the globe (1766–69) and his book about the voyage, which became an international bestseller. Though the chevalier's voyage was quickly overshadowed by Cook's, France continued to honor him as a hero. A commodore in the French Navy during the American Revolution and then a field marshal, Bougainville was one of the few aristocrats to survive the French Revolution with distinction. At 51 he married a famous beauty and fathered four children. After enjoying a long and happy old age, he died in 1811, during the first Napoleonic Empire.*

Nations fallen upon hard times usually indulge in some spectacular gesture to restore their pride at home and their prestige and power abroad. So it was that Louis XV's France, bled white by the Seven Years' War with England, decided in 1766 to sponsor a circumnavigation of the world. This feat had been accomplished at least 13 times before but never by a Frenchman, unless one counted a smuggler named Le Gentil de la Barbinais, who had worked his way round on various ships early in the century. Besides, King Louis was anxious to make up for the loss of his colonies in India and North America with possible discoveries in the Pacific Ocean—that great blue third of the world, still largely unexplored.

To lead the expedition, his majesty chose one of the most brilliant young army officers in France: 36-year-old Louis Antoine de Bougainville. At 22 Bougainville had written a treatise on integral calculus that made him internationally famous. But instead of choosing the life of a mathematician, he had become a Black Musketeer and swashbuckled so successfully that he

became the famous Gen. Louis Montcalm's aide-de-camp in Canada during the Seven Years' War. Returning to France as a much-decorated colonel, Bougainville had then generously colonized the eastern part of the Falkland Islands at his own expense "for the greater glory of France."

Although the chevalier was, strictly speaking, a soldier, not a sailor, Louis XV had no hesitation in giving him command of *La Boudeuse*, a new, 26-gun frigate, and a stout storeship named *L'Étoile*. In addition to 11 officers and a crew of 400, Bougainville had the company of three volunteers: the prince of Nassau-Siegen, an adventure-loving nobleman; Pierre Antoine Véron, a young astronomer; and Philibert de Commerson, a middle-aged naturalist. The latter was attended by his valet, a rather effeminate youth named Baré.

*La Boudeuse* sailed from Nantes on November 15, 1766. If Bougainville felt nervous in his new role as *capitaine*, he was soon put to the test. Hardly had he stood out to sea when a storm cracked *La Boudeuse*'s topmast, forcing him to visit Brest for repairs. *L'Étoile*, at harbor in Rochefort, was damaged, too, so badly that her departure for a rendezvous with *La Boudeuse* in the Falkland Islands was delayed by three months.

The chevalier had a sad diplomatic duty to perform before he quit the South Atlantic for the South Pacific. The Falklands, which he had once dreamed of as France's "step toward the discovery of Southern Lands," were to be handed over to France's new ally, Spain, ruler of nearby Argentina. (In return for the Falklands, Spain had reluctantly allowed Bougainville permission to sail into the Pacific.) Louis XV had decided the islands were too small, too bleak, and too poor to become a prosperous settlement and was confident that Bougainville would discover much richer lands later on in his circumnavigation. "On his crossing to China," commanded the king, "he will examine in the Pacific Ocean as much of, and in the best manner he can, the land lying between the Indies and the western seaboard of America. . . . The area to which M. de Bougainville must pay particular attention is what lies between the two tropics. It is in those latitudes that are found precious metals and spices." Perhaps they would even find the fabled Southern Continent.

The cheerful optimism that usually characterizes the early days of an expedition dulled to boredom as Bougainville waited for his storeship in the South Atlantic. *L'Étoile* took her time about joining him, and it was not until June 1767 that contact was reestablished in Rio de Janeiro. By then the Falklands had been handed over, but additional repairs on *L'Étoile* delayed immediate progress south. The Frenchmen spent some months in Rio as the unwelcome guests of Portuguese colonists and then moved on to Montevideo. By the time Bougainville reached the Strait of Magellan in early December, his expedition was already a year old.

The terrible strait was in one of its fighting moods. The chevalier took four days merely to enter it, in the teeth of a foggy gale that eventually split the foresail. "We having sounded, almost at the same moment, only 20 fathom; the fear of the breakers that extend SSE. off Cape Virgins made me resolve to scud under our bare poles." Once in the strait, the ships proceeded cautiously through a chilly, bleak maze of islands, promontories, bays, and narrows. On December 8 Bougainville anchored in the bay that now bears his name and was greeted on shore by a party of Patagonian Indians.

"They then embraced us, and shook hands with us, crying continually *shawa, shawa.* . . . These good people seemed very much rejoiced at our arrival." Commerson began to collect botanical samples, and they rushed to help him, carefully picking the same plant species that he chose. Tobacco and red cloth were exchanged for pelts of vicuna and guanaco. "At every present we gave them, and at every mark of fondness, they repeated their *shawa*, and cried so that it almost stunned us." When Bougainville gave the order to return on board, the Patagonians serenaded them as they set sail and stood knee-deep in the freezing water, watching the boats pull away. "We did not fail, as we left them, to shout *shawa* so loud that the whole coast resounded with it."

As 1767 passed into 1768, the expedition followed the strait's southwesterly trend. "The weather was intolerable; we had rain, snow, a sharp cold air, and a storm; it was such weather as the psalmist describes, saying, 'Snow, hail, and ice, the breath of tempests.'" (Bougainville was actually quoting the Roman historian Livy, *not* Psalm 148.) At times the decks of both ships whitened under powdery drifts four inches deep.

Seeking shelter on January 6, the explorers played reluctant hosts to another group of Indians, which seemed to devour everything they could lay their hands on. Bougainville found it "rather difficult to get rid of these troublesome and disgusting guests," saying they had "an unsupportable stench about them." A sailor on *L'Étoile* gave some bits of glass as a souvenir to a young

## A Miserable Life at the End of the Earth: The Indians of Patagonia and Tierra del Fuego

During his 52-day trip through the Strait of Magellan, Bougainville had ample time to observe the wretched Indians who lived on both sides of the passage. Capt. James Cook, who later stopped at Tierra del Fuego, the island on the southern side of the strait, wrote: "In a Word they are perhaps as miserable a set of People as are this day on Earth." The Yagan tribe, which lived along the island's coast, managed to survive on the scant number of shellfish they picked up

on the beaches. Always on the move for food, they put up flimsy temporary brush huts, like the one below left, as shelters against the buffeting winds. To dull the discomfort of constant chill, they burned fires day and night, thereby giving the island its name—"Land of Fire."

Inland, the Ona Indians roamed the bush in small bands in search of game and migratory birds, which they hunted with bow and arrow. They, too, lived in huts of twigs and skins and burned the perpetual fires. What little extra warmth they had came from skins of the guanaco, a camel-like mammal with a soft, thick coat. The nomadic Indians living along the northern shore of the Strait of Magellan, on the mainland, were called Patagonians ("big feet") by the Spanish for their habit of wrapping their feet in guanaco skins. They gave Bougainville a warm welcome, and he gave them glass beads. In the illustration at right, the artist has probably exaggerated the height of the Patagonians.

boy who had attracted his attention. The child promptly swallowed them and, on returning to shore, "was all at once seized with spitting of blood and violent convulsions." Bougainville and his surgeon managed to administer a dose of gruel, which calmed the child, much to the admiration of the Indians' witch doctors. But later that night anguished howls were heard on shore, and at daybreak the natives were seen hurrying inland. "They, doubtless, fled from a place defiled by death, and by unlucky strangers, who they thought were come merely to destroy them."

Then, on January 26, after 52 days in the strait, Bougainville was rewarded by the sight that had caused Magellan to cry with joy: ". . . an immense horizon, no longer bounded by lands, and a great sea from the west, which announced a vast ocean to us." A steady wind from the north pushed the ships past Cape Pillar and out into the open Pacific.

Then, for the first time, Bougainville felt the heady freedom and the promise of rich discovery that are adrenalin to every explorer. He had calm water, a steady southeasterly wind, and a healthy crew, thanks to the antiscorbutic (scurvy preventive) vegetation collected on the banks of the Río de la Plata. Day after day as the two ships cruised northwest, *L'Étoile* would sail south of *La Boudeuse* to the farthest limit of visibility, then draw close again as night came on. By this method the two ships covered a much larger area of ocean than they would have in close formation.

To keep his men fit, Bougainville employed established antiscorbutic remedies that were medically sound. They included lacing vinegar water with red-hot bullets and purifying water with daily pints of lemonade prepared from citrus powder. Supplemented by plenty of fresh fish and seawater-kneaded bread, this nutritional program was successful at first, but the lack of fruit and vegetables had its inevitable effect. By the end of March, four sailors were suffering from scurvy, and Bougainville began to look anxiously for signs of land in the midst of the great ocean.

On March 21 somebody caught a tuna, "in whose belly we found some little fish, not yet digested, of such species as never go to any distance from the shore." The following day five islands were sighted, and the flotilla excitedly changed course for the nearest.

"As we approached it," wrote Bougainville, "we discovered that it is surrounded with a very level sand, and that all the interior parts of it are covered with thick woods . . . the verdure charmed our eyes, and the cocoa trees everywhere exposed their fruits to our sight, and overshadowed a grassplot adorned with flowers; thousands of birds were hovering about the shore."

But, alas, this Eden proved to be reef-bound. The other islands were equally inaccessible. Before sailing on, the chevalier was astonished to see groups of tall, bronze-skinned men. "My first conjectures were that some Europeans must certainly have been ship-

**Looked at from outer space,** *the Pacific Ocean seems to cover much of the earth. Actually, it occupies a third of it—64 million square miles, with thousands of widely scattered islands. Navigators could not map it correctly until the late 18th century, when methods of determining longitude were finally perfected. The shining isles just above the center are the Hawaiian group.*

wrecked." But a flourish of spears persuaded him otherwise, and he sailed on in a ruminative mood. "Who can give an account of the manner in which they were conveyed thither? . . . I admire their courage, if they live unconcerned on these little strips of sand, which are exposed to be buried in the sea any moment by a hurricane." He collectively named the islands Dangerous Archipelago, the center of the modern Tuamotu group. Scores of other islands were sighted in the days that followed, but none offered water, food, or shelter. The weather grew stormy, and Bougainville's scurvy list lengthened.

Finally, on April 2, 1768, a different skyline rose on the horizon: "We stood northward in order to make it plain, when we saw another land bearing W. by N. the coast of which was not so high, but afforded an indeterminate extent to our eyes. . . ." Bougainville had sighted Mehetia and then found—but did not discover—the Pacific's most beautiful island—Tahiti.

At first, Tahiti seemed determined to play the part of a seductive siren. It held the Frenchmen off with a dead calm; then vanished behind veils of haze; then presented a surfy, apparently harborless shoreline. Only on April 6 did the expedition penetrate the reefs outside Hitiaa Lagoon. So many welcoming canoes crowded around *La Boudeuse* that the chevalier had difficulty securing a good anchorage.

He also found it difficult "to keep at their work 400

## The "Noble Savages" of Tahiti Provided Bougainville With Evidence for Rousseau's Theory

In 1750, 16 years before Bougainville set out for the South Pacific, Jean Jacques Rousseau published a new social theory of the virtues of the "noble savage" in his treatise *Discours sur les arts et sciences.* Essentially, Rousseau believed that man in his natural state was instinctively good but that contact with society corrupted him. His philosophy questioned the notion of historical progress, the value of property, and the efficacy of religion. His concepts took Paris by storm at a time when people of all classes were dissatisfied with the social conditions of the period. Philosophers discussed his ideas in the drawing rooms, and French aristocrats at Versailles, thinking they were following his precepts, dressed as shepherds and shepherdesses and pranced about the gardens with little lambs.

When Bougainville returned to France in 1769 with a real noble savage, he gave

Rousseau's ideas added support. Ahutoru, friend of the Tahitian king, had joined the expedition the year before as an interpreter and navigator. Bougainville romanticized Tahiti as a bower of bliss, a paradise of ease and joy where hunger, disease, and toil did not exist. The men were well built and handsome (far left), and the women often went bare-breasted, bedecking themselves with flowers and shells (left). According to Bougainville, the Tahitians lived in perfect harmony with nature in their bountiful environment, unspoiled by the trappings of sophisticated society. Their wants being few, they lived happily in communal simplicity. Nevertheless, the

Tahitians did have a strong class system, and social inequalities prevailed. Although peaceful at home, they were fiercely warlike, often launching unprovoked attacks in huge war canoes (above) upon their neighbors. They also took a childlike glee in pilfering watches, eyeglasses, and stockings from the Europeans. As Rousseau might have predicted, soon after Ahutoru arrived in Paris, he became the darling of society, developing a sophisticated taste for fine food and wine, opera, and French women. But in time Ahutoru became homesick. Bougainville arranged for his passage back to Tahiti, but he died of smallpox during the voyage home.

young French sailors, who had seen no women for six months." The canoes were full of girls, "most of them naked," sent to tempt the visitors ashore. One of these "fair females" climbed on board the quarterdeck of *La Boudeuse* while the sailors were still heaving at the capstan below. "The girl carelessly dropped a cloth which covered her and appeared to the eyes of all beholders, such as Venus showed herself to the Phrygian shepherd . . . the capstan was never hove with more alacrity than on this occasion."

During the days that followed, Bougainville used mostly classical similes to describe the beauties of Tahiti. He compared its landscape to that of Paradise, its music to ancient love songs, and its people to Greek deities. He even named the island New Cythera, after the birthplace of the goddess of love. His enchantment was understandable in that Tahiti was indeed one of the most beautiful places in the world. But in romanticizing the natives, he created a myth that persists to this day. The French were much influenced by the "noble savage" philosophy of their compatriot Jean Jacques Rousseau, who believed that life in its purest form was enjoyed by men, women, and children living

in a state of nature. Strolling through green vales to the sound of flutes, accepting gifts of fruit and flowers, Bougainville "found hospitality, ease, innocent joy, and every appearance of happiness." He did not notice the incest, infanticide, and rigid class distinctions that a later and more objective explorer was soon to describe. Even the incessant thievery of his hosts, who would offer bananas with one hand and pick pockets with the other, failed to dim his admiration. "What a country!" he exulted. "What a people!"

It seems that some of Bougainville's men were rather less charmed with the Tahitians than he was. The natives' light morals and light fingers alternately seduced and disillusioned sailors unable to comprehend a way of life totally different from that of Europe. On April 10 an islander was found murdered, and two days later three others were bayoneted by soldiers from *La Boudeuse.* The prince of Nassau arrested four suspects. When Bougainville failed to establish individual guilt, he put the four soldiers in irons and planned to make them draw lots as to who should be hanged in expiation for the crime. The soldiers were understandably reluctant to take part in such a lethal guessing game. At this point the prince of Nassau volunteered a formal apology to Ereti, chief of the Tahitians, and his noble bearing so transcended the difficulties of language that friendly relations were restored.

The Frenchmen soon saw indications that they were not the first Europeans to visit Tahiti. One islander, seeing an arsenal of guns aboard *L'Étoile,* shouted *poo-poo!* and made signs indicating death. Other evidence of the visit of English Capt. Samuel Wallis, only eight months before, turned up, but this did not stop Bougainville from formally claiming the island for France. At the end of his nine-day visit, he planted a ceremonial garden of "wheat, barley, oats, maize, onion, and pot herbs" and near the beach buried an Act of Possession and a bottle containing the names of the officers of both ships. Then, on April 15, he sailed.

Ereti followed *La Boudeuse* out through the reef in his canoe, which was laden with farewell presents and weeping women. As a parting favor he begged Bougainville to take with him his friend Ahutoru, who wished to see the world. The chevalier agreed to accept this living souvenir of Tahiti and welcomed Ahutoru aboard. The young man kissed his girl goodby, "gave her three pearls which he had in his ears, kissed her once more, and notwithstanding the tears of this young wife or mistress, he tore himself from her. . . . Thus we quitted this good people; and I was no less surprised at the sorrow they testified on our departure, than at their affectionate confidence on our arrival."

On May 3, 1768, the expedition, sailing west, came upon a group of islands that Ahutoru promptly assumed must be France (actually it was part of the Samoan chain, discovered by Jacob Roggeveen in 1722). He was greatly disillusioned and asked to communicate with the curious natives who soon paddled out to the ships. Seeing they were naked, the young man stripped off his clothes and spoke to them in Tahitian. "But they did not understand him," wrote Bougainville. "They are no more of the same nation here."

The Samoans proved to be unfriendly and dishonest, and Bougainville, aware his expedition was already a year and a half old, impatiently pushed farther west. He was beginning to worry about his food supplies, which had long since lost their freshness. By the time he reached Quirós' Espiritu Santo group (the New Hebrides) on May 22, his crew was again suffering from the "hot mouths" and swollen gums of scurvy.

Putting ashore on one island, whose diseased natives earned it the name Isle of Lepers (modern Aoba), the French collected a supply of fruits and firewood. They offered baubles and red cloth in exchange, which the natives accepted before suddenly attacking with stones and arrows. Musket fire drove them into the woods, and Bougainville sailed on, not overimpressed with the New Hebrides.

Before leaving the archipelago for good, he was asked to investigate a rumor aboard his ships. It concerned Commerson's effeminate servant, Baré—in particular "his shape, voice, beardless chin, and scrupulous attention to not changing his linen in the presence of anyone." There was strong evidence that Baré was not all he seemed to be. In fact, the Tahitians had guessed at once that something was, so to speak, amiss.

"When I came on board *L'Étoile,* Baré, with her face bathed in tears, owned to me that she was a woman . . . that well she knew when she embarked that we were going around the world, and that such a voyage had raised her curiosity." Bougainville was more amused than angry, aware that Baré was well on her way to becoming history's first known female circumnavigator. "It must be owned, that if the two ships had been wrecked on any desert isle in the ocean, Baré's fate would have been a very singular one."

On May 29 the New Hebrides disappeared from view behind the French ships, and for a week the expedition cruised westward before a favorable wind. During this period of relative inactivity the pangs of hunger became more pronounced. Rather than eat any more of *La Boudeuse*'s decomposing salt meat, Bougainville joined his shipmates in a supper of rats and "found them very good."

At 11 p.m. on the moonlit night of June 4, a long line of breakers was seen ahead, glowing whitely against

## Polynesian Sailors Read the Seas and Skies

The vast open water, uncharted islands, tricky currents, and shifting winds of the Pacific intimidated Europeans. Not so the Polynesians. These fearless navigators knew the ocean and fashioned detailed "maps" (below) that depicted its currents with twigs and its islands with cowry shells. They also understood helpful signs of nature: Stationary clouds on the horizon could signify an unseen volcanic island, and low-hanging, thin formations might denote changing weather. Sailing from Tahiti to Hawaii, more than 4,000 miles away, Polynesians would chart their course by the flight of the golden plover on its annual migration northward. At night, they plotted the way by stars because they knew their shifting seasonal positions. The Polynesian mariners believed that their long voyages were protected by deities and that the kindly rainbow god would lead them safely to their destination. Seaworthy canoes made from dug-out trees transported them over the long stretches. For the most part, the boats were one of two types—outriggers or double canoes. The latter were much like modern catamarans: Wooden planks joined the two halves together, and a cabin on top sheltered food for the trip. Vegetable gum mixed with soil prevented leakage; lateen sails made of thick leaves propelled the boats across the deep. The paddles also served as rudders, stones in baskets were anchors, and wooden scoops were used to bail out water.

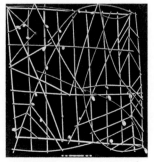

## Mysterious Monuments of Easter Island

Bougaïnville chose not to go to Easter Island, a desolate spot 2,000 miles off the coast of Chile, because its latitude was uncertain. He knew about the island—its mysterious, tall statues of volcanic rock and strange dark-skinned people with reddish hair—from the travels of Jacob Roggeveen, who first sighted the island Easter Sunday 1722. In 1786 Jean La Pérouse, following Bougaïnville's voyage, landed on Easter Island and

examined the bizarre gray monuments with their shoulder-length earlobes and heavy red headpieces (above). He did not think they were "idols, although the Indians have shown a sort of veneration for them." Today, only a few Easter Islanders survive. No one knows where they came from or how they got there. Only the inscrutable stone effigies remain (right), as before.

the dark horizon. This seemed to indicate a reef or sandbank, and Bougainville managed to tack safely past it. But other dangerous-looking shoals soon appeared. "Some of our people even were of opinion they saw a low land to the SW. of the breakers." Bougainville had in fact reached the outskirts of the Great Barrier Reef, and that distant glimmer of land was Australia's Pacific coast.

Now peaks of coral began to bite through the waves, and the chevalier decided to change course for the north. He was not tempted to seek out an opening in the reef, having concluded that "no advantage could be expected" from exploring beyond it.

From then on the fortunes of the expedition deteriorated rapidly. Although New Guinea, whose misty mountains were sighted on June 10, looked fertile and tempting, Bougainville spent two weeks battling against winds and current that sought to sweep him along its southern shore. Terrified of being lost in what looked like a great stormy bay (it was actually Torres Strait, which might have led him smoothly into the

Indian Ocean), the chevalier inched his way back east against almost insuperable odds. Contrary gales loosened the masts, ship-high waves dumped sand and weeds on deck, and dense fogs forced the two vessels to keep in touch by cannon fire. Meanwhile, malnutrition among the men reached such proportions that Bougainville had "to forbid the eating of that leather, which is wrapped around the yards, and any other old leather, as it might have the most dreadful consequences." He himself, one crewmember noted sourly, seemed to have secret supplies of food "and enjoys a most satisfactory fullness of figure, which is something of an insult to the leanness of our faces." As commander, Bougainville was of course entitled to some extra rations, but these consisted only of ancient eggs, goat's milk, and an occasional cup of bitter chocolate. His well-fed appearance was, in fact, due to a natural plumpness, and his cheerful demeanor concealed considerable internal suffering.

At last, on June 26, the flotilla rounded New Guinea's southeastern tip, which Bougainville named Cape Deliverance, and proceeded north, still pursued by storms. Within two days Bougainville sighted what turned out to be the Solomon Islands, discovered by Álvaro de Mendaña de Neyra two centuries earlier. However, since Mendaña had not been to this area of the Solomons, he had not charted them, and Bougainville was uncertain of their relationship. Off Choiseul, swarms of Melanesian natives resisted their visitors with "horrible cries" and volleys of arrows and spears. While fighting them off, Bougainville captured a canoe in which he found "the jaw of a man, half broiled." The sight did not encourage him to linger, and he sailed on in search of a more hospitable anchorage.

This was found off the coast of New Ireland: a deserted bay (modern Kambotorosch Harbor) watered by four fresh streams. Bougainville promptly ordered his men to take on water and firewood and to wash. Unfortunately, the surrounding jungle yielded few antiscorbutic plants, save for latania and cabbage palms swarming with ants. Scorpions and sea snakes made hunting and fishing dangerous. The tropical rain, which had hardly let up since the rounding of Cape Deliverance, eroded morale, rotted bandages, and hampered repair work on the wind-weakened ships. Poor Bougainville was not even allowed to feel the pride of a discoverer: One of his sailors, searching for shells on the beach, uncovered a "piece of a plate of lead, on which we read these remains of English words: '. . . HOR'D HERE . . . ICK MAJESTY'S.'" Not until his circumnavigation was almost completed did Bougainville learn who his predecessor was: the English navigator Philip Carteret, who had landed there several months earlier.

The chevalier's misery was climaxed by an earthquake. The shocks were so violent that they were felt aboard ship, and for two minutes the sea heaved sick-

*Sailors and Scientists*

eningly. It seemed that nature itself was foretelling the doom of his expedition. Eight days in this purgatory were as much as Bougainville could stand, and he put to sea again on July 24, resolving to reach the Dutch Moluccas or starve in the attempt.

He very nearly did starve, and his men with him. By the middle of August what was left of the ships' salt meat was so putrid that only the most dauntless could eat it. "People have long argued about the location of Hell," wrote Bougainville despairingly. "Frankly, we have discovered it." A few days later the first scurvy death occurred. More were sure to follow.

Then, at dawn on August 30, 1768, fires were seen twinkling on the horizon. Shortly after midnight, "a pleasant scent exhaled from the aromatic plants with which the Moluccas abound . . . announced the end of our calamities to us." Next day the emaciated explorers stepped ashore at the little Dutch settlement of Buru Island and were treated to a lavish supper by kindly Dutch colonials. "One must have been a sailor, and

reduced to the extremities which we had felt for several months together, in order to form an idea of the sensation which the sight of greens and a good supper produced in people in that condition."

Although Bougainville had a seven-and-a-half-month voyage still ahead of him, the exploratory part of his circumnavigation was over. Rested, refreshed, and largely restored to health, the Frenchmen continued homeward via Batavia, where many of the crew fell ill with dysentery. Desiring a healthier environment, Bougainville ordered the expedition to continue on to the French colony of Mauritius, in the Indian Ocean, where the sick could be hospitalized and the ships could be overhauled for the voyage ahead. Because the expedition was essentially over, the ships no longer needed to travel together, so, while *L'Étoile* remained in Mauritius to be careened, *La Boudeuse* sailed for France in December. The ship dropped anchor at St. Malo on March 16, 1769, and Bougainville was proclaimed a hero by a proud nation.

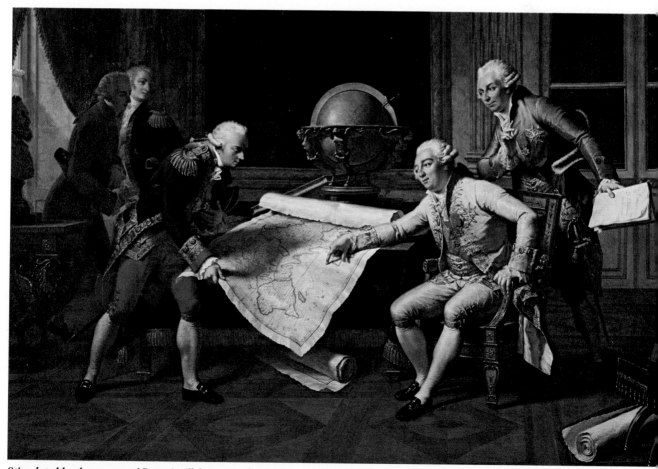

*Stimulated by the success of Bougainville's voyage, the French decided to compete with England in the race for South Sea colonies and control of the sea trade routes. Here Louis XVI (who would be guillotined in the French Revolution) confers with*

*Comte Jean La Pérouse before the latter's expedition to the Pacific in 1785. Unfortunately, the venture was a disaster: La Pérouse and his ships disappeared somewhere in the South Pacific. Years later, wreckage of the fleet was found in Melanesia.*

*Bougainville in the South Pacific*

*From the quarterdeck of the converted* 462-ton *collier* Resolution (*above*), *the flagship of his second and third voyages, Cook mapped the remote islands of Hawaii (top), or "Owhyhee," in 1778. No explorer has excelled Cook in the extent and accuracy of his discoveries. This original chart of the islands is typical of the careful detail that established the Englishman's reputation as a superb cartographer. Many of Cook's maps remained in use for generations after his death. On his second and third voyages, the calculation of longitude, a matter of collating astronomical readings and tables, was made more precise by using the chronometer (right), invented in 1759. Since a knowledge of the correct time is essential to the calculation of longitude, the British government had offered a £20,000 prize for a clock that would not be affected by a ship's rolling motion, dampness, or changes in climate. John Harrison won the prize. Larcum Kendall copied Harrison's chronometer for Cook, who prized it.*

*Capt. James Cook did not become an explorer until he was 40 years old. Nathaniel Dance painted him holding one of his prized maps (above) when Cook was 47, at the height of his fame and shortly before his third and last voyage to the Pacific.*

*Chapter Eighteen. Ordered to search for a southern continent and a northwest passage, a brilliant English navigator makes three long voyages to the Pacific with a company of sailors and scientists. Though he discovers neither continent nor passage, his ability to find and chart coasts reveals the immense ocean in accurate detail for the first time.*

# "Endeavour" and "Resolution": Cook's Three Great Voyages

*Showing a natural aptitude for the sea, James Cook (born in England, 1728) first served on colliers (coal boats) sailing the rough waters off the British Isles. Enlisting in the Royal Navy just before the Seven Years' War (1756–63), he made a difficult coastal survey of the St. Lawrence River and parts of Newfoundland and Nova Scotia, which established his reputation as a superb chartmaker. This attracted The Royal Society and navy to him when a search for the supposed Southern Continent was proposed. Cook's great ability as a leader and diplomat also insured the success of his three voyages. Though he did not "invent" a cure for scurvy, his careful attention to the health of his men, seeing to it that they ate sauerkraut and other antiscorbutic foods and drank fresh water, became a lasting inspiration to all navies.*

June 3, 1769, was a brilliantly hot day in Tahiti. Matavai Bay lay still as glass beneath a cloudless sky, mirroring the squat shape of His Majesty's Ship *Endeavour*. On shore, a group of English scientists and naval officers clustered about two telescopes pitched firmly in the sand. Pieces of smoked glass for looking at the sun were handed around solemnly. Then, at precisely 21 minutes, 50 seconds past 9 on the astronomical clock, an excited shout rang out from the spectators. A slight smudge had appeared on the rim of the sun. Venus was beginning one of its rare solar transits.

Soon the leader of the expedition realized that something was wrong. "We very distinctly saw an Atmosphere or dusky shade round the body of the Planet . . .," he wrote, "and we differed from one another in observing the times of the Contacts much more than could be expected." By 3 o'clock, as Venus was disappearing into the blue again, the observers were puzzled and disappointed. It seemed to the scientists that their entire journey from England—a vital part of international efforts to compute the earth's distance

from the sun—had ended in failure.

Lt. James Cook, commander of the *Endeavour*, was not greatly concerned. His official admiralty instructions made it plain that the Tahiti observation was merely a prelude to something of much greater importance. "When this Service is performed you are to put to Sea without Loss of Time, and carry into execution the Additional Instructions contained in the enclosed Sealed Packet." Then, as his sailors cleared the ship's hull of sea life and spruced her up for departure, he pored over the secret document.

"Whereas there is reason to imagine that a Continent or Land of great extent may be found to the Southward of the tract lately made by Captain Wallis. . . . You are to proceed to the southward in order to make discovery of the Continent above-mentioned, until you arrive in the Latitude of 40°, . . . But not having discovered it, or any evident signs of it on that Run, you are to proceed in search of it to the Westward."

The Southern Continent! Since the time of the ancient Greeks, cosmographers had been discussing the concept of Terra Australis Incognita, a landmass below the Tropic of Capricorn that, they felt, must exist as a counterweight to the crowded continents of the Northern Hemisphere. Without it, the earth would surely have wobbled off its axis long ago, like an unbalanced top. Glimpses of Australia, Tasmania, and New Zealand by various Dutch and Spanish explorers had aroused speculation that the Southern Continent might be a combination of all three. Another theory was that an even vaster land lay farther south, centering perhaps on the pole. Members of the Samuel Wallis expedition, who had discovered Tahiti in 1767, thought they saw southern mountains in the radiance of a Pacific sunset. Alexander Dalrymple, England's most eminent armchair explorer, had gone so far as to calculate the continent's population: 50 million. "There is at present no

## On Tahiti, Cook Found Noble Chiefs, Warring Tribes, Friendly Women, and Bold Thieves

Cook stopped in Tahiti during each of his voyages, anchoring his ships at Matavai Bay (depicted below by William Hodges, an artist on the second expedition) because the climate was warm, food plentiful, and the people genial. On his first visit, Cook was sent to observe the transit of Venus across the sun, calculated to take place on June 3, 1769. He arrived seven weeks earlier to set up an observatory and a fort to protect it—but not without first asking the chief for permission to fell trees to build the fort.

Despite Cook's extreme courtesy, he had problems with the Tahitians, who were friendly but "prodigious thieves." As soon as the observatory was completed, Cook's quadrant—the instrument with which he was to make the astronomical readings—was stolen. It was recovered, however, in ample time.

The Tahitians' notion of property was completely incomprehensible to Cook. One night as he lay awake in his bed, they made off with stockings he had put under his pillow. From Joseph Banks, they stole a white jacket and waistcoat with silver frogs. Threatened with punishment for such thievery, the Tahitians refused to supply Cook's crew with food if reprisal measures were taken.

The crew found their experiences with the Tahitian women more pleasant. Banks, however, was not without complaint. "There were no places of retirement," he wrote. "The houses being entirely without walls, we had no opportunity of putting their politeness to every test that maybe some of us would not have failed to have done had circumstances been more favorable."

trade from Europe thither," wrote Dalrymple, and he painted a glowing picture of a market "sufficient to maintain the power, dominion, and sovereignty of Britain, by employing all its manufactures and ships." It was important to discover the continent before some other European nation did.

This was the real purpose of Cook's voyage. No wonder, given the rewards of such a discovery, that his orders were so shrouded in secrecy. It was a stupendous assignment—in effect looking for an unknown land in an unknown sea—and the lords of the admiralty thought long and hard before choosing Cook to undertake it. In doing so, they not only passed over the head of Dalrymple (who had announced, from his armchair, that he would graciously accept command of the expedition), but also over the heads of many commanders more experienced, and more blueblooded, than the 40-year-old lieutenant. Clearly, he must be something out of the ordinary. About six feet tall, large-boned, with a jutting jaw and decisive mouth, Cook exuded authority. He was a humane, sensible, bluntly spoken man, plain to the point of colorlessness. His only fault as a leader was said to be a volcanic temper, which, however, erupted very rarely.

H.M.S. *Endeavour* was exactly the kind of vessel Cook felt most at home in: a fat, ugly, sturdy collier of 368 tons, seasoned by almost four years of grimy service on the North Sea coal route. He had personally supervised much of the necessary work of conversion: An extra layer of wood, impregnated with nails, was added to her shallow hull to protect against shipworm; cabins were subdivided to house the extra personnel and equipment; enough food was laid on to last 12 months; and 22 guns were installed in case of hostilities at sea. By late summer the ship was ready, the crew recruited, and a distinguished group of scientists, naturalists, and artists welcomed aboard at Plymouth. "All were in excellent health and spirits," wrote Joseph Banks, the expedition's wealthy young botanist, "perfectly prepared (in Mind at least) to undergo with Cheerfulness any fatigues or dangers that may occur in our intended Voyage."

Cook gave the order to sail on the afternoon of August 25, 1768. The *Endeavour*'s stubby nose pushed across Plymouth Sound and out into the English Channel and the Atlantic Ocean. After a stop in the Madeira Islands, she was soon swishing placidly south toward South America, Cape Horn, the Pacific, and Tahiti.

Eleven months later, the observation of Venus was completed, and Cook's secret instructions commanded him to put to sea again "without Loss of Time." Rounding up his crew, not without difficulty (two young marines had "strongly attached themselves" to Tahitian girls), he weighed anchor on July 13, 1769. Natives in canoes that accompanied the ship out of the harbor cried like children as the *Endeavour* moved out to sea. No doubt there were a few tears shed on board, too. Cook wrote an affectionate description of the islanders in his journal: ". . . the men in general are tall, strong-limbed, and well-shaped (one of the tallest we saw measured Six feet 3 Inches and a half), the superior women are in every respect as large as Europeans. . . . Both sexes eradicate every hair from under their armpits, and look upon it as a mark of uncleanliness in us that we do not do the same. They all have fine white teeth, and, for the most part, short flat noses and thick lips, yet their features are agreeable and their gait graceful . . . and their behaviour to strangers and to each other is open, affable, and courteous, and (from all I could see) free from treachery; only that they are thieves to a Man . . . and that with such dexterity as would shame the most noted pickpocket in Europe."

Already, Cook was exhibiting the qualities that were to mark his career as an explorer: a freedom from ethnic prejudice, a willingness to admit the faults of his own race, and a blindspot regarding the free-and-easy Polynesian attitude toward property. Deep within his Yorkshire bones was bred the belief that a man was entitled to keep his own snuffbox. A reasonable belief, perhaps—but it was one day to kill him.

For almost a month the *Endeavour* glided through an enchanting archipelago that Cook named the Society Islands, "as they lay contiguous to each other." His guide was Tupia, a Tahitian priest who had begged to accompany the expedition. When asked for proof of his geographical knowledge, Tupia unhesitatingly reeled off a list of 130 islands, 74 of which he sketched on a map for Cook. "But we cannot find that he either knows or ever heard of a Continent."

After August 9 there were no more islands to be seen, and as the *Endeavour* ploughed on south, the weather began to chill. Day after day lookouts scanned the horizon ahead, but nothing came over it save an endless succession of cold gray swells. The 40th parallel was crossed early in September, by which time Cook was convinced "we had no prospect of meeting with land." He brought to in the teeth of a gale and then, following his official orders, changed course for the west.

After another month of passing through empty water, the sight of seaweed, floating wood, and sea birds indicated that land was being approached. Cook realized that this was New Zealand, which had been discovered a century earlier by the Dutch explorer Abel Tasman. All Tasman had seen, however, was part of its western coast. For all Cook knew, New Zealand might be a massive extension of the elusive Terra Australis.

Forested hills were sighted on October 7, and two days later Cook dropped anchor in a steep-sided bay. "All hands seem to agree," wrote Joseph Banks, "that this is certainly the continent we are in search of."

Smoke rising from various points on shore proved

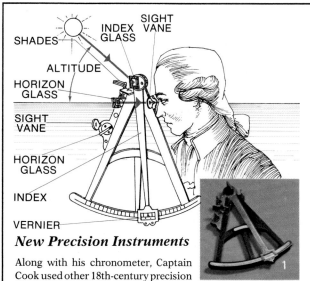

## New Precision Instruments

Along with his chronometer, Captain Cook used other 18th-century precision instruments to map a third of the world. To determine latitude, Cook used a Hadley octant (1). He looked through the sight vane (see diagram above) into an index glass reflecting the sun. Next, he moved the center arm, upon which the index glass was fixed, until the horizon glass on the stationary arm picked up the sun's image. The angle formed between the two arms corresponded to the angle between the sun and the horizon, and the vernier indicated the sun's altitude. Hadley's octant, developed in 1731, proved far more accurate than the quadrant (2), a favorite of mariners for centuries. The azimuth compass (3) was used to locate a star needed as a guidepost by measuring the arc between it and the North Pole, while the inclinometer (4) showed variations in the earth's magnetic field, enabling Cook to calculate true north. Cook used a station pointer (5) to determine his position between two known points and a parallel ruler (6) to help plot courses on Mercator maps.

that the land was inhabited. Cook soon discovered that the "Indians" of New Zealand understood the language of Tupia. But he also discovered that they were considerably less friendly than the Tahitians had been. Cook recounted in his journal: "I rowed round the head of the Bay, but could find no place to land, on account of the great surf, which beat everywhere upon the shore; seeing two boats or Canoes coming in from Sea, I rowed to one of them. . . . Tupia called to them to come along side and we would not hurt them, but instead of doing this they endeavoured to get away, upon which I ordered a Musket to be fired over their heads. . . . Here I was mistaken, for they immediately took to their arms, or whatever they had in the boat, and began to attack us. This obliged us to fire upon them, and unfortunately either two or three were killed."

Some terrified boys who had jumped into the water were hauled on board and taken to the *Endeavour*. There the remorseful Cook saw that they were clothed and treated with the utmost kindness. "To the surprise of everybody, they became at once as cheerful and as merry as if they had been with their own friends."

The hasty killing of the Maori, however, caused a pall of depression to settle over the ship. Cook wrote (and later crossed out) an agonized self-criticism in his journal, and Joseph Banks, who had taken part in the slaughter, described the day as the worst in his life: "Black be the mark for it, and heaven send that such may never return to embitter future reflection."

At dawn on October 11, Cook deposited his young guests ashore but did not dare stay to look for fresh fruit and green vegetables. Worried about the danger of scurvy to his men, he put to sea again, naming his first landing place Poverty Bay, "because it afforded us no one thing that we wanted."

Fortunately, the Maori elsewhere along the coast proved to be more hospitable, and Cook explored as far south as 40° before turning again (at Cape Turnagain) and heading north to the tip of New Zealand. Water, wood, vegetables, and wildfowl were traded in gener-

## In New Zealand, Cook Found the Maori: A Tattooed Tribe With a Taste for Human Flesh

Cook's quest for the unknown Southern Continent took him to New Zealand after navigating the Society Islands. After anchoring the *Endeavour* in Poverty Bay, he met a group of hostile Maori in a canoe (below). Upon landing, the tribesmen did a war dance. Cook wrote: "Then with a Regular Jump from Left to Right . . . they brandished Their Weapons, distorted their Mouths, Lolling out their Tongues and Turned up the Whites of their Eyes Accompanied with a strong hoarse song, Calculated to Cheer Each Other and Intimidate Their Enemies."

Admiring the Maori for their courage, pugnacity, and straightforwardness, Cook noted their physical and cultural likeness to the Tahitians and concluded they were of the same stock. "Indeed many of [their] Notions and Customs are the very same but nothing is so great a [proof] . . . as their Language which differs in a very few words the one from the Other." In addition to the similarity between their tongues, both Tahitians and Maori were tall and well built, with wavy hair and nut-brown skin. They also had similar customs. Both sported tattoos, some tattooing only their faces—such as the native peering over Charles Clerke's shoulder (opposite right)—while others marked various parts of their bodies as well. They used sharply pointed bones or shells to prick flamboyant arabesques and elaborate swirls in their flesh and mixed the soot from their lamps with

water to fill the wounds and color the designs black. One of Cook's crew—a Mr. Stainsby—started the long and noble tradition of tattooed sailors by becoming the first ordinary seaman to undergo the torturous procedure.

Although Cook believed the Maori and Tahitians were descended from a common source, he could not imagine where they originally came from. Today, most scholars feel sure that the Maori are Polynesians who left the Society Islands in two waves, the first about A.D. 1150, the second about A.D. 1350. They made the 2,000-mile journey to New Zealand in canoes, 60 to 100 feet long, bringing along dried fish and fresh water stored in

seaweed bags for the voyage. In addition, they transported sweet potato and breadfruit seeds to plant in their new home, and dogs for livestock. A few rats came, too, as uninvited guests. As for their origin, most ethnologists now believe the Polynesians came from southeastern Asia, while others say they came from India. In apparent support of the India-origin theory, a Maori legend says they came from a dry land called Irihia, which scholars take to be Vrihia, an ancient name for India. Others, such as Thor Heyerdahl of *Kon-Tiki* fame, believe they originally came from the northwest coast of South America, long after having crossed the Bering land

*Sailors and Scientists*

ous quantities for cloth and nails, and the visitors were even permitted to tour a Maori *pa* (fortified village), which impressed them greatly.

Gales and hurricanes buffeted the *Endeavour* as she rounded North Cape in late December. This did not prevent the crew from celebrating Christmas in the traditional English way. "Goose pie was eaten with great approbation," wrote Banks, "and in the Evening all hands were as Drunk as our forefathers used to be upon the like occasion."

Cook then reached New Zealand's west coast and fought his way south to explore it. No matter how squally the weather, he persisted in charting every mile of shoreline he could see. As the spidery dots assembled themselves on paper, New Zealand began to look less and less like a continent and more and more like a scimitar-shaped island, which he was circumnavigating counterclockwise. But when he swung east to complete his great oval, on January 14, 1770, he found himself in a strait, "very broad and deep." More land,

blue-green and mountainous, stretched away to the south. Clearly, New Zealand was more than one island.

Before exploring the land to the south, the *Endeavour* made a recuperative stop in an inlet on its northern tip that Cook named Queen Charlotte Sound. Rich with wild celery and "scurvy-grass," loud with birdsong and tinkling with fresh water, this sanctuary was to become his favorite base in the Southern Hemisphere. Yet here, on January 17, Cook had his first experience of Maori cannibalism.

"Soon after we landed we met with two or three of the Natives, who not long before must have been regaling themselves upon human flesh, for I got from one of them the bone of the fore arm of a Man or Woman which was quite fresh, and the flesh had been but lately picked off, which they told us they had eat. They gave us to understand that but a few days ago they had taken, killed, and eat a Boat's crew of their enemies. . . . To show us that they had eat the flesh they bit and gnawed the bone, and drawed it through their

deserts and rain forests. Artist William Hodges painted the romantic view of Dusky Sound (below) during the second voyage.

It took Cook six months of his first voyage to map New Zealand, narrowly escaping dangerous waterspouts (left) —typhoonlike winds that can destroy a ship in seconds. During those months he spent seven weeks ashore studying the natives, while Banks and Solander collected specimens of flora and fauna. Later, Cook's thorough and insightful observations of the Maori made a profound contribution to the development of ethnology as a science.

Cook recognized that the fertile land of New Zealand held great promise for settlement, but despite his praise, coloniza-

bridge from Asia thousands of years earlier. Heyerdahl points to similarities between the northwest coast Indians and the Polynesians, such as their large dugout canoes, elaborate woodwork designs, and reverence of high carved idols. Wherever they originated, the Maori did not come to New Zealand from Australia and are in no way related to the aborigines who migrated to Australia from Asia around 25,000 B.C.

In addition to the observations that Cook and others made of the Maori, naturalists Daniel Solander and Joseph Banks collected more than 400 species of plants unknown in Europe. There was a striking variety of scenery, from snow-covered mountains and rugged fiords to

tion did not begin for another 70 years. The colonists were mostly middle-class shopkeepers and small farmers looking for a better life than they had in England—a marked contrast to the forced settlement of Australia by British convicts. Settlers began to arrive in New Zealand in the 1830's. In 1841 Great Britain annexed it to the Commonwealth.

The immigrants' desire for property brought them into sharp conflict with the Maori, whose lands they appropriated. The struggle reached its height during the 1860's, a decade with bloody strife known as the Maori Wars. Today, there are 3 million New Zealanders, 14 percent of whom are Maori. Of the latter only 20 percent are fullblooded.

*Among the strange animals found in Australia were the kangaroo (top) and the dingo, a wild dog (above). Baffled when he first saw a roo, Joseph Banks said, "What to liken him [to] I cannot tell." Nevertheless, the crew dined on it, and Cook pronounced it "excellent." Banks brought skins of both animals back to England, where George Stubbs did these fine paintings from them.*

Plants, etc. would thrive here. In short, was this Country settled by an industrious people they would very soon be supplied not only with the necessaries, but many of the luxuries of life."

Cook had now fulfilled all his secret instructions, with largely negative results. "As to a Southern Continent," he wrote, "I do not believe any such thing exists, unless in a high latitude." Far from being disappointed, he actually seemed pleased to refute Dalrymple's theory. The lieutenant was by nature a pessimistic explorer. Unlike the visionary Columbus, who adjusted his discoveries to suit his imagination, Cook never believed anything until he had seen it with his own eyes and had plotted it on paper with his own instruments. He was strongly tempted to return home eastward across the South Pacific, just to make sure the elusive continent was indeed a chimera; but the Antarctic winter was setting in, and his men were beginning to "sigh for roast beef." On March 31 he decided to head in the opposite direction, toward the Cape of Good Hope. He knew, of course, that a gigantic obstacle lay in his path: the unmapped mass of Australia. How near or far that land might be was a mystery, because no European had ever laid eyes on its eastern shore. Well, he would simply sail west until it appeared in the sea ahead of him and then follow it north.

After 19 days of sweeping across the Tasman Sea, a dark blur was seen on the rainy horizon (Cape Everard, near the southeastern extremity of Australia). Cook was prevented by squalls from discovering whether Tasmania was joined to the mainland or not. Instead, he followed the coast toward the north and was pleased to see clumps of green inland: Obviously, Australia was not the bitter desert the Dutch imagined it to be.

On April 28, 1770, the explorer anchored in a bay that he called Sting Ray Harbour, after the multitudes of barb-spined fish found in its warm waters. Later, he changed the name to Botany Bay, "from the great number of new plants collected there." He had the Union Jack raised on shore every day and had the date of the *Endeavour*'s arrival carved into the bark of a gum tree. (He later claimed Australia's entire eastern coast for Britain.) A few naked "Indians" (aborigines) half-heartedly threw darts at the white invaders and showed no interest in the presents laid out for them. Cook wrote, "All they seemed to want was for us to be gone." After recording an admiring impression of the fertility and healthfulness of the bay, Cook continued north on May 6, mapping the coast in minute detail. He noted, but curiously did not explore, a magnificent "Bay or Harbour"—the future port of Sydney.

Late in May, offshore shoals began to interrupt the *Endeavour*'s progress. Without knowing it, Cook was moving into the jaws of the Pacific's most formidable deathtrap: the Great Barrier Reef. Stretching for well over 1,000 miles along the tropical Queensland coast in northeast Australia, it consists of an almost unbroken

mouth, and this in such a manner that plainly showed that the flesh to them was a dainty bit."

The Englishmen took a determinedly scientific view of this savage practice, and Banks went so far as to buy the uneaten preserved head of a victim.

Having taken formal possession of Queen Charlotte Sound for Britain, Cook sailed on eastward through the great strait that now bears his name. Turning south, he circumnavigated the rest of New Zealand in a clockwise direction, thus completing a gigantic figure of eight and proving that "this country, which before now was thought to be part of the imaginary southern continent, consists of Two large Islands."

Back in Queen Charlotte Sound at the end of March 1770, Cook was able to draw history's first map of the New Zealand archipelago—a chart so amazingly accurate that it is still valuable today. His commentary in his journal contained prophetic words: "Although it is a hilly, mountainous Country, yet the very hills and mountains are many of them covered with wood, and the Soil of the plains and Valleys appeared to be rich and fertile . . . all sorts of European grain, fruits,

chain of islands, shallows, and razor-sharp coral. Since he was already walled in on both sides, the explorer had no choice but to continue north at a snail's pace, ceaselessly throwing the lead to gauge his ship's draught. On the moonlit night of June 11, everything seemed to be going well: Visibility was clear, the water calm and deep. Then, shortly before 11 o'clock, there was a jarring shock, and coral crunched through the *Endeavour*'s hull. They had struck an invisible reef. The ship had hardly come to a halt before Cook was on deck, shouting orders. He recorded the action in his journal: "We took in all our sails, hoisted out the boats, and sounded round the Ship, and found that we had got upon the SE. edge of a reef of Coral rocks. . . . We went to work to lighten her as fast as possible, which seemed to be the only means we had left to get her off . . . throwed over board our guns, Iron and stone ballast Casks, Hoops, staves, oil Jars, decayed stores, etc. . . . All this time the Ship made little or no water."

Despite this frantic jettisoning of more than 50 tons, the *Endeavour* could not be budged from her position. The tide fell, causing her to settle more and more heavily upon the dangerous coral. The anguished Cook had nothing to do but throw out anchors and wait for the next tide. But when it came, the ship remained stuck fast to the jagged reef. To make matters worse, she heeled to starboard and began to take in water, "as much as two pumps would free."

At 9 p.m. on June 12, rising seas lurched the *Endeavour* upright again, and the leak began to gain on the pumps. "This was an alarming and I may say terrible Circumstance," wrote Cook, "and threatened immediate destruction to us as soon as the Ship was afloat. However, I resolved to risk all and heave her off in case it was practical, and accordingly turned as many hands to the Capstan and windlass as could be spared from the Pumps. . . . About 20 minutes past 10 o'clock the ship floated, and we hove her off into deep water."

Actually, as Cook later discovered, the ship did not "float" off the reef at all. His desperate crew pulled so strongly upon the anchor cables that a piece of the hill of coral beneath snapped off and was carried away in the *Endeavour*'s woodwork. As such, it acted like a plug, miraculously filling most of the hole it had itself created. Attempting to stem the flooding, Cook bandaged the hull's wound with a fother—a sail padded with wool, oakum, and dirt that was dragged under the keel and sucked into place by water pressure. Then, while her crew reflected on how narrowly they had escaped becoming the first permanent settlers of Australia, the ship limped slowly across to the mainland for repairs, her pumps working rapidly. The sturdy collier had survived an accident that probably would have destroyed a regular naval frigate.

Anchoring at the mouth of a river that he promptly named Endeavour, Cook set his carpenters to work. During the next seven weeks the rest of the crew recovered from their ordeal by hunting, fishing, and botanizing to their hearts' content. The giant local shellfish (one cockle served two people) caused much comment, as did a greyhoundlike "Animal" that the men managed to shoot. Cook described it: "The head, neck, and

**The Great Barrier Reef** (above), a treacherous coral labyrinth extending 1,250 miles down the northeastern coast of Australia, is a formidable obstacle to all ships. Trying to maneuver northward to the shore on its western side, the Endeavour grounded on razor-sharp coral, which gashed her oaken hull. To stop the inrushing water, the crew used a process called fothering: They stretched a sail, smeared it with wool, oakum, and dirt, and used ropes to haul the sail under the ship, where it swelled and covered the hole. Cook then gingerly navigated the crippled ship into the mouth of a river, now called the Endeavour, where the crew labored on the careened vessel (above) for seven weeks, patching the damaged hull with wood and other materials.

*Map for Cook on page 199.*

shoulders of this Animal was very small in proportion to the other parts; the tail was nearly as long as the body. . . . Its progression is by hopping or jumping 7 or 8 feet at each hop upon its hind legs only. . . . The skin is covered with a short hairy fur of a dark Mouse or Grey colour. Excepting the head and ears, which I thought was something like a Hare's, it bears no resemblance to any European Animal I ever saw."

The local aborigines, who put in a shy appearance after three weeks' hesitation, uttered the word *kangoo-roo* when shown the animal. They seemed to resent Cook and his men catching turtles in the estuary and attempted to light a grass fire—a favorite aborigine tactic—around the explorer and his group: "I was obliged to fire a musket loaded with small shot at one of the ring-leaders, which sent them off."

By August 6 the *Endeavour* was patched up sufficiently to continue along the coast. The reef was still an ever-present danger, and during one period of calm the ship drifted within 80 to 100 yards of its coral teeth again. "Between us and destruction was only a dismal Valley the breadth of one wave." But a puff of wind saved her, and she reached Cape York, the northern tip of Australia, on August 21, 1770. Before continuing via Torres Strait into the well-known waters of the East Indies, Cook triumphantly claimed the territory he had discovered. "I now once more hoisted English Colours, and in the name of His Majesty King George the Third, took possession of the whole Eastern Coast . . . by the name of New South Wales."

On the way home he was obliged to put in for more repairs at the Dutch colonial port of Batavia (modern Jakarta). In this steamy, fever-ridden place, all his previous concern for the health of his crew was brought to nothing. No fewer than 73 men fell victim to the vicious mosquitoes and squalor of Indonesia. Seven died of malaria or dysentery before Cook could get away from

Batavia, and 22 more by the time he reached England on July 13, 1771. These were bitter losses to a commander who had not one fatality from scurvy in an expedition lasting almost three years.

However, he could still write, with justifiable pride, "I presume this voyage will be found as complete as any before made to the South Seas." Never was so great an achievement so modestly summarized: The laconic lieutenant had added more than 5,000 miles of coastline to the map of the world.

Mrs. Elizabeth Cook, that most long-suffering of sailors' wives (she was ultimately to lose two sons as well as a husband to the sea), did not have much time to enjoy the company of her returning hero. Within 18 months he was back in southern latitudes, searching for the continent that geographers still determinedly imagined must lurk somewhere in "the large space of Sea" left unexplored on his first voyage. As usual, Cook was pessimistic about such a discovery, but he did not flinch from his orders. These were to "Circumnavigate the Globe in a higher parallel than has hitherto been done"—nothing less than a complete circumnavigation of the Antarctic Ocean. The ships in which Cook faced this awesome assignment were, like the *Endeavour*, stout Whitby-built colliers. His flagship, the *Resolution*, was 462 tons; the *Adventure*, under Capt. Tobias Furneaux, was 340. Both sloops had been lavishly equipped by the admiralty, and Cook was entrusted with four models of a newfangled instrument, the chronometer, that made the calculation of longitude much simpler. Joseph Banks chose not to accompany this second voyage, but a fine artist (William Hodges) and two German naturalists were recruited.

Leaving England on July 13, 1772, in the middle of northern summer, the two ships arrived in Cape Town on October 30, in the middle of the southern spring. After a few weeks ashore, during which Cook made

*After seeing the Antarctic on his second voyage, Cook concluded there was no Southern Continent that could support life other than a few penguins. Finding impenetrable ice, he wrote: "I can be bold to say no man will venture further south than I." But the ice was also an invaluable source of fresh water. It was hoisted aboard the Resolution (left) in hunks and melted on deck to 15 tons of drinkable water at a time. The crew took on ice every week when available, because the water stored in kegs spoiled after 10 days. The penguins' whimsical mien delighted Georg Forster, one of Cook's naturalists, who did this wash drawing of one. The expedition killed many of the flightless birds for provisions.*

*Cook never suspected the exotic* native dancing on Lifuka, a Tongan island encountered on his third voyage, was part of an elaborate plot to murder him. He sat in the center (above) and watched the Tongans, gleaming with oil, move in perfect unison "as if they were one great machine," while flaming torches lit the spectacle and beating drums accented the chanting and dancing. The Lifukans had planned to massacre Cook and his officers during the ceremony and then seize the ships. Fortunately, the Tongan chiefs, unable to decide if it would be possible to capture the ships in the dark, never gave the signal for the attack.

sure his men got plenty of exercise and fresh vegetables, he began his first dip into the Antarctic.

To begin, he headed directly south, searching for a supposed promontory of the Southern Continent that the French explorer Jean Bouvet de Lozier "saw" in 1739 and named Cape Circumcision. As expected, the promontory was not to be found.

On December 14 Cook had his first intimations of the difficulties of Antarctic exploration. "We were stopped by an immense field of ice, to which we could see no end." The explorer cautiously edged his way southeast along the wall, moving into higher and higher latitudes. Thick fog intensified the already aching cold. Soon he was obliged to "set all the Tailors to work to lengthen the Sleeves of the Seaman's Jackets, and to make Caps to shelter them from the severity of the Weather."

On January 17, 1773, the *Resolution* became the first ship in history to penetrate the Antarctic Circle. White petrel and dark gray albatrosses escorted Cook as far south as the 67th parallel, until "the ice was so thick and close we could proceed no further." Climbing to the masthead, the explorer could see no sign of land, only a limitless field of white stretching and shimmering into the hazy distance.

Early in February the ships were separated by a gale. Cook was not unduly worried, since he had arranged a New Zealand rendezvous with Captain Furneaux at Queen Charlotte Sound. Indeed, the Antarctic summer was already beginning to wane, and it was time to seek sanctuary there. On the way east, Cook could not resist another dip into high latitudes of the South Pacific. Again he found no evidence of the Southern Continent. Stopping at Charlotte Harbor for rest and repairs, the *Resolution* found that Furneaux, in the *Adventure*, had arrived there six weeks earlier.

Cook was not a man to be put off by the terrifying sterility of Antarctic exploration. He returned to the white latitudes twice to complete his circumnavigation. Each of these cruises was flanked by two sweeps round the South Pacific, linking together hundreds of islands, many of them unknown to geography. In the process Cook assembled, piece by piece, the vast jigsaw puzzle of Polynesia and Melanesia, showing that two totally different races had mysteriously spread themselves across millions of square miles of ocean.

On the first of these Pacific sweeps (June–October 1773), Cook took his ships to Tahiti, where they were greeted by an armada of canoes filled with fruit, flowers, and girls. Here Captain Furneaux took on a native youth named Omai, who wished to see the world. Swinging west, Cook rediscovered Tasman's delightful "Friendly Isles," Eua and Tongatabu. On the way back to New Zealand, he again lost sight of the *Adventure* in a gale. He awaited her for three weeks in Queen Charlotte Sound and then, impatient to resume his circumnavigation, sailed for the southeast on November 25, 1773. Behind him he left a message concerning his whereabouts for Furneaux in that time-honored sailor's receptacle, a bottle buried under a marked tree.

The Pacific sector of Cook's circumnavigation took him to the highest southern latitude yet recorded by an explorer: 71°10′. He was appalled by the cold: "Our ropes were like wires, Sails like board or plates of Metal, and the Shivers [pulleys] froze fast in the blocks, so that it required our utmost effort to get a Top-sail down and up; the cold so intense as hardly to be endured; the whole Sea in a manner covered with ice, a hard gale and a thick fog."

Finally, they were stopped by a field of ice. Cook wrote in his journal: "I whose ambition leads me not only further than any has been before me, but as far as I think possible for man to go was not sorry at meeting with this interruption."

Tacking north into warmer waters, the explorer began his second island sweep. For eight months the *Resolution* sailed round a great semicircle, covering practically the whole of the Pacific south of the Equa-

tor. Cook was impressed by the gigantic stone statues of Easter Island (March 11); he admired the exquisitely beautiful natives of the Marquesas (April 6) but was so irritated by their thievery that he ordered his officers to fire upon them, and one man was killed; at Tahiti (April 22) he was greeted with the usual ecstatic shouts and a gift of hogs; and at the Tongan island of Nomuka (June 28) some natives treated him with contempt for refusing the gift of a young woman. "The girl certainly did not [lack] beauty," he wrote wistfully.

Instead of following his previous route back to New Zealand, the insatiable explorer continued west to the Quirós Islands (July 16), which he renamed the New Hebrides, and discovered another large archipelago nearby (September 4), which he named New Caledonia. He thought the Melanesian natives ugly and primitive but noted approvingly that they did not steal. Cook was gradually becoming obsessive on this subject, a sign, perhaps, of the exhaustion in leading his tremendous voyage, already well into its third year.

In mid-October 1774 he was back in Queen Charlotte Sound, to find his bottle dug up but no message left by Furneaux in its place. The Maori spoke vaguely of white men in a ship and even more vaguely of certain killings. Not until March 18, 1775, when the *Resolution* had completed her circumnavigation of the Antarctic (by sailing east to the Atlantic at 50° latitude) and was creaking wearily north to Cape Town, did Cook meet a Dutch vessel and hear a firsthand account of the grisly story of what had happened to the *Adventure*.

Furneaux had sent a party of 10 men ashore to fetch vegetables for the *Resolution*. While on land, the men had a meal, during which some Maori snatched at their food. The only Englishman who was armed rashly shot two of the natives in the ensuing quarrel. Instantly, the sailors were attacked by a crowd of Maori, which killed all 10 and cooked them for eating. When the boat did not return, Furneaux sent another party, which found the terrible remains. Shaken by the event, Furneaux ordered the *Adventure* to set sail.

On July 30, 1775, James Cook stepped ashore at Spithead, England, having covered a total distance of 70,000 miles—equivalent to almost three full circumnavigations of the globe. Not one of his crew had died of scurvy and only four by accident or disease. He was given a hero's welcome, a royal reception, a promotion to post-captain, and what the navy considered its major reward: a pensioned retirement as captain at Greenwich Hospital. Even as he settled down to write the official account of his expedition, the 47-year-old Cook felt the claustrophobia that is the lot of all great explorers. "My fate drives me from one extreme to the other," he said sadly. "A few months ago the whole Southern Hemisphere was hardly big enough for me."

The lords of the admiralty took the hint and soon gave Cook another hemisphere to explore. In February 1776, the month he was elected a Fellow of The Royal

*Searching for a northwest passage* in the Arctic, Cook's men shot walruses "huddling one over the other like swine" for meat. Just one 2,000-pounder could keep them well supplied for weeks.

*Sailors and Scientists*

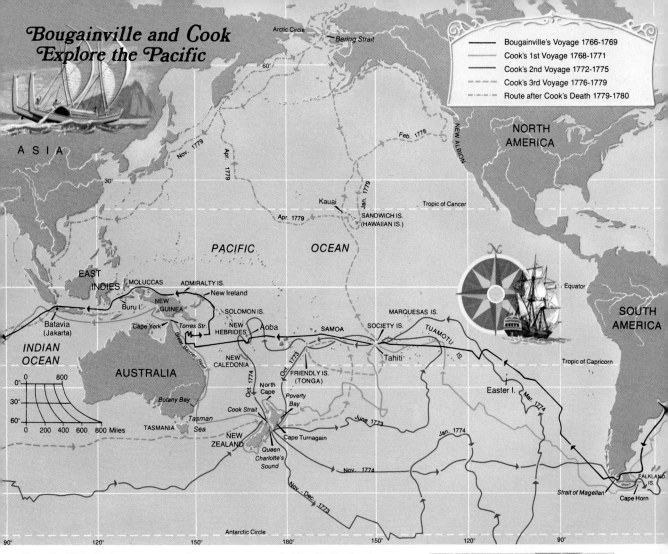

# Bougainville and Cook Explore the Pacific

| | |
|---|---|
| ⸻⸻ | Bougainville's Voyage 1766-1769 |
| ⸻⸻ | Cook's 1st Voyage 1768-1771 |
| ⸻⸻ | Cook's 2nd Voyage 1772-1775 |
| ‑ ‑ ‑ | Cook's 3rd Voyage 1776-1779 |
| ·‑·‑· | Route after Cook's Death 1779-1780 |

Arctic Circle

Bering Strait

60°

Feb. 1778

NORTH
AMERICA

NEW ALBION

A S I A

30°

Nov. 1779

Apr. 1779

Kauai

Jan. 1779

Tropic of Cancer

Apr. 1779

SANDWICH IS.
(HAWAIIAN IS.)

PACIFIC     OCEAN

Equator

EAST
INDIES

MOLUCCAS

ADMIRALTY IS.

New Ireland

SOUTH
AMERICA

Buru I.

NEW
GUINEA

SOLOMON IS.

NEW
HEBRIDES

Aoba

SAMOA

MARQUESAS IS.

SOCIETY IS.

TUAMOTU
IS.

Batavia
(Jakarta)

Cape York

Torres Str.

Great Barrier Reef

Tahiti

INDIAN
OCEAN

Oct. 1773

NEW
CALEDONIA

FRIENDLY IS.
(TONGA)

Tropic of Capricorn

AUSTRALIA

Oct. 1774

North
Cape

Easter I.

Mar. 1774

| 0 | 800 |
|---|---|
| 0° | |
| 30° | |
| 60° | 0  200  400  600  800 Miles |

Botany Bay

Poverty
Bay

Tasman
Sea

TASMANIA

NEW
ZEALAND

Cook Strait

Queen
Charlotte's
Sound

Cape Turnagain

June 1773

Jan. 1774

Nov. 1774

Strait of Magellan

FALKLAND
IS.

Cape Horn

Nov.- Dec.
1773

Antarctic Circle

90°     120°     150°     180°     150°     120°     90°

*Bougainville's single voyage* across the great ocean preceded Cook's first by about two years. Both men eased their ships around the dangerous tip of South America and then sailed northwest to Tahiti. From there, Bougainville headed due west, while Cook, following orders to search for the Southern Continent, sailed south to the 40th parallel and then west to New Zealand. After mapping the coasts of its two main islands, he headed north along Australia's unknown eastern coast, encountering near-disaster on the Great Barrier Reef. Cook, knowing of the Torres Strait, headed home through it. Bougainville, whose French charts gave him less information, beat laboriously around New Guinea before heading west to France. Cook settled the Southern Continent question on his second voyage (box at right), venturing closer to the South Pole than any previous explorer. On his final voyage, in search of a northwest passage, Cook discovered Hawaii, then pressed on to America's northwest coast and up into the ice of the Arctic Circle. The *Resolution* then returned to Hawaii, where Cook was killed.

COOK'S SEARCH FOR THE SOUTHERN CONTINENT 1772-1775

Society, he was called from retirement in order to lead an expedition in search of the Northwest Passage. This mythical link between the northern Atlantic and Pacific Oceans had been a matter of geographical speculation almost as long as the Southern Continent, and once again the explorer's orders were clothed in the utmost secrecy. He was presented with the usual navigational instruments, plus an Eskimo dictionary.

Cook sailed on July 12, once again in the *Resolution*, which was somewhat the worse for wear after a very

inadequate patch-up job in Deptford. Under him was a young officer named William Bligh, who was later to win fame of his own in the South Pacific as captain of the mutinous crew of the *Bounty*. A second ship, the 298-ton *Discovery*, followed three weeks later, under the command of Capt. Charles Clerke.

The two sloops made a rendezvous in Cape Town and swung southeast across the Indian Ocean in December. On the way to Queen Charlotte Sound, Cook visited Tasmania and received an indifferent welcome from

**As symbols of rank,** *Hawaiian chiefs wore brilliantly colored capes made of feathers attached to closely woven fibers.*

**When Tahitians offered a human sacrifice** *to their gods, they chose a vagrant, clubbing him to death before tying him to a pole. Cook, after watching the ritual (he is standing at the right), wrote that victims "are never apprized of their fate till the blow is given."*

the aborigines. He left a few pigs, hoping they would breed, and sailed on to New Zealand past the southern coast, again without determining whether Tasmania was attached to Australia.

Magnanimously, Cook took no revenge on the Maori responsible for the *Adventure* massacre: "I believe they were not a little surprised!" He perhaps assumed that Furneaux's sailors had offended the natives. Moreover, he wished to remain on good terms with the Maori, who could furnish him with food.

On February 25, 1777, he sailed out of Cook Strait for the last time and continued northeast via the Friendly Islands to Tahiti and the Society Islands. There his old indignation at theft flared up again: A native who stole a sextant had his ears chopped off.

Now, as he sailed north in search of Drake's New Albion (America's northwest coast), Cook moved into completely unknown waters. On January 18, 1778, he and his crew became the first white men to lay eyes on the magnificent islands of Hawaii, which Cook named the Sandwich Islands. Stepping ashore at Kauai, he was puzzled by the worshipful attitude of the natives: "The very instant I leaped ashore, they all fell flat on their faces and remained in that humble posture till I made signs to them to rise."

Though he would later be identified with a Hawaiian god, Cook was now simply receiving the homage that the islanders gave their own semidivine chiefs. The Hawaiians even overlooked the shooting of a man by a nervous English officer when a crowd rushed from the beach to help pull in one of the expedition's boats.

Cook wrote a long and admiring description of the Hawaiians in his journal, noting their physical and linguistic resemblance to Tahitians. Sailing on to New Albion in early February, he pondered once again the

mystery of Polynesia. "How shall we account for this nation spreading itself so far over this vast ocean?"

Sighting the coast of present-day Oregon on March 7, Cook cruised slowly north, and the unmapped coastline transferred itself to his meticulous charts, inlet by inlet, bluff by bluff. He was not too impressed with the North American Indians—understandably, since they stole his gold watch and sold him bladders of oil that, after the first pouring, disgorged nothing but water.

The weather grew bitingly cold as he approached Alaska, but no northwest passage presented itself; finally, past the Bering Strait and beyond the Arctic Circle, he was brought to a standstill by ice 12 feet thick at 70°44' N. Vowing to return the next summer, he sailed back to the warmth and flowers of Hawaii.

By the time the *Resolution* and *Discovery* put into Kealakekua Bay on January 17, 1779, they were gaping visibly at the seams. Anticipating a long stay for repairs, Cook was delighted to receive on "Owhyhee" the most ecstatic welcome he had ever known. Only gradually did he realize that he was regarded as some sort of returning god. A red cloth was wrapped around him; his head, arms, and legs were rubbed with coconut; and a piece of well-chewed pork placed respectfully in his mouth. As gifts of hogs and vegetables were arrayed around him, he was praised as Lono, the god of the *makahiki* season, when taxes were settled with the produce of the land, hard work stopped, and war was forbidden. Lono had quit Hawaii centuries before, and it was prophesied that a great ship bearing gifts would bring him back to Hawaii again.

For as long as work continued on the two sloops, the cornucopia of gifts continued. Cook could do nothing to stop it. He soon realized, however, that the islanders were impoverishing themselves with their own generosity. Anxious to be away, he gave the order to sail, rather too hastily, on February 4. That very night a gale split his sails and sprung one of his fragile masts. There was no choice but to put back into Kealakekua Bay, accompanied by the *Discovery*.

The natives received him sullenly. It was plain he had broken faith by returning. Whereas once they lavished gifts, they now began to steal. During the night of February 13, the *Discovery*'s cutter disappeared. This theft of the only large boat on the *Discovery* plunged the 50-year-old Cook into a fatal rage. Storming ashore next morning with a party of marines, he attempted to take the king of Hawaii hostage. This ploy had worked on other islands, and Cook assumed it would here.

An angry crowd collected quickly on the beach; stones began to fly; Cook, provoked, fired a round of small shot and this time killed a man. Suddenly, the air was full of knives and bullets. In the words of a horrified onlooker: "Our unfortunate Commander, the last time he was seen distinctly, was standing at the water's edge, and calling out to the boats to cease firing, and to pull in. . . . Having turned about, to give his orders to the boats, he was stabbed in the back, and fell with his face into the water. On seeing him fall, the islanders set up a great shout. . . .

"Thus fell our great and excellent Commander! After a life of so much distinguished and successful enterprise, his death . . . cannot be reckoned premature; since he lived to finish the great work for which he seems to have been designed."

Both the Hawaiians and the English mourned Cook's death, and the English did not attempt to avenge the murder. Sorrow, more than anger, characterized the expedition's last days in the islands. Cook's lieutenants,

**Paul Revere engraved** *these Raiatean dancers for the 1774 American edition of Cook's book about his first voyage. Recognizing the Englishman's contribution to science, Benjamin Franklin procured safe passage for Cook during the Revolution.*

nevertheless, carried on their captain's plan, again voyaging north of the Bering Strait before heading back to England by way of the Cape of Good Hope.

When the news of Cook's death reached England in January 1780, King George III is said to have wept, and countless thousands mourned the tall, quiet Yorkshireman who had been, for them, the symbol of everything that was good and brave in human nature. Cook was indeed that improbable creature, a perfect explorer. He had great physical strength, a brain capable of making advanced astronomical calculations at the height of a storm, a stomach that could digest sea lions, walruses, dogs, and kangaroos, and that essential quality of all great explorers, an instinct for discovery.

**The English artist** *George Carter did not see Cook's death but painted this version of it from hearsay. Actually, Cook was stabbed in the back as he turned to summon his boats, which were nowhere so near as shown. Had the commander of the launch rushed to Cook's assistance, his life might have been saved. Instead, the inaction sealed Cook's fate as the natives repeatedly attacked him. After Cook's death, the Hawaiians dismembered his body and scraped the bones clean of flesh, except for the hands. Seven days later the remains were returned to the ship and recognized as Cook's by a scar between the thumb and index finger—the result of a powder horn that had exploded in his hand in Newfoundland. Cook's remains were put in a coffin and on February 21, 1779, with flags at halfmast, were buried at sea.*

# Part

## 6

# Crossing the Continents

# Pathfinders in the Wilderness

*Two largely unknown landmasses—North America and Australia—are penetrated by explorers seeking to reveal the limits and natural treasures of their new countries.*

With the death of Capt. James Cook in 1779, the Great Age of Navigation came to an end. The preceding three centuries had reshaped Europe's view of the world. On maps of the time, all the continents except Antarctica were now in place, all the oceans present in roughly their proper size and outline. But what lay deep within the newly discovered continents, especially North America and Australia, was generally unknown. The next era of exploration necessarily turned inward—into the hearts of the new lands.

The settlements that followed closely upon the discovery of North America were mostly clustered along the coasts and the great rivers that emptied into the Atlantic. But the coastal regions soon became thickly populated, and pioneers pushed westward into the back country. The trails they followed had been blazed for them by a new breed of explorer, the pathfinder, whose purpose in exploring beyond the range of settlement was to seek furs to barter from the Indians or to trap himself.

In Canada, about 1658, the swashbuckling French voyageur partners Pierre Radisson and Médard Chouart des Groseilliers established a fur-trading business that extended from Montreal to Minnesota. In 1730 the family of La Vérendrye left their fur-trading post near Lake Superior and began seeking an overland route to the Pacific, discovering Lakes Winnipeg and Manitoba. They also journeyed to the Missouri River and beyond, to the plains of the Northwest. Along with these men—whose exploits were often recorded by the Jesuit missionaries who accompanied them in search of Indian converts—were countless others, many of them nameless, whose patient journeying added by word of mouth to the ever-growing body of knowledge about the new continent.

Below Canada, the English colonies on the Atlantic seaboard of America had few navigable rivers into the interior, and most of the early trailblazing there was accomplished on foot. In the southern settlements, the great barrier of the Appalachians was first probed by traders or their agents. Abraham Wood, captain of the important Virginia trading post, Fort Henry, is alleged to have reached the Ohio and Mississippi Rivers in the 1650's. During the first documented crossing of the Alleghenies, in 1671, the explorers found English letters blazed on the Blue Ridge trees; anonymous frontiersmen had already traveled that way. One of the best recorded expeditions was that of Virginia Gov. Alexander Spotswood, who, accompanied by a party of Virginia gentlemen and servants, crossed the Blue Ridge Mountains in 1716 to claim the country west of the range for England.

It was relations with the Indians that determined the success of most expeditions. Trappers knew Indian languages and customs, and many lived with or married into a tribe. The most famous frontiersman, Daniel Boone, was captured by the Shawnee tribe, who adopted him and renamed him Big Turtle.

At the end of the Seven Years' War (1756–63), when France ceded all of Canada to England, the ownership of the North American continent was divided between Britain and Spain, which claimed all the territory west of the Mississippi and had settled on perhaps 1 percent of it. In the north, English traders pushed into the interior, hoping to take over the fur empire from the French, who still controlled it. Among them was Samuel Hearne, who set out from England in 1770, sent by the Hudson's Bay Company to find a reported source of copper. Accompanied by Indians, he traveled north, becoming the first white man to reach the Canadian Arctic Ocean by land. The remarkable journeys of Alexander Mackenzie, from 1789 to 1793, were undertaken under the auspices of another fur-trading group, the North West Company, also to find a cross-country water passage. Mackenzie reached both the Arctic and the Pacific Oceans, but though he crossed the entire continent, he never found the river thruway he sought.

### From the Atlantic to the Pacific

When President Thomas Jefferson authorized the $15 million purchase of the Louisiana Territory from France (which had recently taken over Spain's holding), he removed forever the threat of a closed French border on the Mississippi and opened up almost the whole of the continent to new U.S. settlement. Yet no one knew either the precise extent of the territory or what lay within its borders. The Lewis and Clark expedition of 1804–06 was the culmination of Jefferson's years-long desire to probe beyond the midcontinent and, even more, to find the water passage that would facilitate U.S. entry into the Northwest fur trade. No water route was found, but the vast size and incredible variety of the continent were clearly revealed, and a U.S. claim to the Oregon territory—first made when Capt. Robert Gray sailed into the mouth of the Columbia River in 1792—was certified.

The discovery of rich beaver country created a new breed of frontiersmen, the fur trappers known as mountain men, whose wanderings helped complete the exploration of the Northwest. They also established the trails over which, shortly, thousands of emigrants would travel. Congress, buoyed by the success of Lewis and Clark's expedition, soon authorized others, many of them headed by young army officers: Zebulon Pike explored the Rockies and the Colorado country in 1806, Stephen Long surveyed the major northwestern rivers in 1819–20, and John C. Frémont covered the area from California to Utah and Nebraska between 1838 and 1845. Within three decades after the triumphant return of Lewis and Clark, most of the North American continent beyond the Mississippi had been explored.

The saga of American exploration ended just as that of Australia was beginning. In 1788 a British ship anchored in Sydney Cove on the eastern coast of Australia. Her cargo was some 750 English convicts, transported to exile in the southern continent; the American colonies were no longer available. No other nation disputed England's colonization of what seemed then a "useless" country, the emptiest of the new lands.

### Challenging Australia's Immensity

When the first convicts landed, almost nothing was known of the size or formation of the continent. Cook had explored its east coast in 1769, and before him, Dutch East Indiamen had sighted the west coast. It was not until 1802 that the continent was circumnavigated: Matthew Flinders, a young naval officer, proved by his voyage that Australia is actually a continent.

The earliest colonies had been built on the southeastern and southern coasts, separated from the interior by dry, grassy highlands that were explored for the first time in 1813. The discovery of passes made the rich grazing country on the other side of the highlands accessible, and Australia's sheep industry boomed. Within three decades, attracted by reports of rich opportunities and by a government "bounty," more than 200,000 Britons had settled in Australia. Yet, because of the arid, forbidding terrain, exploration of the interior was only sporadic in the early 19th century. The first penetration beyond the coast was made by a group led by Gregory Blaxland, who in 1813 crossed the Blue Mountains in New South Wales. Not until 1841 did the explorer Edward John Eyre cross the southern, more settled part of the continent.

In 1851 gold was discovered just north of Melbourne, and a new wave of immigrants surged into the country. But the multiplying population was still confined to the coast, and although some of the rivers flowing from the interior had been explored, very little was known about inland Australia, except that it was hot, dry, and, with some exceptions, almost totally barren. Yet new areas for settlement had to be found, and many Australians dreamed of a promised fertile land somewhere in the north. Exploration of the interior was now a vital necessity. It was hoped that the 1860 south-north expedition of Robert O'Hara Burke would make marvelous discoveries.

Burke and his companion William John Wills died on the return leg of their arduous trek, but rescue parties sent out to search for the missing pair crossed the continent twice more within a year, discovering rich grazing lands in the interior and opening up huge new regions for settlement. By the 1870's an overland telegraph wire, laid along the route of the explorer John Stuart, connected the south coast with the new city of Darwin in the north. Valuable minerals and underground water were found in Australia's center.

The Burke and Wills expedition began, for Australia, the final process of exploration and settlement. Of the remaining continents open to Europeans, only Africa still lay largely unprobed, unmapped, unknown.

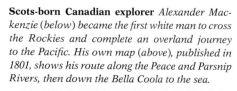

**Scots-born Canadian explorer** *Alexander Mackenzie (below) became the first white man to cross
the Rockies and complete an overland journey
to the Pacific. His own map (above), published in
1801, shows his route along the Peace and Parsnip
Rivers, then down the Bella Coola to the sea.*

**Mackenzie's expedition established** *that it was probably impossible to reach
the west coast of Canada from the east without crossing the Rocky Mountains.
Arduous portages through narrow mountain passes (above) made it obvious
that Mackenzie's overland route to the Pacific would not be practical for trade.
This discovery shattered the hopes of businessmen in Montreal that a transcontinental crossing would lead to a vast increase in their profits.*

*Chapter Nineteen. Three hundred years after its discovery, no explorer has yet crossed the New World north of Mexico. Then a young Scottish fur trader working in western Canada becomes the first to travel by land from coast to coast. En route to the Pacific, he discovers a magnificent virgin wilderness of forests, rivers, and towering mountains.*

# "From Canada by Land": Mackenzie Crosses North America

*Alexander Mackenzie was born in Scotland's Outer Hebrides about 1764. Immigrating to America, he entered the fur trade in Montreal and in 1787 was sent west to operate a trading post at Fort Chipewyan. There he embarked on his brief but fruitful career as an explorer. In 1789, seeking an outlet to the Pacific, he discovered the Mackenzie River and traced it to its outlet in the Arctic Ocean. In 1792–93 he traveled to the Pacific coast. This first crossing of North America opened the way for fur traders, who followed his route and helped establish British claims to the Canadian West. Knighted in 1802, he retired to Scotland in 1808 and died there in 1820. Today the Mackenzie River, Mackenzie Mountains, and District of Mackenzie in the Northwest Territories of Canada all bear the name of this brilliant pathfinder.*

Shrewd, ambitious, eager to learn—Alexander Mackenzie had all the qualities it took to build a future in Canada's bustling fur trade. By the time he was about 23, in 1787, the young Scottish immigrant already was a full partner in the North West Company, the major rival of the all-powerful Hudson's Bay Company. Yet he thirsted for still greater opportunities. When the company's directors selected him to run their operations in the remote Athabasca region, he gave up the comforts of life in Montreal without hesitation.

It was no small decision to make. Lake Athabasca, about midway between Hudson Bay and the Pacific Ocean in what are now northern Alberta and Saskatchewan Provinces, was far beyond the fringes of civilization. Discovered only a decade before by Peter Pond of the United States, the lake was at the center of a vast unmapped wilderness where few white men had ever set foot. But the region's swampy muskegs and wooded uplands were proving to be rich in furs, especially the beavers that Europeans prized so much.

Mackenzie's first job was to establish a permanent outpost, Fort Chipewyan, beside the lake. Then he set about trading with local Indians for furs and exploring the area for water routes that might lead to new, unexploited beaver country. Anxious to find out all he could about the territory, he listened avidly to the tales of Indians and traders. According to legend, the Pacific Ocean was not far to the west, and some claimed it could be reached by river.

The stories whetted the restless young Scot's hunger for adventure. What if he, Alexander Mackenzie, were to discover an interior water route to the Pacific? What if he were to open the way for his company to share in the rich crop of sea otters and seals that Russians were known to be harvesting along the coast?

The idea was a beguiling one, and Mackenzie soon made up his mind to act on it. Early in June 1789 he left his cousin Roderick Mackenzie in charge of Fort Chipewyan and set out into the unknown. In three birchbark canoes he and his companions headed north for Great Slave Lake, whose outlet was rumored to be a river that flowed to the west.

Probing bays along the lake's western shore, he soon found the river. And it did flow west—for a while. Then it veered to the north. For 11 days the party of explorers sped downstream through an increasingly desolate landscape. Gradually, the trees along the banks became more stunted, the wildlife sparser. Soon they reached the treeless tundra, the vast, boggy area of rocks and lichen that borders the Arctic. "This country is one continual morass," Mackenzie observed, "where the ground never thaws above five inches from the surface. I could never force a blade into it beyond a depth of six to eight inches."

When they reached the river's mouth, they found themselves in an ice-choked sea where huge white whales bobbed in the distance. They had reached an ocean, but Mackenzie realized it was the Arctic Ocean,

## Lonely Trading Posts in Backwoods Canada

The American Revolution dealt a severe blow to the Canadian fur trade. The region south of the Great Lakes, previously the most lucrative fur-trading area, fell within the boundaries of the United States. Consequently, Canadian traders had to range farther into the desolate northern and western forests in search of beaver pelts. Outposts were set up in the wilderness where the traders could deposit their furs and reprovision for another season. The station on James Bay in Ontario (above), which was surrounded by a wooden palisade to fend off possible Indian attack, was typical. Because the supplies they could get at the outposts were limited, the traders followed the example of the Indians, seen below hunting moose, and supplemented their diet of pemmican (dried meat mixed with fat) with fresh fish and game. Mackenzie learned to live this way.

not the Pacific. Disgusted, he named the river Disappointment. On modern maps this great 1,120-mile-long waterway is now labeled the Mackenzie River.

It was early September with an autumn chill in the air when the weary party finally got back to Fort Chipewyan. In 102 days they had traveled nearly 3,000 miles through unknown wilderness. They had opened a new route into virgin fur country. But they had not found a passage to the Pacific.

The failure plagued Mackenzie, and he was deter-

mined to try again. The next time, however, he would be better prepared. If his findings were to have any scientific value, he realized that his maps would have to be accurate. And he simply did not know how to take precise readings of his position.

Returning to Montreal in 1791, he took a leave of absence from the company and traveled to England. There, at his own expense, he studied astronomy, navigation, and geography and bought instruments for calculating longitude and latitude. The following spring he returned to Montreal and by fall was back at Fort Chipewyan. Having made his preparations, he was ready to launch his great "voyage of discovery."

This time he planned to set off in an entirely different direction. Instead of heading north, he would follow the course of the broad, placid Peace River, which flows near Lake Athabasca from the southwest. According to neighboring Indians, the Peace arose in the high chain of Rocky or Stony Mountains to the west. From its headwaters, it was supposed to be possible to portage to another river flowing down the western slopes and into the Pacific Ocean.

Mackenzie and his party left Fort Chipewyan on October 10, 1792. Their immediate destination was a point about 200 miles upstream, where they planned to spend the winter and so get a headstart on their journey in the spring. Two men had been sent ahead to fell trees with which to build their winter outpost. Soon after the explorers arrived on November 1, they began constructing a tiny cluster of buildings surrounded by a protective palisade.

Two months later Fort Fork, as Mackenzie dubbed the place, was finally finished, and the men settled down to wait for the spring thaw. Not one to waste time, Mackenzie busied himself with doctoring sick Indians and, mindful of his obligations to the company, trading with them for furs.

He also supervised construction of the specially designed canoe he hoped to paddle to the Pacific. Graceful yet sturdy, the craft was built of large sheets of birchbark stretched over a lightweight frame of cedar ribs. The seams were stitched together with threads made from fine roots of evergreens and then sealed with melted pine gum. Designed to hold 10 men and 3,000 pounds of food, arms, ammunition, and trade goods, the canoe was 25 feet long, 4 feet 9 inches wide, and a shade over 2 feet deep. "At the same time she was so light," Mackenzie noted proudly, "that two men could carry her on a good road three or four miles without resting."

Spring came to Fort Fork with a suddenness that astonished Mackenzie. By mid-April nearly all the snow had disappeared. Within a matter of days "the plains were delightful; the trees were budding, and many plants in blossom." Alexander Mackay, second in command for the expedition, in fact, seems to have suffered a bout of spring fever: On April 20 he brought his leader a bunch of pink and yellow wildflowers.

More important than the appearance of flowers was the state of the river. The ice was breaking up rapidly, and by April 25 the rushing stream of muddy water was completely free of ice. In the days that followed, there was a great flurry of activity at Fort Fork as the men made their final preparations, shipping furs back to Fort Chipewyan, packing their supplies, and loading the canoe. Finally, on May 9, 1793, everything was ready. The canoe bobbed easily on the current despite the huge load of provisions. The 10 men—Mackenzie, Mackay, 6 French-Canadian voyageurs including 2 who had been along on the trip down the Mackenzie River, and 2 Indian hunters and interpreters—clambered aboard. Mackenzie gave the order, and the men cast off, paddling confidently upstream toward the Pacific, which Mackenzie felt certain "cannot, in a direct line, be very far from us."

For the first few days, progress was relatively easy. The river was swollen by melt water from the mountains—Mackenzie noticed that the water level was rising an inch or two each day—and the current was strong. But for the voyageurs this kind of water was strictly routine. Singing and paddling in unison, they worked with the precision of a well-trained team, making 15 miles or so of headway each day.

Their normal schedule was to start out between 3 and 4 o'clock in the morning and continue traveling until 7 in the evening. They stopped now and then to gum up seams that had weakened under the stress of the canoe's heavy load and to patch tears where the boat had brushed against rocks or hidden snags of drift-wood. In the evening they pitched their tents, enjoyed "their usual regale of rum," ate whatever game the Indians had shot that day, then rolled up in their blankets on the bare ground, and arose before dawn.

As they traveled on, Mackenzie was delighted by the "succession of the most beautiful scenery" they were passing through in "this magnificent theatre of nature." Rolling grasslands were interspersed with "groves of poplars in every shape . . . and their intervals are enlivened with vast herds of elks and buffaloes." Obviously, there would be no shortage of fresh meat for their larder. Ever the businessman, he also kept on the watch for signs of beavers—they seemed to be plentiful—and suitable sites for building new trading posts along the way.

On May 17 the party caught its first glimpse of the snow-covered peaks of the Rocky Mountains shining on the western horizon. The sight excited everyone: They were nearing the mountains much sooner than they had expected.

Within a few days, however, their enthusiasm for mountain scenery came to an abrupt end. The river began to narrow, the banks grew steeper, and the placid current gave way to foaming cascades. They were embroiled in the turbulent waters of the Peace River Canyon, a tortuous, 25-mile-long chasm bounded by sheer cliffs as high as 1,100 feet.

Paddles were useless now. The men poled the canoe upstream when they could. Where the water was too deep or too turbulent, they attached ropes and towed the canoe from shore. When the rapids became completely impassable, they unloaded the canoe, carried

## The Voyageur: Hunter, Trader, and Explorer

Fashion in men's hats played an important part in the exploration of Canada. The beaver pelts that had first drawn men to the Canadian wilderness continued for generations to be the most desirable material for hats, such as the trimmed tricorn above. And no group contributed more to Canadian history and legend than the French-Canadian voyageurs, who roamed the woodlands bartering with the Indians for those beaver pelts. These woodsmen would spend two or three years in the wilderness; when they emerged at frontier outposts, they were often dressed and painted like Indians. Many took Indian wives, so that by Mackenzie's time, most of the voyageurs were métis of European-Indian ancestry. In winter they traveled through the frozen north on snowshoes (right), but when spring came, they took to their beloved canoes. As they paddled, they often sang, dipping their blades in time to the rhythm of the music.

Physically, the voyageurs were remarkable men. They would rope themselves together and wade through icy water to drag a canoe through the rapids. If the rapids were impassable, they portaged canoes and supplies. At night they crawled under their canoes and slept on the hard ground. The voyageurs subsisted mostly on a diet of fish, pemmican, and cornmeal mush flavored with salt pork. These meals were habitually washed down with liberal swigs of rum.

Despite the hardships, the life of the voyageur had great romantic appeal. The Beaver Club, a prestigious group of Montreal businessmen that included Mackenzie, expressed its love for the wilderness life in a unique manner. At club dinners members sat on the floor and pretended to paddle a canoe as they sang the songs of the voyageurs.

*Map for Mackenzie on page 224.*

the supplies ahead on their backs, portaged to less dangerous water, reloaded the canoe, and proceeded again "with infinite difficulty" on their "toilsome and perilous progress." Hurled about like a cork on the wild current, the canoe was smashed time and again on rocks, necessitating long delays while gaping holes in the birchbark hull were patched.

After two days of this agony, the men began to mutter among themselves about the futility of going any farther. Mackenzie himself confided to his diary that "I could not but reflect, with infinite anxiety, on the hazard of my enterprise." But he was not yet ready to admit defeat. If he could not make it by water, he would travel by land to the head of the canyon. Mackay and five companions were sent ahead to scout for the best route for portaging.

Mackay's report that evening was not encouraging. The best route to the head of the rapids led up a steep mountain, then across a succession of heavily wooded hills and valleys. Total distance: about nine miles. Even so, "a kettle of wild rice, sweetened with sugar," along with their rum, was enough to revive everyone's spirits. They slept soundly and at daybreak began what Mackenzie described as their "extraordinary journey."

Hacking a path up the mountainside, the men felled the trees so that they would topple downslope to form a sort of railing on each side of the roadway. By pulling from the front with a rope, which they wrapped at intervals around the stumps of the fallen trees, they inched the canoe up the steep slope, then returned to the bottom for their equipment. By midafternoon both the canoe and the supplies were at the mountaintop.

Progress the next day was no easier. Mackenzie, Mackay, and the two Indians cleared a roadway, while

**The Mackenzie River** (*above*) *winds for more than 1,100 miles from Canada's Great Slave Lake to the Arctic Ocean. Mackenzie canoed down it in 1789. He first learned about the river from Peter Pond, a U.S. fur trader, who, nearing the end of his career, imparted his knowledge of the Canadian wilderness to Mackenzie. Pond also inspired the young Scot with his own dream of finding a water route across Canada to the Pacific Ocean.*

the voyageurs trailed behind with the canoe and supplies. The first mile or so was through relatively open woods, but for the next two miles the path went uphill and down through an area that had been burned by a forest fire. Stumbling over a maze of tree trunks that had fallen in every direction, they hacked their way through the dense new growth of shrubs, saplings, and tangled briers. By 5 in the afternoon Mackenzie was more than ready to quit for the day. The men, "in a state of fatigue that may be more readily conceived than expressed," pitched their tents and settled down for the night.

Late in the afternoon of the third day, they finally reached the head of the canyon. Downstream, the water "rushed with an astonishing but silent velocity, between perpendicular rocks . . . [and was] tossed in high, foaming, half-formed billows, as far as the eye could follow it." Upstream, the river was calm and once again navigable by canoe.

For the next week the men progressed steadily up the Peace River through a basin surrounded on all sides by tall, snow-covered mountains. Then, on May 31, they came to a great fork in the river. The branch flowing in from the northwest, now called the Finlay, was broad and calm and seemed to lead in the right direction. The other fork, known today as the Parsnip, was narrow, turbulent, and looked as if it led away from the Pacific. It seemed obvious that they should follow the Finlay.

Although he did not admit it to the crew, Mackenzie himself agreed that the Finlay seemed the logical choice. But, months before, an old Beaver Indian who knew the territory had warned him that the Finlay only led deeper into impenetrable mountains. Far up the Parsnip, on the other hand, the warrior claimed it was possible to portage to another stream flowing west to the ocean. Masking his doubts, Mackenzie ordered his men to proceed up the Parsnip.

The decision seemed utter madness. For the next few days it rained constantly, and the water level rose so rapidly that it was difficult to find dry campsites at night. After two weeks of bitter cold, the weather suddenly became sweltering. Hordes of biting gnats and mosquitoes swarmed about the men's heads, getting into their eyes, their ears, and their hair. For one whole day the only way they could make any progress against the swollen torrent was "by hauling the canoe from branch to branch" of trees lining the banks. The one encouraging sign was the abandoned Indian camps they found from time to time. If only they could meet some of the natives, perhaps they could find out where the river led.

After 10 days of "most laborious exertions," the men were startled one afternoon to smell smoke and then hear voices in the woods. On the riverbank above them two Indians suddenly appeared, "brandishing their spears, displaying their bows and arrows," and screaming threats. Mackenzie realized they were more

*Pathfinders in the Wilderness*

**Mackenzie's canoe founders** *in the turbulent waters of the Fraser River. He and his men often fought white water as they pushed to the Pacific. Their fragile birchbark canoe was constantly in need of repair. Fortunately, Mackenzie's supplies in-* *cluded "a sponge to bail out the water . . . a quantity of gum, bark and watap to repair the vessel." Watap, he noted, was "the divided roots of the spruce fir, which the natives weave into a degree of compactness that renders it capable of containing a fluid."*

frightened than hostile: They had never seen white men before. When his interpreters finally convinced the natives he meant no harm, Mackenzie went ashore and began questioning the two warriors and the rest of their party, which had been hiding in the woods.

The Indians said that they knew of no portage ahead or of any river flowing to the west. Mackenzie persisted. The Indians had a few iron utensils, obviously of European origin. Where did they get them? These, the Indians explained, they got from another tribe 11 days' march away. This tribe in turn journeyed a month to trade with other tribes that traveled the same length of time to reach the "Stinking Lake," as they called the Pacific. There they traded "with people like us, that come there in vessels as big as islands."

This roundabout route was not the one Mackenzie was searching for, and he went to sleep filled with doubts and anxiety for the future. In the morning, however, an Indian lingering near the campfire confessed that he did know of a portage upstream leading to a large river flowing to the west. Mackenzie was elated. He hired one of the Indians as a guide and immediately launched the canoe.

For two days they followed the river as it meandered between steep mountain slopes. It grew steadily narrower and ever more shallow until eventually it led into a long narrow lake. This, Mackenzie correctly surmised, was the southernmost source of the Peace River. The

next day the guide led him to "a beaten path leading over a low ridge . . . to another small lake." Mackenzie noticed with satisfaction that two streams tumbling down a nearby slope flowed into the lake behind him, while two on the other side of the slope fed into the lake just ahead. He had reached the Continental Divide, the high spine of the mountains separating east-flowing from west-flowing rivers.

The men hastily portaged to the second lake and found its outlet, a turbulent stream cascading down the slopes. "We are now going with the stream," Mackenzie declared exultantly.

But traveling with the stream soon proved just as difficult as working against it. The current was swift, and the channel was clogged with rocks and fallen trees, necessitating frequent portages.

The next morning, soon after the party embarked, disaster struck. Scraping a sandbar, the canoe was overwhelmed by the current and began careening sideways downstream. The men had jumped into the icy river to try to straighten the boat but soon were in such deep water that they had to scramble back aboard. By now the canoe was completely out of control. It crashed into a rock and the stern ripped open; then it was hurtled to the opposite bank where, with another sickening crash, the bow tore open. One man, trying to stop the canoe by grabbing an overhanging branch, was hurled ashore. As the canoe skidded diz-

**The northwest coast Indians** *Mackenzie met on the last leg of his journey lived almost entirely on salmon. At the Indian village pictured above, fish can be seen drying on skin-covered wooden* *frames at left. These frames form the sides of the chiefs' lodges. Some tribes in the Pacific Northwest actually had a taboo against eating meat, lest it offend the spirit of the all-important salmon.*

zily down a stretch of rapids, jagged rocks gashed gaping holes in the bottom. A few seconds later they reached calmer water, and the men jumped overboard to guide the rapidly sinking craft ashore.

When "this alarming scene" ended, Mackenzie noted grimly that some, if not all, of his men "were by no means sorry for our late misfortune." They were certain that he would now agree to turn back. The canoe was a wreck, many of their supplies had been lost, and the rest were completely soaked. It seemed impossible to go any farther.

Mackenzie calmly ordered the men to spread everything out to dry and waited until "they had got themselves warm and comfortable, with a hearty meal, and rum enough to raise their spirits." Then he began to lecture, cajole, and encourage them, and once again Mackenzie's calm determination worked. To a man, the crew agreed "to go wherever . . . [he] should lead."

Within a few days the canoe was patched, and the men continued downstream, alternately paddling with the current and portaging around cascades. On June 17 they paddled into a broad river. Travel was easier now, and for four days they sped swiftly downstream.

The explorers made brief contact with a group of unfriendly Indians on July 19. Then, two days later, they were greeted by a volley of arrows fired by a band of angry Indians on shore. From their shouts and gestures, it was obvious they intended to kill the explorers

if they tried to land. But Mackenzie wanted to find out what they knew about the river.

With steely resolve and absolute self-control, he tried a daring scheme. Ordering his men to beach the canoe on the opposite bank, he got out of the boat and slowly, calmly walked along the shore by himself. He would have been an easy target for the Indians, but apparently they were fascinated by the spectacle of this fair-skinned stranger displaying mirrors and other trinkets and gesturing for them to come over. Eventually, two braves got up enough courage to canoe across the river and began to parley with Mackenzie.

Thanks to his calm manner and generous gifts, the Indians soon were convinced of his friendly intentions and agreed to escort him downstream to meet with others of their tribe. As for the river, they confided that it did flow to the ocean, where, they had heard, white men were building houses. But, they added, it was a difficult trip. The distance was far, the meandering river was full of dangerous rapids and difficult portages, and the banks were inhabited by savage tribes who would surely kill the explorers.

Mackenzie was not encouraged. From the Indians' description, he assumed he was on the headwaters of a river that wound far to the south, perhaps even below the recently discovered Columbia River, which empties into the Pacific on the present-day border between Washington and Oregon. In fact, he and his party had discovered the upper reaches of the Fraser River, whose mouth is just north of the modern United States-Canadian border.

There was an alternative, however. Back upstream, the Indians said, it was possible to portage overland a short distance to another river, which would lead them to the coast in just a few days. On June 23 Mackenzie and his party, accompanied by two newly recruited guides, turned around and went back up the Fraser.

By now it was obvious that from a commercial point of view the expedition was a failure. The fierce water and grueling portages they had encountered all along the way meant that their course was hardly a practical trade route to the Pacific. But Mackenzie was obsessed with the dream of setting foot on the western shore of North America. Absolutely certain that the coast could not be far away, he "determined to proceed with resolution, and set future events at defiance."

At the moment, his most pressing concern was the condition of the canoe, which he described as "an absolute wreck." It leaked so badly that one man had to constantly bail out water. Worse still, it had been patched and repatched so often with extra slabs of bark and wads of spruce gum that it was "so heavy . . . two men could not carry her more than a hundred yards, without being relieved." Pausing a few days, the explorers built a completely new canoe, which, Mackenzie noted with satisfaction, "proved a stronger and better boat than the old one."

By July 4 they reached the point where the Indians said the overland journey was to begin. To lighten their loads, the men cached excess food, gunpowder, and supplies and hid the new canoe beneath a heap of brush. Even so, each man had to carry a pack weighing from 45 to 90 pounds, plus his gun and ammunition.

The Indians had assured the men they would reach the coast in six or eight days, but almost two weeks after their start they were still climbing uphill and down across the mountains, guided by friendly tribesmen they met along the way. Late in the afternoon of July 17 they finally came to a village on the banks of a large river now named the Bella Coola. The Indians, who lived on the salmon then migrating upstream to spawn, greeted the explorers with a splendid feast of fish, roe, and berries and loaned them canoes to continue their journey downstream. Passing from village to village, they arrived two days later at a small settlement of houses perched on stilts 25 feet high.

Mackenzie must have slept fitfully that night. From his lofty roost in one of the houses, he could see the fulfillment of his dreams glittering on the horizon: In the misty distance the mouth of the river emptied into a narrow arm of the sea.

Up at the crack of dawn, Mackenzie borrowed a leaky canoe and headed for the ocean. By 8 o'clock in the morning the little band of explorers was paddling through a maze of rocky islands in the Dean Channel, a long narrow inlet of the Pacific that pierces the coast of British Columbia just north of Vancouver Island. Their mission had been accomplished. They had crossed the continent and reached its western shore.

Once the men had tasted saltwater, they were all for beginning the homeward journey immediately. A group of hostile Indians had come out in canoes and had begun threatening them. They claimed that white traders who had recently been there in a ship had mistreated them, and they wanted revenge. Mackenzie was unmoved by the pleas of his frightened crew. He insisted on taking an accurate reading of his location, and he could not do that until the fog lifted. For two days he continued to putter among the islands, his route dogged at every turn by the sullen warriors. Finally, the weather cleared and he was able to take the astronomical readings he so desperately wanted. Then, mixing some vermilion dye with melted grease, he daubed a "brief memorial" on the face of one of the rocky islands. With typical understatement, the message simply read: "Alex Mackenzie from Canada by land 22d July 1793."

And then he headed for home. The trip west had required 10 weeks of grueling labor. Retracing the now-familiar route took only four. On August 24 the haggard band of explorers shot off their muskets as they rounded a bend in the Peace River, triumphantly announcing their safe return to Fort Fork.

### A Proud Claim Inscribed for Later Explorers

When Alexander Mackenzie reached the Pacific, he proclaimed his achievement on a rock (above) in Dean Channel. In 1801 he published an account of his adventures, *Voyages from Montreal . . .*, in which he outlined a plan for a single Canada-based fur-trading company operating on a continental scale. Ironically, one of its most interested readers was the president of the United States, Thomas Jefferson. Partially to protect U.S. interests in the Pacific Northwest against Canadian expansion, he later dispatched Lewis and Clark on their historic journey.

**No wilderness adventure** *had a greater impact on the growth of the United States than the journey of Meriwether Lewis (right) and William Clark (far right). The United States, less than 30 years old, already had ambitions to span the North American continent. After the purchase of the Louisiana Territory from France in 1803, it appeared that they might be realized. When Lewis and Clark's party met a band of Chinook Indians along the Columbia River (above), they knew that their goal, the Pacific Ocean, was not far away. The explorers presented medals (opposite page) to tribal chiefs along the way. The medals bore a portrait of Thomas Jefferson and the clasped hands of an Indian and a white man.*

## Chapter Twenty

When the young United States purchases the Louisiana Territory from France, it acquires a huge and mostly unknown wilderness. Assigned by President Jefferson, two outstanding army officers are sent with an expedition to explore the new land. Their courage leads them past many hazards to the uttermost borders of their continent.

# The Corps of Discovery: Lewis and Clark Open Up the West

*Meriwether Lewis, the brilliant, moody leader of the Corps of Discovery, was born in Virginia in 1774. A neighbor of Thomas Jefferson, he had distinguished himself as an Indian fighter when Jefferson made him his private secretary in 1801. Following the successful cross-continental expedition of 1804–06, Lewis was appointed governor of the Louisiana Territory in 1807. He served ably, with small support from Washington. In 1809 he died mysteriously of a gunshot wound on his way to the nation's capital. Also an Indian fighter and Virginia-born (1770), William Clark grew up in a family of soldiers. He drew the expedition's maps and sketches and organized the diaries for publication. Later made superintendent of Indian Affairs and then governor of the Missouri Territory, he died in St. Louis in 1838.*

Thomas Jefferson never traveled much farther west than his home near Charlottesville, Virginia, but he had a restless mind and a thirst for knowledge. The puzzle of what lay in the vast, uncharted span of North America between the Mississippi River and the Pacific coast tantalized him beyond measure. Over the course of 20 years he had tried several times to send explorers into the area, but none had gotten very far. In 1803, as president of the United States, Jefferson decided the time had come to make an official probe into the region.

In mid-January he sent Congress a confidential message requesting $2,500 to finance the project. The secrecy was necessary for the very good reason that he was proposing a venture on foreign soil—most of the land between the Mississippi and the Rocky Mountains belonged to France. Congress agreed to the plan "for the purpose of extending the external commerce of the United States," but Jefferson prudently preferred to describe the expedition as an innocent "literary" pursuit, purely scientific in nature.

The man he chose to lead the expedition was his 29-year-old friend and personal secretary, Capt. Meriwether Lewis. Young Lewis certainly had the "courage, prudence, habits and health adapted to the woods, and some familiarity with the Indian character" that Jefferson considered necessary for the job. As for the "perfect knowledge of botany, natural history, mineralogy and astronomy" that the ideal leader should also possess, Jefferson sent his protege to some of the best minds in America for cram courses in the sciences.

Lewis immediately and enthusiastically set about the task of organizing the expedition. After consulting with scientists and cartographers, he began to buy scientific instruments, arms, Indian trade goods, and all his other supplies. Since he intended to live primarily off the land, his provisions included little more than dried corn, flour, salt, pork, and "portable soup," a not very appetizing type of dried soup for use in emergencies. His medicine chest, on the other hand, was well equipped with bandages, lancets, syringes, 30 different drugs, and dozens of cure-all pills received from Dr. Benjamin Rush of Philadelphia and known as Rush's Thunderbolts. Like most experienced frontiersmen, Lewis knew how to remove bullets and set broken bones. He had also learned a great deal about herb remedies from his mother, who was well known for her skill in folk medicine. This expertise would be put to good use countless times in the next three years.

Jefferson had intended to have just one man lead his Corps of Discovery. But Lewis, aware of the size of the responsibility, invited his old friend William Clark to share the command, along with "its fatigues, its dangers and its honors."

Clark, who was four years older than Lewis and had once been his commanding officer, was then retired from the army and settled on a farm in Louisville, Kentucky. Like Lewis, he had spent much of his career in the West and, in accepting his friend's offer, was under

*Map for Lewis and Clark on page 224.*

no illusions. "This is an immense undertaking, fraught with numerous difficulties," he replied, "but my friend I can assure you that no man lives with whom I would prefer to undertake and share the difficulties of such a trip than yourself."

Jefferson was pleased with the arrangement. And well he might have been—Lewis and Clark developed one of the most harmonious partnerships that has ever existed in the annals of exploration. Though totally different in many respects, their personalities seem to have complemented each other perfectly. Lewis was dark, introspective, and something of a loner; Clark was redheaded, outgoing, and amiable. Lewis was imaginative; Clark was practical. Lewis admitted to an insatiable wanderlust, while Clark preferred a comfortable domestic life. Yet during their long, trying months in the wilderness, they seldom disagreed.

Lewis spent July 4, 1803, at the White House and received meticulously detailed instructions from the president. "The object of your mission is to explore the Missouri River," Lewis had been told, "and such principal stream of it as . . . may offer the most direct and practicable water communication across this conti-

loss of yourselves," wrote Jefferson, "we should lose also the information you will have acquired. . . . To your own discretion, therefore, must be left the degree of danger you may risk." With typical thoroughness, Jefferson even wrote a personal letter of credit with which his Corps of Discovery might purchase homeward passage should they encounter any merchant ships when they reached the Pacific.

Lewis left Washington at dawn on July 5 and headed for Pittsburgh, where he collected the bulk of his supplies. There he received a letter with astounding news from the president. For some months the U.S. minister in Paris had been negotiating with Napoleon in an attempt to purchase the port city of New Orleans. (Jefferson realized that whoever controlled the river's mouth controlled the entire Mississippi Valley.) In a surprise move, Napoleon offered to sell not just New Orleans but the entire Louisiana Territory. And at the bargain price of $15 million—less than 3 cents an acre.

The astonished Americans had accepted immediately, and with the stroke of a pen, the United States was about doubled in size. So it was no longer necessary to travel under the guise of a literary pursuit. Now

## An Amazing Air Gun Was "Great Medicine" to the Indians

One of the first items that Lewis purchased for the expedition was the air gun pictured above. Similar weapons were in use in Great Britain but were a rarity in the United States. Although the gun was not as accurate as a rifle at long range, it had one great advantage: No gunpowder was needed to fire it. Compressed air in the bulb on its underside forced the bullet out of the barrel. Several bullets could quickly be fired before the bulb needed to be repumped, and consequently, the air gun could fire much more rapidly than a rifle but with less power. Up to 40 shots could be loaded at one time. Indians constantly demanded that the explorers shoot the weapon. "My air gun," Lewis recorded, "astonishes them very much; they cannot comprehend its shooting so often and without powder; and think that it is great medicine, which comprehends everything that is to them incomprehensible."

nent, for the purposes of commerce." But Jefferson's boundless curiosity did not stop with potential water routes to the Pacific. The explorers were also to map the terrain; check on the fertility of the soil; make daily observations of temperatures, winds, and rainfall; keep an eye open for mineral deposits; collect specimens of any new plants and animals they discovered; and, of particular interest to the president, find out everything they could about the western Indians. In short, they were to overlook nothing.

Jefferson was also a practical man. He instructed Lewis to write all his observations in duplicate, with one copy to be written "on the paper of the birch, as less liable to injury from damp than common paper." As for Indians, the explorers were to "treat them in the most friendly and conciliatory manner." But if they should find their way blocked by warlike tribes, they were to give up the expedition and return home. "In the

there was an added urgency to the need to explore the newly acquired territory. To all the expedition's other duties was added the new one of diplomacy. The explorers were to woo the Indians they met with promises of friendship from their new "fathers" in Washington.

From Pittsburgh, Lewis sailed down the Ohio River with a few recruits to rendezvous with Clark at Louisville. Then, with Clark's tall black slave, York, and nine Kentucky volunteers—"robust healthy hardy young men," Clark called them—they continued on to St. Louis. They spent the winter of 1803–04 in a camp on the banks of the Mississippi, opposite the mouth of the Missouri River. By spring the army recruits had been welded into a fairly well-disciplined, smoothly functioning team. The Corps of Discovery then numbered 29 soldiers in the permanent party, plus 16 temporary hands who were to accompany it during its first year.

At last, on May 14, 1804, a swivel gun fired, and the

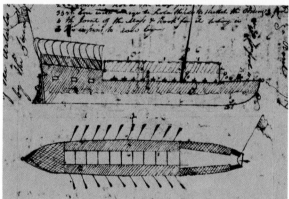

**Navigating the Missouri River** *was one of the most formidable tasks that Lewis and Clark faced. The treacherous current and sunken trees called sawyers posed the most dangerous hazards. The picture above, entitled "Snags—Sunken Trees on the Missouri," illustrates the river's perils, as risky for later steamboats as for Lewis and Clark's small flotilla. "Set out early and had not proceeded far e'er we wheeled on a sawyer which was near injuring us very much," a journal entry noted. The entry went on: "The river rising, water very swift . . . a very bad place; moving sands, we were nearly being swallowed up by the rolling sands over which the current was so strong that we could not stem it." The expedition's keelboat, however, shown at left in a diagram by Clark, withstood the unpredictable Missouri waters. It was 55 feet long and could be sailed, rowed by 22 oars, poled along, or towed by ropes.*

expedition, in Clark's words, "proceeded on under a jentle brease up the Missourie." (For the sake of clarity, the two explorers' highly imaginative spelling has mostly been updated in extracts in this chapter.) Leading the way were two flat-bottomed pirogues (dugouts). In their wake cruised a 55-foot-long keelboat, the largest craft yet to navigate "Big Muddy." This shallow-draught supply boat, which had a deck in the bow and a cabin in the stern, was the best type available for maneuvering in the river's tricky currents. It was fitted with a sail for use when the winds were right. When they were contrary, it could be rowed with its 22 oars, propelled by poles, or even towed from shore.

All that was missing was the expedition's leader: Lewis was still in St. Louis attending to last-minute business and saying goodby to "fair friends." He joined his men six days later at St. Charles, a short distance upriver. The fleet left St. Charles the next day. On May

25 the explorers camped at La Charette, the last white settlement they would see for more than two years.

It would be quite some time before they passed into totally unknown territory, however; fur traders—mostly French—had probed well up the lower Missouri and its tributaries. Jefferson had even supplied the corps with a crude map of the river as far as the Mandan Indian settlements in modern North Dakota. Throughout the summer the keelboat would regularly pass fur traders drifting downstream toward St. Louis on rafts and pirogues piled high with precious pelts.

But the country was all new to the Corps of Discovery, and the men were amazed at the fertility of the lower Missouri Valley—a "fine, rich land, and well watered." Cottonwoods and willows lined the riverbanks, while the rolling uplands were cloaked with inviting groves of oak and blue ash.

Although the landscape was almost monotonously

Lewis and Clark's party, *like the group of frontiersmen shown in the 19th-century painting at left, made camp at night along the banks of the Missouri, though sometimes the expedition would settle on a sandbar in the middle of the river. The main meal of the day was eaten in camp, and the expedition's hunters had their work cut out for them to satisfy the enormous appetites of the crew of 45 men. Lewis recorded: "It requires four deer, an elk and a deer, or one buffalo to supply us plentifully for 24 hours." His favorite meal was beaver's tail, "a most delicious morsel." Along with the other men, Lewis also loved a concoction called white pudding, which was made of chopped meat, kidney suet, pepper, salt, and flour. The ingredients were stuffed into a buffalo intestine, boiled, and then "fried with bear's oil until it becomes brown, when it is ready to assuage the pangs of a keen appetite."*

"butifull," the spring-swollen river that snaked across it was a constant challenge. Unpredictable currents, shifting sandbars, floating logs, and debris—all impeded progress. Most dangerous were the sawyers, whole sunken trees that bobbed slowly up and down with the current. Without warning, a sawyer could pop up in seemingly safe water and rip open the bottom of a boat. The explorers quickly learned the rivermen's trick of putting the heaviest load at the rear of the keelboat so that it could ride up on a sawyer with less chance of damage.

Even when the men were on shore, the river posed endless hazards. Meandering across the plains, it constantly changes course by undermining the clay bluffs that line much of its course. Without warning, great chunks of riverbank, trees and all, will often give way and slide into the rushing current. At one point the whole expedition was almost lost when, in the middle of the night, Clark awoke and realized that the sandbar on which they were camped had begun to wash away. Everyone was hurried into the boats, and by the time they made shore, the entire sandbar had dissolved in the swirling currents of Big Muddy.

The men toiled on upstream week after week. Perspiration streamed over skin blotched with insect bites as they alternately pulled at their oars, pushed on their poles, and tugged on ropes from shore. Despite all the difficulties, the expedition managed to maintain a steady pace of about 15 miles a day.

On July 19 the corps reached the sandbar-clogged mouth of the Platte River, a little south of present-day Omaha, Nebraska. By then they were well into the seemingly limitless, undulating expanse of the Great Plains, verdant with "leek green grass."

For the first weeks the expedition had seen no Indians. Their first native parley was with the Oto tribe in early August. After exchanging gifts of meat, flour, and meal for luscious watermelons, the explorers delivered a message of friendship from the "great chief of the seventeen great nations of America." The Indians listened impassively but were greatly intrigued when Lewis demonstrated his air gun, which could fire several shots in succession. After bestowing more gifts of gunpowder, whisky, and medals, the explorers continued upriver with full Indian approval.

At the end of August, Lewis and Clark met ceremoniously with Sioux chieftains, who requested ammunition and a little "milk of great father"—their euphemism for rum. Though slightly hostile, they proved less dangerous than their reputation and treated the explorers to their first tastes of roast dog.

In the cooling days of September, the keelboat labored into modern South Dakota. There the explorers, who earlier in the season had been impressed by "gangs" of 200 or 300 bison, gazed in disbelief at "vast herds of buffalo, deer, elk and antelopes" that were "feeding in every direction as far as the eye of the observer could reach."

The zoologist in Lewis found this the most exciting part of the trip. Besides the pronghorn antelope, which were new to science, he took special note of badgers, white-tailed jackrabbits, coyotes, and black-billed magpies. He especially marveled at the little animals he called barking squirrels. (One sergeant preferred to call them prairie dogs, and the name has stuck.) The high-pitched yapping of these creatures, living by the hundreds in vast underground cities, was audible for miles in the prairie. Lewis found them hard to catch, and his men spent a whole day toting water from the river to flush one prairie dog from its burrow. But in the end they succeeded, and Lewis dutifully caged the sodden animal to send back to President Jefferson.

As the Corps of Discovery probed deeper into South Dakota, cultural differences between the Plains Indians and their visitors became more apparent. At the wattle villages of the Arikara tribe, the Indians refused gifts of liquor. They "are not fond of spiritous liquors," wrote Clark, "nor do they appear to be fond of receiving any or thankful for it." The Arikaras also disapproved of flogging, and when a mutinous soldier was sentenced to 75 lashes, the chief protested that his people "never whipped even their children."

Clark's slave, York, was surprised to find himself a center of attention with the Arikara squaws. Never having seen a black man, they wet their fingers and rubbed his skin to see if the "paint" would come off. "They were the handsomest women in the world," Clark reportedly told an acquaintance years later.

By this time the men had long since been issued flannel shirts, leaves had fallen from the trees, and there had been repeated morning frosts. It was time to look for winter lodgings.

Early in November the explorers built a log encampment on the banks of the Missouri in what is now west-central North Dakota. They named the place Fort Mandan after the Mandan Indians who lived nearby. Before long the keelboat was frozen in, and the men settled down for the long, cold wait for spring.

By then the Corps of Discovery had navigated 1,600 miles up the Missouri River and nearly reached the limit of penetration by white fur traders. They had seen for themselves the immensity of the Great Plains, the fertility of its soil, the plenitude of its game. And all this had been accomplished with the loss of just one life: Sgt. Charles Floyd had died late in August, apparently of a ruptured appendix. (Amazingly, he was to be the only casualty of the entire expedition.) Lewis and Clark had plenty to describe in the long reports and maps

---

## The Mysterious Mandans: A Tribe of "Welsh" Indians on the Banks of the Missouri River

Near the point where the Knife River joins the Missouri, the Corps of Discovery built a winter settlement, which they named Fort Mandan after the neighboring Indians. On New Year's Day 1805, Clark visited a Mandan village "to allay some little misunderstanding," and York, his black servant, added to the occasion by dancing, "which amused the crowd very much and somewhat astonished them that so large a man should be so active." York's skin color was equally astonishing, and the chief of the Hidatsa, a neighboring tribe, attempted to rub the black off York's body (right). The Mandans were objects of equal curiosity for the white explorers. A popular myth had identified them as descendants of a Welsh prince, Madoc, who was reputed to have planted a colony in America in the 12th century. The Mandans' appearance encouraged the romantic story of their origins. They were light-skinned,

some had chestnut or red hair, and many had blue or gray eyes. Mandan men, moreover, grew beards, and both sexes had white hair in old age, characteristics uncommon among other Indian tribes. More important, a few words in the Mandan language resembled the corresponding words in Welsh, and in addition, the Mandans built round, skin-covered boats (left), similar to the Welsh coracle. John Evans, a Welsh clergyman, spent the winter of 1795 or 1796 with the Mandans. Evans, however, en-

countered no Welsh-speaking Indians and concluded: ". . . from the intercourse I have had with Indians from latitude 35° to 49° I think you may with safety inform my friends that they have no existence." Twenty years later, after spending a winter with the Mandans, Lewis and Clark agreed with Evans' conclusions. However, before the mysterious origins of the Mandans could be examined in greater detail, tragedy struck: Smallpox almost entirely wiped out the tribe by the end of the 19th century.

---

that they were preparing for President Jefferson.

The camp was still being constructed when, one day, a French-Canadian fur trader, Toussaint Charbonneau, wandered into it. He soon was followed by his young Indian wife, Sacajawea ("Bird Woman"), and the two offered their services as interpreters. When Lewis

**Clark carried** *this pocket compass across the continent; Jefferson had instructed the party to chart the Missouri "by the compass" and to note its variations "in different places." The instrument was also occasionally used by Clark to impress Indians with its "magic."*

learned that Sacajawea was a Shoshone, he hired them immediately. Sacajawea would be invaluable once the expedition reached her tribe's territory in the foothills of the Rocky Mountains.

In February, with the help of an old Indian inducement—a little crushed rattlesnake rattle mixed with water—Sacajawea gave birth to her first child. Charbonneau named the boy Jean-Baptiste, but Clark affectionately dubbed him Pomp, the Shoshone word for eldest son. He was a sturdy baby, destined to journey all the way to the Pacific strapped to his mother's back. Along the way, the pair would convince strange tribes of the corps' peaceful intentions—no war party ever traveled with a woman and child.

By late March signs of spring were unmistakable, and on April 7, 1805, the Corps of Discovery abandoned Fort Mandan. Twelve men returned to St. Louis in the keelboat and a canoe with a heavy load of reports, maps, and cages and crates of specimens for the insatiably curious Jefferson. Included in the cargo were dried plants, animal skins and skeletons, Indian artifacts, a live prairie dog, a sharp-tailed grouse, four

squawking magpies, and scores of "sundery articles."

The rest of the expedition pushed off upriver in six canoes and the two pirogues. From the first, the two leaders resumed the respective roles they had established the previous summer. The gregarious Clark stayed mostly with the boats, surveying and making maps. Lewis, who needed frequent solitude, spent much time ashore, hunting and exploring.

Admiring his little flotilla as it set out, Lewis observed that it was "not quite so respectable as those of Columbus or Capt. Cook." But, he added, it was "still viewed by us with as much pleasure as those deservedly famed adventurers ever beheld theirs." And the men, he declared, were "in excellent health and spirits, zealously attached to the enterprise, and anxious to proceed . . . with the most perfect harmony." Harmony was indeed essential. They were about to cross a totally unknown, uncharted area "at least two thousand miles in width, on which the foot of civilized man had never trodden." They would encounter Indian tribes that had never seen a white man. Some of them might be hostile.

Six days after setting out, the explorers noticed the tracks of an enormous animal on the riverbank and realized they must have been made by a grizzly bear, a beast few white men had ever seen but one tremendously feared by Indians. It was not until April 29 that Lewis shot his first grizzly, near the mouth of the Yellowstone River in Montana. Walking along the shore, he was suddenly confronted by two bears and fired at them both. One escaped, but the second chased him 70 or 80 yards before he was able to reload and kill it. "They are by no means as formidable or dangerous as they have been presented," he confidently declared.

Within a few days, however, one of the party's hunters was chased by a grizzly that he had shot clean through the lungs. Lewis found the bear two hours later—still alive—in a "grave" two feet deep dug with its

**The Corps of Discovery** *rapidly learned respect for the giant grizzly bear. Lewis noted "the difficulty with which they die, when even shot through the vital parts." On one occasion Clark and George Drouilliard, the chief scout and best hunter of the expedition, shot a bear so strong that 10 musket balls were needed to bring it down. The beast swam halfway across the Missouri before dying on a sandbar. "This animal," Clark remarked, "is the largest of the carnivorous kind I ever saw." It was more than 8 feet tall, measured nearly 6 feet around the chest and 4 feet around the neck, and weighed 500 to 600 pounds. Its lethal talons were nearly 5 inches long. The talons were highly prized by the Indians, who also dreaded the great bear.*

**Probably looking much like** *this French trapper and his Indian wife, Toussaint Charbonneau and his bride, Sacajawea, a Shoshone, or Snake, Indian, joined the Lewis and Clark expedition at Fort Mandan. Sacajawea's skill as an interpreter and guide* *soon made her one of the party's most valued members. Clark grew so fond of the Shoshone woman that he nicknamed her Janey, and Lewis in appreciation of her crucial services named a river Sacajawea, "after our interpreter, the Snake woman."*

own claws. It took two more shots through the skull to kill it. "These bears being so hard to die, rather intimidate us all," he now confessed. "I do not like the gentlemen, and had rather fight two Indians than one bear."

Besides grizzly bears, the men faced other dangers. Clark was nearly bitten by a rattlesnake. One night a buffalo ran amok through camp, nearly trampling the heads of some sleeping men. And on May 14 there was a mishap that Lewis could never think of afterward without "the utmost trepidation and horror."

Lewis and Clark were both ashore when a sudden squall struck the pirogue carrying their precious scientific instruments, books, papers, medical supplies, "in short almost every article indispensably necessary to . . . insure the success of the enterprise." The boat was blown over on its side, and only the deck awning resting on the water kept it from being turned "completely topsaturba." Yelling unheard orders into the wind, Lewis was about to jump into the icy water and swim to the boat when he realized "I should have paid the forfeit of my life" in such a futile attempt.

Fortunately, the men in the pirogue succeeded in righting it and bailing out the water. Even more fortu-nate, Sacajawea had the presence of mind to scoop up most of the light articles before they were washed away. In Lewis' opinion, she proved herself of "equal fortitude and resolution, with any person on board at the time of the accident."

No doubt reflecting on the unforeseen hazards that could end the expedition at any time, the corps pushed resolutely westward. By late May, when they were more than 2,000 miles from the Missouri's mouth, many men were beginning to wonder if they would ever reach its end. No wonder that, on May 26, Lewis felt "a secret pleasure" when he climbed a hill and saw the snow-capped Rocky Mountains glistening on the horizon. At last, they were nearing the headwaters "of the heretofore conceived boundless Missouri."

A few days later the expedition passed into a stretch of truly spectacular scenery. The White Cliffs section of the river is bounded by towering sandstone ramparts that have been eroded into "a thousand grotesque figures." The intricately sculpted formations reminded Lewis of "elegant ranges of lofty freestone buildings" topped with parapets and embellished with columns, statuary, and long galleries.

**Meeting with the timid** *Shoshone Indians, who mistook the explorers for a hostile war party, was crucial to the expedition. "If we do not find them or some other nation who have horses," Lewis wrote, "I fear the successful issue of our voyage will be very doubtful." An advance party headed by Lewis finally encountered some frightened squaws and persuaded them to accept presents of beads, pewter mirrors, and paints. In return for these gifts, the women led them to a Shoshone camp. Lewis had established good relations with the Indians by the time Clark and Sacajawea arrived. In the picture at left, Sacajawea embraces a long-lost friend after many years, while Clark, in a fur cap, observes her joyful reunion with her native tribe.*

This enjoyment soon gave way to uncertainty. On June 2 the expedition reached a fork in the river. Which was the Missouri? A short reconnaissance up each branch proved inconclusive, but the two leaders instinctively felt the south fork was the correct route into the mountains. Another, longer trip up the north fork proved them right. Naming that branch Maria's River, Lewis headed south on foot to look for the great falls that Indians said identified the Upper Missouri.

On the morning of June 13, his "ears were saluted with the agreeable sound of a fall of water," and soon he glimpsed "the spray arise above the plain like a column of smoke." The sound increased to a tremendous roar when he reached the brow of a hill and saw before him "the grandest sight I ever beheld . . . a perfect white foam which assumes a thousand forms in a moment." That night he celebrated his discovery of the Great Falls of the Missouri with a feast of "buffalo's humps, tongues, and marrow bones, fine trout, parched meal, pepper and salt, and a good appetite."

When the rest of the expedition caught up, Lewis was alarmed to learn that Sacajawea was seriously ill. Her life was extremely precious, since the corps was counting on her help in obtaining horses from the Shoshones to carry them across the mountains. Luckily, Lewis was able to work his usual medical miracle with doses of bark and opium and lots of water from a nearby sulfur spring. Soon Sacajawea's pulse improved, her pain and fever abated, and in no time at all she was eating buffalo soup and broiled buffalo meat.

Lewis was then free to devote his attention to another pressing problem. The falls—that "truly magnificent and sublimely grand object, which has from the commencement of time been concealed from the view of civilized man"—also presented a serious obstacle. It took 12½ agonizing days to transport the expedition across an 18¼-mile portage around the 10 miles of cataracts and rapids that make up the Great Falls.

The men felled a cottonwood and sawed it into crude wheels to transform the canoes into makeshift carriages. Even so, the going was rough. Wheels and axles were constantly breaking. Sweltering heat alternated with thundershowers, hailstorms, even a cyclone. Insects bit their faces, and prickly pear thorns pierced their moccasins. Limping, exhausted, some of them were so fatigued that they fell asleep instantly at every rest stop. The only easy moments came when the wind was right and the men were able to hoist sails on the canoes. "This," noted Clark with amusement, "is sailing on dry land in every sense of the word."

On July 15 the Corps of Discovery embarked again on the waters of the Missouri. They had now left the plains behind and were traveling in the shadows of the Rocky Mountains. Although this was Shoshone country, a ghostly silence hung over the land. Passing 40 recently abandoned Indian camps, the explorers guessed that the timid Shoshones had gone into hiding.

On July 22 Sacajawea began to recognize hills and other landmarks. She had lived there as a girl, she said, before being kidnaped by Minnetaree Indians and carried off to the Great Plains. Lewis was surprised at her lack of emotion on seeing her native country again. "If she has enough to eat, and a few trinkets to wear, I believe she would be perfectly content anywhere."

Three days later the mighty river they had been following for 14 months and some 2,300 miles finally branched out into three source tributaries. Lewis and Clark named the western fork the Jefferson, the middle fork the Madison, after the secretary of state, and the eastern fork the Gallatin, after the secretary of the treasury. On July 30, after a few days' rest at the Three Forks, the expedition began to travel wearily up the Jefferson. Lewis, impatient as usual, set off on foot in advance of the main party. Thirteen days later he and three companions were overjoyed to see an Indian on horseback. But when Lewis attempted to speak to him,

## *Great Landscapes of "Visionary Enchantment" Confronted the Expedition on Its Way West*

Experienced woodsmen, Lewis and Clark nonetheless were moved by the scenic grandeur they encountered on their 8,000-mile journey. The level country where the Musselshell River joins the Missouri (top right) gave the explorers an early opportunity to observe the landscape. "I ascended the highest hill I could see," Clark wrote, "from the top of which I saw . . . the meanderings of the Missouri for a long distance." As the expedition made its way upriver, the men were entranced by the White Cliffs area of the Missouri, where towering sandstone ramparts have eroded in fantastic shapes (middle left). "As we passed on," Lewis noted, "it seemed as if those scenes of visionary enchantment would never have an end." At the Great Falls of the Missouri (bottom left), the scenery was so overpowering that Lewis felt his prose was insufficient to record the spectacle. After composing an "imperfect description" of the falls, he "was so much disgusted" with his writing that he decided "to draw my pen across it and begin again." At a magnificent Missouri River gorge that Lewis named Gates of the Rocky Mountains (top left), the explorer captured the drama of the setting: "Every object here wears a dark and gloomy aspect. The towering and projecting rocks in many places seem ready to tumble on us." Making their way through the snow-covered Bitterroot Mountains, however, gave the men little chance to appreciate the area's swift-running streams and waterfalls (top center). In fact, the group became so short of water that they drank melted snow. Winter was closing in as the party arrived on the Oregon coast (bottom right). The men noted the vastness of the Pacific and "the roaring or noise made by the waves breaking on the rocky shores."

the Indian whipped his horse about and disappeared.

The next day, following a little side stream of the Jefferson, Lewis reached a spot where it narrowed to a trickle. Jubilant, one of his men "exultingly stood with a foot on each side of this little rivulet and thanked his god that he had lived to bestride the mighty . . . Missouri." Over the next ridge they found another stream flowing to the west. "Here," commented Lewis, "I first tasted the water of the great Columbia River." The explorer had actually discovered the source of one of the Columbia's many tributaries but was correct in assuming that he had just crossed the Continental Divide. From here on, all streams flowed toward the Pacific.

The following day Lewis and the three soldiers finally managed to make contact with the Shoshones. He came upon three Indian women who had not noticed the approaching white men, Lewis explained, because "the short and steep ravines which we passed concealed us from each other until we arrived within 30 paces. A

young woman immediately took to flight, an elderly woman and a girl of about 12 years old remained." Lewis convinced the terrified squaws that he was not one of the Shoshones' dreaded enemies, the Blackfeet or the Minnetarees, by rolling up his sleeve and revealing his white skin. The squaw they had frightened returned, and after receiving some gifts, the three women escorted Lewis to the Shoshone camp. There they met a party of warriors that greeted them affectionately.

Cameahwait, the dignified chief of the Shoshones, welcomed the explorers and shared his starving tribe's meager fare of dried berries. Though his people feared Lewis was luring them into an ambush, he reluctantly agreed to go back to the Jefferson River to meet the rest of the expedition.

There the explorers witnessed a happy reunion. Called on to interpret, Sacajawea looked at Cameahwait, then suddenly burst into tears, ran to him, and wrapped him in her blanket. The chief, it turned out,

**Crossing the Bitterroot Mountains** *proved the most arduous part of Lewis and Clark's long journey. Guided by a Shoshone Indian nicknamed Toby, the expedition struggled over narrow mountain passes where treacherous climbing was made even trickier by the newly fallen snow (left). Shod only with thin moccasins, the party had to cling to tree branches on the steeper slopes. Both men and horses constantly lost their footing and tumbled into deep ravines, but miraculously, they generally escaped injury. In the opinion of one soldier, these were "the most terrible mountains I ever beheld." Hardship increased as game became more scarce. Before long the men were reduced to eating the detested "portable soup" that the expedition carried in its supplies. And at one point, they made a meal of bear's oil and wax candles. Finally, in desperation, they slaughtered several of their precious horses so that the party would have enough food to survive. On the return trip, hunger again plagued the party as it toiled through the Bitterroot passes, some as much as 6,000 feet above sea level. Clark recorded that "our meat being exhausted, we issued a pint of bear's oil to a mess which with their boiled roots made an agreeable dish." Rugged and snow-capped, the Bitterroot Mountains rise abruptly above Lake Como in Montana (above), looking as formidable today as they did to Lewis and Clark and the Corps of Discovery more than 150 years ago.*

was none other than her brother. Thanks to this stroke of luck, the explorers had relatively little trouble in obtaining a guide, Toby, and 29 horses from the Shoshones. (A little reconnoitering had quickly convinced Lewis that the rivers flowing to the west were far too turbulent to attempt by canoe.)

At the end of August the Corps of Discovery said goodby to the Shoshones and followed Toby into the Bitterroot wilderness of the Rocky Mountains in western Montana. The next month proved to be the most difficult time the party had yet endured.

The weather was growing cold, and all knew they had to escape the mountains before winter trapped them. Rain gave way to hail and then to snow. On September 16, six to eight inches of snow fell, obliterating all signs of a trail. Clark, who declared he was as "wet and as cold in every part as I ever was in my life," added that "indeed I was at one time fearful my feet would freeze in the thin moccasins which I wore."

Even in good weather, progress would have been difficult. Up and down steep, rocky slopes the men clambered, hacking their way through dense underbrush and across fallen logs. Horses were constantly losing their footing and tumbling into deep ravines. (Miraculously, they generally escaped "but little hurt.")

Aside from a few squirrels and grouse, game was almost nonexistent. By September 18 provisions were so low that Clark and a few men moved on ahead of the rest to search for game. That night he camped "on a bold running creek . . . which I call *Hungry* Creek, as at that place we had nothing to eat."

Two days later, with great relief, Clark sighted a large tract of level country and soon learned from some Indians that the river flowing through it (the Clearwater) fed eventually into the Columbia River. On September 22 the rest of the weary corps joined him in the Nez Perce village of the chief they called Twisted Hair, near the present Washington-Idaho border. Though suffer-

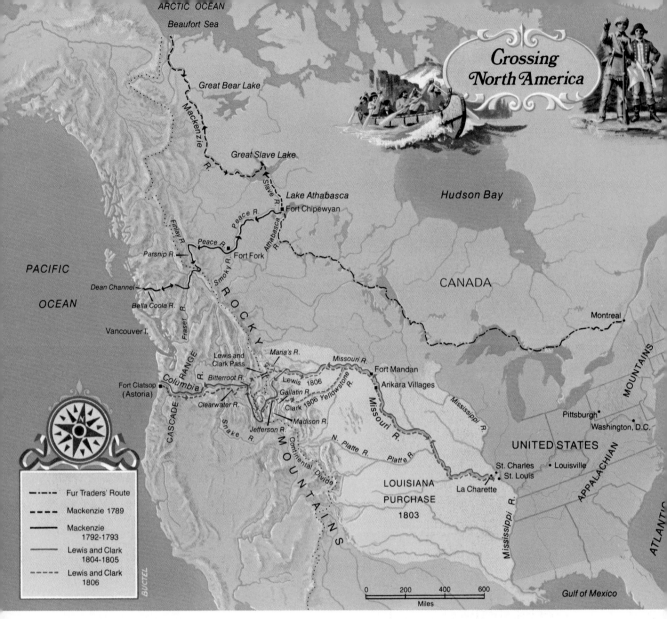

## Crossing North America

Mackenzie

ARCTIC OCEAN
Beaufort Sea

Great Bear Lake

Great Slave Lake

Slave R.

Lake Athabasca
Fort Chipewyan

Peace R.

Athabasca R.

Finlay R.

Peace R.
Fort Fork

Parsnip R.

Smoky R.

Dean Channel

Bella Coola R.

Vancouver I.

Fraser R.

ROCKY

Hudson Bay

CANADA

Montreal

PACIFIC

OCEAN

Lewis and
Clark Pass

Maria's R.

Missouri R.

Fort Mandan

Arikara Villages

Bitterroot R.

Lewis 1806

Gallatin R.

Clark 1806 Yellowstone R.

Columbia

CASCADE RANGE

Fort Clatsop
(Astoria)

Clearwater R.

Snake R.

Jefferson R.

Madison R.

Missouri R.

RANGE

MOUNTAINS

Continental Divide

N. Platte R.

Platte R.

Mississippi R.

Pittsburgh

Washington, D.C.

UNITED STATES

APPALACHIAN

St. Charles
Louisville
St. Louis

La Charette

LOUISIANA
PURCHASE
1803

Mississippi R.

MOUNTAINS

ATLANTIC

Gulf of Mexico

BUCTEL

- · – · –  Fur Traders' Route
- – – –  Mackenzie 1789
- ———  Mackenzie 1792-1793
- ———  Lewis and Clark 1804-1805
- – – –  Lewis and Clark 1806

0    200    400    600
Miles

**Though merchant ships** *had long been plying the northwest coast of North America, no man had yet crossed the huge continent by land when Alexander Mackenzie reached the mouth of the Bella Coola in 1793. His 1789 attempt to reach the Pacific had* *ended at the Beaufort Sea. The Lewis and Clark expedition was far more ambitious than Mackenzie's. It sought to explore and map many thousands of miles in the United States' new lands and to beat the British to the mouth of the Columbia River.*

ing from fatigue and malnutrition, everyone no doubt shared Lewis' jubilation at "having triumphed over the Rocky Mountains."

Gorging on dried salmon, camas roots, and berries, almost everyone immediately fell ill with dysentery. Lewis himself was too sick to move for 12 days. "Desperate diseases require desperate remedies," said Clark, as he administered heavy doses of Rush's Thunderbolts, salts, and other medicines. By September 27 some of the men were well enough to start building the canoes that would take them on the last leg of their journey to the sea. The Nez Perces agreed to look after their horses until they returned.

On October 7 the corps set off down the Clearwater, which led them, by way of the Snake River, into the Columbia nine days later. Then the flotilla passed through a belt of flat, dry country so barren of trees that Indians sometimes burned dried salmon for fuel. The explorers met with no hostility. "Sacajawea's mere presence," wrote Clark, "reconciles all the Indians as to our friendly intentions."

Toward the end of October, yet another wall of peaks confronted the surprised explorers, who now realized that not one but two mountain ranges separated the Louisiana Territory from the Pacific Ocean. These—the Cascade Range—are named for the long series of dizzy-

**Among the Chinooks** (*right*), *who lived near the Columbia River, a flattened forehead was a sign of free birth. To achieve this effect, the Indians compressed their infants' heads between two boards. Ironically, white men applied the name "Flathead" not to the Chinooks but to a rival tribe that used captured Chinooks as slaves.*

ing rapids that the Columbia River has carved through the rock as it plunges toward the coast.

Beyond the Cascades the explorers found an entirely different world of lush rain forests inhabited by slope-headed, salmon-fishing Chinooks. Alarmed at their dwindling supplies, the explorers lost no time in pushing on down the Columbia. By this time the ebb and flow of tide was perceptible in the river, and sea otters swam around the canoes. Although the cold, green river broadened steadily, the men had trouble finding places on its banks flat enough to camp, dry their rotting buckskins, and kill the fleas that "are very troublesome and hard to get rid of."

On they went in fog and driving rain, until at last they entered Gray's Bay at the mouth of the river and heard the distant roar of waves crashing on rocky shores. "Ocean in view! Oh! The joy!" Clark wrote in his notebook on November 7, 1805. "We are in view of the ocean . . . this great Pacific Ocean which we [have] been so long anxious to see."

Clark's joy was premature, since 25 miles of bay still separated him from the ocean proper. After a week of rain, spent in sodden camps, the explorers settled near the site of present-day Astoria, Oregon. There they built a winter camp, Fort Clatsop, and settled down to watch for a ship to take notes and specimens back to Jefferson. They knew from the sailors' clothing, pistols, brass kettles, and other goods owned by local Indians that British and American trading vessels did visit these parts, and they were much amused to hear the Indians reciting such terms as "damned rascal."

But months passed and no ship appeared. Ceaseless rain poured down, confining the men to their quarters. They had little to do but eat, sleep, and stare at the logjammed sea, "more raging than Pacific." Finally, on March 23, 1806, the weather cleared, and Lewis gave the order to begin the long journey back.

Collecting their horses from Chief Twisted Hair on May 7, the explorers retraced their route to the Bitterroot River Valley near modern Missoula, Montana. There the corps divided into two groups. Some, under Clark, continued on through the now-familiar Shoshone country and down the Jefferson River to the Three Forks, where a few men proceeded by canoe down the Missouri. The rest continued overland to the unexplored Yellowstone River and boated downstream to its confluence with the Missouri.

Meanwhile, Lewis headed overland from the Bitterroot on an Indian shortcut to the Missouri, exploring Maria's River to see if it linked up with fur territory in Canada. During this excursion he had his only bloody encounter with Indians. Meeting a party of the dreaded Blackfeet, he managed to convince them he was friendly and invited them to share his camp for the night. Toward daybreak, he was awakened by the sounds of a scuffle. The Indians had been caught trying to steal off with a haul of guns. In the fight that followed, one Blackfoot was stabbed and another shot.

To make matters worse, Lewis was subsequently shot in the buttocks by his navigator, Cruzat, who was blind in one eye and mistook him for an elk. For weeks Lewis was unable to sit down and write in his journal.

On August 12 all members of the expedition were reunited on the Missouri River near the mouth of the Yellowstone. Two days later they reached the Mandan villages, where the explorers said a sad goodby to Charbonneau, Sacajawea, and Pomp, who was then 19 months old and the best traveled baby in America. Continuing on down the Missouri, the party arrived at St. Louis on September 23, 1806, where they "received a hearty welcome from its inhabitants."

In the two years and four months they had been away, the Corps of Discovery had traveled nearly 8,000 miles. They had not discovered a water route to the Pacific, but they had proved the continent could be crossed. They had also brought home a wealth of information about the new territories to the west, information that would prove immensely valuable to the fur traders—and settlers—who soon would follow.

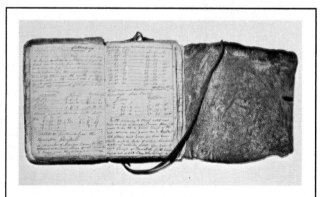

### Clark's Diary Records a Momentous Venture

Lewis was so eager to preserve accurate records that he ordered each sergeant to keep a diary of "all passing occurrences . . . worthy of note." Several of the men wrote accounts, but it is Lewis and Clark's *Journals* that give the fullest narrative of the expedition. The two made rough jottings in field notebooks, like Clark's diary above, and later transcribed them into a more formal version, which was widely read. The *Journals*, originally published in 1814, have become an American classic, despite their unorthodox grammar and spelling. Lewis, for example, once noted: "I saw a Mosquetor [mosquito] to day."

Robert O'Hara Burke (left, above) and William John Wills (below) left Melbourne in 1860 with the best equipped expedition ever to assault the Australian outback. In addition to horses and a specially designed amphibious cart, the party had camels to cross the bleak Australian desert (above). The camels were generally used to haul baggage, but Wills noted that riding one was a "much more pleasant process than I had anticipated." Several animals escaped, and many of the wild camels that roam the Australian desert today are descendants of these runaways. No sooner had the expedition started out than Burke and Wills found themselves racing another party of explorers to be the first to cross the Australian continent. To speed progress, Burke decided to lead an advance party to Cooper's Creek (below), from which an even smaller party would make a dash for the coast. A support party with food and equipment was to follow. The creek's tranquil waters give no hint of the dramatic events that took place along its banks when Burke and Wills returned and camped there in the remote isolation of the Australian wilds.

## Chapter Twenty-One

In the middle of the 19th century, the interior of the Australian continent is still largely a mystery. No one has succeeded in crossing its hostile terrain from south to north. Then two young immigrants accept the challenge to lead such an expedition, achieving their goal before tragedy develops at a lonely oasis halfway home.

# Cooper's Creek:
# Burke and Wills Cross Australia

Born in County Galway, Ireland, in 1820, Robert O'Hara Burke was trained as a professional soldier, serving in Austria before he enlisted in the Irish Constabulary. Immigrating to Australia at the height of the gold rush, he was soon employed as a police inspector. When Burke was chosen to command the south-to-north expedition, some critics were surprised because the impetuous Irishman was not an experienced bushman, and a few recalled that he had once gotten lost along a well-marked trail outside Melbourne. By contrast, Englishman William John Wills, who was 13 years Burke's junior, was of a meticulous, studious nature. Since coming to Australia as a teenager to work in the goldfields, he had wanted to explore the interior. Self-trained in science, he kept an invaluable diary of the fated expedition.

An early geographer once described the Australian outback—or interior—as "either a desert or a deluge." In some years it only rains three inches, and daytime temperatures soar into the 100's. In others, torrential storms turn the arid terrain into sandy swamps. Consequently, few early European settlers dared explore this fickle environment of stagnant backwater and stunted eucalyptus trees.

But by the late 1850's, when the whole Australian coastline had been charted from the sea, and when Sydney, Melbourne, and Adelaide were already sprawling settlements, colonists continued to cast their eyes toward the unexplored outback. After all, mineral-rich mountains, fertile oases, and grazing lands might be found beyond those veils of shimmering heat. The Royal Society of Victoria raised £12,000 for a well-organized expedition from Melbourne to explore territory not reached in several previous attempts. Melbourne newspapers duly carried advertisements for a leader, and 14 men replied. One was Robert O'Hara Burke, a bearded, 39-year-old Irish immigrant. Al-

though a strict disciplinarian, Burke did not appear to have the qualifications of a true explorer: He had a fierce temper and an impatient, impulsive nature. He also was a bit of a romantic, enjoying poetry and courting Julia Matthews, the prima donna of a touring light opera company.

Yet the Victoria Exploration Committee, charmed no doubt by Burke's attractive and gentlemanly manner, confidently elected him to lead the best equipped and best financed expedition that Australia had seen.

Chosen as second in command was George James Landells, a heavily built and somewhat sullen Englishman. The committee promptly sent Landells to India to buy camels, the most suitable beasts for crossing desert country. While there, he met John King, a 21-year-old Irish soldier who had been recently discharged from the Indian Army. Since King could handle camels, Landells brought him back to Melbourne, where he was hired to join Burke's 14-man force. Other members included three men of German descent: William Brahe, a bushman; Ludwig Becker, a red-bearded naturalist, geologist, and artist, whose beautiful watercolors were to faithfully record the early part of the journey; and Herman Beckler, a doctor and botanist. Another member was William John Wills, a surveyor, who soon became Burke's devoted companion.

Preparations went on apace throughout June, July, and August of 1860—winter in the southern latitudes. On August 20 a crowd of 10,000 turned out to see the expedition off. Assembled in Royal Park in Melbourne were 27 camels, their three attendants (called sepoys), 28 horses, several wagons, 14 men, and enough salted meat, vegetables, flour, and lime juice to keep the explorers alive for a year and a half. Among the 21 tons of baggage were sufficient weapons, fishing lines, wide-brimmed hats, and tents for all to live off the land and be protected from the elements. In addition, Dr. Beckler took surgical instruments and four gallons of medicinal brandy, while Landells insisted on bringing 60 gallons of rum for the camels, which he said would keep them free of scurvy. There was even a portable library of works of former Australian explorers who had penetrated the interior. Just before 4 o'clock Burke, dressed in a conical black hat and mounted on his gray charger, Billy, led the way out of the park through a cheering crowd.

Burke's instructions from the committee were to proceed through settled districts directly to Menindee, a settlement on the Darling River, marking his route on trees at regular intervals. There he was to set up a base and establish a line of communication to Melbourne. From Menindee he was advised to "follow the watercourses and the country yielding herbage" to Cooper's

**With great fanfare,** *the Burke and Wills expedition departed from Royal Park, Melbourne (above). In the festive atmosphere, Burke confidently told an excited crowd that "no expedition has ever started under such favorable circumstances as this."*

Creek and then continue on to the Gulf of Carpentaria by any route he saw fit.

The first days of the journey were trying. Heavy rains doused campfires and caused overloaded wagons to bog down in the mud. Horses and camels shied nervously at one another. Yet no amount of discomfort deterred Wills from keeping meticulous account of their position and Becker from making faithful sketches of leaping wallabies and pink-breasted cockatoos along the way.

The expedition reached Swan Hill, 230 miles from Melbourne on September 6, two and a half weeks after their departure. There Burke, anxious to outpace a competitive expedition being organized in Adelaide, dumped some stores in the hopes of making better time. He also hired an extra hand, a stout, middle-aged ex-sailor named Charles Gray.

By September 15 the expedition had reached Balranald, a sparsely populated outpost on the Murrumbidgee River, where Burke dropped another load of stores and dismissed a fractious foreman and several

other malcontents. Spirits temporarily improved as they approached the great Darling River, en route to Menindee 160 miles farther north. In this more fertile country, the landscape was brightened by groves of eucalyptus, yellow-blossomed acacia, and colorful parrots that filled the air with their cries.

But six miles from Menindee, friction between Burke and Landells erupted when Kinchega sheepshearers broke into the camels' rum cache one night and went on a drunken rampage. Burke lost his temper and flatly refused to carry the liquor any farther, and Landells immediately resigned. Burke found himself without a second in command.

By early October the expedition had finally reached Menindee, the last outpost before entering the unexplored interior. Here Burke promoted Wills to Landells' position, William Brahe to foreman, and put King in charge of the camels and their three sepoys. He also recruited William Wright, an illiterate bushman with some knowledge of the north country, to act as third in command.

By then it was midspring. Burke realized that once summer arrived the country that lay ahead would be too parched to sustain his slow-moving caravan and decided to split his party in two. He would make a fast 400-mile dash north to Cooper's Creek with Wills, Brahe, King, Gray, three assistants, 16 camels, a sepoy, and 15 horses. Wright would lead them to Torowoto Swamp, more than half of the way to the creek. The others would establish a base camp seven miles up the Darling from Menindee.

Leaving Menindee on October 19, 1860, Burke led his advance group through an increasingly arid landscape. The desert was relieved only by an occasional waterhole surrounded by clumps of hop vines and gum trees. Scattered families of aborigines sometimes crept up to stare curiously at the camels. Traveling at a rate of 20 miles a day, the explorers reached Torowoto Swamp without incident. On October 29 Wright turned back to Menindee, taking a letter to be forwarded to the committee requesting his confirmation as third officer. This done, Wright was supposed to round up the supplies and the remaining men in Menindee and proceed immediately to Cooper's Creek.

The days grew fiercely hotter as Burke and the seven men moved nearer to one of the driest spots on earth. With immense relief they sighted the welcome waters of Bulloo Hole, an aborigine camping ground. The waterhole's ample supplies of fish made a welcome change from salt meat, and the explorers ate their fill. Then, pushing on across a series of rocky, bruising ridges, they arrived after a 23-day journey from Menindee at Cooper's Creek, halfway across the continent. They had been gone from Melbourne for almost three months and were about to pass into unexplored territory to the north.

Weary and filthy, they encamped on the grassy banks

of a mile-long waterhole. Wills noted in his journal that the creek teemed with fish and mussels and that its banks were "densely clothed with gum trees and other evergreens." But, in spite of the water, the air was dry and hot, with temperatures reaching 109° in the shade. The men were plagued by flies "so that one can do nothing without having a veil on; and while eating the only plan is to wear goggles," Wills noted in a letter to his sister.

While awaiting the arrival of Wright and the remainder of the supplies, Burke sent several parties out to reconnoiter a well-watered route to the Gulf of Carpentaria, no easy task in the desert. Wills demonstrated remarkable stamina on these forays, covering 90 miles one day without finding water and returning the last miles on foot when his camel escaped him. Because they could not find a suitable route directly north, Burke decided to veer a bit to the northwest and start out on the course of a previous explorer, Charles Sturt. This route would take them across the Stony Desert; from there the country was uncharted.

After a month's wait Burke was impatient to get started; yet there was still no sign of Wright. In mid-

**Enormous anthills** (*left*) *were among the strange sights encountered by Burke and Wills on their expedition. Australia's "white ants," actually termites, construct the wedgelike mounds with the narrow sides aligned along a north-south axis. This unusual characteristic explains why the mounds are often called magnetic anthills.*

December, encouraged by the sight of heavy thunderclouds stretching north, Burke decided to use the rainy season to make a "quick" 1,500-mile sprint to the gulf and back. He would take Wills, King, Gray, six camels, his horse, Billy, and three months' provisions with him. The others were to remain at the creek under Brahe's command and build a stockade (Depot LXV) in preparation for Wright, who must be coming soon. Upon his arrival, they were to search for a better return route to the Darling River.

At last, the most crucial part of the expedition was about to get under way. At 6:40 a.m. on December 16, 1860, having instructed Brahe to wait for him on the creek for three months or as long as his supplies lasted,

**Less than a month** *after the expedition started out, German-born artist Ludwig Becker painted the group at one of their campsites (above). Becker also did the portrait at right of "Dick, the Brave and Gallant Native Guide." With two companions, Dick tried to get a message to Burke and Wills as the explorers advanced from Menindee toward Cooper's Creek. Near starvation, Dick turned back for help, but his companions died en route.*

Burke set off for the sea, 750 miles away. As the party proceeded, Wills carefully noted their positions on his pocket compass, while Gray led the horse and watched the birds of the area in order to find waterholes. Behind marched King and his camels. The beasts carried 800 pints of emergency water and enough food to provide each man with a pound of flour and a pound of dried meat daily. To keep loads light, such creature comforts as tents had been left behind. Underfoot, rock-hard clay or oozing mud made the going difficult over sparsely timbered plains punctuated by sand ridges and viciously sharp stones. Following Cooper's Creek west for the first few days, the explorers were exposed to the relentless sun, then heavy rains, then skin-lacerating windstorms that filled their eyes with burning red dust. Meanwhile, with a diet of only meat, starch, and tea, they kept scurvy at bay by steadily consuming boiled portulaca, a wild green succulent.

After passing a series of creeks and lagoons, the four

started crossing the 20-mile stretch of Stony Desert to the northwest on December 22. The little band pressed on until Christmas Eve 1860, when they came upon the welcoming sight of "a delightful oasis in the desert." Here Golah, one of the camels, "gave decided hints about stopping by lying down under the trees." Unable to budge him, Burke called a halt, and the explorers celebrated Christmas in the rare luxury of shade.

The next leg of the journey was north across luxuriant plains. In early January the party crossed the Tropic of Capricorn and a series of hills (the Standish and Selwyn Ranges) from which the camels emerged "bleeding, sweating, and groaning." Approaching the site of modern Cloncurry on the river of that name, they entered a fertile green plain even more lush than what they had seen before. A landscape of dry spiny grass, dotted with palm trees and thousands of enormous anthills, stretched before them on the horizon.

At the end of January the four men finally reached

## An Ancient People Successfully Adapted to a Harsh Land

Until the mid-19th century only aborigines managed to survive in the bleak interior of Australia. With their intimate knowledge of the desert's changing seasons, these nomadic natives traveled constantly to different sources of fresh water. They carried almost no possessions with them. Both sexes went naked and slept in hastily built windbreaks or out in the open. Their diet consisted largely of roots, berries, and grubs, as well as snakes and lizards. Food often was eaten raw. From a flour of pounded nardoo seeds, women made small cakes that added bulk but little nourishment to their meager fare. When hunting was good, men supplemented this fare with game, usually an emu or a kangaroo. They also fished.

Hunters drew pictures of the prey on bark shields (above) to insure a plentiful

supply of game. They also mimicked animal behavior in ritualistic dances (below left), like the one observed by British naturalist Charles Darwin in 1836. "One man," he wrote, "imitated the movements of a kangaroo grazing in the woods whilst a second crawled up, and pretended to spear him." Burke and Wills were invited to join an aboriginal dance, but they refused. They were less hesitant, however, about using aborigines as guides, one of whom Ludwig Becker sketched (right). Expeditions into the outback signaled the end of the aborigines' way of life. Smallpox and tuberculosis took a great toll among them.

Greater damage was done by the culture shock when European civilization was imposed on their primitive existence. White settlers unknowingly violated sacred sites, aboriginal hunting grounds became enormous sheep runs, and traditional laws were replaced by codes the natives did not understand. To defend their dying world, some aborigi-

nes opposed armed white intruders with their Stone Age spears (below right), but few could re-create the simple existence that Captain Cook had described in 1770. "They may appear to some," Cook observed, "to be the most wretched people on earth, but in reality they are far happier than we Europeans; being wholly unacquainted not only with the superfluous but with the necessary conveniences so much sought after in Europe, they are happy in not knowing the use of them."

**Ironic twists of fate** *haunted Burke and Wills even at their moment of greatest triumph. After enduring the most severe trials on their transcontinental trek, Burke and Wills were never rewarded by the sight of the open sea. Sloshing amid drenching rains through coastal salt marshes near their goal, the weary men were tantalized by the smell of the ocean and the brackish-tasting water. Nearly within view of the Gulf of Carpentaria (left), the explorers were prevented from reaching their destination by mangrove swamps too dense to penetrate.*

the Flinders River. Now in the tropics, they were a mere 30 miles from the Gulf of Carpentaria. The ground grew so boggy that Golah got stuck and had to be abandoned. Afraid of losing any more precious camels in the swampy terrain, Burke and Wills decided to leave Gray and King behind to watch them, while they completed the trek to the gulf with the horse, Billy, and three days' rations. Following a native path through dense tropical forest, they eventually came upon an open expanse of salty marshland. Its reedy waters were alive with flocks of wild geese, plover, and pelicans. Splashing on north for three miles, the explorers discovered a tidal channel that swelled encouragingly with the influx of the still hidden sea. But rain and impassable mangrove swamps cheated Burke and Wills of their longed-for sight of the gulf, and they had to be content with deep lungfuls of salty air. "It would be well," wrote Burke sadly, "to say that we reached the sea, but we could not obtain a view of the open ocean, although we made every endeavor to do so."

On February 12, 1861, Burke and Wills rejoined Gray and King. After marking their position on trees and burying a package of books as proof of their transcontinental crossing, they tried to hurry back to Cooper's Creek because two-thirds of their rations were gone.

Rain poured down for the entire first week, soaking relentlessly into their skin, inflaming their tired bones with rheumatic pains. There was no respite from the elements, and by February 23 the men's progress had been reduced to a snail's pace. Then, on March 3, Burke was suddenly attacked with dysentery, having rashly devoured the meat of a snake more than eight feet long. This debilitating illness lasted three days, by which time the party had reached the healthier climate of the desert. But by that time Gray, too, was ailing. The explorers were still only halfway to Cooper's Creek when, on March 25, Wills discovered Gray hiding behind a

tree eating stolen gruel. (According to Wills, "many things have been found to run unaccountably short.") Gray weakly explained that he had to have the flour to relieve his dysentery, whereupon Burke flew into a rage, gave Gray "several boxes on the ear," and removed him from his job as custodian of the stores.

The four men were soon so short of food that a camel had to be sacrificed for its meat. "Employed all day in cutting up, jerking, and eating Boocha," wrote Wills on March 30. Burke's "gallant charger," Billy, met the same fate 11 days later. After a while only two camels remained, and the weary explorers took turns riding them. Eventually, Gray became so ill he had to be strapped on. Then, on April 17, he died, just south of the Stony Desert. Although desperately weak, the others spent a whole day digging his grave, a compassionate act that cost them valuable time and energy.

Abandoning all gear that couldn't be packed on the camels, the three ragged men struggled on toward Cooper's Creek, still 70 miles away. Desperate to reach their headquarters, they covered the last 30 miles in one day, arriving outside Depot LXV late on the evening of April 21. The place seemed fearfully silent. Burke feebly called out the names of the men he had left there more than four months earlier. There was no reply: The camp was deserted.

In the moonlight Wills managed to make out a message, freshly carved on the giant coolibah tree. "DIG 3 FT. NW." Two feet below ground they found a box of food and a bottle containing a letter from Brahe saying that the depot party had returned to the Darling since no supplies had come up from there.

On a tree in the camp were blazed the dates "Dec. 6 '60-Apr. 21 '61." Brahe had left Cooper's Creek that very morning.

Burke collapsed in utter dejection. In the cache was enough food for about 40 days, but no replacements for

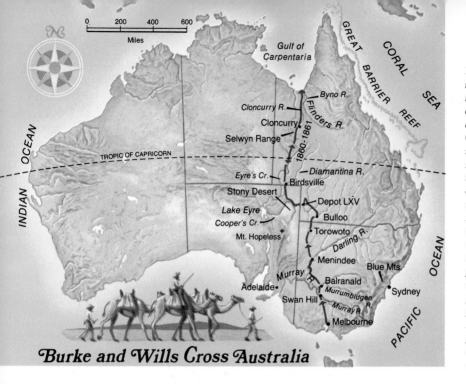

Byno R.
Gulf of
Carpentaria
Cloncurry R.
Cloncurry
Selwyn Range
Flinders R.
1860-1861
GREAT BARRIER REEF
CORAL SEA
TROPIC OF CAPRICORN
Eyre's Cr.
Diamantina R.
Birdsville
Stony Desert
Lake Eyre
Cooper's Cr.
Mt. Hopeless
Depot LXV
Bulloo
Torowoto
Darling R.
Menindee
Blue Mts.
Adelaide
Murray R.
Balranald
Murrumbidgee R.
Sydney
Swan Hill
Murray R.
Melbourne
INDIAN OCEAN
PACIFIC OCEAN
Miles
0 200 400 600

**Burke and Wills Cross Australia**

*Many explorers had ventured into the inhospitable interior of Australia before the Burke and Wills expedition of 1860–61, but none had made a south-north crossing of the great island continent. (In 1813, in the first exploration of the interior, an expedition led by Gregory Blaxland had crossed the Blue Mountains. Then, in 1841, Edward John Eyre crossed the southern part of the continent from east to west.) When the weary Burke and Wills party reached Cooper's Creek on their way north, their pleasure in the relatively sylvan region was short-lived. Thousands of rats appeared and proceeded to eat everything within reach—saddles, shoes, tents, and food—forcing the campers to move to a less infested site downstream called Depot LXV. This incident was typical of the persistent natural hazards that eventually wore down the explorers' strength and resulted in their tragic deaths.*

their wornout clothing and boots. Burke had no way of knowing that Brahe, whose camels and horses were not in as good condition as he thought, had stopped for the night a mere 14 miles away. The three abandoned explorers, exhausted as they were, might have caught up with Brahe if he had said he would be moving slowly.

Burke decided not to take the 400-mile return path to the Darling base because they didn't have enough food to reach their destination. Instead, he recommended heading toward a sheep station at Mount Hopeless, 150 miles to the southwest, which he thought they could make in 40 days. From there they could continue through settled country to Adelaide. Wills and King tried to dissuade him from his decision, arguing that the route to the Darling was at least familiar and offered their only hope of rescue, but Burke prevailed. On April 23, fortified by hearty meals of porridge and sugar, the three set off down the south bank of the creek after Burke had left a note regarding their destination in the cache. But they failed to indicate their visit to the depot on that tree.

Meanwhile, Brahe, who was progressing steadily east by southeast, was shortly to encounter the recalcitrant Wright, who was on his way at last. When the two parties met on April 28, 80 miles south of Cooper's Creek, Wright glibly explained that sickness and death among his ranks had caused his six-month delay. Actually, he had also been leisurely awaiting confirmation of his appointment as third officer while mismanaging affairs at the base camp. Once he had finally left the Darling on January 26, it took him 92 days to cover the same ground that Burke had crossed in 19.

Before returning together to Menindee, Brahe and Wright decided to go back to Cooper's Creek in a last

attempt to find Burke and Wills. On May 8 they reached Depot LXV. Here they were affected by an extraordinary, and still unexplained, myopia. Not noticing the broken letter bottle, not bothering to check whether the box of provisions had been dug up, and even dismissing fresh ashes as the remains of natives' fires, they turned right around and rode back to the others without leaving any sign of their visit. Shortly thereafter, Wright left Brahe to continue to Melbourne to report their leader's disappearance.

While all this was going on, Burke, Wills, King, and their two remaining camels had traveled some 50 miles down Cooper's Creek, to the point where they had to strike southwest across a wasteland toward Mount Hopeless. Misfortune continued to plague them. One camel, Landa, got stuck in quicksand and had to be shot. Watercourses they hopefully followed all ran dry, constantly forcing them back to Cooper's Creek. After two weeks of such frustrating activity, their food supplies had substantially diminished, and they had to depend on friendly aborigines for gifts of fish, "nice fat rats," and nardoo cakes that, although filling, were not very nourishing. Conditions inspired Wills to note on May 6: "The present state of things is not calculated to raise our spirits much. The rations are rapidly diminishing; our clothing, especially the boots, are all going to pieces, and we have not the materials for repairing them properly. The camel is completely done up, and can scarcely get along, although he has the best of feed and is resting half his time. I suppose this will end in our having to live like the blacks for a few months."

The last camel died on May 7 and shortly thereafter came yet another bitter blow. Suddenly, without warning, the natives disappeared and with them went all chance of prolonged survival, for the explorers hadn't yet learned the source of the nardoo seed, their fish hooks were too large to snare the local fish, and game was not plentiful. The three emaciated men made a final, desperate 45-mile sortie toward Mount Hopeless, but they failed as before. After six days they were forced to return yet again to the Cooper, where they at last discovered the source of the nardoo seed.

There was nothing to do now but live on nardoo cakes and hope for rescue. Acting on a desperate hunch that a relief party might be at Depot LXV, Wills made an exhausting trip there. Burying his precious journals in the cache, along with a note indicating their position along the creek, Wills began to voice recriminations: "The depot party having left, contrary to instructions, has put us in this fix. . . ." The desolate wanderer retraced his steps to his companions only to find that during his absence a cooking fire had gotten out of control and destroyed their *gunyah* ("native dwelling") and all their remaining possessions. Only a revolver and a gun had been saved from the flames.

Wills was never to recover from his emotional and physical ordeal. "Unless relief comes in some form or other," he wrote on June 21, "I cannot possibly last more than a fortnight." Then, on the 23rd: "The cold plays the deuce with us from the small amount of clothing we have." Three days later: "Nothing now but the greatest good luck can now [sic] save any of us; and as for myself I may live four or five days if the weather continues warm. My pulse is at forty-eight, and very weak, and my legs and arms are nearly skin and bone."

In the end only King survived. Burke died on about June 28, leaving King his watch and a notebook in which he had written: "I hope we shall be done justice to. We fulfilled our task but we were [crossed out] not followed up as I expected, and the depot party abandoned their post." Wills died about the same time.

Stunned with grief and loneliness, King wandered aimlessly for days, finding nothing but some nardoo and a few birds to live on. Attracted by the sound of King's gun, a group of natives eventually appeared. They kindly cooked his birds for him and offered him shelter for the night. Too weak to fend for himself, King came to depend utterly, in the weeks that followed, upon the hospitality of the aborigines.

Finally, about a month after his companions' deaths, the long-delayed miracle occurred.

After much lobbying by Wills' worried father, the Royal Society of Victoria had organized a relief expedition in Melbourne to search along Cooper's Creek, while three other expeditions were organized to search other regions where the explorers could have been lost. Accompanied by nine men, including Brahe, the expedition, under the competent Alfred William Howitt, left Melbourne on July 4, 1861. With the expedition to the creek went letters of concern from the committee and an affectionate note to Robert Burke from his favorite

opera singer, who signed herself "C. Cupid."

Moving swiftly, the group arrived at Depot LXV on September 13, 1861. The site looked, said Brahe, as undisturbed as he had left it. Moving on down the creek, Howitt came upon some tracks, which appeared he said, "as if stray camels had been about during the last four months." Two days later, as the party pushed on farther, natives on the alert for the "white fellows" called out to them from a sandbank. When one horse bolted toward them, all of the blacks scattered and left a sun-scorched, skeletal figure kneeling on the ground. It was John King, "half demented by starvation and loneliness." Although he could hardly talk, he managed to croak his name.

The natives were generously rewarded with food and trinkets, and within two days King was sufficiently restored by a bland diet to be able to direct Howitt to Wills' grave, seven miles along the creek. There they found his last diary buried intact. King's instructions

 **Burke's corpse,** *wrapped in a Union Jack, was first buried near Cooper's Creek (above), but public grief was such that the bodies of both Burke and Wills were returned to Melbourne and reburied there. At Cooper's Creek a tree carving of Burke (left) done in 1898 is a haunting reminder of his tragic end.*

then led them to Burke's corpse, eight miles up the creek. Howitt dug fresh graves for the two heroes before gently escorting King back toward Menindee.

Burke and Wills were later reinterred in a public ceremony in Melbourne. A government committee assigned to study the expedition found that Burke in many instances had acted with "more zeal than prudence," that he made an error in selecting Wright, and that "many of the calamities might have been averted . . . had Mr. Burke kept a regular journal and written instructions to his officers." Nevertheless, both Burke and Wills are recognized as heroes of exploration.

# Part

# 7

# Penetrating Darkest Africa

# Revealers of the Sources

*Determined to bring commerce and Christianity to the mysterious continent, European explorers seek the sources of the great rivers that flow from its interior.*

"The houses of Kilwa are high like those of Spain. In this land there are rich merchants, and there is much gold and silver and amber and musk and pearls. Those of the land wear clothes of fine cotton and of silk and many fine things, and they are black men." So wrote a contemporary of Portuguese mariner Pedro Álvares Cabral's visit to the thriving city of Kilwa on Africa's east coast in 1500. Within a decade of Cabral's visit, Kilwa had been laid under tribute to the Portuguese, who also seized and occupied Mombasa and other coastal cities. The hold of the Portuguese on the coast was never strong, however, and at the close of the 17th century they were expelled from Oman by Arabs. At the same time the coastal cities suffered a series of raids by primitive tribes from the interior. The nations of the West lost touch with the area, and for centuries most of Africa was thought of as the Dark Continent, an enigma whose only value came from the gold and ivory taken from there and from its most sinister product—the legions of natives snatched from its shores and carried in chains, first to Europe and then ultimately to provide a labor force in the New World.

The first slaves to be shipped to Europe were criminals or slaves within their own communities. But as the demand increased, African slavers scoured deeper into the interior, raiding for slaves with their new European firearms. To maintain a steady supply of captives, African states warred on one another. Whole communities were totally destroyed or, to evade the slavers, migrated en masse. The slave trade, finally, caused the disintegration of entire societies. In the meantime, the main thrust of European exploration was concentrated in the newly discovered lands of America and the Pacific area. Africa, once it had been circumnavigated in the reach for India, was neglected.

Thus, at the beginning of the 19th century, Africa, alone of all the great continents, remained largely unknown to the West. The new worlds that Europe had discovered and conquered over the previous three centuries, and the oceans between them, were now named, mostly explored, and in the process of settlement. Yet the interior of the Dark Continent was still a blank on the increasingly detailed maps of the world. But now a powerful new motive for exploration appeared: The antislavery movement in England wished to root out the evil and convert Africans to Protestant Christianity. Along with this there was the powerful incentive of trade, for England had become an industrial nation with goods to export. In 1807 England declared slave trading illegal for British subjects and began an antislaver blockade of the west African coast.

The antislavery movement found its strongest ally in the new enthusiasm in Britain for Christian missionary work—the desire to preach the Gospel to all the peoples of the world and especially to the abused blacks of Africa. But before missions could be established, it was first necessary to end the almost total ignorance about what lay inside the continent. The great rivers of Africa seemed to be the key to its interior.

Geographically, the continent presented difficult obstacles to exploration. Africa is largely high plateau, sloping steeply to narrow coastal plain. The rivers leading from the interior are blocked at their mouths by sandbars, farther inland by rapids. But in the early 19th century, little was known of these great streams that could possibly carry European religion and trade into the heart of Africa. The source of the White Nile was still a mystery. As for the Niger, although some Europeans had heard of it, only Mungo Park had ever seen it or knew which way it flowed.

In 1795 the African Association, a wealthy English group of humanitarian and curious gentlemen, had financed an expedition to the Niger led by the Scottish physician Mungo Park. Park solved the main mystery of the Niger, the direction of its flow, in two hazardous and heroic journeys, before he was drowned in 1806 in the river he had discovered.

Mungo Park's discovery was one of the first scenes in the drama of modern African exploration. Others—some tragic, almost all triumphant—quickly followed. The Englishmen Hugh Clapperton, Dixon Denham, and Walter Oudney crossed the Sahara to discover Lake Chad in 1823. In 1828 the innovative French explorer René Caillé, posing as an Arab, was the first European to reach the fabled city of Timbuktu and return alive. In 1830 two brothers, Richard and John Lander, completed Mungo Park's journey, traveling down the Niger from Bussa to the sea. The German Heinrich Barth plotted the middle section of the Niger and explored the vast triangle of desert between Tripoli, Lake Chad, and Timbuktu from 1845 to 1855.

### English Scholars and Adventurers

It was the English who mainly completed the exploration of Africa. In 1830 the prestigious and powerful Royal Geographical Society was established and became, in effect, Parliament's unofficial exploring body. The society sent the scholar and linguist Richard Burton, with his friend John Hanning Speke, to Tanganyika in 1857. Speke discovered Lake Victoria on that journey and on another trip in 1862 found the source of the White Nile, which flows from the western side of the great lake. Two years later, the indomitable Samuel White Baker and his wife, Florence, traveling at their own expense, discovered Lake Albert, which also contributes to that mighty river.

Exploration became a popular Victorian avocation. Would-be explorers were offered such guidebooks as *The Art of Travel* by Francis Galton. Enormously popular, this book went through many editions. Mr. Galton offered advice on what to wear in the jungle (dressing gown and slippers for relaxing in the evening) and noted: "Before going among a rich but semi-civilized people, travellers sometimes buy a few small jewels, and shut them up into a little silver tube with rounded edges, then making a gash in their skin, they bury it there, allowing the flesh to heal over it. By this means, should a traveller be robbed of everything, he could still fall back on his jewels. I fear, however, that if his precious depot were suspected, any robbers into whose hands he might fall would fairly mince him to pieces in search of further treasures." It was the books written by the great explorers themselves, however, that created the huge public interest in exploration that emerged in the 19th century.

### Missionaries and Empire Builders

The Scottish missionary David Livingstone, perhaps the greatest explorer of the "dark interior," spent three decades crisscrossing the southern third of the continent. His book *Missionary Travels and Researches* (which within a few weeks of its publication had sold an astounding 30,000 copies) inspired mass adulation for the man and his work. "I go back to Africa," said Livingstone in one of the lectures that drew thousands to hear him, "to make an open path for commerce and Christianity." And the paths this dauntless, fanatic man hewed out of the African interior did indeed carry Christians. By 1901 the Church Missionary Society alone had 510 male missionaries, 326 unmarried women, and 365 ordained native pastors working in the field in Africa; they had accounted for 270,000 newly baptized members of the Christian faith.

But commerce—the "legitimate trade" that Livingstone hoped would oust the slavers and bring civilization to Africa—did not develop in quite the way he had imagined. The journalist Henry Morton Stanley made his career and his fortune by "finding" the ailing Livingstone in an African village in 1871. From 1874 to 1877, Stanley, starting in Zanzibar, fought his way across the vast Congo Basin country to the west coast. He returned to the area two years later as the agent of Belgium's King Leopold II to create the Congo Free State as the king's possession.

As a result of Leopold's incursion, the nations of Europe, meeting at the 1884–85 Berlin West Africa Conference, divided most of Africa among themselves. The exploration of the great continent, begun in a spirit of humanitarianism and simple curiosity, thus ended in the outright annexation of almost all of Africa. And yet in 1890, when the writer Joseph Conrad made his journey up the Congo River, he described Africa as an unknown planet, harboring "a black and incomprehensible frenzy"; and the new white rulers as the possessors of an "accursed inheritance, to be subdued at the cost of profound anguish and of excessive toil." It was still seen as the Dark Continent by Europeans and would remain so in the Western vision, until, in the 1950's, its nations began to achieve independence.

**Three arduous years** *after their unorthodox expedition left Cairo, Samuel and Florence Baker discovered Lake Albert (above). The British government had not financed their journey, but it eagerly recognized the Bakers' exploits. "Baker has done us a very great honour," wrote one politician, ". . . and hë has achieved his work without costing the State a shilling."*

**Arab superstition** *held that Thursday, December 18, was a lucky day for a start, but when the Bakers' expedition left Khartoum (above), the date seemed unlucky. At the last minute, a government official insisted that Samuel Baker pay an exorbitant bribe. Baker refused the demand and threatened the official. To add to the confusion, a government boat collided with Baker's craft, smashing its oars. Once these were replaced, a yardarm on one of the boats snapped in two and another stop was needed to fix it. Delay also preceded Baker's meeting with the ruler in Bunyoro (right), the most powerful African kingdom the travelers came upon. The ruler, caught in a tribal war and afraid the Bakers were allies of his rivals, kept the party waiting three weeks before granting an interview.*

*Revealers of the Sources*

## Chapter Twenty-Two

*The most famous husband and wife team in the history of exploration venture into unknown Africa to find the source of the world's longest river. Their extraordinary determination sees them through great hardships and dangers, including warring tribes, illness, predatory animals, and a royal offer to buy Mrs. Baker.*

# An Ancient Riddle:
# The Bakers Hunt for the Source of the Nile

*Samuel Baker (1821–93) typified the exuberant self-confidence of Victorian England. "I could not conceive that anything in this world had power to resist a determined will," he wrote, "so long as life and health remained." Son of a wealthy landowner and shipping magnate, Baker craved adventure. As a young man he went to Ceylon, where he indulged his fondness for hunting while overseeing family estates. Baker's first wife died after they returned to England, and he was soon on the move again. He hunted big game in Asia Minor and supervised the building of a railroad in Hungary, where he met his second wife, Florence (1842–1916). Together they planned their Nile exploration of 1862–65. Samuel Baker later returned to Africa (1869–74) and eventually retired to England to write about his extraordinary adventures.*

"The three vessels rode into the middle of the river, and hoisted sail; a fair wind, and strong current, moved us rapidly down the stream; the English flags fluttered gaily on the masts, and amidst the shouting of farewells, and the rattling of musketry, we started for the sources of the Nile."

So wrote Samuel White Baker of his departure from Khartoum on December 18, 1862, on an incredible expedition through the Sudan and central Africa that would transform the 41-year-old Englishman from an obscure traveler and big game hunter into a world-famous explorer. Physically robust, intellectually curious, independently wealthy, and linguistically gifted, he was ideally suited to his self-imposed task. He meant not only to settle once and for all the 2,000-year-old question concerning the sources of the White Nile, but also to find his old friend John Hanning Speke, who had disappeared in central Africa while trying to prove that the White Nile rose in Lake Victoria.

Standing at Baker's side on the deck of the cabin boat, called a *diahbiah*, was his wife, Florence, an exquisite Hungarian blond, just 20 years old. Far from dreading the rigors that lay ahead, she welcomed the chance to escape from "miserable, filthy, and unhealthy" Khartoum. The Bakers had spent more than a year in the Sudan and Abyssinia (Ethiopia), tracking the Blue Nile and learning Arabic before moving to Khartoum. There they spent six months hiring personnel for their expedition. Since Khartoum, like Zanzibar, was one of the main centers of the illegal but flourishing trade in African slaves, the explorers were widely suspected of being British spies, and the local officials—nearly all of whom were involved in the trade to some degree—had been less than eager to grant them the necessary escort for their journey to the interior. The Bakers were a determined pair, however, and they had spent lavishly to recruit 45 soldiers, 40 sailors, and 11 personal servants for the expedition. Determined that he should lack for nothing in equipment or supplies, Baker had acquired the best guns, scientific instruments, and food. In the *diahbiah*'s wake floated two open sailboats, called *nuggars*, crammed with 4 camels, 4 horses, and 21 donkeys.

The Bakers' initial destination was Gondokoro, a former mission village but by then a thriving slave-trading center, a thousand miles up the White Nile in the southern Sudan. The journey was dreary in the extreme; for 500 miles endless desert stretched away on both sides, relieved only by an occasional anthill.

Toward the end of December, the little fleet began to nudge its way through the steamy, mosquito-ridden marshes of the Sudd. One of the world's greatest swamps, the Sudd is a vast sea of immense papyrus reeds and floating islands of vegetation. A tribe living there was "so emaciated that they have no visible posteriors . . . and their long thin legs and arms give them a peculiar gnat-like appearance." Masses of papyrus, in dense thickets 18 feet high, transformed the river into an "entangled skein of thread." "It is not surprising," Baker remarked, "that the ancients gave up the exploration of the Nile when they came to the countless windings and difficulties of the marshes."

On February 2, 47 days after leaving Khartoum, the explorers emerged from the fetid air of the Sudd and arrived at Gondokoro. There they had to leave the Nile, for above the town were some 80 miles of cataracts. Fringed with hills and citrus groves, the old mission station was a welcome sight to eyes "accustomed to the dreary flats of the White Nile."

At the time of the explorers' arrival, Gondokoro's population was swollen by a seasonal influx of 600 slave traders; judging by Baker's description, its atmosphere must have resembled that of a California mining camp in the brawling days of the gold rush: "The greater number [of slavers] were in a constant state of intoxication. . . . It was their invariable custom to fire off their guns in the first direction prompted by their drunken instincts; thus, from morning till night, guns were popping in all quarters, and the bullets humming through the air. . . . On more than one occasion they struck up the dust at my feet. Nothing was more probable than a ball through the head by *accident*. . . . A boy was sitting upon the gunwale of one of the boats, when a bullet suddenly struck him in the head, shattering the skull to atoms. *No one had done it.* The body fell into the water, and the fragments of the skull were scattered on the deck."

Despite this threatening atmosphere, the Bakers established themselves in Gondokoro with the imperturbable calm of true Victorians. It was not long, however, before they faced the first real crisis of the expedition. A discontented soldier, in an effort to incite mutiny, began to complain about his rations. But he was no match for the Bakers. Samuel Baker described the incident: "To stop his blow, and to knock him into the middle of the crowd, was not difficult; and after a rapid repetition of the dose, I disabled him, and seizing him by the throat, I called . . . for a rope to bind him, but in an instant I had a crowd of men upon me to rescue their leader. . . . As the scene lay within ten yards of my boat, my wife who was ill with fever in the cabin witnessed the whole affray, and seeing me surrounded, she rushed out. . . ." Florence Baker's sudden appearance had "a curious effect." She gathered several of the "least mutinous" men around her and went to her husband's side. He, in turn, sternly ordered all the men to fall in, which they did. The ringleader was led forward and, at Florence Baker's request, forgiven. It was a compromise that "completely won the men."

On February 15, the Bakers' 13th day at the station, gunshots were heard in the distance. The explorers looked up excitedly. Two white men were approaching: It was the long-lost Speke and his companion, James Grant, who had finally made their way northward from Lake Victoria to Gondokoro. Infected by Baker's obvi-

**Hungarian-born** *Florence Baker, the explorer's second wife, displayed courage equal to her husband's throughout the trip. Baker claimed that he begged her to remain behind, but "she was resolved, with woman's constancy and devotion, to share all dangers and to follow me." Twenty-one years younger than her husband, Mrs. Baker was also adept at organizing the details of camp life.*

ous delight, his men let off a salvo of rifle salutes, accidentally shooting one of the donkeys. Tall, blond, and thin as a rake, the exhausted Speke had "a fire in the eye" and announced triumphantly that the "Nile Question" was finally settled. He had discovered that Lake Victoria spilled out through a northern bottleneck, which he had named Ripon Falls, and, although he had not followed the river thus formed very far downstream, he was certain it was the Nile.

Baker was bitterly disappointed to hear that his ambition had been thwarted. "Does not one leaf of the laurel remain for me?" he asked. Yes, said Speke, one did. He and Grant had not followed the river's course after it veered westward at the Karuma Falls; weariness, waning supplies, and tribal fighting had prevented them from exploring farther before heading north to Gondokoro. Handing Baker his map, Speke suggested that he trace this missing link of the Nile and investigate native stories of another lake known to them as Luta N'zigé, which presumably interrupted the river on its circuitous way to Gondokoro.

This was all the encouragement the Bakers needed. At the end of March, after seeing Speke and Grant off in three of their boats, they set off overland on horseback with 17 porters, the camels, and the donkeys. Ahead of them, to the southeast, lay totally unexplored country.

Florence Baker had by now abandoned her heavy skirts and was dressed like her husband in a shirt, loose trousers, belt, and gaiters. Though she suffered from occasional bouts of malaria, she was an enormous asset to the party: Not only did she plan meals, supervise the servants, and treat the sick, but her temperament was ideal for the hazards of life in the bush. As her husband observed, she was "not a *screamer*." If she sensed danger, even at night, she would merely reach out and touch Baker's arm to alert him. Her patience, tact, and persuasive charm ideally balanced his imperious decisiveness; together they were formidable.

The first part of the route from Gondokoro lay through treacherous ravines. Burdened with 700-pound loads, the camels often stumbled, shedding their baggage of pots, pans, and boxes. Precious sacks

*Revealers of the Sources*

of rice, salt, and coffee began to leak and had to be patched with any rags that came to hand. One day Florence's pet monkey, riding a camel laden with *kisras* (a kind of pancake used in place of bread), helped himself to as many as he could eat and threw the rest away. That night everyone went to bed supperless. Next day, however, they easily resisted the temptation to join a party of natives that was cooking a decomposed boar's head. Baker reported: "The skull becoming too hot for the inmates, crowds of maggots rushed *pêle-mêle* from the ears and nostrils like people escaping from the doors of a theatre on fire. The natives merely tapped the skull with a stick to assist in their exit, and proceeded with their cooking until completed; after which they ate the whole, and sucked the bones."

Although Luta N'zigé was said to be only two weeks' march from Gondokoro, the Bakers spent the next nine months in a frustrating, aimless meander through the wilderness. They were unable to get porters to take them to their first objective, the kingdom of Bunyoro (in present-day Uganda), because of a civil war between its ruler, Kamrasi, and his brother Rionga. Their progress was also impeded by native suspicion: The Africans often took the white strangers for slavers, just as the slavers were afraid that they were British spies trying to suppress the trade. Nevertheless, Florence Baker, who was worried by their inability to defend themselves, undertook to seek the protection of a well-armed Turkish caravan of slaves and ivory. Although Baker chafed at traveling with the traders—"they convert every country into a wasp's nest," he wrote—conditions forced them to remain with the caravan until they reached Kamrasi's headquarters.

May found the Bakers and the traders moving south through forested mountains lush with wildflowers, grapes, custard apples, and yellow plums. By June, Florence was ill again and had to be carried in a litter covered with two tanned hides, so that even in torrential rains she was kept snugly dry and warm. Baker himself was also battling constant bouts of malaria, and their quinine supply had all but run out. "I am thoroughly sick of this expedition," he despaired, "but I shall plod onwards with dogged obstinacy."

They did not plod far. By July the party had only reached the village of Obb, where they had to remain for six months. As described, the village was not very salubrious: "The hut was swarming with rats and white ants, the former racing over our bodies during the night. . . . Now and then a snake would be seen gliding within the thatch, having taken shelter from the pouring rain. The smallpox was raging throughout the country, and the natives were dying like flies in winter."

The civil war in Bunyoro dragged on unceasingly. Not until early 1864 were the Bakers able to leave Obb and resume their march toward the lake. Their horses were long since dead, and they rode on the backs of oxen wistfully named Beef, Steak, and Suet. On January 23

they reached Speke's Nile, the portion of the river now known as the Victoria Nile, near the Karuma Falls. Across it lay Kamrasi's kingdom, and its inhabitants lined the riverside to watch the explorers approach.

Knowing that his predecessor had been popular in Bunyoro, Baker diplomatically sent a man to explain that "*Speke's brother* had arrived from his country to pay Kamrasi a visit, and had brought him valuable presents." The reply was, "Let us look at him!" So, having hastily changed into a tweed suit similar to Speke's, Baker climbed a high rock and waved his cap at the crowd. "I looked," he said, "almost as imposing as Nelson in Trafalgar Square."

Bunyoro, like neighboring Buganda (also in present-day Uganda), was a considerable kingdom, and the Bakers' party was welcomed with due ceremony by handsome natives wearing togalike robes of bark cloth. Gourds of plantain wine and beds of straw were provided for the tired visitors. The next morning in the Bakers' large hut, Florence created a sensation by

---

## A Reed Marsh Blocked the Way Up the Nile

For centuries the Sudd, a vast swampy area in the Sudan, had stopped travel along the Nile (right). But with characteristic determination, Samuel Baker decided to challenge the marshy barrier. Baker, in fact, pushed through the enormous swamp on two journeys: The first time, he discovered Lake Albert; on the second African trip, from 1869 to 1874, he tried to suppress the slave trade in the Sudan. On the latter trip, Baker's weary men hauled two steamboats through miles of dense tropical vegetation teeming with dangerous crocodiles and malarial mosquitoes (below). "The work is frightful," Baker wrote, "and great numbers of my men are laid down with fever; thus my force is physically diminished daily, while morally the men are heart-broken. Another soldier died; but there is no dry spot to bury him."

---

"dressing her hair at the doorway, which, being very long and blond, was suddenly noticed by some natives. . . . The hut was literally mobbed by the crowd of savages eager to see the extraordinary novelty."

Impatient for permission to proceed through Bunyoro to the lake, the Bakers sought an audience with Kamrasi at his headquarters at M'rooli on Lake Kyoga. By the time they arrived there on February 10, however, Baker was prostrated by fever and had to be carried to the king's presence on a stretcher. Kamrasi received them seated on a copper stool placed on a carpet of leopard skins. Baker was struck by his prominent eyes and "carefully-attended" nails; the monarch in turn admitted that he was relieved by Baker's evident weakness, which proved he had not come to plunder. Gifts were exchanged: a Persian carpet, a cashmere cloak, scarlet Turkish shoes, a red silk sash, socks, a gun, ammunition, and a "great heap of first-class beads" for the king; 17 cows, 20 pots of plantain cider, and bunches of unripe plantains for Baker.

The explorers soon realized that this was only the first round of long negotiations. Each day, Kamrasi came to their hut for more presents. He particularly coveted Baker's sword, watch, compass, and one of his rifles. Although Baker badly needed Bunyoro guides and porters, he refused to part with these possessions.

By way of gentle persuasion, his majesty then sent an emissary, who solemnly laid out 24 pieces of straw, explaining that Speke had given that many presents, whereas Baker had given only 10. The Englishman was thoroughly exasperated by this "miserable, grasping, lying coward," who was nevertheless a king on whose goodwill the success of his expedition depended.

The traders' caravan departed on February 21, leaving the Bakers alone with their "little party." They started for the lake two days later, after a final encounter with Kamrasi, who came "to peel the last skin from the onion." He told Baker, "I will send you to the lake . . . but, *you must leave your wife with me!*" Baker instantly drew his revolver. He later recounted: "Looking at him with undisguised contempt, I told him, that if I touched the trigger, not all his men could save him. . . . My wife, naturally indignant, had risen from her seat, and maddened with the excitement of the moment, she made him a little speech in Arabic (not a word of which he understood) . . . . With an air of complete astonishment, he said, 'Don't be angry! I had no intention of offending you by asking for your wife; I will give you a wife, if you want one, and I thought you might have no objection to give me yours. . . .' This very practical apology I received very sternly, and merely insisted upon starting."

Just a few days' trek brought the explorers to a crossing of the Kafu River, a floating "bridge" of matted water grass that they had to negotiate on foot. Baker recounted: "The river was about eighty yards wide, and I had scarcely completed a fourth of the distance and looked back to see if my wife followed close to me, when I was horrified to see her standing in one spot, and sinking gradually through the weeds, while her face was distorted and perfectly purple."

Florence Baker had been felled by sunstroke. Unable

## *The Very Model of the Great Hunter, Samuel Baker Chased and Was Chased by Big Game*

Big game hunting was one of the overriding passions of Samuel Baker's life. Baker, an avid sportsman in the English tradition, set a standard for generations of big game hunters. His books on Africa give vivid details of his shooting adventures, with many illustrations from his own drawings. The explorer (right) was never in too great a hurry, for example, to abandon his caravan for an elephant chase through the bush. On the occasion pictured above, Baker's horse bolted as

he fired his gun, and the tables were turned on the avid sportsman, who was pursued by his quarry for several miles. "In a life's experience in elephant hunting," Baker noted, "I never was hunted for such a distance." Baker surprised a lion (above) when he was only 10 yards from the beast. He fired, and the lion "gave a convulsive bound but rolled over backwards; before he could recover himself, I fired the left hand barrel. It was a glorious sight." Crocodiles presented a constant threat as Baker's party traveled

to stop because they could find no food along the river, the men carried the unconscious woman for two days "through valleys of tall papyrus rushes, which . . . waved over the litter like the black plumes of a hearse." For another week she lay raving with delirium. Sick himself, Baker watched over her for seven days and nights before collapsing from exhaustion. Anticipating the worst, the porters prepared to dig a grave. But on the eighth day, when Baker awoke, he saw that Florence's eyes were miraculously "calm and clear."

On March 14, 1864, the indomitable couple crossed a deep valley and approached a high ridge. Spurring his ox, Baker rode on ahead of the main party. He later wrote: "The glory of our prize burst suddenly upon me! There, like a sea of quicksilver, lay far beneath the grand expanse of water, a boundless sea horizon on the south and south-west, glittering in the noon-day sun; and on the west at fifty or sixty miles distance blue mountains rose from the bosom of the lake to a height of about 7,000 feet above its level."

They had at last reached the Luta N'zigé. Baker promptly named it Albert N'yanza (Lake Albert), in honor of England's late prince consort. The explorers tottered weakly down the hillside, Baker supporting himself on a bamboo pole and his wife clinging to his shoulder. Soon they reached the shore. Gentle waves lapped at Florence's feet as her husband rushed into the water. "With a heart full of gratitude," Baker later recalled, "I drank deeply from the Sources of the Nile.

"It was with extreme emotion that I enjoyed this glorious scene. My wife, who had followed me so devotedly, stood by my side pale and exhausted—a wreck upon the shores of the great Albert Lake that we had so long striven to reach. No European foot had ever trod upon its sand, nor had the eyes of a white man ever scanned its vast expanse of water. We were the first; and this was the key to the great secret that even Julius Caesar yearned to unravel, but in vain."

Baker believed that Lake Albert was the Nile's main source, and nothing could mar his heady triumph that day. (Speke's theory that Lake Victoria was the source would be hotly debated for years to come, though it eventually was proved correct.)

It was time to turn back toward Gondokoro and take a trading boat north to Khartoum. But the Bakers had as far to go as they had come, and there was exploration yet to do before they could consider their journey complete. After obtaining canoes from local fishermen, they set off at once from the eastern shore of the lake, where they had first sighted it, and headed toward its northern tip. But their men were far from expert rowers. "Round and round we pirouetted, the two canoes waltzing and polking [sic] together in their great ball-room, the Albert N'yanza."

As they traveled northward, food was once again in short supply. "To my taste, nothing can be more disgusting than crocodile flesh," complained Baker, with its "combined flavour of bad fish, rotten flesh, and musk." To make matters worse, they were soon caught up in a full-scale lake storm.

Baker recounted: "In a short space of time a most dangerous sea arose, and on several occasions the

on the Nile. Once, freeing his boat from a swamp, his men "felt something struggling beneath their feet. They immediately scrambled away in time to avoid the large head of a crocodile." The crocodile, Baker noted, "had not exactly fallen into the hands of the Royal Humane Society," and the men immediately killed it (below). Baker's boats were also charged by a hippopotamus (right, top) that "attacked us without ceasing with a blind fury that I have never witnessed in any animal except a bull-dog." The rhinoceros (right, bottom) surprised Baker's party when they were out shooting antelope. "We heard a sharp whistling

snort with a tremendous rush through the high grass and thorns close to us," he explained, "and at the same moment two of these determined brutes were upon us in full charge." A giraffe was

hardly as formidable as a rhinoceros, but Baker nonetheless found it difficult to hunt. The long-legged animal usually outdistanced his horse before he could get off a shot. Although he failed to bag any of the giraffes pictured above, Baker consoled himself with the pleasure he derived from the chase. "Never mind, it was a good hunt—first rate." Big game was so abundant in Baker's time few sportsmen could foresee that many African species would be endangered today because of wanton slaughter by hunters.

**Samuel Baker** *was forced to ride oxen when his horses expired in the African bush. Here he portrayed himself astride one of the lumbering beasts, followed by his soldiers and bearers. Dancing* *about the column are tribesmen dressed in leopard or lion skins and antelope horn headdresses. Eventually, all of the expedition's sturdy oxen succumbed to the virulent flies of the area.*

waves broke against the arched covering of the canoe. . . . Everyone was at work bailing with all their might; I had no idea that the canoe could live. Down came the rain in torrents, swept along with a terrific wind. . . .'' On the 13th day, after further storms, they finally reached Magungo at the head of the lake, where their porters and pack animals had gone to await them. Here, where the Victoria Nile enters the lake from the east and flows out again a few miles to the north (at what is now called the Albert Nile), the couple had their first recorded disagreement. Baker wanted to explore only the portion of the river to the east, then head overland to Gondokoro from the Karuma Falls. Florence, while perfectly willing to go with him, also "wished, if possible, to return and follow the Nile from the lake down to Gondokoro!" Amazed at his young wife's tenacity in her state of exhaustion, Baker refused, saying the extra journey was impossible and unnecessary.

They set off eastward in early April, still traveling by canoe. After an upriver journey of 18 miles, the banks narrowed dramatically into a gorge walled in by 200-foot cliffs. Presently, they came upon "the greatest waterfall of the Nile," a snowy foam of water plunging about 130 feet through a 19-foot-wide funnel of rock. Baker named the cataract Murchison Falls after Sir Roderick Impey Murchison, president of the Royal Geographical Society. His admiring contemplation of it, however, was rudely interrupted. "A tremendous com-

motion took place in the rushes, and in an instant a great bull hippopotamus charged the canoe, and with a severe shock striking the bottom he lifted us half out of the water. . . . Crocodile heads of enormous size were on all sides, appearing and vanishing rapidly as they rose to survey us; at one time we counted eighteen upon the surface. Fine fun it would have been for these monsters had the bull hippo been successful in his attempt to capsize us." Despite the presence of the crocodiles, Baker calmly made a drawing of the falls while his men steadied the boat in midstream.

At a village downriver the explorers collected their pack animals, brought there by the porters, and then headed overland toward Gondokoro. After a few days the oxen "succumbed to the flies," however, and the Bakers, weakened by fever, had to be carried. The entire countryside was deserted because of the continued civil war in Bunyoro, and no food was available. Meals generally consisted of "a mess of black porridge of bitter mouldy flour, that no English pig would condescend to notice, and a large dish of spinach." In place of tea, the Bakers drank water boiled with wild thyme and sweetened with wild honey, when they could find it. Starving, they talked of the food at home. "My idea of perfect happiness was an English beefsteak and a bottle of pale ale," recounted Baker. Reduced to "perfect skeletons," they began to give up all hope of ever reaching Gondokoro and decided to return to

Kamrasi's headquarters, where they could obtain food. Reaching it five months later, Baker discovered that the "king" he had lavished so many presents on earlier was actually a younger brother of Kamrasi's called M'Gambi. Apparently, the real Kamrasi had been afraid to expose himself to these unknown white visitors in case they turned nasty. After sending the half-starved explorers gifts of a cow, calf, sheep, and cider, he consented to see them in person. Wearily, Baker dressed up again, this time in a Scottish Highlander's full dress. The king was greatly impressed and gave him more presents of food.

Meanwhile, the local wars dragged on for month after month, making progress north impossible. To pass the time, the explorers made dozens of cheeses, each one "about the size of a six-pound cannon-shot," from their cow's surplus milk. Every week, the king sent them an ox and flour, and soon "the whole party grew fat." One morning an agitated Kamrasi appeared at the Bakers' hut, warning them that an attack—this time from the powerful kingdom of Buganda to the south—was imminent. His majesty was dressed in a short blue kilt (a present from Speke), and Baker complimented him on its practicality for fighting. "Fighting!" shrieked Kamrasi. "I am not going to fight! I have dressed lightly in order to be able to run quickly!"

That attack never occurred. But in the face of another invasion, the Bakers took flight with Kamrasi to the safety of a nearby district, one with immense fields of sweet potatoes. Here, while waiting for the hostilities to end, the ingenious Baker built a distillery, which produced four or five bottles of "good spirit" a day. "I found an extraordinary change in my health from the time that I commenced drinking the potato whisky," he remarked. "I became strong . . . my fever left me."

The invasion soon forced Kamrasi to retreat north, and the explorers took the opportunity to move with him. Joining forces with the same caravan with which they had first traveled to Kamrasi's headquarters, they reached Gondokoro in February 1865. Mounted on oxen, the Bakers entered the town amid suitable pomp, flags flying and guns firing, but their dramatic entrance was somewhat lost on the inhabitants. Not a single European remained in Gondokoro to greet the explorers, who had long ago been given up for dead. Instead, the Bakers were greeted by an outbreak of bubonic plague. Hastily hiring and fumigating a boat, they set sail once again upon the Nile and arrived in Khartoum on May 5.

It was not until the explorers reached the English hotel at Suez in October 1865 that Baker at last slaked his thirst with a long draught of ale. In Cairo, their last stop before sailing for home, he learned that the Royal Geographical Society had awarded him its coveted Victoria Gold Medal. On the way to England, Baker began to wonder if all the dangers and excitement of the past three years had been a fantastic dream. But, as he later wrote: "It was no dream. A witness sat before me; a face still young, but bronzed like an Arab with years of exposure to a burning sun; haggard and worn with toil and sickness, and shaded with cares, happily now past; the devoted companion of my pilgrimage to whom I owed success and life—my wife."

In England the unflappable "Baker of the Nile" and his gallant wife were greeted with tremendous adulation. Their adventures were the stuff of romantic fantasy, and the British public lapped it up; Baker's book *The Albert N'yanza, Great Basin of the Nile* quickly went through three editions. Soon after his return, Baker was knighted, and Lady Baker, no longer a haggard wraith, was fashionable and elegant once more.

## The Riddle of the Nile Was Solved by Speke and the Bakers

Since ancient times men had speculated on the source of the Nile, the world's longest river. The river has two branches, the Blue Nile and the White Nile, which unite at Khartoum. Europeans, however, did not verify the source of the Blue Nile until 1770, when an eccentric Scotsman named James Bruce traced the river to its origin in the Ethiopian highlands. The White Nile, the longer of the two branches, remained a mystery for almost another century. John Hanning Speke (left) confidently announced that his discovery of Lake Victoria settled the problem of the Nile. But many sceptics remained unconvinced because Speke had not been able to follow the river for a substantial distance as it emerged from Lake Victoria. Further exploration, however, proved Speke was correct. Samuel and Florence Baker discovered the points at which the Nile flows into and out of Lake Albert and followed the river up to foaming Murchison Falls (far left).

**Scottish missionary** *and explorer David Livingstone (above) was revered by his contemporaries as a protector of the African and a fierce opponent of the slave trade. His reputation grew even more during the solitary wandering of his last years in Africa. Many people were convinced that Livingstone was dead when an American newspaper editor sent an ambitious young journalist, Henry M. Stanley, to find the explorer. Their famous meeting at Ujiji on the shores of Lake Tanganyika is shown below. Stanley, whose reports on Livingstone created a great sensation when they were published, was the last white man to see the famous explorer alive.*

**Livingstone was** *the first European to see the great falls of the Zambezi (above), which are up to 350 feet high. He named the magnificent cataract Victoria Falls, after the queen of England. "The falls are singularly formed," he noted. "They are simply the whole mass of the Zambezi waters rushing into a fissure . . . made right across the bed of the river."*

*Revealers of the Sources*

*Chapter Twenty-Three. A solitary Scottish missionary travels thousands of miles looking for a navigable river to bring Christianity and commerce into Africa. Hating slavery, he is forced to travel with slavers. He maps a huge tract of previously unknown territory before he disappears into the bush, where he is later sought by a determined journalist.*

# Seeking God's Highway:
# Livingstone Explores Africa

*At 10, David Livingstone (1813–73) was already working in a Scottish textile mill. The boy had a determination that set him apart from the other factory hands: He balanced a book on a spinning jenny (a machine for spinning many strands of yarn) so he could read while he worked, and after an exhausting 14-hour day, he attended Latin class at a village school. His father, a strict Calvinist, encouraged him to become a missionary. However, when David read a pamphlet about medical missionaries, he decided that he would study medicine first and then enter a missionary society, hoping to go to China. After completing his studies at Anderson's College, Glasgow, he was accepted by the London Missionary Society. In 1840 the unknown young doctor was sent to Africa, where he would die 33 years later, one of the most famous and admired men of the Victorian Age.*

November 10, 1871, dawned bright as usual over the African village of Ujiji on the east shore of Lake Tanganyika. With equatorial speed, the sun climbed high, steaming the dew from the palm trees. The morning was already scorchingly hot when Her Majesty's Consul for Inner Africa, a frail-looking middle-aged man in a faded blue cap, limped out of his hut.

After 30 years of exploration, during which he had tramped across the continent and had seen some of the grandest spectacles in nature, Dr. David Livingstone still found delight in the everyday sights and sounds of an African marketplace. He would record in his journal every detail that caught his eye—a squawking bunch of upside-down chickens, two little girls selling roasted white ants. But today, as he settled slowly and painfully onto a mud bench in the shade, his two African servants, Susi and Chuma, saw the doctor's tired face glaze over with the familiar symptoms of depression.

Livingstone had ample reason to feel dejected. Only a few weeks before, returning from an expedition to the Lualaba River, he had arrived in Ujiji half starved and afflicted with dysentery. Desperate for food, medicine, and especially for letters—he had heard nothing from the outside world for more than two years—he asked the town's Arab merchants if supplies for Dr. Livingstone had yet arrived from Zanzibar. Yes, said the Arabs kindly, but in his absence all the goods, including his mail, had unfortunately been sold. "I felt in my destitution as if I were the man who went down from Jerusalem to Jericho, and fell among thieves; but I could not hope for Priest, Levite, or Good Samaritan to come by on either side."

As he sat on his mud bench listening to the dull slap of waves from the lake, Livingstone must have felt that his extraordinary career in Africa was at an end. So, too, it seemed, was his life: All he had left in the world was a few yards of calico, enough to trade for perhaps one month's food supply.

What he wanted was one more year. Just one, to make up for the failures of his first 58.

The explorer whom Florence Nightingale called "the greatest man of his generation" was born in abject poverty in Blantyre, Scotland, on March 19, 1813. His home was a 24-room tenement housing 24 families, owned by the firm that operated the local cotton mills. For the first 14 years of his life, young David shared a 10- by 14-foot space with his parents, three brothers, and two sisters. The effect of this claustrophobic atmosphere was to instill in him a permanent lust for open space that only the vastness of Africa would eventually satisfy.

He was a sullen, plodding, introspective boy, "aye lyin' on his belly readin' a book," as a childhood acquaintance later noted. Sent out to work in the mills at 10, he devised a way to prop his books on the frame of the spinning jenny so that he could read a sentence at a time as he walked up and down the machine. Although

## Slave Caravans Were Often the Safest Way for an Explorer to Travel in Unknown Territory

The slave trade was not new to Africa. The first captive Africans had been brought to Portugal in 1441, and for centuries Arab traders had been making slave raids. But by the 1870's, moral indignation, stimulated by such missionaries as Livingstone, focused new attention on the grisly commerce in human lives. English explorers, such as Richard Burton, John Hanning Speke, and Samuel and Florence Baker, wrote with profound distaste about the horrors of slaving. Ironically, lack of porters and supplies often forced explorers, Livingstone included, to join the very slaving caravans they deplored. On these caravans, male captives were yoked together with forked sticks, which were known throughout Africa as slave sticks (right).

Women and children had their arms bound. Captives who could not keep pace with the caravan were often abandoned or killed. "We passed a woman tied by the neck to a tree and dead," Livingstone wrote. "The people of the country explained that she had been unable to keep up with the other slaves in a gang." Most of the slave trains were headed for the notorious Zanzibar slave market. Here the trade in human beings was a degrading spectacle. "The teeth are examined . . . and a stick is thrown for the slave to bring," Livingstone commented. "Some are dragged through the crowd by the hand and the price is called out incessantly. . . ." The description

Livingstone wrote of the bloody massacre at Nyangwe, where at least 400 Africans were murdered by slavers, was instrumental in ending the largest slave market: The British government successfully pressured the sultan of Zanzibar into closing down the island's infamous slave bazaar.

he worked from 6 a.m. to 8 p.m. six days a week, he somehow found the strength to follow his labors with two hours of school, then two hours of reading in bed. Significantly, the boy's favorite subjects were natural history and exploration. His fanatically religious father considered such interests "trashy," and Livingstone developed a lasting guilt about them. Not until his early twenties was he able to reconcile his longing for far horizons with his religious conscience: He decided to invest his carefully hoarded savings in study for the career of a medical missionary.

When Livingstone obtained his medical certificate from Glasgow University in 1840, he was a reticent, humorless young man of 27, handsome in a rather toothy way, with a short thick body and big feet. He spoke haltingly in a working-class Scots burr that education had failed to eradicate. Yet there was something quietly formidable about him, even a kind of awkward charm, and he was accepted by the London Missionary Society for service at Kuruman in Bechuanaland, which was then South Africa's remotest mission.

In April 1841 Livingstone arrived in Port Elizabeth, South Africa, 450 miles east of the Cape of Good Hope. As his ox wagon rumbled over a range of stony hills into the seemingly empty interior, the young doctor felt his soul expand. Everything he saw filled him with delight: the dry swirls of dust through the bush, the watery shimmer of heat haze on distant rocks, the three-

foot piles of "mud" that his guide informed him were elephant droppings. At night, under a sky almost white with stars, he lay listening to the guttural conversations of black men. Although he could not understand a word, he felt as if he were already one of them and that he had, in some mysterious way, "come home."

Kuruman, which Livingstone reached after a two-month trek, lay at the edge of the African heartland, a vast territory virtually unknown to Europeans that stretched thousands of miles northward to the Sahara. A neat enough little village, it supported a few missionary families and an African congregation of 350—although only 40 of these were baptized communicants. To the new arrival, it was a disappointment; he found it too tame, too underpopulated, and altogether too dominated by its chief missionary, Robert Moffat, who was also a Scot. Revealingly, Livingstone wrote home to his family: "I would never build on another man's foundations. I shall preach the gospel beyond every other man's line of things."

By September the restless Livingstone had set off with another missionary northeast through Bechuanaland's arid wastes to find a suitable site for a new mission. A more dismal cradle for Christianity could scarcely be imagined; bordering on the Kalahari Desert, the whole region was flat, thorny, and so hot "the very flies sought the shade." Undeterred, the missionaries chose Mabotsa, 200 miles northeast of

Kuruman, and there they settled early in 1843.

In the little village of Mabotsa, Livingstone threw himself into the study of native dialects so enthusiastically that his English soon grew rusty. "I am becoming more and more of a barbarian," he noted with satisfaction. But as time went by, he discovered that even life in this remote settlement did not suit him. He was frustrated by the difficulty of converting Africans, who found Christianity at odds with their tribal traditions. They, in turn, were mystified by Livingstone's insistence that they must give up polygamy—in their tightly knit tribal society many wives meant many children, many hands to grow food and tend cattle, and, above all, considerable prestige.

Although Livingstone could never admit it, at heart he was already far more of an explorer than a missionary. He was never so happy as when he was trudging through the bush in 100° heat, meticulously noting the shape of the land, the structure of anthills, the texture of rocks and leaves. Even a near-fatal attack by a lion in 1844 was an event to be described with detachment:

". . . I was upon a little height; he caught my shoulder as he sprang, and we both came to the ground below together. Growling horribly close to my ear, he shook me as a terrier dog does a rat. The shock produced a stupor. . . . It was like what patients partially under the influence of chloroform describe, who see all the operation, but feel not the knife. . . . This peculiar state is probably produced in all animals killed by the carnivora; and if so, is a merciful provision by our benevolent Creator for lessening the pain of death."

Livingstone was saved by the quick thinking of an African assistant, Mebalwe, whose shots diverted the beast; but the doctor's upper left arm was shattered, and for the rest of his life he was unable to raise it above shoulder level.

While recuperating in Kuruman, he proposed to Robert Moffat's daughter Mary, a plain but sturdy young woman whose upbringing on a remote mission station had well prepared her for the hardships of life in Africa. They were married in January 1845, and together they established other missions, including one at Kolobeng, north of Mabotsa. These, too, were a failure. Livingstone did make the one convert of his career at Kolobeng—Chief Sechele of the Bakwena tribe—but the newly baptized Christian found himself unable to abandon the delights of polygamy. (He later underwent another, lasting, conversion.)

To Livingstone, this was a bitter blow. It also reinforced his growing conviction that an alien religion, such as Christianity, could never flourish in Africa until tribalism and all its traditions were utterly rooted out, no matter what the cost. To effect this, a healthy infusion of British commerce was needed; it would radically alter the tribesmen's subsistence economy, and as the Africans shed their savage ways, they might learn to accept the white man's God.

But first of all, Livingstone persuaded himself, a navigable waterway connecting the African interior with either the Atlantic or the Indian Oceans must be found—a river that could be transformed into a great highway of British trade. On one of his expeditions, in July 1849, he had crossed the eastern part of the Kalahari Desert and discovered that a great sheet of water (Lake Ngami) lay to the north of it. Local natives assured him that a tributary river of the lake was connected by swamps and streams to "a country full of rivers" somewhere in central Africa. This phrase mysteriously excited Livingstone, who was to become obsessed with his notion of a watery paradise where commerce and Christianity would flower side by side.

On August 3, 1851, after a 700-mile trek across country so dry he was obliged to drink the dungy slush in wild beasts' waterholes ("and no stinted draughts of it either"), Livingstone was rewarded by the sight of a river so clear and beautiful it brought tears to his eyes. Fully 500 yards across, it flowed smoothly eastward until it was lost in the distant haze. The explorer guessed this must be the same Zambezi River that spilled into the Indian Ocean via the Portuguese colony of Mozambique. He had found "God's Highway."

The Makololo tribe, which inhabited the swampy triangle between the Zambezi and its tributary the Chobe, welcomed Livingstone and agreed to let him establish a mission and trading center among them. (To them, of course, trade meant guns, and the presence of whites meant protection from their enemies.) But before moving in with the Makololo, the doctor had to divest himself of his rapidly growing family, all of whom he had inexplicably brought along with him. Mrs. Livingstone, whom he rather unkindly called the "great Irish manufactory," had an irritating habit of giving birth during expeditions. With sorrow and relief, he put her and the children on a homebound steamer at Cape Town in April 1852. Exultant at being free and full of grandiose visions for the future, Livingstone hurried back to the Zambezi to continue exploring.

Puffing contentedly on their cannabis pipes, the puzzled Makololo listened politely to Livingstone's theories about "opening up" central Africa to British commerce and religion. Although they had no idea what he meant by "oceans" and "paddle steamers," they agreed to supply 27 porters, oxen, and ivory for a trial expedition to the coast. If he returned with firearms and other goods, they would be happy to enter into trade agreements with his "chief" (Queen Victoria), even though she *was* a woman. Joyfully, Livingstone set off from the Makololo town of Linyanti on November 11, 1853.

For reasons best known to himself, he headed not east down his broad Zambezi "highway" toward Mozambique, but northwest into the steamy jungles of Barotseland and Angola. Presumably, he was seeking a land route for traders to follow inland from the Atlantic coast—despite the fact that the distance from the

**Two Europeans**—*the artist Thomas Baines and a companion, James Chapman—crouch in a canoe while two Africans pole them across the Zambezi on an 1862 expedition. Baines, who had* been with Livingstone's 1858 Zambezi Expedition, was inspecting the waters near Victoria Falls, discovered by Livingstone in 1855. Falls and rapids make the Zambezi unnavigable.*

Angolan ports to Linyanti was well over a thousand miles through extremely difficult terrain. Possibly, the doctor's head was already turned by malaria—that dizzying, chilling fever that was to prostrate him many times before he reached the coast.

During the next six months Livingstone fought his way through hideous country—curtains of slippery vines, swamps gray with mosquitoes, bogs that rotted his trousers, and prairies stiff with razorlike grass—but his inexorable forward motion never slackened. He was not the swiftest of explorers, but he was the most relentless, vowing that "I shall not stop till my breath does." At times, he was so weak with fever and dysentery that he had to cling to the wet back of an ox; at others, he could do nothing but lie in the bottom of a canoe and vomit into the water.

Every tribe he encountered en route demanded payment of the customary *hongo*, or "passage dues." The usual request was for an ox or a gun, but one day Livingstone heard the ominous alternative, ". . . or one of your men." With a sense of revulsion, he realized that, even this far inland, central Africa was contaminated by the slave trade. His terrified porters begged his permission to turn back, but Livingstone paid extra *hongo* in cloth and beads and forced them onward.

By the time he reached settlements in Angola in April 1854, Livingstone was paying his way in shirts and living off manioc and ox meat. Sympathetic Portuguese traders gave him food and medicine, but his health continued to decline. Descending onto the coastal plain near Luanda, he was attacked by clouds of ferocious mosquitoes, whose sharp sting felt like "a nail through the heel of one's boot."

When the palms of the Atlantic coast rose up on the horizon, Livingstone was near death. But he could still touchingly observe the awe of his Makololo porters as they gazed for the first time at the sea.

In describing their feelings afterward, they remarked, "We marched along with our father, believing that what the ancients had always told us was true, that the world has no end; but all at once the world said to us, 'I am finished, there is no more of me!'"

On May 1, 1854, Livingstone was carried into Luanda and deposited in the bed of the town's only English resident. "Never shall I forget the luxuriant pleasure I enjoyed in feeling myself again on a good English couch, after six months' sleeping on the ground."

For weeks David Livingstone lay struggling for his life. He was too weak to hold a pen and had to dictate his official report to the London Missionary Society. When this letter reached England in early August, accompanied by some amazingly detailed sketch maps, it created an instant sensation. The obscure missionary's thousand-mile march was hailed as "one of the greatest geographical explorations of the age."

Livingstone, however, knew that the same feat had been performed before by at least two Portuguese slave traders, and although he conveniently forgot to mention it in his letter, this knowledge tortured him. Refusing a free trip home to England, he announced his intention to return to Linyanti the way he had come—and then to continue along the Zambezi to the Indian Ocean. Ostensibly, this was to give British commerce a choice of routes to the interior, but Livingstone's private reasons were obvious: He wanted to become the first European to cross the entire African continent.

It very nearly killed him. On the way back he vomited quantities of blood, was almost blinded by a sharp branch, and partially lost his hearing from an attack of rheumatic fever. But he considered giving in to weakness "effeminate" and continued to make meticulous geographical observations, dragging himself shivering from bed at 2 a.m. to take sightings of the moon.

The Makololo gave him a hero's welcome when he arrived in Linyanti on September 13, having been away almost two years. Chief Sekeletu was so delighted with Livingstone's gift of a Portuguese army uniform that he forgave him for having brought no guns and having spent all the expedition's ivory profits on *hongo*. More than a hundred porters were immediately recruited to accompany the doctor down the Zambezi.

By November 3, 1855, Livingstone was ready to resume his 2,500-mile transcontinental journey. Paddling down the Chobe and into the broad Zambezi, he found

himself gliding east toward a phenomenon he had long heard tales of but had never seen. The Makololo, who called it Mosioatunya, "the smoke that thunders," had never dared approach it before. On November 17 Livingstone began to hear a dull roaring noise and saw columns of vapors rising above the river. At his publisher's suggestion, he later penned a glowing description of the falls for his book *Missionary Travels and Researches*: "The snow-white sheet seemed like myriads of small comets rushing in one direction, each of which left behind its nucleus rays of foam."

At the time, however, he was less than enchanted by the obstacle posed by this wall of water some 300 feet high and a mile wide, which he dutifully named after Queen Victoria. Here, barely 50 miles down God's Highway, was a formidable roadblock indeed. Praying that the Zambezi would flow freely for the rest of its long journey to the sea, the explorer pressed on.

He was pleased to discover that the plateau on the river's north bank was high, fertile, and free of fever. Birds sang in the trees, and herds of fat buffalo grazed on the silvery grass. Surely, a British colony could flourish here, spreading Christianity across central Africa and purifying it of superstition and slavery.

Impatient to reach the coast and communicate his good news to the London Missionary Society, Living-

**Even after being badly mauled** *by an attacking lion (top), Livingstone continued to explore. Extremely ill, he was carried on the shoulders of an African through flooding swamps (above).*

*Above, his boat is forced between dense reeds. "Nothing earthly will make me give up my work in despair," the discoverer wrote. "I encourage myself in the Lord my God, and go forward."*

**The steamship** Ma-Robert—*named African-fashion for Mrs. Livingstone, mother of Robert, the explorer's oldest son—was intended to speed exploration of the Zambezi River. However, the ship, transported in sections from England, did not have* *sufficient power to fight the river's swift current. The engine, Livingstone complained, was "evidently made to grind coffee in a shop window." The boiler wheezed and coughed so insistently that the hapless ship was soon nicknamed* The Asthmatic.

stone headed southwest across open country in order to bypass a loop of the Zambezi. It was one of the worst mistakes he ever made, for by taking this shortcut, he failed to discover the Quebrabasa Rapids, a 30-mile-long caldron of boulders and foam—proof positive that God's Highway was not navigable.

Fever struck again, viciously, when Livingstone arrived at the river port of Tete, Mozambique, in early March 1856. The local Portuguese nursed him with the same care as their counterparts in Angola, refusing to accept payment for food or clothing and offering to look after his Makololo porters if he wished to continue downriver and sail for home. Promising to return within a year to take his African attendants back to Linyanti (a promise he delayed two years in keeping, by which time the Makololo had been seduced by the pleasures of town life), Livingstone set off in a canoe on the last 270 miles of his journey with eight men. The usual clouds of mosquitoes rose to greet him as he entered the slimy swamps of the lower Zambezi; by the time he reached Quelimane, a few miles from the coast (May 20, 1856), he was again desperately ill with fever.

The 43-year-old explorer did not know it, but he was already famous. Reports of his epic continental crossing had long since reached England, and H.M.S. *Frolic* came to take him home to a hero's welcome.

It must have been painful for the older man, sitting on his mud bench at Ujiji in 1871, to remember the years following his triumphal return to England. At first, there had been medals, a royal reception, and editorials praising him as the greatest British explorer since Sir Francis Drake. But there had also been an icy letter at Quelimane from the directors of the London Missionary Society (from which he would soon part company), stating that the society would no longer sponsor expeditions "connected only remotely with the spread of the Gospel." Praised as a selfless, devoted missionary who had converted thousands, Livingstone could not bring himself to admit that his sum total of saved souls in Bechuanaland was one. His book *Missionary Travels and Researches* had sold 30,000 copies and had made him embarrassingly rich. Worst of all, his wife had taken to drink during their long separation, and his children were almost strangers to him.

Then there had been the long, bitter, government-sponsored Zambezi Expedition (1858–63), which ended in total failure. Livingstone had returned to Quelimane at the head of a seven-man team to make a scientific survey of God's Highway. But the seething rapids of Quebrabasa had blocked his little steamer, destroying his bright vision of a river filled with Christian shipping. Frantically, he went on to explore the Shire, a

*Revealers of the Sources*

northern tributary of the Zambezi. It, too, proved to be choked with rapids, but by now Livingstone could not stop. "I will go anywhere," he wrote, "provided it be forward." Continuing up the riverbank on foot, he was overwhelmed by the sight of 11,600 square miles of water—the legendary Lake Nyasa, which had been described to him by the Portuguese.

Although the beautiful landscape around the lake was littered with piles of forked slave-taming sticks, used to secure the necks of captives, Livingstone transferred his colonial dreams there and recommended that a party of British missionaries be sent out. No sooner had seven unsuspecting recruits arrived, however, than they were swept up in a vortex of tribal wars and slave raids. Three reverend gentlemen lost their lives, adding to the burden of guilt on Livingstone's soul. (A similar fate had befallen a mission established among the Makololo, with Livingstone's encouragement, in the late 1850's; almost all the missionaries and their families had been quickly wiped out by fever.) Then, on April 27, 1862, Livingstone's wife, who had come out with the missionaries' families, died. The doctor was devastated. "For the first time in my life," he wrote in his journal, "I feel willing to die."

Meanwhile, the health and morale of the Zambezi Expedition's members steadily deteriorated. Livingstone, who had been extremely successful in his dealings with African natives and was usually gentle and patient with them, found himself incapable of controlling a group of quarrelsome, fever-ridden Europeans. Tortured by chronic dysentery, he would sink into moods of gray melancholy and for weeks would do nothing but stare into space, humming to himself. At other times he would fly into hysterical rages and shriek what John Kirk, the expedition's botanist and medical officer, called "the most abusive filthy language ever heard in that class of society." In the privacy of his journal, Livingstone wondered if he were not losing his mind.

The inevitable letter of recall from the Foreign Office arrived in July 1863. "I don't know whether I am to go on the shelf or not," he wrote miserably. "If so, I make the shelf Africa."

Livingstone was back there sooner than he expected. Thanks to the lobbying of Sir Roderick Murchison, president of the Royal Geographical Society, he was assigned to Zanzibar in 1865 in the unofficial capacity of Her Majesty's Consul for Inner Africa.

In April 1866 Livingstone landed at Rovuma Bay (on the border between modern-day Tanzania and Mozambique) to begin searching for the key to an ancient mystery: the source of the Nile. His plan was to lead a small expedition to the unknown country west of Lake Nyasa and seek out a lake called Bangweulu, rumored to be the source of a northward-flowing river that he thought might be the Nile. He had already dismissed Richard Burton's and John Speke's claims for Lakes Tanganyika and Victoria as the Nile's sources, and he was fascinated by the theories of Herodotus, who had written in the fifth century B.C. that deep in the heart of Africa rose "the fountains of the Nile, which it is impossible to fathom: Half the water runs northward into Egypt: half to the south." Livingstone had already explored the southern flow, assuming it to be the Zambezi; now he had only to explore the northern, and his immortality would undoubtedly be assured.

**Thomas Baines painted** *Livingstone's party at the Quebrabasa Rapids (right). In the bottom righthand corner of the picture, a photographer, undoubtedly Livingstone's younger brother Charles, records the scene (enlarged below). Livingstone had proposed Charles for the expedition, claiming that he had learned photography while a student in the United States. Charles, in addition, was appointed "moral agent" of the expedition, although he seems to have been more expert at creating disharmony. Baines, who had become friendly with some Portuguese traders that Charles considered "degenerate," was a particular target of his wrath.*

*Charles accused Baines of pilfering a lot of sugar from the expedition's supplies. Nothing was missing, but Baines was dismissed from the exploration party.*

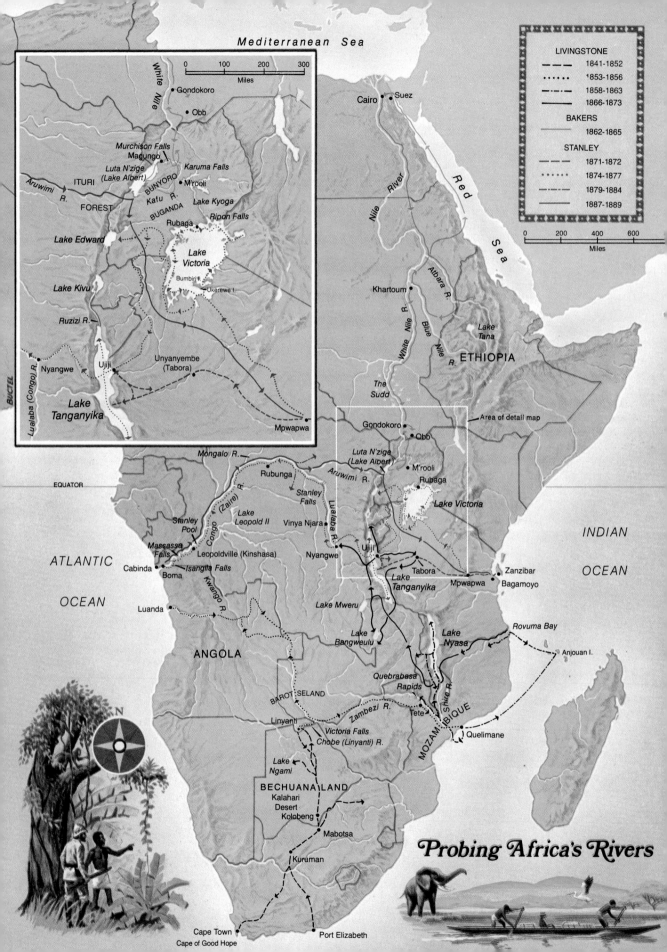

Mediterranean Sea

**Inset map (detail):**

White Nile

Gondokoro
Obb

Murchison Falls
Magungo

Karuma Falls

Luta N'zige
(Lake Albert)

ITURI

M'rooli

Aruwimi R.

BUNYORO

Kafu R.

FOREST

BUGANDA

Lake Kyoga

Rubaga

Ripon Falls

Lake Edward

Lake Victoria

Lake Kivu

Bumbiri I.

Ukerewe I.

Ruzizi R.

BUCTEL

Lualaba (Congo) R.

Nyangwe

Ujiji

Unyanyembe
(Tabora)

Lake
Tanganyika

Mpwapwa

0   100   200   300
Miles

**Legend:**

LIVINGSTONE
- - - 1841-1852
····· 1853-1856
-·-·- 1858-1863
——— 1866-1873

BAKERS
——— 1862-1865

STANLEY
- - - 1871-1872
····· 1874-1877
-·-·- 1879-1884
——— 1887-1889

0   200   400   600
Miles

Cairo   Suez

Nile River

Red Sea

Atbara R.

Khartoum

White Nile R.

Blue Nile R.

Lake Tana

ETHIOPIA

The Sudd

Gondokoro
Obb

Luta N'zige
(Lake Albert)

M'rooli

Rubaga

Area of detail map

Mongalo R.

EQUATOR

Aruwimi R.

Rubunga

Stanley Falls

Lualaba R.

Lake Victoria

INDIAN OCEAN

ATLANTIC OCEAN

Stanley Pool

Congo (Zaire) R.

Lake Leopold II

Vinya Njara

Nyangwe

Ujiji

Massassa Falls

Leopoldville (Kinshasa)

Cabinda
Boma

Isangila Falls

Kwango R.

Tabora

Zanzibar
Bagamoyo

Mpwapwa

Lake Tanganyika

Luanda

Lake Mweru

Lake Bangweulu

ANGOLA

Lake Nyasa

Rovuma Bay

Anjouan I.

BAROTSELAND

Quebrabasa Rapids

Shire R.

Zambezi R.

Tete

MOZAMBIQUE

Linyanti

Victoria Falls
Chobe (Linyanti) R.

Quelimane

Lake Ngami

BECHUANALAND

Kalahari Desert
Kolobeng

Mabotsa

Kuruman

## Probing Africa's Rivers

N

Cape Town
Cape of Good Hope

Port Elizabeth

## The Persistent Victorian Discoverers

In the middle of the 19th century, most of the African continent's 11.5 million square miles was still a mystery to Europeans. The heart of Africa, particularly the vast area between Kolobeng in the south and Gondokoro in the north (outlined opposite right, enlarged opposite left), was virtually unexplored. The Portuguese had long held commercial enclaves along the coast, and Arab slave traders had regularly penetrated the interior for centuries; but they had kept their discoveries to themselves. Thus, in 1841, when Livingstone first arrived in Africa, the major part of its interior was labeled "unknown" on maps.

It was the British who pioneered the exploration of Africa; but it was not until the 1850's, when the news of Livingstone's discoveries began to reach England, that their efforts begin in earnest. In 1849 Livingstone had discovered Lake Ngami, and in 1852–56 he had explored the Zambezi River, discovered Victoria Falls, and become the first known European to traverse Africa (from Luanda on the west coast to Quelimane on the east coast). Now famous, he returned to Africa in 1858 as head of an official British government expedition. Livingstone's main purpose then—a proposed navigation of the Zambezi River by steamer—was thwarted at the Quebrabasa Rapids. Abandoning the Zambezi, he navigated the Shire and discovered Lake Nyasa (1859). On his final expedition (1866–73), Livingstone sought to find the elusive source of the White Nile, despite the contention of John Hanning Speke that he had indeed done so with his discovery of Lake Victoria in 1862.

The 1862–65 expedition of Samuel and Florence Baker had also expanded Europe's knowledge of the Nile's source by the discovery of Lake Albert and the Murchison Falls. Nevertheless, it was felt that Livingstone could clear up whatever doubts remained. When there had been no news from him in five years, an expedition was sent from London to find him, and the New York *Herald* newspaper sent one of its own, led by a journalist named Henry Morton Stanley. Stanley found the ailing Livingstone at Ujiji on Lake Tanganyika on November 10, 1871. Stanley returned to England with his news, while Livingstone, his health somewhat restored, set out south to explore the basin of the Lualaba River. (He died during this trek on May 1, 1873.)

Stanley returned to Africa in 1874 with a large expedition, reaching Lake Tanganyika in 1876. From there he traveled overland to the Lualaba River. Launching his portable boat, *Lady Alice*, he sailed down to the confluence with the great Congo River. Then ensued one of the great adventures in the exploration of Africa. Braving the unknown river, Stanley sailed almost its entire length, reaching Boma on the west coast three years after leaving Zanzibar. In 1879, working for Belgian King Leopold, Stanley returned to the Congo, discovering Lake Leopold II and founding the city of Leopoldville. His 1887–89 expedition to the Congo was aimed at "rescuing" Emin Pasha, the governor of Equatoria.

There is no doubt that the aging doctor in these final years of his life was for long periods half crazed. Burning with dysentery, bewildered by instruments that failed to work and guides who confessed themselves lost, he took increasing refuge in his fantasy of Herodotus' bubbling, bottomless fountains. Susi and Chuma, his two faithful servants, noticed sadly that the doctor was not the man he had been. He was becoming vague and querulous, and he seemed indifferent when porters abused their pack animals, stole supplies, and deserted one by one. Only his fabulous endurance remained—he marched as compulsively as ever.

Lake Bangweulu, which Livingstone reached on July 18, 1868, proved to be a putrid swamp teeming with leeches. By now the doctor was so short of men and supplies that he was obliged to join forces with an Arab slave caravan that happened by. This humiliation, for one who still saw himself as a missionary, was painful, but at least he could go on exploring.

For most of 1869 and 1870 the Arabs, who regarded Livingstone as an amusing eccentric, escorted him through a landscape of death. Nothing he had seen in the Portuguese colonies had prepared him for the horrors of the Arab slave trade. Skeletons of captives abandoned by previous expeditions littered the bush, and Africans screamed with terror whenever they saw the caravan approach—those same Africans who, as Livingstone well knew, often sold captives from their own intertribal wars to the Arab slavers.

Moving ceaselessly back and forth between Lakes Nyasa, Bangweulu, Tanganyika, and Mweru, the caravan increased its haul of slaves to more than a thousand. The sight of these files of cruelly yoked blacks marching beside him inspired Livingstone, in his *Last Journals*, to put down one of the most perceptive, moving passages ever written about Africa:

"The strangest disease I have seen in this country seems really to be broken-heartedness, and it attacks free men who have been captured and made slaves. . . . They endured the chains until they saw the broad River Lualaba roll between them and their free homes; they then lost heart. . . . Eight, with many others still in chains, died in three days after crossing. They ascribed their only pain to the heart. . . . Some slavers expressed surprise to me that they should die, seeing they had plenty to eat and no work. One fine boy of about twelve years was carried and when about to expire, was kindly laid down on the side of the path, and a hole dug to deposit the body in. He, too, said he had nothing the matter with him, except pain in the heart."

The Lualaba River, with its strong northerly flow, began to look more and more like the upper Nile to Livingstone (it is actually the upper Congo). For six months in 1870 he tried to reach it on his own, until crippled by muscle-eating ulcers on his feet. Compelled to remain inactive for another six months, he read the Bible four times from cover to cover. When he could

walk again, he set out once more for the Lualaba, and in March 1871 he finally reached it at Nyangwe (in present-day Zaire). At this point the river still flows northward, and Livingstone began to plan a canoe expedition to see if the Lualaba or any of its tributaries had as their source the mysterious fountains of his growing obsession.

But before Livingstone's plans were completed, a hideous event drove them from his mind—the infamous Massacre of Nyangwe on July 15, 1871. Following a trifling dispute between a native merchant and three armed Arabs over the price of a chicken, there was a sudden, senseless explosion of violence in which at

**Livingstone faithfully** *kept a journal, writing on scraps of old newspapers and in the margins of books when there was no other paper. When his supply of ink ran out, he made some "with the seeds of a plant called by the Arabs Zugifaré." At left is a page from his 1855 journal with rough map sketches. The entry was written during his transcontinental expedition.*

least 400 defenseless Africans were shot down by the town's Arab slavers. That evening, a shaken Livingstone wrote in his journal: "As I write I hear the loud wails on the left bank [of the Lualaba] over those who are slain. . . . Oh let Thy Kingdom come! No one will ever know the exact loss on this bright sultry summer morning, it gave me the impression of being in Hell."

The massacre haunted Livingstone's dreams for the rest of his life and convinced him that he could never again accept Arab charity. Marshaling his few remaining porters, he left the slavers to begin the long march to Ujiji, where he hoped to find desperately needed supplies and mail awaiting him.

Now, as the old man sat dreaming in Ujiji's midday heat, a single rifle shot suddenly broke the stillness. More shots followed. Then Susi came running across the square, his long robe streaming out behind him, screaming, "An Englishman! I see him." Dazed, the doctor stood up and hobbled out into the sun.

Excited natives jostled in the square. From up the main street came the sounds of laughter and singing. Presently, Livingstone saw a flag bobbing above the heads of the crowd. The Stars and Stripes? The crowd parted, and a magnificent caravan marched into the square. Tin baths, copper pots, and huge kettles flashed in the sun. "This must be a luxurious traveller!" Livingstone later remembered thinking.

Now the caravan's leader stepped into view. He was a stocky young white man, very well dressed in freshly ironed flannels and freshly waxed boots. He was also very nervous. A hush fell as he approached the elderly figure standing alone, took off his helmet, and bowed.

"Doctor Livingstone, I presume?"

"Yes!"

"I thank God, Doctor, that I have been permitted to see you."

The supreme drama of this meeting, perhaps the most poignant in the history of exploration, has long since become a subject of cartoons and jokes. But at high noon in Ujiji on November 10, 1871, Henry Morton Stanley knew that only the purest formality could control the emotions on both sides. As it was, Livingstone had tears in his eyes when he took the young man's hand. Later, as Livingstone fell with sudden appetite upon Stanley's celebration breakfast—champagne, cakes, curry, kabobs, fricasseed chicken, white rice, plums, honey, jam, and tea—he told his rescuer over and over, "You have brought me new life!"

Eighteen months later, Livingstone was dead. Susi and Chuma found him kneeling over his camp bed on the southern shore of Lake Bangweulu, where he had gone on a renewed quest for the sources of the Nile. He

*Revealers of the Sources*

had been stiff and cold for many hours. The date was May 1, 1873. Among his papers was one of the saddest documents ever penned: an announcement of the "discovery" of the fountains of the Nile, with only the latitude and longitude left blank.

By that time Stanley had returned to civilization, where he was lauded for having come to Livingstone's aid when all British attempts to find him had failed. The fame he brought upon Livingstone, however, vastly eclipsed his own. Overlooking Livingstone's faults, Stanley in his dispatches to the New York *Herald* re-created the doctor as a saint who had fought, ill and alone, against the slave trade in Africa. No Victorian could resist such a figure of heroic virtue, least of all Stanley, who was admittedly awed by the older man (and who, in fact, shared many of his qualities, including courage, touchiness, and obstinacy).

Thus was founded, on the rocklike base of mass publicity, the Livingstone myth. After his death, an act of incredible devotion by his servants Susi and Chuma served to add even more luster to the doctor's legend. They cut out and buried Livingstone's heart and viscera and dried his body in the sun. Then, with infinite care, they wrapped the corpse in layers of calico and bark and sewed it into a piece of sailcloth. After lashing this improvised shroud to a pole, they began the difficult and dangerous task of carrying Livingstone's body all the way to the coast—a walk of more than a thousand miles, much of it through hostile territory, which took them nearly a year to accomplish. On the coast at Bagamoyo, the body was taken by ship to Zanzibar and then to England, where services were held at Westminster Abbey on April 18, 1874.

All England mourned on the day of Livingstone's funeral, but in recent years the myth of the selfless missionary-explorer has undergone considerable revision. Unquestionably, Livingstone *was* a failure in his mission work; and as a man he could be arrogant, suspicious, irascible, and indifferent to others' sufferings (as, indeed, he usually was to his own). His obsession with discovery repeatedly led him to endanger the health and even the lives of his family and of his colleagues in missionary work and exploration. Also, despite his genuine love of Africans, on many occasions he simply forgot his promises to help those who had provided him with supplies and porters for his expeditions. But his very singlemindedness, ill suited as it may have been to a missionary, gave him much of his greatness as an explorer.

In fact, the more Livingstone's faults are examined, the more his stature grows. He was unquestionably a great man, superhuman in his endurance, totally individualistic, and genuinely dedicated in his own way to what he called "the alleviation of human misery." Few words had greater impact on the comfortable Victorian conscience than a letter Livingstone gave to Stanley that described in detail the horrors he had witnessed at Nyangwe. The letter was duly published in the *Herald*, and the furious indignation it aroused, together with other accounts of the effects of slavery, forced the sultan of Zanzibar to close the island's slave market permanently. The concluding sentence of a later letter to the *Herald* was engraved on Livingstone's tomb at Westminster Abbey: "All I can say in my solitude is, may Heaven's rich blessing come down on everyone, American, English or Turk, who will help to heal this open sore of the world." Even here, Victorian sentimentality was allowed to distort Livingstone's true feelings. Instead of "solitude," the original letter, as printed in the *Herald*, read "loneliness."

## Black Man's Burden: Livingstone's Loyal Servants Carried His Body 1,000 Miles for Burial

When Livingstone was too sick to walk, his devoted porters Chuma (right) and Susi (left) bore him on a stretcher, similar to the modern African carving below. After he died, they carried his body more than 1,000 miles to the coast. The two men met a Livingstone search party sent by the Royal Geographical Society, and its leader urged them to bury the body on the spot. Susi and Chuma, however, would not be dissuaded from their mission. In addition to Livingstone's body, they also carried the explorer's valuable journals to be returned to his countrymen. Susi and Chuma were later brought to England to help with the editing of these journals. The compiler of the journals noted, ". . . I found them actual geographers of no mean attainments. In one instance, when in doubt concerning a particular water-shed, to my surprise, Susi returned a few hours afterwards with a plan of the whole system of rivers in the region under examination." Susi and Chuma each received a medal from the Royal Geographical Society, after which the two men returned to Zanzibar and became popular caravan leaders.

Stanley's career as an explorer did not end with his discovery of Dr. David Livingstone. He led three additional African expeditions, and his exploration of the Congo River (above) and his part in founding the Congo Free State made him the most celebrated adventurer of his day. At right, he is shown before embarking on his momentous 1874–77 crossing of the continent with Kalulu, an African boy he had brought back to England after the Livingstone expedition. Below right, Stanley's fleet of canoes pushes down the unexplored Congo River. Just before departure, Stanley showed a European companion a blank piece of paper, explaining: "Never has white paper possessed such a charm for me as this has and I have already mentally peopled it, filled it with the most wonderful pictures of towns, rivers, countries and tribes." The Congolese tribes signaled Stanley's progress with hugh drums (opposite). Among them were the Bakuba, noted for their expressive sculpture, such as this wooden statue.

*Chapter Twenty-Four. In one of the most spectacular adventures in the history of discovery, a daring journalist crosses Africa by way of its second longest river, fighting hostile tribes and dangerous, unexplored waters. His great journey thrills the world and opens the way for European domination of the Dark Continent in the early 20th century.*

# *Bula Matari:*
# *Stanley Conquers the Congo*

*Henry Morton Stanley was born in Denbigh, Wales, on January 28, 1841, the illegitimate son of John Rowlands and Elizabeth Parry. Christened John Rowlands, he lived with relatives until he was six. He was then put in the St. Asaph Union Workhouse, where he spent the next nine years. Escaping from the cruel master of this grim place, he shipped as a cabin boy on a freighter bound for New Orleans. Luckily, in that city a merchant named Henry Stanley befriended the penniless youth. He later adopted the boy and gave him his own name. As a young man, Stanley fought in the Civil War (on both sides), then became a journalist, traveling across the United States and to Asia Minor. Editor James Gordon Bennett, Jr., sent him to find David Livingstone and thus launched him on the career that made him famous.*

On a spring day in 1874, a few weeks after the burial of David Livingstone in London's Westminster Abbey, the Welsh-born American reporter who had found the explorer in Africa strolled over to the *Daily Telegraph* offices on Fleet Street. One of the newspaper's proprietors, Edward Lawson, recognized him at once and greeted him with respect. Stocky little Henry Morton Stanley, with his hard gray eyes and perpetual scowl, was already an international celebrity. Although few Englishmen liked him—he was aggressive, vulgar, and suspiciously secretive about his origins—editors ignored him at their peril. Stanley was, in the trade phrase, "hot copy." His dispatches from Africa had been read by millions, and his book, *How I Found Livingstone*, was an international bestseller. Now the ambitious explorer-correspondent had another journalistic coup to propose.

"Much remains shrouded in mystery in Dark Africa," Stanley told Lawson portentously, and then proceeded to sketch his plan for a new African expedition. What he intended was to finish the work begun by Living-

stone, John Hanning Speke, and Richard Burton: First he would circumnavigate Lakes Victoria and Tanganyika to determine their extent and relationships and to finally establish whether the Nile rose in either of them; and then he would strike westward to the Lualaba River and follow its course wherever it might lead—to the Nile, the Niger, or the Congo. If the river flowed westward, so much the better, since most of the continent's western half remained to be explored.

Lawson, who was suitably impressed, expressed his willingness to help finance the expedition if Stanley's publisher, James Gordon Bennett, Jr., of the New York *Herald*, agreed to share the expenses. Bennett had been the man behind the search for Livingstone, and when Lawson cabled him that day in New York, he promptly cabled back a terse "Yes Bennett."

Thus, on a single afternoon in 1874, the most ambitious and far-reaching expedition of the century was launched. Stanley, with characteristic impatience, flung himself into preparations. Bales, boxes, trunks, barrels, and sacks of provisions soon clogged the *Telegraph*'s offices. A British boatbuilder was commissioned to make a portable cedar boat "of sufficient capacity to convey up any river a force of twenty-five men, with a month's provisions." The finished craft, christened *Lady Alice*, was divided into five eight-foot-long sections, so that porters could carry it inland and assemble it when they reached navigable water. Meanwhile, Stanley was devouring as many books on east and central Africa as he could find—more than 130 in all—and going through the more than 1,200 applications he had received from would-be adventurers eager to accompany the expedition. In the end he rejected all these petitioners and picked out three obscure working-class youths as his assistants: Francis (Frank) John and Edward Pocock, 24 and 22, fisherman's sons from Kent, who were said to be reliable and skilled with small

## The "Lady Alice": A Reliable Boat Named for a Fickle Fiancé

trip, also wrote to her, although delivery of his letters depended on caravans going to the coast. "The very hour I land in England," he promised, "I should like to marry you." But as his journey became longer, Stanley worried about Alice's pledge: "Let us hope cheerfully that a happy termination to this long period of trial of your constancy and my health and courage await us both." However, by the time Stanley wrote these encouraging words, Alice was already married. "I have done," she confessed, "what millions of women have done before me, not been true to my

promise. But you are so great, so honoured and so sought after, that you will scarcely miss your once true friend and always devoted admirer." Nonetheless, at the time of his tumultuous reception in Paris, one of the few friends to whom Stanley had told the story wrote: "He was evidently suffering acutely from a bitter disappointment; what that was I could well guess, but need not disclose." The boat named after Alice proved to be a reliable sailer on the great river, but Stanley had to abandon it near the end of his exhausting journey when the Congo rapids made the river impassable.

Before leaving London in 1874, Stanley had commissioned the building of a portable boat (right) that could be carried in sections and reassembled with ease. Christened *Lady Alice*, the craft was named for Alice Pike (above), the daughter of a wealthy American businessman. Stanley had secretly become engaged to her before his departure. On July 12 the two signed a pact: "We solemnly pledge ourselves to be faithful to each other and to be married to one another on the return of Henry Morton Stanley from Africa." Stanley, who carried two pictures of Alice throughout his

---

boats, and a London hotel clerk named Frederick Barker, whose only apparent qualification was a passionate longing to see Africa. These three seemed strange selections for a world-renowned explorer, but, as Stanley remembered only too well, he himself had come from a poor family and had been lifted out of obscurity in his youth by the kindness of a stranger.

Now, at 33, Stanley was a restless bundle of ambition and nervous energy, ready for the greatest exploit of his career. On his arrival in Zanzibar in September 1874, he was promptly besieged by islanders who had been with him on the Livingstone expedition. Although he had marched them off their feet three years earlier, they remembered him as a fair and generous man and seemed anxious for more adventures with him.

Spending his sponsors' money freely, Stanley soon assembled an expedition that he proudly termed "the best organized and best equipped of any that ever left the seacoast of East Africa." When he landed on the mainland at Bagamoyo (in present-day Tanzania) on

November 13, he was accompanied by 356 porters and guides, mostly Moslem blacks from Zanzibar, and had assembled eight tons of supplies; 30 men alone were required to carry his boat, *Lady Alice*, now subdivided into eight sections (not 12, as it is shown above).

Before leaving the island of Zanzibar, Stanley dashed off dispatches to the *Herald*, which read in part: "What I may discover along this lengthy march I cannot at present imagine. . . . After I leave the Unyanyembe road the first news you will receive from me will be, I hope, via the Nile."

The "road" to the interior, the route of the slave and ivory caravans, was nothing more than a narrow footpath. Advancing in single file, the expedition stretched out half a mile from its leading guide to its last trailing porter. Despite the caravan's unwieldiness and its considerable burden of supplies, Stanley maintained an almost military discipline and soon confirmed his reputation as the swiftest of African explorers. Stanley and his men covered the route to Mpwapwa, usually re-

*Map for Stanley on page 252.*

garded as a four-month march, in just 25 days.

The town of Unyanyembe (modern-day Tabora, Tanzania) was the traditional gateway to the great lakes of central Africa. Burton and Speke had passed that way en route to the discovery of Lake Tanganyika in 1858; Stanley himself had parted from Livingstone there in 1872. Now, however, he was so impatient to reach Lake Victoria that he bypassed the town and struck northwest into unknown country, a parched, thorny plain called Ukimbu. This was a mistake.

During December the expedition struggled through inhospitable plains, where dry streambeds suddenly turned to raging torrents in fierce storms and temperatures could drop from 96° to 69° in minutes. Lack of food and water soon crippled the expedition's speed; by early January three men had died of hunger and exhaustion, and the weaker porters, laboring under their heavy loads, had begun to lag miles behind. Starvation became an increasing threat. The local natives, when they sold food to the expedition at all, demanded 10 times its normal cost.

On the next phase of the journey, in a swampy country known as Ituru, the inhabitants proved overtly hostile. By January 21, 89 of Stanley's men had deserted and 20 were dead, including young Edward Pocock, who had contracted typhus. Some 30 others had become too lame to withstand Stanley's relentless pace. There were no longer enough men to carry all the supplies, and some goods had to be burned.

Morale began to improve when the expedition descended into the sweet grasslands near the southern shore of Lake Victoria. Inexplicably, the natives here were as friendly as the inhabitants of Ituru had been hostile; smiling villagers came out of their huts to greet Stanley as he passed. On February 27, 1875, after a journey of more than 700 miles, he at last stood at the edge of Victoria, the world's second largest freshwater lake. "As I look upon its dancing waters," Stanley wrote in one of his dispatches, "I long to launch the *Lady Alice* and venture out to explore its mysteries."

Stanley was determined to settle "once and forever" whether Victoria was one lake or several by the simple process of circumnavigating it in *Lady Alice*. Leaving

**Tippu Tib** (*left*), *the most notorious central African slaver, escorted Stanley on part of his 1874–77 expedition. Named Hamed bin Mohammed, Tib's nickname came from a nervous affliction. "He had a fine intelligent face,"* Stanley noted, *"with a nervous twitching of the eyes, and gleaming white, perfectly formed teeth." Despite Tib's reputation, Stanley concluded that "this Arab was a remarkable man."*

Frederick Barker at the base camp, he launched his boat on March 8, 1875, with 11 reluctant "volunteers."

Rowing and sailing by turns, Stanley and his crew soon discovered that Victoria's immense size (27,000 square miles) made it as dangerous to navigate as any ocean. As they explored the lake's eastern shoreline, the little boat was swept up in a storm so violent that the waves collided above it.

On the island of Ukerewe, the natives informed Stanley with evident relish that "people who preferred to feed on human beings" lived farther up the coast; fishermen at a nearby village insisted that a full circumnavigation of the lake would take eight years. But Stanley was enjoying himself far too much to be turned back by such warnings.

"We were frequently chased by hippopotami; crocodiles suddenly rose alongside, and floated for a mo-

## Buganda's King Mutesa: The Most Promising Man in Africa

Mutesa (left), the kabaka (ruler) of Buganda, ruled the most powerful and technically advanced tribe in central Africa. "Their cloths are of finer make," Stanley noted, "their habitations are better and neater; their spears are the most perfect, I should say, in Africa." Below right, Mutesa's bodyguard welcomes Stanley at a town on the shores of Lake Victoria. "Numerous kettles and bass drums sounded a noisy welcome," the explorer noted. He glowingly described Mutesa as "of all men in Africa, the most promising." His enthusiasm for the wily chief grew, no doubt, from Mutesa's apparent readiness to accept Christian missionaries in Buganda. But after the missionaries had arrived,

Mutesa tired of their preaching and returned to mass human sacrifice to propitiate the souls of his ancestors. Mutesa himself died in 1884, but his successors ruled Buganda until the mid-1950's. The last of Mutesa's line, King Mutesa II became the first president of independent Uganda in 1963 but died in exile.

**Stanley witnessed** *an impressive victory dance by the warriors of a chief named Mazamboni during the 1887 Emin Pasha expedition. A thousand warriors formed an immense square, and "each man was forcefully stamping the ground and taking for-* *ward steps not more than six inches long. . . . There was simultaneous action of the bodies, and as they brought the tremendous weight of seventy tons of flesh with one regular stamp of the feet on the ground, the firm and hard earth echoed the sound."*

ment side by side, as though to take the measure of our boat's length. The natives of Utiri [on the east coast] fell into convulsions of laughter as they looked on the novel method of rowing adopted by us. When we hoisted the sail, they ceased mocking us and ran away in terror. Then we laughed at them!"

After swinging westward past the Ripon Falls—the foaming bottleneck through which Victoria spilled its waters into the White Nile—Stanley arrived on the shores of the kingdom of Buganda (in present-day Uganda) on April 5 and prepared himself for an audience with the most powerful ruler in central Africa.

White men were no strangers to Mutesa, the kabaka (ruler) of Buganda. As long ago as 1862 he had received John Hanning Speke, who had been appalled by his habit of ordering human sacrifices on the slightest whim. In the intervening years, however, the ruler had refined his considerable political talents, and by the time Stanley met him, he was well aware of the advantages of establishing links with the outside world. As Stanley was escorted to the kabaka's hilltop palace in the Bugandan capital of Rubaga, he admired the 150-foot-wide highway Mutesa had built "for the good time that is coming when some charitable European will send him any kind of a wheeled vehicle."

Pages in white cotton robes led the explorer past

ranks of kneeling chiefs and into the imperial presence. He was expected; only the night before, Mutesa's mother had dreamed of a boat approaching "like a fish-eagle, over the Nyanza [lake]," with a white man. The kabaka rose, advanced with a peculiar gait (meant to imitate that of a lion), and shook hands with Stanley. Then, in accordance with Bugandan protocol, the two men sat down and stared at one another in silence. Stanley later recorded his impressions:

"In person, Mtesa [Mutesa] is slender and tall, probably six feet one inch in height. He has very intelligent and agreeable features, which remind me of some of the faces of the great stone images at Thebes and of the statues in the Museum at Cairo. He has the same fulness of lips, but their grossness is relieved by the general expression of amiability, blended with dignity, that pervades his face, and the large, lustrous, lambent eyes that lend it a strange beauty."

The explorer, who was not physically vain, was well aware of the way *he* looked to Mutesa:

"The equatorial sun had painted my face of an intense fiery hue, while my nose was four times peeled, and my eyes were as bloodshot as those of the most savage Andalusian *toro* [bull] ever a matador killed."

If the kabaka was amused by his short, red-faced visitor, he gave no sign. They began to converse in

Swahili, discussing "Europe and Heaven," and Mutesa showed special interest in the subject of angels. (He had learned long ago that the quickest way to ingratiate himself with Europeans was to let them talk about their religion.) Stanley, who was quite taken with Mutesa, decided to prolong his stay for several days.

One afternoon the kabaka, bored with theology, interrupted a Bible reading to say, "Stamlee, I want you to show my women how white men can shoot." Accompanied by his numerous ladies—Stanley estimated that there were about 900 of them—Mutesa led the way down to the lake shore.

"The ladies formed a crescent line, Mutesa in the midst, and amused themselves by criticising my personal appearance—not unfavorably, I hope! It was, 'Stamlee is this,' and 'Stamlee is that,' from nine hundred pairs of lips. . . . An admiral with a fleet of canoes searched for a crocodile, at which I might take aim. They discovered a small specimen, sleeping on a rock at the distance of a hundred yards.

". . . I am happy to say that my good luck did not desert me. The head of the young reptile was nearly severed from the body by a three-ounce ball, and this feat was accepted as conclusive and undeniable proof that all white men were dead shots!"

Perhaps because of this impressive demonstration of "white power," Stanley was given permission to send for missionaries from England. Mutesa also agreed to let him return to Buganda with his entire expedition

after he had finished his circumnavigation of Lake Victoria and promised to provide him with an escort for an expedition to Lake Albert.

On May 6, 1875, Stanley was back at his base camp on Victoria's southern shore. His 1,000-mile circumnavigation had taken just 57 days, and it confirmed Speke's claim that the lake was indeed a single sheet of water and the true source of the White Nile. But the explorer's triumph was soured by the news that Frederick Barker had died of fever in his absence. Stanley's deep melancholy was reflected in his next dispatch:

"Thus two out of four white men are dead. I wonder who next? . . . We could not better ourselves by attempting to fly from the fatal land; for between us and the sea are seven hundred miles of as sickly a country as any in Africa. The prospect is fairer in front, though there are some three thousand miles more to march."

Having obtained a fleet of canoes from a local chief, Stanley managed to transport his entire expedition to Buganda in July 1875. On the way there, he savagely attacked the natives of Bumbiri Island, who had tried to bar his passage during the circumnavigation. His own account of this massacre of 42 warriors armed only with spears and stones ("I then ordered the canoes . . . to fire as if they were shooting birds") caused a public furor when it finally reached London a year later, and there were even demands that Stanley be brought back and tried for murder. However, he was well out of reach.

**Bangala tribesmen mounted** *the most serious attack that Stanley's party faced on the Congo River. "This was our thirty-first fight on the terrible river," he noted, "and certainly the most determined conflict." Despite the great number of attackers (63 large canoes full of men, many with muskets), the explorer's fleet fought through the barrier with their superior repeating rifles.*

**Shooting the Congo rapids** (*right*) *was the most hazardous part of Stanley's 1874–77 expedition across Africa. When the cataracts were impassable, cables were fastened to the canoes and exhausted men hauled them along the shore. Sometimes, however, the falls loomed so unexpectedly that men and canoes were swept into the maelstrom before they had a chance to get out of danger. Stanley, caught in such a whirlpool, described his reaction: "Oars were only useful to assist the helm, for we were flying at terrific speed past the series of boulders which strangled the river. Never did the rocks assume such hardness, such solemn grimness and bigness, never were they invested with such terrors and such grandeur of height as while we were the cruel sport and prey of the brown-black waves, which whirled us round like a spinning top, swung us aside, almost engulfed us in the rapidly subsiding troughs and then hurled us upon the white rageful crests of others." Stanley and his crew were luckily thrown clear of the whirlpool, but others were not so fortunate. Frank Pocock, the last of Stanley's European companions, drowned in the Congo's rapids, as did Kalulu, the African boy Stanley had adopted. Carried over the falls, Kalulu's canoe "plunged down into the depths, out of which the stern presently emerged pointed upward, and we knew that Kalulu and his canoemates were no more." And immediately after Kalulu's canoe was lost, another boat was carried over the rapids "to apparent, nay almost certain destruction. . . . Nine men lost in one afternoon." Stanley and his men fashioned new canoes from giant tree trunks (below), but there could be no replacement for human lives lost amid the Congo's cataracts. Stanley was so grief-stricken about the deaths of his companions and the others that he contemplated suicide.*

After spending some months at Mutesa's court—where his attempts to explore Lakes Albert and Edward were balked by sudden faintheartedness on the part of his Bugandan escort—Stanley had headed southward once more. In June 1876 he launched *Lady Alice* on Lake Tanganyika, and in less than two months he confirmed what Speke had earlier guessed: The lake has no northward-flowing outlet. By August, the time of the outcry against him in London, he had struck northwestward from Tanganyika's shores to begin what he called "the grandest task of all"—a voyage down the Lualaba.

On October 17 Stanley for the first time saw the majestic river. A mass of slow-moving silver, fully 1,400 yards wide, it was flowing steadily northward. Deeply moved, Stanley mustered his men—many of whom were fearful of the unknown country ahead—and made a speech:

"This great river has flowed on thus since the beginning through the dark wild lands before us, and no man . . . knows whither it flows; but I tell you solemnly that I believe the one God has willed that this year it shall be opened throughout its whole length and become known to all the world. You, my people, will therefore make up your minds that I am not going to leave this river until I reach the sea. You promised at Zanzibar, two years ago, that you would follow me wherever I wanted to go. . . . I promise you that we shall reach the sea before the year is out. All you have to do, then, is to say, 'In the name of God,' and follow me."

Fifty young men stepped forward immediately, but their elders were still reluctant. Another 10 days' march would bring them to Nyangwe (in modern-day Zaire), where Livingstone had been a witness to a bloody massacre five years earlier. They knew that "Stamlee," for all his confident words, was leading them into a country barely explored even by Nyangwe's Arab slavers. In the end, it was to the latter that Stanley turned for help: For a price of $5,000, the region's chief slaver, a wily old Zanzibari known as Tippu Tib, agreed to provide the explorer with an armed escort of his own slaves for the first leg of the journey. These men would see to it that all the members of the expedition kept going until, as Stanley put it, "the seductions of Nyangwe would be left far behind."

With his enlarged expedition—which now numbered 854 people, including Tippu Tib and his men—Stanley set off northward along the Lualaba's east bank. He proposed to keep to the land until his reluctant companions were too far from Nyangwe to find their way back and then launch his boat on the river. But he was now heading through true jungle where every step was a struggle. Stanley noted in fascination: "It appalled the stoutest heart; it disgusted me with its slush and reek, its gloom and monotony."

On November 21, 1876, at a point some 40 miles north of Nyangwe, Stanley finally boarded *Lady Alice* with an advance party of 36 men and set off downstream. The appearance of the unfamiliar craft greatly alarmed the natives of the region, and Stanley soon heard weird

One of the most dramatic *moments of Stanley's first Congo expedition came when a canoe overturned, and Zaidi, one of the chiefs, was marooned on a rock in the middle of the rushing torrent. Another canoe was secured by strong vines, and two men tried to reach the stranded Zaidi in it; but Zaidi was swept over the cataract. Miraculously, however, he did not drown but managed to swim to a rock outcropping some yards from shore where the rescuers, who were also marooned, pulled him from the water. Here darkness forced the three to spend the night precariously perched amid the swirling currents of the Congo. In the morning the men were able to make their way safely to shore, inching hand over hand along a cable that had been tossed out to them. "The cheers we gave them were so loud,"* the explorer later recalled, that all the Africans who lived along the riverbank *"must have known . . . that we had passed through a great and thrilling scene."*

howls echoing through the jungle ahead of him. He knew what the calls meant: The river tribes were passing along the signal "Beware of strangers afloat."

"At every curve and bend they 'telephoned' along the river the warning signals; the forests on either bank flung hither and thither the strange echoes; their huge wooden drums sounded the muster for fierce resistance; reed arrows, tipped with poison, were shot at us from the jungle as we glided by. To add to our distress, the small-pox attacked the caravan and . . . victims of the pest were flung daily into the river. What a terrible land! Both banks, shrouded in tall, primeval forests, were filled with invisible, savage enemies; out of every bush glared eyes flaming with hate; in the stream lurked the crocodiles to feed upon the unfortunates; the air seemed impregnated with the seeds of death!"

After four weeks afloat, during which the land caravan struggled vainly to keep up with him, Stanley halted near a village called Vinya Njara and built a fortified camp. All friendly overtures to the riverside tribes had come to nothing; what Stanley called their "unreasonable hate of strangers"—which may well have been sheer terror—increased as the expedition moved deeper into the wild. All through the night of December 18, the village's inhabitants poured a rain of poisoned arrows against Stanley's fortifications, and a pitched battle began the next day. It lasted 72 hours, and Stanley was saved only by the arrival of Tippu Tib's armed escort. With their help, he captured 36 native canoes, enough to continue downriver with his 149 remaining men. Tippu Tib and his slaves refused to continue, but Stanley no longer needed them.

As the canoe flotilla followed *Lady Alice* out into midstream, the men from Nyangwe sang a farewell dirge from the riverbank. Stanley's own companions, aware that he might soon lead them to their deaths, wept. "It was," Stanley later recalled, "one of the saddest days I remember to have spent in Africa."

There were to be many sadder. On January 4, 1877, Stanley was halted by the first of a series of seven cataracts that now bear his name (Stanley Falls). Five men died as they dragged their heavy canoes past fall after fall under incessant attack by natives. Miles of roads had to be hacked through the riverside jungle before the water opened out wide and calm again.

Near the end of January, Stanley noticed with a surge of excitement that the Lualaba's flow was beginning to veer westward. The river began to look more and more like the Congo or, just possibly, the Niger. But there was little time for speculation: Attacks were now coming by water as well as by land. No fewer than 54 native canoes, with an estimated 2,000 warriors aboard, awaited Stanley at the confluence of the Aruwimi. Since the river there is swollen to a width of nearly three miles, the ensuing battle (on February 1) took on almost naval proportions. As usual, the explorer's rifles won the day, but Stanley was feeling increasingly desperate about the steady erosion of his once-proud expedition. "We were still only in the middle of the continent, and yet we were being weeded out of existence, day by day, by twos and threes . . . the hour of utter exhaustion was near."

For the moment, it was the river itself that saved them. So wide does it become as it rolls lazily westward across table-flat country that Stanley was able to hide his flotilla among the midstream islands. But he knew that stones and spears would fly whenever he went to the mainland in search of food.

Finally, after hundreds of miles of paddling and no less than 32 separate battles, the expedition moved into a more hospitable region known as Rubunga. In the village of that name the chief welcomed the nearly starved Stanley with such warmth that the explorer "almost crushed his hand, making him hop, out of pure love." A solemn ceremony of blood brotherhood was concluded; then:

" 'What river is this, chief?' I asked.

'The River,' he replied.

'Has it no name?'

'Yes, the Great River.'

'I understand; but you have a name, and I have a name, your village has a name. Have you no particular name for your river?'

'It is called Ikutu Ya Kongo.'

The River of Congo!"

Secure at last in the knowledge that he was on his way to the Atlantic, the explorer led his flotilla onward. The lush Congo Basin became increasingly populous; one town they passed stretched along the riverfront for fully two miles. But on February 14, when they reached the confluence of the Mongala River, Stanley's expedition received unpleasant proof that "civilization" had reached this far inland in the form of guns, no doubt secured from European traders on the coast:

"Sixty-three canoes of light, even elegant make approached. . . . When they were about three hundred yards off I held a crimson cloth up to view in one hand and a coil of brass wire in another, and by signs offered it to them. My answer was from three muskets, a shower of ironstone slugs, and four of my boat's crew and one in my canoes wounded. . . . We formed our usual close line, and allowed the canoes and boat to float down, every rifle and revolver being required here. . . . The battle lasted from twelve o'clock to near sunset. We had floated down ten miles during that time. . . . At sunset our people sung the song of triumph; the battle was over. We continued floating down in the darkness."

As it turned out, Stanley had been saved by a fortuitous circumstance: The tribe that had attacked him, the Bangala, had plenty of muskets but no proper ammunition—they used jagged bits of iron and copper that were effective only at very close range. This battle, apart from one minor skirmish, was the last Stanley had to fight on the river.

By now the Congo was curving southwest, and Stanley sensed that his voyage was nearing its end. He had been five months on the river and calculated that *Lady Alice* had already covered 1,400 miles. But a 180-mile-long gorge looming ahead, just beyond a wide, calm portion of the river now known as Stanley Pool, was to prove the worst obstacle of the entire expedition.

For nearly five more months the bone-weary party dragged the boats past waterfalls, whirlpools, and rapids, up nearly impassable cliffs, and over improvised bridges across the deep chasms between them. At one time a 1,200-foot mountain had to be negotiated. So many canoes were lost that new ones had to be hollowed out of green wood.

During this period, in May, an ugly situation threatened to develop in the Mowa area, where the natives had initially been quite friendly to the expedition. They

**The most popular** *of Stanley's books,* In Darkest Africa *inspired this vivid turn-of-the-century advertisement for electric light bulbs. Ironically, the book, which sold 150,000 copies, described his least successful venture, the "rescue" of Emin Pasha, the German-born governor of the Sudanese province of Equatoria. Stanley's party crossed the Ituri rain forest, an area so densely vegetated that large parts still remain uninhabited. "Ever before us rose the same solemn and foodless Forest," he wrote, "the same jungle to impede and thwart our progress." Stanley described "streams choked with snags, chilling mist and icy rain, thunder-clatter and sleepless nights and a score of other horrors." Food became so scarce that the explorers resorted to eating grubs, slugs, caterpillars, wild roots, and even ants. "Several of our followers," he noted, "lost heart, became mad with hunger and wild forebodings, tossed the baggage into the bush and fled from us, as from a pest."*

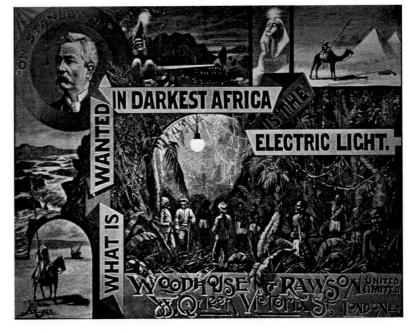

**Here Stanley greets** *Emin Pasha (see page 267). To his dismay, Stanley discovered that Emin had little desire to evacuate Equatoria. In fact, he hoped to hold the province in the face of a religious rebellion by the followers of a Moslem leader called the Mahdi. Stanley's expedition was too weak to support Emin's troops. Fearing the Mahdi's strength, Emin's troops revolted, and he was forced to flee with his loyal followers. Born Eduard Schnitzer, Emin had converted to Islam while a medical officer in Turkey. After his "rescue," he led a German expedition to central Africa, where he was murdered by Arab slavers in 1892.*

suddenly turned hostile after they saw Stanley "making medicine on paper" (that is, writing, which they considered a dangerous magical art), and demanded that he hand over his notebook for burning. Stanley nervously produced a volume of Shakespeare, whose binding was similar to that of his notebook. "Is this what you want?" "Yes, burn it!" So the Bard was consigned to the flames, and the explorer's precious journal—on which his immensely popular book *Through the Dark Continent* was to be based—was saved.

It was also during this last part of the journey that Frank Pocock, Stanley's only surviving white companion, tried to shoot the Massassa Falls and was sucked to his death in the boiling pot below. He had become the explorer's valued second in command and was known to everyone as the Little Master. His death so grieved Stanley that he briefly contemplated suicide. Eight other men also died in accidents during this period.

By July 31 the expedition was out of food, and five more falls still separated it from the low coastal plain. "Enough," said Stanley, and he ordered his men to abandon *Lady Alice* and the boats.

On August 4 the expedition, now reduced to a straggling line of 116 emaciated bodies, reached a native village a few miles from the trading post of Boma, where Stanley knew there were European residents. The exhausted explorer immediately sat down to write a desperate appeal for help "to any gentleman who speaks English at Embomma [Boma]" and sent four of his strongest men ahead with it. (The message had a postscript: "You may not know me by name: I therefore add, I am the person that discovered Livingstone in 1871.—H.M.S.")

Stanley and his men, who were riddled with dysentery, ulcers, and scurvy, were met two days later on the road to Boma with plentiful food supplies from the town's European merchants. The latter were agog with excitement at the news of the famed explorer's approach—they did, indeed, know him by name. After his first hearty meal in months, Stanley sent ahead a deliriously grateful letter to his benefactors:

"August 6, 1877—Gentlemen. . . . I am unable to express, just at present, just how grateful I feel. . . . For the next twenty-four hours we shall be too busy eating to think of anything else much; but I may say that the people cry out joyfully, while their mouths are full of rice and fish, 'Verily our master has found the sea and his brothers, but we did not believe him until he showed us the rice and the pombé [rum].' "

Two days later Stanley reached Boma, where he was given the nearest equivalent to a royal reception the small trading post could provide. By August 11 he was at Cabinda on the coast, where he wrote a dispatch to the *Herald* dramatically announcing God's deliverance of his expedition "from the mouth of hell and the jaws of death" and describing himself as "an old man in my 36th year" (his thick black hair had become gray).

Of the 356 people who had started off with Stanley's expedition, only 108 survived the journey across Africa and the voyage home to Zanzibar—a voyage on which Stanley, remembering his promise to see his men safely home, accompanied them. The price of his three-year odyssey had been enormous, yet it is fair to say that it accomplished more than any single African expedition that had been made up to that time. Not only were the relationships of the central African lakes and rivers at last clearly established, but the immense region bordering the Congo, Africa's second longest river, was no longer a blank on the map.

When Stanley returned to Europe in early 1878, he was hailed as the greatest of living explorers, the conqueror of a continent. After triumphal stops in Marseilles and Paris, Stanley went to England to write (in less than five months) *Through the Dark Continent*, a two-volume account of his Congo journey. He then made a tour of the fashionable European resorts, but "lounging" bored him. Back in England, he repeatedly tried to convince the government that Britain should undertake the commercial development of the Congo Basin, but to no avail.

King Leopold II of the Belgians, however, was keenly interested in commercial exploitation of the region, and that year he offered Stanley a job: to go back to the Congo, open a safe route inland from the Atlantic coast, and secure trading concessions from the native rulers along the great river. Having been rebuffed by the land of his birth, Stanley accepted Leopold's commission. From 1879 to 1884 he battered his way inland, building a road that linked the coast with the Congo's navigable portions, establishing a string of fortified trading stations along 1,400 miles of the river, and conducting endless trade negotiations with the region's African chiefs. His savage energy as a roadbuilder earned him the Swahili nickname Bula Matari, the "Rock-Breaker," a title that pleased him more than all the decorations showered on him in later life.

Although Stanley had not intended it, his opening up of the Congo Basin set the scene for the most vicious colonial exploitation in Africa's history—the so-called Congo Free State founded by King Leopold for his personal profit. But, in fairness to the explorer, it was not until the year following his departure from the Congo that Leopold's empire was formally established, and he took no part in its abuses.

Stanley returned to the Congo region once more in 1887, leading an expedition sponsored by private British interests. Ostensibly, its purpose was to rescue Emin Pasha, the beleaguered governor of Equatoria, who was being threatened by an Arab revolt in the Sudan. (Emin was actually Eduard Schnitzer, an eccentric German-born naturalist and physician, who had changed his name after adopting the Moslem faith.) Stanley knew that Emin and his garrison of Egyptian and Sudanese soldiers were somewhere near Lake Albert; it is not clear why he chose to travel from west Africa through nearly impassable jungles to reach them, but it seems likely that he was under secret instructions from both British and Belgian interests to look into central Africa's commercial possibilities.

In any case, the expedition was a nightmare from the first. Losses from disease and native attacks were appallingly heavy; Stanley bullied his men relentlessly and commonly ordered floggings of 300 lashes for relatively minor offenses. In the end he found Emin, but their meeting was to have a comic-opera aspect: The German had wanted reinforcements, not rescue, and proved distinctly reluctant to leave central Africa. Eventually, Stanley persuaded him to depart for the safety of the east African coast, and the explorer was as loudly acclaimed for the "rescue" of Emin as he had been for the finding of Livingstone. But his behavior during this expedition gave him a reputation for ruthlessness that haunted him for the rest of his life.

Stanley's later years in England were heaped with honors. In 1890, at the age of 49, he published an account of the Emin expedition, *In Darkest Africa*, which became a bestseller in six languages. That year he also married a noted artist, Dorothy Tennant, and was granted honorary degrees by the Universities of Oxford, Cambridge, and Edinburgh. He settled in a suitably grand country house, became a British subject once again, and in 1895 entered Parliament. Finally, in 1899, the onetime "workhouse brat" from Wales was awarded Britain's highest honor, a knighthood.

Stanley's health, however, had been undermined by his African travels. In April 1904 he became ill with pleurisy, and his condition worsened steadily. On May 10, 1904, Henry Morton Stanley, the greatest African explorer of his age, died in London. The explorer's tombstone, chosen by his wife, lies in the village churchyard near his English country home at Pirbright. It is a six-ton boulder of granite, chiseled with the words: "Henry Morton Stanley, Bula Matari, 1841–1904, Africa."

## A Hero Who Was Shy With Women and Ashamed of His Past

Stanley's wife, artist Dorothy Tennant, painted the portrait of him at right. He had asked Dolly, as she was called, to marry him before he left on the Emin Pasha expedition, but she had refused. Her refusal intensified his lifelong shyness with women, which had markedly increased after Alice Pike jilted him. "The fact is," he confessed, "I can't talk to women. In their presence I am just as much of a hypocrite as any other man." However, despite his misgivings, Stanley did not turn Dorothy away when she sought to renew their friendship upon his return from Africa, and the two were married on July 12, 1890, in Westminster Abbey. Dolly, afraid that Stanley would return to Africa, persuaded him to stand for Parliament. But, before running for office, Stanley had to reassume British citizenship. In 1885 he had secretly become an American citizen, so he could profit from the substantial United States royalties on his books. Ironically, years earlier, after the Livingstone expedition, Stanley had tried to obscure the fact that he was a British subject. Remembering his unhappy youth in Wales, he had steadfastly maintained that he was an American. Although he finally admitted his origins, Stanley always preferred to remain elusive about his youth. After his death in 1904, Dolly, who completed his *Autobiography*, bought and destroyed letters and articles that detailed Stanley's early years.

# Part

# 8

## Striving for the Poles

---

## Heroes of the Arctic and Antarctic

*Two remote unconquered points of the globe— the North and South Poles— become the goals of resourceful men facing awesome obstacles.*

The polar region of the Arctic is a sea, two-thirds covered by drifting ice, edged at its outer limits by the coasts of the northern continents and the islands lying on the continental shelf. Antarctica, by contrast, is a desolate landmass larger than Australia. Almost completely covered by a continental ice sheet, it can support only limited plant and animal life. Yet these forbidding places remained to be explored.

The great efforts to reach the North and South Poles really began at the turn of the 20th century. The nations of Europe and America had finally run short of new worlds to explore, and national pride, as well as the popular press, needed new achievements to cheer. The poles themselves were useless places, devoid of treasure, arable land, or people. At the North Pole, polar bears and foxes roamed the bleak ice, occasionally pursued by Eskimos. The South Pole area was almost entirely lifeless, though its borders were home to the penguin—"little old gentlemen in evening dress," according to the 19th-century French explorer Jules Dumont d'Urville.

For centuries the almost insuperable obstacles of ice, wind, and cold allowed little more than a tentative skirting of the fringes of the frozen regions. There was small profit to be gained by sailing into the high latitudes, and when men did, it was almost always because they were searching for a new and better route to some more desirable part of the globe.

In the 16th century, when Spain and Portugal had effectively monopolized the only known sea routes to Asia, the northern nations of Europe began to probe the edges of the Arctic for a China passage through the icy fringes of Siberia or over the unknown crest of North America. During the following two centuries, expeditions were dispatched regularly into northern waters, especially by Britain and Russia. The British government posted a standing £5,000 reward for the first ship reaching 89° N (the reward was never claimed, 89° being one degree short of the North Pole), and £20,000 for the discovery of a navigable passage.

The 18th century's greatest explorer, James Cook, penetrated far into the ice regions, both north and south. In 1773 he made the first known crossing of the Antarctic Circle, and in 1778 Cook sailed through the Bering Strait, seeking an ice-free passage east or west but failing to find one.

By the beginning of the 19th century, almost nothing was yet known of the Arctic coastline of North America. Despite the failures of two centuries of exploration, the conviction that an Arctic passage could be found was as intense as ever. In 1818, in a wildly optimistic venture, four English ships set out in pairs, two to go east over Siberia, two to sail westward over Canada, all four to meet halfway around the world in the Bering Strait. The expedition met the same fate as its predecessors. The Siberia-bound ships were turned back by ice and fierce gales off Spitsbergen. The westward-bound pair suffered what was becoming a common experience for vessels that dared the Arctic seas: The ships were trapped in the ice, in this case at Melville Bay. "... Every support threatened to give way, the beams in the hold began to bend ... while the ice, which was more than six feet thick, broke against the sides," wrote the captain, John Ross.

When the ice loosed its grip, the atmospheric conditions peculiar to the far north made navigation almost impossible: Mists and shifting ice produced the illusion of land, open channels became rock-enclosed bays, and passages through the ice-laden waters would close almost under the ships' keels. The expedition, for which much had been hoped, turned back to England. But Ross' second in command, Edward Parry, returned the next year and fought his way through the ice to 112°—farther west than any ship to the Arctic had ever sailed from the east. Parry became the foremost British Arctic explorer of his century. The techniques he developed for contending with the far north, especially his method of sledging boats over drifting ice to the next stretch of open water, became standard practice in Arctic exploration. And John Ross' nephew, James Clark Ross, who served under Parry, became in his turn the greatest 19th-century Antarctic explorer.

### Searching for Ships in the Arctic

Tragedy was of course a constant theme of polar exploration. But most of the ships sent out into northern waters returned sooner or later. The Franklin expedition did not. Two ships, the *Erebus* and the *Terror*—both newly fitted with steam-driven propellers, which, it was hoped, would force a way through the ice—left England in 1845 under the command of Sir John Franklin. They were never seen again. From 1848 to 1858, 40 search expeditions scoured thousands of miles of Arctic territory seeking some sign of Franklin and his ships and, in the process, discovered more about the high northern latitudes than had been learned in all the years of previous discovery. (Although Franklin was never found, the graves of three of his crew were discovered on Canada's Arctic coast; his ships had been icebound for two years, and despite a desperate attempt to escape on foot, the entire 129-man party had died.) Not until 1909 was the North Pole conquered by Robert Peary, an American, in a controversial journey by dogsled over the Arctic pack ice. Since then, other men have reached the pole, and thousands have flown over it.

In the years after Cook's voyages, a few ships had attempted to sail farther south than he had done, but all were turned back by the impassable ice barrier. It was only in 1840 that the ice was finally breached by James Clark Ross—fresh from his Arctic explorations and commanding two sturdy naval vessels, both strong enough to withstand the fracturing ice pressures. Ross' voyage through the great icepack took five days, and when the ships emerged, it was to find an open, ice-free

sea (the Ross Sea) and the continent itself. Ross' expedition proved that strong ships and perfect seamanship together can conquer even the formidable polar ice. (Although luck is a necessary ingredient as well: Ross' ships were the very same *Erebus* and *Terror* that took Sir John Franklin to his Arctic death five years later.)

### Discovering a Frozen Continent

At the turn of the century, four separate expeditions attempted to explore the Antarctic interior. British, German, and Swedish teams pioneered in mastering the arts of life near the pole—wintering over in their ships or in rough stone huts, using dogs or manpower to pull their sledges over the ice. Capt. Robert Scott's British team sledged to within 500 miles of the pole in 1903. A companion on that journey, Ernest Shackleton, was to come within 97 miles six years later and to spend the rest of his life in an endurance test with the Antarctic. In 1915, three years after Scott's tragic race to the South Pole against Roald Amundsen, Shackleton's ambitious plan to cross the continent ended when his ship was crushed by ice. He and a few companions then made an epic trip to seek help—in an improvised open boat across 800 miles of the most ferocious stretches of ocean in the world.

The men who pioneered in early modern polar exploration—Fridtjof Nansen, Peary, Amundsen, Scott—opened territory that had never before been invaded by man, using traditional methods and tools. But exploration techniques changed fundamentally when the airplane replaced the ship. Richard E. Byrd flew over the North Pole in 1926 and the South Pole in 1929. In 1937 the Soviet Union airlifted a scientific station onto the drifting ice near the North Pole. After World War II, new equipment was created to counter the severe polar climate and conditions—snow tractors, insulated clothing, dehydrated foods, prefabricated shelters. A new era of exploration began, culminating in the International Geophysical Year of 1957–58.

For that 18-month-long event, scientists from 67 nations joined forces to expand and exchange terrestrial knowledge, especially of the polar regions. More than 50 year-round polar stations were established; many of them are still in existence. Scientific studies ranged from the analysis of ancient snow cores to the charting of wind and weather patterns. The vast mineral wealth, particularly of the lands around the Arctic, was accurately assessed for the first time. New techniques were devised for living comfortably, and for long periods, where men had until then barely subsisted. During that Geophysical Year the Englishman Vivian Fuchs, with a small party of dog-hauled sledges, became the first man to walk across Antarctica—an incredible 2,000-mile, 99-day journey. And during that year the nuclear submarine U.S.S. *Nautilus* made its undersea Arctic crossing, surfacing at the pole, and brought the great era of polar exploration to a triumphant end.

**Fridtjof Nansen,** *who resembled his Viking ancestors, was 32 when he set off for the North Pole in 1893. He returned three years later— when this photo was taken—a national hero.*

**Nansen tried to reach** *the North Pole by locking his ship, the* Fram, *into the Arctic pack ice (top) and letting her drift with the pack. When he realized the* Fram—*specially designed to withstand the frozen ocean's crushing pressure— would pass to the south of the pole, he left her and tried to reach his goal on foot. Nansen, also a poet and artist, drew the sketch (above) of an Arctic night. To him, it was a "dreamland, painted in the imagination's most delicate tints."*

*Heroes of the Arctic and Antarctic*

## Chapter Twenty-Five

*Determined to be the first explorer to reach the desolate North Pole, a young Norwegian carefully plans a unique assault on his goal. After coming closer to the pole than anyone had before, he and a companion make an amazing return journey on foot and by kayak across hundreds of miles of dangerous ice and freezing ocean.*

# Beneath the Northern Lights: Nansen in the Arctic

*A man of many talents, Fridtjof Nansen achieved fame as an explorer, a scientist, and a statesman. He was born near Oslo, Norway, in 1861 and earned a Ph.D. in 1888, while curator of zoology at the Bergen Museum. In May of 1888 he led an expedition across Greenland on skis and in 1893 set out on his most famous adventure: an attempt to drift to the North Pole in his icebound ship, the* Fram. *In later years he became a recognized zoologist and oceanographer, headed Norway's delegation to the League of Nations, and directed massive international relief programs after World War I. Nansen was awarded the Nobel Peace Prize in 1922 for his humanitarian efforts. Throughout his life, his literary talent made him a popular author. He died at his home near Oslo in 1930, honored as one of his country's heroes.*

In November 1884, Fridtjof Nansen, a young Norwegian scientist, was intrigued by an article he noticed in his daily newspaper. According to the report, debris from the *Jeannette*, a ship wrecked three years earlier on an Arctic expedition, had just been discovered on the southwestern coast of Greenland. Yet the ship had not gone down anywhere near Greenland. It had sunk off the coast of Siberia, 2,000 miles away, on the other side of the Arctic Ocean. How had the wreckage gotten from one side of the North Pole to the other?

The author of the report, a prominent meteorologist, theorized that some uncharted current must have carried the debris across the Arctic. It was a daring notion. At that time no one knew whether the North Pole was covered by land or sea. The theory appealed to Nansen, who knew that driftwood from Siberian trees had turned up on the Greenland coast. So had a wooden weapon of a type made only by Alaskan Eskimos.

A polar current seemed the only logical explanation, a current powerful enough to carry something slowly but surely across the Arctic Ocean. If such a current did

exist, Nansen felt it could help polar exploration. Several years were to pass before he could act upon his idea. Meanwhile, Nansen gained experience in the Arctic exploring Greenland.

His first proposal—to ski from coast to coast across the unknown interior of Greenland—had struck most of his countrymen as a harebrained publicity stunt. "Exhibition!" jeered a writer in Bergen's comic paper. "Fridtjof Nansen, curator of the Museum, will give an exhibition of ski running . . . in Greenland. Good seats in the crevasses. Return tickets unnecessary."

Nansen was undaunted. When the Norwegian government refused to finance the expedition, he went to Denmark to raise the necessary funds. Then, in the summer of 1888, he and five companions set out aboard a sealer and were put ashore on the desolate eastern coast of Greenland. More than two months and 400 miles later, the weary party stumbled into the primitive port of Godthaab on the west coast. They had accomplished what no man had ever done before—crossed the barren cap of perpetual ice and snow that covers most of Greenland's interior.

When they returned to a hero's welcome in Norway the following spring, Nansen made the most of the opportunity. He realized that at last the time was ripe for acting on an even more audacious plan he had been mulling over ever since reading about the discovery of wreckage from the *Jeannette*. So, in February 1890, the 28-year-old scientist appeared before the Christiana Geographical Society to present his proposal.

Nothing could have been simpler—or more daring. He suggested that instead of trying to reach the North Pole on foot or by dogsled, why not let the suspected polar current do the work? Build a special ship, Nansen proposed, freeze her into the ice off Siberia, and simply let her drift northward across the pole. The journey, which he estimated might take anywhere from two to

**Members of the De Long expedition** *froze to death trying to reach the North Pole in 1881. Although ice devastated their ship, one boatload of survivors returned in spring to identify these corpses (above). Nevertheless, the disaster gave Nansen the idea of trying to float across the pole on the westward ice drift.*

be lifted up by the pressure instead of being crushed—or so Nansen hoped.

Snug and compact, the 128-foot-long vessel was just large enough to hold 13 men and fuel and provisions to last for five years. In addition to sails, the trim three-master had a steam engine for auxiliary power. There was a power plant to provide light during the long Arctic winter—a dynamo that could be driven by the ship's engine, by hand, or by a windmill on deck. Space was provided for a woodworking shop, a mechanic, a blacksmith, a sailmaker, a tinsmith, and a shoemaker. As Nansen explained, "There was nothing, from the most delicate instruments down to wooden shoes and axe handles that could not be made on board."

Finally, on October 26, 1892, the ship was ready. Thousands of spectators gathered at Colin Archer's shipyard that crisp clear morning to watch as Nansen's wife broke a bottle of champagne on the ship's hull and christened her *Fram*, the Norwegian word for "forward." The stays were released, and the *Fram*

five years, would be an ideal opportunity for ferreting out some of the secrets of that vast unknown region.

Again there were skeptics. One critic scoffed at the value of "amateur nautical expeditions." Another dubbed the proposal "Dr. Nansen's illogical scheme of self-destruction." But his novel approach definitely fired the public's imagination. It just might work, people agreed. Possibly, this was the way for Norway to snare the honor of being the homeland of the first man to reach the North Pole.

This time, with national pride at stake, financing for the expedition came easily. The Norwegian government supplied most of the money, but in a unique expression of popular enthusiasm for exploration, Norwegian citizens contributed more than a third of the funds Nansen needed. Even Norway's monarch, King Oscar, donated 20,000 kroner to the cause.

With money in hand, Nansen's first priority was to build his special ship, a ship strong enough to withstand any amount of ice pressure. "This and this alone," he commented, "was the dominant idea which guided her construction."

The problem was not the drift ice—the free-floating chunks of ice that dot the fringes of the Arctic Ocean during the summer thaw. The real challenge would be the pack ice—the jumbled mass of huge ice blocks found nearer to the pole. Shifting, drifting, heaving with the tides, the sea here is a "continuous mass of ice-floes in constant motion, now frozen together, now torn apart, or crushed against each other." This was the ice that could smash an ordinary ship to pieces.

Nansen went to Colin Archer, a prominent Scottish shipbuilder, for assistance. Together they designed a short, broad ship with rounded hull, fore and aft, and thick curved sides reinforced with heavy beams and braces. "Bow, stern, keel—all were rounded off so that the ice could not be able to get a grip on her anywhere," wrote Nansen. "The object was that the whole craft should be able to slip like an eel out of the embrace of the ice." As the pack ice closed in on her, the ship would

*Heroes of the Arctic and Antarctic*

glided easily down the slipway and into the water.

Though the ship was completed, much work remained to be done. Crew, supplies, and equipment had to be chosen. (Applications to join the expedition poured in by the hundreds, but the crew was to be limited to 13 men including Nansen, all of them first-rate sailors or scientists.) Experts had to be consulted. Food depots were established on islands off the coast of Siberia in case the crew had to abandon ship or simply turn back. A rendezvous was established for picking up 34 sledge dogs the expedition would need for exploring the polar ice once the ship was frozen in. It was a bold and exciting venture, this Norwegian voyage to the North Pole, but it was also the most painstakingly organized Arctic expedition up to that time.

Thus, nine months had passed in completing final preparations before the *Fram*, on June 24, 1893, nosed out to sea and began her northern voyage.

To the men on board, it seemed as if all Norway wanted to wish them well. As they cruised up the coast, passing ships dipped their flags and fired off cannon. Steamers came out from ports, their decks crowded with people who sang and saluted the explorers. Peasants on shore and fishermen in their boats shouted and waved farewells. Whenever they stopped for supplies, the men were honored with banquets and celebrations.

Late in July the ship rounded the northernmost tip of Norway and headed into the polar sea. For weeks she plowed steadily eastward, threading among ice floes and fighting stiff headwinds. Then, about three-quarters of the way along the coast of Russia, as the ship approached the New Siberian Islands, she veered sharply to the north and headed into the unknown.

The sea was free of ice here, and for 10 days the ship sped toward the pole. "On to the north, steadily north," Nansen exclaimed, "with a good wind, as fast as steam and sail can take us, the open sea mile after mile . . ."

But the ice was closer than he thought, and the sea was not clear. The very next day, looming on the horizon, he saw "the edge of the ice, long and compact,

## Built to Withstand the Crushing Power of Arctic Ice, the "Fram" Brilliantly Rose to Her Task

The *Fram* is considered by many navigators and explorers to be one of the greatest discovery ships in the history of exploration. Nansen designed the *Fram* as a short, three-masted schooner with a rounded bow and stern. (The ship is one-third as broad as she is long.) He then commissioned Colin Archer, a Scottish shipbuilder, first to build a model and then to construct the vessel.

Preserved today in the specially constructed Fram Museum (opposite) near Oslo, Norway, the *Fram* was made to withstand the ice's crushing pressure when the Arctic Ocean froze around her. When the hull was completed, it "assumed a plump and round form," the sides were round, the bottom flat (see cross-section below right). It responded to the pressure created by the expansion of the freezing water by lifting the ship on top of the forming pack ice. The hull was very strong (the sides were 24 to 28 inches thick) and extremely smooth, so the ice could not get a grip on the sides. Pitch pine boards, 4 to 8 inches wide, lined the inside of the hull. Next were two layers of 3-inch oak planking, and on the outside was what Nansen called an "ice-skin." It was a smooth covering of greenheart, a durable South American evergreen. The ice-skin was 6 inches thick at the waterline—the ship's most vulnerable area—and 3 inches thick at the keel.

To reinforce the hull (1), the lower deck was constructed slightly below the waterline (see diagram right), where the pressure from the ice would be the greatest. The keel (2), made of two American elm logs each 14 inches square, was sunk in the planking and protruded only 3 inches below the bottom—a precaution against the keel forcing the ship over to one side once she was on top of the ice. Strengthened with oak and pitch pine beams, the hold (3) looked like a "cobweb of balks, stanchions, and braces." It was designed to carry a four-month, 380-ton supply of coal, and cargo to last 13 men and 34 dogs five years. The amount of coal needed was minimal, because the ship was to be carried on the drift ice for the majority of the trip.

Nansen wanted the rigging to be simple and strong because there would only be 13 men to operate it. The mainmast was 80 feet high, and the crow's nest was 102 feet above water so that a lookout would have a good view "when it came to picking our way through the ice." In addition, the ship had a triple-expansion, 220-horsepower engine that could be regulated by adjusting the cylinders.

The good spirits and health of the crew owed much to the *Fram*'s airtight walls, insulated with tarred felt, cork, and linoleum. The ceiling was insulated with an 11-inch layer of reindeer hair and other materials, and the floor with an extra 6 inches of cork. On previous Arctic voyages, condensation had always formed on the walls and usually ran down—often into the men's bunks where it froze. But on this voyage the crew was snug and comfortable. Nansen proudly wrote, "When a fire was lighted in the saloon there was not a trace of moisture on the walls, even in the sleeping cabins."

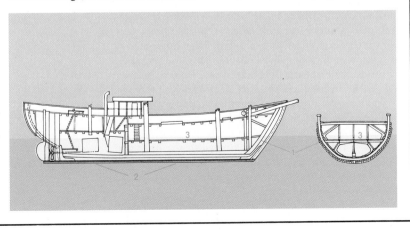

**Life aboard the "Fram"** *was grim for the expedition's 34 Siberian huskies. Chained to the deck day and night, the "splendid animals" were almost drowned by the stormy seas. Yet during Nansen's practice drive on the ice, they raced back to the ship "at lightning speed" and dumped him at the refuse heap (above), where they tried to scavenge food. "I tugged, swore, and tried everything I could think of" to start them up, wrote Nansen. Then the dogs were off again, "merrily" dragging him over the ice.*

shining through the fog." The test of the *Fram*'s construction was about to begin. Finding an opening among the drifting floes, Nansen nosed the ship into the pack ice, shut down the engines, and waited.

"We were closely surrounded on all sides by tolerably thick ice," he noted on September 24. "Between the floes lies slush ice, which will soon be quite firm. . . . It looks as if we were being shut in."

"Frozen in faster and faster!" he exulted the next day. "Winter is coming now."

So was the moment of truth. Soon no water at all was visible. On all sides the ship was surrounded by a vast rumpled plain of ice, and the crewmen waited apprehensively for the packing to begin. They knew that at any time, the huge, slowly shifting floes could collide, slide atop one another, and pile up into jagged pressure ridges of jumbled ice blocks 15, 20, or even 25 feet high.

Then on October 9 it happened. The entire crew was belowdecks, "sitting idly chattering," when the world seemed to explode. "A deafening noise began, and the whole ship shook." All hands rushed to the deck and for the first time saw the awesome power of the pack ice. Trembling as in an earthquake, it heaved and squeezed in on the *Fram*.

But she was not crushed. The ice simply lifted her up,

as Nansen had predicted, and then when the pressure eased, she sank slowly back down again.

Day after day the assaults of the ice continued, but the *Fram* escaped unscathed. "Now we are in the very midst of what the prophets would have had us dread so much," Nansen commented. "The ice is pressing and packing round us with a noise like thunder. It is piling itself up into long walls, and heaps high enough to reach a good way up the *Fram*'s rigging; in fact, it is trying its very utmost to grind the *Fram* into powder.

"But," he added smugly, "here we sit quite tranquil, not even going up to look at all the hurly-burly, but just chatting and laughing as usual."

Reassured that the *Fram* could indeed withstand the pressure of the ice, the crew settled down to the routine they would follow for months, perhaps years, as they waited for the sturdy craft to drift across the North Pole. When the weather was fair, they trekked across the ice to hunt polar bears or simply to marvel at the splendor of the northern lights that flickered endlessly in the Arctic night. They played cards, they sang, they read books, they had special feasts to celebrate holidays—including the *Fram*'s birthday.

Above all, they had the serious work of the expedition to do. They took weather readings every four hours and astronomical observations every other day. They measured the ocean's temperature, salt content, depth, and currents, and dredged up samples from its floor. And they carefully charted the *Fram*'s course.

Some of the findings were disturbing. Originally, Nansen had believed the Arctic Ocean was shallow. But it was turning out to be even deeper than his 1,000-fathom sounding line could reach. Nansen realized that such great depths must mean the current, which he was counting on to carry the *Fram* across the pole, was weaker than he had assumed and that the influence of the wind would be much stronger.

Most disturbing of all was the map of the *Fram*'s progress. Although the ship's course over several months was generally northwest, her progress was erratic, full of stops and even southward movements. Discouraged, Nansen realized that the voyage, initially estimated to take two to five years, might well take seven or eight years. Even worse, it looked as if the

**A scientist by training** *and a researcher by profession, Fridtjof Nansen tracked his course, recorded the weather, measured the thickness of the ice, took the water temperature, and analyzed sea currents with great precision. Sigurd Scott-Hansen manned the meteorological station (left). He took the temperature—often as low as −40° F—every four hours and astronomical observations every other day to establish the ship's position.*

*Heroes of the Arctic and Antarctic*

## The Northern Lights: A Glittering Cloak of Heavenly Light

To Nansen, poet and artist as well as scientist and explorer, the northern lights were a magical phenomena expressing the mystery of the universe. In awe of their mystical beauty, he portrayed them in a woodcut (far right) and wrote about them in his diary: "The aurora borealis shakes over the vault of heaven its veil of glittering silver—changing now to yellow, now to green, now to red. It spreads, it contracts again in restless change; next it breaks into waving, many-folded bands of shining silver, over which shoot billows of glittering rays, and then the glory vanishes. Presently it shimmers in tongues of flame over the very zenith, and then again it shoots a bright ray right up from the horizon, until the whole melts away in the moonlight, and it is as though one heard the sigh of a departing spirit. Here and there are left a few waving streamers of light, vague as a foreboding—they are the dust from the aurora's glittering cloak. But now it is growing again; new lightnings shoot up, and the endless game begins afresh. And all the time this utter stillness, impressive as the symphony of infinitude. I have never been able to grasp the fact that this earth will some day be spent and desolate and empty. To what end, in that case all this beauty, with not a creature to rejoice in it? Now I begin to divine it. This is the coming earth—here are beauty and death. But to what purpose? Ah, what is the purpose of all these spheres? Read the answer, if you can, in the starry blue firmament."

Today, scientists know that the northern lights, or the aurora borealis (photo below), are caused by electrically charged particles, discharged from the sun, bombarding gases high in the atmosphere. The particles from the sun approach the earth at a speed of 600 miles per second and are captured by the earth's magnetic field. The colorful lights occur only in high latitudes, yet when exceptionally strong, they can be perceived as far south as Mexico City. Al-

though they appear almost every night, they are most beautiful in fall and spring. An aurora's hue depends upon the molecule in the atmosphere that is being bombarded. For example, yellow-green—the most common color—arises from the reaction of the sun's particles with oxygen. Red, like the aurora at left, occurs during magnetic storms. Auroras take many shapes—they can be arcs, rays, veils, or patches—but most are long wavy bands of many folds extending from an altitude of 70 to 500 miles in the sky.

*Fram* might miss the North Pole entirely.

As their first winter in the ice gave way to summer and the summer sun began to set again, Nansen grew increasingly restless. "This carefree life, this passive existence oppresses me," he confided in his diary. "Ah! the very soul freezes. What would I not give for a single day of struggle—for even a moment of danger!"

Even as he fretted over "this irksome inactivity," a plan began to form in his mind, a plan that might well involve all the struggle and danger he could cope with, for he was determined to reach the pole even if the *Fram* did not. So as the second Arctic winter closed in on the expedition, he laid his plan before Otto Sverdrup, his second in command on the *Fram*. Why not make an overland expedition from the drifting boat to the North Pole, he proposed. With one companion he would travel on skis, snowshoes, dogsleds, and kayaks and then return to civilization by way of Franz Josef Land, a scattering of islands a few hundred miles to the south. It could not be much worse than his trip across the Greenland Ice Cap, he reasoned. February or March seemed the best time to start, for he had observed the year before that the ice was smoothest then and best suited for travel by dogsled. By May, when the warming sun began to melt the ice, progress would be

hampered by long stretches of water that would open between the drifting floes.

The crew was enthusiastic about the idea. Several men volunteered to accompany Nansen, but he finally chose Hjalmar Johansen, a reserve naval officer who had been so eager to join the *Fram* expedition that he had signed on as a stoker. With customary care, Nansen tested every piece of equipment that was to be used on the trek to the pole. He and Johansen moved out on the ice and began living there. They tried out different kinds of footgear, clothing, food, tents, sleeping bags. They tested sleds and dogs. Then on March 14, 1895, after two false starts, they set out with their equipment and supplies lashed to three dogsleds. At this point the *Fram* was just 350 miles from the North Pole—closer than any ship had ever been before.

At first, the going was easy. Encountering vast plains of smooth ice "which seemed as if they must stretch right to the Pole," they often covered 14 miles or more in a day. "If this goes on," Nansen noted, "the whole thing will be done in no time."

Before long, however, they found themselves trapped in a maze of towering pressure ridges, with the intervening level areas strewn with blocks of ice rubble. Driving the dogs to their utmost, the men themselves

**"Nahnook," the polar bear,** *is lord of the Arctic's icefields. All other animals—Nansen and Johansen included—have feared the skull-crushing swack of its paw. To reach the pole, Nansen had planned to cross 350 miles of the desolate white icefields like this* one, *varied only by ridges of ice and howling winds. For him, the icefields had a "weird beauty, without feeling, as though of a dead planet, built of shining white marble . . . [where] the soul bows down before the majesty of night and death."*

had to tug and strain to haul the heavily laden sledges over every jagged ridge that blocked their route. "Lanes, ridges, and endless rough ice," Nansen despaired. "It looks like an endless moraine of ice blocks; and this continual lifting of the sledges over every irregularity is enough to tire out giants."

Just as bad were the pools of fresh water that formed by day and froze over during the night, when the temperature regularly plummeted to −40° F. Soon the "damp exhalations of their bodies" had transformed their clothing "into complete suits of armor." Their clothes "were so hard and stiff that if we had only been able to get them off they could have stood by themselves, and they crackled audibly every time we moved." Before long, deep bloody wounds circled Nansen's wrists where the frozen cuffs chafed them.

The toil continued, and as Nansen described it, "we became more and more worn out with the never-ending work of helping the dogs, righting the sledges every time they capsized, and hauling them, or carrying them bodily, over hummocks and inequalities of the ground. Sometimes we were so sleepy in the evenings that our eyes shut and we fell asleep as we went along. My head would drop, and I would be awakened by suddenly falling forward on my snowshoes."

By the first week of April, Nansen began to lose hope of ever reaching the pole. "The ice seems to be getting worse and worse," he commented, "and I am beginning to have doubts as to the wisdom of keeping northward too long." He was also puzzled by the seeming lack of progress. Although the two men traveled several miles each day, his astronomical observations in the evening showed that they were scarcely any farther north than they had been the night before. Then he realized what was happening. They were on a giant treadmill; the floes they struggled so desperately to cross were drifting south nearly as fast as they were moving north. Nansen, the coolly objective scientist who always strove to work *with* the forces of nature, now found himself working against them.

His journal entries for the next few days are a record of growing disillusionment:

*April 3:* "Beginning to have doubts as to the wisdom of keeping northward too long."

*April 5:* "I begin to think more and more that we ought to turn back before the time we originally fixed."

*April 6:* ". . . this morning I had almost decided to turn back. . . . I am rapidly coming to the conclusion that we are not doing any good here."

On April 8 he finally gave in. Going ahead of Johansen to scout the route, Nansen climbed the highest hummock he could find and saw only "a veritable chaos of ice-blocks, stretching as far as the horizon." That night, at the latitude of 86°14', the men pitched their tent on their northernmost camping ground. In 26 days they had traveled 124 miles and come within 224 miles of the North Pole. Although they had not reached their goal, they had come closer to it than any man ever had before. The next morning they took one last look at their monotonously forbidding surroundings and set out on their homeward journey for Franz Josef Land, some 400 miles to the south.

The homeward journey proved even worse than the race toward the pole. Day after day they struggled over the same sort of ice they had endured ever since leaving the *Fram.* "It is hard to go on hoping in such circumstances," Nansen commented, "but still we do so; though sometimes, perhaps, our hearts fail us when we see the ice lying before us like an impenetrable maze of ridges, lanes, brash, and huge blocks thrown together, pell-mell, and one might imagine one's self looking at suddenly congealed breakers. There are moments when it seems impossible that any creature not possessed of wings can get farther. . . . But then, in spite of everything, one finds a way."

The onset of spring also created problems. As the midnight sun rose higher and higher in the sky, temperatures inched up toward the melting point. The accumulation of fresh snow on the ice rubble turned to knee-deep slush, and progress became more difficult than ever. Huge cracks, sometimes miles long, opened between the slowly drifting floes, then froze over with skins of ice too thin to support their sledges but thick

### A Lonely Winter Spent on an Arctic Island

Their improvised hut of stone, moss, and walrus hide protected Nansen and Hjalmar Johansen from the villainous winter on Franz Josef Land. They lived on polar bear flesh and warmed themselves with the great beasts' skins. Because it often was too cold to go out, they slept—sometimes 20 hours a day. "It was a strange existence. . . . How we longed for a book!"

enough to rip their kayaks to shreds if they attempted to launch the boats. Unable to cross these leads in the ice, the men had to make detours around them.

Worse still, provisions were running low, especially food for the dogs. The solution was, in Nansen's words, "a horrible affair," but the men had no choice. One by one they killed off the weakest dogs and fed their flesh to the survivors. By mid-June, with only three dogs still alive, the two men had to fashion harnesses for themselves and pull side by side with the dogs as they hauled the sledges across the ice.

There were a few hopeful signs. Now and then they came across the tracks of an Arctic fox. Occasionally, a polar bear lumbered within firing range and so replenished their larder. As summer progressed, gulls and other waterfowl soared overhead more and more frequently. Surely, all this wildlife had to mean that land could not be far away.

And yet it eluded them. They no longer even knew exactly where they were. Not until July 24, after three and a half months of traveling southward, did they finally spot an island on the horizon. Nansen was jubilant: "At last the marvel has come to pass—land, land! and after we had almost given up our belief in it!"

His elation was short-lived. Two weeks of "inconceivable toil" followed as they struggled to reach the open water surrounding the island. "We never could go on with it were it not for the fact that we *must,*" Nansen noted grimly.

When at last they did reach the edge of the pack ice and launched their kayaks, they left without their two remaining faithful sled dogs. (They had killed and eaten the other along the way.) It was a difficult decision, but again they had little choice. Once they began traveling by boat, the dogs would be more hindrance

**Built of bamboo and canvas,** *kayaks were strong and light and could store provisions for three months. If sailed alone, the boats overturned too easily when walruses attacked. But two lashed together (above) carried Nansen and Johansen, their sledges, and gear across frigid and dangerous Arctic seas to Franz Josef Land.*

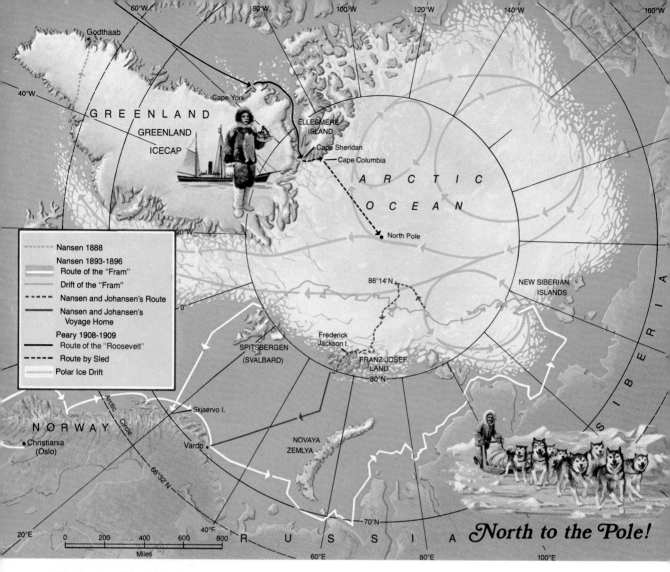

The following map legend appears on the illustration:

Nansen 1888
Nansen 1893-1896
　Route of the "Fram"
　Drift of the "Fram"
Nansen and Johansen's Route
Nansen and Johansen's
　Voyage Home
Peary 1908-1909
　Route of the "Roosevelt"
　Route by Sled
Polar Ice Drift

*North to the Pole!*

**The Arctic, unlike Antarctica,** *is not a landmass; it is simply a vast, constantly shifting area of pack ice and drift ice. Since a deep ocean flows beneath the ice, it gradually changes shape in response to the sea's currents (indicated by the green lines). These currents cause the ice to flow in circular patterns around the pole. The North Pole, the "top" of the axis around which the earth rotates, became a challenging goal for explorers in the late* *19th century. Fridtjof Nansen was the first to conceive the idea of locking a ship into the ice and drifting with the moving pack. Nansen's* Fram *failed to reach the pole in this fashion, so the explorer and a companion attempted to reach it on foot—a venture that also failed but brought them closer than anyone had been before. It was Robert Peary who in 1909 became the first to reach the frozen goal in a well-planned dash by dogsled.*

than help. Regretfully, they destroyed the animals and set out across the sea.

What they found was not one island, but a whole maze of them. They had done the impossible; they had reached Franz Josef Land. For three weeks they scouted the shores, landing here and there to revel in the feel of solid rock beneath their feet and the sight of poppies blooming in crevices.

But the brief Arctic summer was waning rapidly now. By the end of August the ice was closing in on all sides, blocking every possible route to the south. The ordeal of the ice was over, and now they were faced with a new one: wintering in this impossible place.

A few days later Nansen watched wistfully as two

geese passed overhead, flying south. "With what longing I looked after them as they disappeared," he wrote, "only wishing that I could have followed them." Curiously, however, neither he nor Johansen seems to have doubted for a moment that they could survive the winter at their isolated outpost. They immediately began hunting walruses to build up a supply of tough hides for shelter and oily blubber for fuel. They shot the polar bears that came almost daily to gnaw at the abandoned walrus carcasses and before long had more than enough meat to carry them through the winter and warm bearskins to sleep on. Then, improvising tools from odd bits of wood and walrus bones and tusks, they built a tiny hut of stones chinked with moss and roofed over with thick, waterproof walrus skins.

Late in September they moved into the hut and settled down to their winter routine. Although they took turns cooking, they seldom varied their menu: bear meat soup for breakfast, fried bear steak for dinner. Their diet, combined with enforced idleness, must have been nourishing. The next summer they would be surprised to discover that in some 15 months since leaving the *Fram*, Nansen had gained about 22 pounds and Johansen more than 13 pounds.

So they wiled away their third winter in the Arctic night, venturing out, when the weather was calm, to hunt, walk on the snow, or watch breathtaking displays of northern lights and shooting stars. When gales blasted over the plains and snow swirled around their shelter, they remained inside, huddled near their oil stove, and slept, sometimes for as many as 20 hours a day. When they were awake, they talked for hours on end. They dreamed of food—"great platters full of cakes, not to mention bread and potatoes." They reminisced over the luxury of Turkish baths with lots of soap and hot water—"what a magnificent invention soap really is." They yearned for the sight of bright shops filled with warm soft clothing—"Ugh, the clothes we lived in were horrible!"

But spring was on the way. Their spirits soared when on February 25 they saw the first birds winging in from the south. "The first greeting from life," Nansen called them, then added, "Blessed birds, how welcome you are." Clearly, the time had come to prepare for what they hoped would be the last leg of their journey home. "Our hut," Nansen commented, "was suddenly transformed into a busy tailor's and shoemaker's workroom." Unraveling thread from a canvas bag, they stitched together their ragged clothes, made new ones from their blankets, and fashioned a new lightweight sleeping bag from bearskins.

By May 19 everything was ready. They loaded their kayaks with supplies, lashed them to the sledges, and began hauling them across the ice or sailing when they came to stretches of open water. For a month they continued southward, making their way from island to island. They endured dunkings in icy water, attacks by walruses, cold nights in a sodden sleeping bag, and all the other hazards and discomforts of exploration.

On June 17, 1896, almost three years to the day since their departure from Norway, they were camped on the ice near a rocky island. Nansen was preparing breakfast when the mist shrouding the island's interior began to lift. Curious about the land, he left Johansen behind and wandered off to look at it. Thousands of birds wheeled overhead, filling the air with song. "Arctic majesty," thought Nansen, this land "unseen by any human eye and untrodden by any human foot."

Suddenly, a dog barked in the distance.

Nansen could hardly believe his ears. Then his eyes. As he made his way across the ice, a man approached.

"I'm immensely glad to see you," the stranger said.

"Thank you; I also," Nansen replied, recognizing Frederick Jackson, an English Arctic explorer.

Jackson stared at the bedraggled Norwegian, hesitated, then blurted out, "Aren't you Nansen?"

"Yes, I am."

"By Jove!" Jackson declared, "I am glad to see you!"

Ironically, Jackson was in Franz Josef Land on an expedition seeking a new land route to the North Pole, a possibility that Nansen's journey had already disproved. For the next few weeks Nansen and Johansen basked in the luxuries of Jackson's well-equipped camp, waiting for his supply ship to arrive from Norway. As soon as it came in and was unloaded, the two explorers clambered aboard and headed for home.

Within a week of their arrival in Norway, Nansen's triumph was complete. He received a telegram from the man in charge of the *Fram*: "Fridtjof Nansen: *Fram* arrived in good condition. All well on board. Shall start at once for Tromso. Welcome home! Otto Sverdrup."

So Nansen had proved his theory. The *Fram* had continued her drift just as he had predicted. Although she had missed the pole, she had come across the polar

**Nansen was so thankful** *for his chance encounter (reenacted above) with Frederick Jackson, an English traveler in the Arctic, that he named the barren island where they met in his honor.*

sea without the slightest mishap and had finally broken out of the pack ice off the coast of Spitsbergen, an island group to the west of Franz Josef Land.

All Norway was dazzled by the exploits of Nansen and his crew and greeted them with wild celebrations. But for Nansen, the greatest satisfaction was to be home again with his family. Standing on the beach in his native town one evening, he listened to the waves lapping at his feet and reflected on his accomplishment. "The ice and the long moonlit polar nights, with all their yearning, seemed like a far-off dream from another world—a dream that had come and passed away," he recalled. "But what would life be worth without its dreams?"

**Robert Edwin Peary was** *52 when he discovered the North Pole in 1909. The following year he posed for a portrait (below) with snowshoes and sextant—items that allowed him to advance to the earth's apex over the Arctic icepack (above) and measure his position. When he returned, though relatively young in years, his face was that of an old man, ravaged by cruel winds and freezing temperatures. As soon as word reached the press that Peary had attained his goal (right), he was hailed as a hero. He had "won the last great geographical prize, the North Pole, for the credit of the United States." The Stars and Stripes (opposite page), handmade by Peary's wife, had waved over the top of the world.*

 Over fathomless waters at the top of the world floats the frozen goal of a generation of explorers. Surrounded by more than 1,000 miles of treacherous ice, it is one of the last unconquered places. After years of preparation, an American finally attains it in a daring, headlong thrust that brings him international acclaim.

# Planting the Flag: Peary Reaches the North Pole

*Consumed by a passion for fame, Robert Edwin Peary sought and found it in the Arctic. Born in Cresson, Pennsylvania, in 1856, he grew up in Maine and graduated from Bowdoin College. On his first trip to Greenland, in 1886, he only traveled about 100 miles inland across the icecap, but in 1891–92 he reached Greenland's northern coast after a 1,300-mile journey and proved that it was an island. In the following years Peary continued to explore the great island, mapping much of its northern coast. His first attempt to reach the North Pole (1893–94) failed when he was forced to turn back at 84° 17' N. In 1905–06 he came within 174 nautical miles of the pole, setting a new world's record for "farthest north." After reaching the pole on his 1908–09 expedition, he retired to an island in Maine. He died in 1920.*

Almost a month out of New York City, the steamer *Roosevelt* plowed steadily northward along the western coast of Greenland. The commander, Robert Edwin Peary, squinting from beneath dense, bushy eyebrows, scanned the coast for familiar landmarks. Just ahead, on August 1, 1908, far to the north of the Arctic Circle, he sighted the snowcapped headland of Cape York plunging to the sea.

It seemed a barren, lifeless place—just rocky cliffs "encircled and guarded," as Peary put it, "by an enormous squadron of floating icebergs." Yet at the foot of the cliffs there was a tiny Eskimo settlement. As the *Roosevelt* nosed in toward shore, an excited band of hunters paddled out in sealskin kayaks to meet the steamer. "You are like the sun," one of them greeted Peary. "You always come back."

It was true. In the 22 years since his first trip to Greenland, when he had decided to make Arctic exploration his life's work, Peary had returned to these frozen wastes seven times. Twice, his wife, Josephine, had accompanied him, so becoming the first white woman

to spend a winter in the Arctic. On her second expedition, she had given birth to their daughter, Marie Ahnighito, the "Snow Baby," the first white child to be born so far north.

At first, Peary's motives had been purely scientific: to explore Greenland's interior icecap and to map the unknown coasts of far northern islands. But ever since childhood he had been haunted by dreams of glory. Gradually, his scientific motives gave way to a more compelling one—to become the first man to set foot on what he called "the last great geographical prize, the North Pole."

On his most recent expedition, in 1905–06, he had nearly made it. He was within 174 miles of the pole when he was forced to turn back. It was the closest any man had ever come to that elusive goal. But that was small consolation to Peary. Commenting later on the expedition, he wrote: "It seemed to me then that the story of my life was told and that the word failure was stamped across it."

Yet here he was, back in Greenland, ready to try once more. He realized that this was his last chance at the pole. At 52 he was no longer young, and two decades of battling the Arctic's elements had taken their toll. Though he was still trim and athletic, his face was weathered and deeply lined. His reddish hair was beginning to gray. His years in the Arctic were reflected even in his peculiar sliding gait: On one expedition his feet had been so severely frostbitten that all but two of his toes had to be amputated.

But his experience was greater than that of any other Arctic explorer, and experience he considered an explorer's greatest asset. Nor had he ever before gone north so well prepared for the challenge of polar exploration. The *Roosevelt*, already the veteran of one Arctic voyage, had been refitted and was more powerful than ever. Peary had designed the stubby 184-foot-

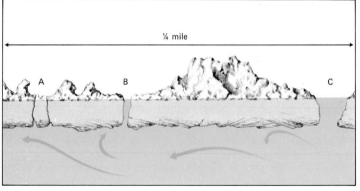

**A midnight sun glows** *over the Greenland icefield as Peary's sleds lurch onward. This 1894 scene was painted by Frank Stokes, who traveled with Peary and sketched barehanded, sometimes in −40° F weather. The permanent Greenland icefield was easy to cross compared to the frozen Arctic Ocean. The pressure of the ocean's iceblocks freezing together each year creates forbidding hummocks (see diagram left) often 50 feet high, in addition to cracks (A) and crevasses (B). To avoid open water Peary made his dash before the spring thaw. Nevertheless, he was often temporarily stopped by a lead (C), the separation of iceblocks by high winds and tides.*

long ship himself, not only to survive the crushing pressure of polar ice floes—her heavily braced wooden sides were as much as 30 inches thick—but also to thread adroitly through narrow passages between the masses of ice. There were sails for emergencies, but the main power source was massive steam engines strong enough to make the craft a floating battering ram, one that could plow through ice that would have been impenetrable by any other ship.

His crew, the best he had ever chosen, included several men who had been with him on earlier expeditions. Among them was his indispensable assistant, Matthew Henson, the black explorer who had shared in nearly all his Arctic exploits for the past 18 years. Peary's

*Heroes of the Arctic and Antarctic*

knowledge of the Arctic people, moreover, would enable him to choose the best of what he affectionately termed "my Eskimos" for the time when he would set off across the frozen sea toward the pole itself.

He knew the geography. He knew the men. He knew the obstacles. He was finally ready to begin his "last and supreme effort."

After pausing briefly at Cape York to take on a few Eskimo families and sled dogs, the *Roosevelt* continued north, stopping here and there to pick up more recruits. By August 18 the ship was crowded with the entire party that would spend the winter with Peary: 69 human beings, including 49 Eskimos, and 246 dogs. "The *Roosevelt*, as usual," he noted laconically, "was loaded almost to the water's edge." Besides all the bustling human life and howling dogs, the decks were heaped with 300 tons of coal, 70 tons of whale meat, and the flesh of nearly 50 walruses. Belowdecks, supplies brought north from civilization included such items as 8 tons of flour, 5 tons of sugar, 15 tons of pemmican (a concentrated, high-energy food made of pounded dried meat mixed with fat and flavorings), and even 1,000 pounds of smoking tobacco.

The final 350 miles of the voyage were the hardest test the *Roosevelt* had to face. The route was through the narrow channel between Greenland and Ellesmere Island. And the channel was almost solidly packed with high slabs of ice up to 100 feet thick. Despite the "stupendous" ice and "villainous" weather, however, by early September the *Roosevelt* had battered her way to Cape Sheridan at the head of the channel. She had set a record, for this was the farthest north any ship had ever steamed under her own power.

As the long Arctic night began to close in, Peary's men settled down to their winter regimen. A top priority was to hunt for polar bears and musk-oxen to supplement the larder: Peary believed in living off the land as much as possible.

Whenever the full moon lit the landscape with a feeble glow, sledging parties hauled supplies to Cape Columbia, 90 miles away on the northernmost shores of Ellesmere Island. This was to be the jumping-off point for Peary's assault on the pole in early spring.

The Eskimo women, meanwhile, earned their keep by stitching up clothing for the men: fawnskin shirts, deerskin parkas with fox tails fringing the hoods, hareskin stockings, shaggy bearskin trousers, sealskin boots, and fur mittens. Warm and windproof, animal skins were, in Peary's opinion, the ideal clothing for work in the Arctic—as centuries of use by the Eskimos had amply demonstrated.

Just as Peary used Eskimo clothing, he felt dogsleds were the only efficient means of Arctic travel. They would transport his party over 413 miles of frozen sea from Cape Columbia to the North Pole.

By late February everything was ready. Although the sun was still below the horizon, the sky glowed for 12 hours each day with a pale twilight just bright enough for travel. Gathering at their tiny cluster of igloos at Cape Columbia, the men loaded up their sleds and prepared to head north.

Peary's "Northern party" consisted of 24 men, 19 sleds, and 133 dogs. He divided them into six divisions, each headed by an American with three Eskimo assistants. The "pioneer divison" was to travel a day ahead of the main party, breaking trail. A second division also would travel in advance, laying down caches of supplies. The other four divisions made up the main party, with Peary bringing up the rear where he could keep an eye on everything—and conserve his strength for the final spurt for the pole.

The pioneer and supply divisions left Cape Columbia on February 28, and on March 1, 1909, the remaining divisions set out one by one onto the frozen surface of the Arctic Ocean, where they were immediately engulfed in a haze of swirling snow driven up by a vicious wind howling in from the east.

Even with a trail broken by the men of the pioneer division, who had hacked away the worst irregularities in the ice with pickaxes, the going proved rough. Sleds immediately began to break and often overturned as they slammed against jagged ice hidden under the drifted snow. Matthew Henson, at the head of the main division, described the agonies of repairing his broken sled that first day: "Cold and windy. Undo the lashings, unload the load, get out the brace and bit and bore new holes, taking plenty of time, for, in such cold, there is danger of the steel bit breaking. Then, with ungloved hands, thread the sealskin thongs through the hole. The fingers freeze. Stop work, hand under your armpit, and when you feel it burning you know it has thawed out. Then start to work again."

Although the main party advanced only about 10 miles that day, Peary found reasons to be cheerful. Some of the 9-foot-long Eskimo sledges had suffered

### A World of Ice and Spirits

The ice world of the Eskimos was alive with spirits. Tools, clothes, water, hunger, animals—all had their own "souls." The dancing spirits of stillborn children, for instance, lit the northern lights. At night a man's spirit left him sleeping to wander about and bring him dreams. To prevent evil spirits from bringing disaster to their homes and families, Eskimos carved driftwood masks (above). There were also benevolent deities, such as the god of ice, who allowed safe passage across the icepack, and helpful spirits, such as those of the sled dogs, who could bring a man safely to his destination. Some Greenland Eskimos, especially, feared Tornarsuk, cannibal god of the north, who guarded the pole area. Peary had some difficulty recruiting men because of this fear.

badly, but the 12-to-13-foot-long models he had designed were holding up well. Because of their extra length, each sledge's 500-pound load of provisions could be spread out more evenly, thus lowering the center of gravity. As a result, the sledges were less likely to overturn on rough ice.

Settling in for the night, the men first built igloos of blocks of snow for shelter, a task four men could complete in an hour. (Here again Peary relied on Eskimo methods. Tents would mean extra weight on the sledges, and igloos were infinitely warmer and more windproof.) Then they fed the dogs, ate their own suppers of pemmican, dried biscuits, and tea, and with their clothes still on, curled up to sleep on fur robes spread on the igloo floors.

Travel the second day proved just as difficult as on the first. The Arctic Ocean, as Peary was fond of pointing out, is not "a gigantic skating pond with a level floor over which the dogs drag us merrily." Its frozen surface is in slow but constant motion—pulled by currents, pushed by winds, stretched and crushed by tides. Where high slabs of ice collide and pile up atop each other, the surface is scarred by pressure ridges, long, jumbled windrows of jagged ice piled up as high as 50 feet. To cross these barriers, the men had to hack out trails as best they could, then push and tug to help the dog teams haul the sledges "over hummocks and up acclivities whose difficulties sometimes seem likely to tear the muscles from one's shoulder-blades."

Even worse were leads—long, dangerous stretches of open water where winds and tides had cracked the ice apart. They might form anytime, at any place, and without warning, even through an igloo as one slept. It was sometimes possible to cross narrow leads by using one of Peary's extra sleds as a bridge. Or, on other occasions, a slab of ice could be hacked out and used as a raft. But at really wide leads the only course was to wait for winds and tides to bring the two sides crashing together or for the surface of the open water to freeze enough to support the sledges. Peary called leads the Arctic traveler's "ever-present nightmare." He was grimly aware that they could make or break an expedition by causing lengthy delays or, worse still, by stranding a party offshore on its return to land.

## *"Sturdy, Magnificent" Dogs Pulled Peary to the North Pole*

Peary stands on the snow-covered deck of his exploration ship, the *Roosevelt*, with some of the sled dogs that pulled him to world fame (right). "They are sturdy, magnificent animals," he wrote. "There may be larger dogs than these, there may be handsomer dogs; but I doubt it. Other dogs may work as well or travel as fast and far when fully fed; but there is no dog in the world that can work so long in the lowest temperatures on practically nothing to eat." Fearlessly, they struggled over the Arctic icefields against winds, "enveloped in the white cloud of their own breath."

The Eskimo huskies are as remarkable as Peary described. Weighing as much as 100 pounds each, dogs in teams of 8 to 12 can pull a fully loaded sled and a man over hundreds of miles of treacherous ice. Today, Eskimos often drive their dogs in pairs, as in the contemporary photograph below, but Peary drove his in fan-shaped teams. When Eskimos used splayed traces, they let the lead dog pick the route, but Peary chose his course himself, directing the dogs where he wanted to go.

Dog driving is an art. Although 25-foot whips are used, even they are often not enough to make the dogs take off. The skill of driving the dogs lies in snapping the thong in the air above their heads, but never touching them, while coaxing them with the voice. Peary's dogs were harnessed around the chest and shoulders, Eskimo-style, with traces made by Eskimo women. Equally important as the dogs were the 19 sleds that carried the gear, without which the men would

have starved and frozen. Peary designed the sledges to be 12 to 13 feet long (above), about 3 feet longer than those of the Eskimos. Made of willow, they were both light and strong, packed carefully to keep the center of gravity low and to prevent overturning. On the bottom were red tins of pemmican for the dogs, then blue tins of pemmican for the men, as well as cans of biscuits, alcohol, condensed milk, snowshoes, and a pickax and saw for cutting iceblocks for igloos. Peary used 40 dogs pulling five such sledges in his final dash to the pole.

Peary had reason to be apprehensive. Late on their second day out, he noticed "a dark ominous cloud" up ahead. Such clouds were sure signs of leads, for the evaporating surface water quickly condensed in the frigid −50° F air. "When the wind is blowing just right," he noted, "this forms a fog so dense that at times it looks as black as the smoke of a prairie fire."

Peary gave the order to camp and, to his great relief, awoke the next morning to the roar of the two sides of the lead grinding together. The whole party breakfasted in a hurry, then quickly made for the other side, using chunks of ice as rafts and floating stepping-stones. "If the reader will imagine crossing a river on a succession of giant shingles, one, two, or three deep and all afloat and moving," Peary later wrote, "he will perhaps form an idea of the uncertain surface over which we crossed this lead."

As they continued north that day, the men were cheered to see "a flaming blade of yellow light" illuminating the southern sky. The returning sun was skimming along just beneath the horizon. In a few days it would be visible once more, and the long Arctic night would be over.

Their elation was short-lived. The next day they were favored by relatively smooth ice—Henson called it "the best traveling sea ice I had ever encountered"—but Peary kept an apprehensive eye on a broad band of clouds stretching across the horizon. Before long, about 45 miles north of Cape Columbia, they were halted by a lead of open water a quarter of a mile wide and stretching endlessly east and west. And there on the ice, waiting for them, sat Bob Bartlett, captain of the *Roosevelt*, and the rest of the pioneer division, who had not been able to proceed any farther.

Although leads are normal occurrences in the Arctic, Peary called this gigantic gash in the ice the Big Lead. He had encountered one like it in this same area three years earlier, and it was the obstacle he feared most from the beginning of this expedition. A "familiar unwelcome sight," Peary called it with disgust, ". . . the white expanse of ice cut by a river of inky black water, throwing off dense clouds of vapor which gathered in a sullen canopy overhead, at times swinging lower with the wind and obscuring the opposite shore."

Day after day the party waited for the lead to close or freeze over. The sun now rose briefly above the horizon each day, but it did little to raise anyone's spirits. "Intolerable inaction," Peary lamented, "and still the broad line of black water spread before us." Angry and frustrated, he paced back and forth at the water's edge, fretting about the future.

Peary was also concerned about a shortage of fuel for the party's cookstoves. Many cans had sprung leaks when sleds overturned, and the supply was getting dangerously low. Peary had sent one party and then another back to Cape Columbia for more fuel. They should have caught up with the main group by then.

## Matthew Henson: "Brother" of the Eskimos

Matthew A. Henson was the first black man to reach the North Pole. Peary had met Henson 22 years earlier in a Washington, D.C., hatshop. On his way to Nicaragua with a U.S. Navy expedition, he hired Henson on the spot as his personal servant. At the time, Henson was 21 and Peary 31, but the younger man had already earned his sea legs at the age of 13 on a ship out of Baltimore. Throughout his two decades with Peary, Henson was indispensable. Because of his skin color, the Eskimos thought he was their brother. He learned their language fluently, was accepted in their homes, and even adopted an Eskimo son. They, in turn, taught him how to build sledges, drive dogs, and construct igloos, so that Henson came to oversee these tasks during the expeditions. The Eskimos were particularly impressed by Henson's skills as a hunter and dog driver. Due to their profound admiration for him, Henson was able to rally them when morale was low with a gentle pressure that Peary was never capable of. Although Henson received little acclaim for his accomplishments, Peary praised his bravery and intelligence. After two decades of polar exploration, Henson went to work in a Brooklyn garage and then as a messenger in a U.S. customshouse. He died in Harlem in 1955 at the age of 89, still remembered as a friend by the Eskimos of Greenland.

Yet there was no sign of them. In desperation, Peary began calculating how far he could proceed if he were forced to burn the sledges for fuel. What he did not know was that both supply parties, replenished with ample fuel, at that moment were blocked by another lead a few miles away.

There were other problems, too. "The Big Lead," Matt Henson commented, "has no attraction for the Eskimos." Gathering in dispirited groups, they muttered nervously among themselves or complained to Peary of imaginary illnesses. Exasperated, he finally sent two of the worst men back to shore with orders to leave the expedition entirely.

"Altogether," Peary concluded, "I think that more of mental wear and tear was crowded into those days than into all the rest of the fifteen months we were absent from civilization."

Finally, after wasting seven days of exceptionally fine weather, the Big Lead froze over. Fuel or no fuel, Peary could lose no more precious traveling time. Early on the morning of March 11, he ordered the party to cross the thin young ice, hoping desperately that it would hold and that the supply divisions would catch up soon. Three days later they did.

Now Peary drove his men northward as rapidly as possible. They hauled over pressure ridges and rough ice. They crossed leads on rubbery new ice so thin that

**Peary and his four Eskimo companions**—*Ooqueah, Ootah, Egingwah, and Seegloo—stood on the pinnacle of the earth while Matthew Henson took their photograph. Peary had just planted the American flag that his wife had made for him years before. As an incentive for the Eskimos to go with him, Peary gave each man two rifles, a shotgun, knives, spearheads, tobacco, oil, and a whaleboat. Each had his own reasons for going, but one fought his way to the pole to win his sweetheart.*

it buckled under the weight of the sledges. Once, trying to cross a lead, an entire dog team fell into the water, nearly dragging the sledge in with it. On another occasion, a lead formed right through the middle of a camp, briefly stranding half the party on a drifting floe. Even so, the expedition managed to advance 10, 15, and sometimes even 20 miles a day.

It was then, also, that Peary started sending the support divisions back to Cape Columbia, thus beginning the process of eliminating the weaker men and dogs. They would be sent back group by group until only those Peary judged to be the best remained for the final assault on the pole. "My theory," he explained, "was to work the supporting parties to the limit, in order to keep the main party fresh." The returning parties also were to keep the trail open so that the polar party could get back to land as quickly as possible.

Thus on March 14 the first support party turned back. Another headed south on March 15, the third on March 20, and the fourth on March 26. On March 28, still including Henson, Bartlett, and their Eskimos, the group surpassed Peary's "farthest north" record of 1906. Then, on April 1, Bartlett too turned his sleds south and began his return to land.

And so, on April 1, at 87°47′ N, the polar party prepared for the final drive. Peary, Matt Henson, and the Eskimos Ootah, Egingwah, Seegloo, and Ooqueah stood at their sleds in the then perpetual Arctic day-

light, ready to cross the remaining 133 miles of ice and water to, as Henson put it, "unlock the door which held the mystery of the Arctic." There was no more broken trail before them, no more supply depots or igloos. With five sleds and 40 dogs, they were ready to set out, with Peary for the first time taking the lead.

His goal was to advance 25 miles a day for the next five days. Through superhuman effort, the handpicked party of men and dogs managed to average 26 miles a day. Though the full moon and consequent high tides posed the constant threat of opening impassable leads, they encountered long stretches of smooth young ice and hard-packed snow. And the dogs, Peary noted with satisfaction, seemed to have "caught the high spirits of the party. Some of them even tossed their heads and barked and yelped as they traveled."

Not that polar travel is ever easy. Henson later recalled only the "toil, fatigue, and exhaustion" of those last few days, when he and the Eskimos were allowed only a few hours sleep at a time and Peary seemed to sleep not at all. At one point Henson almost drowned in a frigid lead, and Peary, too, endured repeated dunkings in the icy Arctic waters. During their grueling dash for the pole, Peary pulled his belt in another notch—the fourth time he had done so since leaving land. At the end of the expedition, he would discover that he had lost a total of 25 pounds.

At 10 a.m. on April 6, 1909, Peary called the column to a halt. Then, at high noon, he took a sighting on the sun. Their latitude, he announced, was 89°57′ N. They were just three miles from the exact top of the world.

"The Pole at last," Peary exulted triumphantly. "The prize of three centuries. My dream and goal for twenty years. Mine at last!" Then, with disarming candor, he added, "I cannot bring myself to realize it. It seems all so simple and commonplace."

Peary, in fact, was so spent that, as he later confessed, "with the Pole actually in sight I was too weary to take the last few steps. The accumulated weariness of all those days and nights of forced marches and insufficient sleep, constant peril and anxiety, seemed to roll across me all at once. I was actually too exhausted to realize at the moment that my life's purpose had been achieved."

"The Commander gave the word," Henson recalled. "'We will plant the stars and stripes—*at the North Pole!*' and it was done. . . . Another world's accomplishment was done and finished."

The flag was one Mrs. Peary had made for her husband years before. The explorer had carried it wrapped around his body on all his northern expeditions, leaving pieces at each of his successive "farthest norths." Before parting, he would cut a diagonal strip from the flag and leave it in a bottle with notes claiming the North Pole for the United States.

To confirm his location and make sure he passed near the pole itself—there is, of course, nothing to mark

*Heroes of the Arctic and Antarctic*

that precise theoretical point—Peary marched due north for 10 miles. His observations then showed that he was beyond the pole, heading south. It was strange, he reflected, that in that short distance he had "passed from the western to the eastern hemisphere." While traveling in a straight line, he had first been moving due north, then suddenly had passed a point where he was moving due south. "East, west, and north had disappeared for us," he went on. "Only one direction remained and that was south."

During the 30 hours the explorers spent at the North Pole, Peary took six separate sets of solar observations to reconfirm their location. (Peary had already sent back Captain Bartlett, the only other person qualified to make independent corroborative readings.) Then the explorers hitched up their dog teams and started on the homeward trail. "Though intensely conscious of what I was leaving," wrote Peary, "I did not wait for any lingering farewell of my life's goal. . . . One backward glance I gave—then turned my face toward the south and toward the future."

With an open trail and igloos already built along the way, the trip back was swift, much faster than the northward trek. Leaving the pole on April 7, the weary explorers arrived at Cape Columbia on April 23. A few days later they were safely back aboard the *Roosevelt*. By mid-July the ship had broken free of the ice and was steaming toward home. On September 5, 1909, the *Roosevelt* at last reached a northern outpost of civilization, and Peary exultantly flashed out telegrams to the world with his electrifying news: "Stars and Stripes nailed to the Pole."

## Dr. Cook and His Bitter Controversy With Peary, or Who (*If Anyone*) Got to the Pole First?

After reaching the North Pole on April 6, 1909, Robert Peary rushed south to the nearest telegraph office, 1,500 miles away in Labrador, to announce he had nailed the Stars and Stripes to the top of the world. He did not know that one Frederick Cook claimed to have reached the North Pole a full year earlier, on April 21, 1908, and had announced his conquest only five days before Peary did his. Traveling with two Eskimos, a few huskies, a canoe, and sled, Cook said it took him a year to get to a telegraph office. Peary's news reached the Labrador wire station more quickly because he had organized an entourage of 24 men in relay stations across the icecap, and his ship, the *Roosevelt*, was waiting for him off the northern coast of Ellesmere Island. Peary, when he learned of Cook's claim, bitterly tried to disprove it. Peary's challenge of Cook's claim set off a worldwide debate—memorialized in a pro-Cook postcard of that period (right)—that to this day has not been settled. The information is inconclusive: No one actually knows which, if either, man reached the pole. One skeptical examiner of both men's records said: "If it is true, as Peary would like us to believe, that Cook has given us a gold brick, then Peary has offered a paste diamond."

Frederick Cook, an unsuccessful Brooklyn doctor, first went to the Arctic with Peary in 1891 as the ship's doctor. Then, in the fall of 1907, a wealthy sportsman named John Bradley asked Cook to be his guide on an Arctic hunt. Cook went and, leaving Bradley off Devon Island, allegedly made his 2,000-mile dash to the North Pole. Later, he floridly described the achievement in his book, *My Attainment of the North Pole:* "We all were lifted to the paradise of winners as we stepped over the snows of a destiny for which we had risked life and willingly suffered the tortures of an icy hell. The ice under us, the goal for centuries of brave, heroic men, to reach, which many had suffered terribly and terribly died, seemed almost sacred. Constantly and carefully I watched my instruments in recording this final reach. Nearer and nearer they recorded our approach. Step by step, my heart filled with a strange rapture of conquest.

"At last we step over colored fields of sparkle, climbing walls of purple and gold—finally, under skies of crystal blue, with flaming clouds of glory, we touch the mark!"

Peary had his supporters, but so had Cook, among them men whom Peary had alienated on his past expeditions. The New York *Herald* was Cook's greatest ally and published his story for $25,000; the *Times* was Peary's. Whereas Cook was poor and always in need of money, Peary was well known and had influential backers. As one Cook supporter put it: "Cook was a liar and a gentleman. Peary was neither." Although Peary never disproved Cook's claim, Cook did some damage to Peary's. He maintained that Peary never got to the North Pole but, thinking he had, turned back 100 miles short of it. The controversy could never be settled because neither man took along a companion who knew how to use a sextant and could confirm their astronomical readings.

TWO DAUNTLESS AMERICANS WHO REACHED THE GOAL OF A THOUSAND YEARS AND PLANTED THE STARS AND STRIPES UPON THE AXIS OF THE WORLD.

**Norwegian Roald Amundsen** (*left*) *was the most outstanding polar explorer of his time. He completed the first successful navigation of the Northwest Passage through frigid Arctic waters strewn with gigantic icebergs like the one pictured above. A leading Antarctic explorer as well, Amundsen, in a dramatic race with Englishman Robert Falcon Scott, became the first man to reach the South Pole. On his Antarctic expedition, Amundsen applied many of the lessons of cold weather survival that he had learned from Eskimos in the Arctic. He and his men, for example, dressed Eskimo-style in loose-fitting fur garments, which were light, warm, and waterproof. Scott's party, in contrast, wore heavy woolen clothing, which became damp and uncomfortable in the cold. When Amundsen's party reached the South Pole, they proudly raised the Norwegian flag with the words: "We are planting you, dear flag, at the South Pole, and we name this area, where the South Pole is found, The Land of King Haakon VIIth." The Norwegian party celebrated with a special dinner, but "there was no champagne," Amundsen noted. "We were content to eat the meat of a seal and outside we could hear the flag fluttering." Before they departed, a member of the expedition passed out cigars to his weary but triumphant comrades "as a memory of the South Pole."*

# Determined to Succeed: Amundsen Reaches the South Pole

*Few explorers have met with such spectacular success in both the Arctic and Antarctic as Roald Amundsen (1872–1928). Training himself from childhood to be a polar explorer, he always approached his expeditions with iron determination and meticulous preparation. Sailing in the* Gjoa, *he finally realized a goal of generations of explorers when he navigated the Northwest Passage in 1903–06. On December 14, 1911, he became the first to reach the South Pole, beating Scott's expedition by only 35 days. In 1918–20 he was the first to follow Baron Nordenskjold on a successful Northeast Passage. After failing to fly over the North Pole by plane in 1925, Amundsen finally made the trip in a dirigible, the* Norge, *in 1926. Two years later he died in an Arctic search for Umberto Nobile, the Italian commander of the* Norge.*

The South Pole is a lonely place. Stretching away in every direction is a scene of utter desolation: just a flat, windswept expanse of ice and snow, blindingly white in the bright Antarctic summer, shrouded in inky black through the long south-polar night. Uninviting. Inhospitable. And challenging.

Late in the afternoon of December 14, 1911, the all-enveloping silence at the southern end of the earth's axis was shattered for the first time by the sound of human voices. Where no man's foot had trod before, Roald Amundsen and four Norwegian companions congratulated each other. They were the first men ever to reach the South Pole.

It was one of the great achievements in the history of exploration. Yet Amundsen's reaction was subdued. "The goal was reached, the journey ended," he later wrote. "I cannot say—though I know it would sound much more effective—that the object of my life was attained. That would be romancing rather too barefacedly. I had better be honest and admit straight out that I have never known any man to be placed in such a diametrically opposite position to the goal of his desires as I was at that moment. The region around the North Pole—well, yes, the North Pole itself—had attracted me from childhood, and here I was at the South Pole. Can anything more topsy-turvy be imagined?"

These reflections were the thoughts of a man of strong purpose who viewed life not as one adventure but as many. As he himself admitted, he had not become an explorer by chance. "My career," he once explained, "has been a steady progress toward a definite goal since I was fifteen years of age. Whatever I have accomplished . . . has been the result of lifelong planning, painstaking preparation, and the hardest kind of conscientious work."

The spark of Amundsen's ambition was ignited when, as a boy, he read an account of England's great Arctic explorer Sir John Franklin, whose unsuccessful search for the Northwest Passage had met with astonishing hardships. The tale of courage in the face of adversity, said Amundsen, "thrilled me as nothing I had ever read before."

Determined to prepare himself for a life of adventure in the Arctic, he continued to read voraciously everything he could find on the subject of polar exploration. The boy began sleeping with his bedroom windows opened wide, even in the depths of winter. (When his mother protested, he told her he liked fresh air; later he was to explain, "of course it was really part of my conscientious hardening process.") Whenever he could get away from school, he took to the hills and mountains that surround Oslo, "increasing my skill in traversing ice and snow and hardening my muscles for the coming great adventure."

Amundsen considered service in the Norwegian Army the next logical step in his training. His eyesight was so poor that he knew he could not pass the army's physical examination, but with characteristic determi-

## Amundsen's "Gjoa," First Ship to Sail the Northwest Passage

The 19th century witnessed renewed interest in the Northwest Passage, a navigable water route across the top of North America linking the Atlantic and Pacific Oceans. Great Britain, fearful that Russian exploration of the North Pacific threatened Canada, took the lead in the search for the fabled passage. Parliament, in fact, offered cash prizes for Arctic exploration to stimulate the search. As a result, British expeditions in the early 19th century succeeded in charting large regions of hitherto unexplored polar waters. Paradoxically, the most significant of 19th-century British Arctic ventures, the Franklin expedition, ended in total failure. Sir John Franklin and his crew of 129 men aboard the ships *Erebus* and *Terror* were never heard from again after they left England in 1845.

The search for the Franklin party, however, led to the most extensive exploration of the Canadian Arctic that had ever been undertaken. One search party, in fact, under Sir Robert McClure, com-

pleted a northwest passage, but only after abandoning their ship and traveling across the ice on sledges. Even before Roald Amundsen's historic voyage, the quest for the fate of the Franklin party had yielded so much information on Arctic waterways that it was possible to chart a theoretical route through the polar icecap. All that remained, as Amundsen himself admitted, was to test whether such a theoretical route was actually navigable. "We knew there was a sea passage round North America," he wrote, "but we did not know whether this passage was practicable for ships and no one had yet navigated through it."

In his converted herring boat, the *Gjoa*, seen at right riding out an Arctic storm, Amundsen and his crew of six pushed their way through ice-clogged Arctic waters and became the first men to navigate the Northwest Passage successfully. The Norwegian explorer described the joy with which his crew broke through the ice that blocked the last leg

of their historic voyage through the passage: "It seemed as if the old *Gjoa* knew she had reached a critical moment. She had to tackle two large masses of ice that barred her way to the Northwest Passage; and now she charged again into them to force them asunder and slip

---

nation, he decided to try it anyway. And there his years of exercise paid off. At the induction center, the examining physician was so impressed by the young recruit's splendid physique that he called in a group of officers from another room to show off this find of his—a stark naked and very embarrassed Roald Amundsen. "In his enthusiasm over the rest of my physical equipment," Amundsen reported with amusement, "the good old doctor entirely forgot to examine my eyes. Consequently, I passed with flying colors and got my training in the army."

His progress was briefly interrupted by his mother's wish that he become a doctor. Though he had no interest in such a career, Amundsen dutifully began to study medicine. By the time he was 21, however, both his parents had died. Amundsen immediately dropped his medical studies and openly announced his intention to become an explorer.

He soon learned that it was to be no easy life. At 22, he and his brother set out on a training expedition in the dead of winter to cross a range of mountains west of Oslo on skis. Ill-equipped and poorly provisioned, before they were done the two had been frozen, starved, snowbound, frightened, and thoroughly defeated. They returned home lucky to be alive. "Think of it!" wrote Amundsen with dismay as he summed up the whole adventure. "It was part of my preliminary training for my polar career . . . [yet it was] severer than the experience for which it was preparation, and well-nigh ended the career before it began."

But Roald Amundsen learned his lesson. Never again did he launch an expedition unprepared. Indeed, for the rest of his life, careful planning was to be a hallmark of all his explorations.

Amundsen had been struck by what he called "one fatal weakness common to many of the preceding Arctic expeditions": Their leaders were seldom ship captains. As a result, once they set sail, the expeditions were under divided command. Amundsen decided he had better qualify as a licensed mariner and in 1894 signed on as a seaman aboard a whaling vessel.

Three years later, at age 25, he became first mate of the *Belgica*, the ship of a Belgian-sponsored Antarctic expedition. With international membership and the best of intentions, the group sailed from Antwerp in August 1897 on what was to be a brief probe of the coast. The result was disaster. Woefully inexperienced Antarctic explorers, the leaders of the expedition allowed the south-polar winter to surprise them and freeze the ship in. Before long, the *Belgica* was a speck of black surrounded by a seemingly endless white desert, broken only by a few channels of water that ended in walls of ice farther off.

In May 1898, two months after they became locked in the "vise of this ice field," the men saw the Antarctic sun set for the winter. It did not rise again until the end of July. Without winter clothes or rations, seamen and scientists alike soon feared for their lives. Two men actually went insane in the months that followed, and all but three came down with scurvy.

*Heroes of the Arctic and Antarctic*

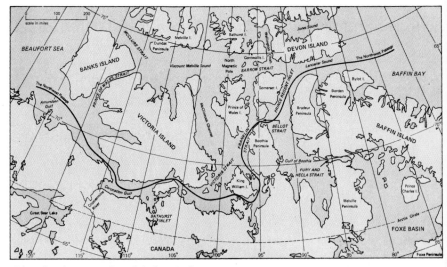

through. The lads attacked the ice on both sides with boat hooks, a tough desperate fight. The ice yielded a fraction of an inch at a time, but at last it gave way. A wild shout of triumph broke forth as the vessel slipped through. The barrier was broken. We were out in open waters with a clear homeward track before us." The map above shows Amundsen's 1903–06 route through the passage.

In 1969 the specially constructed icebreaker *Manhattan* made the most ambitious transit of the Arctic seas since the voyage of Amundsen's *Gjoa*. The *Manhattan* plowed through ice-obstructed water in an attempt to prove that the Northwest Passage is a viable route for international trade. Though the *Manhattan* completed her voyage, the conditions are too difficult to allow for regular runs by commercial ships.

When even the captain fell deathly ill, Amundsen suddenly found himself in command of the apparently doomed ship. Rising to the occasion, he calmly and methodically sent parties out to hunt for seals and penguins and set the men to work making warm clothing out of blankets.

Eventually, after months of agonizing labor, the few able-bodied crewmen were able to dig, hack, and blast a pathway through the frozen polar sea to an open lane of water. Even then the *Belgica* was not completely free. For a month more, she was caught at the end of her sealane by an unexpected pack of ice that would not yield to blasting or digging. Beyond it, the open sea rose and fell, tossing the floes against the trapped ship.

On March 28, 1899—some 13 months after she had become entrapped—the *Belgica*, under Amundsen's command, finally broke through the barrier and set sail to the north. She had been the first ship ever to winter in the Antarctic—however unintentionally.

"I got my skipper's license," wrote Amundsen of the following year, "and began making definite plans for my first expedition."

Such resilience was typical of Amundsen. Whether he experienced triumph or defeat, discovery or disaster, he was always ready to respond with another plan for another expedition. His new proposal was to search for the famed (and perhaps fabled) Northwest Passage that his boyhood hero, Franklin, had sought in vain.

Amundsen realized that his expedition would need a scientific purpose as well as an explorer's goal if he was to gain financial backing. Polar magnetism, he decided, would be a suitable subject, and with the same deliberation that characterized all his actions, he traveled to Hamburg to master the science. Nor was that the only task he set himself over the next three years. Besides studying terrestrial magnetism, he practiced navigation in the North Sea, worked out careful plans for his expedition, and raised money to pay for it.

In Norway he purchased the *Gjoa*, a 47-ton, shallow-draft fishing smack 72 feet long and 11 feet wide. He chose a six-man crew of skilled sailors and scientists. He selected scientific instruments, food, clothing, and gear. By the time he was ready to set out, the ship's hold was packed so tightly with supplies and the decks were piled so high with boxes that the *Gjoa* barely rode above the waterline.

By now Amundsen owed so many people so much money that he found himself confronted with "a supreme crisis." On June 16, 1903, the creditor to whom he owed the most threatened to have Amundsen arrested unless he was paid within 24 hours. "The ruin of my years of work seemed imminent," Amundsen recalled. Desperate, he "resolved upon a desperate expedient." Hastily summoning his crew, he set sail from Christiania (Oslo) at midnight in a torrential downpour. By dawn, the *Gjoa* was on the open sea, and Amundsen's great adventure was underway.

From Norway, the *Gjoa* crossed the North Atlantic and sailed up the west coast of Greenland to the northern end of Baffin Island. There she headed west into

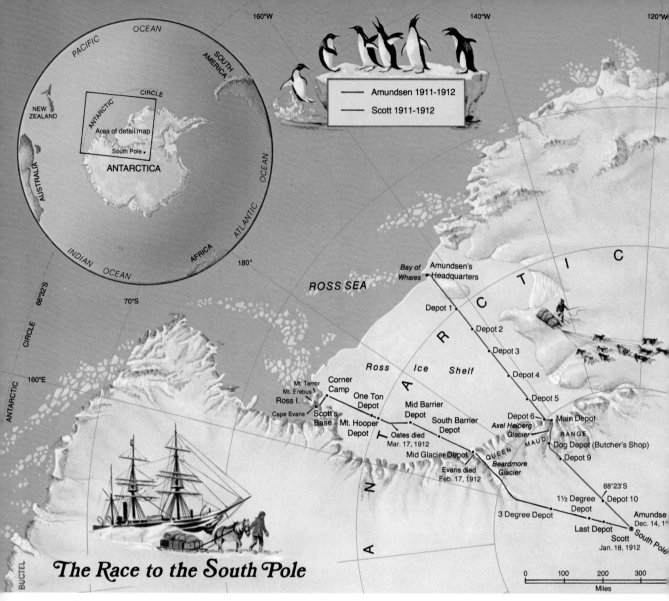

Amundsen 1911-1912
Scott 1911-1912

## The Race to the South Pole

**Both Amundsen and his rival,** *the English explorer Robert Scott, approached the South Pole from bases on the Ross Sea, but Amundsen's base at the Bay of Whales was 60 miles closer to the pole, an important factor in a land where every mile traveled required great effort. Both explorers also crossed the Ross Ice Shelf, but Scott's party, which left two weeks after Amundsen's,* encountered repeated snowstorms, while the Norwegians had relatively easy going. Amundsen's party had more difficulty ascending the Queen Maud Range than Scott's did the Beardmore Glacier, but once on the great central plateau, Amundsen's journeys to and from the pole were quick. Scott's fatigued party, however, met with disaster on the way back and ultimately perished.

Lancaster Sound and began to thread her way southward among the maze of islands beyond the Canadian mainland. Shallow water, fog, and raging winds made for slow going, but by summer's end, Amundsen found a natural winter harbor on King William Island, to the northwest of Hudson Bay. Besides being "a veritable haven of rest for weary travelers," the harbor was close enough to the north magnetic pole to permit precise scientific observations.

The men named the harbor Gjoa Haven and in September 1903 set about establishing the base that would be their headquarters for the next two years. They built their observatories and equipped them with instru-

ments so delicate that they had been packed in crates held together with copper nails rather than standard steel nails, which might have thrown the magnetic apparatus out of kilter. They built kennels for the sled dogs they had taken on board in Greenland, and they built a house that Amundsen called "warm and weatherproof," with "every convenience we needed." "When all was done," he declared, "we could not have been more snugly housed anywhere in civilization."

As the months wore on, the men hunted, traded with Eskimos, and explored nearby islands. After many lessons from friendly Eskimos, Amundsen learned to drive a team of dogs, an experience that convinced him dogs were invaluable for polar exploration. He also noted the clothing the natives wore and made a complete collection of Eskimo outfits. Weapons, food, customs—all were of great interest to Amundsen, for he realized that these people were the true masters of survival in polar regions.

The expedition's two years of scientific work included observations so precise and thorough that the data the men were to bring home would give the experts on polar magnetism material for 20 years' evaluation—a fact in which Amundsen never ceased to take pride. After all, a few years before he had known nothing of the science; now he was a major contributor to it.

On August 13, 1905, with observations of the north magnetic pole completed, the *Gjoa* resumed her westward passage through fog and drifting ice. Along the way, the ship passed a place where two casualties of the ill-fated Franklin expedition were buried. Amundsen remembered his boyhood hero, "and with colors flying in honor of the dead we went by the grave in solemn silence . . . honoring our unfortunate predecessors."

Slowly, carefully, the ship groped her way westward through uncharted waters that grew ever more shallow. Surrounded by drifting chunks of ice and blanketed by dense fog, Amundsen was forced to lower a boat to scout ahead of the *Gjoa* and take soundings. At one point, Amundsen exclaimed, "we had just an inch of water to spare beneath our keel!"

Tension mounted as the boat proceeded to the west. As everyone on board was well aware, they soon would be sailing into well-known waters charted by ships probing eastward past Alaska. If their way was not blocked by shallow water, land, or ice, the last link in the Northwest Passage soon would be completed.

Amundsen, pacing the deck, became so excited he could scarcely sleep or eat. "Day after day," he recalled, "we crept along, sounding our depth . . . trying here, there, everywhere to nose into a channel that would carry us clear to the known waters of the west." At last, on the morning of August 26, his second in command burst into his cabin shouting, "A sail! A sail!"

"What a glorious sight that was," Amundsen exulted, "the distant outline of a whaling vessel in the west. It meant the end of years of hope and toil . . . all doubts of our success in making the Northwest Passage were at an end. Victory was ours!"

The passage was not yet quite complete, however. Before long, the *Gjoa*—along with a dozen whaling ships in the area—was frozen into the Arctic ice for another winter. Amundsen, bursting with the news of his great conquest, refused to remain on board. On October 24 he set out by dogsled for Eagle City, Alaska, 500 miles away, where he knew there was an army post with a telegraph office. The trip, which involved crossing a mountain range 9,000 feet high, was his first experience with long-distance sledding. But on December 5, 1905, he arrived at Eagle City and broadcast his news to

the world: A dream of explorers since the discovery of the New World had at last come true.

The following year he sailed the *Gjoa* triumphantly to Nome, Alaska, and then to San Francisco, where cheering crowds welcomed him as a hero. He spent the next two years lecturing to audiences all over the world, raising enough money to pay off all the creditors he had evaded that rainy midnight when he was so close to being jailed.

With his Northwest Passage and north magnetic pole projects completed and paid for, 36-year-old Roald Amundsen began to prepare for the greatest of all Arctic adventures—discovery of the North Pole. Since he was now a famous man, raising funds was no longer a problem. He planned to drift over the pole in a ship frozen into the ice that covers the Arctic Ocean, an exploit that had been attempted in the mid-1890's by the illustrious Norwegian explorer Fridtjof Nansen. He even arranged to use Nansen's stout history-making ship, the *Fram*.

Then, late in 1909, Amundsen's Arctic plans were suddenly sent into a spin. That year the tenacious American Robert Edwin Peary cabled out the news that he had reached the North Pole. "At that same instant," wrote Amundsen, "I saw quite clearly that . . . if the expedition was to be saved, it was necessary to act quickly and without hesitation. Just as rapidly as the message had traveled over the cables I decided on my change of front—to turn . . . to the South," for now the South Pole was the only polar conquest that remained. Since the Englishman Robert Falcon Scott was known to be preparing for his second try at it, Amundsen decided there was only one thing to do—he must beat Scott to the South Pole.

Amundsen kept his change of plan a secret from his financial backers, even from the members of his crew. Claiming he still intended to drift over the North Pole for purely scientific purposes, he set sail from Norway on August 9, 1910. (The *Fram*'s cargo of 100 Greenland sled dogs and materials for building a hut big enough to house 10 bunks and a kitchen should have been obvious enough clues that he planned an overland trek from a land base.) As soon as the *Fram* crossed the Equator, the men were informed that they were heading south for Antarctica.

The new year, 1911, found the *Fram* in a nook on the fringe of the Ross Ice Shelf, a vast expanse of ice that covers the sea in a huge indentation in the Antarctic mainland. Amundsen had chosen this spot—the Bay of Whales—because he knew it was 60 miles closer to the pole than Scott's base at the far end of the ice shelf. He immediately established the expedition's headquarters some two miles inland on the ice, and the men began transporting equipment and supplies ashore.

In February the Norwegians were visited by members of Scott's expedition. The meeting was cordial enough, but both groups knew, as Scott himself put it,

## Antarctica, the Earth's Last Unconquered Continent, Is a Wilderness of Mountains and Ice

Unlike the Arctic, which is an ocean covered by floating ice, Antarctica is a mountainous continent of almost 5.5 million square miles. All but small parts of it is covered with an ice shelf up to 4,000 feet thick. Surrounded by the roughest seas in the world, it is also the colder of the two polar areas: The lowest temperature ever recorded on earth, −126.9° F, was recorded in Antarctica.

Pack ice (1) and icebergs (5) surrounding the continent kept early explorers from landing on its frozen shores. Much of that shoreline is covered with precipitous walls of glacial ice like the area near Palmer Station on the Antarctic Peninsula (3), a long finger of land that points toward the southern tip of South America. Yet for all its forbidding cold and the darkness that envelops it for half a year, Antarctica is a land of awesome beauty, particularly when sunsets (7) backlight its mountains, some of which range well over 15,000 feet.

Despite the harsh environment, Antarctica has a variety of animal life and even some vegetation, especially on its rocky island fringe. Fur seals (2) attracted some of the area's earliest explorers in the 19th century. Penguins, like those dwarfed by a giant iceberg (4), and sea birds (6) nest by the shores, and the ocean itself is home to the now-endangered baleen whale. Today at least eight nations, including the United States, maintain Antarctic bases.

*Heroes of the Arctic and Antarctic*

"that Amundsen's plan is a very serious menace to ours." Besides being closer to the pole, Amundsen, with dog teams, would be able to start his journey earlier in the season than Scott could with the ponies he planned to use for hauling his sleds.

Through February and March, Amundsen's men laid out seven supply depots and trailmarkers on the ice shelf for their journey to the pole the following spring. The *Fram* and her skeleton crew sailed off to New Zealand, not to return until the next year. In April the sun disappeared for the season, and the land party settled down to make scientific observations, improve the land base, and build sleds and equipment.

The sun reappeared in August, but for nearly two months the weather remained too cold for traveling. Finally, on October 19, 1911, the race for the pole began. Mounted on skis, Amundsen and four companions started south across the ice shelf. They drove four lightweight sleds, each one pulled by 13 dogs. A network of deep, dangerous crevasses in the ice shelf caused occasional delays, but with a marked trail and supply depots already laid out along the way, the party made good time. The dogs were in such fine condition that Amundsen frequently tied a rope to a sled and was towed along behind. "Yes, that was a pleasant surprise," he commented. "We had never dreamed of driving on skis to the Pole!"

Once they reached the mainland, progress was abruptly slowed by the mountainous barrier of the Queen Maud Range. Inching their way to the top via the Axel Heiberg Glacier took days of agonizing toil. Pushing the sleds, pulling with the dogs, they made their way around hidden crevasses, over huge hummocks, across endless waves of ice frozen so hard they had to use rock-climbing equipment to move on it. Time and again, men, dogs, and sleds were nearly lost down gaps in the surface that seemed to drop off into bottomless space. At one point, when Amundsen called ahead to ask, "What does the crevasse look like?" the answer came back, "Oh, as usual, no bottom."

At the top of the mountains, a vast, gently rising plateau stretched away to the south. With the worst of the pulling now past, all the dogs were no longer necessary. At a camp the men named the Butcher's Shop, Amundsen had about two-thirds of the animals shot to conserve food and to supply meat for both the men and remaining dogs. It was a grim business, but it was all part of Amundsen's plan.

On December 7 the party reached 88°23' S, the "farthest south" record set by Ernest Shackleton in 1909. Amundsen, skiing ahead of the rest, had given the order to fly the Norwegian flag the moment they reached that latitude. Suddenly hearing a rousing cheer, he looked back to see the banner flapping in the wind. "No other moment of the whole trip affected me like this," he confessed. "The tears forced their way to my eyes; by no effort of will could I keep them back. It

**A member of Amundsen's party** *is pictured above at the South Pole with the sledge dogs that contributed so greatly to the Norwegian explorer's triumph over Scott's party. Amundsen began his journey with 52 dogs. The weaker animals, however, were slaughtered to provide meat for the others, and Amundsen returned from the pole with only 11 of his sledge dogs left alive.*

was the flag yonder that conquered me and my will. Luckily I . . . had time to pull myself together and master my feelings before reaching my comrades."

The men were now within 97 miles of their goal. Down to 17 dogs and 3 sleds, they lightened their load by establishing their last supply depot (Depot 10) nearby. (To make sure they found it on the way back, they planted a long line of black sticks east and west across their trail.) Then they continued on their way, meters on the sleds ticking off the miles traveled toward their destination each day.

Suddenly, the weather cleared and the surface became smooth and unobstructed. It was, thought Amundsen, as though the elements had anticipated them. And yet there was always that gnawing doubt as to what they would find at the pole. At the rate they were traveling, wrote Amundsen, "we must reach the goal first, there could be no doubt about that. And yet—and yet . . ."

By December 13 they knew they had only a few more miles to go. "It was like the eve of some great festival that night in the tent," recalled Amundsen, who "had the same feeling that I can remember as a little boy on the night before Christmas Eve—an intense expectation of what was going to happen."

The next morning they were up early and on their way. Straining their eyes to spot any signs of life on the horizon, they saw only "the endless flat plain ahead." Finally, at 3 p.m. on December 14, 1911, they were there—90° S, the South Pole. "Thus," wrote Amundsen, "the veil was torn aside for all time, and one of the greatest of our earth's secrets had ceased to exist."

They stayed at the pole almost four days, alternating celebration with the business of completing scientific observations. They put up a small tent with a Norwegian flag fluttering from its pole and left two notes inside, one for Scott and another for the king of Norway, which they asked Scott to take back in case they did not return. "It was a solemn moment when we bared our heads and bade farewell," Amundsen recalled. "We drove at once into our old tracks and followed them. Many were the times we turned to send a last look. . . . The vaporous white air set in again, and it was not long before our little flag disappeared from view."

On January 25, 1912, they arrived back at their base camp. They had journeyed 1,860 miles in 99 days. Their dogs were down to 11, and the men had suffered frostbite, windburn, snow blindness, and exhaustion. But they had triumphed. They were the first men ever to reach the South Pole.

Weary and weatherbeaten, the five explorers lumbered aboard the *Fram*, which had returned to the Bay of Whales just two weeks earlier. And no one even mentioned the South Pole! The seamen were embarrassed to ask for fear that Amundsen had failed; the explorers did not want to boast. Finally, in the most casual way, someone asked, "Have you been there?" And then at last, with all the men of the expedition together again, there was cheering, laughter, and one great final celebration of their achievement.

Amundsen soon decided to launch another expedition, this time to his beloved Arctic. His plan once again was to repeat Nansen's attempt to drift by ship over the North Pole. Since he disliked the business of fundraising, he decided to spend his own money (all of it, as it turned out) to outfit the venture. Supplies, food, dogs, clothing—he would have the best. He even designed and built his own ship, the *Maud*, and christened her, not with champagne but with a block of ice. "I want you from the beginning to get a taste of your true element," he announced at the launching ceremony. "For you have been built for the ice, you are to spend the best years of your life in the ice, and there you are to fulfill your destiny."

The *Maud*'s destiny, as it happened, was one disappointment after another. Embarking from Tromso, Norway, in 1918, she sailed into the Arctic Ocean, only to spend her first two winters helplessly frozen into shore ice. She was abandoned by many of her crew, soon required extensive repairs, and wherever she went, seemed to be the scene of accidents. Amundsen returned to Norway, where his doctor advised him to give up exploring before it cost him his life.

The voyage of the *Maud* had already cost him his fortune, but Amundsen was not about to quit. His newest idea was to be first to fly a plane over the North Pole. But he had no more money, and over the next two years his finances worsened. It seemed, he mused, "as if the future had closed solidly against me, and that my career as an explorer had come to an inglorious end." He was 52 years old, broke, and so deeply in debt

---

## Crossing the North Pole by Balloon, Airplane, or Dirigible Was a Dangerous Undertaking

Air travel ushered in a new era of polar exploration. One of the pioneering attempts to fly over the polar icecap, however, ended in failure. In 1897 Salomon August Andrée, pictured on the Swedish stamp on the opposite page (column two, top), perished while attempting to balloon over the North Pole. Despite such early disasters, Roald Amundsen was enthusiastic about air reconnaissance of the polar regions. "Certainly human power and skill had overcome and conquered vast tracts of this unknown whiteness," he wrote, "but enormous tracts remained unexplored—tracts which could now be reached from the air."

Amundsen and wealthy American sportsman Lincoln Ellsworth unsuccessfully attempted a flight over the North Pole in 1925, but engine malfunction forced their two Dornier-Wal flying boats to land on the ice just 90 miles from the pole (near right). The following year, however, two successful flights over the North Pole were made. On May 9, 1926, Americans Richard Byrd and Floyd Bennett piloted their tri-motored Fokker airplane over the pole and back. The picture opposite (column three) shows the two men returning to base on the Spitsbergen islands (now Svalbard).

Recently, questions have been raised about whether Byrd and Bennett actually made a crossing of the pole. Some experts have calculated that they would have needed an absolute minimum of 20 hours for the flight. Byrd and Bennett, however, took only 15½ hours to complete their round-trip journey.

On May 11, two days after Byrd's flight, Amundsen, Ellsworth, and Italian Umberto Nobile took off in the dirigible *Norge* (column two, bottom), and on the following day, Lincoln Ellsworth's birthday, they passed over the North Pole. When the Norwegian, Italian, and American flags were dropped from the dirigible to the ice below, Ellsworth experienced "an extraordinary, quite indescribable feeling. . . . When again will a man plant the flag of his country at the Pole on his birthday?" In 1928 Nobile again attempted a transpolar flight in the dirigible *Italia*. It crashlanded, and Amundsen led a search party. Nobile was rescued, but Roald Amundsen vanished in the far north that he had loved so well.

*Heroes of the Arctic and Antarctic*

that he calculated it would take another 52 years to raise all the money he needed.

His problem was solved when, alone one night in a hotel room in New York, he received a phone call from a total stranger. The caller was a wealthy young American, Lincoln Ellsworth, who, to Amundsen's amazement, offered to finance the polar flight. On May 21, 1925, the two took off in two planes from Spitsbergen, their destination Alaska. But by early the next morning, one plane had sprung a leak in its fuel tank, and the other had developed engine trouble. Both planes went down on the ice about 90 miles from the pole, and one was damaged beyond repair. It was not until June 15 that the expedition's crew was able to repair the other, hack a runway across the rough ice, and get airborne again. Overloaded with the weight of all the men, the plane headed directly back for land but crashed in the sea off Spitsbergen, and the explorers had to be rescued by ship.

Strangely, this most unsuccessful of adventures caught the imagination of the world. Once again a hero, Amundsen was sought after everywhere. His return to Oslo, with hundreds of boats coming out to meet him, throngs of people in the streets for the parade in his honor, dinner at the royal palace with the king himself—all this Amundsen described as "the undying memory of the best in a lifetime."

Though disenchanted with planes, Amundsen was convinced that a continent-to-continent flight across the pole was possible—by dirigible. Such an airship was obtained by Amundsen and Ellsworth, after some negotiation, from the Italian government. Christened the *Norge*, it took off from Spitsbergen on May 11, 1926. On board were Amundsen, Lincoln Ellsworth, and Umberto Nobile, the craft's designer and pilot. The next day at 1:25 a.m., the men jubilantly dropped the Norwegian, American, and Italian flags on the North Pole. Then, on May 14, they set down in the little village of Teller, Alaska, 50 miles from Nome. They had flown 3,391 miles in 72 hours and had been the first men to travel from Europe to North America by air.

Now began the most triumphant tour of Amundsen's life. In the United States, Norway, and Japan, crowds cheered him as never before. But trouble had been brewing between Amundsen and Nobile. Shortly after the flight, when the crew arrived in Seattle, Amundsen and Ellsworth still wore their rough work clothes as they greeted the crowds; Nobile appeared in a brilliant dress uniform. Since weight had been so important that only essentials were to be taken aboard the *Norge*, resentment arose. In time, Amundsen began to criticize Nobile's design of the airship, and Nobile began to disparage Amundsen's role in the flight. Before long, a feud developed.

Even so, on May 28, 1928, when 56 year-old Amundsen learned that Nobile's new dirigible, the *Italia*, had gone down in the Arctic, he set out without hesitation to rescue his former colleague. Months later, a float from his seaplane was found off northern Norway, but Amundsen was never seen again. (Nobile and his party were rescued on June 22.)

Thus the man who since his youth had been irresistibly attracted to the Arctic found his final resting place there. His old friend Fridtjof Nansen no doubt echoed the sentiments of many when he wrote of Amundsen: "He found an unmarked grave under the quiet ice, but surely his name will long shimmer like our northern lights. He came to us, a blazing star that burst upon the darkened heavens. Then, suddenly, the star went out, and we are left, gazing sadly at the empty spot."

**Beaten in the race for the South Pole,** *Capt. Robert Scott (above) became as famous in defeat as Roald Amundsen did in victory. Scott's party left vivid records of their adventures in the pictures of expedition photographer Herbert Ponting and the watercolors of Dr. Edward Wilson. At left is a Ponting photograph of the* Terra Nova, *Scott's ship, taken from the cavern of an iceberg. Below, Wilson painted some of Scott's men harnessed to the sledges they hauled across the Antarctic vastness. Untrained in driving dog teams, Scott had concluded on his previous 1901–04 Antarctic expedition that dogs were unreliable for transport. He also disliked the idea of killing the dogs for food when their usefulness was over, a tactic Scott wished to avoid. Scott's expedition published a small newspaper, the* South Polar Times. *The coat of arms with two penguins (opposite) appeared on the title page of the first edition.*

*Chapter Twenty-Eight. In a dramatic race to reach the South Pole ahead of Amundsen's rival expedition, an English naval officer leads his men across hundreds of miles of frozen desolation. Exhausted and disappointed at their goal, the group displays great courage and loyalty on the fatal return trip, enduring misfortune and foul weather to the end.*

# Destined to Command: Scott in the Antarctic

*Robert Falcon Scott (1868–1912) was a giant of the Heroic Age of Antarctic exploration, the first two decades of the 20th century. A British Navy career officer, Scott led his first Antarctic venture from 1901 to 1904. His expedition did not reach the South Pole, but he was given a hero's welcome when he returned to Great Britain. Promoted to the rank of captain, he married artist Kathleen Bruce in 1908 and was the father of a son (Peter) when he left on his second voyage in 1910. He was eager to better the mark of Ernest Shackleton, who served with his first expedition. In 1908 Shackleton had led his own Antarctic party, which fell only 97 nautical miles short of reaching the South Pole. Scott, however, left England unaware that Roald Amundsen planned to challenge his intention to be the first explorer to reach the South Pole.*

Robert Falcon Scott's destiny in the frozen wastes of Antarctica was sealed a quarter of a century earlier beneath a blazing tropical sun. The year was 1887, and Scott, a midshipman in the British Royal Navy, was on training maneuvers at the Caribbean island of St. Kitts. Watching his every move was Sir Clements Markham, who was visiting his cousin, Scott's commanding officer. An influential member of the Royal Geographical Society, Markham was even then beginning to lay the groundwork for a future British Antarctic expedition.

Markham, who was in time to earn recognition as the father of British polar exploration, was firmly convinced that youth was more important than experience in the leader of an expedition. A young man, he believed, would be more open to new ideas, better able to improvise in emergencies. "How," he snorted, "can novel forms of effort be expected from stiff old organisms hampered by experience!" Scott, he concluded, had just the combination of stamina and resilience he was looking for. He was "the destined man to command the Antarctic expedition."

Clearly a man who could keep a secret, Markham never mentioned his plans to Scott when they met from time to time over the next 12 years—not until they happened upon each other one June day in 1899 on a crowded London street. Scott, by then a lieutenant in the navy, crossed the street to greet his old friend, now president of the Royal Geographical Society, and the two fell into casual conversation as they threaded their way toward Sir Clements' home.

"That afternoon I learned for the first time that there was such a thing as a prospective Antarctic expedition," Scott confessed, adding that "two days later I wrote applying to command it, and a year after that I was officially appointed." This was exactly the sort of dangerous assignment that Scott, perhaps subconsciously, was looking for.

With zest and enthusiasm, he threw himself into the task of organizing the expedition and overseeing every detail in its preparation. On August 5, 1901, his specially designed ship, the *Discovery*, steamed out into the English Channel and headed for the south. By the time it returned in 1904, Scott, at 36, was a seasoned veteran of Antarctic exploration. He had successfully weathered two winters there. He personally had made the first balloon flight over the frozen continent. With two companions he had sledged to 82° 17′ S, establishing a new "farthest south" record. His men had mapped and made topographical surveys of large areas, gathered hundreds of geological specimens, collected masses of data on weather and climate. Scott, in short, had observed, mapped, and explored the forbidding southern continent as no one ever had before. He came home to England a national hero.

In the years that followed, Scott resumed his career in the navy, married, and became a father. But the lure of the South Pole persisted. Gradually, he resolved to return again to Antarctica, this time on his own. The

**Pounded by ice floes,** *Scott's ship, the* Terra Nova *(above), weathered punishing Antarctic storms. "I have become strangely attached to the* Terra Nova," *he wrote. Struggling onward to the south, "she seemed like a living thing fighting a great fight."*

the ponies for hauling heavy loads. He had been advised time and again to use dogs and only dogs, but he knew from bitter experience that many of them would be doomed to die from starvation, exhaustion, exposure, or accident. Even more repugnant to Scott was the commonly used system of killing off weak dogs, one by one, to feed both men and remaining dogs. "One cannot calmly contemplate the murder of animals which possess such intelligence and individuality," he explained, "which have frequently such endearing qualities, and which very possibly one had learnt to regard as friends and companions."

But there was something more than sentimentality involved. In the final stages of his journey, Scott planned to rely exclusively on man-hauling—pulling the loaded sleds by hand—which he regarded as more noble and manly no matter how exhausting it would be for the men. "In my mind," he once had written, "no journey ever made with dogs can approach the height of that fine conception which is realized when a party of men go forth to face hardships, dangers, and difficulties with their own unaided efforts, and by days and

next trip would be financed not by some learned scientific society but by public contributions. True, he planned once again to carry out a full program of scientific studies. (He recruited a formidable team of scientists, including biologists, geologists, a meteorologist, a physicist, and three medical doctors.) But as Scott himself publicly announced, his main objective was "to reach the South Pole, and to secure for the British Empire the honour of this achievement." It was the last of the great geographic goals.

His preparations took on an added air of urgency when in January 1909 Ernest Shackleton, who had been with Scott on his 1903 "farthest south," set a new record—he came within 97 nautical (111.6 statute) miles of the South Pole. It was just the sort of feat the public loved to read about in newspapers, which gave full coverage to each new polar exploit. And the newspapers duly noted the event when 42-year-old Scott's new ship, the *Terra Nova,* set out in June 1910 to test British manhood in the great unknown.

When the *Terra Nova* docked at Melbourne, Australia, in October, Scott's plans received an unexpected jolt. Awaiting him was a telegram from the Norwegian explorer Roald Amundsen: "Beg leave to inform you proceeding Antarctica. Amundsen." Apparently, the Norwegian, whose lifelong ambition to be first at the North Pole had recently been forestalled by Robert Peary, had set his sights on the South Pole instead. So there was to be a race.

Concerned but undeterred, Scott continued on his way. In New Zealand he took on the last of his supplies, including 19 shaggy Manchurian ponies and 33 Siberian sled dogs. Scott also had three experimental motorized sleds on board, but he planned to rely mainly on

### Scott's Unlucky Ponies

Trouble with the ponies began in their stalls aboard the *Terra Nova.* Despite Lieutenant Oates' constant care (right), two of them died during a storm. The surviving ponies spent the winter stabled behind the expedition's quarters. Scott recorded the antics of one who habitually took great mouthfuls of snow. "When the snow chills his inside he shuffles about with all four legs and wears a most fretful and aggrieved expression." The ponies, however, proved woefully inadequate for hauling supplies. They could not withstand the fierce Antarctic blizzards. Miserable when the wind-whipped snow penetrated their shaggy coats (below), the ponies died one by one or were killed to end their suffering. Strangely, Scott, who was revolted at the thought of eating dog meat, had no such scruples about ponies. "We have all taken to horse meat," he casually noted in his journal, "and are so well fed hunger isn't even thought of."

*Heroes of the Arctic and Antarctic*

## A Memorial to the Lost Expedition, Scott's Hut Still Stands Below the Summit of Erebus

More than 8,000 men applied to become members of Scott's second Antarctic expedition. The final party of more than 20 was mainly English but also included the Australian scientists Frank Debenham and T. Griffith Taylor and Canadian geologist Charles S. Wright. The expedition built winter quarters on Cape Evans, near Mount Erebus, an active volcano rising 13,202 feet from the Antarctic coast (right). Scott described their dwelling, called the Hut, in glowing terms: "The hut is becoming the most comfortable dwelling place imaginable. We have made unto ourselves a truly seductive home, within the walls of which peace, quiet and comfort reign supreme. . . . The word hut is misleading. Our residence is really a house of considerable size, in every respect the finest that has ever been erected in polar regions; 50 feet long by 25 feet wide and 9 feet to the eaves." Scott was equally enthusiastic about the grandeur of the Antarctic scenery that encircled the Hut: "As for our wider surroundings, it would be difficult to describe their beauty in sufficiently glowing terms. Cape Evans is one of many spurs of Erebus and the one that stands closest under the mountain, so that always towering above us we have the grand snowy peak with its smoking summit." In 1971, almost 60 years after the Hut had been abandoned, Sir Peter Scott, the explorer's son, recorded the scene on visiting his father's Antarctic home: "The Cape Evans hut is perhaps the most beautifully situated of all. . . ." Though snow had filled the Hut in the intervening years, nothing had decayed. The drifts had been moved by a New Zealand Antarctic party in the 1950's, exposing the long-abandoned furniture, utensils, supplies, and even personal possessions of the expedition. New Zealand still maintains Scott's Antarctic Hut as a historic monument.

weeks of hard physical labor succeed in solving some problem of the great unknown. Surely in this case the conquest is more nobly and splendidly won."

By January 1911, after a stormy passage from New Zealand and a difficult crossing of the barrier of floes and icebergs that wreathes Antarctica in summer, the *Terra Nova* landed at Cape Evans on Ross Island, near Scott's old headquarters for his *Discovery* expedition. Dominated by the smoking volcanic peak of Mount Erebus and its dormant twin, Mount Terror, Ross Island lies at the fringe of the floating, apronlike expanse of the Ross Ice Shelf. Beyond, the mountainous mainland of Antarctica itself rises abruptly, and to the south, on a high plateau, is the South Pole, about 800 miles from Ross Island.

It was across this landscape, on much the same route Shackleton had taken, that Scott intended to make his dash to the pole the following Antarctic spring. His immediate task, once his winter quarters had been built on Cape Evans, was to haul some of his supplies inland on the ice shelf and cache them for use in the spring. His plan was to deposit about a ton of food, fuel, and fodder at 80° S on the ice shelf. But because of bad weather, this crucial One Ton Depot had to be laid short of his goal—about 20 miles farther north than he planned. "We shall have a good leg up for next year,"

Scott noted with satisfaction at the time. In fact, the shortfall was to have tragic consequences when the time came to rely on One Ton Depot.

Meanwhile, as part of Scott's crew struggled to haul supplies to One Ton Depot, some of his men sailed the *Terra Nova* east to reconnoiter land at the far end of the ice shelf. To their amazement, they came across Amundsen's ship, the *Fram*, anchored in the Bay of Whales, an indentation in the face of the ice barrier. The Englishmen and the Norwegians—the only men on the entire desolate continent—were cordial, if a bit restrained, in their greetings. But it was disturbing news the *Terra Nova* brought back to Cape Evans: The Norwegians were definitely racing for the pole.

Surprised and somewhat rattled, Scott tried to evaluate this new development. The Bay of Whales was 60 miles closer to the pole than Cape Evans. The Norwegians had 100 sled dogs, all in excellent condition, and they were experts at driving them. They had no qualms about using the animals as a sort of traveling larder, to be killed off one by one for food. And Amundsen, Scott now realized, "can start his journey early in the season—an impossible condition with ponies." On the depot-laying journey the animals had suffered terribly, and a few had already died of exposure. Despite their thick woolly coats, fine, storm-

## *Herbert Ponting's Camera Recorded Life at the Base Camp*

Time passed pleasantly in the Hut during the Antarctic winter. Despite close quarters, tempers remained good. "Undoubtedly a very powerful reason," one member of the expedition noted, "was that we had no idle hours; there was no time to quarrel." Supplies were transferred from the *Terra Nova* to the Hut. Some of the boxes bore the names of the commercial firms that donated their products (below right). The men repaired sleeping bags and tents and made crampons, provision bags, and other equipment necessary for the dash to the pole. Three nights a week, selected expedition members gave lectures. The highlight of the series was photographer Ponting's talk on his trip to Japan, illustrated by his own magic lantern slides. On other nights Scott noted, "The gramophone is usually started by some

kindly disposed person." The instrument is pictured at left, eyed by a curious dog. A special celebration (above) was held on Midsummer's Day, June 22, 1911. Since this was the heart of the Antarctic winter, the men renamed the holiday Midwinter's Day. The celebration included a homemade Christmas tree and presents for all. By the time this picture was taken, Scott and his men knew of Amundsen's plans.

driven snow penetrated right down to their skins as they floundered belly-deep through drifts. "It is clear that these blizzards are terrible for the poor animals. . ." Scott noted unhappily. "It makes a late start *necessary for next year.*"

All in all, Amundsen was clearly a formidable rival. "I think that two parties are very likely to reach the Pole next year," concluded one of Scott's men, "but God only knows which will get there first."

Despite the odds against him, Scott himself decided

to stick to his original plan. As he evaluated the situation, "One thing only fixes itself definitely in my mind. The proper, as well as the wiser, course for us is to proceed exactly as though this had not happened. To go forward and do our best for the honour of the country without fear or panic."

Scott and his men spent the winter snug in their quarters at Cape Evans and with the return of the Antarctic spring set out on their trek to the pole. The first advance party, traveling on the motorized sleds, left

Ponting's photographs have preserved an intimate record of life in the Hut. Above, Scott works in his private cubicle. Behind him are pictures of his wife and infant son. At top right, scientists Debenham and Taylor analyze Antarctic rock. At right, Dr. Wilson works on one of his watercolors. Below right, a group of men rest in their bunks, which they nicknamed the Tenements.

the cape on October 24, 1911. (Within a few days the sleds broke down, and the crew was forced to man-haul the heavy loads.) On November 1, Scott and the rest of the support parties, carrying supplies to be cached en route for the return journey, followed in its tracks. (Amundsen, with four companions and 52 dogs, had left the Bay of Whales nearly two weeks before, on October 19.)

The first leg of the journey, across the Ross Ice Shelf, was sheer agony for men, dogs, and ponies. Hauling the sleds over sastrugi—windswept, icy crests of frozen snow—then floundering through the deep, soft drifts between the ridges, soon began to take its toll of the ponies. Within five weeks the few that had not died of exposure had to be shot for meat. Repeated snowstorms also impeded progress. "Our luck in weather is preposterous," Scott declared. From December 4 to December 8 a howling blizzard pinned the entire party in their little tents, consuming not only precious time but carefully rationed food and fuel as well.

**Lieutenant Bowers took the picture** *at left of the polar assault party harnessed to its sledge. From left to right the picture shows Evans, Oates, Wilson, and Scott. Sledge hauling was made even more difficult by terrible Antarctic blizzards. New snow seldom falls during these storms; instead, winds of terrifying force whip the surface snow into blinding clouds. Wilson's painting above shows one of Scott's men entering a tent during such a storm. Amundsen had good luck with the Antarctic weather on his run to the pole. Scott, on the other hand, was constantly plagued by storms. "Our luck in weather is preposterous," he wrote in his diary.*

By December 9 the men reached the foot of the Beardmore Glacier, a broad, rough avenue of ice leading up the range of mountains that marks the continent's true coastline. After setting up a supply depot on the lower slopes, the last of the dogs were sent home with a no-longer-needed support party. Man-hauling the loaded sleds up the glacier—a jumbled mass of huge ice blocks crisscrossed by gaping crevasses—proved slow going for the expedition. But Scott found reason for optimism. On December 14 he wrote in his diary, "It is splendid to be getting along and to find some adequate return for the work we are putting into the business." (Late that same afternoon, far to the south, Amundsen and the Norwegians planted their flag at the South Pole.)

It took nearly two weeks to reach the top of the glacier, but by Christmas the men were well out on the high polar plateau. On January 4, 1912, when he was just 150 miles short of his goal, Scott sent the last of his support parties back to the base camp. The four men he chose to go with him on the final dash to the pole were Dr. Edward Wilson, an old friend and a veteran of the *Discovery* expedition; cavalry officer L.E.G. Oates; Petty Officer Edgar Evans; and naval lieutenant Henry Bowers, whose willingness to work had so impressed

Scott that he added him to the polar party at the last minute. (This impulsive change of plan may have been Scott's most disastrous error: His tents were designed for four people, and food and fuel had been rationed out for a party of four. Bowers, moreover, had cached his skis at the glacier and had to tramp along, wearily, on foot, slowing the party down.)

Alone now, the five men struggled desperately to advance at least 10 miles a day. One wonders what Scott thought of the "nobility" of man-hauling now as, on foot and on skis, whipped by the wind and numbed by subzero temperatures, the men valiantly, hopefully dragged their sledge up and down the crests of sastrugi that rippled endlessly to the south.

Day after day they ticked off the miles that brought them ever closer to their goal. On January 9, 97 nautical miles from the pole, they reached Shackleton's 1909 "farthest south." By January 15 Scott estimated "that two long marches would land us at the Pole." But then doubt crept over him as he added, "It ought to be a certain thing now, and the only appalling possibility is the sight of the Norwegian flag."

The next morning all of Scott's hopes and dreams collapsed forever. Still 11 miles from the pole, the men found a black flag tied to a sledge bearer, the remains of a camp, ski tracks, and dog prints in the snow. "This told us the whole story," Scott wrote bitterly. "The Norwegians have forestalled us and are the first at the Pole. It is a terrible disappointment, and I am very sorry for my loyal companions."

The following day, January 17, 1912, Scott and his party reached their goal. "THE POLE," he wrote in his journal. "Yes, but under very different circumstances from those expected . . . great God! This is an awful place and terrible enough for us to have laboured to it without the reward of priority." Then, ominously, he added, "Now for the run home and a desperate struggle. I wonder if we can do it."

Nearby, on January 18, the weary, dispirited men found Amundsen's tent surmounted by the Norwegian flag, odds and ends of equipment, and a letter addressed to Scott. "We built a cairn," says Scott, "put up our poor slighted Union Jack and photographed ourselves—mighty cold work all of it. . . . Well, we have turned our back on the goal of our ambition and must face our 800 miles of solid dragging—and good-bye to most of the daydreams!"

Heading north again in their old tracks, the men enjoyed a spell of fair weather. When the wind was at their backs, they were able from time to time to hoist a mast and sail to help propel the sled. But everyone was beginning to show signs of weakening. Exhaustion, hunger, frostbite, snow blindness—all were beginning to take their toll. Scott's notes for the next week begin to take on a grim pattern. "Oates is feeling the cold and fatigue." "I think about the most trying march we have had." "There is no doubt Evans is a good deal run down." "Things beginning to look a little serious." "A bad march . . . we covered 7 miles."

On January 25 he wrote, "It's time we cleared off this plateau. . . . Oates suffers from a very cold foot; Evans' fingers and nose are in bad state and tonight Wilson is suffering tortures from his eyes." (That same day Amundsen and his companions arrived safe and healthy at their base camp on the Bay of Whales.)

Injuries also slowed progress as the men groped their way from depot to depot, straining in their traces as they hauled the sled over rugged terrain. Wilson's leg became swollen and inflamed from a pulled tendon. Scott fell and injured his shoulder. Evans, who lost two fingernails from his frostbitten hands, hurt his head seriously in a couple of bad falls.

By February, with the brief Antarctic summer already on the wane, temperatures began to plummet. "The temperature is 20° lower than when we were here

## A Photo of Doomed Men: Scott's Party After Finding Amundsen Had Beaten Them to the Pole

Scott's arrival at his goal turned into his bitterest defeat, for Amundsen had reached the pole first. Above, Scott's men inspect Amundsen's tent, with the Norwegian flag flying above it. At right, the British expedition posed in front of the Union Jack at the South Pole. From left to right, the picture shows Oates, Bowers, Scott, Wilson, and Evans. Bowers took the photograph with a string attached to the camera's shutter. The film was found eight months later along with the frozen bodies of Scott and his companions. Crucial differences of temperament between Amundsen and Scott help to explain the Norwegian's triumph. Amundsen was single-minded in the pursuit of his objective. "We agreed to shrink from nothing in order to reach our goal," he wrote after slaughtering many of his dogs to feed both his men and the other animals. Scott, on the other hand, was periodically gripped by deep fits of depression that seem to have affected both his resolve and his judgment. "I can't describe what overcomes me," he wrote of his melancholic moods. "I'm obsessed with the view of life as a struggle for existence and then forced to see how little past efforts have done to give me a place in the struggle." When he was tormented by such a period of self-doubt, Scott questioned his own ability to lead other men. In a letter to his wife detailing the early setbacks of the expedition, he commented with perception: "The root of the trouble was that I had lost confidence in myself. I don't know if it was noticed by others consciously, but it was acted on unconsciously."

**Several days before Oates walked** *to his death in a howling blizzard (above), Scott realized his comrade could never survive the journey. ". . . Oates is very near the end," he noted. And then, interestingly, Scott added a sentence that showed he might have been anticipating Oates' stoic suicide: "What we or he will do, God only knows." At this time, Scott wrote, "I practically ordered Wilson to hand over the means of ending our trouble to us. Wilson had no choice between doing so and our ransacking the medicine case. We have 30 opium tablets apiece and he is left with a tube of morphine." Later, however, the three surviving men decided to struggle on. Two days before a final blizzard sealed their fate, Scott wrote: "We are 15½ miles from the depot and ought to get there in three days. What progress! We have two days' food but barely a day's fuel. All our feet are getting bad—Wilson's best, my right foot worse, left all right. . . . Amputation is the least I can hope for now." Wilson's picture of three men huddled in a small tent (left), drawn on Scott's 1901–04 expedition, suggests the last days of Scott and his two companions.*

before," Scott noted one day, and on another, "Our faces are much cut up by all the winds we have had. . . . I am indeed glad to think we shall so soon have done with plateau conditions."

Once on the Beardmore Glacier, the weather did improve slightly. The mountains enclosing the slope shielded the men somewhat from the ferocious plateau winds, and temperatures rose a bit. But picking their way down the jagged, jumbled face of the glacier was cruel work. Scott's journal for the next few days abounds with vivid, telling phrases: "the worst day we have had during the trip"; "the worst ice mess I have ever been in"; "arrived in a horrid maze of crevasses and fissures." In spite of it all, the scientist in Scott

found time to pick among exposed rock on the mountainsides and add some 30 pounds of geological specimens to the already heavy sled.

As they neared the bottom of the glacier, Evans became Scott's chief worry. Dazed from his head injuries, growing steadily weaker, he was no longer able even to help with camp chores. Time and again he fell behind, forcing the others to wait as he staggered to catch up. At midday on February 17, he fell so far behind that the rest of the men skied back to find him. "I was the first to reach the poor man and shocked at his appearance," reported Scott. "He was on his knees with clothing disarranged, hands uncovered and frostbitten, and a wild look in his eyes." Back in the tent, Evans fell into a

Map for Scott on page 292.

deep coma, and during the night he died.

Continuing across the ice shelf, Scott, Oates, Wilson, and Bowers struggled on, sometimes making 9 or 10 miles a day, more often only 5 or 6 over a surface that was "really terrible . . . like pulling over desert sand." "God help us," Scott despaired, "we can't keep up this pulling, that is certain. Amongst ourselves we are unendingly cheerful, but what each man feels in his heart I can only guess."

It was no longer a race against Amundsen, he realized, but a race against time and their own weakening condition. "There is no doubt," he wrote, "the middle of the Barrier [shelf] is a pretty awful locality." Temperatures were regularly plunging to −40° F. Fuel, vital for heat and cooking, was running short. At each depot they found the oil cans only partially full, the fuel apparently having evaporated or leaked out. All the men by now were suffering from scurvy, and Oates' feet were so badly frostbitten that he could scarcely get his boots on in the morning.

No longer able to help pull the sled, he staggered painfully behind, growing weaker and weaker each day. By March 15, aware that he was slowing progress and threatening everyone's chances of survival, Oates begged to be left behind. The men refused, and he struggled on for a few more miles. On March 16 or 17 (Scott was beginning to lose track of time), it was "tragedy all along the line." Waking to a blizzard, Oates told his companions, "I am just going outside and may be some time." With that he left the tent and disappeared forever in swirling clouds of snow.

"We knew that poor Oates was walking to his death," commented Scott, "but though we tried to dissuade him, we knew it was the act of a brave man and an English gentleman." Then, grimly, he added, "We all hope to meet the end with a similar spirit, and assuredly the end is not far."

Making painfully slow progress, Scott, Wilson, and Bowers continued north against gale force winds and −40° F temperatures. All three now had frostbitten feet. "Amputation is the least I can hope for now," noted Scott. Low on food and fuel, by March 20 they reckoned themselves only 11 miles from the vast hoard of lifesaving supplies at One Ton Depot—the depot that, because of bad weather, had been established 20 miles north of Scott's goal the preceding spring.

But the three were unable to make a final dash for it as, once again, a blizzard pinned them down in their tent. Day after day they planned to start out, and day after day the whirling, gusting storm continued without letup. On March 23 Scott wrote, "Blizzard bad as ever . . . tomorrow last chance—no fuel and only one or two days of food left—must be near the end."

Finally, on March 29, he wrote, "Since the 21st we have had a continuous gale. . . . Every day we have been ready to start for our depot *11 miles* away, but outside the door of the tent it remains a scene of whirling drift. I do not think we can hope for any better things now. We shall stick it out to the end but we are getting weaker of course and the end cannot be far. It seems a pity but I do not think I can write more—R. Scott." Then, with faltering strokes, he added, "Last Entry. For God's sake look after our people."

Eight months later, in November 1912, a search party found Scott's last camp. The three men lay in their final rest, Wilson and Bowers in closed sleeping bags, Scott with sleeping bag and coat thrown open, his arm flung across Wilson, his friend and companion on two Antarctic expeditions.

Scott's diaries and photographic films were complete and intact. In his last few days he had also written a series of letters—one addressed "To My Widow," others to his mother, to Wilson's wife, to Bowers' mother, to friends, even a "Message to the Public" concisely analyzing the expedition's disaster.

The search party removed the tent poles, leaving the frozen bodies as they had found them, and covered the spot with a cairn of snowblocks. As a final memorial, the survivors of the expedition erected a wooden cross, on a hill overlooking Cape Evans, inscribed with a line from Tennyson's "Ulysses." It was a line that Scott himself might have chosen as his epitaph: "To strive, to seek, to find, and not to yield."

**Scott's reputation grew** *after his tragic death, thanks in part to the eloquent letters and diary (his last entry is shown below). In a "Message to the Public," composed during his last days, Scott wrote: "I do not regret this journey which has shown that Englishmen can endure hardships, help one another and meet death with as great fortitude as ever in the past."*

we shall stick it out
to the end but we
are getting weaker of
course and the end
cannot be far.
It seems a pity but
I do not think I can
write more —
R Scott
Last Entry
For God's sake look
after our people

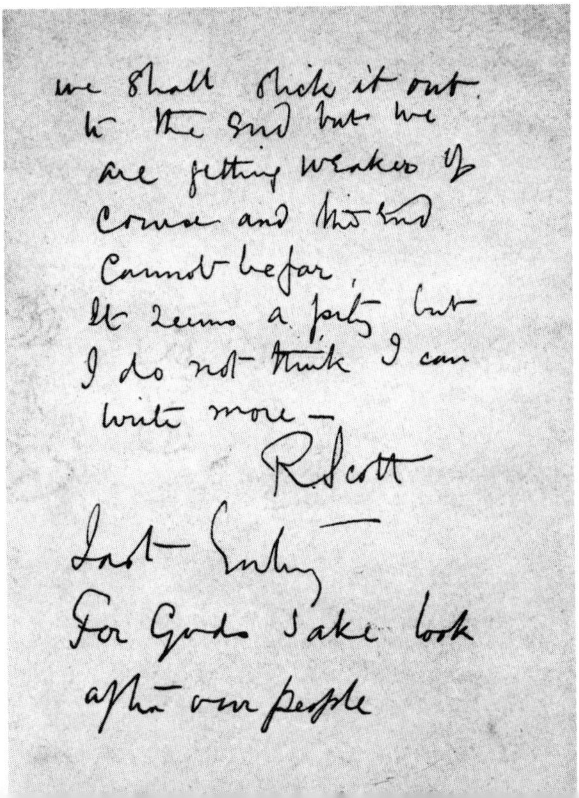

# Part 9

# Reaching for the Beyond

## Adventurers Below and Above

*In the 20th century,
with most of the earth discovered,
explorers face the challenge
of the deepest seas,
the highest mountains,
and the
universe itself.*

By the middle of the 20th century, most of the earth had been "discovered" by Western man, and his civilization had spread far beyond Europe and the Americas. There were skyscrapers in Australia and paved highways in Africa, movie theaters in India and democracy in Japan. True, there were still relatively unexplored places: the northern forests and tundra of Canada and Siberia, the jungles of New Guinea and the upper Amazon River area, various pockets of wilderness here and there. But the West's 500-year odyssey of exploring the surface of the earth had almost been completed. Now man's urge to explore inevitably began to be directed at the oceans and the mountains and even to outer space itself. As Russian space pioneer Konstantin Tsiolkovsky, whose work in the late 19th and early 20th centuries laid the foundation for modern space technology, wrote: "The earth is the cradle of the mind, but you cannot live in a cradle forever."

As Tsiolkovsky predicted, 20th-century technology was called upon to conquer the natural obstacles presented by hitherto inaccessible areas, for the new frontiers are inimical to human life. Men wearing oxygen masks ascended the rarefied atmosphere of the world's highest peaks. Other men in life-protecting capsules descended into the murky depths of the ocean or rocketed to the moon. In this new age of discovery, man was linked to machine as never before.

### The Planet's Last True Frontier

Covering more than two-thirds of the earth's surface, the oceans present the planet's last true frontier. For millennia, men had wanted to descend deep into the sea to discover its wonders, to retrieve sunken treasure. Yet below about 100 feet, water pressure and lack of oxygen killed quickly, and the average depth of the ocean floor is 12,450 feet—four and a half times the average height of the earth's land surface above water.

From the days of the Greek philosopher Aristotle, who recorded sponge divers descending to depths of 100 feet with diving bells, various underwater apparatuses were invented and used with little success. The diving helmet and suit, developed in 1819, enabled divers to descend deeper than ever before and opened millions of square miles of relatively shallow seabed to salvagers, pearlfishers, and construction men.

But what lay in the great ocean deeps, the home of sea monsters and unimaginable mysteries? Until 1930, no human being had ever dived deeper than 600 feet, less than one-twentieth of the average depth of the oceans of the world. Then, from 1930 to 1934, two Americans made a series of dives into the sea near Bermuda. The men were William Beebe and Otis Barton, and the device they made their descents in was called the bathysphere. Their 1930 dives in this insulated steel sphere plunged them down as far as 1,426 feet. There, "below the level of humanly visible light," Beebe observed "a world as strange as Mars or Venus." Strange marine creatures that had never been seen before swam past the bathysphere's double quartz windows. These dives, terminating in one of 3,028 feet in 1934, opened the door to the undersea world.

Only 26 years later, Jacques Piccard and Donald Walsh lowered their highly sophisticated bathyscaphe *Trieste* into the deepest known point of the earth's oceans: Challenger Deep of the Mariana Trench, southwest of Guam in the Pacific. The *Trieste* went down to 35,800 feet, 252 feet from the bottom. The water pressure there was 16,000 pounds *per square inch.* (The pressure on Beebe's bathysphere during its deepest dive was 1,360 pounds per square inch.)

Today, governments and industries are engaged in widespread research into undersea development. Despite the achievements of Beebe and Piccard, the oceans' depths are still virtually unexplored, but thanks to them, they are no longer totally unknown.

Mountains have always towered above men but until the late 18th century were regarded as obstacles rather than goals. Then, in 1771, a Swiss scholar offered a prize to the first man to climb Mont Blanc. The 15,771-foot peak was finally conquered 15 years later, and the tradition of mountaineering was begun. Some people have found mountain climbing an inexplicable and dangerous activity, but it surely springs from the same human spirit that has always sent men and women off on journeys of discovery. With the conquest of Mount Everest in the Himalayas in 1953, the world's tallest peak (29,028 feet) had been scaled.

### The Discovery of the Universe

The most dramatic and significant frontier of modern discovery and exploration is the universe itself. In the latter half of the 20th century, man for the first time realized an age-old dream: to propel himself to the moon. At 4:17 p.m.(EDT) on Sunday, July 20, 1969, the lunar module of the great Apollo 11 spacecraft touched the surface of the moon. At 10:51 p.m. American astronaut Neil Armstrong emerged from the module and gingerly climbed down the ladder to the moon's surface, 238,857 miles from the earth. As he set a historic foot on the ground, he said, "That's one small step for a man, one giant leap for mankind." Much of mankind, in fact, saw him make the step and heard his words, for hundreds of millions of men, women, and children throughout the world were watching the spectacular lunar landing on live television.

Like the North and South Poles, the moon itself offered no immediate riches to its discoverers: It is an airless, dust-covered sphere incapable of sustaining unprotected life. But like the poles, it represented a great goal attained, a triumph of the human will against staggering odds.

It was modern science and technology that brought men to the moon; the exploration of the universe will be inextricably linked with sophisticated machines. Yet the evolution of space travel has occurred over an astonishingly short period of time. The United States effort began on a Massachusetts farm in 1926, when a New England physics professor named Robert H. Goddard launched the first liquid-fuel rocket. The rocket was 10 feet high and when set off rose only 40 feet in the air before falling back to the ground. Its maximum speed was 60 mph. Only 43 years later, the United States launched a Saturn 5 rocket that stood 281 feet high and weighed 3,000 tons. It sent three men and tons of equipment to the moon, more than a quarter of a million miles away, at speeds of many thousands of miles an hour. The years between those two flights are one of the great chapters in the history of discovery.

Men had been experimenting with balloons and high-altitude aircraft flight for years before Goddard's experiment. But Goddard realized that it was the rocket, which does not depend on the earth's atmosphere for flight, that would provide the means for space travel. Yet this idea was not shared by the public or the U.S. government. For years Goddard worked in relative obscurity, supported by his wife and a handful of farsighted men. Experimenting in the New Mexico desert in the 1930's, he gradually developed larger and more successful rockets.

The German rocket scientists who were brought to the United States after World War II freely acknowledged Goddard's work as one of their main sources. To Wernher von Braun, Goddard had been a childhood hero. The great American died in 1945, on the eve of the U.S. space program, but today he is acknowledged as the father of American rocketry.

The U.S. space effort, sparked by Von Braun, gradually developed more efficient rockets throughout the 1950's. Then, in 1957, the U.S.S.R. stunned the world by sending the first manmade satellite, Sputnik I, into orbit. The United States admitted it was "behind" the U.S.S.R. and intensified its own efforts. The space race was on. In 1961 the Soviets triumphed again when the first man, cosmonaut Yuri Gagarin, orbited the earth. That same year Alan Shepard became the first American in space, and the next year John Glenn made the first U.S. orbital flight around the earth.

In the ensuing years both the U.S.S.R. and the United States have made great strides, sending unmanned flights to Mars, Venus, and even the Sun. The two nations, in addition, have moved toward greater cooperation, notably in the combined orbiting space lab experiments. This progress in space research promises a new era of exploration—other galaxies may even be discovered. "A future of infinite promise lies ahead," predicts writer Arthur C. Clarke. "We may yet have a splendid and inspiring role to play, on a stage wider and more marvelous than ever dreamed of by any poet or dramatist of the past. For it may be that the old astrologers had the truth exactly reversed, when they believed that the stars controlled the destinies of men."

**Their bathysphere suspended** *over the barge* Ready *(above), William Beebe and Otis Barton are about to be lowered into the Atlantic to begin their record-breaking dive into the ocean. "These descents of mine beneath the sea seemed to partake of a real cosmic character," Beebe wrote. "First of all there was the complete and utter loneliness and isolation, a feeling wholly unlike the isolation felt when removed from fellow men by mere distance. . . . It was a loneliness more akin to a first venture upon the moon or Venus."*

**Beebe** *(far left) peers through one of the bathysphere's quartz windows. Gazing out of these portholes in depths where light could not penetrate, he found many fish that produced their own radiance with luminous body organs. The* astronesthes gemmifera *(left) "glistened like tin-foil."*

# In Dangerous Depths:
# Beebe's Oceanic Descent

*Naturalist and explorer, William Beebe (1877–1962) crammed sufficient adventure for several men into his event-filled life. In 1899, shortly after his college gradua- tion, Beebe was appointed curator of ornithology at the New York Zoological Society, and he maintained his association with the organization until his death. In the early 1900's he led a scientific party to Mexico, the first of many such expeditions that would take him to South American jungles, the Galapagos Islands, and Asia to pursue his interest in ornithology. Beebe wrote fascinat- ing accounts of his journeys, which made his exploits well known to the general public as well as to fellow naturalists. He was already a scientist of international reputation when, at the age of 51, he and bathysphere designer Otis Barton made their 1930 dives off Bermuda.*

One evening early in this century, the young zoologist Dr. William Beebe discussed ways and means of deep- sea diving with his good friend President Theodore Roosevelt. Although both men longed to know what mysterious creatures might lurk below the shallow layer of water so far explored by man, they were per- plexed by the age-old problem of pressure. They knew that the sheer weight of the sea is enough to make an unprotected diver unconscious at 200 feet. If he sank much farther, he would be crushed to pulp. Before abandoning the discussion, Beebe sketched a cylinder as the ideal form of diving chamber, while Roosevelt drew a sphere. In 1930 the president's theory was proved correct by Beebe himself.

By then Roosevelt had been dead for a decade, and Beebe was director of the Department of Tropical Re- search at the New York Zoological Society. At 51 he was tall, balding, and vigorous, a witty man who combined scientific passion with a poetic temperament. His fa- vorite author was Lewis Carroll, with whom he shared a fascination for strange and exotic animals. He had

made hundreds of ocean descents, outfitted in diving suit and helmet, in search of marine creatures. Accord- ing to his diving colleague, however, Beebe had "no feeling for machinery," and this constantly hampered his search for an effective deep-sea chamber.

His lack of success was not for want of proposals. Over the years the director had been presented with so many plans—none of them workable—that he began to suspect that every other unemployed person in Amer- ica was designing diving tanks. Then, in 1928, an inge- nious young engineer named Otis Barton walked into his office and spread a blueprint on his desk. "My idea is very simple," said Barton, "just a hollow steel sphere on the end of a cable."

The design struck a chord in Beebe. He knew that pressure was distributed most evenly along the surface of a sphere. The sphere's simplicity was deceptive; as Barton explained the sophisticated engineering that had gone into the plan, the director grew more and more convinced that here, at last, was his ideal vessel. When built, the steel ball would have a diameter of four feet nine inches and a deadweight of two and a half tons. Set into its one-and-a-quarter-inch-thick walls would be three round eight-inch windows made of fused quartz, one of the strongest and most transpar- ent substances known to man. Opposite the windows would be the doorway, a bolted steel lid so heavy it would have to be lifted on and off by block and tackle. A 3,500-foot, nontwisting steel cable almost an inch thick, with a breaking strain of 29 tons, would lower and raise the ball, and the communications link with the outside world would be a solid rubber hose carry- ing electric light and telephone wires.

As soon as he won the director's approval of his in- vention, Barton, who was independently wealthy, con- tracted with a New Jersey hydraulic company to con- struct it at his own expense. There remained the problem of what to call it. After careful consideration, Beebe settled on "bathysphere," after the two Greek words for "deep" and "ball."

By the spring of 1930, Beebe was ready to begin man's first exploration of the ocean's unknown interior. He chose to dive at a point 10 miles south of Nonsuch, a tiny island of the Bermuda group, where he had already established a full-time oceanographic research station. In early June a huge barge bearing the bathysphere was towed out to sea by a tugboat. Accompanying Beebe was Barton, who would join him in the dive, and a team of 26 assistants.

The underwater mountain that is Bermuda dropped rapidly away below the barge. When the ocean depth reached one and a half miles Beebe signaled a halt, and a series of dummy tests began. Everyone on board was well aware of the risk that the divers would be taking. The bathysphere had no fail-safe capability: Since it lacked buoyancy, it could never return automatically to the surface. If its slender supporting cable snapped, it would plunge to the bottom of the sea with no hope of rescue. (Beebe's wife later wondered why both the sphere and the cable had not been enclosed in an enormous, precautionary steel net. The answer was simple:

**The 13th-century picture** *above shows Alexander the Great, king of Macedon, suspended underwater in a glass diving barrel. According to legend, his intense desire to observe undersea life was amply rewarded: He saw a sea monster so enormous that it took three days and three nights to pass in front of him.*

Nobody seems to have thought of it at the time.)

June 6 dawned calm and clear—perfect weather for the bathysphere's first manned descent. At about noon Beebe and Barton wriggled through the 14-inch doorway, bruising themselves on its projecting steel bolts, and coiled up on the chilly floor of the observation chamber. Beebe sat beside the windows (only two contained quartz; the third held a steel plate); Barton squatted near the door where he could keep an eye on the instruments. Both divers wore telephone headsets, which left their hands free. Zoologist Gloria Hollister would note down their telephone observations from the depths. They were to relay information to her every five seconds, thus assuring those on deck of their continuing safety in the ocean depths.

In spite of all the equipment crammed into the bathysphere—oxygen tanks, chemical trays, searchlight, switchboxes, communications systems, and tools—the divers announced that they "had room and to spare."

Satisfied, Beebe gave the signal to proceed with sealing, and the 400-pound lid was hoisted onto its bolts. To take up any possible slack in the screw threads, each of the 10 great nuts was tightened with a combination of wrenches and hammers. Inside the bathysphere the noise was so tremendous that Beebe worried that the quartz windows might split. But the glass held, and the hammering stopped. Barton tested the searchlight and adjusted valves so that oxygen would flow from two tanks at a rate of two liters a minute. "A palm-leaf" electric fan kept the fresh air circulating, while trays of soda lime removed exhaled carbon dioxide, and ones of calcium chloride absorbed surplus moisture.

At precisely 1 p.m. the winch creaked, and the bathysphere was swung high to the yardarm and then out over the sides of the barge to begin its descent toward the surface. Beebe, deceived by the amazing clarity of the quartz windows, imagined that the sphere was swinging much too close to its parent vessel. "Gloria wants to know why the director is swearing so," said a voice over the wire. Beebe replied that any language was justified, since the side of the barge was only a yard away. Reassurance came promptly: The clearance was, in fact, a safe 15 feet.

The bathysphere hit the water with a splash, yet the divers hardly felt its impact. As foam bubbled up over the glass, the world inside and out turned green. The hull of the barge floated into view: Beebe described it as "a transitory, swaying reef with waving banners of seaweed, long tubular sponges, jet-black blobs of ascidians, and tissue-thin plates of rough-spined pearl shells." Soon the keel passed out of sight above him. At 50 feet down, Beebe noted that this was the deepest he had ever been in a diving helmet. At 100 feet, as they moved farther from the sun's rays, the green light that illuminated the sea began to dim.

At 300 feet Barton gave a sudden shout of alarm. He had felt something wet. Beebe flashed his light at the

*Adventurers Below and Above*

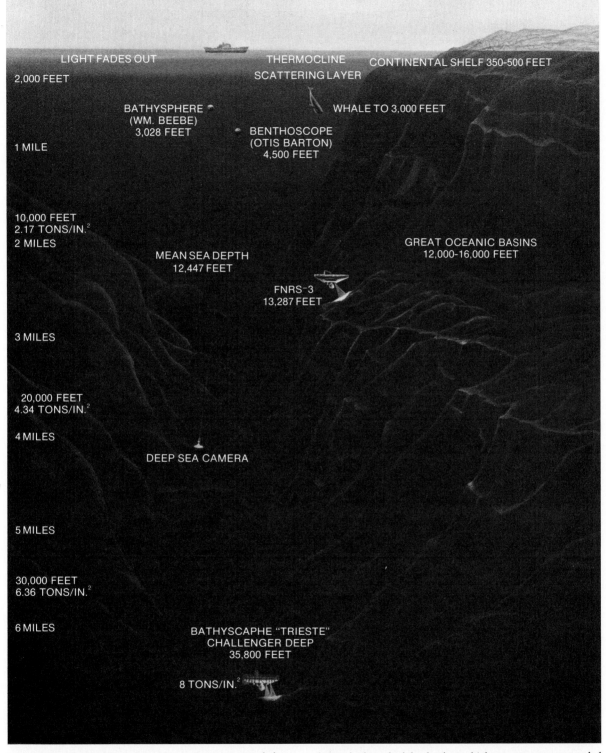

LIGHT FADES OUT

2,000 FEET

THERMOCLINE
SCATTERING LAYER

CONTINENTAL SHELF 350-500 FEET

BATHYSPHERE
(WM. BEEBE)
3,028 FEET

WHALE TO 3,000 FEET

BENTHOSCOPE
(OTIS BARTON)
4,500 FEET

1 MILE

10,000 FEET
2.17 TONS/IN.$^2$
2 MILES

MEAN SEA DEPTH
12,447 FEET

GREAT OCEANIC BASINS
12,000-16,000 FEET

FNRS-3
13,287 FEET

3 MILES

20,000 FEET
4.34 TONS/IN.$^2$

4 MILES

DEEP SEA CAMERA

5 MILES

30,000 FEET
6.36 TONS/IN.$^2$

6 MILES

BATHYSCAPHE "TRIESTE"
CHALLENGER DEEP
35,800 FEET

8 TONS/IN.$^2$

**Since Beebe's 1934 dive,** *a host of new deep-sea records have been set, culminating with the 1960 dive of the bathyscaphe Trieste to 35,800 feet in the deepest known part of the ocean. No diver, however, has expressed the wonder of descending better than Beebe, who wrote: "Thousands upon thousands of human beings had reached the depth at which we were now suspended and had passed on to lower levels. But all of these were dead, drowned victims of war, tempest or other Acts of God. We were the first living men to look out at the strange illumination and it was stranger than any imagination could have conceived."*

## Into the Depths of Bermuda's Blue Waters

Beebe's memorable bathysphere dives were made in the sparkling Atlantic Ocean off the Bermuda coast. Embarking from a research station on tiny Nonsuch Island (bottom), a tug hauled the barge *Ready*, with the bathysphere, to an area to the south that Beebe called "the magic circle," eight miles in diameter. Here, in the deep sea, free from the treacherous coral reefs that ring the Bermuda shore, the bathysphere made its deepest descents (see map). If both wind and water conditions were satisfactory, the decision on the exact location to submerge could be quite arbitrary. "Choosing a favorable spot under such conditions is like looking around and trying to decide the exact location of the North Pole," Beebe wrote. "I looked about, could detect no unusually favorable swell or especially satisfying wave so I reached a temporal decision and at exactly 9 o'clock ordered the *Gladisfen* [Beebe's tugboat] to stop. We headed up wind and up swell, and lowered the bathysphere." Within minutes, it disappeared and sank into the dark depths.

BERMUDA

NONSUCH ISLAND

CONTOUR DIVES

door and saw a trickle of water seeping in. There was already about a pint on the floor. Knowing that air pressure would soon cause the leak to self-seal, Beebe gave the order to be lowered more quickly, and the trickle abated.

Five hundred feet was passed. The bathysphere was now sinking into totally unexplored regions of the sea. At 700 feet Beebe, dazed by the beauty all around him, called a temporary halt. It crossed his mind that until now only dead men had plummeted to these depths. The light had changed to "an indefinable translucent blue . . . which seemed to pass materially through the eye into our very beings." For the first time during the descent, the beam of the bathysphere's electric searchlight became visible, "a pale shaft of yellow—intensely yellow—light," in the blue.

As the descent continued, the blue radiance darkened. At 800 feet "some mental warning" told Beebe he should sink no farther on this trip. Without hesitation, he gave the order to be raised back up to the barge. "Coming up to the surface and through it was like hitting a hard ceiling—I unconsciously ducked, ready for the impact, but there followed only a slather of foam and bubbles, and the rest was sky."

One by one the 10 bolts were wrenched loose, and the divers tumbled out onto the deck, stiff and sore. They had been imprisoned in the bathysphere for exactly one hour. Beebe, utterly absorbed, had sat on a monkey wrench throughout the dive and carried the imprint on his buttocks for several days.

Four days later, the leaky door had been plugged with white lead, and the divers began their second descent. But at 250 feet, the telephone went suddenly, terrifyingly dead. "We had neither of us felt before quite the same realization of our position in space as we did now. We had become veritable plankton." The bathysphere was hurriedly winched up, and the descent postponed for repairs.

At 10 a.m. on June 11, the divers were once again lowered into the water south of Nonsuch Island. This time Beebe intended to make a serious study of creatures he had only half-seen in the excitement of his first descent. Tied to the bathysphere were the flags of the Explorers Club and Beebe's Department of Tropical Research; a decomposing squid wrapped in cheesecloth hung temptingly just below the observation windows, surrounded by baited luminous hooks.

As the bathysphere sank, Beebe made a scientific study of the changing colors of the sea. Red and orange light disappeared first at 150 feet, and yellow at 300 feet. At 350 feet approximately half the spectrum was blue-violet, a quarter green, and the remaining quarter a colorless pale glow. At 450 feet only violet and a fraction of green could be seen on the spectroscope. By the time they reached 800 feet, there was nothing left but a narrow line of pale grayish white.

Then, far beyond the reach of the sun's rays, Beebe began to experiment with his powerful searchlight. But its bright beam disturbed him: Most of the time he preferred to watch the creatures swarming outside his window by the light of their own luminescence. With his extraordinary gifts of observation and seemingly instinctive knowledge of all sea life, he had already learned to look beyond the bright spots of deep-sea creatures to determine the dim shapes around them.

Microscopic plankton and copepods, the sea's most abundant organisms, constantly swirled about at all depths. Most fish sighted at 200- to 300-foot levels were of the carangid family, such as jacks, pompanos, and pilot fish. At these depths also lived delicate, lacy siphonophores, schools of jellyfish, and clouds of flying snails with gossamer-thin shells. At 400 feet glowing lantern fish and bronze eels floated by, followed at 550 feet by the ghostly larva of a sea eel, "a pale ribbon of transparent gelatine with only the two iridescent eyes to indicate its arrival."

At 150 feet farther down, Beebe saw a jellyfish bump against his window, "its stomach filled with a glowing mass of luminous food." It was hard to believe that such fragile-looking creatures were able to bear a pressure great enough to crush a man. Here Beebe became the first human being to see a school of tiny silver hatchetfish alive and swimming freely, their sides dazzling with tinselly lights.

Passing their previous limit of 800 feet, the divers then continued on to 1,200 feet, where the searchlight picked out the snakelike form of a golden-tailed serpent dragon with transparent fins. Beebe knew this creature had at least 300 light organs, but unfortunately none was visible in the beam.

At 1,426 feet, more than a quarter of a mile down, the total pressure on the bathysphere had reached 6.5 million pounds, or 3,366.2 tons. Yet Beebe felt a dangerous urge to open the hatch and swim out. He wrote: "The baited hooks waved to and fro, and the edge of one of the flags flapped idly, and I had to call upon all my imagination to realize that instant, unthinkable instant death would result from the least fracture of glass or collapse of metal. There was no possible chance of being drowned, for the first few drops would have shot through flesh and bone like steel bullets."

As the two explorers dangled in the abyssal blackness, they felt as isolated as atoms floating in outer space. Although Beebe felt no mental warning this time, he asked to be raised. Forty-three minutes later, after almost two hours down, the men were back on deck with "the memory of living scenes in a world as strange as that of Mars."

It was not until two years later that Beebe and Barton were able to make their next diving expedition. The bathysphere was essentially unchanged except that a quartz window had been inserted in the third porthole.

**One of Beebe's closest brushes** *with death came, ironically, on the* Ready*'s deck. Springing a leak on a 1932 test dive, the bathysphere filled with water under tremendous sea pressure. When Beebe opened the craft's door, the strength of the water jet that spewed out (above) could have killed anyone in the way.*

Since the explorers intended to plunge farther than ever before, the sphere was first sent down empty almost three-fifths of a mile. This was a fortunate precaution, for the new window proved to be insufficiently sealed. When the bathysphere reappeared, it was packed with deep-sea water, and the pressure was so terrific that the central door bolt, when loosened, tore from Beebe's hands and exploded across the deck like a cannonball. It gouged a scar half an inch deep in the steel winch 30 feet away and was followed by a screaming jet of water. "If I had been in the way I would have been decapitated," remarked Beebe.

The original steel plate was put in place of the glass, and at 1:15 p.m. on September 22, 1932, the divers once

---

## Exploring in the Bathysphere: "The Longer We Were in It, the Smaller It Seemed to Get."

When the bathysphere was exhibited at New York's American Museum of Natural History, a skeptical visitor inquired: "Is *that* the thing in which they went down in the ocean?" The small steel

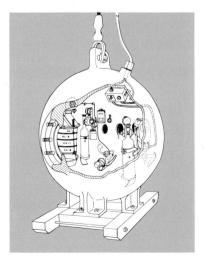

sphere, however, proved admirably suited for marine exploration. "I had no idea," Beebe wrote, "that there was so much room in the inside of a sphere only four and a half feet in diameter." But, he added, "the longer we were in it, the smaller it seemed to get." Equipment inside the bathysphere was sparse but adequate. The cutaway diagram at left shows the main power switch on the ceiling, temperature and humidity gauges, and the headset with which Beebe and Barton communicated with the *Ready*. On the left of the craft, there were four trays, two containing calcium chloride and two with soda lime to keep the bathysphere's atmosphere fresh. Two oxygen tanks provided the men with enough air for eight hours. Beebe, in addition, took a lesson from the master escape artist Houdini: "I remembered what I had read of Houdini's method of remaining in a closed coffin for a long time and we both began conscientiously

regulating our breathing and conversing in low tones." Once the men had crawled through the tiny porthole (below), a 400-pound lid was lifted into place and made fast with 10 oversize steel bolts.

again curled up on the familiar floor. This time a live lobster was attached outside as bait. The crew played out the cable slowly, giving Beebe and Barton little sense of movement as they sank. After an hour and a half of absorbed contemplation of the darkening scene outside, they heard the sound of tugboat whistles through their earphones signaling the passing of 1,426 feet, their 1930 record. Shortly afterward, Miss Hollister reminded Beebe that for the next 30 minutes everything he said would be broadcast to the world by

NBC. Completely fascinated by the sight of two bronze eels, he soon forgot this advice and continued to recite the zoological names of species he recognized, which were incomprehensible to most listeners.

At 1,650 feet the sea was already pitch-black, except for "a school of brilliantly-illuminated lantern fish with pale green lights." Fifty feet lower, the darkness inside the bathysphere seemed almost palpable. Beebe had attained one of the chief aims of his expedition: ". . . to get below the level of humanly visible light. I was be-

*Adventurers Below and Above*

## A Bizarre World Is Seen for the First Time

A scientist as well as an adventurer, Beebe aimed to observe marine life in his record-breaking dives. Biologists had brought some deep-sea creatures to the surface in nets, but Beebe and Barton were the first to observe denizens of the deep in their natural habitat. What they saw through the fused quartz windows of their sphere (below) is summarized in this painting of the bathysphere surrounded by an array of creatures that the divers saw at various levels of their descent. Although several six-foot giants were sighted, most deep-sea fish were smaller, measuring less than two feet in length. Intricate luminescent markings, however, made these small creatures spectacular sights. Their brilliance, in fact, was so overwhelming in the pitch-black ocean that Beebe noted he "had learned to ignore light as soon as possible and look to left or right of it . . . so the sudden flashing out of lights is less blinding." In the upper left corner of the picture, avocet eels glide in back of a constellationfish, named by Beebe for its beautiful, glowing patterns. "In my memory," he wrote, "it will live throughout the rest of my life as one of the loveliest things I have ever seen." Below the constellationfish, several pale yellow fish Beebe described as "ghostly-looking" and "corpse-hued" swim by. At the top right, two saber-toothed viperfish feed on a school of scarlet arrow worms, while above a jellyfish, several hachetfish glide past. With elongated telescopic eyes, the silver hatchetfish are decorated with hundreds of colored lights that mark their presence in the enveloping darkness. The eyes of the anglerfish in the bottom right corner, in contrast to those of the hatchetfish, are nearly useless. The fish attracts prey with the luminescent lure extending above its upper jaw. At the center of the picture, an orange-lighted finger squid captures brightly glowing lantern fish in its tentacles. In the left-hand corner, a scarlet flamethrower shrimp sprays out a mist of radiant fluid to blind a pursuing dragonfish. Dragonfish are so ferocious that Beebe speculated on their resemblance to mythical dragons of much larger size. Below the dragonfish hover four brilliantly colored small fish with

slender, stiff bodies and sharply protruding jaws. Because Beebe admired the flamboyant red, yellow, and blue color of their tiny, four-inch bodies, he wrote: "Rainbow gars is the only name we can think of for these fish." Beebe had to give names to many of these strange new creatures.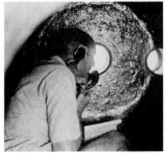

yond sunlight as far as the human eye could tell, and from here down, for two billion years there had been no day or night, no summer or winter, no passing of time until we came to record it."

Beebe had then been down for two and a half hours, and his descriptions were becoming more and more inarticulate. Most of the creatures passing the windows had been seen neither dead nor alive: They therefore had no names. He did, however, recognize one monster that charged the quartz headlong, baring long fangs

and flashing hexagonal scales. It was the 10-inch-long saber-toothed viperfish, which feeds eagerly on fish almost as large as itself.

Suddenly, at 1,950 feet, the bathysphere's mother vessel far above began to roll in a heavy swell, jerking the cable. Beebe was thrown against the window, cutting his lip and forehead, and Barton banged his head on the door. Still, the director could not bring himself to stop the descent. Finally, at 2,220 feet, Beebe and Barton decided to return to the surface.

ness of the sea as compared to the ever-changing earth.

At 4 p.m. the bathysphere surfaced, and the winching team noticed with surprise that its tethered lobster, long since presumed dead, was still wriggling indignantly. The hardy crustacean had withstood tons of deep-sea pressure.

Another two years went by. In 1934 the National Geographic Society offered to sponsor a third expedition. The bathysphere, which was on exhibit in Chicago's Hall of Science, was removed for a thorough overhaul. New windows, oxygen tanks, chemical trays, electric blower, and earphones were installed. When the face-lift was completed, little was left of the old vessel but its dark blue shell.

At 9:41 a.m. on August 11, the bathysphere hit the sea six and a half miles southeast of Nonsuch Island and quickly sank out of sight. Within, Beebe and Barton gazed at familiar hosts of siphonophores, yellow tails, and blue-banded jacks. At 800 feet came arrow worms and swarms of copepods, hotly pursued by voracious round-mouths. The blue spectrum once again faded to gray, and at 1,500 feet Beebe saw a new fish, at least two feet long, with fins like "ghostly sails." With his usual imaginative flair he called it the Pallid Sailfin.

Tug whistles signaled yet another new record as the bathysphere plunged to 2,300 feet. Still, the dive continued. Resting at 2,500 feet for 30 minutes, Beebe caught in his searchlight beam "a strange quartet" of fish that he called Abyssal Rainbow Gars. They were four inches long and swam in tight formation, almost upright. Their jaws and heads were bright red, their bodies rich blue, and their tails yellow. Beebe remarked how wasted these brilliant colors seemed to be in the eternal blackness of the deep.

After an extended photography session, the explorers felt tiredness coming on and asked to be raised. Their timing was fortunate, for at 1,900 feet an extraordinary leaf-shaped fish appeared. Its flat brown body was starred with rows of yellow and purple lights. Beebe called it the Five-lined Constellationfish and said it was "one of the loveliest things I have ever seen."

Beebe and Barton's last and deepest dive together in the bathysphere took place four days later, on the morning of August 15, 1934. Going down merely to break records had no meaning for the director: His only ambition was the discovery of new species and the observation of strange behavior. At 1,680 feet he had ample opportunity for the latter. He wrote: "I saw some creature, several inches long, dart toward the window, turn sideways and—explode. At the flash, which was so strong that it illuminated my face and the inner sill of the window, I saw the great red shrimp and the outpouring fluid of flame. . . . The fact that a number of the deep-sea shrimps had this power of defense is well known. . . . It is the abyssal complement of the sepia smoke screen of a squid at the surface."

At 2,450 feet the explorer was surprised when a huge,

## Tons of Pressure "Piled Up in All Directions"

Otis Barton (left), who designed the bathysphere, and William Beebe stand beside the diving craft after their record descent of 3,028 feet. At the deepest point, the bathysphere successfully withstood 1,360 pounds of pressure per square inch, more than half a ton. "Each window," Beebe marveled, "held back over nineteen tons of water, while a total of 7,016 tons were piled up in all directions upon the bathysphere itself."

Even the ascent held fresh surprises. At 2,100 feet a tray of calcium chloride pitched to the floor, distracting Barton's attention. Beebe, as usual, had more important things on his mind and kept right on with his observations, as Barton recalled with chagrin. "A deep-sea dragon at least six feet long crossed before the window and a moment later returned with its mate. Until that time scientists had doubted the presence of such large fish in the mid-depths. This was the only big dragon on record, and I had missed seeing it." Beebe named his important discovery *Bathysphaera intacta* (the Untouchable Bathysphere Fish).

At 1,900 feet a giant female anglerfish swam by, two feet long "with enormous mouth and teeth" and a tentacle rising from its head. Beebe knew that this fish, like many others he had seen, had been the same for hundreds of millions of years. As the bathysphere continued to move slowly up, Beebe pondered the changeless-

*Adventurers Below and Above*

dim, 20-foot outline swam effortlessly past the end of the searchlight beam. Beebe surmised it must be a small member of the whale family, since they have "a special chemical adjustment of the blood which makes it possible for them to dive a mile or more, and come up without getting the 'bends.'"

Barton, who had missed seeing the whale, soon managed to make a significant discovery of his own—the first living *Stylophthalmus*, "one of the most remarkable of deep sea fish." Its eyes are on the ends of periscope stalks nearly a third the length of its body.

At 11:12 a.m. the bathysphere finally stopped at 3,028 feet. Beebe and Barton were more than half a mile down and had reached a record depth that would not be surpassed until 15 years later, by Barton himself. As Beebe sat musing in his lonely sphere, he sensed, through the absolute blackness around him, the purity of the water and felt a kinship between the luminescent bodies in the depths of the sea and the planets, suns, and stars of outer space.

---

## Ingenious New Vessels Explore the World Below the Waves

The bathysphere's dives were limited by the length of the steel cable that connected the craft with its mother ship. Swiss scientist Auguste Piccard, however, designed a diving vehicle, the bathyscaphe, which could descend and resurface unhampered by cables. The upper part of the bathyscaphe (above right) consisted of huge tanks, some filled with air and others with gasoline, a fluid lighter than water, which kept the bathyscaphe afloat. To descend, the bathyscaphe's air tanks were opened and flooded with water, forcing the craft downward. To ascend, lead ballast, held in storage compartments, was released, and the bathyscaphe rose to the surface. The diving craft's occupants were housed in the circular cabin, a spherical, 10-ton observation gondola suspended beneath its giant tanks.

The bathyscaphe *Trieste* (right), purchased by the United States government, made the deepest dive ever recorded. On January 23, 1960, Piccard's son Jacques and American Donald Walsh took the *Trieste* to the bottom of Challenger Deep, the deepest part of the huge Mariana

Trench off the Pacific island of Guam. The two men descended 35,800 feet, well over six miles beneath the water's surface. Since this remarkable feat, undersea research has concentrated on how human beings can live and work in the ocean depths. Frenchman Jacques-Yves Cousteau has pioneered in the development of undersea habitats, where divers have spent several weeks living underwater. They could emerge from their research station to explore the ocean floor in a minisub. The United States Navy has also developed a program for divers (called aquanauts), among them former astronaut Scott Carpenter, to live in an undersea station called Sealab (left). In 1965 Carpenter and Navy physician Robert Sonnenburg each spent 30 days in Sealab 2 at a depth of 205 feet. In addition to prolonging the period of time human beings can stay underwater, future research will concentrate on exploiting the mineral wealth of the sea.

**Mount Everest** (*above*), *a plume of snow swirling from its summit, rises over the crests of smaller Himalayan peaks. The first man to reach the summit was the New Zealander Edmund Hillary (below).*

**Edmund Hillary** (*above left*) *and his Sherpa companion Tenzing Norkay (right) toil slowly and laboriously up to Everest's 29,028-foot summit. "We climbed because nobody climbed it before—it was a mountain to climb," Hillary would later explain. "But even now the danger adds something to it. If Everest were just a mountain that you plugged to the top without any danger, it would be the world's biggest bore."*

*Adventurers Below and Above*

## Chapter Thirty

*Towering above the tiny Himalayan kingdom of Nepal is the tallest mountain in the world, almost five and a half miles high. It has defied, and sometimes killed, some of the world's greatest mountaineers. In 1953 a British team of climbers finally conquers the great peak in a thrilling display of skill and indomitable courage.*

# At the Top of the World: Hillary Climbs Mount Everest

*Born in Auckland, New Zealand, in 1919, Edmund Hillary became interested in mountain climbing as a young man while vacationing with a friend in the New Zealand Alps. In 1951 he was invited to join a New Zealand expedition to the Himalayas, and subsequently, he was included in a British reconnaissance party to Everest and a 1952 British attempt to climb Cho Oyu, a major Himalayan peak. His performance on these expeditions won him a place on the 1953 British Everest team and marked him as a potential "summiter." After his successful climb, Hillary was knighted by Queen Elizabeth II. From 1955–58, Hillary led the New Zealand unit of the British Commonwealth Transantarctic Expedition. On January 4, 1958, after crossing 1,200 miles of icecap, he and his party became the first to reach the South Pole in 46 years.*

As the peers of the realm waited to proceed into Westminster Abbey for the coronation of Queen Elizabeth II, they seemed to give more attention to a headline in the London *Times* than to the pageantry all around them. The story that so absorbed them on that June morning in 1953 was the sensational news that Everest, the unconquerable mountain, had been conquered—and by a British expedition. This glorious achievement, coming as it did on the eve of the coronation of the young queen, was heralded as appropriate for the beginning of a second Elizabethan Age.

At 29,028 feet, Everest is the highest mountain in the world. Named by the British in honor of a 19th-century surveyor general of India, the Himalayan peak is better known locally as Chomolungma, "Goddess Mother of the World." Looming between Tibet and Nepal and flanked by other immense peaks, it appears unassailable and inaccessible. As the English mountaineer George Mallory said before his pioneering expedition in 1921, "It would be necessary in the first place to find the mountain." Mallory found Everest but lost his life

in a 1924 attempt to scale it. During the next three decades no fewer than nine other expeditions were defeated by its awesome difficulties: precipitous rock faces, deep powdery snow, tearing gales, severe penetrating cold, and sheer, lung-starving altitude.

Yet, when 42-year-old Col. John Hunt was appointed by the Royal Geographical Society and the Alpine Club to be leader of the British expedition to Mount Everest in 1953, hundreds of mountaineers offered their services. Only 10 were chosen. These were Charles Evans, 33, a sandy-haired brain surgeon; Charles Wylie, 32, a quiet major in the Brigade of Gurkas; Alfred Gregory, 39, a small, dapper travel agent; Wilfrid Noyce, 34, a shy schoolmaster; Tom Bourdillon, 28, a huge but nimble physicist; Michael Westmacott, 27, a statistician with a superb mountaineering technique; and George Band, 23, a former president of the Cambridge University Mountaineering Club whom Hunt regarded as "the most brilliant climber in Britain." For the last three members of his climbing pary, Hunt, needing experienced snow-and-ice men, looked outside the British Isles. Two New Zealanders exactly fitted the bill: lanky George Lowe, 28, a man of almost superhuman stamina; and Edmund Hillary, 33, a beekeeping bachelor from Auckland, who stood six feet four in his size 12 boots and climbed, he said, "for the fun of it." A later addition was a veteran of five previous Everest expeditions, Tenzing Norkay, 39, a member of the Sherpa tribe of Himalayan hillmen. Although he could neither read nor write, Tenzing had the unmistakable air of a man who knows his worth. While the rest of the Everest team practiced in Wales and New Zealand, Tenzing toted a knapsack full of heavy stones up and down the hills near his home in India. "This is the time you must do it," he silently vowed. "You must do it or die."

In the first week of March 1953, members of the Everest expedition converged on Katmandu, a city of

### Mountaineering for Sport Began in the Alps

The modern sport of mountaineering owes its development to 18th-century Swiss scientist Horace-Bénédict de Saussure, who offered a reward for the first man to climb Mont Blanc in the Alps. The peak was first scaled in 1786, and the following year De Saussure himself reached its formidable summit. Above, De Saussure's party is pictured descending Mont Blanc.

gods they believed to inhabit Chomolungma. Everest's summit was visible from a ridge just above the monastery, snow streaming from its triangular silhouette like a panache of ostrich feathers.

Then began three weeks of rigorous training and acclimatization. Groups fanned out in all directions, practicing mountaineering skills. Lungs stretched and muscles tautened as the climbers ventured higher and higher, preparing for their ascent of the great mountain's southern face. The seven topographical features of that face were already well known to them: the curving, rubble-strewn Khumbu Glacier; the precipitous Icefall; the Western Cwm, a hidden valley of ice between Lhotse Mountain and Mount Everest; the terrifying, near-vertical Lhotse Face; the wind-whipped saddle of the South Col, which rises to 26,200 feet; the South Peak, towering 28,700 feet high; and finally the untrodden ridge that led to the summit and was known only from aerial photographs.

Acclimatization to heights of 20,000 feet had to be done gradually. The men needed time for their bone marrow to manufacture extra oxygen-bearing red corpuscles. Beyond 20,000 feet bottled oxygen became increasingly necessary: Lack of it could cause nausea, rapid pulse, blurred vision, and dangerous lightheadedness. Hunt experimented with two different systems:

**Natives of Nepal** *tell tales of the yeti, or Abominable Snowman, a mythical apelike creature whose supposed footprint can be seen in the snow beside an ice ax. The stocky, nocturnal creature allegedly stands about six feet tall. But no yeti has ever been sighted, and the print is believed to be that of the Tibetan blue bear, which roams the snowy slopes of the Himalayas.*

temples and palaces in the wooded valley of Nepal. Here the climbers were joined by Tenzing and by a doctor, a physiologist, a cameraman, and a correspondent from the London *Times*, which had bought exclusive rights to the story of the ascent.

By March 10 the expedition had begun its 170-mile trek east to the first Base Camp at Thyangboche Monastery. Swelling the ranks were a group of experienced Sherpas, destined for high-altitude work, and 350 temporary porters. Some of these were women with multicolored aprons and high felt boots. They made a lively addition to the party.

As they marched, Hunt's men were confronted by the blaze of spring rhododendrons in the valley. The expedition began to snake up into the mountains, and more and more high peaks revealed themselves. Swinging northward, the party passed through the little Sherpa capital of Namche Bazar. Ten miles above it, at an altitude of about 13,500 feet, lay the Buddhist sanctuary of Thyangboche. Here, surrounded by some of the loveliest scenery on earth, Hunt and his men pitched 20 tents of various shapes and colors in a yak field.

The monastery, a large building topped with a knob of gold, stood amid fields of blue primula and forests of juniper. Pheasants, partridges, and musk deer roamed at will, for no living creature, not even the fabled dreaded yeti, could be killed there. The monks spent their days brewing a clove-scented rice spirit, popularly known as lama's milk, and worshiping the

the familiar open-circuit, in which air breathed out was lost for good, and the new closed-circuit, in which exhalations passed through soda lime, which removed carbon dioxide, and then were rebreathed along with pure oxygen.

By the third week in April the Base Camp had been moved to an altitude of 17,900 feet on the Khumbu Glacier. This "avenue" of stones and ice was inhabited by a few tailless rats, high-altitude spiders, and crowlike choughs. Its head, at the very base of Everest proper, was the formidable, constantly shifting Icefall, a frozen cataract 2,000 feet long.

Here Hillary, Lowe, Band, and Westmacott began to hack out a "staircase" safe enough for Sherpas carrying heavy loads. It was difficult and treacherous work, complicated further by snowstorms, avalanches, and shifts in the glaciers. Blocks of ice as big as houses and pinnacles as high as steeples had to be scaled with rope

*Adventurers Below and Above*

ladders. Deep crevasses too wide to jump had to be bridged by poles and aluminum ladders. Certain particularly attractive passages soon earned names to describe their charm. "Hillary's Horror" (steps cut above a chasm) and "Hell Fire Alley" (a stretch of iceblocks moving with the glacier) were among these.

Camp II, consisting of two three-foot tents, was established halfway up the Icefall, at 19,400 feet; Camp III followed at 20,200 feet, and the effects of high altitude were soon felt in the form of befuddled thinking and lagging enthusiasm. There James Morris, the *Times* correspondent, first realized that Hillary "had a strain of greatness in him." Watching the big man tirelessly hacking steps out of the ice, Morris described his energy as "almost demonic." He also had "a tremendous bursting, elemental, infectious, glorious vitality about him . . . but beneath the good fellowship and the energy there was a subtle underlying seriousness."

Camp IV—Advance Base—was set up on the Western Cwm, Camp V below the towering Lhotse Face, and Camps VI and VII at 23,000 and 24,000 feet, respectively, on the face of Lhotse itself.

While all this work was being done, a potentially brilliant partnership was developing between Hillary and Tenzing. They were an odd-looking couple, the one tall and angular, the other short and wiry. On April 26,

during their first climb together, Hillary rashly leaped across a crevasse in the Icefall with Tenzing roped behind. Hillary described the incident: "It was too much for the overhanging lip and with a sharp crack it split off and descended into the crevasse with me on top of it. I didn't have much time to think. I only knew that I had to stop being crushed against the ice by the twisting block and I threw my cramponed feet hard against one wall and my shoulders against the other. Next moment the rope came tight and the block dropped away underneath me. Tenzing's reaction had been very quick. . . . His rope work was first class, as my near-catastrophe had shown. Although not perhaps technically outstanding in icecraft, he was very strong and determined and an excellent acclimatizer. Best of all, as far as I was concerned, he was prepared to go fast and hard." Back at Base Camp, Hillary confessed, "Without Tenzing I would have been finished today."

Six days later, in another experimental climb, Hillary and Tenzing went from Base Camp to Advance Base and back, using open-circuit oxygen. This was regarded as a three-day trip, but Hillary and Tenzing returned, in spite of a great blizzard, that evening. This extraordinary performance singled them out as the most energetic climbing pair in the expedition.

On May 2 Hunt ordered a few days' rest at low alti-

## Nepal: Lofty Land of Sherpas and Dwelling Place of Gods

Site of soaring Himalayan peaks, Nepal was the birthplace more than 2,000 years ago of Siddhartha Gautama, who became known as Buddha, the Enlightened One (below). Buddhism has become one of the world's great religions, but today, as a result of centuries of migration from India, Nepal is 90 percent Hindu. Yet, in the small kingdom, religions exist harmoniously together. At the shrine of Swayumbhunath (right), near the capital of Katmandu, statues of Jesus, Buddha, and Mahatma Gandhi, father of Indian independence, stand next to those of various Hindu gods.

Buddhism retains its strongest hold among the Sherpas, who migrated centuries ago to the Himalayan foothills of Nepal from their ancestral homes in Tibet. At monasteries like Thyangboche, which many Everest parties have visited on their trek to the base of the mountain, red-robed lamas twirl prayer wheels with the sacred Buddhist benediction *Om mani padme hum*—"Behold, the jewel is in the lotus." The Sherpas believe that the huge mountain peaks surrounding their villages are inhabited by deities. After descending from Everest, Hunt's party was asked by the abbot of Thyangboche if the climbers had seen gods on the summit. When the reply was negative, the abbot responded that they probably hadn't reached the summit.

The Sherpas never attempted to scale neighboring Himalayan peaks until foreign expeditions tried to do so in the 20th century. However, living and working at heights up to 15,000 feet, they acclimatized easily to the demanding tasks of porters. Moreover, the climbing expeditions have brought many changes to Sherpaland. Under the direction of Sir Edmund Hillary, at least 17 schools and 2 hospitals have been constructed in the

Sherpas' native provinces of Solu and Khumbu. "When you go into the Sherpa villages with the eyes of the West," Sir Edmund has said, "you can't help seeing what they lack and what can be done for them." Tragically, Hillary's wife and a teenage daughter were killed in a 1975 plane crash in Nepal while he was supervising the building of a Sherpa hospital.

## Everest Challenged the Most Daring and Skillful Climbers

When the 1953 Everest party attacked the world's highest peak, seven Englishmen, one Sherpa (Tenzing himself), and Swiss climber Raymond Lambert had already come within 1,000 feet of its summit. Of this elite group, the best known were George Leigh Mallory and Andrew Irvine, who vanished on the slopes of Everest in 1924, after being observed higher on the mountain's northeast ridge than any men had ever gone before. When Hillary and Tenzing reached the summit, one of their first

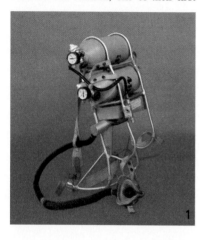

acts was to look for any sign that Mallory and Irvine might have reached the top before plunging to their doom on Everest's icy slopes. However, there was no evidence that Mallory and Irvine had scaled the peak. "It was romantic to suppose," wrote 1953 expedition leader John Hunt, "that some spell had been cast over the final keep."

Actually, Mount Everest is not a particularly difficult peak to climb from a mountaineering point of view. Other mountains, in fact, require more technical work, such as using pitons to provide hand- and footholds on their sheer faces. In addition, Everest rises only 12,000 feet from its base on the 17,000-foot-high Tibetan plateau, while Mount McKinley in Alaska extends upward for 19,000 feet from its base. Tenzing rated the ascent of India's Nanda Devi East as the most difficult climb of his entire career. However, it is the combination of tricky weather and high altitude that makes Everest's summit so difficult to reach. The weather severely limits the time of year when an attempt on Everest is feasible. The winter gales, whipping the summit with 100-mile-per-hour winds, make climbing impossible. The summer

monsoons, bringing desperately needed rain to the Indian subcontinent, deposit layers of fresh snow on Everest, which make climbing difficult and avalanches an ever-present danger. Attempts on the mountain have to be timed between the end of the winter winds and before the onset of the monsoons—a period in May and early June lasting little more than a

---

tude for all except Lowe and Band, who were still on Lhotse hacking a route up to the South Col. Congregating in a valley six miles below Base Camp, the mountaineers drank in the sight of grass and flowers, a necessary tonic before the assault began in earnest.

On May 7 they returned to Base Camp for a briefing by their leader. Perched on boxes or sprawled on sleeping bags, they waited with bated breath to hear what roles they would play in the last act of the drama. First, Hunt announced, Lowe, Band, and Westmacott would complete cutting the route up Lhotse Face by May 15. Noyce and Wylie would then establish Camp VIII at almost 26,000 feet on South Col, a broad, windswept, inhospitable ridge of stones and ice. From there, Evans and Bourdillon would make the first attempt on the summit. Their main objective was to survey the South Peak, 328 feet below the actual summit but separated from it by the ridge that no climber had ever seen. Only if the weather held and oxygen reserves were sufficient were they to go for the top.

If they failed, Hillary and Tenzing were to follow within 24 hours from the South Col, picking up en route a small tent and supplies that Gregory and Hunt would dump at 28,000 feet. They were then to establish Camp IX as near to the summit as possible, making

their final assault after a recuperative night's sleep.

The team's doctor, Michael Ward, 27, voiced the only objection to Hunt's scheme. He was strongly against the leader going so high. More than anyone, Ward understood the telltale lines of strain on Hunt's face. "You've done too much already," he said. Hunt thanked him, but the plan was not changed.

At 5 the next evening, Lowe, using the radio, reported from Lhotse Face that Band was ill and would have to come down. Meanwhile, helped intermittently by Sherpa Ang Nyima, Ward, and Noyce, Lowe continued to hack at Lhotse, determined to keep a route open in high wind and heavy snow. By the time the work was completed, Lowe had spent 10 consecutive nights at more than 23,000 feet. Griffith Pugh, the physiologist, worried about the possible effect on Lowe's mind. The feat would, said Hunt, "go down in the annals of mountaineering as an epic achievement of tenacity and skill." Toward the end, according to Noyce, Lowe was so exhausted that he fell asleep during a meal, with a sardine hanging from his mouth.

On May 21 Noyce and a Sherpa, Annulla, accomplished the first "lift" up Lhotse Face to Camp VIII on the Col. "I have been in many wild and lonely places in my life," said Tenzing about the site, "but never any-month. Even during this favorable period, wind and gales push men to the limit of their endurance. The altitude combines with the weather in a grueling test of strength. The physical disabilities caused by elevations over 25,000 feet include blurred vision, racing pulse, and extreme muscular fatigue. Every movement seems to require immense effort. To minimize the effects of the altitude, Hillary and Tenzing used open-circuit oxygen apparatus (picture 1) on their summit ascent. Oxygen from the set, carried on the climber's back, combined with air in his face mask to supply him with enough oxygen to function in the rarefied atmosphere. However valuable, the weight of the sets was an enormous drawback. Each set, with a reserve can of oxygen, weighed $28\frac{1}{2}$ pounds. In addition, because one-third of the oxygen cannisters had arrived from England too

damaged to be used, the party tried to conserve the remaining supply. Hillary recalled that he was constantly calculating how long their supply would last on the summit climb.

With the exception of the concern for oxygen supplies and altitude sickness that occurred at the higher levels, the lower slopes of Everest presented some of the trickiest aspects of the ascent. The Khumbu Glacier with its shifting snow and ice was particularly treacherous. Huge crevasses tore jagged gashes in the snow (picture 2). Some were so large that a portable aluminum ladder was used to bridge them (picture 3). Colored flags,

which can be seen in Camp III (picture 4), were used to mark safe passages on the unstable surface.

The trek up to Camp III was made even more difficult by the heavy loads the climbers and their Sherpa porters carried. More than three tons of supplies were hauled to Camp III as the men picked their way up the dangerous Icefall. Some 20 years later, Hillary disapproved of the way the men disposed of their supplies during the ascent. "We just chucked the trash out," he noted. "Our old junk is still on the ice on Everest. We should have taken it down with us or disposed of it in a deep crevasse."

---

where like the South Col. Lying at 25,850 feet between the final peaks of Everest and Lhotse, it . . . is simply a bare frozen plain of rock and ice, over which the wind roars with never a minute's stop."

From Camp VIII on May 26, the first attempt on the summit was made. The appointed day dawned clear and bright. Evans and Bourdillon, carrying closed-circuit oxygen, set out up the great couloir, a snowy gully more than 1,000 feet high that led to the South Peak of Everest. Later that morning, the men on the Col spotted the two distant figures going strongly toward the peak. There was great excitement in the camp. George Lowe reported that only Tenzing, normally given to yodeling and whooping when he was happy, "lost his smile. . . . The idea that anybody but Tenzing should reach the summit was not pleasurable to him."

At 1 p.m. Evans and Bourdillon stepped onto the South Peak. At 28,700 feet, this was the highest point ever climbed by man. Both men were eager to continue along the last ridge, which swooped downward before ascending to the summit. But it was late in the day, and Evans estimated that they would need five hours to get there and back, let alone return to the South Col. Besides, their oxygen supply was running low, and they were more exhausted than they realized.

Utterly spent, they tumbled part of the way down the couloir, arriving in Camp VIII at 4:30 p.m., "their faces frost-covered, looking," wrote Hunt, "like strangers from another planet."

That night the temperature dropped to −13° F. Crammed into three tents without enough of the oxygen sleeping sets they called "night oxygen" to help them sleep, everybody was uncomfortable. "The wind," said Lowe, "slammed over the Col and worried the tents, whining, roaring and snapping incessantly." Evans and Bourdillon were in bad shape next day, and Hunt, though extremely reluctant to leave Hillary and Tenzing, had to help them down to a lower altitude. High winds continued to buffet the tents, compelling the second assault team to postpone their attempt until the following day. On the 28th the wind dropped. At 8:45 a.m. Lowe, Gregory, and Ang Nyima set out to prepare the route up the couloir. About an hour later Hillary and Tenzing followed. They were using open-circuit oxygen, which Tenzing preferred because "there was less bad effect when you had to turn it off."

At midday the climbers and the support party met up on a high ridge. Continuing on to 27,350 feet, they picked up the tent and supplies dumped by Hunt and Gregory two days earlier. (The leader had been too

SUMMIT · SOUTH SUMMIT · IX · VIII · VII · VI · To V · IV · III · II · BASE

CHINA

HIMALAYA

TIBET

MOUNTAINS

INDIA

NEPAL

Mount Everest
(29,028 ft.)

Katmandu

**The British pioneered** *a new route up Everest (above) in their 1953 assault. Before World War II, expeditions had begun from Tibet and ascended the mountain from the northeast. However, after the 1951 Communist Chinese takeover of Tibet, climbers approached the mountain through Nepal, which had recently opened its borders to foreigners. From Base Camp at 17,900 feet on the Khumbu Glacier, the British party established Camp II halfway up the treacherous Icefall. Camp III stood at the top of the Icefall, and Camp IV, called Advance Base Camp, was in the Western Cwm, a windswept valley enclosed by the peaks of Everest and neighboring Lhotse. Camp V was pitched at the foot of Lhotse Face; Camps VI and VII were on the face itself; and Camp VIII, at 25,800 feet, was on the South Col. Hillary and Tenzing pitched Camp IX at 27,900 feet, from where they started their summit ascent. The map at left shows Everest on the border of Tibet and Nepal.*

*Adventurers Below and Above*

spent to go up to 28,000 feet, as he had planned.) Their loads were now cripplingly heavy, weighing between 50 and 63 pounds. At 2:30 p.m. they reached a level of approximately 27,900 feet. Here the two parties split. As he watched his colleagues descend out of sight, Hillary confessed to "a certain feeling of loneliness."

Hillary and Tenzing spent the next few hours clearing a six-foot platform (Camp IX) beneath a bluff of rock for their tent. The site was made uncomfortable by being at two levels, one a foot higher than the other. In spite of strong winds, the climbers managed to anchor their guy ropes to oxygen bottles sunk in the surrounding snow. Tenzing made a supper of hot soup, sardines, thawed-out canned apricots, dates, biscuits, jam, honey, and huge quantities of tea, and a drink made of powdered lemon juice, sugar, and warm water. (In the high altitudes, standard camp fare had little appeal. The climbers lost their appetites at the same time as they became enormously thirsty and wanted greater quantities of liquids.) About 6 p.m. they settled into their sleeping bags, Tenzing on the lower level, and the lanky Hillary squeezed half-lying, half-sitting on the upper. Tenzing never forgot their discomfort that night.

"Lying in the dark," he later said, "we talked of our plans for the next day. Then, breathing the 'night oxygen,' we tried to sleep. Even in our eiderdown bags we both wore all our clothes, and I kept on my Swiss reindeer boots. . . . Hillary, on the other hand, took his off, and laid them next to his sleeping bag. The hours passed. I dozed and woke, dozed and woke. And each time I woke, I listened. By midnight there was no wind at all. God is good to us, I thought. Chomolungma is good to us. The only sound was that of our own breathing as we sucked at our oxygen."

At 3:30 a.m. Tenzing peered out through the tent flap. In the dawn light Thyangboche Monastery was just visible some 14,000 feet below. He hoped that the monks were praying for them. After a quick breakfast of more sardines, biscuits, and lemon juice, both men were ready for the greatest challenge of their lives. But when Hillary reached for his boots, he found they were frozen solid. Thawing them out over the stove took an hour and filled the tent with the smell of scorching leather. Finally, at 6:30 a.m., swathed in so many layers of clothing their limbs looked dropsical, they turned on their oxygen and set off toward the South Peak. Tenzing led until Hillary was sure of his boots.

The slope was snowy and slippery. At one point Hillary fell so heavily he wondered aloud if it were safe to continue. "Just as you wish," came Tenzing's reply. Without another word, they continued climbing. The climbers soon found themselves pushing up an increasingly narrow ridge to the site where Evans and Bourdillon had cached precious bottles of oxygen for Hillary and Tenzing. "The narrow ridge," Hillary remembered, "led up to a very impressive steep snow face running to the South [Peak]. Evans and Bourdillon had ascended the rocks on the left and then descended the snow on their return. Their tracks were only faintly visible and we liked neither route. We discussed the matter and decided for the snow. We commenced plugging up in foot deep steps with a thin wind crust on top and precious little belay for the ice axe. It was altogether most unsatisfactory and whenever I felt feelings of fear regarding it I'd say to myself, 'Forget it! This is Everest and you've got to take a few risks.' Tenzing expressed his extreme dislike but made no suggestion regarding turning back. Taking turns we made slow speed up this vast slope. After several hundred feet the angle eased a little and the slope was broken by more rock outcrops and the tension eased."

**Originally a porter,** *Sherpa Tenzing Norkay won a place as a full-fledged climber on the 1952 Swiss Everest expedition and the 1953 British climb due to his mountaineering skill. Above, Hillary's photograph of Tenzing on the summit. Hillary, unfortunately, did not have his picture taken at the top of the world, since Tenzing had never used a camera and Hillary could not teach him how to at the top of the mountain.*

**From Everest's summit,** *Hillary photographed the breathtaking Himalayan scenery to prove conclusively that the two climbers had reached the mountain's top. Above left, to the northwest wends West Rongbuk Glacier, the approach to Everest taken by all assault expeditions before World War II. And, above right, to the southeast looms Makalu, the world's fifth highest mountain at 27,824 feet. From the top of Everest, Hillary speculated on a route to Makalu's summit, which was not scaled until 1955.*

At 9 a.m. Hillary and Tenzing cramponed onto the South Peak and saw stretching ahead the final ridge to the summit. "We looked with some eagerness on the ridge ahead as this was the crux of the climb. . . . Both Tom and Charles [Bourdillon and Evans] had expressed comments on the difficulties of the ridge ahead and I was not feeling particularly hopeful." The ridge was an "impressive and even rather frightening" sight, Hillary recalled. "On the right, great contorted cornices, overhanging masses of snow and ice, stuck out like twisted fingers over the 10,000-foot drop of the Kangshung Face. Any move onto these cornices could only bring disaster. From the cornices the ridge dropped steeply to the left until the snow merged with the great rock face sweeping up from the Western Cwm. Only one encouraging feature was apparent. The steep snow slope between the cornices and the rock precipices seemed to be composed of firm, hard snow. If the snow proved soft and unstable, our chances of getting along the ridge were few indeed. If we could cut a trail of steps along this slope, we could make some progress at least."

The snow, luckily, was firm. With Tenzing belaying him, Hillary ventured out along the ridge, patiently cutting out step after step. "To my surprise," he found, "I was enjoying the climb as much as I had ever en-joyed a fine ridge in my own New Zealand Alps."

At about 10 a.m. they reached a formidable obstacle that Hillary had been dreading since he had first sighted it through binoculars at Thyangboche. It was an immense rock some 40 feet high, which he at first thought was "beyond our feeble strength to overcome." Too smooth-faced to climb directly, it was impassable on the left, and on the right there was only a deep, narrow crack between the rock and a cornice of frozen snow. Squeezed in this "chimney," Hillary, digging his crampons backward into the snow and clutching at every nook or cranny he could find, gradually eased his way up the rock and onto a safe ledge. Tenzing followed. Hillary felt "the fierce determination that nothing now could stop our reaching the top." On they went, slowly cutting steps up the interminable slope.

Hillary wrote: "Our original zest had now quite gone and it was turning more into a grim struggle. I then realized that the ridge ahead, instead of still monotonously rising now dropped sharply away, and far below I could see the North Col and the Rongbuk Glacier. I looked upward to see a narrow snow ridge running up to a snowy summit. A few more whacks of the ice axe in the firm snow, and we stood on top."

Tenzing told it this way. "A little below the summit Hillary and I stopped. We looked up. Then we went on. The rope that joined us was thirty feet long, but I held most of it in loops in my hand, so that there was only about six feet between us. . . . We went on slowly, steadily. And then we were there. Hillary stepped on top first. And I stepped up after him." It was 11:30 in the morning of May 29, 1953.

Hillary's first feeling was one of profound thankfulness that he had no more steps to cut. Behind his oxygen mask, Tenzing grinned. The two men shook hands

*Adventurers Below and Above*

formally. But this was not enough for the exuberant Sherpa. "I waved my arms in the air, and then threw them around Hillary, and we thumped each other on the back until, even with the oxygen, we were almost breathless." Unfurling the flags of the United Nations, the United Kingdom, India, and Nepal from his ice ax, Tenzing then posed while Hillary took his photograph.

As they gazed down from the roof of the world, Hillary thought of all the men who had died to stand where he stood. He even looked for signs of the lost Mallory and his companion, Andrew Irvine, but saw nothing. Tenzing dug a little hole in the snow, in which he placed an offering of chocolate, candy, and biscuits for the gods of Chomolungma. Hillary, for his part, buried a small, white crucifix that somebody had mailed to Hunt. Fifteen minutes passed, during which Hillary took more pictures. Then, aware that they had a limited supply of oxygen for the descent from the summit to South Peak, they started down, cramponing carefully in the steps so laboriously carved on the way up. In an hour they reached the South Peak, where they picked up the spare oxygen bottles cached there.

After a swig of fruit juice, they continued on. Both men were extremely tired now. One sharp gust, one careless move, could topple them headlong into the Kangshung Glacier, 10,000 feet below. With this constantly in mind, Hillary packed each step safely before he and Tenzing lowered themselves onto it.

Pausing for a hot drink at Camp IX, they changed their oxygen bottles and wearily added mattresses and sleeping bags to the loads on their backs. As they hacked their way down the icy couloir, they could see the flapping tents of Camp VIII far below them. At 200 feet above the camp George Lowe was waiting with hot soup for the stiff-legged climbers. "Well, we knocked the bastard off!" said Hillary, grinning. Just short of the tents, his oxygen ran out.

The following day the victorious party made its way down the Lhotse Face to the Western Cwm, where Hunt sat tensely waiting for news. Suddenly, somebody spotted the climbers, and an eager crowd emerged from the tents. Not until they were within 50 feet of the camp did Lowe wave triumphantly toward the summit. Westmacott and Hunt rushed toward them, followed by Gregory in his pomponed cap, Bourdillon in his suspenders, and Evans in an upturned hat. Hillary lifted his ax; Tenzing flashed a brilliant smile. Laughing and crying, everybody shook hands and embraced.

"How did you feel when you stood on the summit?" asked James Morris later.

"It was a great relief to me," said Hillary, eating a leathery omelet.

"Very excited, not too tired, very pleased," beamed the delighted Tenzing.

### Garlands for Victors

Jubilant Nepalese decked Hillary (left), Hunt (center), and Tenzing with flowers after their Everest triumph. Since 1953, at least 35 men have scaled the peak, including a 1963 U.S. expedition on which six climbers reached the top. In 1975, a 35-year-old mother, Junko Tabei, member of an all-female Japanese expedition, reached the mountain's top.

**Men have long dreamed of** *traveling to the moon, but that dream became a reality on July 20, 1969, when Neil Armstrong and Col. Edwin Aldrin flew their tiny lunar module,* Eagle, *from the command ship,* Columbia, *to the moon's surface. The lunar module was named after the American eagle; an eagle is shown landing on the moon on the astronauts' arm patch (opposite). The name* Columbia, *said Neil Armstrong, "was an attempt to reflect the sense of adventure and exploration and seriousness with which Columbus undertook his assignment in 1492." From the window of the* Columbia, *Lt. Col. Michael Collins, who piloted the command ship while his two companions investigated the lunar surface, captured the drama of space exploration in his photograph of the earth rising over the barren lunar landscape (above). His picture shows the* Eagle, *with Armstrong and Aldrin aboard, returning from the moon to the mother ship. At right, Armstrong photographed Aldrin walking on the surface of the moon. Armstrong and the lunar module are reflected in Aldrin's face mask. The astronauts left a metal plaque at the lunar landing site inscribed, "We came in peace for all mankind."*

*Adventurers Below and Above*

## Chapter Thirty-One

*Reaching an ancient goal of mankind, two U.S. astronauts land their space vehicle on a lunar landscape after a voyage of almost 239,000 miles. There, in a barren and hostile environment, they initiate a new age of discovery. Meanwhile, hundreds of millions back on earth watch them via television, uncertain of their safe return.*

# "One Giant Leap for Mankind": Apollo 11 Lands on the Moon

*The U.S. space effort was jolted into action by news of the U.S.S.R.'s lofting of the first satellite, Sputnik 1, on October 4, 1957. The following year the United States orbited a satellite and founded the National Aeronautics and Space Administration (NASA). Sufficient progress had been made in space technology by 1961 for President John F. Kennedy to announce: "This nation should commit itself to the goal, before this decade is out, of landing a man on the moon and returning him safely to earth." The three astronauts who were finally chosen for the great task eight years later were Neil Armstrong, Michael Collins, and Edwin ("Buzz") Aldrin. All three had been born in 1930 and had extensive experience as pilots and astronauts. By July 1969, their training for the flight was completed, and their rocket was ready for them.*

"T minus two minutes and counting," said the flat voice of Mission Control. As the final seconds ticked away toward 9:32 a.m.*—lift-off time—the Saturn 5 rocket sat on its pad as huge and seemingly immovable as a 36-story skyscraper. The date was July 16, 1969, and three men encapsulated on the tip of that rocket were about to blast off for the moon.

More than a million spectators clustered under the palms of Cocoa Beach, Florida, gazing across the Banana River at an oddly peaceful scene. Hot sunshine poured down on the concrete emptiness of Cape Kennedy. The only movement, apart from some distant lines of surf, was the lazy curl of what appeared to be smoke forming around the sides of the rocket. Actually, this was an ice mist caused by the extreme coldness of Saturn's interior, where 6 million pounds of liquid hydrogen, liquid oxygen, and kerosene froze in supercool chambers, awaiting the electric shock that would soon transform them into white heat.

"T minus ninety seconds and counting." The crew of Apollo 11 lay side by side on their parallel couches,

facing directly up to the sky. Neil Alden Armstrong, the blond civilian whom a combination of luck, ambition, and expertise had destined to be the first man to tread the surface of the moon, occupied the commander's couch, on the left next to the abort handle. His small-boned, 5-foot 11-inch body fitted comfortably into its small allotted space; the interior of the Apollo command module was about as large as a station wagon's, and much of it was given over to computer hardware.

With an easy, practiced sweep, Armstrong's eyes raked the glimmering mass of dials surrounding him. At 38, he had been checking cockpit dials for almost a quarter of a century and had been obsessed with flight for as long as he could remember. As a small boy in Wapakoneta, Ohio, he used to dream of hovering weightless. ("I neither flew nor fell. . . . There was never any end to the dream.") Now, as a pale, taciturn adult, he was about to begin his second journey into the regions of "zero gravity," a journey infinitely more dangerous than that of March 1966, when his Gemini 8 spacecraft had begun to roll and yaw sickeningly while in earth orbit. Armstrong, who had been known as one of America's best test pilots before he became an astronaut, had calmly coaxed his wild thrusters into submission, saving his own life and that of his crewmate. This display of steel was thought to have influenced his selection as leader of the moon mission.

Michael Collins, also 38, lying on the right-hand couch, was as breezy and garrulous as his commander was quiet. Throughout the mission this lanky Air Force officer was to provide most of the humor that enlivened the terse broadcasts from space. His role was pilot of Apollo's command module, *Columbia*, remaining in orbit above the moon while his colleagues made their descent to the surface in the lunar model, *Eagle*. After West Point—where his motto had been "stay casual"—he had joined the Air Force because it seemed "more

*Eastern Daylight Time. All times cited in this chapter are EDT.

331

## Jules Verne's Prophetic Voyage to the Moon

In 1865 the great French science fiction writer Jules Verne published *From the Earth to the Moon*, the story of a manned lunar voyage that anticipated the Apollo 11 shot with uncanny accuracy. Verne's fictional spacecraft, *Columbiad*, carrying three passengers, was launched by a 900-foot cannon from Tampa, Florida, little more than 100 miles from the Apollo 11 launch site at Cape Kennedy. Moreover, Verne gave a detailed description of the condition of weightlessness that the astronauts were to encounter during space flight. Unlike the Apollo 11 crew, however, Verne's space travelers ate gourmet meals accompanied by wine at a table set with a linen cloth. Illustrations from Verne's book depict the multistage rocket being readied for launch (top left); the blast-off into space from the mouth of the enormous cannon (top right); the *Columbiad* about to land on the moon (above left); and the recovery of the craft and its passengers (above right). The *Columbiad* splashed down in the Pacific Ocean and was retrieved by ship, a procedure that paralleled the method actually used to pick up the Apollo 11 crew a century later. In a televised broadcast from the spacecraft on the day before its Pacific splashdown, Apollo 11 commander Neil Armstrong began his reflections on the meaning of the epic flight with the words: "A hundred years ago, Jules Verne wrote a book about a voyage to the moon." Earlier, *From the Earth to the Moon* had inspired the father of American space technology, rocket builder Dr. Robert H. Goddard. Fascinated by Verne's book as a boy, Goddard resolved to turn stories of space travel into real scientific achievements.

exciting and more innovative than the Army." Sent to France to fly F-86's, he had developed a taste for good food and wine and probably suffered more than the other astronauts from NASA's infamous space rations. However, he proved to have a precise technical mind and a gift for articulating complex flight procedures in what he called "agricultural terms."

Lying between Armstrong and Collins was Col. Edwin Eugene Aldrin, Jr. (39), who since his Montclair, New Jersey, childhood had answered to the nickname Buzz. A natural athlete, with a burly body and lightning reflexes, he was also blessed with brains. "If you don't understand what Buzz is talking about today," said Collins, "you will tomorrow or the next day." Aldrin's 1962 doctoral dissertation at MIT on space rendezvous dynamics was so revolutionary that aspects of it were incorporated into NASA flight plans. His mental and physical energy had made him a textbook astronaut—tireless, serious, an infallible master of machines. Few guessed that of the three men to fly to the moon on Apollo 11, Buzz Aldrin would return the most changed.

"It's been a real smooth countdown," intoned the loudspeakers at Cocoa Beach. "Forty seconds away." Priests at the Vatican gazed at their television sets. "Thirty-five seconds and counting." Farmers in Australia pressed transistor radios to their ears. "We are still go with Apollo 11." Merchants in Pakistan squatted mute beneath public address systems rigged in dusty squares. "T minus fifteen seconds, guidance is internal." Jan Armstrong, floating in a boat on the Banana River, peered at the distant white bullet that contained her husband. "Twelve, eleven, ten, nine, eight, seven, ignition sequence starts. Six, five, four, three, two, one, zero, all engines running."

The first burst of light beneath Saturn was, surprisingly to most observers, silent. Orange flame, blinding in its brilliance, spread out so fast that all sound was obliterated. Then a series of thunderclaps hit Cocoa Beach, and all Florida seemed to tremble underfoot. Yet for one second and a quarter the rocket remained motionless atop its own explosion, secured by giant clamps, as eight engines built up 1.3 million pounds of thrust. The clamps flipped back. "Lift-off. We have a lift-off, thirty-two minutes past the hour."

The thunderclaps blurred into a coughing roar as Saturn rose from its pad. The rocket seemed reluctant to move, although it had already consumed 85,000 pounds of fuel; but in less than a minute it was traveling at well over the speed of sound. The sunburst of its exhaust faded into the sky, and its roar gradually diminished. Presently, a flash was seen in the southeast, indicating that the rocket's first stage had burned out and was dropping into the Atlantic.

While all this was going on, the three men inside the Apollo spacecraft lay strapped like mummies, listening to their only contact with the receding world, the voice of Launch Control. The first few seconds of their flight, which they knew were the most dangerous, were also the most unreal. ". . . We didn't sense the movement of lift-off," Aldrin remembered afterward. ". . . There was a slight increase in the amount of background noise, not at all unlike the sort one notices taking off in a commercial airliner. . . ." But as the rocket broke free of its escape tower, it began to sway and swing, reminding him of a train trying to settle onto its rails. Then, suddenly, all was glassy smoothness, and the crew felt earth's gravity dragging at them as Saturn accelerated. The drag never exceeded 4g's (or four times normal gravity), since in the words of Collins, "the Saturn is a gentleman, and will not plaster us into our couches."

Within three minutes the first-stage engines ran dry, and the astronauts lolled forward against their straps as the giant rocket momentarily slowed; then the second stage took over, forcing them back onto their seats again. Six minutes later, at an altitude of 100 miles, that stage, too, burned out and dropped away, and yet another engine blasted Apollo to a velocity of 25,500 feet per second. Eleven minutes, 42 seconds after lift-off, the third stage shut down, and the spacecraft was in silent orbit around the earth.

Although the astronauts found themselves suspended upside down, they were able to enjoy side-window views of earth. "From space," Aldrin wrote afterward, "it [earth] has an almost benign quality. Intellectually one could realize there were wars underway on earth, but emotionally it was impossible to understand such things. The thought occurred and reoccurred that wars are generally fought for territory or are disputes over borders; from space the arbitrary borders established on earth cannot be seen."

During the first hour of orbit the astronauts were busily preparing for Translunar Injection (TLI)—the final burn with which Saturn would thrust Apollo into outer space and toward the moon. It was scheduled to take place halfway through the second orbit. Working their way rapidly through a long sequence of "chores," they floated around the light gray cabin, throwing switches, taking star sightings, checking out the navigation systems. By the time Apollo 11 was over Australia, the spacecraft had been converted "from a passive payload to an active orbiter."

The astronauts saw their second dawn of the day—a

**Twentieth-century science fiction** *stimulated interest in space exploration and foreshadowed scientific developments in the field. In 1931 the cover of* Amazing Stories *(above), one of the earliest science fiction magazines, showed a mechanized lunar monster remarkably similar to the Apollo 11 landing vehicle.*

curving, incandescent horizon—as they swept on across the Pacific and approached Baja California. Whizzing over the United States, Apollo 11 passed Florida, completing its first earth orbit. Less than an hour now to TLI. The crew strapped themselves back onto the couches. Once again, the South Atlantic, Africa, and the Indian Ocean rolled by the spacecraft windows. Then, from NASA's relay station in Australia, came formal permission for man's most momentous journey. "Apollo 11, this is Houston. You are GO for TLI." "Apollo 11, thank you," responded Collins, as calmly as if he were accepting a business card. They moved out over the Pacific, and the three astronauts braced themselves for Saturn's last blast, which was to fling them, like a stone escaping a whirled sling, toward the moon.

TLI came, with computerized precision, at 12:16 p.m. For 5 minutes 47 seconds the liquid oxygen and hydrogen detonated at temperatures exceeding 4,000° F, hurling the 48-ton spacecraft eastward along an arrow-straight trajectory. As the curve of the earth

**This 19th-century** *photograph of the moon was one of the first to be taken through the lens of a high-powered telescope. It shows the lunar surface pockmarked by craters. Astronomers call the vast plains between craters "seas," although they contain no water. The lunar seas are crisscrossed by trenches referred to as rilles, as well as by ranges of lunar mountains.*

*Before attempting to land* on the moon, man first had to prove his ability to function in space. Accordingly, on June 3, 1965, astronaut Edward B. White II emerged from his Gemini 1 spacecraft for a 21-minute walk 100 miles above the earth. Secured to the spacecraft by a 27-foot umbilical cord, White held a self-maneuvering unit to enable him to move about in the weightless environment. Orbiting at 17,500 miles per hour, White covered 6,000 miles during his pioneering space walk.

dropped away, Neil Armstrong made what was for him an emotional remark. "Hey Houston, the Saturn gave us a magnificent ride." "It looks like you are on your way now," Mission Control responded.

Then Collins performed a tricky transposition and docking maneuver. First, he disconnected the command module *Columbia* from Saturn and floated a short way off, exposing the lunar module (LM) *Eagle* tucked like a chrysalis in the body of the rocket. Turning *Columbia* gently around, he nosed back toward the LM, docked with it, and heard the loud click of latches as the two modules slotted into each other. Then he triggered springs that freed the LM from its rocket cocoon. Apollo 11 was now reduced to its basic binary form, an ungainly combination of streamlined *Columbia* and spidery *Eagle*. Locked together, the two spacecraft sped on toward the moon at seven miles a sec-

ond, leaving the Saturn's remains to drift into space.

With nothing much to do until the time for mid-course corrections came the next day, the astronauts could relax. They climbed gratefully out of their bulky space suits and changed into comfortable, two-piece cabin garments. Understandably, the departing earth occupied much of their attention. Although it seemed to remain in closeup at first, they began to notice a gradual shrinkage every time it reappeared in the window. (The spacecraft was rotating very slowly, like a barbecue spit, to "spread" the heat of the sun's rays.) Aldrin devised an ingenious way of looking at the earth clearly and steadily through a small monocular telescope: "It was an intriguing process: in order to minimize any manual disturbances and compensate for the vibrations we could feel, I'd very carefully remove my hand from the monocular and leave it floating, weight-

*Adventurers Below and Above*

less, in front of the window. I'd then look through it, and for the several seconds before it drifted away from pointing at the earth we had a greatly improved view."

Through the floating telescope the world seemed "fragile, above all else" to Mike Collins. "From space there is no hint of ruggedness to it; smooth as a billiard ball, it seems delicately poised in its circular journey around the sun."

On the second day of the voyage, Houston's computer banks calculated that Apollo 11 was aimed so

**A Soviet stamp** *commemorates Yuri Gagarin, the first man in space. On April 12, 1961, he orbited the earth for an hour and 29 minutes in his spacecraft, Vostok 1. In 1968 Gagarin was killed during a training flight.*

accurately at the moon that only one minor mid-course correction would be needed. This burn took place without mishap, and the crew, relaxed and happy after a night's deep sleep, found themselves actually enjoying their space rations.

All food was packaged in plastic sachets to prevent the danger of stray morsels floating weightlessly around the cabin and clogging vital systems. Although there were some solids, such as baby shrimp and crackers, most food came in powder form and had to be mixed within the sachet by adding water and kneading. The resultant mush was then sucked through a tube.

Like all explorers venturing into the unknown, the astronauts maintained a watch through the night, rotating positions each rest period. While two men slept in light mesh sleeping bags, the third would doze on his couch with his earphones on, available for any midnight colloquy with Houston. But Mission Control remained almost silent, wanting the crew to arrive at the moon fully relaxed and in top physical condition.

Since the spacecraft's motion was not powered, its trajectory was affected by three different gravitational forces—those of the sun, the moon, and the earth. During the first two days of flight, the last was by far the most powerful, tugging at Apollo until its TLI speed of seven miles a second was slowed to less than one mile a second. Then, as the halfway mark was passed on Thursday afternoon, the pull of the other two celestial bodies took over, and Armstrong's speed needle began to creep upward again.

Later that day, and again on Friday, television viewers on earth were treated to magnificent views of their own planet, relayed to them from the cabin of Apollo 11. At one point the mischievous Collins decided to give the human race vertigo. He spun the television

camera 180 degrees, saying, "O.K., world, hang on to your hat. I'm going to turn you upside down!"

After their third "night" in space, the crew became serious astronauts again. Since the looming moon now screened off the sun, they stilled Apollo's "barbecue" rotation and swung the spacecraft around to bring their destination into closeup for the first time. The moon looked more frightening than beautiful. With a nervous attempt at humor, Armstrong said, "It's a view worth the price of the trip." Collins called it "the most awesome sphere I have ever seen." Huge, dim, and craggy, surrounded by the halo of the sun, it seemed near enough to touch. The spacecraft was accelerating steadily now and would continue to do so until its first Lunar Orbit Insertion burn (LOI-1) in the early afternoon. This six-minute firing would brake Apollo enough to allow the moon to drag it into orbit.

"Apollo 11, this is Houston," said the voice of Mission Control shortly after 1 p.m., as the spacecraft shot past the left-hand side of the moon. "All your systems are looking good going round the corner, and we'll see you on the other side." With that, the astronauts lost radio contact with the world. LOI-1 was scheduled for 1:22 p.m., and if the retrorocket failed to fire, there was nothing Houston could do to prevent three brave men from vanishing into space.

The climactic moment arrived, and Apollo's big engine burst into life. It thundered reassuringly for six minutes, slipping the spacecraft into a lopsided orbit of 71 miles by 194½ miles from the lunar surface. Less than half an hour later it curved around the right side

### *Apollo's Crew: A Civilian and Two Colonels*

Civilian Neil Armstrong (left) and Air Force officers Michael Collins (center) and Edwin Aldrin (right) were announced as the Apollo 11 crew on January 9, 1969, six months before the historic flight. All three had participated in the Gemini flights, the two-man space shots that had preceded the Apollo program. Armstrong had successfully performed the first docking in space between a Gemini capsule and its Agena rocket.

**One of the largest structures** *in the world, the Vehicle Assembly Building at Cape Kennedy is 525 feet high and has a floor space of 1.5 million square feet. If the building were not air-conditioned, moisture that would condense inside could form rain clouds under the roof of the main rooms. In this building, enormous cranes assembled the parts of the Saturn 5 rocket and the spacecraft that rode on top of it. Outside the mammoth structure, the completely assembled Apollo 11 stands on top of a 3,000-ton, diesel-powered tractor known as a crawler. This motorized platform, 113 feet long and 114 feet wide, crawled the 3.5 miles to the Apollo launch site at a speed of a mile an hour. It moved over a road called the crawlerway, specially constructed with an eight-foot-thick stone roadbed to bear the enormous weight of the rocket. When it arrived at the launch site, the crawler carefully transferred the giant NASA Apollo 11 to its launch pad and moved the service tower into place. Only then did technicians begin to fuel the rocket for the lunar flight.*

of the moon, and Collins was able to reply to the anxious calls of Mission Control.

*Houston:* "Apollo 11, Apollo 11, this is Houston. How do you read?"

*Collins:* "Read you loud and clear, Houston."

*Houston:* "Roger. . . . Could you repeat your burn status report?"

*Collins:* "It was like—it was like perfect."

The world breathed easier, but the astronauts, faced in four hours with a second, even trickier burn (LOI-2), were still as tense as wires. That burn, intended to place them in a closer, near-circular orbit, was, as Aldrin later recalled, "critically important. . . . It had to be made in exactly the right place, and for exactly the correct length of time. If we overburned for as little as two seconds we'd be on an impact course with the other side of the moon." But LOI-2 occurred with split-second promptness, and the spacecraft glided down until it was orbiting at an altitude of only 60 miles. Rolling beneath them the astronauts saw a curving, cratered landscape of barrenness: Dry, airless, too sterile even for color, it awaited the imprint of its first human foot.

Saturday, July 19, became Sunday, July 20—scheduled date of the lunar landing—and the three men sank into an exhausted sleep. Apollo 11 continued its soundless revolutions through space, moving from lunar day to lunar night and back again every hour. Armstrong had wisely covered up the windows of the cabin, so that the bright glare of the moon and the softer rays of earthshine did not disturb the crew as they slept.

"Apollo 11, Apollo 11, good morning from the Black Team." It took the groggy Collins 20 seconds to find his microphone button and answer, "Good morning, Houston. . . . You guys wake up early." "Yes. . . " replied Mission Control cheerfully, "looks like you were really sawing them away."

The bleary astronauts ate breakfast, helping it down with sachets of lukewarm coffee. Then came the complicated process of "suiting up." Aldrin and Armstrong donned liquid-cooled tubular underwear, climbed into their stiff space suits, clamped on their helmets, and strapped on their backpacks. Armstrong was ready first and crawled through the docking hatchway into the LM. Collins helped stuff them through, like two large laundry bags into a washer. Then the sound of slamming hatches sealed off the two lunar explorers from the man who would wait for them in orbit. "You cats take it easy on the lunar surface," said Collins over the radio. He flipped a switch, and the LM began to float away, its foil wraps twinkling in the sun. "The *Eagle* has wings!" shouted Aldrin triumphantly. It was 1:47 p.m., July 20, 1969.

The separation of the *Columbia* and *Eagle* took place behind the moon. When the two spacecraft emerged into "view," they were still close together, but by the time they disappeared again, Collins had performed a separation burn, putting 1,100 feet between them. Eight minutes later the LM's descent engine fired and began to power Aldrin and Armstrong steadily downward toward their landing target—the great pale plain named Mare Tranquillitatis, "Sea of Tranquillity," by an Italian Jesuit astronomer in 1651.

Strapped to the cabin's walls in standing positions, the astronauts were too busy to notice that they were gradually "gaining weight" as the moon's gravity strengthened. Aldrin, shouting a stream of computer display figures at his commander, was dimly aware that to bewildered listeners on earth he must sound as if he was "chattering like a magpie." Armstrong, watching his instruments like a hawk, was his usual taciturn self. His heart, however, was galloping at 156 beats a minutes, twice as fast as normal.

Suddenly, a yellow light flashed, and Armstrong's calm voice announced, "12 02, 12 02." Of all the millions of figures in Apollo 11's flight program, these were the ones Mission Control least wished to hear: "12 02" was the alarm code, signaling that *Eagle*'s computer was finding the task of landing men too great a strain.

After a few seconds of hesitation, the Houston flight controller, his mind working even faster than the computer, calculated that the problem would neutralize itself electronically and advised Armstrong he was still "go" for landing. *Eagle*'s engine was performing perfectly, but as the thin-legged craft plummeted at 129 feet per second, with only a mile between it and the moon, Armstrong became seriously alarmed by the

---

## NASA's Marvelous Machines for Exploring an Alien World

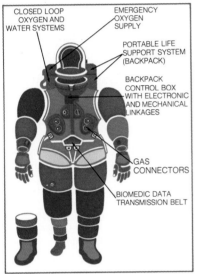

CLOSED LOOP OXYGEN AND WATER SYSTEMS

EMERGENCY OXYGEN SUPPLY

PORTABLE LIFE SUPPORT SYSTEM (BACKPACK)

BACKPACK CONTROL BOX WITH ELECTRONIC AND MECHANICAL LINKAGES

GAS CONNECTORS

BIOMEDIC DATA TRANSMISSION BELT

The Saturn 5 rocket (far right), 281 feet long, consisted of three stages with a combined weight of 6.5 million pounds. Stage 1 burned for two and a half minutes after lift-off and boosted the rocket's speed to 6,200 miles per hour. At 41 miles above the earth's surface, Stage 1 dropped off, and Stage 2 raised the speed to 15,400 miles per hour. At 116 miles up, Stage 2 was jettisoned, and Stage 3 increased the speed to 17,400 miles per hour. If any malfunction had occurred during lift-off, the Launch Escape System atop the Apollo 11 spacecraft would have blasted it free of the huge rocket. Since no such maneuver was needed, the Launch Escape System was jettisoned after lift-off.

Three hours and 17 minutes into the flight the Saturn 5's Instrument Unit was also jettisoned, and three minutes later a protective shield that surrounded the lunar module during lift-off was dropped. Sometime later the command module and the service module that held its engine separated from the third stage. Both then turned around and redocked with the lunar module. The Apollo 11 spacecraft, with the lunar module in the front, now weighed just over 96,000 pounds. The lunar module (below) made up about 33,000 pounds of this total. The landing craft was more than a lunar landing vehicle: Its descent stage served as a launch pad to blast Armstrong and Aldrin back to the command module after their stay on the moon. During the moon walk, the astronauts wore space suits with more than 500 different parts (left). Each garment had an oxygen-inflated inner layer covered by two outer layers of tough cloth. Pipes inside the suit circulated water to keep the men's body temperature comfortable. With the backpack containing the Portable Life Support System (each man's oxygen supply), each suit weighed 183 pounds. But in the moon's one-sixth gravity, the suit was a mere 30 pounds.

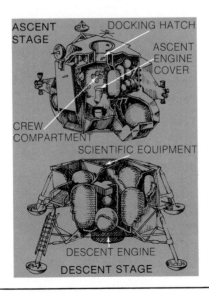

ASCENT STAGE

DOCKING HATCH

ASCENT ENGINE COVER

CREW COMPARTMENT

SCIENTIFIC EQUIPMENT

DESCENT ENGINE

DESCENT STAGE

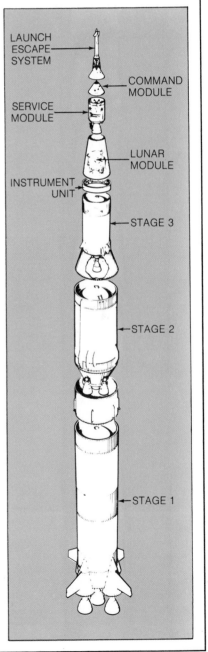

LAUNCH ESCAPE SYSTEM

COMMAND MODULE

SERVICE MODULE

LUNAR MODULE

INSTRUMENT UNIT

STAGE 3

STAGE 2

STAGE 1

---

terrain the computer was leading him into. ". . . We were quite certain that we would land a little 'long' [that is, downrange of the ideal landing site]. . . . As we dropped below a thousand feet, it was quite obvious that the system was attempting to land in an undesirable area in a boulder field. . . . I was surprised by the size of those boulders; some of them were as big as small motorcars. And it seemed at the time that we were coming up on them pretty fast."

Now the icy cool that Armstrong had cultivated for years as a test pilot steadied his hand as he reached out and deliberately overrode the computer. With only 500 feet to go, he took control of the sinking spacecraft and nudged it toward a clear area beyond the boulders. Houston warned him urgently that he had 60 seconds of fuel left: If it ran out before touchdown, *Eagle* would crash lifeless onto whatever rocks loomed beneath. Aldrin kept firing off descent rates and angles. "Forty feet, down two and one-half. Picking up some dust. Thirty feet, two and one-half down. Faint shadow. . . . Drifting to the right a little." The priceless fuel drained

away—only 30 seconds' worth left now—as *Eagle* hovered over a cloud of gray dust. Millions of radio listeners on the distant earth held their breath. But then *Eagle*'s footpad sensors, poking down through the churning dust, felt the surface of the moon, and Armstrong switched off. "Houston," he said, "Tranquillity Base here. The *Eagle* has landed."

It was 4:17 p.m. on Sunday, July 20, 1969. The two astronauts barely had time to slap each other's backs before beginning a countdown for emergency lift-off. Should Mission Control, which was "probing" the LM all over, like a doctor checking a patient's life signs, decide an abort was necessary, Armstrong could be ordered to fire his ascent engine and rejoin Collins in lunar orbit. But with relief he heard Houston announce that *Eagle* was "STAY" on the moon.

Neil Armstrong gazed out of *Eagle*'s windows at the territory he would soon explore. It was an eerie chiaroscuro of harsh light and inky dark, extending a mere four miles in all directions to the close lunar horizon. He could see a number of craters from 5 to 50 feet in

After Apollo 11's Florida lift-off (above), Mission Operations Control Room at the Manned Spacecraft Center in Houston (left) was the nerve center of the flight. Four different groups of flight controllers worked in shifts around the clock to monitor the progress of the spacecraft and relay complicated computer instructions to the Apollo 11 crew. In addi-

## Technicians and Computers Carefully Monitored the Flight

tion to this vital scientific information, the controllers also provided the crew with national and local news briefings, complete with baseball scores, stock market quotations, and messages from the astronauts' families. Doctors at Mission Control could monitor the crew's physiological reactions through delicate sensors attached to the men's bodies before lift-off. At one point the doctors noted from Aldrin's heart rate that he was doing exercises in the *Columbia*, although the astronaut himself had not

reported the fact. The jargon that Mission Control used in talking with the crew was made necessary, in part, by the problems of radio communication. "We copy," for example, transmitted more clearly than "we understand." The latter often became garbled. On the return flight, Mike Collins paid tribute to the splendid work of Apollo 11's supporting cast: "All you see is the three of us," he said, "but beneath the surface are thousands and thousands of others and to all those . . . thank you very much."

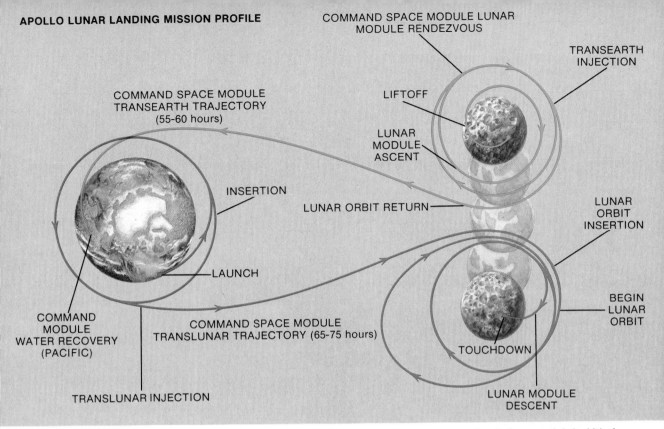

COMMAND SPACE MODULE LUNAR
MODULE RENDEZVOUS

TRANSEARTH
INJECTION

COMMAND SPACE MODULE
TRANSEARTH TRAJECTORY
(55-60 hours)

LIFTOFF

LUNAR
MODULE
ASCENT

INSERTION

LUNAR ORBIT RETURN

LUNAR
ORBIT
INSERTION

LAUNCH

COMMAND
MODULE
WATER RECOVERY
(PACIFIC)

COMMAND SPACE MODULE
TRANSLUNAR TRAJECTORY (65-75 hours)

BEGIN
LUNAR
ORBIT

TOUCHDOWN

TRANSLUNAR INJECTION

LUNAR MODULE
DESCENT

**The diagram above shows** *the Apollo 11 flight plan. The path from earth to moon is charted in red, and the return trip is drawn in blue. After the launch, Apollo orbited the earth to check its systems and then fired its rockets for Translunar Injection, which* *headed the craft to the moon. After the lunar module had lifted off from the moon and reunited with the command module, another rocket firing, Transearth Injection, directed the Apollo spacecraft on a path back to earth for its Pacific splashdown.*

radius, some ridges, and a distant hill. The "plain" he had selected as a landing site was pocked with thousands of tiny craters, some of them as small as a foot across. Grays were the only intermediate tints between the whiteness of the sun and the blackness of the shadow: chalky grays, dark grays, grays that were smooth and shiny, grays that were rough and opaque.

After performing a complicated sequence of navigational alignments, Armstrong and Aldrin were free to enjoy four hours of rest before venturing out to explore the moon. With minute quantities of wine and bread from his Personal Preference Kit, Aldrin, a Presbyterian elder, celebrated Communion on the moon, feeling a sudden need for privacy. He then sent a radio message back to earth: "Houston, this is the LM pilot speaking. I would like to request a few moments of silence. I would like to invite each person listening in, wherever or whoever he may be, to contemplate for a moment the events of the last few hours and to give thanks in his own individual way."

Nevertheless, Armstrong found himself longing to get out. As he said later, ". . . the surface looked very warm and inviting. It looked as if it would be a nice place to take a sunbath." Too excited to rest, the astronaut requested permission to begin his historic moon walk three hours early. So, at 10:51 p.m., the Apollo

commander, having "bled" all the air out of the lunar module, opened its hatch and struggled out into the vacuum. Moving sluggishly lest he tear the fabric of his suit against a jutting piece of metal, he descended the *Eagle's* ladder. On the way down, he pulled the lens cap off *Eagle's* outboard television camera, and viewers on earth, who up to now had no visual report of surface proceedings, suddenly saw man about to set foot on the moon. The last rung of the ladder was a good three feet from the ground. Armstrong announced, "I'm going to step off the LM now." The blurry white figure sank as gently as a diver toward the floor of the ocean. "That's one small step for a man," he said as he touched the moon, "one giant leap for mankind."

The surface of the moon felt very soft under his cleated boots, but when he tried to collect a sample of soil he found hard rock beneath. Bouncing gently up and down in the weak lunar gravity (his suited-up "earth weight" of 360 pounds there measured a mere 60 pounds), he had little difficulty moving around.

"That looks beautiful from here, Neil," said Aldrin, waiting impatiently inside *Eagle's* cabin. "It has a stark beauty of its own," agreed Armstrong. "It's like much of the high desert of the United States." After relaying a few geological observations back to Houston, he

*Text continued on page 342.*

*Map for Apollo 11 on page 339.*

## Millions Watched the First Men on the Moon

Few moments in human history have matched the drama of Neil Armstrong's first step on the moon (top left). As countless millions watched on television, Armstrong scooped up a handful of dust and rock into a special pocket of his space suit. This contingency sample insured that even if unforeseen hazards abruptly terminated the moon walk, samples of lunar material would be brought back to earth. Fortunately, no problems materialized, and 19 minutes after Armstrong emerged from the lunar module, Edwin Aldrin slowly climbed down the craft's ladder (middle left). He recalled his emotions as he joined his fellow astronaut on the moon: "Neil and I are both fairly reticent people, and we don't go in for free exchanges of

sentiment. Even during our long training we didn't have many free exchanges. But there was that moment on the moon, a brief moment in which we sort of looked at each other and slapped each other on the shoulder—that was about the space available—and said, 'We made it. Good show.'" The astronauts soon found the most effective way to move around on the moon, where gravity is only one-sixth that of the earth. "You have to cross your foot over to stay underneath where your center of mass is," Aldrin advised Armstrong. Aldrin later described their slightly slumped forward stance as "tired ape" posture. The two men methodically began to perform the tasks that they had rehearsed for so long during their training. Setting up a U.S. flag was more difficult than the men anticipated because of the hard subsurface beneath the top layer of moon dust. They needed a hammer to pound it into place. When the flag was upright (a special metal strip woven into the fabric made it "fly" without wind), Aldrin stepped back and saluted it (bottom left). In addition to collecting rock samples, the men set up two important scientific experiments: The first, a passive seismometer (above), measured quakes and tremors on the moon; the second, a solar wind screen, trapped gas particles emitted by the sun. The astronauts left the seismometer on the moon but brought the solar wind screen back with them for scientific analysis. Ironically, one of those most interested in the moon walk was unable to see any of Armstrong and Aldrin's activities. Mike Collins, orbiting some 60 miles above them in the *Columbia*, had to rely on descriptions of his colleagues' actions relayed to him by Mission Control in Houston.

*Apollo 11 Lands on the Moon*

## A Precision Splashdown by Spacecraft 107

Reentry into the earth's atmosphere gave the astronauts their last nervous moments. The angle at which the spacecraft descended was all-important. If the incline was too shallow, the craft would bounce off the earth's atmosphere and perpetually orbit in outer space. If, on the other hand, the reentry angle was too steep, friction created by the contact of the ship with the atmosphere would cause it to be consumed in flames. A special plastic heat shield that reached temperatures of up to 4,200° F protected the capsule

during the critical reentry period. At about 23,300 feet from earth, special parachutes called drogues were released to slow the spacecraft's speed, and at about 10,500 feet the Apollo's main parachutes were deployed (above left). As soon as the capsule hit the water, helicopters from the recovery ship U.S.S. *Hornet* carried Navy swimmers to the site. They attached a flotation collar to the spacecraft (above right) to keep it upright until the crew could disembark. After the crew had emerged from the *Columbia*, they were scrubbed down with a powerful disinfectant to kill any alien bacteria that they might have carried back from the moon.

Then the astronauts donned Biological Isolation Garments, which they wore until they reached the Mobile Quarantine Facility aboard the *Hornet*. As a result, the Apollo 11's crew had to accept congratulations from behind a glass window (below) and couldn't receive any visitors. The isolation continued for two more weeks in a specially constructed Lunar Receiving Laboratory after the astronauts reached Houston's Manned Spacecraft Center. Quarantined with the men was their space capsule, on which command module pilot Collins wrote: "Spacecraft 107—alias Apollo 11—alias Columbia. The best ship to come down the line. God Bless Her."

guided his partner out of the LM and down the ladder to join him. "Beautiful. Beautiful!" repeated Aldrin, gazing around in ecstasy. Afterward, he confessed to feeling goose pimples when his boots touched the ground. "I was particularly struck by the contrast between the starkness of the shadows and the desertlike barrenness of the rest of the surface. It ranged from dusty gray to light tan and was unchanging except for one startling sight: our LM sitting there with its black, silver, and bright yellow-orange thermal coating shining brightly in the otherwise colorless landscape. I had seen Neil in his suit thousands of times before, but on the moon the unnatural whiteness of it seemed unusually brilliant, a contrasting white like no white I had ever seen before."

Both men were fascinated by the fine, powdery lunar surface. Since there was no air, grains kicked up as they walked flew straight as projectiles before dropping down in neat patterns. "Isn't this fun?" said Armstrong, sounding more like a little boy than an explorer in the most hostile environment yet encountered.

Portable air-conditioning units cooled the astronauts as they loped, kangaroolike, about their duties, setting up a seismometer to register lunar shocks, a laser reflector to monitor earth-moon distances, and a panel to measure the solar wind. They also collected some geological samples and hammered a U.S. flag into the rock-hard ground. It stood, but only just, "flying" stiffly in an imaginary breeze (thanks to a metal strip across the top), and the two men paused to salute it solemnly.

Despite the low gravity of the moon, they found themselves tiring rapidly. Armstrong had spent two hours and 20 minutes on the moon, Aldrin about two hours, and both men were glad to complete their work. With a final gaze at the lunar landscape and the "beckoning oasis" of the earth, they reentered the LM. Exhausted, they sealed themselves up again and relaxed in their dusty space suits, but found it difficult to sleep. Sixty miles above them, Collins slept deeply in the spacious isolation of *Columbia*'s cabin.

The unspoken fear that no doubt disturbed the repose of Neil Armstrong and Buzz Aldrin was allayed at 1:54 p.m. the following day, Monday. Precisely on time, *Eagle*'s Ascent Stage engine fired with a heartwarming roar, and the little capsule lifted off, leaving its spider-legged Descent Stage behind as a permanent monument to the lunar visit. Affixed to the latter was a plaque engraved with the three astronauts' names and that of President Richard M. Nixon, and a message reading: "Here men from the planet Earth first set foot upon the moon July 1969 A.D. We came in peace for all mankind." As Aldrin had uncovered the plaque, he found himself wondering when human eyes would next read those words. *Eagle* then rocketed up to a flawless rendezvous with *Columbia*—and a triumphant return to earth, 195 hours and 18 minutes after lift-off, half a minute ahead of schedule.

*Adventurers Below and Above*

## Amazing New Ships for Discovery: Skylab and Space Shuttle

Five additional U.S. moon landings followed Apollo 11's historic mission. Later astronauts carried out increasingly complex experiments and even ventured several miles from their landing vehicles in the lunar rover, a small car with a top speed of seven miles per hour. The Apollo missions were succeeded by the even more ambitious Skylab project. Launched by a Saturn 5 rocket, Skylab (right), 118 feet from end to end, was designed to remain in earth orbit as three separate astronaut crews docked their Apollo capsules with the space lab.

The painting below shows an Apollo spacecraft positioned beneath the Skylab's solar panels. Damaged during launch, the solar panels that provided power for Skylab's batteries were re-

as filet mignon and lobster Newburg. Other amenities aboard Skylab included a small shower, an air-suction toilet, and sleeping bags placed in specially designed, individual compartments.

Skylab experiments performed by the three crews provided scientists with important information on the sun's chemical reactions as well as detailed pictures of the earth itself. Some of these amazing pictures indicated untapped mineral and oil deposits, new sources of geothermal energy, and potentially rich fishing grounds. Moreover, Skylab demonstrated man's ability to function for prolonged periods in zero gravity with only minor physiological changes, a requirement for interplanetary space travel. With no gravity, body fluid was not

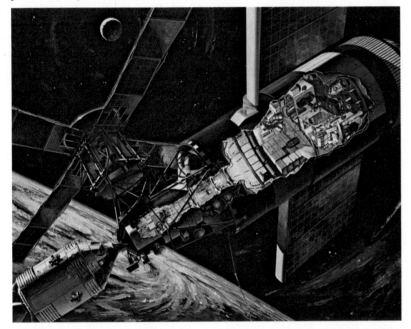

tugal. The four-and-a-half-day joint maneuvers made few technical breakthroughs but pointed the way to future international cooperation in space exploration. The United States' next major space venture, the Space Shuttle, is scheduled for the early 1980's. Launched like a rocket, the Shuttle will orbit the earth and land like an airplane. A reuseable craft, it will be much less expensive to operate than earlier spaceships. The Shuttle will launch interplanetary probes and service orbiting scientific laboratories similar to Skylab, which are now being designed. Space shuttles, in the future, can ferry people to man-made space colonies that such scientists as Princeton University professor Gerald O'Neill forecast for the next century. The scientific world is following O'Neill's theories with interest. After all, only 100 years ago Jules Verne's *From the Earth to the Moon* seemed to be nothing more than pure fantasy.

paired in a daring space walk by the first astronaut crew. The first Skylab crew spent 28 days aboard the laboratory, the second crew 59 days, and the third set an astounding record of 84 days in orbit.

Skylab gave each three-man crew far more living and working space than the cramped Apollo capsule. The walls of the huge workshop seen in the painting were 27 feet long by 22 wide and contained storage tanks for food and water. One end of the workshop was sectioned off as a small wardroom for the crew, with a table containing a unit for heating food. The Skylab astronauts had a more elaborate menu than was possible on the Apollo flights, featuring such delicacies

pulled down to the lower limbs, and the crew developed rounder faces, flabby cheeks, and an appearance one crewman called "our Chinese look." Without the pull of gravity, each man's spine lengthened about an inch. However, all crews returned to normal height and appearance when they came back to earth.

Little more than a year after the last crew left Skylab on February 8, 1974, the United States embarked upon another pioneering space venture—the linkup of a Soviet and an American spacecraft (right). On July 17, 1975, at 12:09 p.m., a U.S. Apollo capsule and a U.S.S.R. Soyuz spaceship joined together above the Atlantic Ocean, about 650 miles off Por-

# Part 10

# Mapping the World

## A Biographical Atlas of Exploration

On the following pages you will find more than 100 biographical and geographical descriptions of the great discoverers and their discoveries that were not included in the text of this book. The entries are in alphabetical order, under the explorer's name. Each entry is accompanied by a map that contains all of the major place names associated with the exploration it illustrates. To aid students and others interested in the exploration of particular regions, the listing on this page also identifies explorers by region. Heavier type indicates explorers covered in the preceding chapters. For further research on the history of exploration, consult the card catalog of your local public library.

(Asterisks in the text copy designate explorers whose biographies also appear in this atlas or who have been included in the preceding chapters.)

### AFRICA
**Baker, F.**
**Baker, S.**
Barth
Binger
Brazza
Bruce
Burton
Caillé
Cameron
Clapperton
Grandidier
**Hanno**
Laing
Lander, J.
Lander, R. L.
**Livingstone**
Nachtigal
Park
Rohlfs
Schweinfurth
Speke
**Stanley**
Thomson

### ASIA
Burckhardt
Doughty
Garnier
Hedin
Niebuhr
**Polo**
Przhevalsky
Richthofen
Stein
Yermak Timofeyevich
Younghusband

### AUSTRALIA
**Burke**
Dampier
Eyre
Flinders
Leichhardt
Stuart, J. McD.
Sturt
**Wills**

### NORTH AMERICA
Alvarado
Ayllón
Becknell
Bridger
Cabeza de Vaca
Cabot, J.
Cartier
**Champlain**
**Clark**
**Coronado**
**Cortés**
De Soto
Fraser
Frémont
Gomez
Gray
Hearne
**Hudson**
Hunt
**La Salle**
**Lewis**
**Mackenzie**
Marquette
Pike
Ponce de León
Radisson
Stuart, R.
Thompson
Ulloa
Vancouver
Verrazano
Vizcaíno
Walker

### NORTHERN PASSAGES
**Amundsen**
Baffin
Barents
Chancellor
Davis
Franklin
Frobisher
McClure
Nordenskjold

### PACIFIC
**Balboa**
**Bougainville**
**Cook**
Dumont d'Urville
La Pérouse
Malaspina
Mendaña de Neyra
Quirós
Roggeveen
Saavedra
Tasman
Torres
Urdaneta
Wallis

### POLES
**Amundsen**
Bellingshausen
De Long
Fuchs
Greely
Kane
**Nansen**
Parry
**Peary**
Ross
**Scott**
Shackleton
Weddell

### SOUTH AMERICA
Almagro
Berrio
Cabot, S.
Cabral
Fawcett
Humboldt
Le Maire
Orellana
Pinzón
**Pizarro**
Schomburgk
Solís

### OTHER
Alaminos: Gulf Stream

**Aldrin:** Moon
**Armstrong:** Moon
**Beebe:** ocean depths
**Bering:** Bering Strait
**Collins:** Moon
**Columbus:** New World

Covilhã: Indian Ocean monsoons

Dezhnev: Bering Strait

**Dias:** Cape of Good Hope

**Drake:** global circumnavigation

**Eric the Red:** Greenland

**Gama:** Cape of Good Hope to India

**Henry the Navigator:** inspired New Age of Discovery

**Hillary:** Mt. Everest / South Pole

**Leif Ericsson:** New World

**Magellan:** global circumnavigation

**Pytheas:** Iceland / theory of tides

**Tenzing Norkay:** Mt. Everest

Vespucci: New World

*Special Consultant: John A. Church*

## ALAMINOS, Antonio
*Spain 16th century*
**Atlantic Ocean: discovered Gulf Stream.**
While serving as chief pilot for Juan Ponce de León* in 1513, Alaminos noticed that as his ships cruised south down the east coast of Florida, they were caught in a northbound current so strong that it drew them backward against the wind. He had discovered the Gulf Stream.

In 1519 Hernando Cortés* sent Alaminos from Mexico to Spain with urgent letters for the king. Recalling what he had observed six years earlier, Alaminos made for the tip of Florida, where he entered the Gulf Stream again. This time sailing *with* the powerful current, he was carried rapidly northeast until he caught the prevailing westerlies that blow toward Europe. (He made excellent time for the crossing.)

After Alaminos' discovery, mariners utilized the Gulf Stream and the prevailing westerlies of the northern latitudes when sailing from America to Europe.

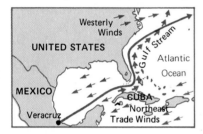

When sailing to America, they continued to take advantage of the northeast trade winds blowing toward America in equatorial latitudes. For his achievement, Alaminos was made pilot general of Spain for the Gulf of Mexico.

## ALMAGRO, Diego de
*Spain 1475–1538 Peru*
**South America: explored northern Chile.** Although Almagro was one of Francisco Pizarro's* first partners in the conquest of Peru, Pizarro considered him a rival. However, Almagro's appointment as governor of Chile postponed the inevitable conflict between the conquistadors.

Setting out to explore his new territory in 1535, Almagro left Cuzco, Peru, with a few hundred men and took the Inca highway south over the Andes Mountains. At altitudes of over two miles many men and beasts died of cold; later travelers found them standing as they had perished, men leading their horses, frozen in ice.

By early 1536 Almagro had reached the Chilean coastal plain near Copiapó. There his followers might have settled and prospered, but they wanted nothing but gold, for which they ransacked the

country as far south as present-day Valparaiso. Finding none, they persuaded their leader to take them back to Peru. This time Almagro traversed the lowlands west of the Andes, not knowing he would encounter deserts so dry that in places rain has never been known to fall. Many in his party died of thirst before the expedition reached Cuzco in 1537.

Embroiled in fighting with Hernando Pizarro in 1537–38, Almagro was killed before he could revisit the southern land he had been the first to explore.

## ALVARADO, Pedro de
*Spain 1485–1541 Mexico*
**Central America: explored Guatemala, El Salvador.** A brave and trusted captain of Hernando Cortés,* Alvarado is famous for his heroism during the *noche triste* ("night of sorrow"). He was the last Spaniard to leave Tenochtitlán (Mexico City) on that terrible night in 1520 when the Aztecs expelled Cortés' men, using his lance to pole-vault to safety over a break in the causeway.

At Cortés' command, in 1523 Alvarado invaded Guatemala and El Salvador, where no European had yet ventured. Like other conquistadors, he explored the land while conquering it. From the

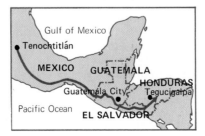

capital that he founded near modern Guatemala City, his expeditions in search of gold and slaves took him into every part of the country. In 1527 rivals in Mexico, envious of his success, brought him into court on charges of embezzling the king's share of the riches he had captured. Appealing his case to Spain, he not only cleared himself of the accusations but also won the governorship of the lands he had conquered. To these he soon added Honduras.

Twice, at the Spanish king's order, Alvarado built a fleet to cross the Pacific to the Spice Islands—the Moluccas in Indonesia—but the voyages were canceled. In 1534 he sailed instead to Ecuador in an unsuccessful effort to win a share of Francisco Pizarro's* conquests. On his second try, in 1541, he interrupted his voyage to the Orient, landing in Mexico to help put down an Indian rebellion. He was killed in battle there at the age of 56.

## AYLLÓN, Lucas Vásquez de
*(see VERRAZANO)*

## BAFFIN, William
*England c. 1584–1662 Persia*
**North America: searched for Northwest Passage, discovered Baffin Bay.** Like most English explorers of his day, Baffin was seeking a seaway through Canada

when he made his two voyages of discovery to North America. As pilot to Robert Bylot, he made a careful survey of Hudson Strait in 1615. Returning to the area in 1616, he sailed north through Davis Strait. On this second trip, he entered the bay between western Greenland and Baffin Island, which now bears his name. Sailing 370 miles farther north than John Davis* had, he reached 77°45′ N, a latitude record that remained unsurpassed for 236 years. Although Baffin did not find the Northwest Passage, he did locate the mouth of Lancaster Sound, which is, in fact, the eastern entrance to the long-sought waterway.

Both a master navigator and a scientist, Baffin made some of the earliest serious attempts to determine longitude by lunar observation at sea. The remarkable accuracy of the surveys he made with the crude instruments of his age have been verified by recent investigators, and his magnetic observations were still in use as late as 1865.

Later joining the British East India Company as a captain, Baffin was killed in action when the company, cooperating with the Persian (now Iranian) government, attacked Hormuz and expelled the Portuguese.

### BARENTS, Willem
*Netherlands c. 1550–97 At sea*
**Arctic: discovered Spitsbergen.** In the late 16th century Portugal monopolized the Indian Ocean route to the Orient by force. Initially, rather than fight the Portuguese, the Netherlands sought an alternate northern route to east Asia. Aided by their government, Dutch merchants dispatched two expeditions (in 1594 and 1595) to pioneer the Northeast Passage to the Pacific. Barents was cap-

tain of one of the four ships on the first expedition and one of the seven on the second.

Both ventures were unsuccessful. Large islands off the coast of Russia —Novaya Zemlya and Vaigach—bar the way east. On his first voyage Barents attempted to sail north of Novaya Zemlya. On his second he tried to pass between Vaigach and the mainland. Each time he had to turn back when he encountered impenetrable masses of floating ice.

In 1596 the merchants made one last effort, this time without the government's assistance. Barents, the chief pilot of two ships, again sailed as far north as he could. By doing so, he discovered on June 19 the islands of Spitsbergen (now part of Norway) and sailed

around them before turning to the east.

At this point the second ship deserted him because the captain feared the pack ice. Proceeding alone, Barents rounded northern Novaya Zemlya. But then the pack ice surrounded him, and his vessel froze in.

The Dutch wintered on Novaya Zemlya's bleak eastern coast in a hut built of driftwood. They suffered greatly from exposure and malnutrition, and Barents fell ill with scurvy. In mid-June 1597, when they found they could not free their ship from the ice, the men started the rigorous journey back in small boats.

On June 20 Barents died, but the survivors were rescued by Russian ships near the mainland. Almost 300 years later, in 1871, explorers found the hut in which the expedition had wintered and, in 1875, recovered part of Barents' journal.

### BARTH, Heinrich
*Germany 1821–65 Germany*
**Africa: explored Lake Chad area, Niger River.** One of the most remarkable figures in the history of exploration, Barth was outstanding as a geographer, linguist, anthropologist, historian, and friend of Africa and the Africans. The British government had sent the explorer James Richardson on an official mission to negotiate trade treaties with African sheikhs and persuade them to discontinue their slave trade. So Barth and another German, Adolf Overweg, were retained to accompany him, because Germans had not dealt in slaves and it was thought they might be valuable intermediaries on the mission. Barth was instrumental in changing the main purpose of the expedition from trade to exploration, although he promoted British commerce during his travels as well.

The party left Tripoli, Libya, for Lake Chad in 1850. When Richardson died in 1851, Barth took charge. Starting in the east, he and Overweg stayed a month at the commercial center of Kano. Then they moved on to Kukawa, in northeastern Nigeria, where they explored a vast area around Lake Chad.

In October 1852 Overweg died. Barth continued alone and spent five years traveling south of the Sahara. On one trip he located the upper Benue River and established that neither the Benue nor the Niger connects with Lake Chad. His discoveries were among the greatest achievements in African geography of the 19th century. But as important, everywhere he went, Barth made meticulous studies of political organizations,

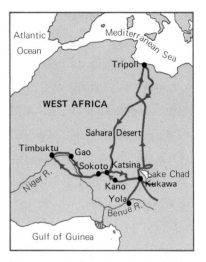

history, natural resources, production, and trade. In these exhaustive labors he was aided by his extraordinary gift for languages and by his ability to get along with Africans.

In November 1852 Barth traveled westward and after a stay at Sokoto continued on to Timbuktu, which he reached about a year later. There he spent many months, often in great danger from religious fanatics who infested the ancient city and persecuted non-Moslems. But the Tuareg sheikh El Bakey befriended him, risking his own life to protect him, and finally led the armed guard that escorted Barth to safety several hundred miles down the Niger. The two men parted with sincere regret. On this return trip Barth surveyed the middle Niger, for while Mungo Park* had already traversed it, his records had been lost when he was drowned.

After a last visit to Kukawa to finalize a trade treaty, Barth recrossed the Sahara to Tripoli, arriving in August 1855. His records, *Travels and Discoveries in North and Central Africa*, published in five volumes two years after his return, remain almost unrivaled for their accuracy, variety, and scope of information.

### BECKNELL, William
*U.S.A. 1790–1832 U.S.A.*
**North America: discovered Santa Fe Trail.** If Becknell's wagons were not "the first wheels to roll on the Central Plains," they were the first to do so successfully. With his pioneer wagon train Becknell opened a new route between St. Louis, Missouri, and Santa Fe, in present-day New Mexico.

Encouraged by several profitable trading trips through Spanish territory in the American Southwest, in 1822 Becknell collected $5,000 worth of merchandise in St. Louis to take to Santa Fe to sell. He planned to use wagon transport—something no one had done before—instead of the usual pack mules. And he intended to find a shorter route than the previous trail, which had led through Kansas to central Colorado and then south down the Rio Grande.

With 21 men and 3 wagons, Becknell followed the old trail into western Kansas, but then left it to cut southwest toward Santa Fe through unexplored territory. Unaware that he was entering desert country, he carried very little

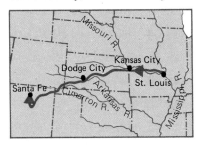

water. Soon his men grew so thirsty that they killed their dogs to drink their blood. Fortunately, they reached the Cimarron River in time to save their lives.

The Cimarron Valley, they discovered, led almost directly to Santa Fe. Becknell had found the shortcut he was seeking. The route he had pioneered at such risk became the famous Santa Fe Trail.

### BELLINGSHAUSEN, Fabian von
*Estonia 1779–1852 Russia*
**Antarctica: circumnavigated the continent.** When Bellingshausen sailed to the Southern Ocean in 1819, many Russians believed Czar Alexander I had sent him to recover the Philosopher's Stone. This legendary object, thought capable of changing lead into gold, was believed to be located in a cave on an unknown Atlantic islet. But, in fact, Bellingshausen

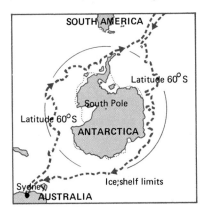

was commanding an official expedition to the southernmost latitudes to advance both science and Russian prestige.

In the 18th century James Cook* had almost destroyed the 2,000-year-old myth of a habitable Antarctic continent. Yet gaps in Cook's surveys left room for speculation. A devoted admirer of Cook, Bellingshausen set himself to complete the work of the great Englishman. Circumnavigating the continent now known as Antarctica, he entered areas south of New Zealand and Africa where Cook had failed to follow the polar ice. Bellingshausen hugged the ice floes so closely that only his consummate seamanship kept his ships from disaster. When he had finished, no one could doubt that all the far south could offer was bare rock, ice, and snow. The region was clearly uninhabitable.

Although Bellingshausen's voyage was second in importance only to Cook's in early Antarctic exploration, like Cook he failed to get credit for discovering Antarctica. Ironically, he probably was the first person to see the Antarctic mainland but described the heights he had sighted off what is now Ellsworth Land in 1820 as icebergs rather than mountains, not realizing that what he saw was the continent.

### BERRIO, Antonio de
*Spain 1520–97 Trinidad*
**South America: explored Colombia, Venezuela.** After 40 years of active service in Spanish armies, Berrio went to Colombia to retire. He planned to settle

near Bogotá on land inherited from Gonzalo Jiménez de Quesada, a relative by marriage. Upon arriving in South America, he learned that the bequest became his only if he continued Jiménez de Quesada's search for Eldorado, a legendary country believed to lie somewhere in the lowlands of Colombia or Venezuela.

Berrio accepted the challenge. In 1580 and in 1586–88 he made two arduous expeditions eastward from Bogotá through unexplored country to the Orinoco River.

On his second return to Bogotá, in 1588, he learned that he had been named royal governor of the rumored Eldorado. During a third trip into the same region, Indians told him that Eldorado was far to the east, near modern Guyana, but, already exhausted by his efforts, he and his party abandoned the search. Descending the Orinoco almost to its mouth, they hurried overland to the coast and sailed to the nearest Spanish settlement, Margarita Island.

There authorities who wanted Eldorado for themselves tried to block Berrio. They intercepted his correspondence with the king and killed some of his men. Going to Trinidad, at the mouth of the Orinoco, Berrio was captured and briefly imprisoned by the English corsair Sir Walter Raleigh, who was also looking for Eldorado. Although Berrio died in Trinidad without attaining the golden reward he had hoped for, he is honored as the first explorer of the Orinoco River Basin.

### BINGER, Louis Gustave
*France 1856–1936 France*
**West Africa: explored Ivory Coast, Ghana.** Second only to Heinrich Barth* among explorers of west Africa in his scientific knowledge, his breadth of interests, and his cordial relations with Africans, Binger was an important pioneer of the area between Bamako, Mali, and Grand Bassam, Ivory Coast.

Starting from Bamako on an official exploring expedition in 1887, Binger traveled almost two years through unknown country, most of the time without European companions. He finally reached the Ivory Coast in 1889. For the first five months of his journey he traveled in a war zone between embattled African factions. It was a region depopulated by slave raids and starvation, its farms laid waste and its ruined villages noisome

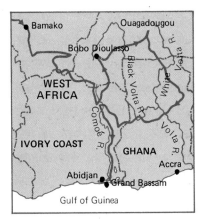

with unburied dead. Although often in danger, he never used weapons. Once, threatened by some 200 tribesmen, he disarmed his own men rather than risk any violence and made peace with his attackers through skillful negotiation.

An army officer with official powers, he concluded treaties of friendship with many chiefs. He also surveyed the region and discovered the sources of the Volta, one of Africa's major rivers. Perhaps his most important achievement was to amass a veritable encyclopedia of information about the peoples of west Africa, their social and political systems, production, and trade.

After joining in the Ivory Coast-Ghana boundary survey in 1892, Binger was made governor of the Ivory Coast and later became a minister in the French government.

### BRAZZA, Pierre de
*Brazil 1852–1905 Senegal*

**Africa: explored area of Congo and Gabonese Republics.** Born an Italian (on shipboard in Rio de Janeiro harbor),

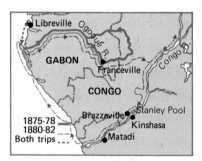

Brazza became a naturalized French citizen during his youth. He began his African explorations for France in what is now the Gabonese Republic (Gabon) and was the first to ascend the Ogooué River to its source in 1875. Brazza then cut through the jungle into the area of the modern Congo Republic, where he discovered important northern tributaries of the Congo (Zaire) River. He returned to France in 1878.

The French government commissioned Brazza to explore Nigeria in 1880 but then changed its plans and sent him to the Congo instead. There, on the north bank of the river, he founded Brazzaville, capital of the present-day People's Republic of the Congo, and claimed for France the land north and west of the great river. Hearing that Henry Stanley* was nearby, he paid him a visit. The American explorer was greatly chagrined to learn of Brazza's

presence, for he had intended to add the area north of the river to the Belgian Congo, which he had already annexed for his own employer, Leopold, king of the Belgians. Brazza remained another 18 months in the French Congo exploring France's new possessions.

Having been made French high commissioner in Brazzaville some years later, Brazza was noted for his justice and kindness. "Let there be no arms," he once warned a subordinate. "No military escorts. Do not forget that you are the intruder who was not invited."

### BRIDGER, James
*U.S.A. 1804–81 U.S.A.*

**North America: explored Far West.** Although Bridger was illiterate, his skill as a guide and his almost intuitive knowledge of the landforms and river systems of the far western United States justify his reputation as a geographer. A Virginian by birth and raised in Missouri, Bridger first entered the wilderness as a trapper in 1822 at the age of 18. For 50 years he roamed the West, coming to know the area as few others ever have.

In 1824, while he was leading a party of trappers on Bear River, in present-day Utah, an argument arose about the river's outlet. Bridger, who already knew that most of the waters of Utah do not drain to the ocean, made a bet that the Bear River flows into a salt lake or marsh. To prove his point, he took a perilous ride down the Bear River Canyon in a makeshift canoe and emerged on Great Salt Lake. Thus he discovered the lake and won his wager.

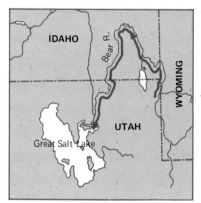

Bridger is sometimes credited with discovering the geysers of Yellowstone Park. The region's original name—Colter's Hell—suggests that John Colter found it first, but Bridger undoubtedly was the second man there and the first to investigate it thoroughly.

It was Bridger who opened the Oregon Trail. South Pass, in modern Wyoming, was discovered by Robert Stuart* in 1812, but in 1830 Bridger took the first wagons across it. For decades thereafter he served as guide and protector to thousands of immigrants who crossed the pass to settle the West.

### BRUCE, James
*Scotland 1730–94 Scotland*

**Ethiopia: explored Blue Nile source.** A Scottish laird, rich, handsome, and commanding, Bruce was well received when

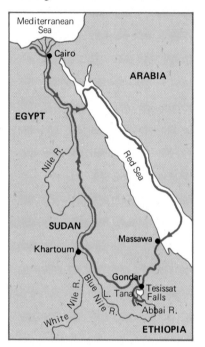

he presented himself to the royal court of Ethiopia at Gondar in 1770. Although without official British connection—he was simply traveling to satisfy his curiosity about the world—he was made a cavalry officer in the Ethiopian king's army. In his glittering mail and bright robes he must have made a brave show.

Bruce had come to Ethiopia to explore the Blue Nile, which he believed was the main branch of the Nile. To assist him, the prime minister appointed him a government official in the area around Lake Tana. Often fighting for the king in the tribal warfare that wracked the country, Bruce managed nevertheless to visit the spring of the Abbai River, then considered the Blue Nile source; Lake Tana, its actual source; and the Tesissat Falls, where the Blue Nile flows from the lake. He was not the first European to see the river, the lake, and the falls, but he was the first to survey them with scientific instruments. Besides doing the research for a map of the area, he collected a vast amount of information about Ethiopia. He found time, too, for pleasure: When he left after two years in that country, pretty ladies from the court followed him for days, begging him to return.

Reaching the confluence of the Blue and White Niles at Halfaya, near Khartoum, Sudan, Bruce was chagrined to observe that the White Nile is the larger and therefore the main branch. In London his account of Ethiopia met with disbelief and derision, and Bruce became deeply embittered. Yet later travelers confirmed substantially all he had told of that fascinating country.

### BURCKHARDT, Johann
*Switzerland 1784–1817 Egypt*

**Arabia: explored Mecca-Medina area.** When Burckhardt undertook to explore west Africa for the British Africa Society, he first settled in Aleppo, Syria, and mastered Arabic and the Koran, planning to disguise himself as a Moslem as

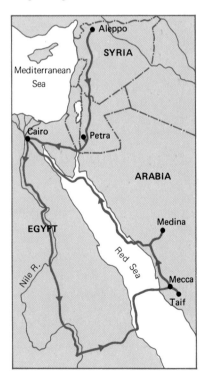

he crossed the Sahara. In two years, calling himself Sheikh Ibrahim ibn abd Allah, he passed an examination and was pronounced a learned doctor of Islamic religion and law. Although he never reached west Africa, he later made good use of this achievement.

Traveling to Cairo, Egypt, in 1812, he visited Petra, in present-day Jordan, and wrote the first modern description of that astonishing ruin—an abandoned city of classic times, much of it hewn in the pink sandstone walls of desert canyons.

In 1813 he started south for the Niger River via the Sudan, only to find that there was no feasible route to west Africa in that direction. Rather than return to Cairo without accomplishing anything of importance, he turned east through the desert, crossed the Red Sea, and made the Moslem pilgrimage to Mecca and Medina, Arabia.

Burckhardt was not the only impostor to visit Islam's holy cities, but he was probably the most scholarly. Trained in many sciences, he surveyed the area around Mecca and Medina and made a detailed report, which is still valuable, on its appearance and climate, its people and their economy. Rarely has an explorer left so little for others to complete and rarely has a Westerner been able to accomplish so much, unmolested, in an area that is still a difficult one for Westerners to investigate.

Falling ill, Burckhardt returned to Cairo in 1817 and died there soon afterward, although not before he had sent his records back to his English sponsors.

### BURTON, Richard
*England 1821–90 Italy*

**Africa: discovered Lake Tanganyika.** A gifted linguist and a man of great courage, Burton first captured public attention by making the Moslem pilgrimage to Mecca. He visited the holy city in 1852 disguised as an Afghan gentleman, an imposture that would have cost him his life if he had been detected. Sent to explore Somalia in 1854, he made an even bolder trip to another sacred city—Harar, Ethiopia—that had never before been seen by a European. Unable to disguise himself this time, since he was on official business for the British government, Burton left his companions in Somalia and traveled the last 150 miles alone. He was well received by the local ruler, who favored an alliance with Britain, but after he rejoined his party, natives drove them from Somalia.

Accompanied by John Hanning Speke,* who had also been with him in Somalia, Burton led an expedition into east Africa in 1856–59. Opposed by Arab slavers, who feared British interference, and tormented by malaria, the Englishmen took eight months to cover the 600

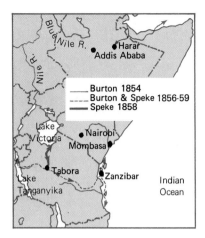

miles from Zanzibar to Lake Tanganyika, which Burton discovered in 1858. His hopes that he had found the source of the Nile fell when Speke, a surveyor, showed that the lake was below the known altitude of the upper Nile.

During their return to Zanzibar, Burton authorized Speke to travel alone to a lake that Africans told them lay to the north—and so forfeited to his colleague the honor of discovering Lake Victoria, the Nile's actual source.

Joining the British Foreign Service, Burton did minor exploratory work in west Africa when stationed there in the 1860's. He was British consul in Trieste when he died in 1890.

### CABEZA DE VACA, Álvar Núñez
*Spain c. 1507–59 Spain*

**North America: first European to cross continent.** Cabeza de Vaca arrived in North America as treasurer of an ill-fated expedition under Pánfilo de Narváez, a Spaniard who had been sent to settle in Florida. From modern-day Tampa,

where the settlers landed in 1528, they went north on foot looking for suitable land. Losing contact with their ships, they were almost overwhelmed by hostile Indians. Near present-day St. Marks, Florida, they built crude barges, hoping to sail to safety in Mexico. However, most of the barges foundered, and only Cabeza de Vaca and a few others survived to be beached near the site of present-day Galveston, Texas, and captured by Indians.

The Indians who enslaved him were a wretched lot, Cabeza de Vaca reported, so poor they ate spiders and deer dung "and other things I omit to mention." His own lot was even more wretched. He was forced to spend his days grubbing barehanded for food and his nights tending fires for his captors.

Cabeza de Vaca gradually improved his situation by trading skillfully on the Indians' behalf. Five years later he managed to escape and headed west with three fellow castaways. Persuading Indians they met on the way that he had magical powers, he kept his party safe and well fed. He eventually crossed Texas to the Pecos River, entered Mexico, and reached Ures, Sonora, in 1536 to become the first European to cross the continent. At Ures, he was welcomed back to civilization by a Spanish slave-raiding expedition.

## CABOT, John
*Italy c. 1451–98 Unknown*
**Western Hemisphere: rediscovered North America.** Believed to be of Genoese origin like Christopher Columbus,* Cabot rediscovered the North

American continent in 1497, one year before Columbus discovered the South American continent. And like Columbus, Cabot believed he had reached Asia.

When Columbus' earlier discoveries in the "Indies" failed to produce great riches, Cabot, a skilled navigator, tried to interest the Spanish and Portuguese crowns in a northern voyage, which he thought would lead directly to Asia. Rebuffed, he found a patron in Henry VII of England. In 1497 he sailed from Bristol, England, probably to Maine or southern Nova Scotia, which he claimed for King Henry. Although the king awarded him £10 and a pension for the discovery, Cabot was disappointed: Nova Scotia

was plainly not Cathay or Japan. He had, indeed, discovered riches—the huge codfish that then swarmed in unbelievable numbers on the Grand Banks of Newfoundland—but that was not the sort of treasure he and his backers were seeking.

In 1498 John Cabot sailed again, with five ships—and disappeared. Little is known about this second voyage. There is evidence that Cabot intended to sail in a southwesterly direction along what he thought was the coast of east Asia to the tropical latitudes, searching for Cathay. But no report by John Cabot or any of his companions has been found to support these theories, and his route remains a mystery to this day.

## CABOT, Sebastian
*Italy c. 1482–1557 England*
**South America: explored Río de la Plata Basin.** A boaster and exaggerator who is not much better known to us than his father, John,* Sebastian Cabot nevertheless deserves credit for opening up the Río de la Plata system—a gateway to the South American interior.

Brought to England from Italy as a child, Sebastian accompanied his father to North America in 1497. After John's death, Sebastian claimed he himself had led his father's expedition, boasting of his accomplishments so persuasively that he received a royal invitation to come to Spain. There he became a naval captain and, eventually, chief pilot.

In 1526 Cabot led a flotilla bound for the Orient through the Strait of Magellan. On his way across the Atlantic he ignored his pilots and had to seek help from Spain's bitter rivals, the Portuguese, at Pernambuco, Brazil, before he could continue. Cruising down the Brazilian coast, he met survivors of Juan Díaz de Solís'* last expedition, who tantalized him with tales of a mountain of silver in the interior of South America. Soon afterward, he lost his flagship, primarily because of his poor seamanship. Using this as an excuse, he abandoned his voyage to the East Indies in favor of searching for the rumored treasure nearby. Entering the Plata, he built a fort near its mouth.

For more than two years Cabot explored the Plata tributaries as far north as modern-day Asunción, Paraguay. He obtained stray Inca gold objects from Indians but never found the silver mountain—Potosí, in present-day Bolivia.

Once more in Spain in 1530, he produced the first world map to include the Plata region. His reports precipitated

Spanish penetration and settlement of Argentina, Paraguay, and Uruguay through waterways he had pioneered.

Returning to England in 1548, Sebastian Cabot founded the "company of merchant-adventurers" (later known as the Muscovy Company, for which Hugh Willoughby and Richard Chancellor* sailed in 1553) and became its governor.

## CABRAL, Pedro Álvares
*Portugal 1467–1520 Portugal*
**Western Hemisphere: sighted and claimed Brazil for Portugal.** If Christopher Columbus* had not discovered America on his way to Cathay in 1492, Cabral would have discovered it on his way to India in 1500. Leaving Lisbon in command of a fleet of 13 ships, Cabral planned to sail around the Cape of Good Hope, then cross the Indian Ocean to the coast of India. If a mariner hugged the coast around the bulge of west Africa, he met doldrums in the Gulf of Guinea. Since the northeast trade winds are constant in these latitudes, his best strategy

was to let them carry him south by west from the Cape Verde Islands halfway across the Atlantic and then turn southeast, keeping the trades on his left side while he made a long tack toward the tip of Africa.

This is what Cabral did in 1500. However, there were no instruments in those days to measure how far west he sailed daily, so he inadvertently went farther across the Atlantic than he intended. At about the time he was ready to turn southeast, his lookouts had sighted land on his right. He had sailed as far as America, almost running his ships aground on the Brazilian coast near modern-day Caravelas. Landing, he set up a wooden cross on shore, and on this basis Portugal laid claim to Brazil, although it had already been sighted by Vicente Yáñez Pinzón* and Amerigo Vespucci.*

### CAILLÉ, René Auguste
*France 1799–1838 France*

**West Africa: was first European to visit Timbuktu and return.** A prize of 10,000 francs offered by the Paris Geographical Society to the first Frenchman to visit

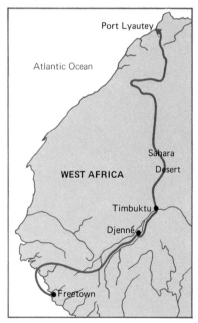

Timbuktu and return induced Caillé to make the attempt. After working in Freetown, Sierra Leone, to earn money for his expedition, Caillé first spent several months among the Berbers of west Africa, studying Arabic and the Koran, so he could disguise himself as a Moslem.

In Guinea in April 1827, he assumed the role of an Egyptian and joined a caravan bound for Timbuktu. Traveling

with it, he soon collapsed from fever and scurvy. So ill that he prayed for death, he was saved only by the care of a kindly old African woman. By early 1828 he was able to walk to Djenné, on a tributary of the Niger River, 500 miles away. There he boarded a riverboat to Timbuktu.

Timbuktu, which Caillé entered in April 1828, was a bitter disappointment to him. He found its people unfriendly and its buildings "a heap of badly built adobe houses." Staying two weeks, he joined an Arab caravan and crossed the Sahara north to Morocco, where he took a ship to France.

In Paris the Geographical Society awarded him the coveted prize and a bonus of 1,000 francs for making the most important discovery of the year.

### CAMERON, Verney Lovett
*England 1844–94 England*

**Africa: explored Congo River watershed.** Lieutenant Cameron's exploration of Africa began with an attempt to aid

David Livingstone.* Sent by the Royal Geographical Society in 1873, he started upcountry from Zanzibar only to meet a party of Africans bringing Livingstone's remains to the coast.

After retrieving some of Livingstone's papers, Cameron remained in Africa another two years. Local hostilities prevented him from descending the Congo River as he had planned, so he devoted himself to mapping its southern watershed, traveling slowly westward despite dire misfortunes: His associate shot himself while delirious from fever, and he himself was robbed and mistreated by almost everyone that he dealt with. Although wracked by scurvy and half starved, he managed to reach Benguela on the Angola coast. Preceding Henry Morton Stanley* by almost two years, he was the first European to cross equatorial Africa from sea to sea. Cameron's book, *Across Africa*, suggested opening up the continent to commercial development, which Cameron later promoted.

### CARTIER, Jacques
*France 1491–1557 France*

**North America: discovered St. Lawrence River.** First sent to America in search of gold and a route to Asia, Cartier attempted the first settlement of Canada and is hailed by French Canadians as its "discoverer and founder."

A survey of the Gulf of St. Lawrence, which Cartier began on his first trip in 1534 and continued during his second in 1535–36, led to his discovering the St. Lawrence River. He gave the name St. Lawrence to a bay on the western coast of Newfoundland where he anchored on August 10, 1535, the feast day of that saint.

Exploring the St. Lawrence River in 1535, Cartier searched its shores for treasure and a route to Asia. When Indians reported an imaginary Kingdom of Saguenay where gold was plentiful farther inland, he made great efforts to find it. Anchoring two ships near modern-day Quebec, he took the third up the St. Lawrence as far as Lac St. Pierre, where the river becomes shallow. He went on by longboat as far as Montreal, "Mount Royal"—as he named the rocky height dominating the river there. Unable to surmount the rapids that bar the river, he then turned back.

After wintering near Quebec, Cartier returned to France with a captive Indian chief, a dozen gold nuggets, furs, and the rumor of Saguenay. His story of Saguenay, reinforced by the chief's eloquence,

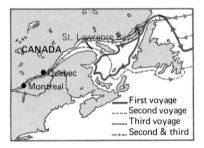

persuaded the king to dispatch a third expedition to Canada. In 1541 Cartier set out again with several shiploads of colonists to prepare a base for the conquest of the Kingdom of Saguenay.

The colony was a failure. After overseeing construction of a fortified village near Quebec and sending home several reports of gold ore and jewels, Cartier went up the St. Lawrence River to examine the rapids for an attempt to clear them the following spring. Beyond the rapids, he felt sure, was Saguenay. Returning, he found the Iroquois hostile.

That winter more than 35 Frenchmen were killed in Indian skirmishes, so in the spring Cartier embarked with the survivors and went back to France.

Meanwhile, beaver pelts, Canada's real source of wealth, were not in demand in Cartier's day, so their enormous potential was overlooked. After his attempt, French colonization of the New World lapsed for another half century.

### CHANCELLOR, Richard
*England ?–1556 At sea*
**Arctic Ocean: searched for Northeast Passage.** Chancellor's ship was the only one of a three-vessel fleet to survive the earliest search for the Northeast Passage, the sea route north of Siberia that connects Europe with eastern Asia. Commanded by Sir Hugh Willoughby, the expedition was organized by a London group of "merchant-adventurers" that wanted a share in the wealth of the East Indies without having to fight the Spanish and Portuguese for use of the southern sea routes.

Neither Sir Hugh nor any of the men who set out with him from England on May 20, 1553, had any idea of the distances or conditions they would encounter. The ships became separated in a gale off Norway's Lofoten Islands. Due to poor seamanship, Willoughby's and the second ship wandered in the Barents Sea for a month, then wintered near present-day Murmansk, U.S.S.R. Unprepared for winter, all men in both ships perished.

Chancellor had proceeded to Vardo, the designated rendezvous on the northern coast of Norway. When the other ships did not arrive, he then entered the White Sea and landed near what is now Archangel, U.S.S.R. Resolved to turn a profit in some way, he traveled to Moscow and contrived to interest Czar Ivan IV ("the Terrible") in a trade treaty with Queen Mary of England ("Bloody Mary"). The resultant treaty and the discovery of the convenient port of Archangel opened Russian trade and led to the formation of the Muscovy Company.

Returning from a second trip to Archangel in 1556, Chancellor was shipwrecked off Scotland and drowned.

### CLAPPERTON, Hugh
*Scotland 1788–1827 Nigeria*
**West Africa: discovered Lake Chad, explored Nigeria.** If the riddle of the Nile was its origin, the riddle of the Niger was its outlet. Did the Niger eventually join the Nile—or the Congo? Did it dry up in the Sahara—or go underground to the Mediterranean?

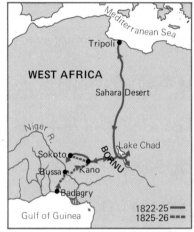

Clapperton correctly guessed that the Niger runs to the Gulf of Guinea but was unable to prove it during his lifetime. With a party that included Dr. Walter Oudney and Dixon Denham, Clapperton crossed the Sahara from Tripoli, Libya, to Bornu, Nigeria, in 1822. The men had been sent by the British government to promote trade and explore. En route to Bornu, they discovered Lake Chad, and Denham left the group to investigate it. From Bornu, Clapperton and Oudney went west toward the Niger. Oudney died in January 1824. Continuing alone, Clapperton was stopped at Sokoto, in what is now Nigeria, by Sultan Muhammad Bello, because the sultan feared European encroachment on his territory. Casually revealing that the Niger was merely a few days' march to the west (it was only 150 miles away), the sultan refused to let Clapperton proceed. So Clapperton returned to England with Denham via Tripoli in 1825.

That same year Clapperton revisited Nigeria, this time landing at Badagry. He and his servant, Richard Lander,* reached Sokoto in 1826, crossing the Niger at Bussa where Mungo Park* had died. Again Sultan Bello detained Clapperton because he was at war with Bornu and knew the men meant to go there. When refused permission to continue exploration, Clapperton was disappointed and gradually lost his health, succumbing to dysentery before he could set out to prove his theory.

### COVILHÃ, Pedro da
*Portugal c. 1456– c. 1526 Ethiopia*
**Indian Ocean: visited Eastern ports.** Portugal's early reconnaissance along the Middle East coasts may have been influenced by the report of this great Jewish explorer, who traveled to Asia and Africa in the late 1400's as a secret agent for King John II.

Disguised as an Arab, Covilhã went first to Aden, in southern Yemen, a thriving international marketplace at that time. Learning from merchants that Calicut was the greatest of the Indian ports, he went to investigate it, and from there visited the rich seaports of Goa, India; Hormuz, Iran; and Sofala, Mozambique. The Arab ships in which he journeyed relied exclusively on the monsoon, the steady wind that blows throughout the Indian Ocean from Africa to Asia during the summer and reverses itself during the winter. A seasoned traveler, Covilhã must have noticed this reversing wind, a novelty to a European, and observed that the ablest Arab mariners considered the ocean unsafe in other months.

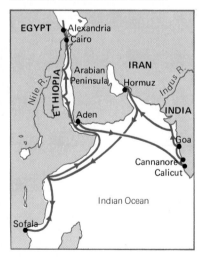

From Cairo, Egypt, Covilhã sent a report to King John in 1490, and then at the king's command, proceeded to Ethiopia, where he remained the rest of his life. Whether his report reached Portugal is uncertain, but there is evidence that it did. Vasco da Gama* timed his voyage of

*Mapping the World*

1498 to cross the Indian Ocean with the monsoon and made straight for Calicut. Among the places Covilhã spied out, Portugal seized Sofala in 1505, Goa in 1510, and Hormuz in 1514; only an attempt to seize Aden in 1513 proved unsuccessful.

## DAMPIER, William
### England 1652–1715 England
**Australia: explored coast, nearby islands.** Dampier passed much of his early career as a buccaneer preying on Spanish shipping. Since none of his victims was British, his government had no objection; in fact, his account of his adventures, published after his return to England in 1691, attracted favorable attention and was very popular.

In 1699 the British Admiralty sent Dampier to explore Australian waters. After surveying the Shark Bay area of Western Australia and pronouncing it unfit for human habitation, he skirted the north coast of New Guinea—then considered part of Australia—and discovered New Britain and New Ireland. Because his ships were in poor condition, he was unable to explore the islands thoroughly and reported them to be one (the strait between them was discovered by Philip Carteret, Samuel Wallis'* lieutenant, in

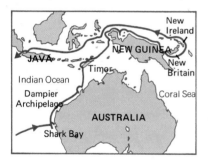

1767). On the way home his ship foundered while in the harbor at Ascension Island in the Atlantic, but he and his men were rescued.

In 1703–07 Dampier commanded a pair of privateers—privately owned vessels commissioned to harry Spanish shipping in the Pacific. During this long cruise he marooned a Scottish captain, Alexander Selkirk, on one of the Juan Fernández Islands, near Chile. Later, when piloting a British round-the-world privateering expedition in 1708–11, Dampier rescued Selkirk and brought him home. Selkirk's story became the basis of Daniel Defoe's famous novel about the survival of the castaway on a desert island, *Robinson Crusoe*.

## DAVIS, John
### England c. 1550–1605 East Indies
**North America: searched for Northwest Passage, discovered Davis Strait.** Although humble by birth, John Davis became one of England's outstanding mariners. Backed by a group of English

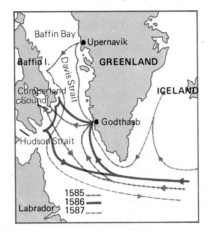

nobles and merchants, Davis made three voyages to northern Canada between 1585 and 1587 to seek the Northwest Passage. During his third trip he reached Upernavik, Greenland, almost directly across Baffin Bay from Lancaster Sound, which is the actual entrance to the passage as Roald Amundsen* proved in his voyage of 1903–06. But thick pack ice and bad weather prevented Davis from approaching or even seeing the sound.

A student of navigation, Davis devised the Davis quadrant, used to determine latitude as late as 1731. He also wrote *The Seaman's Secrets*, a book on navigation that was "the Bible to English mariners in the next century." He was noted as well for his humane treatment of his crews and of the Eskimos he dealt with. Yet Davis died a poor man. While many of his contemporaries were knighted, he went unrewarded. Although Davis Strait (between Greenland and Baffin Island) bears his name, his later disastrous expeditions brought him ruin.

## DE LONG, George Washington
### U.S.A. 1844–81 Siberia
**Arctic: tried to reach North Pole.** Two 19th-century theories about the Arctic led De Long to try to reach the North Pole through the Bering Strait: One was that Greenland extended over and beyond the pole, almost touching Siberia near the strait; the other was that a warmwater current from the Pacific flowed north through the strait, keeping

the water ice free around this imaginary landmass.

Financed by New York publisher James Gordon Bennett, Jr., and with help from the United States Navy, De Long sailed to the Arctic from San Francisco in July 1879. Within a year he proved both theories wrong—the first by sailing right through the supposed land of the north, the second by getting his ship caught in the polar pack ice.

Before and after freezing in, he discovered several small islands, but his greatest achievement was to show that the whole mass of Arctic ice is in motion, circling slowly but steadily westward. It was this discovery that was the inspiration for Fridtjof Nansen's* famous voyage in the *Fram*. Unable to free his ship, De Long was carried almost 1,000 miles west before the vessel was finally crushed by the floes and sunk.

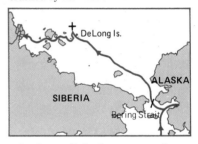

De Long died of exposure after a grueling journey over ice and by open boat to the Siberian coast. However, a few of his men survived, and his logbooks, which contributed much to our knowledge of the Arctic, were saved.

## DE SOTO, Hernando
### Spain c. 1500–42 North America
**North America: discovered Mississippi River.** When De Soto heard about Álvar Núñez Cabeza de Vaca's* journey across North America, he suspected that the continent was much richer than his fellow countryman had made it seem. Dreaming of finding treasure, he obtained royal permission to occupy what is now the U.S. coast of the Gulf of Mexico. He spent a fortune on a fleet of 10 ships and recruited about 620 soldiers. In 1538 he sailed from Spain and, after a stay in Cuba, landed his force near Tampa Bay, Florida.

De Soto found no precious metals in Florida, and the Indians there, enraged by previous raids of Spanish slavers, held the expedition under such constant attack that it took the men six months to force a path overland to the site of modern Tallahassee. Hearing of gold and silver in what is today the state of Georgia, De Soto marched his column northeast to the Savannah River in 1540. The local Indians were friendly, but they produced no treasure: Their "gold" turned out to be large quantities of spoiled freshwater pearls. De Soto turned southwest.

In the Alabama area another Indian onslaught began. Soon a quarter of De Soto's troops had been killed. Informed of the arrival of his supply ships on the gulf, De Soto abandoned his plan to meet them, fearing that his exhausted men would desert him. Not wishing to return to his ships emptyhanded, he ordered the expedition inland, then west to search for gold and silver. They passed a second winter in the deep forest—cold, hungry, and preyed upon by the Indians.

Early in April 1541, the Spaniards reached the banks of the Mississippi River. They were the first Europeans to see the huge stream—part of a system that drains almost half of the United States. It cost them a pitched battle to cross to its west bank.

Still seeking gold, the weary men fought their way northwest to the Arkansas River (near modern Little Rock), where they passed one more winter. By the spring of 1542 their condition was desperate: Ceaseless warfare had drastically cut their numbers by a half; their equipment and clothing were worn out; their gunpowder was almost gone. Admitting failure at last, De Soto returned

Before death of De Soto - - -
After death of De Soto ——

to the Mississippi, but it was too late: He died of exhaustion soon after he got there. Fearing that the news of their leader's death would encourage the Indians to attack, De Soto's officers secretly sank his body deep in the Mississippi.

The survivors decided to head for Mexico. Not sure which direction to take, they first traveled westward some 450 miles. Finding the country increasingly barren, they then struggled back to the

Mississippi. Forging nails out of their stirrups, they put together seven crude vessels, and on July 2 they set off downriver. For seven days they fought off Indians who swarmed after them in canoes. Finally entering the Gulf of Mexico, they coasted west and south for two months. Late in the year the wretched survivors, hardly half of their original number, reached their destination—the Spanish settlement of Tampico, Mexico.

### DEZHNEV, Semyon
*Russia 1605– c. 72 Russia*
**Siberia: discovered Bering Strait.** Dezhnev's great discovery bears another man's name: In 1648 Dezhnev discovered Bering Strait. His report, duly filed in the archives of Yakutsk, Siberia, remained unnoticed until an historian found it by chance in 1736—eight years

after Vitus Bering* had sailed through the strait on his first expedition.

Dezhnev was a Cossack who traded with the Chukchi aborigines of the Kolyma valley, in northern Siberia, for fur and walrus ivory. Like many fellow Russians, he believed in the existence of a mythical Pogicha River still farther east, where the Chukchis got their ivory, and he set out to find it in 1647. In three flatboats his party sailed down the Kolyma River to the Arctic Ocean, then followed the north coast of Siberia to its eastern tip. Between June 20–23, 1648, the three vessels sailed through the Bering Strait. Then they cruised the coast for three months searching for furs and walrus ivory. One vessel ran aground and had to be abandoned. (The crew was taken aboard Dezhnev's craft.) When sailing became dangerous in the autumn weather, the Russians tried to land near the Anadyr River, but Chukchis drove them back to their ships. Then the two vessels became permanently separated in a storm.

In October another storm wrecked Dezhnev's ship near the Anadyr estuary.

When the 26 survivors reached shore, they were attacked by Russian prospectors who had somehow managed to reach this remote region to hunt for furs and walrus tusks. The fight ended in a stalemate, and both sides entrenched themselves in improvised fortifications.

A messenger from Dezhnev managed to pass the prospectors and equally hostile Chukchis and reached the governor in Yakutsk, where he requested help for Dezhnev's party. The governor dispatched two Cossacks and plenty of volunteers, who scattered the prospectors. Then Dezhnev and his men constructed a fortified trading post on the Anadyr River, completing Russian penetration of Siberia from east of the Ural Mountains to the Pacific Ocean.

Bering Strait retains Bering's name, but the easternmost tip of Siberia is named Cape Dezhnev in honor of this adventurous and intrepid Cossack.

### DOUGHTY, Charles Montagu
*England 1843–1926 England*
**Arabia: explored northwest.** Originally planning only a brief journey to investigate ancient ruins in the desert north of Mecca, Doughty left Damascus, Syria, in 1876 to enter what was then a lawless country infested by brigands. For his safety he had little more to trust than his utter poverty. Doughty ended up spend-

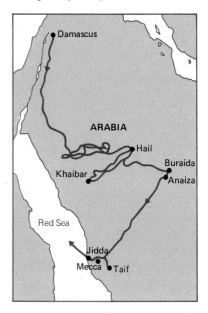

ing almost two years in Arabia, drawn by his curiosity about a land from which few European visitors had returned.

After he had completed his archeological studies, Doughty traveled for eight months as the guest of desert Bedouins, following them on their ceaseless rounds in search of fresh pasture. A geologist and surveyor, he recorded all he observed. While speaking the language and wearing the dress of his Moslem hosts, he never concealed his Christianity. This did not matter to the nomads, but when he left the tent dwellers in the autumn to visit the towns, his faith almost cost him his life several times. Religious intolerance in Arabia was at its worst among the idle poor of the cities, who superstitiously blamed their miseries on non-Moslem foreigners. Doughty could have escaped danger by pretending conversion to Islam, but his honor forbade it.

At Hail, a former provincial capital, Doughty was well received by the king, but the townsfolk became so enraged by his presence that the king could not control them and had to tell him to leave. Beaten and robbed, he eventually reached Buraida. Doughty was probably the first European to see Buraida and its neighbor, Anaiza, and they were very nearly the last places he ever saw. Although accepted by the rulers, he was once more beset by a mob and barely escaped after suffering brutal indignities.

Heading with a caravan for the port of Jidda, he had to pass close to the forbidden Mecca, where he had his closest brush with death. Some Moslem merchants discovered Doughty carrying a concealed pistol, at which point they accused him of treachery. But Doughty's knowledge of Moslem customs saved his life: Seizing a breadcrust from the man next to him, he devoured it and then claimed the Arab's protection, since they had shared bread and salt. Reluctantly bowing to age-old custom, the stranger helped him to safety at the court of the sherif of Taif, a humane gentleman who sent him under armed escort to the sanctuary of the British consulate at Jidda, where he arrived in mid-1878.

Doughty provided the first accurate description of the geography of northern Arabia. And, despite the barbarous treatment he suffered there, he wrote a detailed and sympathetic memoir that remains an enduring record of Arabia and its people.

### DUMONT D'URVILLE, Jules
*France 1790–1842 France*

**Pacific Ocean: explored islands, Antarctic coast.** Dumont d'Urville's previous record as second in command of an official round-the-world cruise and his distinction as a naturalist won him leader-

ship of an expedition to explore the southwest Pacific in 1826–29.

Recognizing that the major features of Pacific geography were already known, Dumont d'Urville applied himself to correcting and completing previous surveys. In 1828 he learned that traces of the Adm. Jean La Pérouse* expedition, missing since 1788, had been found on Vanikoro in the Santa Cruz Islands. He sailed there at once, learned what had happened to the expedition, and obtained some relics.

During a second voyage, in 1837–40, Dumont d'Urville visited Antarctica, where he claimed for France the Adélie Coast. He then devoted the rest of the cruise to completing his Pacific survey.

Dumont d'Urville's accomplishment is virtually the modern map of the southwest Pacific—he charted several million square miles of dangerous waters studded with low-lying atolls and reefs. If his many discoveries were only tiny islets and submerged rocks, their accurate location on his charts has proved invaluable for mariners ever since.

### EYRE, Edward John
*England 1815–1901 England*

**Australia: made first east-west transcontinental crossing.** Immigrants settling around Perth, in southwestern Australia,

in the early 1800's faced a food-supply problem. There was little grazing land there, and salted meat, which had to be imported from Adelaide in the southeast, was expensive. As an alternative, eastern cattlemen proposed to drive herds across the continent from Adelaide to supply fresh beef to the newcomers, hoping to discover new pasturelands on the way. Eyre, an experienced stockman, doubted that cattle could survive crossing Australia's arid south coast. He offered, instead, to prospect new grazing lands northwest of Adelaide.

Eyre's party rode north in early 1840, discovering the large, brackish Lake Eyre but no good cattle country. Unwilling to return with so little to show for his effort, Eyre then decided to cross the continent. After a coastal rendezvous in July with a supply boat from Adelaide, he and his English foreman, his native servant, and two native guides started west.

Months of thirst and hunger followed, and then catastrophe: Returning to camp one night, Eyre found that the guides had murdered his foreman and escaped with his weapons and most of the food. Only the timely appearance of a whaling ship off the coast saved him. Resupplied and rearmed by the whalers, he and his servant struggled on, still desperately short of water. They reached Albany, Western Australia, in July 1841, having conclusively proved that cattle could not be driven over the route they had traveled. In so doing, they were the first persons to cross that unexplored part of the Australian continent.

### FAWCETT, Percy Harrison
*England 1867–c. 1925 Brazil*

**South America: explored Bolivian borderlands.** Although best known for his masterly survey of the Bolivian bound-

ary early in the 20th century, Fawcett was even more dedicated to his search through South America for traces of the fabled lost continent of Atlantis.

An army officer, Fawcett was lent by the British Army to the government of Bolivia to chart its frontiers. From 1906 to 1914 he led six surveying expeditions through mostly unexplored jungle beset by jaguars, 30-foot anacondas, spiders bigger than dinner plates, and Indians armed with poisoned darts. For this work he received the Royal Geographical Society's highest award.

Then began the second phase of Fawcett's career. Convinced that Brazil had originally been colonized by highly civilized people from the ancient continent of Atlantis, he believed that in its forests he would find ruins of cities grander than classic Rome. He made two journeys to find them: in 1920–21 and 1925. He did not return from the last trip. Many expeditions went in search of Fawcett, but no trace of this daring and romantic adventurer has ever been found.

## FLINDERS, Matthew
### England 1774–1814 England

**Australia: explored coast.** While Britain and France were at war in the opening years of the 19th century, French and British surveyors were concurrently

- —— 1798
- – – 1801-03
- ···· Homeward voyage 1803

mapping the Australian coast, once even meeting for a friendly exchange of greetings. Flinders, the Englishman, had a French safe-conduct pass guaranteeing his ship *Investigator* against French capture; the Frenchman Nicolas Baudin carried a similar British document.

By the time Flinders took command of *Investigator* in 1801, he had already circumnavigated Tasmania, proving it to be an island. Now commissioned to survey the entire coast of Australia, he had nearly completed mapping the southern shoreline when he met Baudin in 1802. Keeping ahead of Baudin, he continued his work, sailing north along the east coast of the continent, then making a careful examination of the Gulf of Carpentaria. There his ship became unseaworthy—the timbers had rotted—and he had to discontinue his survey. First calling at Timor for emergency repairs, he

returned to Sydney via the west coast of Australia as fast as possible. His charts, despite his haste, were of such quality that they have required little correction.

Returning to England as a passenger on the British ship *Cumberland*, Flinders was captured by the French, who imprisoned him until 1810, claiming that his pass had been valid only for the *Investigator*. Until Flinders was freed, Baudin was credited with much of the work that the Englishman had done first, and for some years maps of Australia bristled with French names. Flinders lived just long enough to see the error corrected.

## FRANKLIN, John
### England 1786–1847 Canada

**North America: searched for Northwest Passage.** John Franklin's last voyage was one of the most productive failures in the history of exploration. A sailor most of his life, Franklin entered the British Navy at the age of 14. He served under his cousin Matthew Flinders* on his coastal survey of Australia from 1801–03 and was second in command on an Arctic cruise in 1818. He also led two long overland surveys in the Canadian Arctic in 1819–22 and 1825–27.

Thus he was the natural choice to command an expedition sent by the British Admiralty to renew the search for the Northwest Passage. In May 1845 his sailing ships *Erebus* and *Terror* left England and were last seen entering Lancaster Sound in July. Nothing more was heard of them for 14 years.

When a message from members of Franklin's expedition was found on a cairn on King William Island in 1859 by

- —— Before Franklin's death
- —— After Franklin's death

one of the many expeditions sent in search of Franklin and his crew, the world learned that the ships had wintered in Barrow Strait in 1845–46. Then, sailing south, they became icebound off King William Island late in 1846 and

never got free again. Provisioned for three years, the party waited for the ice to break up. Franklin, already 59 when he left England, died in 1847. Early in 1848, their provisions depleted, the crew started for the mainland on foot. Eskimos who saw the starving, exhausted men said, many years later, that some practiced cannibalism to keep alive. If so, it was useless. None survived.

Their disappearance touched off one of the greatest search-and-rescue operations in history. During the next six years more than 40 expeditions searched for the men or their remains, only to find a few scattered graves, skeletons, and odds and ends from the ships. Because almost all these rescue ventures were well-equipped scientific expeditions, their combined efforts managed to survey more than 10,000 miles of Canadian coastline and added an enormous area to our map of the world. Indirectly, then, Franklin accomplished a great deal. The Arctic archipelago and Boothia and Melville Peninsulas are named the District of Franklin in his memory.

## FRASER, Simon
### U.S.A. 1776–1862 Canada

**Canada: explored British Columbia.** Appointed to explore and establish trading

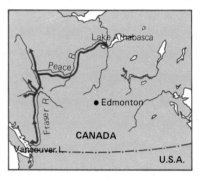

posts in the Canadian Rockies for the North West Company, the New Yorker Simon Fraser led a party of trappers and traders from Alberta's Peace River district into British Columbia in 1805. Beyond the Rocky Mountains, well north of the region soon to be covered by his English colleague, David Thompson,* he came upon a river that is now called the Fraser. Like Alexander Mackenzie,* who had seen it before him, he mistakenly believed that it was part of the Columbia.

In 1808, after spending three years exploring British Columbia and establishing trading posts, Fraser decided to canoe down the river. Indians told him it was impossible because of the many rapids, and they were right. The banks were so steep the men could not even portage their canoes and had to abandon them. Undeterred, Fraser led them on foot to where the river becomes navigable again. After bargaining with friendly Indians for new canoes, they paddled south, only to be stopped again by rapids and canyons. After another hundred miles the river turned west and became navigable. In a few days Fraser reached tidewater near modern-day Vancouver. Knowing the Columbia's mouth was much farther south, Fraser realized he was not on that river.

Prevented by hostile Indians from actually entering the Pacific, Fraser knew it could not be far away. Thus he was able to fix the position of the Fraser River mouth within a very few miles, before returning the way he had come.

### FRÉMONT, John Charles
U.S.A. 1813–90 U.S.A.

**United States: explored Far West.** At a time when the United States was preparing to assert claims to what is now its Far West, Frémont, an army officer from

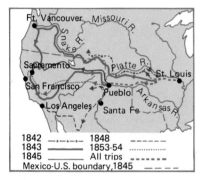

1842 —·—·— 1848 — — — —
1843 _____ 1853-54 ················
1845 _____ All trips
Mexico-U.S. boundary, 1845 — — —

Georgia, was sent on three official expeditions to gather geographical and military information about the area. On all three trips he was accompanied by Kit Carson, the renowned guide and frontier fighter of that day, and on his third trip he was joined by Joseph Walker* as well.

On his first two missions, in 1842 and 1843, Frémont led U.S. Army units over the Oregon Trail from St. Louis, Missouri, and surveyed most of the historic roadway for the first time. At Fort Vancouver, in present-day Washington, his survey connected with one made previously by the U.S. Navy. Instead of turning east, Frémont marched his men south, deliberately crossing what was then the Mexican border when he entered Nevada. Daring a dangerous midwinter crossing over the mountains into central California, he made his way from

Sacramento almost to Los Angeles before returning to St. Louis.

With the United States on the brink of war with Mexico, Frémont was dispatched to California again in 1845. Seeking a direct route from St. Louis, he ascended the Arkansas River to Pueblo, in present Colorado, and proceeded northwest and then west through mountains and deserts to Sacramento. War with Mexico broke out after he arrived, and Frémont took an active part in the fighting. After the U.S. victory, however, he was accused of disobedience and mutiny and sent under arrest to Washington, D.C., in 1847. Convicted by a court-martial, he was later pardoned by President James Polk but resigned his commission.

In 1848 Frémont was retained by railroad interests to find a suitable central transcontinental route between St. Louis and San Francisco. The attempt was disastrous. Anxious to locate an all-weather road, Frémont timed his ascent of the Arkansas River to arrive at Pueblo in November. From there he plunged straight west into impassable country. In a few weeks half his men died of cold and starvation. The survivors limped down to Santa Fe, New Mexico, and Frémont reached California by a southern route of no interest to his backers.

Another effort in 1853–54 also ended in failure. Better prepared than previously for the rigors he had to endure, Frémont managed to cross Colorado during the winter. Although this time he brought his party through to California in safety, he had to report that his route would be useless to the railroads in cold weather.

### FROBISHER, Martin
England c. 1539–94 England

**North America: searched for Northwest Passage, discovered Frobisher Bay.** A career as a pirate helped Frobisher win command of an early English attempt at American exploration. His backers sent him out to find the Northwest Passage, hoping its discovery would open up a new route to the profitable Orient trade. Frobisher's fighting reputation as well as his expert seamanship qualified him to be chosen for this venture into Eastern waters where he might well encounter armed Portuguese merchant ships.

Making three transatlantic voyages between 1576 and 1578, Frobisher never got farther than southeastern Baffin Island, where he entered the bay now named for him in the hope of discovering the passage. Unfortunately, he became convinced that black stones he found there

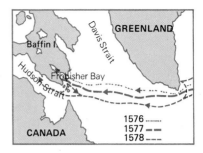

1576 ············
1577 — — —
1578 — · — ·

contained gold, and his voyages of exploration deteriorated into futile treasure hunts ending in failure and discredit.

Knighted for valiant service fighting against the Spanish Armada, Frobisher resumed piracy in his fifties. Preying on the Spanish treasure fleets from America, he died possessed of a small fortune.

### FUCHS, Vivian
England 1908–

**Antarctica: crossed the continent.** To mark the International Geophysical Year of 1957–58, Fuchs determined to cross Antarctica by way of the South Pole, an endeavor unsuccessfully attempted by Ernest Shackleton* in 1914. A doctor of science and an experienced explorer (of Greenland and east Africa), Fuchs was well qualified for the job. His second in command was Edmund Hillary,* conqueror of Mount Everest.

Esteeming Shackleton as the greatest of Antarctic explorers, Fuchs adopted his plan in full. From the Ross Sea, Hillary ascended the coastal mountains and established supply depots between the sea and the pole. Starting from the Shackleton Base area on the Weddell Sea, Fuchs crossed to the pole, making careful sci-

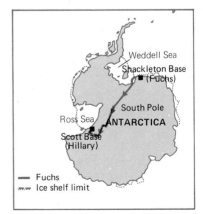

— Fuchs
······ Ice shelf limit

entific observations as he slowly progressed. Using tractors and aircraft, communicating by radio, always able to rely on the huge U.S. base at the pole itself, the expedition was a far cry from the often desperate ventures of earlier explorers. Yet there were moments of danger when aircraft strayed in the fog or tractors slipped into crevasses.

Early in 1958 Fuchs and Hillary reached the South Pole. Hillary, who had arrived there first (January 4), was flown out, while Fuchs, who arrived on February 22, continued across the continent to the Ross Sea. By their efforts they had amassed a great body of important scientific data, and Fuchs was knighted when he returned to England.

### GARNIER, Marie Joseph
*France 1839–73 Indochina*
**Southeast Asia: surveyed Mekong River.** In 1866, when the French government adopted Garnier's plan to survey the Mekong and open it to traffic between Indochina (Vietnam) and China, Garnier himself was considered too young to take charge. Yet Garnier was chiefly responsible for the expedition's

achievements, although he was only second in command.

Traveling upriver from Saigon, first by steamer, then by native canoes, and finally on foot, the expedition took more than a year to reach the northern Laos-Burma border. The party surveyed not only the Mekong but its major tributaries as well. Sometimes attacks of malaria halted them. Reports of a revolt in the south, which threatened to cut them off from their base, caused them to wait while young Garnier made a dash to Pnompenh. After traveling through country held by the rebels, he returned with the welcome news that the French had regained control. This trip, early in 1867, took Garnier through 1,000 miles of hitherto unexplored territory.

As the expedition continued to ascend the river, rapids often obstructed progress. These stretches of white water, which no vessel could navigate, ended Garnier's dream of using the Mekong as a great river trade route. Forced by an outbreak of civil war to leave the watercourse near the Chinese border, the French went overland to Kunming. There Garnier managed to get letters of introduction to the insurgents in the war zone. As the expedition headed back toward the Mekong, its leader, Capt. Douant de Lagrée, fell ill and died. Taking charge, Garnier reached the rebel capital of Tali—only to find himself suspected of being a Chinese government spy. He was forbidden access to the river and was finally made to return by the way he had come. Reluctantly, he abandoned the project and led his party down the Yangtze River to Shanghai in 1868.

Disappointed in his hopes that the Mekong could be a highway of commerce and thwarted in his ambition to trace the great river to its source, Garnier had still achieved impressive results: He had traveled more than 3,600 miles through previously unexplored country from Pnompenh to Tali and made an accurate survey of more than 100,000 square miles of the area.

### GOMEZ, Estevan
### (*see* VERRAZANO)

### GRANDIDIER, Alfred
*France 1836–1921 France*
**Africa: explored Madagascar.** Destined to find his name inseparably linked with Madagascar, the young Grandidier originally planned to explore Tibet disguised as a Buddhist monk. But while studying Buddhism in Ceylon, he contracted malaria. While recuperating, he visited Madagascar. So interested did he become in what he observed there that he soon abandoned his plans to explore Asia in order to study Africa's largest island, which was then mostly unknown.

Between 1865 and 1870 Grandidier traveled almost continuously through the interior of Madagascar, making careful surveys and collecting specimens of animals, plants, and minerals. Among other accomplishments, he precisely fixed the positions of 26 large towns by astronomical observations. Often suspected of sorcery because of his scientific activities, he twice saved his life from superstitious islanders by persuading local chieftains to become his blood brothers in a ceremony in which each

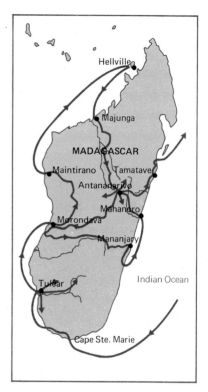

man cut his wrist and mixed the other's blood in his vein.

When Grandidier left Madagascar in 1870 to fight for France in the Franco-Prussian War, he had amassed enough information to map the enormous island for the first time. The last 50 years of his long life scarcely sufficed to publish the results of his pioneer labors.

### GRAY, Robert
*U.S.A. 1755–1806 U.S.A.*
**North America: discovered Columbia River.** Two centuries after Sir Francis Drake* had made his first probes for the Pacific entrance to the Northwest Passage, mariners were still seeking it along the American northwest coast. Gray looked for it during a trading trip to China. Leaving Boston in 1787, he planned to buy furs from Pacific coast Indians, sell them in China, and reap a profit in Boston with a return cargo of tea. His three-year voyage was a financial failure but a geographic success: While collecting furs, Gray explored more of the Alaskan and Canadian coastlines than had all his predecessors, including Capt. James Cook.*

A second trading trip to the Pacific Northwest in the ship *Columbia* in 1790 was more successful. Trade prospered in spite of an Indian attack that caught Gray with his ship beached and his guns ashore. Still looking for the passage, he sailed south past what is now the state of Washington to investigate a large bay he had heard of. He was almost forestalled by George Vancouver,* whom Gray met at sea after the English explorer had sailed past the river mouth, which he had failed to see because of bad weather.

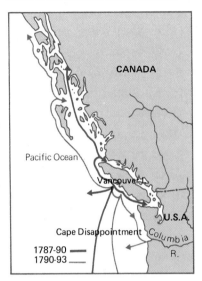

CANADA

Pacific Ocean

Vancouver I.

U.S.A.

Cape Disappointment
Columbia R.

1787-90 ———
1790-93 ———

Rounding Cape Disappointment May 11, 1792, Gray entered the mouth of the mighty Columbia River. Soon aware that it was not a strait, he named the stream for his ship. (The area was later claimed by the United States on the basis of his discovery.) Then, getting back to business, Gray crossed to China, and this time returned to Boston with a handsome profit from his fur sales.

## GREELY, Adolphus Washington
*U.S.A. 1844–1935 U.S.A.*

**Arctic: explored Greenland, northern Canada.** The United States joined several other nations to coordinate scientific and

Arctic Ocean

Lockwood I.

Lincoln Sea

Greely Fjord

Hall Basin

Ellesmere Island

Kane Basin

GREENLAND

Baffin Bay

geographic observations in the Arctic during the International Polar Year of 1882–83. Lieutenant Greely was appointed to head the U.S. expedition, which was to be the country's first participation in an international scientific effort.

In August 1881 Greely and an army detachment were taken to the Canadian shore of Hall Basin, on Ellesmere Island, opposite Greenland, to prepare for the year's work ahead. Erecting a substantial prefabricated building, Fort Conger, they settled in for two years, expecting a supply ship in 1882 and transportation home the year after. While the group's chief duty was to make scientific and geographic observations, exploration was not overlooked. In the first winter a party examining the north coast of Greenland discovered Lockwood Island, establishing a "farthest north" record for that area that stood for many years.

Misfortune struck in 1882; ice kept the supply ship from arriving. Yet Greely continued working and explored western Ellesmere Island, discovering Greely Fjord. No relief came in 1883: One ship was wrecked, and another turned back before reaching the explorers. In August, Greely led his men south until, unable to travel farther, they built a hut out of their boat on the shore and crowded into it to await rescue—or death. Of the 23 men who began the third winter, only Greely and 6 others survived to be rescued in June 1884 by a U.S. naval vessel.

## HEARNE, Samuel
*England 1745–92 England*

**Canada: explored Northwest.** A veteran of 10 years' active service in the British Navy, the 20-year-old Hearne joined the Hudson's Bay Company in 1766. In 1769 he was assigned to the company's post at Churchill, on Hudson Bay, where he was employed in exploration. From Churchill he made three expeditions to locate a copper deposit in the Northwest, which Indians had reported.

The first two trips ended in failure: Robbed and abandoned both times by his Indian guides, Hearne had to return emptyhanded and starving to Churchill. On his third try, in 1770–72, guided by a Chipewyan Indian chief, he found a copper deposit, but it was almost worthless. However, he became the first European to stand on the shore of the Canadian Arctic, which he reached at Coronation Gulf at the mouth of the Coppermine River. Winter approaching, his guide led him south via Great Slave Lake, which

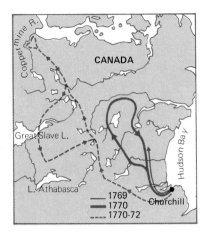

Coppermine R.

CANADA

Great Slave L.

Hudson Bay

L. Athabasca

1769 ———
1770 ———
1770-72 ----

Churchill

he was the first European to see.

Although the copper mine turned out to be of little value, the Canadian Northwest, which Hearne had opened up, proved to be the richest fur-trapping territory yet discovered in North America. Hearne was made manager of the Hudson's Bay post at Churchill as a reward. In 1782, during the American Revolution, he was captured by Adm. Jean La Pérouse* and did not reach England until 1787.

## HEDIN, Sven
*Sweden 1865–1952 Sweden*

**Central Asia: explored Sinkiang, Tibet.** While still a child, Hedin made up his mind to explore central Asia. Accordingly, as he grew up, he mastered the natural sciences of his time and learned surveying. In his twenties he obtained the financial backing of the Swedish king and the Nobel family.

On his first expedition to central Asia, in 1893–98, Hedin began his work in the

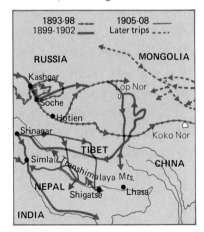

1893-98 ➤➤➤    1905-08 ———
1899-1902 ———    Later trips ----

RUSSIA        MONGOLIA

Kashgar

Lop Nor

Soche

Hotien

Srinagar

Koko Nor

Simla

TIBET

CHINA

NEPAL

Himalaya Mts.

Shigatse

Lhasa

INDIA

mountains and deserts of Sinkiang, China. Avoiding the tracks of previous travelers, such as Nikolai Przhevalsky,* he covered an enormous area previously unknown to Western geographers. In 1896 he entered Tibet and trekked east 600 miles across its unexplored northern borderland, emerging at Lake Chinghai (Koko Nor), western China, and from there he made his way to Peking.

Hedin returned to central Asia in 1899, determined to visit Lhasa, the capital of Tibet, which was then forbidden to non-Buddhists. After further exploration in Sinkiang and northern Tibet, he made a dash for the holy city in 1901 disguised as a Mongol pilgrim. Unfortunately, he was recognized, and Tibetan troops stopped him. Forced to leave Tibet, he managed to travel west through unexplored land and reached Kashmir in 1902.

Hedin's third trip, in 1905–08, was geographically his most productive. When he left Tibet in 1902, he had observed a vast mountain system parallel to the Himalayas and north of them. (He named it the Transhimalaya, and it is now called the Kailas and Nyenchen Tanglha.) On this trip he crossed the chain eight times, sometimes over passes as high as 19,000 feet. He established its great extent—the range is more than 1,400 miles long—and mapped most of it for the first time. He also discovered the sources of the Brahmaputra, Indus, and Sutlej Rivers.

Almost 30 years later (1927–35), Hedin directed a large Chinese-Swedish expedition to Sinkiang and Tibet, which mapped the area for the Chinese government. He will always be remembered as the principal explorer of central Asia.

### HUMBOLDT, Alexander von
*Germany 1769–1859 Germany*
**Americas: explored Colombia, Ecuador, Mexico, Venezuela / General: founded physical geography.** A man of towering intellect and virtually universal interests, Humboldt mastered all the scientific

disciplines of his age and made lasting contributions to many of them. He

founded the science of physical geography, which deals with the structure of the earth's crust and the circulation of earth's waters and atmosphere.

Humboldt's most important field trip was in Central and South America from 1799 to 1804. For variety, accuracy, and sheer volume of observation, it has seldom been equaled. It took him 23 years to publish his findings, which were noteworthy for their marked originality of interpretation.

Among his achievements, Humboldt discovered and surveyed the Casiquiare River, which connects Venezuela's Orinoco River and Brazil's Amazon River systems. Investigating the northern Andes Mountains, he provided the first correct geological description of the area and obtained evidence supporting his theory, revolutionary in those days, that volcanoes mark faults in the earth's crust. His analysis of the formation of tropical storms laid the foundation of modern meteorology. Earth magnetism, ocean currents, glaciers—these are but a few of the many scientific subjects that were profoundly influenced by Humboldt's exploration and study. The Humboldt Current (also known as the Peru Current) in the Pacific Ocean west of South America and the Humboldt River, Nevada, are among many geographical features named in his honor.

### HUNT, Wilson Price
*U.S.A. 1782–1842 U.S.A.*
**North America: discovered western part of the Oregon Trail.** An ambitious scheme to develop the fur trade in the United States led to the discovery of the Oregon Trail. Planning to establish western headquarters for his Pacific Fur Company at the mouth of the Columbia River, in Astoria, Oregon, John Jacob Astor needed a good overland route to connect it with the center of the fur trade at St. Louis, Missouri. Working independently, two partners in the company, Wilson Price Hunt and Robert Stuart,* each explored about half of what later became the Oregon Trail.

Hunt commanded the first expedition from St. Louis to Oregon in 1811. Traveling up the Missouri River into South Dakota, he then left it and headed west to avoid the dangerous Blackfoot Indians reported by one of Lewis* and Clark's* men to be living on its upper course. Across South Dakota and Wyoming he found the wilderness almost impassable. But entering southern Idaho, Hunt discovered something important—the na-

tural highway of the Snake River Valley that leads toward the Pacific.

Unprepared for the barren country ahead of them, his men suffered agonies as they traveled down the Snake. So near did they come to starvation that Hunt feared his men would resort to cannibalism, but game became plentiful as they neared Oregon. Leaving the Snake in western Idaho, Hunt cut northwest to the Columbia and reached Astoria by way of that river early in 1812.

Hunt's route from about Idaho Falls to Astoria became the western half of the Oregon Trail over which passed an enormous American emigrant traffic during the 19th century.

### KANE, Elisha Kent
*U.S.A. 1820–57 Cuba*
**Arctic: tried to reach North Pole.** Kane's North Pole expedition, the first attempted by an American, failed 700 miles short of its goal but established the route over which Robert Peary* succeeded

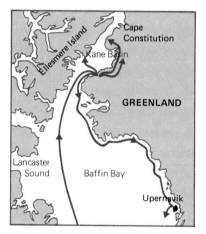

more than 50 years later. Privately financed and with some U.S. Navy assistance, the venture was announced as an attempt to find John Franklin,* who had been missing in Arctic waters since 1845. Believing the Englishman dead, Kane secretly planned to try for the pole.

Sailing to Baffin Bay in 1853, Kane did not turn west as Franklin had done, but continued north until he was stopped by

*Mapping the World*

ice. He anchored in late August in what is now called Kane Basin, between Greenland and Ellesmere Island, Canada. In April 1854 he began his march along Greenland's coast to the pole. The march ended anticlimactically: Kane had vastly underestimated the difficulties and had to return to his ship after covering only 160 miles. On a later expedition a subordinate reported sighting open water farther north: This was the passage that Peary later followed to the polar icepack before starting his triumphant sledge trip in March 1909.

Finding his vessel hopelessly icebound, supplies short, and his men ill with scurvy, Kane led his party southward in 1855. Luckily, they met a Danish trading ship, which carried them to a U.S. rescue expedition sent to find them.

### LAING, Alexander Gordon
*Scotland 1793–1826 Mali*
**West Africa: explored Timbuktu.** Preparing to cross the Sahara to Timbuktu in 1825, Laing, a British officer on a mission to explore the Niger River, stayed long enough in Tripoli, Libya, to fall in love with and marry the daughter of the British consul. Two days later he left his bride with his father-in-law and resumed his journey. The couple never met again.

Laing's caravan was attacked by desert nomads. Badly wounded and the sole survivor, Laing rode his camel 400 miles to the village of a friendly sheikh, where he recovered.

Laing reached Timbuktu on August 18,

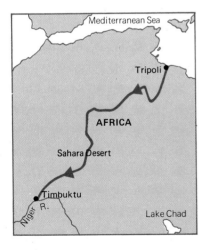

1826, and was the first European to visit there. From a dispatch to his father-in-law dated late September, we know that his reception there was unfriendly. What happened next is not known. Natives

offered conflicting accounts: One was that he turned back north by the way he had come; another was that he had started westward to begin his river survey. The only certainty is that he was murdered not far from Timbuktu, probably by the caravan leader with whom he was traveling. Neither his journals nor his effects were recovered.

### LANDER, Richard Lemon
*England 1804–34 Equatorial Guinea*
### LANDER, John
*England 1807–39 England*
**Africa: traced Niger River to its mouth.** In an age when Europeans did not usually feel that servants were worthy of

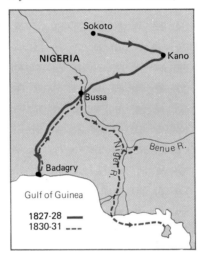

honors, Richard Lander, Hugh Clapperton's* valet, won the first royal medal ever awarded by the Royal Geographical Society for his exploration of the Niger. After Clapperton died in Nigeria in 1827, Lander, prevented from following his master's plan to go down the Niger River and discover its outlet, had traveled overland to the Nigerian coast. The trip was dangerous: Once, suspected of spying for British businessmen, he was captured and tried by a Yoruba chief, who made him drink poison, announcing that if he died his guilt would be proven. Lander drank it but, running to his tent, was able to vomit it, thus saving his life and regaining his liberty.

Lander's report of this journey, which he published together with Clapperton's account of the expedition, interested the British government. Soon it employed him to make another attempt to trace the Niger to its mouth. His brother John volunteered to go with him.

The brothers landed at Badagry, Nigeria, in 1830 and pushed through the jun-

gle to reach the Niger at Bussa, where Mungo Park* had drowned. Starting where Park's survey ended, they went down the river by canoe, making a rough map of its course. When they emerged at its mouth on the Gulf of Guinea in 1831, they had solved the riddle of the Niger and had charted the lower part of its course. Their achievement was all the more remarkable, considering that Richard Lander had been grossly underpaid and John not paid at all, so the expedition was poorly equipped. Richard Lander was awarded the royal medal in the following year.

### LA PÉROUSE, Jean François
*France 1741–88 Santa Cruz Islands*
**Pacific Ocean: charted east Asian coast, discovered islands.** With handwritten instructions from his sovereign, Louis XVI, Admiral La Pérouse sailed from France for the Pacific in 1785 to make a three-year ocean survey intended to enhance French prestige in the scientific world. He hoped to equal the achievements of Capt. James Cook,* whom he admired.

He began his work near Cape Horn by searching for two mythical coastlines long shown on maps of the southern oceans and often thought to be parts of

continents resembling Australia: They were "Isla Grande" in the Atlantic and "Drake's Land" in the Pacific. Passing through their reported positions, La Pérouse proved that there could be nothing larger than small islands within many hundreds of miles east and west of South America. He sailed next to Alaska in 1786, intent on exploding another supposed geographical myth: the Northwest Passage through Canada. Daunted by the labyrinthine northwestern coastline of North America (which later took George Vancouver* three years to survey), he was utterly disheartened when an accident cost the lives of 21 of his men, many of them sons of old friends. After the catastrophe he abandoned that project and crossed the Pacific.

La Pérouse's exploration of the north-eastern coast of Asia ranks as his major original geographic work. Beginning off the coast of what is present-day North Korea, he followed the shoreline northward to the narrows between the Russian mainland and Sakhalin. There shoal water prevented La Pérouse's further progress, but not before he had determined that Sakhalin is an island.

After a call at Petropavlovsk, La Pérouse visited Polynesia in 1787, where he made some discoveries. In Samoa he was ambushed by islanders who killed 12 of his company. His last port of call was at the site of what is modern Sydney, Australia. There he sent home his records and a letter announcing his intention of exploring islands to the northeast.

Then the Frenchmen sailed away, and no Westerner ever saw them again; for decades their whereabouts remained a mystery. At last, in 1826, Peter Dillon, an Irish trader, found some traces of them, and little by little their story was reconstructed: Shipwrecked on Vanikoro in the Santa Cruz group not long after leaving Australia, many were killed by natives as they went ashore. Then the survivors, possibly led by La Pérouse, built a boat from salvaged materials and put out to sea again. Their final destination remained unknown until, in 1840, a native of Ponape in the Carolines confessed that many years earlier a boatload of Europeans had landed there and his people had murdered them all. Such, probably, was the fate of the expedition and, perhaps, of La Pérouse.

In addition to clearing the map of imaginary features, La Pérouse contributed much to Pacific geography: He corrected some of Cook's measurements, discovered islands in the Hawaiian and Samoan groups, and made the first reliable chart of the east Asian coast facing Japan.

### LEICHHARDT, Friedrich
*Germany 1813–48 Australia*
**Australia: explored northeast.** Leichhardt was the first explorer to successfully lead an expedition overland from southern to northern Australia. Unknown and almost penniless when he first presented his scheme, he managed to solicit contributions of a few hundred dollars through the press. Leaving Brisbane for Port Essington in 1844, he explored 3,000 miles along a route roughly parallel to the coast. The journey, planned for 6 months, stretched to 14. The well-equipped expedition moved leisurely up the east coast, each man

pursuing his own scientific interest on the side. Warlike aborigines killed one member near the Gulf of Carpentaria, and Leichhardt lost most of his botanical collection near Port Essington in 1845.

Leichhardt was momentarily famous for reaching Port Essington, but then came anticlimax and tragedy: An attempt at a pioneer east-west crossing of the continent from Darling Downs to Perth in 1846 ended in disaster when his party suffered an outbreak of fever. Returning unsuccessful and discredited but determined to vindicate himself, Leichhardt started on the same route again in 1848—and disappeared. Perhaps he and his party were killed by aborigines or engulfed in sandstorms or floods. No trace of them has ever been found.

Despite his failures, Leichhardt contributed much to Australian geography, notably the discovery of vast pasturelands in the northeast.

### LE MAIRE, Jakob
*Netherlands 1585–1616 At sea*
**South America: first to navigate Drake Passage.** Seeking a way to Java through the southern tip of South America, Le Maire pioneered a great trade route from

the Atlantic to the Pacific. In 1615–16, when he sailed, maps showed a vast archipelago south of the Strait of Magellan. But because Magellan's strait is difficult to navigate, Le Maire looked for an easier passage farther south. Cruising 200 miles southeast, he discovered a short seaway between Tierra del Fuego and land to the east that he thought was a southern continent and named Staten Landt. Beyond stretched the open water of Drake Passage through which Le Maire entered the Pacific, rounding Cape Horn, which he named for Hoorn, the Netherlands, the birthplace of his pilot, Willem Schouten.

Although first to navigate Drake Passage, Le Maire is not credited with its discovery: Sir Francis Drake* first saw it in 1578. Le Maire did not understand what he had accomplished. His Staten Landt, as we now know, is not a continent but the tiny Isla de los Estados, which Le Maire Strait separates from southeastern Tierra del Fuego. South of the island lies the ocean—not more land, as Le Maire thought.

But Le Maire deserves credit for leading others to Drake Passage and around Cape Horn. Progress was slow at first, but well before 1700, pilots had virtually abandoned the Strait of Magellan for the southern ocean where a sailing ship has room to tack against contrary winds. An enormous commerce passed that way before the Panama Canal opened in 1914.

### MALASPINA, Alejandro
*Italy 1754–1810 Italy*
**Pacific Ocean: charted coasts, islands.** Ranking with Capt. James Cook* and

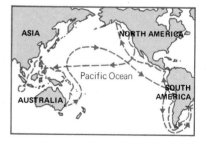

Adm. Jean La Pérouse* among leaders of outstanding 18th-century scientific expeditions, Malaspina has been almost forgotten, for his record was suppressed because of government disapproval of his liberal sympathies.

An "adopted son of Spain," as he called himself, he joined the Spanish Navy and rose to high rank. In 1789 he took command of what was intended to be Spain's greatest contribution to geography—a detailed study of its colonial areas throughout the world. Old charts were to be updated, and ocean currents, climate, and natural resources thoroughly investigated.

Rounding Cape Horn, Malaspina spent a year mapping the South American west coast before sailing to Alaska, where he made a thorough northern survey and unsuccessfully searched for a northwest passage to connect Spain with its colonies. His next assignment—an examination of the southwestern Pacific and eastern Indian Oceans—ended when he was recalled to Spain in 1794 because of the outbreak of war with France.

Although a nobleman, Malaspina was devoted to republican principles. In his report of his voyage he advocated sweeping reforms of Spanish colonial policy, based on what he had observed during his cruise. As a result, he was judged subversive by the ultraconservative Spanish government and imprisoned. When released eight years later, he was deported to his native Italy. His report was never made public, and he remains almost unknown.

### MARQUETTE, Jacques
*France 1637–75 North America*
**North America: explored Mississippi River.** Interested in learning whether the Mississippi led to the Pacific Ocean, the

intendant of New France, Jean Talon, sent Jacques Marquette and Louis Jolliet to explore that great waterway in 1673. Jolliet, a trapper and trader, was the leader; Marquette was the obvious choice to accompany him. A frontier missionary inured to wilderness life, Marquette was loved by his Indian converts and was fluent in six of their languages. To him fell the delicate work of forging good relations with Indian tribes on the way down the river.

The pair embarked on the Mississippi in southern Wisconsin in June 1673.

Later that month they reached the Missouri River. Observing its great size, they realized that it must drain a vast area of the West, and they began to suspect that they were nowhere near the Pacific. At the mouth of the Arkansas River in July, Indians told them that the Mississippi flows on southward, not west, and added that there were Spaniards at its delta. Feeling confident that the Mississippi flowed to the Gulf of Mexico but fearful of being captured by the Spanish, the explorers turned back 700 miles short of the river's mouth and arrived at Lake Michigan in September 1673. Their journey had, in effect, paved the way for Robert La Salle,* who later followed the Mississippi to the gulf.

On his way to Quebec, Jolliet lost all his notes in an accident, so it is chiefly to Marquette's journals that we owe our record of this journey.

### McCLURE, Robert John
*Ireland 1807–73 England*
**North America: first to traverse Northwest Passage.** Three hundred and fifty-six years after John Cabot* first sailed north to find Asia, McClure traversed the Northwest Passage. An officer in the British Navy, McClure sailed to the Canadian Arctic in the *Enterprise* under James Ross* in 1848, the first mission sent to find John Franklin's* lost expedition. Ross entered Barrow Strait west of Baffin Bay but was blocked by pack ice.

In 1850–54 McClure commanded *Investigator* in another search for Franklin, this time entering northern Canadian waters through Bering Strait to the west.

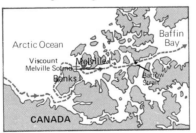

McClure sailed east until he could see Viscount Melville Sound and was the first person to prove the existence of a continuous waterway north of Canada. Again blocked by ice, he wintered in the area. Finding the ice still impassable when summer came, he returned to Banks Island in the west. There *Investigator* froze in for a second winter, and there she remained: Her crew could not free her during the summer of 1852. McClure went by sledge north to Melville Island

and left a message there. Providentially, a search party sent out by Sir Edward Belcher's rescue expedition found it, and Belcher's party located McClure and his men the following spring. While making the final leg of the trip east to Belcher's vessels, McClure crossed the Barrow Strait icepack on foot, thus completing the crossing of the Northwest Passage. The strait north of Banks Island is named for McClure.

### MENDAÑA DE NEYRA, Alvaro de
*Spain 1541–95 Santa Cruz Islands*
**Pacific Ocean: discovered Solomon, Marquesas, and Santa Cruz island groups.** Four centuries ago Mendaña heard the legend of the pre-Columbian Inca, Tupac Yupanqui, who crossed the

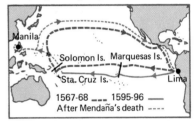

Pacific Ocean on a raft and returned with a fortune. Inspired to repeat his exploit, Mendaña sailed from Callao (Lima's harbor), Peru, in 1567. Although he discovered the Solomon Islands, he came back to Peru emptyhanded.

Almost 30 years passed before Mendaña convinced the crown to support another venture. Reembarking from Callao with a shipload of emigrants, he planned this time to colonize a Pacific island where he would be king and his wife, Isabel, queen. With his pilot, Pedro de Quirós,* he discovered the Marquesas Islands and then the Santa Cruz group, where he landed his people.

His little settlement was unsuccessful. Mendaña died, and Isabel tried to carry on. But food ran short, and fighting erupted between the islanders and the Spaniards. With the faithful Quirós as pilot, Isabel sailed to Manila to get help. There she married Don Fernando de Castro, a relative of Mendaña's. They refitted and supplied the ship and returned to Acapulco, Mexico, in late 1596 after a voyage of incredible hardship.

Thinking Mendaña's discoveries might be sources of treasure, Spain kept them secret—and then forgot them. The Solomons and the Santa Cruz group were rediscovered in 1767 by Philip Carteret, second in command to Samuel Wallis.* In our own century the Norwegian Thor

Heyerdahl crossed the Pacific on a balsawood raft alleged to be an exact copy of the one sailed by the fabled Inca.

## NACHTIGAL, Gustav
*Germany 1834–85 At sea*

**West Africa: explored Sahara.** In the 19th-century European race for African colonies, Germany was delayed a year or more because of Nachtigal's interest in the wonders of the Sahara, through which he traveled. Leaving Tripoli, Libya, in 1869, he was supposed to deliver eight camel loads of gifts from the king of Prussia to the sheikh in Bornu, an area which has been partitioned between Cameroon and Nigeria. Ostensibly, his mission was to express appreciation of

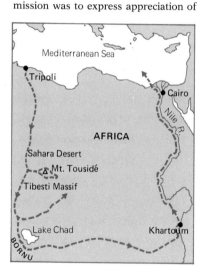

the African ruler's kindnesses to Heinrich Barth* and other German explorers; actually, it was to prepare the way for German annexation of Bornu.

But for Nachtigal, scientific investigation took priority. The first modern European to see the Tibesti highland of the eastern Sahara, he explored it thoroughly and studied its mysterious Tebu tribesmen, a race of unknown origin possibly dating back 15,000 years to the last ice age. He finally arrived in Bornu in 1870 and, after delivering his gifts, departed eastward through Sudan to the Nile. By the time Nachtigal reached Khartoum in 1874, he had been given up for lost. His account of his trip was hailed as a major addition to African geography.

## NIEBUHR, Karsten
*Germany 1733–1815 Denmark*

**Yemen: first comprehensive exploration.** The sole survivor of a royal Danish scientific expedition to the Middle East,

Niebuhr is best remembered for his masterly presentation of his deceased colleagues' work. He was a peasant's son who had worked his way through school in an age when long working hours and social discrimination made this almost impossible. His specialties were surveying and mapmaking.

Niebuhr sailed to Alexandria, Egypt, with four other scientists in 1761. The party's destination was Arabia, which they were to investigate, but the men had hardly reached Mocha, Yemen, when two died of tropical diseases. Traveling for about a year throughout Yemen, Niebuhr saved his own life, he believed, by adopting local habits of diet and dress. As well as he could, he performed the scientific duties of his deceased colleagues. His two other companions died on the way home, and Niebuhr reached Copenhagen alone in 1767.

Niebuhr's edition of the expedition's results provides a record of Yemen that later explorers have hardly been able to add to or improve. If Niebuhr's report reflects credit on his colleagues, it reflects even more credit on the man himself. An historian later wrote: "If he was not the most brilliant of the party, if any

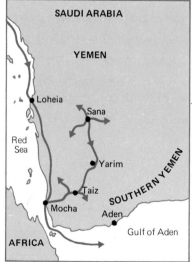

of his fellows surpassed him in energy, courage, and endurance, in intelligence or in his measure of the scientific temper ... then a more remarkable expedition was never dispatched to any land."

## NORDENSKJOLD, Nils Adolf
*Finland 1832–1901 Sweden*

**Arctic Ocean: first to traverse Northeast Passage.** First to sail through the Northeast Passage along the European and Siberian coasts from Norway to the Ber-

ing Strait, Nordenskjold was also first to sail completely around Europe and Asia. Born in Helsinki, Nordenskjold was deported for opposing the Russian government of Finland and became a naturalized Swede. He gained his first Arctic experience during expeditions to Spitsbergen and Greenland. Making a first attempt to find the Northeast Passage in 1875–76, he sailed east along the coast of Siberia as far as the Yenisei Delta before turning back.

In 1878 he set out again from Sweden in the steamer *Vega*, rounded Cape Chelyuskin, the northernmost point of the Asian mainland, and almost reached the Bering Strait before becoming frozen in for the winter. Released by the summer thaw, he continued east and then south through Bering Strait. Nordenskjold had finally sailed completely through the Northeast Passage 326 years after Sir Hugh Willoughby and Richard Chancellor* had made the first attempt. He returned to Sweden via Japan, Ceylon, and the Suez Canal in 1880.

Nordenskjold was made a baron after his 1878–80 expedition. He remained active in Arctic exploration, becoming the first man to take a ship through the Arctic pack ice east of Greenland.

## ORELLANA, Francisco de
*Spain c. 1490–c. 1546 Brazil*

**South America: first to go down Amazon River.** Orellana was second in command under Gonzalo Pizarro (half brother of Francisco Pizarro*) on an expedition in 1541 to locate a region rich in cinnamon, rumored to exist in eastern Ecuador. During months of fruitless wandering in the jungles east of the Andes Mountains, the Spaniards so antagonized the Indians on

*Mapping the World*

whom they depended for food that the Indians finally refused to supply them with any more. Desperate, Pizarro sent Orellana with a small party by boat down a tributary of the Napo to forage. That was the last Pizarro ever saw of his lieutenant. Going overland to the designated rendezvous, Pizarro discovered Orellana had gone on downstream; so he struggled back to Quito after fearful losses from starvation.

Although Orellana obtained supplies from friendly Indians only 12 days' journey downstream, he made no attempt to return to Pizarro, blaming the strong river current for his failure to do so. He went down the Napo River and entered the Amazon near the site of modern-day Iquitos, Peru, in February 1542, not knowing what river it was or where it would lead. The men halted briefly and built a small ship to replace their boat, improvising tools and materials with great ingenuity. Sailing on, they encountered Indians on the forested riverbanks whose armed women fought alongside their men in battle: The river was named Amazon—the female warrior of ancient Greek mythology—from the Spaniards' accounts of them.

Reaching the mouth of the river in August, the explorers sailed to a Spanish settlement at Cubagua Island, west of Trinidad. Orellana returned to Spain, where he obtained royal permission to colonize the Amazon Basin. However, upon his return to South America, his boat capsized, and he drowned in the delta region before he could carry through his ambitious plan.

## PARK, Mungo
*Scotland 1771–c. 1806 Nigeria*
**West Africa: explored Niger River.** For more than 2,000 years geographers had been hearing of the existence of a great west African watercourse—the Niger, or "Black," River—that was said to flow south of the Sahara. No explorer had seen it. No one even knew whether it ran eastward or westward. In 1795 the African Association sent Mungo Park to investigate it.

Park started inland from a village upstream from Bathurst, in modern-day Gambia, in 1795 with two servants and a meager stock of provisions and trade goods. Petty chieftains whose lands he passed through soon robbed him of most of his possessions, and on the border of the Sahara he was seized by "Moors"—the fierce Tuareg tribesmen of west Africa. Threatened with death because he

was not Moslem and given barely enough food and water to exist, Park endured captivity for four months. After he had escaped with only his clothes, his horse, and a pocket compass he had hidden from his captors, he made his way south and again nearly died of hunger and thirst. Park reached the Niger at Ségou. He was the first European ex-

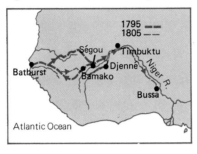

plorer to see and describe the mysterious river and the first to discover that it flowed eastward. He traveled downstream for 80 miles, but then, unable to buy food and his horse worn out, he turned back. In spite of illness and almost incredible hardships, he traced the Niger's course 300 miles upstream, to Bamako, Mali. There he met a friendly Moslem slave trader who nursed him back to health. When he finally reached England again, not long before Christmas 1797, he learned that he had been given up for dead.

In early 1805 Park returned to west Africa on a British mission to follow the Niger to its mouth. Starting again from near Bathurst, Park took a party of 40 Britons with him. By the time he reached the Niger at Bamako, 29 had died from dysentery and malaria, and all but 4 of the rest died before he set off downriver.

Park and the four survivors converted log canoes into a flatboat, which he named H. M. schooner, the *Joliba* (the great water). In November 1805 he sent a guide back to Bathurst with his records to that date and embarked on the Niger. He was never heard from again.

Later explorers—Hugh Clapperton* and Richard Lander* among them—learned his story. On his way down the river Park was attacked many times, perhaps because he neglected to make friendly overtures to the chiefs through whose territory he passed. At Bussa, Nigeria, his boat was ambushed. A last terrible battle ensued, and Park and his remaining companions were drowned. A few of his personal effects were recovered years later, but his records of the middle course of the Niger were lost.

## PARRY, William Edward
*England 1790–1855 Germany*
**Arctic: explored Canada, polar area.** Second in command of an 1818 British naval expedition seeking a northwest passage through Canada, Parry strongly criticized his superior for failing to enter the ice-strewn channels west of Baffin Bay. Commanding his own expedition in 1819–20, he was the first explorer to force his wooden sailing ships through heavy pack ice into Lancaster Sound and beyond. He reached Melville Island—chief of his many discoveries—before being stopped by solid ice just 300 miles short of completing the passage. Making other trips to the area in 1821–23 and 1824–25, he again failed to get through but made valuable surveys north of Hudson Bay.

A keen observer and ready innovator, Parry was the first to propose the use of Eskimo dogsleds for polar exploration. Attempting to reach the North Pole from Spitsbergen in 1827, he also experimented with amphibious vehicles: boats on sleigh runners, to be pulled by men when they reached pack ice. During this trip he was the first to note the drift of the Arctic pack ice, later confirmed by George Washington De Long*: At one point he realized he was being *carried*

southwest almost as far as he could travel northeast every day. He attained 82°45′ N, 500 miles from the pole.

During his later career Parry was instrumental in converting the British Navy to steam power. For his achievements, Parry was knighted in 1829, and many places in Canada and Greenland now bear his name.

## PIKE, Zebulon Montgomery
*U.S.A. 1779–1813 Canada*
**North America: explored Rocky Mountains area.** Dispatched by Gen. James Wilkinson, first governor of the Territory of Louisiana, to explore the country west of St. Louis, Missouri, Pike had secret

orders to spy in Spanish territory, which then included the U.S. Southwest. (Wilkinson and Aaron Burr, a well-known political figure of the day, were plotting to occupy Spanish land and found an independent country of their own. Pike was to get them information about the area.)

Lieutenant Pike left St. Louis in 1806 with surveying instruments and a detail of 20 men. Following an early route of the Santa Fe Trail, he crossed Missouri and parts of Arkansas and Kansas, country that had often been traversed but that Pike was the first to map. Reaching central Colorado in November, he discovered Pikes Peak.

Pike then led his men south into Spanish territory, where Spanish troops promptly arrested them. Wilkinson had double-crossed Pike: Knowing the party would be taken to Santa Fe if captured and wanting Pike to examine that area, he had warned the Spanish authorities of Pike's approach. Conditionally released on parole, Pike made a careful examination of the city. The Spanish took Pike and his men to old Mexico and then to the U.S.-Mexican border. Pike later claimed credit for exploring the Spanish land he passed through because the Spanish had prohibited outsiders from investigating their territory, although they were familiar with it themselves. He and his party were repatriated in 1807 at Natchitoches, Louisiana. By then Wilkinson and Burr had been discredited and had no use for his information.

However, Pike's reports were the first ones of the Mexican provinces he had passed through and were of great value to the U.S. government and to traders. Pike's exploratory work resulted in the establishment of the Santa Fe Trail from St. Louis to the Pacific.

A brigadier general during the War of 1812, Pike was killed in action.

## PINZÓN, Vicente Yáñez
*Spain c. 1460–c. 1523 Spain*
**South America: discovered Brazil.** Captain of the *Niña* on Christopher Columbus'* epoch-making voyage of 1492–93, Pinzón went on to become a noted explorer in his own right.

After Columbus had discovered South America during his third transatlantic trip, Pinzón got private backing for an expedition in 1500 to establish the size of the new continent. Sailing well south of his predecessor's track, his first landfall was the northeastern tip of Brazil. (He beat Pedro Álvares Cabral* there by three months.) As he cruised from there along the north coast of South America, he entered an area where the seawater was fresh enough to drink. Realizing that he was off the mouth of a great river, he entered it. It is widely believed that he had discovered the Amazon, although it has been suggested that it was the Orinoco that he entered. In any case, Pinzón thought it was the Ganges in India. Pinzón then continued to Costa Rica, linking up his survey with Columbus', before turning toward Spain.

As joint commander with Juan Díaz de Solís* of an official expedition in 1508–09, Pinzón took part in the first exploration

of the Yucatan coast. But credit for this achievement properly belongs to his partner who was commander at sea, while Pinzón was in charge of landing operations.

On his return to Spain, Pinzón retired with a modest fortune and a reputation as one of Spain's ablest pilots.

## PONCE DE LEÓN, Juan
*Spain c. 1460–1521 Cuba*
**North America: discovered Florida.** The legend that Ponce de León was seeking a magical "fountain of youth" when he found Florida seems to be based on fact. He had obtained royal permission to "discover and settle Bimini," and there is

a spring on one of the Bimini Islands, Bahamas, with a reputation for its life-giving powers. Ignorant of the whereabouts of the island when he sailed from Puerto Rico in 1513, the Spaniard reached the mainland near modern-day St. Augustine. He named his discovery for a recently passed feast day—*Pascua Florida* ("feast of flowers")—Easter. As he sailed down the coast, he came within 40 miles of the Bimini Islands, but he never saw them.

Returning to Puerto Rico the same year by a roundabout route, Ponce de León may have sighted Mexico's Yucatan Peninsula (a route not shown on this map). After exploring it west of the point Juan Díaz de Solís* had reached in 1509, he named it Bimini, thinking he had attained his goal.

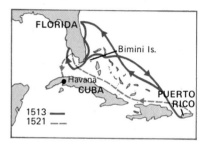

In 1521 Ponce de León again embarked from Puerto Rico, this time with two shiploads of settlers. Entitled governor of Bimini and Florida, he was authorized to establish colonies in both places. He landed his emigrants on an island off the west coast of Florida, from where they planned to invade the mainland. But they were surprised and badly mauled by an Indian war party. The survivors fled to Cuba, where Ponce de León died of a wound received in the fighting.

## PRZHEVALSKY, Nikolai
*Russia 1839–88 Russia*
**Central Asia: explored Mongolia; Sinkiang, China; Tibet.** In 1856 Lieutenant Przhevalsky asked the Russian Army to

transfer him to Siberia because he was interested in exploring in Asia. He was disciplined for his show of independence. Persisting, nevertheless, he eventually won permission to lead an expedition through Mongolia.

The first scientific explorer of central Asia, Przhevalsky devoted his life to its study. His first trip, in 1870–73, took him from Kyakhta, near Ulan Bator, across the Gobi Desert to Peking, through Inner Mongolia, and into eastern Tibet. There he located the headwaters of the Yangtze River of China while fending off attacks of the murderous Tangut tribesmen who inhabited the area. On a second expedition, in 1876–77, he entered Sinkiang, China, from western Siberia and became the first European to view the enormous A-erh-chih, or Astin Tagh, the northern mountain wall of the Tibetan plateau. (It is almost 1,000 miles long and averages over 20,000 feet in height.) In 1879–80 he reentered Tibet. Heading south toward its capital, Lhasa, then a sacred city forbidden to non-Buddhists, Przhevalsky was stopped by Tibetan militia not far from his goal and forced to retreat. Undeterred, he returned to northeastern Tibet in 1884–85 and discovered the sources of China's great Yellow River.

Starting out on another expedition in 1889, Przhevalsky died of typhoid fever while still in Russia. His legacy is an encyclopedic mass of information about an area of the world still relatively unknown. Punished in his youth for his high ambition, he was honored after death for its fulfillment: His government renamed Karakol, the little town in Kirghiz S.S.R., where he died, Przhevalsk in his honor.

## QUIRÓS, Pedro de
*Portugal 1565–1615 Panama*
**Pacific Ocean: discovered Tuamotu Archipelago, New Hebrides.** Chief pilot of Álvaro de Mendaña de Neyra's* ill-fated expedition to the Santa Cruz Islands in 1595, Quirós returned to Spain convinced of the existence of a rumored southern continent, which he believed was not far from the Marquesas, Solomon, and Santa Cruz Islands that Mendaña had sighted. Since Quirós was a naturalized Spaniard, it was to the Spanish crown that he turned for money to enable him to discover the continent.

Successful in getting generous backing, Quirós sailed from Callao (Lima's harbor), Peru, in 1605 with three vessels. Carried by the trade winds, he cruised through the Tuamotu Archipelago of the central Pacific, becoming the first European to sight many of its low-lying atolls. In 1606 he discovered the New Hebrides, near Australia. Mistakenly, he thought these mountainous islands were head-

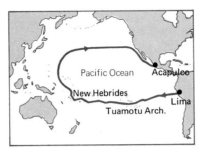

lands of the continent he was seeking. But he had no chance to find out. Leaving the New Hebrides, the ships became separated in a storm, and Quirós proceeded to the designated rendezvous at Santa Cruz. Unable to locate the island, he returned to Acapulco, Mexico. One of his captains, Luis Vaez de Torres,* led his other ships on westward and discovered Torres Strait, north of Australia.

Fearing exploitation of the South Pacific by other nations, Spanish authorities kept Quirós' logbooks secret and eventually forgot all about them. Louis Bougainville* revisited the New Hebrides in 1768.

## RADISSON, Pierre Esprit
*France 1636–c.1710 England*
**North America: explored Midwest, far north.** Kidnaped by marauding Mohawks in 1652 while hunting near his

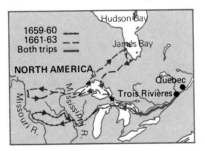

home in Trois Rivières, Quebec, Radisson was adopted by an Indian couple and learned wilderness lore while living with their tribe. After his escape some years later, he returned to the wilderness as a trapper and guide.

Defying the governor of New France, who illegally demanded half of Radisson's profits as the price of a trapping permit, Radisson made his first exploring trip with his brother-in-law, Groseilliers, in 1659–60 to seek new sources of fur, Canada's main export at that time.

From Trois Rivières they went up the St. Lawrence River and crossed the Great Lakes to Wisconsin, where they discovered the upper Mississippi and followed it toward its source in Minnesota. Continuing westward, they were the first Europeans to enter the Dakotas and northern Nebraska. Their tactful dealings with the Indians opened the area to their compatriots, who were soon trapping and trading throughout it.

On Radisson and his partner's return in 1660, the governor confiscated their cargo of 100,000 pelts (which was worth about $1 million in today's money), because the trappers had not obtained a license. Retaliating, Radisson defected to England, where he provided information on which the founders acted in establishing the Hudson's Bay Company. That enterprise soon took over the valuable bay area and all the lands draining into it.

Radisson later claimed that he set out again in 1661 and pioneered an overland route to Hudson Bay in the next two years. Some scholars doubt the validity of this claim.

## RICHTHOFEN, Ferdinand von
*Prussia 1833–1905 Germany*
**China: compiled country's first modern atlas.** While Richthofen was making his survey of China, the country's inhabitants were seething with hatred of Europeans. They had recently been defeated in war by France, Great Britain, and Russia, and troops led by a British general had just put down the popular Taiping uprising, inflicting great loss of life. Yet Richthofen, a German scientist, tra-

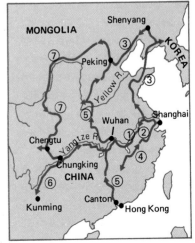

versed the length and breadth of the country for five years without incident, gathering material for the first modern atlas of China. Patient, courteous, and immensely learned, he charmed and impressed Chinese officials, who readily gave him the help and protection he needed.

Aided financially by the Bank of California, with the agreement that he would report his findings to the Chamber of Commerce in Shanghai, Richthofen made seven trips (see map) through the war-torn land from 1868 to 1872, surveying, making geological studies, and collecting economic data. His most important trip, in 1870 (marked 5 on map), took him through provinces where the Taiping forces had been strongest and the anti-foreign feeling most intense. Undismayed, he prospected the route for the railroad that was later built linking Canton and Hankow (one of the tri-cities of the Wuhan area). Another journey took him through the Shantung Peninsula (3); his report led to its virtual annexation by Germany in 1897.

Returning to Germany, Richthofen spent seven years preparing his great atlas of China, which established him as one of Europe's foremost geographers.

## ROGGEVEEN, Jacob
*Netherlands 1659–1729 Netherlands*
**Pacific Ocean: discovered Easter Island.** Honorably retired after serving as a lawyer in Dutch-ruled Indonesia (Java),

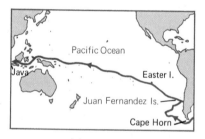

Roggeveen was requested, at the age of 62, to lead a Pacific expedition for the Dutch West India Company. The voyage plan—to search for a southern continent supposed to lie between South America and Australia—was one that his father had originated many years earlier.

Roggeveen left the Netherlands with three ships in 1721 and reached the Pacific by rounding Cape Horn. After calling at Más a Tierra—Robinson Crusoe's island in the Juan Fernández group—he turned west and on Easter Sunday 1722 discovered an island.

Easter Island, as Roggeveen named it, is more than 1,000 miles from the nearest land. Yet it is dotted with enigmatic stone statues, which were erected by Polyne-

sians. How they reached this remote island in their frail canoes remains a mystery. Roggeveen paid the island scant attention, for it was not the continent that he was looking for. He continued his search for several months, only giving up and putting in at Batavia (modern Jakarta) in Java, after one of his ships was wrecked and two-thirds of his crew had died of scurvy. Lonely Easter Island lapsed into obscurity until it was rediscovered by a Spanish naval captain, Don Felipe González, in 1770.

## ROHLFS, Friedrich Gerhard
*Germany 1831–96 Germany*
**Africa: explored Sahara.** A high school dropout at 18 and soldier of fortune until he was 30, Rohlfs was noted more as an

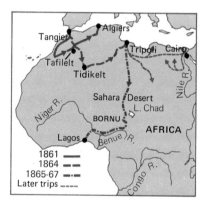

adventurer than a scientific explorer. On his discharge from the French Foreign Legion in 1861, Rohlfs disguised himself as an Arab, intending to explore west Africa. He went first to Tafilelt, Morocco, previously seen only by René Auguste Caillé,* whose account was too general to be of use to him. Unwisely showing his money to his guide, Rohlfs was robbed and maimed one night as he left the oasis alone. Undaunted, he penetrated to Tidikelt in the Tuat oases of southern Algeria in 1864 and was the first European to see them. However, he was suspected of impersonation and had to flee to Tripoli.

In 1865–67 Rohlfs crossed the Sahara from Tripoli, Libya, to explore the Ouadai oases of Chad. Barred from Ouadai by the sultan, Rohlfs went on to Lagos, Nigeria, becoming the first European to cross Africa from the Mediterranean to the Gulf of Guinea. Later, during the 1870's, Rohlfs led two large German expeditions to Egypt and Libya.

Rohlfs' accomplishments were impressive. He provided the first good accounts of Tafilelt and Tidikelt, two ancient Saharan trade centers, and was the

first to fix the latter's position. Of Rohlfs' transafrican journey, August Petermann, the most noted geographer of his time, declared that the results "far exceeded the accomplishments of his predecessors, [Heinrich] Barth* . . . not excluded."

## ROSS, James Clark
*England 1800–62 England*
**Antarctica: discovered Ross Sea.** An able shipmaster experienced in five polar expeditions before he was 30, Ross was without doubt the best qualified man of his time to command the Antarctic expedition that the British Admiralty dispatched in 1839 to investigate the south magnetic pole.

Provided with two specially reinforced wooden sailing ships, the *Erebus* and *Terror*, Ross had instructions to reach, if possible, the Antarctic mainland south of Australia. Using his ships as battering rams, he repeatedly charged the ice barrier head-on, until after five days he broke through to Ross Sea. He then penetrated to 78° S, a latitude not previously reached in that area or reached again for 60 years. After spending almost five

years in Antarctic waters, Ross was knighted on his return in 1843.

When John Franklin* disappeared in the Arctic, Ross led the first unsuccessful search for him in 1848–49. By a twist of fate, the ships in which the Franklin expedition had sailed to the north were Ross' former ships, *Erebus* and *Terror*.

## SAAVEDRA, Álvaro de
*Spain 15th century–1529 At sea*
**Pacific Ocean: explored islands.** The first explorer to sail to the Orient from America, Saavedra was sent by his kinsman Hernando Cortés,* at the king's command, to assist the survivors of an earlier expedition to the Philippines. (At that time Portugal barred the way through

the Indian Ocean by force, so Saavedra sought a route across the Pacific.)

Saavedra made a rapid crossing from Mexico to the Philippines in 1527, sailing with the trade winds, which blow perpetually toward Asia in tropical latitudes. Turning south to Tidore, Indonesia, he met other Spaniards, including Andrés de Urdaneta,* who had come from Spain via the Strait of Magellan and the Pacific. They told him that it was impossible to sail back to America against the trade winds.

Seeking favorable winds for the trip back to America, Saavedra made two northern cruises. He discovered the Marshall Islands in 1529 during the second, just before becoming fatally ill. After his death his crew returned to Tidore, having turned back several hundred miles short of the Temperate Zone's west winds, which blow toward America.

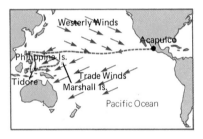

Despite the relative unimportance of Saavedra's discoveries, his work was by no means in vain. He had shown how easy it was to sail the trade winds from Mexico to the Far East. Furthermore, his search for a homeward route inspired Urdaneta's later success in finding the westerly winds farther north.

## SCHOMBURGK, Robert Hermann
*Germany 1804–65 Germany; naturalized British subject*

**South America: surveyed Guyana.** A humanitarian response began Schomburgk's career as an explorer. On a trip in 1831 to the British Virgin island of Anegada, he saw a slave ship strike an uncharted rock and sink, drowning 135 Africans. Horrified by the tragedy, Schomburgk made a survey of the nearby waters on his own initiative. The British government paid him nothing for his charts but was obviously impressed by their excellence, for when it needed a survey of British Guiana, now Guyana, Schomburgk was hired for the job.

The first scientifically trained man to enter Guyana's interior, Schomburgk ranks as its first explorer. He spent almost five years there in the wild and

mountainous interior, traveling mostly through country that had been visited only by slave raiders. Schomburgk claimed as much territory as possible for Great Britain. Besides mapping the intricate channels of the Essequibo River and its tributaries, he traced its watershed, which Britain claimed formed the country's southern and western borders. Asserting, on the contrary, that the river itself was the frontier, the Brazilian and

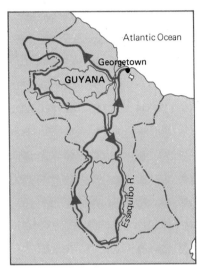

Venezuelan governments promptly tore up boundary posts that Schomburgk had installed. Yet most of the borderlines that Schomburgk established still exist.

## SCHWEINFURTH, Georg August
*Latvia 1836–1925 Germany*

**Africa: explored Sudan, Congo.** The first European to cross the watershed between the Nile and Congo (Zaire) River

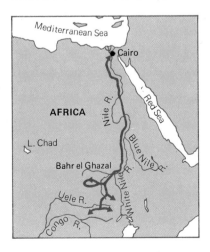

basins, Schweinfurth was also the first to confirm the existence of African pygmies

mentioned by the Greek historian Herodotus in the fifth century B.C.

From 1869 to 1871 Schweinfurth explored central Africa, backed by a German scientific foundation. He first explored the Bahr el Ghazal region of southwestern Sudan, about which very little was then known. From there, he crossed the highlands to the south, where he discovered the Uele River. This he considered a Niger tributary, not realizing that it forms part of the Congo River system, the enormous extent of which was as yet unknown. On the banks of the Congo he observed the primitive Akka forest pygmies, whose average height he estimated to be under five feet.

One of Schweinfurth's chief interests was to trace the migrations of peoples by the study of human bones found in various places. Accordingly, he let it be known that he was looking for human skulls for his research. The Mangbettu, a tribe of average-sized people living nearby, promptly sent him 200—some still warm from the cook-pot. Unwittingly, he had ventured among Africa's most inveterate cannibals.

Having lost his instruments in a fire as he was returning to Khartoum in 1871, Schweinfurth could measure his route only by counting his steps. (The remaining distance was 1.25 million paces.)

Schweinfurth founded the Egyptian Geographical Society in 1875 and resided in Cairo until his retirement in 1888.

## SHACKLETON, Ernest
*Ireland 1874–1922 At sea*

**Antarctica: tried to reach South Pole.** Shackleton's initial Antarctic experience on Robert Scott's* 1901–04 expedition ended when he collapsed from scurvy and had to be sent home. Undeterred, he raised money for his own South Pole expedition, which he launched in 1908.

A bold experimentalist, Shackleton took an automobile with him—the first in Antarctica—and substituted Manchurian ponies for sled dogs. His early model car was of little use, but the ponies did well and only the accidental loss of one of them robbed him of the glory of being first to reach the South Pole.

Shackleton made his polar dash from the Ross Sea coast with four ponies that hauled sledloads of food. His strategy was to kill a pony periodically, using part of the carcass to feed his party and storing the rest to serve as food on the way back. But so closely had he calculated that when the last animal fell with its sled down a deep crevasse 97 miles from his

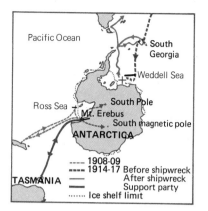

goal, Shackleton realized that he would have to turn back. Yet he had accomplished much. No other explorer had so greatly outdistanced the one before him toward either pole. In addition, parties directed by him had climbed the 13,370-foot volcanic Mount Erebus and had located the south magnetic pole. For those achievements, Shackleton was knighted in 1909.

By 1914, when Shackleton's next expedition was ready, his objective was no longer simply to reach the South Pole, since Roald Amundsen and Scott had already been there. Instead, Shackleton planned to cross Antarctica from Weddell Sea to Ross Sea by way of the pole. A support party was sent ahead, but just before Shackleton himself sailed with the main group, the First World War broke out. The First Lord of the British Admiralty—Winston Churchill—had to personally order Shackleton not to cancel the whole project in favor of combat duty.

Shackleton's second voyage proved disastrous. Arriving in Weddell Sea, his ship was crushed by ice and sank with most of his supplies. Only by feats of almost unbelievable bravery and endurance, including an 800-mile winter journey over the Antarctic Ocean in a 22-foot open rowboat, was Shackleton able to get his men to safety.

On another expedition to Antarctica in 1921–22, Shackleton died of a heart attack off the island of South Georgia, where he is buried.

## SOLÍS, Juan Díaz de
*Spain c. 1470–1516 Uruguay*
**Americas: explored Yucatan coast, discovered Río de la Plata.** Trained as a pilot by the Portuguese East Indies Department, Solís was welcomed in Spain because it needed experienced ocean navigators. Such was his reputation that

when the government gave Solís and the Spaniard Vicente Yáñez Pinzón* joint command of an expedition in 1508, Solís was put in charge of its marine operations, although Pinzón was also renowned as a pilot. His position cost him dearly: When the expedition (sent to find a strait through Central America to the Pacific) ended in failure, Solís was jailed upon his return. But the voyage was not without results, for the two men had explored the coast north to the tip of Yucatan, 400 miles farther than Christopher Columbus* had sailed in 1503. Having been released from prison, Solís became chief pilot of Spain when Amerigo Vespucci* died in 1512.

Solís made another search for a strait to the Pacific in 1515. This time he followed Pinzón's 1500 route to the northeast point of Brazil. Coasting far to the south, he discovered the vast estuary of the Río de la Plata, which he ascertained to be freshwater and therefore not a strait. Unwisely landing to trade with some Indians on the north shore, he was killed and eaten in sight of his men. But his records, brought back to Spain, proved useful to Ferdinand Magellan* on his voyage to the Pacific.

## SPEKE, John Hanning
*England 1827–64 England*
**Africa: discovered White Nile source.** Until his death Speke asserted correctly that Lake Victoria is the principal source of the White Nile. His former friend Richard Burton* retorted, equally correct, that Speke did not have sufficient evidence to prove his theory.

Exploring east Africa with Burton from 1854 to 1859, Speke, while briefly separated from Burton, discovered Lake Victoria. Without exploring it or even locating its outlet, he pronounced it to be

the main source of the Nile. Burton challenged his statement.

To resolve the dispute the Royal Geographical Society commissioned Speke to reexplore Lake Victoria in 1860. After many delays, Speke reached the lake,

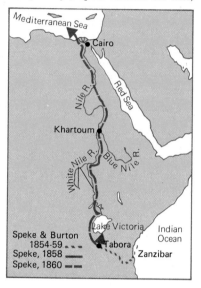

found its outlet, and followed the stream 50 miles north. Threatened by hostile Africans, he struck out across country until he reached the Nile again in Sudan.

Back in England, Speke repeated his claim of having discovered the source of the Nile. Although the Geographical Society awarded him its founder's medal, Burton and other geographers soon attacked him, pointing out that he could not prove the waters of the stream he abandoned near Lake Victoria were the same as the river he had reached in Sudan. The dispute grew acrimonious, and Burton and Speke became bitter enemies. On the day the two men were to meet in public debate, Speke was killed in a hunting accident.

## STEIN, Mark Aurel
*Hungary 1862–1943 Afghanistan*
**Central Asia: explored in Sinkiang; Tibet; and western Kansu, China.** An outstanding explorer, archeologist, and

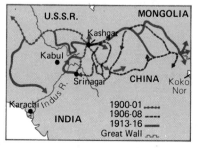

geographer, Stein has left us a unique record of central Asia. A naturalized British subject, he spent many years as a teacher in India before obtaining government sponsorship for a series of expeditions in 1900–01, 1906–08, 1913–16, and again in 1930.

Combining all his skills, Stein traced the way of the ancient and long-disused Silk Route between China and the West, excavating many sites. He also located the forgotten, sand-buried, westernmost reach of the Great Wall of China, an earthen barrier 200 miles long in western Kansu, and discovered the Caves of the Thousand Buddhas, which held priceless ancient Buddhist manuscripts.

In the mountainous Pamirs in southwest Sinkiang and in the northeast corner of Tibet, Stein made meticulous surveys, filling in gaps left by previous explorers, such as Francis Younghusband* and Sven Hedin,* as well as contributing to our knowledge of the geology and wildlife of these regions.

At the age of 80, Stein obtained permission to explore the remote and then almost unknown land of Afghanistan. Traveling to Kabul, he fell ill and died at the U.S. legation. He is buried in the Kabul Foreigners' Cemetery.

## STUART, John McDouall
*Scotland 1815–66 England*

**Australia: pioneered the major modern south-north transcontinental route.** In 1859 the South Australia legislature offered a reward of £2,000 sterling to the first person to cross interior Australia from south to north. Stuart was among those who accepted the challenge.

Stuart had been with Charles Sturt* on his attempt to penetrate the geographical center of Australia 15 years earlier, and he decided to run his transcontinental route through the point they had sought unsuccessfully together. Like Sturt, he started from Adelaide. Profiting from his previous experience, Stuart avoided the worst of the terrain they had earlier encountered, and he reached the center on his first trip, in 1860. He named the peak nearest to it Central Mount Stuart. (It has since been renamed Central Mount Stuart.) Upon reaching desert country, Stuart's party was increasingly hampered by lack of water, failing supplies, and then scurvy. A savage onslaught by aborigines caused Stuart to turn back at Attack Creek.

Returning over the same route the following year, Stuart pressed on to New-

castle Waters before being thwarted again by shortages, sickness, and native hostility. Making a third heroic effort, in 1861–62, he finally reached the Indian Ocean shore near modern-day Darwin.

Although Stuart won the reward, he was not the first to cross the continent. Coming back to Adelaide, sick and exhausted, he was just in time to see the funeral procession of Robert Burke* and William Wills* on its way to Melbourne. They had made the crossing in 1860–61 but had died on the trip, although this had not been known when Stuart set out.

To Stuart's everlasting credit goes the selection of his route for the first transcontinental telegraph line. Completed in 1872, it connected southeastern Australia to the undersea cables already laid from Darwin to Asia and Europe. A major modern road-and-rail link now also follows the track he pioneered.

## STUART, Robert
*Scotland 1785–1848 U.S.A.*

**North America: discovered eastern part of Oregon Trail.** Like Wilson Price Hunt,* who pioneered the western half of the Oregon Trail in 1811–12, Stuart was a partner in John Jacob Astor's Pacific Fur Company. And, like Hunt, he shared an interest in finding an overland route

between its western headquarters at Astoria, Oregon, and the center of the U.S. fur trade at St. Louis, Missouri.

In charge of a group heading east from

Astoria in 1812, Stuart backtracked Hunt up the Columbia River, crossed southeast to the Snake, and followed that stream into eastern Idaho. There he followed Hunt's route through the Teton Mountains into northwestern Wyoming. Following an Indian guide's advice, Stuart left Hunt's route and headed southeast along the flank of the Wind River Mountains and discovered South Pass, one of the most remarkable features of the U.S. Continental Divide. (The slope of both sides of this 20-mile-wide gap is so gradual that, though it is 7,743 feet in altitude, it is difficult to distinguish its crest, making it an ideal wagon road.) From South Pass, Stuart followed the Platte and Missouri Rivers by a safe and easy route, finally reaching St. Louis in 1813. Thus Stuart discovered the portion of the Oregon Trail between St. Louis and eastern Idaho.

## STURT, Charles
*India 1795–1869 England*

**Australia: explored southeast.** When British colonists first settled around present-day Sydney in the late 1700's,

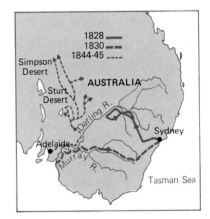

they noticed that many of the rivers rising near the southeastern coast flow inland. This led them to believe that they emptied into an inland sea—an "Australian Mediterranean." On Sturt's first two exploring trips he saw that these waters are drained by the Darling River, which he discovered in 1828. In 1830 he located the confluence of the Darling and the Murray, which he followed to its outlet in the Indian Ocean near modern Adelaide.

Knowing of several more northern rivers that also flow toward the west, Sturt made another search for an inland sea in 1844–45. This time he tried to reach the geographical center of Australia, an attempt that almost cost him his life. From

Adelaide he went up the Murray and then the Darling River for a short distance and turned northwest to the Grey Range. There he set up permanent camp. Making excursions farther north and northwest, he discovered the Sturt and Simpson (Arunta) Deserts, but thirst and exhaustion repeatedly turned him back from his goal. Scurvy attacked the company; one died, and by the time the party returned to Adelaide, Sturt's health was broken and he was nearly blind. But his efforts had prepared the way for later, more successful explorers.

### TASMAN, Abel Janszoon
*Netherlands c. 1603–c. 1659 Indonesia*
**Southwest Pacific: explored Tasmania, New Zealand, island groups.** Tasman has been called "the greatest of the Dutch navigators." Since Tasman spent most of his life in Batavia (now Jakarta,

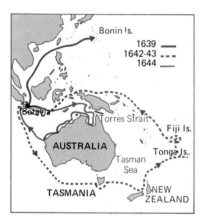

Indonesia), the Dutch East India Company sent him on three voyages between 1639 and 1644 to find sources of profit in nearby waters. On his first trip he searched for "islands of gold and silver" east of Japan. His second trip, in 1642–43, was the most productive: He proved Australia was not joined to a reputed Antarctic continent by sailing almost completely around it, and he discovered Tasmania, New Zealand, and the Tonga and Fiji Islands. On his last trip, he charted the northwest Australian coast.

In retrospect, much of Tasman's work seems marred by haste. He did not sail around Tasmania but annexed it for the Netherlands thinking it part of mainland Australia. Cruising almost the whole length of New Zealand, he did not investigate it but reported it as the western coast of a southern continent. Sighting Torres Strait but never entering it, he charted it as a bay, so that until Capt.

James Cook* traversed this waterway in 1770, New Guinea and Australia were believed to be joined.

The reason for these lapses is not difficult to understand: Tasman and his company were traders and privateers, and Tasman was looking for sources of silks and spices. The coasts he prospected plainly yielded no riches of these kinds.

Making a fortune in trade in later years, Tasman died one of the richest men in Batavia. Tasmania, among other geographical features, is named for him.

### THOMPSON, David
*England 1770–1857 Canada*
**North America: explored Northwest.** A surveyor for the North West Company in the early 1800's had to combine his mapmaking with trading. In Thompson's long service with that company, he proved exceptionally able at both jobs. Traveling more than 50,000 miles, mostly through unexplored country, he surveyed a large area of the Northwest.

From 1797 to 1805 Thompson crisscrossed the wilderness between Lake Superior and the Rocky Mountains, from the Missouri River to Hudson Bay, winning much praise for both the accurate maps and the ample revenues that he produced. He was appointed in 1806 to explore the area west of the Rockies. On his first trip out from Rocky Mountain House in 1807, he reached the upper Columbia River and, going upstream, discovered its source. He returned to Rocky Mountain House in 1809 from a second trip, which had taken him into Idaho and Montana. In 1811 he set out for the Columbia again, determined to reach its mouth before Wilson Price Hunt* of the

rival Pacific Fur Company. Arriving at the river's northern bend, he traced it upstream to the point where he had

reached it before and then canoed down its course to the Pacific—only to find Hunt already there. His trip was a successful one, nevertheless: He finished mapping the Columbia and had collected a small fortune in furs.

### THOMSON, Joseph
*Scotland 1858–95 England*
**Africa: explored eastern parts.** On an 1878–80 expedition deep in unexplored Tanganyika (part of modern Tanzania), Thomson suddenly found himself in charge of his caravan when the expedition's leader died in 1879. Despite his youth (he was 21) and almost total inexperience (he had never been to Africa before), Thomson led the group for another year. Traveling 3,000 miles through country infested with Arab slavers and embattled Africans without losing a man or firing a shot in anger, he traced the Lukuga outlet of Lake Tanganyika and discovered Lake Rukwa.

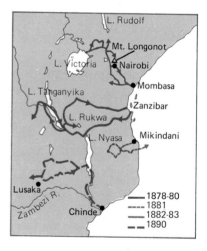

After a second venture into the same area, in 1881, to map a coal deposit, Thomson turned his attention to Kenya. In 1882–83 he crossed the lands of the Masai, who were notorious for their hostility toward strangers. When they captured him and subjected him to terrible indignities, Thomson kept his temper and avoided bloodshed. His discoveries on that trip include Mount Longonot and Lake Baringo, near modern-day Nairobi. On the border of Mozambique in 1890, Thomson was fired on by Portuguese fearful of British encroachment in the area, but got his men away without loss or return fire.

Much of the modern map of east Africa can be attributed to Thomson's efforts. And at a time when European intrusions into Africa were generally marked by conflict, Thomson's achievements in diplomacy were as remarkable as his contributions to geography. Wherever he had been, "explorers and administrators who followed him discovered that Thomson's example made their own tasks easier to accomplish."

### TORRES, Luis Vaez de
*Spain 17th century*
**Pacific Ocean: discovered Torres Strait.**
A storm raised Torres to the rank of explorer. A subordinate of Pedro de Quirós,* Torres sailed with him from Callao (Lima's harbor), Peru, in 1605 in search of a southern continent in the South Pacific. He was captain of one of the expedition's three ships. By the time the vessels reached the New Hebrides, the crew was sick with scurvy and quarrelsome from skirmishes with islanders. Quirós ordered the expedition to return to America; but the ships were separated in a storm, and Torres managed to keep control of his crew and sail on.

Sighting the large island of New Guinea, the Spaniard coasted along its southern shore and passed through the strait between New Guinea and Australia that now bears his name. Reaching its western outlet, he sailed north to Manila, where he arrived in desperate condition, his ship rotted and waterlogged.

Ironically, Torres never saw the continent he and Quirós had hoped to discover, since he had kept too far to the north of Australia while passing through the strait. His report was suppressed by the Spanish government to avoid en-

couraging English and Dutch penetration of the area. In 1764 Torres' account came to light, and his name was later given to his discovery. Capt. James Cook* rediscovered the strait in 1774.

### ULLOA, Francisco de
*Spain 15th-16th centuries Unknown*
**Mexico: explored Baja California.** After an expedition that Hernando Cortés* had led to colonize the Baja California peninsula ended in failure and near-

starvation, Cortés sent a trusted officer, Ulloa, to search the region for a better site for a settlement.

In the summer of 1539 Ulloa sailed from Acapulco into the Gulf of California. Keeping chiefly to its eastern shore, he penetrated to the head of the gulf and discovered the mouth of the Colorado River. Cruising down the gulf's western side in the autumn, he examined the peninsula's coast and its offshore islands. Although few of the Indians there had seen Europeans before, they were unfriendly; while making a landing, Ulloa was attacked and gravely wounded. He reported the region as nearly barren and unfit for Spanish settlement. After rounding the tip of the peninsula, he followed its outer coast about 700 miles. In April 1540 he sent a ship back to Acapulco with his records. Then, according to the historian Prescott, "the bold navi-

gator held on his course to the north, and was never more heard of." (Other historians indicate he *returned* to Spain.)

Ulloa's voyage marked the first successful exploration off the North American west coast. He showed that Baja California is a peninsula, not an island.

### URDANETA, Andrés de
*Spain 1508–68 Mexico*
**Pacific Ocean: discovered key to its sail navigation.** As Urdaneta learned by bitter experience, early 16th-century mariners knew how to cross the Pacific Ocean in one direction only. In 1525 he accompanied Spanish traders to Indonesia via the Strait of Magellan. Carried westward across the Pacific by the trade winds blowing from America to Asia in tropical latitudes, they found they could not return the same way. The trades never change, and for the Spaniards to tack their clumsy vessels against them for so vast a distance would have taken more than six months, risking the loss of all hands

from scurvy. The only other known route homeward was across the Indian Ocean and around Africa, but the Portuguese barred that way, claiming it their monopoly. Therefore, the Urdaneta expedition was marooned on Tidore, in modern-day Indonesia, and Urdaneta didn't return to Spain until 1536.

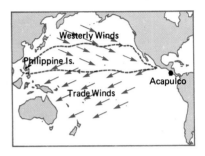

In 1565 Urdaneta, by then a monk, navigated a Spanish fleet from Acapulco, Mexico, to Cebu, in what is now the Philippine Republic. This time he showed genius. Returning, he set out not east but *north*, to the latitudes of Japan, where he discovered the westerly winds of the Temperate Zone, which are about as regular as the trades but blow in the opposite direction. After a quick crossing, he reached California near Cape Mendocino and coasted southeast to Acapulco.

Thus Urdaneta had discovered the key to Pacific sailing: the combination of the northeast trades of the tropics and the westerlies farther north. Until the days of steam, all Pacific navigation followed the "Passage of Urdaneta."

### VANCOUVER, George
*England 1757–98 England*
**North America: explored northwest coast.** Vancouver was determined to confirm the disputed claim of his former commander, James Cook,* who had said that there was no Northwest Passage south of the Arctic. Knowing that the North American northwest coast was

still largely unexplored, Vancouver accepted command of a British expedition there in 1791. To prove his point, he surveyed the area with such precision that some of his charts are still in use.

At first, his expedition was dogged by bad luck. Because of inclement weather, he missed the mouth of the Columbia River when he sailed past it in 1792. Arriving at Juan de Fuca Strait, he was chagrined to learn that others had preceded him through that entrance to Puget Sound. Nevertheless, Vancouver entered the sound and minutely surveyed the vast watery network of modern-day northwest Washington State. While circumnavigating Vancouver Island, he mistook the mouth of the Fraser River for just one more inlet of Canada's intricate western shoreline.

Wintering each year in Hawaii, Vancouver spent two more seasons examining every mile of the Pacific northwest coastline north to the Aleutian Islands. In August 1794 he set sail for England, having effectively established that the west coast of the Americas, from the Bering Strait to the Strait of Magellan, forms a continuous barrier between the Atlantic and Pacific Oceans.

### VERRAZANO, Giovanni da
*Italy c. 1485–c. 1528 West Indies*
### GOMEZ, Estevan
*Portugal c. 1483–1528 South America*
### AYLLÓN, Lucas Vásquez de
*Spain c. 1475–1526 North America*
**North America: explored east coast.**
Within a span of four years the reports of these three explorers virtually ended Spain's interest in America north of Mexico, leaving most of the area free for development by Britain and France.

Verrazano, the first of the three to explore, led a transatlantic expedition for France in 1523. His mission was to explore the area north of Florida, a region then so little known that geographers disputed whether it was open ocean, a new continent, or an extension of Asia.

From present-day North Carolina, Verrazano cruised northward to Canada. Aware when he first sighted land that he had not sailed far enough to reach Asia, he overestimated his distance nevertheless. Hence, when he saw Pamlico Sound, near Cape Hatteras, separated from the Atlantic only by narrow sandspits, he thought it was the Pacific. Unaccountably, he did not enter it, and the sound was labeled "Sea of Verrazano" on maps for a century. Farther north he

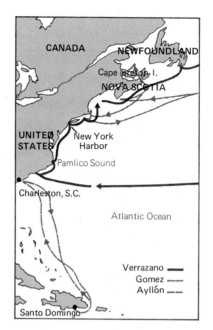

discovered New York Harbor, where a great bridge now bears his name. Still following the coast, he reached Newfoundland in 1524 and returned to France to report that he had found no passage to Asia through North America and had discovered no gold.

Later in 1524, the Spanish king, fearful of losing ground to France, dispatched Gomez to explore the same coastline. A Portuguese immigrant who had already discredited himself by deserting Ferdinand Magellan* during his great voyage, Gomez did nothing on this trip to improve his reputation. His only contribution to geography was to discover the Strait of Canso, which separates Cape Breton Island from Nova Scotia. He dismissed the Gulf of St. Lawrence, which he entered in midwinter, as unnavigable because of the ice he encountered there. Coasting south as far as Rhode Island, he landed on the way and captured some Indians to sell as slaves. When he returned to Spain in 1525, he was censured and the Indians were released.

Finally, Ayllón, Justice of the Supreme Court of Santo Domingo, tried to colonize the North American coast. In 1526 he led some 600 Spaniards to what is now South Carolina, where he founded a settlement. But Indian attacks, a hard winter, and disease brought his enterprise to disaster. Only 150 of his followers survived to flee back to Santo Domingo.

Studying the results of these efforts, the Spanish authorities concluded that there was no northern strait to the Pacific

Ocean and that most of North America was a wasteland not worth exploiting. The way was free for their rivals.

Ironically, all three explorers ended their lives in misfortune. Ayllón died of malaria in South Carolina. Gomez was killed by Indians in Paraguay while on an expedition to Argentina in search of gold and silver. On a later voyage to the Antilles, Verrazano was killed and eaten by cannibals on Guadeloupe.

### VESPUCCI, Amerigo
*Italy 1454–1512 Spain*
**Western Hemisphere: explored South American coast.** Although the American continents are named for Amerigo Vespucci, he was not their discoverer. A businessman representing an Italian company in Spain in the 1490's, Vespucci became interested in the tales of Christopher Columbus'* voyages and, eventually, visited the New World himself.

Considerable mystery surrounds Vespucci's first voyage, partly due to the loss of his records. A letter attributed to him, dated 1504 and addressed to a colleague in Florence, Italy, tells of a transatlantic voyage from Spain with a fleet of four ships in 1497. Vespucci—if he was the writer—claimed that he discovered a

continent, having sighted land at 16° N, 75° W of the Canary Islands. This would have put him in the Pacific Ocean west of Mexico. Assuming that he got his longitude wrong (navigators often did in those days), he might have been in the Caribbean Sea off Honduras. Then, he stated, he cruised 3,500 miles northwestward—a course that would have taken him through the heart of North America. Thus scholars today doubt Vespucci's claims.

*Mapping the World*

It is now generally agreed that Vespucci's first trip was made in 1499, not 1497, and that he sailed as a "gentleman volunteer" under a reckless freebooter named Alonzo de Ojeda, whose only purpose was to rob the South American Indians of gold and pearls. Ojeda reached the coast of present-day French Guiana with his little fleet and then sailed northwest, stopping frequently to ransack the coastlands for treasure. He entered the Orinoco River (already reported by Columbus), and later discovered Lake Maracaibo, which he named Venezuela—"Little Venice"—because the Indians there lived in houses built on pilings over the water. After sharing many adventures, Vespucci left Santo Domingo with Ojeda and returned to Spain.

In 1500 Vespucci moved to Portugal, and in the following year he accompanied an official expedition under Capt. Gonzalo Coelho sent to investigate the Brazilian coast, where Pedro Álvares Cabral* had just landed. Making a landfall near Cape São Roque—the northeastern tip of Brazil—Coelho's flotilla of three ships sailed south to what is now the harbor of Rio de Janeiro. From there they went on down the coast, but we do not know how far. Vespucci seems to have asserted that they reached 72°30′ S, which is within the Antarctic continent. Another interpretation of his reports suggests that they went nearly to the Strait of Magellan. But the lands that Vespucci described were tropical, and he did not mention the Río de la Plata, although its fresh, muddy water can be seen 80 miles out at sea. The expedition got back to Portugal in early 1502.

Sailing as a captain of one of six Portuguese ships, again under Coelho in 1503, Vespucci once more skirted the coast of Brazil, traveling from Salvador south to Cape Frio, near present-day Rio de Janeiro, and returning to Lisbon in 1504.

Vespucci's "voyages of discovery" were really other men's achievements. Yet his published accounts of them were noteworthy for calling attention to the size and importance of South America. Perhaps Vespucci's best claim to fame is that he was the first to call South America "a new world" (although he probably thought it was attached to Asia). The first man to call the New World "America" was Martin Waldseemuller, a German geographer and cartographer at St.-Dié, France, in his 1507 *Introduction To Universal Geography*.

Making his permanent home in Spain

after 1505, Vespucci was appointed chief pilot of that country in 1508 and held the post until his death four years later.

## VIZCAÍNO, Sebastián
*Spain c. 1550–c. 1629 Mexico*
**North America: explored west coast.** After an English privateer had looted and burned the galleon carrying Vizcaíno from Manila to Acapulco in 1587, the Spaniard found himself a castaway in uninhabited Baja California. Organizing the other survivors, Vizcaíno salvaged the galleon's hulk and managed to reach Acapulco in it. He later undertook to explore California, partly as a haven for Spain's Pacific galleon traffic.

Vizcaíno sailed from Acapulco in May 1602 with three vessels. By November he had reached San Diego Bay, which he named for his flagship. (He was unaware that it had been entered in 1542 by João Cabrillo, a Portuguese navigator in Spanish employ, whose report had been misplaced in the government's archives.)

A month later Vizcaíno discovered Monterey Bay. Encountering bad weather in that latitude just as Francis Drake* had, he and his partners were separated and the ships were driven north of the present-day California-Oregon border before their masters could regain control of them. The battered vessels were barely able to get back to Mexico in 1603 with a crew disabled by scurvy. Strange though it may seem, none of the captains saw the Golden Gate, although they sailed past it twice. It was discovered only in the next century.

Despite Vizcaíno's favorable report of the lands he had discovered, he could raise no more funds for colonial exploration, and Spanish settlement of California lapsed for another 150 years.

## WALKER, Joseph Reddeford
*U.S.A. 1798–1876 U.S.A.*
**North America: explored Far West.** A trapper, trader, and noted guide, this

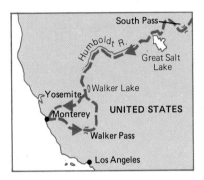

Tennessee-born frontiersman spent his life roving the United States west of the Rocky Mountains. Few men have ever known this area as well as Walker did.

Exploring a new track westward into central California in 1833, Walker discovered Yosemite Valley, whose enormous trees he was the first to describe. On his way back east that year, he found his usual route through the Sierra Nevada blocked by early snow. Looking for another trail, he discovered Walker Pass, only 5,250 feet high and clear in all seasons. Over this pass, 10 years later, Walker guided one of the first immigrant wagon trains to enter California.

The route he discovered became part of the California Trail. (It branches off the Oregon Trail west of South Pass, Wyoming, and leads southwest from watercourse to watercourse through Utah and Nevada. Then it crosses over the Sierra Nevada through several passes into California's central valley.)

## WALLIS, Samuel
*England 1728–95 England*
**Pacific Ocean: explored Tuamotu Archipelago, discovered Tahiti.** For at least

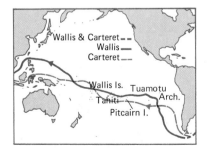

two centuries, until James Cook* and Fabian von Bellingshausen* proved the contrary, geographers believed in the existence of a great, temperate, and fertile continent in the South Pacific. They argued that such a landmass was necessary to counterbalance all the land in the Northern Hemisphere. Beginning with Pedro de Quirós* in 1605, many navigators had reported sighting it, and in 1766 Captain Wallis was sent from England to find it.

Trying to cross the Pacific westward in the latitude of the Strait of Magellan, Wallis was driven north by contrary winds, but not before he had sailed 1,000 miles southwest of any previous European navigator in the southern ocean. Thus he vastly reduced the area in which the supposed continent might be found. Continuing around the world, Wallis discovered several islands of the Tuamotu Archipelago, including Tahiti. He also discovered the Wallis group.

Meanwhile, Wallis' consort, the sloop *Swallow*, had accidentally separated from him near Tierra del Fuego. Crossing the Pacific alone, Philip Carteret, the captain, made independent discoveries, the most important being Pitcairn Island, in the Tuamotus.

### WEDDELL, James
*Belgium 1787–1834 England*
**Antarctica: discovered Weddell Sea.** Born in Belgium of British parents,

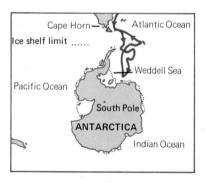

Weddell spent his youth in the Royal Navy, and after the end of the Napoleonic Wars he became master and part owner of a seal hunting ship. Believing that every British merchant captain should explore for his country in the course of his business, Weddell spent large sums on surveying instruments and seldom returned from a voyage without new map data. The seal hunting ground he frequented, a dangerous area of rocky islets and submerged reefs between South America and Antarctica, had not yet been thoroughly charted. Whenever

his men went ashore to club their prey, Weddell made careful surveys, few of which have required correction.

As the seal population dwindled under their attack, the hunters ventured farther south. In 1823 Weddell, bolder than most, made his way through masses of floating ice into unknown waters southeast of Cape Horn. He discovered Weddell Sea and sailed into it to 74°15′ S, surpassing James Cook's* southernmost record by 200 miles. A modest man, he named the area for his sovereign, George IV, but geographers gave his own name to it in 1900.

### YERMAK TIMOFEYEVICH
*Russia ?–1584 Siberia*
**Asia: explored western Siberia.** Yermak, an illiterate soldier of fortune, became the first person to explore Siberia. A wealthy Russian merchant, Maxim Stroganov, had obtained royal permission to seize as much of Siberia from the Mongols as he could and develop its trade in furs and walrus ivory. Stroganov chose Yermak to lead his pioneering expedition of 1581.

The 800 men whom Yermak assembled near Perm were wild Cossacks like himself, mostly fugitives wanted for violent crimes. As it turned out, he needed such men: When he crossed the Ural Mountains into the forests and swamps of western Siberia to winter in Tyumen, he was attacked by barbarous Mongols, descendants of Genghis Khan's horsemen who had conquered Asia 350 years earlier. And the Cossacks needed Yermak: He held out prospects of government pardons if they were successful.

During 1581–82 Yermak fought four pitched battles with the Mongols and finally subdued them. Near modern-day

Tobolsk he occupied Sibir, the stronghold of the Mongols' chieftain.

Before his death in a fresh outbreak of warfare with the Mongols in 1584, Yermak had covered much of western Siberia. A greater achievement was the impetus that his expedition gave to settlement there. Russians, mostly Cossacks, penetrated Siberia from the Urals to the Bering Strait during the next 60 years.

### YOUNGHUSBAND, Francis
*India 1863–1942 England*
**Central Asia: explored Pamir region.** Now usually remembered for leading a British military invasion of Tibet in 1904, Younghusband was well known in his own day as an explorer, whose advice such men as Sven Hedin* and Mark Aurel Stein* valued. While stationed with the British Army in India, Younghusband got his early exploring experience by taking long leaves to make walking tours of the Himalayan foothills—a practice the army encouraged because hikers brought back information about unknown country.

Younghusband's first long expedition followed a visit to China in 1886. Returning to India by way of central Asia, the last part of his journey led him from western Sinkiang, China, over the Pamirs, a region with some of the tallest mountains in the world. Situated at the juncture of modern-day Afghanistan, China, Pakistan, and the U.S.S.R., the area had not yet been explored.

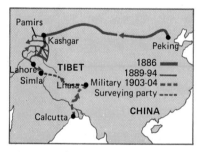

In the Pamirs again in 1889 and in 1892–94, Younghusband made the earliest and perhaps the greatest contribution to our knowledge of that area. In 1904, while leading a British-Indian incursion into Tibet to negotiate trade and frontier issues, he also directed a survey of 40,000 square miles of Tibet's south.

Younghusband made his last contribution to exploration in the 1920's and 1930's when, as president of the Royal Geographical Society, he organized all the early British attempts to climb Mount Everest.

# Index

Page numbers in regular type refer to text and captions; those in **bold** type refer to maps.

# ACKNOWLEDGMENTS

**Introduction:** *The Age of Reconnaissance* by J. H. Parry. Praeger Publishers, Inc., 1969; © 1963 in London, England, by J. H. Parry. **Part I, Ch. 1:** *Beyond the Pillars of Hercules* by Rhys Carpenter. Copyright © 1966. Reprinted by permission of Delacorte Press. Pub. in Great Britain by Universal-Tandem Publishing Co. Ltd. *Lodestone and Evening Star* by Ian Cameron. E. P. Dutton & Co., Inc., 1966; Hodder & Stoughton Ltd., 1965. *The Histories* by Herodotus. Penguin edition, trans. by Aubrey Selincourt, 1954. **Ch. 2:** *Norse Atlantic Saga* by Gwyn Jones. Copyright © 1964 by Oxford Univ. Press. *A History of the Vikings* by Gwyn Jones. Oxford Univ. Press, 1964. **Ch. 3:** *Travels of Marco Polo* reprinted from *The Travels of Marco Polo*, revised from Marsden's Translation and ed. by Manuel Komroff. Copyright 1926 by Boni & Liveright, Inc. Copyright 1930 by Horace Liveright. Copyright renewed 1953 by Manuel Komroff. **Part II, Ch. 4:** *Chronicle of the Discovery and Conquest of Guinea* by Gomes Eannes de Azurara. Ed. by R. Beazley and E. Prestage. Copyright The Hakluyt Society, London, 1896. *Travel and Travelers of the Middle Ages*. Ed. by A. P. Newton. Barnes and Noble, 1968; Rutledge & Kegan Paul Ltd., 1968. *The Voyages of Cadamosto* by G. R. Crone. Copyright The Hakluyt Society, London, Series 2, No. 80, 1937. **Ch. 5:** *Journals and Other Documents on the Life and Voyages of Christopher Columbus*, pub. by The Limited Editions Club and The Heritage Club. Copyright © 1963 by Samuel Eliot Morison. Used by arrangement with The Heritage Press, Avon, Conn., and by permission of Admiral Morison as translator and editor. *Journey of Christopher Columbus*. Select documents illustrating the four voyages of Columbus. Ed. by Cecil Jane. Copyright The Hakluyt Society, London, 1930. Reproduced with the permission of The Hakluyt Society, London. *Life of the Admiral by His Son, Ferdinand*. Trans. and annotated by Benjamin Keen. Rutgers State, 1959; Folio Society, London, 1960. **Ch. 6:** *The Lusiads* by Camoens. Trans. from the Portuguese by Leonard Bacon. Copyright The Hispanic Society, 1950. *A Journal of the First Voyage of Vasco da Gama*. Ed. by E. G. Ravenstein. Copyright The Hakluyt Society, London, 1898. *Sea Road to the Indies* by Henry Hart. Macmillan Pub. Co., Inc., 1950; William Hodge & Co. Ltd., 1952. **Ch. 7:** *The Voyage of Magellan: The Journal of Antonio Pigafetta*. Trans. by Paul Paige. © 1969 The William L. Clements Library. Pub. by Prentice Hall, Inc. *The Longest Voyage* by Robert Silverburg. Bobbs Merrill, 1972. *Magellan* by Ian Cameron. Saturday Review Press, 1973; George Weidenfeld & Nicolson, Ltd. *So Noble a Captain* by Charles McKew Parr. Thomas Y. Crowell, 1953; Robert Hale & Co., 1955. *The European Discovery of America: The Southern Voyages* by Samuel Eliot Morison. Oxford Univ. Press, 1974. *Conqueror of the Seas* by Stefan Zweig. Viking Press, 1938. **Part III, Ch. 8:** *Balboa of Darién* by Kathleen Romoli. Doubleday & Co., Inc., 1953. *Natural History of the West Indies* by Gonzalo Fernandez de Oviedo y Valdes. Trans. by Stirling A. Stoudemire. Univ. of North Carolina Studies in the Romance Languages and Literature, 1959. *Life and Letters of Vasco Núñez de Balboa* by Charles L. G. Anderson. Flemina H. Revell Co., 1941. **Ch. 9:** *The Bernal Diaz Chronicles* by Albert Idell. Doubleday & Co., Inc., 1956. *Cortés: The Life of the Conqueror of Mexico by His Secretary Lopez de Gomara*. Ed. and trans. by Lesley B. Simpson. Univ. of California Press, 1964. *Cortés and the Downfall of the Aztec Empire* by Jon M. White. St. Martin's Press, Inc., 1971. *Narrative of Some Things of New Spain* by the Anonymous Conqueror. Trans. by Marshall H. Saville.

Cortés Society, New York, 1917. **Ch. 10:** *Reports on the Discovery of Peru* by Xeres. Ed. by C. I. Markham. Copyright The Hakluyt Society, London, 1872. **Ch. 11:** *Narratives of the Coronado Expedition* by George P. Hammon and Agapito Rey. Univ. of New Mexico Press, 1940. *Spanish Explorers in the Southern United States* by Frederick W. Hodge. Charles Scribner's Sons, 1907. *Coronado: Knight of Pueblos and Plains* by Herbert E. Bolton. Univ. of New Mexico Press, 1964. *Conquistadors in North American History* by Paul Horgan. Farrar, Straus & Giroux, Inc. 1953; Macmillan, Ltd., London, 1963. **Part IV, Ch. 12:** *Francis Drake, Privateer* by John Hampden. Univ. of Alabama Press, 1972. Reprinted also by permission of A. P. Watt & Son, London, the Estate of John Hampden and Eyre Methuen Ltd. *New Light on Drake*. A collection of documents relating to his voyage of circumnavigation, 1577-80. Ed. by Zelia Nuttall. Copyright The Hakluyt Society, London, 1914. *The World Encompassed by Sir Francis Drake*. Ed. by W.S.W. Vaux. Copyright The Hakluyt Society, London, 1854. Reproduced with the permission of The Hakluyt Society. *Drake* by Llewellyn Powys. Harper & Row, 1929. *Narratives of New Netherland* by J. Franklin Jameson. Barnes and Noble, 1909. **Ch. 14:** *The Works of Samuel de Champlain* by H. P. Biggar. The Champlain Society, Toronto, 1924. *Samuel de Champlain: Father of New France* by Samuel Eliot Morison. Little, Brown & Co., 1972. **Part V, Ch. 16:** *Bering's Voyages* by F. A. Golder. Vol. II. American Geographical Society, 1925. *The American Expedition* by Sven Waxell. William Hodge & Co. Ltd., 1952; The Macmillan Pub. Co., Inc., New York, 1952. **Ch. 17:** *French Explorers in the Pacific* by John Dunmore. Vol. I. Oxford Univ. Press, 1965. **Ch. 18:** *The Journals of Captain James Cook on His Voyages of Discovery*. Ed. by J. C. Beaglehole. Copyright © The Hakluyt Society, 1955-64. Reproduced with the permission of The Hakluyt Society, London. *The Life of Captain James Cook* by J. C. Beaglehole. Copyright © 1974 by J. C. Beaglehole. Reprinted by permission of Stanford Univ. Press and A. & C. Black, Ltd. *Explorations of Captain James Cook in the Pacific (1768-1799)*. Ed. by A. Grenfell Price. Used by arrangement with The Heritage Press, Avon, Conn. *Endeavour Journal of Joseph Banks 1768-1771*. Ed. by J. C. Beaglehole. Angus & Robertson Publishers, Ltd., Sidney, 1962. **Part VI, Ch. 19:** *The Journals and Letters of Sir Alexander Mackenzie*. Ed. by W. Kaye Lamb. Copyright © The Hakluyt Society, London, 1970. Reproduced with permission of The Hakluyt Society, London. **Ch. 20:** *The Journals of Lewis and Clark*. Ed. by Bernard De Voto. Houghton Mifflin Co., 1953. *The Westward Crossings* by Jeannette Mirsky. Univ. of Chicago Press, 1970. *Lewis and Clark: Partners in Discovery* by John Bakeless. William Morrow & Co., 1947; McClelland & Stewart Ltd. *The Taming of the Canadian West* by Frank Rasky. McClelland & Stewart Ltd., 1967. *History of the Expedition Under Lewis and Clark*. Ed. by Elliott Coues. Dover Publications, Inc., 1965. *European Discovery of America: The Northern Voyages* by Samuel Eliot Morison. Oxford Univ. Press, 1973. **Ch. 21:** *Australian Explorers*. Ed. by Kathleen Fitzpatrick (1958). Oxford Univ. Press. Reprinted by permission of the publisher. *Cooper's Creek* by Alan Moorehead. Harper & Row, 1963; Hamish Hamilton Ltd. *The Fatal Impact* by Alan Moorehead. Hamish Hamilton Ltd., 1966. *Dig* by Frank Clune. Angus & Robertson Ltd., 1937. **Part VII, Intro.:** *The African Past* by Basil Davidson. Little, Brown & Co., 1964 **Ch. 23:** *Living-*

*stone* by Tim Jeal. G. P. Putnam's Sons, 1973. *Livingstone and Africa* by Jack Simmons. Macmillian Pub. Co., Inc.; English Universities Press, Ltd., 1955. *Livingstone's African Journal 1853-56*. Vols. I & II. Ed. by I. Schapera. Univ. of California Press; Chatto & Windus, London, 1963. *Livingstone's Missionary Correspondence 1854-56*. Ed. by I. Schapera. Univ. of California Press; Chatto & Windus, London, 1961. **Ch. 24:** *Stanley's Despatches to the New York Herald*. Ed. by Norman R. Bennett. Boston Univ. Press, 1970. *Stanley, an Adventurer Explored* by Richard Hall. Houghton Mifflin Co., 1975. **Part VIII, Intro.:** *To the Arctic!* by Jeannette Mirsky. Alfred A. Knopf; McClelland & Stewart Ltd., 1948. **Ch. 25:** *Farthest North* by Fridtjof Nansen. Copyright 1897. Pub. by Harper and Row, New York; Constable & Co. Ltd., London; H. Aschehoug & Co., Oslo. *The Saga of Fridtjof Nansen* by Jon Sorensen. Trans. by J. Watkins. Pub. by W. W. Norton, New York; Geo. Allen & Unwin, London, 1932. Originally pub. by Gyldendal Norsk Forlag, Oslo. **Ch. 26:** *The North Pole* by Robert E. Peary. Frederick A. Stokes & Co., 1910. *A Negro Explorer at the North Pole* by Matthew A. Henson. Copyright 1912 by Frederick A. Stokes & Co. Reprinted by permission of J. B. Lippincott Co. **Ch. 27:** *The Northwest Passage* by Roald Amundsen. Copyright 1907 by Roald Amundsen. Pub. by H. Aschehoug & Co., Oslo; Constable & Co., Ltd., London; E. P. Dutton & Co., Inc., New York. *My Life as an Explorer* by Roald Amundsen. Doubleday & Co., Inc., 1927; Gyldendal Norsk Forlag, Oslo. *The South Pole* by Roald Amundsen. John Murray, London, 1913; Gyldendal Norsk Forlag, Oslo. *Roald Amundsen, Explorer* by Charles Turley. Methuen & Co. Ltd., 1935. *Our Polar Flight* by Roald Amundsen and Lincoln Ellsworth. Dodd, Mead & Co., 1925. *First Crossing of the Polar Sea* by Roald Amundsen and Lincoln Ellsworth. Doubleday & Co., Inc., 1927. **Ch. 28:** *Scott's Last Expedition* by Robert F. Scott. Pub. by Dodd, Mead & Co.; John Murray, London. *Scott's Last Voyage* by Ann Savours. © 1975 Ann Savours and reprinted by permission of Praeger Publishers, Inc.; Sidgwick & Jackson. *Captain Scott and the Antarctic Tragedy* by Peter Brent. Saturday Review Press, 1974; George Weidenfeld & Nicolson, Ltd. *Scott of the Antarctic* by Reginald Pound. Coward-McCann & Geoghegan, 1967; Cassell & Co. Ltd., 1966. *Scott of the Antarctic* by George Seaver. John Murray, London, 1953. **Part IX, Ch. 29:** *Half Mile Down* by William Beebe. Reprinted by permission of Elswyth Thane Beebe. *The World Beneath the Sea* by Otis Barton. Thomas Y. Crowell Co., Inc.; Longmans Green & Co., Ltd., 1953. **Ch. 30:** *The Conquest of Everest* by Sir John Hunt. Copyright John Hunt. Reprinted by permission of Hodder & Stoughton, Ltd. Pub. in the U.S. by E. P. Dutton & Co., Inc. *Man of Everest* by Tenzing Norgay and James R. Ullman. Copyright. All Rights Reserved. Reproduced by kind permission of George G. Harrap & Co., Ltd., and Intercontinental Literary Agency. Pub. in the U.S. as *Tiger of the Snows* by G. P. Putnam's Sons. *High Adventure* by Sir Edmund Hillary. Copyright © Edmund Hillary. Reprinted by permission of Hodder & Stoughton, Ltd., and John Farquharson, Ltd. Pub. in the U.S. by E. P. Dutton & Co., Inc. *Nothing Venture Nothing Win* by Sir Edmund Hillary. © 1975 Edmund Hillary. Reprinted by permission of Coward-McCann & Geoghegan, Inc.; Hodder & Stoughton, Ltd.; and John Farquharson, Ltd. *Coronation Everest* by James Morris. Faber & Faber, Ltd.; E. P. Dutton & Co., Inc., 1958. *Because It's There* by George Lowe. Cassell & Co. Ltd., 1959. **Ch. 31:** *First on the Moon: A Voyage with Neil Armstrong, Michael Collins, and Edwin E. Aldrin, Jr.* Written with Gene Farmer and Dora Jane Hamblin. Copyright © 1970 by Little, Brown & Co. Pub. in the U.K. by Michael Joseph, Ltd. *Carrying the Fire* by Michael Collins. Copyright © 1974 by Michael Collins. Reprinted with permission of Farrar, Straus & Giroux, Inc. *Return to Earth* by Col. Edwin E. "Buzz" Aldrin with Wayne Warga. Copyright © 1973 by Aldrin-Warga Associates. Reprinted by permission of Random House, Inc. *Appointment on the Moon* by Richard Lewis. The Viking Press, 1969.

# PICTURE CREDITS

*The initials AMNH are for the American Museum of Natural History, New York; BM, for the British Museum, London; NMM, for the National Maritime Museum, Greenwich, London; NYPL, for the New York Public Library.*

Page **12** *top* Lotti/Grimoldi; *lower left* Vatican Museum/Grimoldi; *bottom* BM. **13** NYPL, Picture Collection. **14** *lower* Bjorn Landstrom from *Bold Voyages and Great Explorers* published by Interbook Publishing. **16** *left* UPI; *right* Hirmer Fotoarchiv, München. **17** *left* Murray Miller. **18** BM. **19** *left* National Archaeological Museum, Athens/Baylor Trapnell; *center* NYPL, Map Div. **20** *top left* The Pierpont Morgan Library; *center* Universitetets Oldsaksamling; *bottom* & **21** Ted Spiegel/Black Star. **22** *left* Norwegian Information Service; *right* & **23** *right* Ted Spiegel/Black Star; *left* Swedish Information Service. **26** *lower* Reprinted by permission of Yale Univ. Press from *The Vinland Map and the Tartar Relation* by R. A. Skelton, Thomas E. Marston, and George D. Painter, © 1965 by Yale Univ. **27** *lower* John Pope. **28** *top left* Bodleian Library, Oxford/Angelo Hornak; *top right* Jerry Cooke; *center* Freer Gallery of Art, Smithsonian Institution; *bottom* Collection of the National Palace Museum, Taipei, Taiwan, Republic of China. **30** Topkapu Saray Museum/Ergin Turkish Public Relations Service. **31** Bibliothèque Nationale, Paris. **32** *right* Freer Gallery of Art, Smithsonian Institution. **33** Metropolitan Museum of Art, Gift of the Dillon Fund. **35** *right* Bodleian Library, Oxford/Angelo Hornak. **36** *upper left* Museum of Arts and Crafts, Hamburg/Beatrice Constantinescu-Frehn; *top center* Church of St. Mark, Venice; *right* Chase Manhattan Bank Numismatic Collection; *lower left* Dorothy Woodman Collection. **37** *top* Collection of the National Palace Museum, Taipei, Taiwan, Republic of China; *lower* Bodleian Library, Oxford/Angelo Hornak; *right* Courtesy of the Museum of Far Eastern Antiquities, Stockholm. **42** *left* Biblioteca Nazionale Marciana/Angelo Hornak; *top right* BM; *center right* The Granger Collection; *lower right* Museu Nacional de Arte Antiga, Lisbon. **43** Victoria and Albert Museum. **44** *left* Metropolitan Museum of Art, the Cloisters Collection; *right* Bibliothèque Nationale, Paris. **45** Museo Episcopal/Oronoz. **46** *top* S. Clyde/FPG; *bottom* Ergin Turkish Public Relations Service. **47** *left* NMM; *right* Biblioteca Estense, Modena/Umberto Orlandini. **48** *upper* M. P. Kahl; *lower* John R. Freeman & Co. **49** *left* Ron Jones; *right* Bjorn Landstrom from *Bold Voyages and Great Explorers* published by Interbook Publishing. **50** *right* Eric Morris. **51** Harrison Forman. **52** *top* Museo Navale, Pegli/Scala; *lower left* Metropolitan Museum of Art, Gift of J. Pierpont Morgan; *lower right* Museum of Seville/Photri. **53** Museo Navale, Pegli/Scala. **54** *upper* BM; *lower* Germanishches Nationalmuseum, Nürnberg. **55** Convento Retrato de los RR. CC. **56** *Santa Maria:* Bjorn Landstrom from *The Ship* published by Interbook Publishing; cross-section of *Santa Maria:* Bjorn Landstrom from *Columbus* published by Interbook Publishing. **57** The Bettmann Archive. **58** NYPL, Rare Book Div. **61** The Granger Collection. **63** Alcazar de Sevilla/Photri. **64** Drawn by Lima de Freitas for The Heritage Press edition of *Journals and Other Documents on the Life and Voyages of Christopher Columbus*, © 1963 and reproduced by permission of The Heritage Club, Avon, Conn. **65** *upper* The Mansell Collection; *lower* Palacio de Alba, Madrid. **66** *upper* Museo Naval, Madrid/Photri. **67** *top* Museo Navale, Pegli/Scala; *center* NYPL, Picture Collection; *bottom* Metropolitan Museum of Art, Gift of James Hazen Hyde. **68** *upper* Fernand Bourges, Courtesy of French & Co., Inc.; *lower left* BM/Angelo Hornak; *lower right* Academy of Science, Lisbon. **69** Schatzkammer of the Residenz, München. **70** Lauros-Giraudon. **72** *top* BM; *center* Academy of Science, Lisbon. **73** *bottom* Museo Naval, Madrid/Oronoz; *left* Harrison Forman; *right* Lynn McLaren/Rapho/Photo Researchers. **74** Museu de Marinha, Lisbon. **75** BM. **76** National Museum of Antique Art, Lisbon. **78** *top* Bibliothèque Nationale, Paris; *lower left* Michael Holford Library; *lower right* The Bettmann Archive. **79** NYPL, Rare Book Div. **80-81** Museo de America, Madrid. **82** NYPL, Rare Book Div. **83** *top* Tony La Tona; *lower left* Palacio de los Duques de Alba, Madrid/Oronoz. **85** *left* Science Museum, London; *right* By permission of the Houghton Library, Harvard Univ. **86** BM. **90** *top* Photri; *center right* The Granger Collection; *center left* Metropolitan Museum of Art, Rogers Fund; *bottom* Museo Militar, Barcelona/Photri. **91** Walter R. Aguiar. **92** NYPL, Rare Book Div. **93** Carl Frank/Photo Researchers. **94** *left* Museum of the American Indian; *remainder* Walter R. Aguiar. **95** *center* Museum of the American Indian; *remainder* Walter R. Aguiar. **97** Bradley Smith. **98** *top* Juan O'Gorman; *bottom left* Armeria Real, Madrid/Oronoz; *bottom right* & **99** **BM**. **100** *left* Hospital de Jesus, Mexico City/Bradley Smith; *upper right* Biblioteca Nacional, Madrid; *bottom center* Bradley Smith. **101** Bodleian Library, Oxford/Angelo Hornak. **102** *top* Photri; *lower left* National Archives, Mexico; *lower right* AMNH. **103** Bradley Smith. **104** *left* Museo Nacional de Antropología, México, D.F./Photri; *right* Bradley Smith. **105** *above* Museo Nacional de Antropología, México, D.F.; *below* Germanisches Nationalmuseum, Nürnberg. **106** & **107** *below* BM/Angelo Hornak. **108** *top* British Embassy, Mexico City; *lower right* BM/Angelo Hornak. **110** *top* Loren McIntyre; *lower left* Museo America, Madrid/Oronoz; *bottom* BM. **111** Institut d'Ethnologie, Paris. **113** *left* Francisco Erize/Bruce Coleman, Inc.; *center & right* Loren McIntyre. **114** *left* By gracious permission of His Grace, the Duke of Wellington, KG; *right* & **115** *left & upper center* Loren McIntyre; *lower center* Museum of Primitive Art/Elizabeth Little; *center right* Univ. Museum, Univ. of Pennsylvania; *far right* AMNH. **117** *right* NYPL, Rare Book Div. **118** *top left & right* Loren McIntyre; *bottom left* Institut d'Ethnologie, Paris; *bottom center* William Franklin; *lower right* Museum & Institute of Archeology, Univ. of San Antonio, Abad, Cuzco/Loren McIntyre. **119** *left* Loren McIntyre; *right* NYPL, Rare Book Div. **120** *top* Loren McIntyre; *lower left* Giorgio Gualco/Bruce Coleman, Inc.; *lower right* Institut d'Ethnologie, Paris. **121** Photri. **122** *top* The Curtis Project; *center* BM; *bottom* Ray Atkeson. **123** AMNH. **124** *upper* Castello de Chapultepec/Photri; *lower* David Muench. **125** Remington Art Museum. **126** *upper* Frans Halsmuseum, Haarlem; *lower* Amon Carter Museum of Western Art. **127** BM. **129** *left* Courtesy of the Kennedy Galleries; *right* Bill Ratcliffe. **132** The Golden Hinde Company, Ltd.; *inset* Kunsthistorisches Museum, Vienna/Photo Meyer. **133** & **134** City Art Gallery, Plymouth/Anglo Hornak. **135** *left* Published by permission of the British Library Board; *center* Museo Naval, Madrid/Oronoz; *right* NMM. **136** *top* The Golden Hinde Company, Ltd.; *bottom* ship by George Kelvin, figures by Howard Koslow; *bottom left* & **137** *top right* Faith Herbert; *remainder* The Golden Hinde Company, Ltd. **138** Courtesy of Mrs. Catherine Palmer. **139** *upper* Hispanic Society of America; *lower* & **140** NYPL, Rare Book Div. **141** *top left* San Francisco Chronicle; *lower left* Courtesy of the Bancroft Library; *right* Peter D. Capen. **142** *lower right* Courtesy of the American Numismatic Society, New York. **143** *left* City Art Gallery, Plymouth/Angelo Hornak; *right* Ian Yeomans/Susan Griggs. **144** *top left* The Granger Collection; *top right* National Gallery of Art, Washington, Gift of the Avalon Foundation; *bottom* NMM. **145** BM. **146** NMM. **147** *left* Library of Congress; *top right* Stadelsches Kunstinstitut, Frankfurt am Main/Kunst-Dias Blauel; *lower right* American Heritage Publishing Co., Inc. **148** *top left* Rijksmuseum, Amsterdam; *lower left* NYPL, Rare Book Div.; *right* BM. **149** *left* Bodleian Library, Oxford/Photo Nicholas Servian, FLIP, Woodmansterne, Ltd.; *right* The Granger Collection. **151** Tate Gallery/John Webb. **152** *top & bottom right* NYPL, Rare Book Div.; *bottom left* Smithsonian Institution. **153** NYPL. **154** The New-York Historical Society. **155** Huntington Library, San Marino, Calif. **157** *right*, **158**, & **159** NYPL, Rare Book Div. **161** Musée de Québec. **162** *top* Yale Univ. Library, Map Collection; *bottom* Musée du Louvre, Paris/Giraudon. **163** Nouvelle Librairie de France, Paris. **164** *upper* Museum of the American Indian, Heye Foundation; *bottom* Courtesy of D. B. Quinn, Univ. of Liverpool.

Picture Editor: Robert J. Woodward